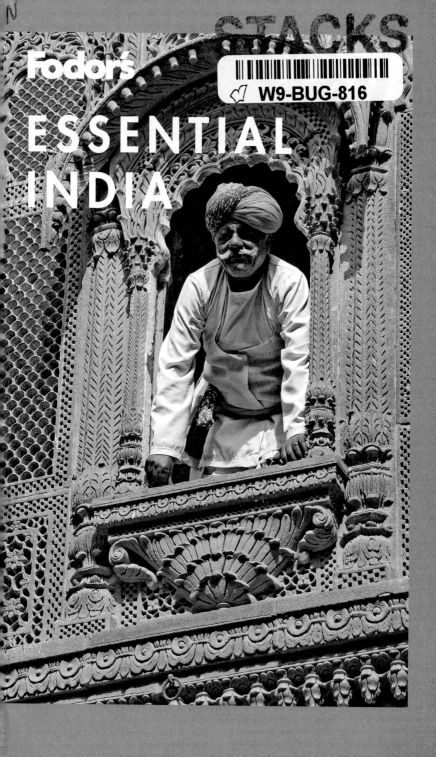

Fodor's

ESSENTIAL
INDIA

WITHDRAWN

WELCOME TO INDIA

India is a soulful, soul-stirring country, overflowing with cultural treasures, spiritual wonder, and natural beauty. A wondrous land of crowded megacities, Himalayan monasteries, and ancient fishing villages, India sweeps you up in a confounding and beautiful tide of humanity. Float along Kerala's famous backwaters, take a camel ride through Rajasthan, or find peace at the holy Ganges. And whether you drink *chai* (tea) from the source in Munnar, or savor Marwari cuisine in Jaipur, the land of spices and its remarkable people will linger long in your memory.

TOP REASONS TO GO

★ **Sacred Spaces:** Temples, shrines and holy *ghats* evoke ancient spiritual traditions.

★ **Food:** Rich curries, creamy *daals*, spicy street snacks: India's variety delights.

★ **Architecture:** Delhi's Jama Masjid, the iconic Taj Mahal, Udaipur's Lake Palace.

★ **Beaches:** Palm-fringed golden coastline beckons in Goa, Kerala, and even Mumbai.

★ **Markets:** Jewelry, leather, vibrant fabrics, pungent spices—bargains are plentiful.

★ **Music and Dance:** Bollywood, Bhangra, and festivals like Diwali make a joyful noise.

Fodor's ESSENTIAL INDIA

Publisher: Amanda D'Acierno, *Senior Vice President*

Editorial: Arabella Bowen, *Editor in Chief*; Linda Cabasin, *Editorial Director*

Design: Tina Malaney, *Associate Art Director*; Chie Ushio, *Senior Designer*; Ann McBride, *Production Designer*

Photography: Jennifer Arnow, *Senior Photo Editor*; Jennifer Romains, *Photo Researcher*

Production: Linda Schmidt, *Managing Editor*; Evangelos Vasilakis, *Associate Managing Editor*; Angela L. McLean, *Senior Production Manager*

Maps: Rebecca Baer, *Senior Map Editor*; Mark Stroud (Moon Street Cartography), *Cartographers*

Sales: Jacqueline Lebow, *Sales Director*

Marketing & Publicity: Heather Dalton, *Marketing Director*; Katherine Punia, *Publicity Director*

Business & Operations: Susan Livingston, *Vice President, Strategic Business Planning*; Sue Daulton, *Vice President, Operations*

Fodors.com: Megan Bell, *Executive Director, Revenue & Business Development*; Yasmin Marinaro, *Senior Director, Marketing & Partnerships*

Writers: Malavika Bhattacharya, Margot Bigg, Vaihayasi Pande Daniel, Michael Edison Hayden, Chandrima Pal, Snigdha Poonam, Vandana Verma

Editors: Róisín Cameron, John Rambow

Production Editor: Elyse Rozelle

3rd Edition

ISBN 978-1-101-87808-8

ISSN 2164-2222

All details in this book are based on information supplied to us at press time. Always confirm information when it matters, especially if you're making a detour to visit a specific place. Fodor's expressly disclaims any liability, loss, or risk, personal or otherwise, that is incurred as a consequence of the use of any of the contents of this book.

SPECIAL SALES

This book is available at special discounts for bulk purchases for sales promotions or premiums. For more information, e-mail specialmarkets@penguinrandomhouse.com

PRINTED IN THE UNITED STATES OF AMERICA

10 9 8 7 6 5 4 3 2 1

CONTENTS

CONTENTS

ABOUT THIS GUIDE

Fodor's Recommendations

Everything in this guide is worth doing—we don't cover what isn't—but exceptional sights, hotels, and restaurants are recognized with additional accolades. **Fodor's Choice** ★ indicates our top recommendations; and **Best Bets** call attention to notable hotels and restaurants in various categories. Care to nominate a new place? Visit Fodors.com/contact-us.

Trip Costs

We list prices wherever possible to help you budget well. Hotel and restaurant price categories from **$** to **$$$$** are noted alongside each recommendation. For hotels, we include the lowest cost of a standard double room in high season. For restaurants, we cite the average price of a main course at dinner or, if dinner isn't served, at lunch. For attractions, we always list adult admission fees; discounts are usually available for children, students, and senior citizens.

Hotels

Our local writers vet every hotel to recommend the best overnights in each price category, from budget to expensive. Unless otherwise specified, you can expect private bath, phone, and TV in your room. For expanded hotel reviews, facilities, and deals visit Fodors.com.

Top Picks	Hotels &
★ **Fodor's Choice**	**Restaurants**
	🏨 Hotel
Listings	⤴ Number of
✉ Address	rooms
✉ Branch address	❌ Restaurant
☎ Telephone	✑ Reservations
🖷 Fax	👔 Dress code
⊕ Website	▭ No credit cards
✐ E-mail	$ Price
🎫 Admission fee	
⊙ Open/closed	**Other**
times	⇨ See also
Ⓜ Subway	☛ Take note
✛ Directions or	⚑ Golf facilities
Map coordinates	
	❗ Meal plans

Restaurants

Unless we state otherwise, restaurants are open for lunch and dinner daily. We mention dress code only when there's a specific requirement and reservations only when they're essential or not accepted. To make restaurant reservations, visit Fodors.com.

Credit Cards

The hotels and restaurants in this guide typically accept credit cards. If not, we'll say so.

EUGENE FODOR

Hungarian-born Eugene Fodor (1905–91) began his travel career as an interpreter on a French cruise ship. The experience inspired him to write *On the Continent* (1936), the first guidebook to receive annual updates and discuss a country's way of life as well as its sights. Fodor later joined the U.S. Army and worked for the OSS in World War II. After the war, he kept up his intelligence work while expanding his guidebook series. During the Cold War, many guides were written by fellow agents who understood the value of insider information. Today's guides continue Fodor's legacy by providing travelers with timely coverage, insider tips, and cultural context.

EXPERIENCE INDIA

WHAT'S WHERE

The following numbers refer to chapters.

3 Delhi. The capital of India is really two cities: the architecturally planned Central (New) Delhi (including South Delhi), is characterized by broad tree-lined avenues. Old Delhi, by contrast, features labyrinthine alleys and narrow lanes.

4 Delhi Side Trips. Uttar Pradesh, the state neighboring Delhi, has several worthwhile attractions, most notably the Taj Mahal, in Agra. Just west of Agra is the former Mughal capital of Fatehpur Sikri, noted for its urban planning and architecture. In eastern Uttar Pradesh the holy city of Varanasi draws a constant stream of pilgrims to bathe in the river's holy water. The famous Hindu temples at Khajuraho are west of here in Madhya Pradesh.

5 Rajasthan. The "Land of Kings," once 18 princely kingdoms, is probably India's most-visited state. Historic palaces and forts are the prominent attractions here, along with the Pink City of Jaipur, the Jain temples in Ranakpur and Mount Abu, the enchanting lake-city of Udaipur, and Jaisalmer Fort.

6 Mumbai. This spirited city by the sea—still Bombay to locals—in many ways sets the tone for the rest of the country with its masala of markets, cafés, art galleries, shops, food carts, and street hawkers. Aurangabad, the base for exploring the caves of Ajanta and Ellora, is about 250 km (150 miles) east of Mumbai.

7 Goa. This former Portuguese colony is blessed with a bright blue coastline stretching down to sparkling, palm-lined beaches along the Arabian Sea. It's as popular for its laid-back values as its legendary seafood and beautiful views.

8 Kerala. On the southwest Malabar coast, Kerala is known for beaches, lush greenery, and ayurvedic massages. Scenic coconut groves and palm trees in places like Alapuzha offer a rustic paradise, while Trivandrum and Kochi preserve a rich culture and vestiges of a colonial past.

9 Kolkata (Calcutta). The former capital of British India, Kolkata has long been at the center of East India's cultural and intellectual life. This city characterized by grandiose architecture and lively markets is best known outside India as the place where Mother Teresa did her charitable work.

INDIA PLANNER

When to Go

The weather in India is best from November to March, and most tourists come in the first half of this high season. Delhi, a city of extremes, is often scorching from mid-April through June, and damp and cold—sometimes freezing—in December. The monsoon's daily rains, sweeping up from the southwest, usually arrive in Mumbai in June and hit Delhi a month later. Although you can work around the monsoon rains, they can lead to flooding, which makes traveling slow and sometimes even dangerous. The five days of Diwali, one of India's biggest festivals, fall in mid-October and mid-November; make reservations well in advance if you're visiting during this time or around Christmas.

The Foreigner Ticket Tax

As is common throughout India, admission to many of the country's museums and sites is often 10 times higher for foreign tourists than it is for locals. While this can be annoying, remember that in order for these sights to be accessible to the not-so-well-to-do general public, institutions and authorities need to make up revenues elsewhere.

Getting Here

Delhi's huge new airport terminal is helping ease congestion at the busiest airport in the country. Flying into Mumbai is also an option, though long-needed improvements there are still a few years off. You'll need to take a taxi or have a driver pick you up from either airport: public transportation isn't a realistic option. Delhi's airport is about 30 minutes from the city center; it can take two hours to reach Mumbai's center from the airport. Allow lots of extra time for the transfer, especially if you arrive during the day, as roads are prone to bottlenecks and other delays. If you haven't arranged transportation in advance through your hotel, head to the prepaid government-approved stands past immigration and customs, and ignore touts offering other options.

Getting Around

Flying between major destinations can save lots of time, as long as everything stays on schedule. It's definitely worth planning for at least one train ride, though—it's a signature India experience. Between some well-traveled destinations, the higher-end buses are faster and have better schedules than trains. Cars (which nearly always come with drivers) can help you get off the beaten path, and can also help you pack an extra village or temple or two into your itinerary. For trips within cities, taxis must often be prearranged, and the zippy, slightly manic auto-rickshaws are often more convenient. If you're only traveling a short distance you may even be able to try a bicycle rickshaw, which runs on its inevitably wiry driver's formidable muscles. Delhi's Metro provides safe, convenient air-conditioned service throughout the city and while Mumbai's commuter trains can be hot and crowded, they offer a fast and culturally immersive way to traverse the length of the city.

Dining

In a place as obsessed with food as India, unshowy neighborhood restaurants that cater to locals are often standouts. Luxury and business-class hotels often have so-called coffee shops; these are open 24 hours and always have a variety of cuisines, including a selection of Western dishes. Unless we mention otherwise, the restaurants we list are open daily for lunch and dinner. However, it's common for restaurants to close from roughly 3 to 6 pm, and they also stop serving by 11 pm or midnight. Only the most popular and heavily touristed restaurants, such as Delhi's Bukhara, require a reservation, although it's never a bad idea, and similarly it's only the highest-end restaurants that would have a dress code that requires a jacket or tie.

Packing Essentials

Go for loose, breathable, sturdy fabrics. Pants are better than shorts: they protect from the sun, and they won't make you stick out. (Shorts are inappropriate for most religious sites, in any case). Women should opt for pants or skirts or dresses that go below the knee. Pack light but sturdy walking shoes that are easy to take off (you'll need to do so to enter temples), strong sunscreen (the good stuff is costly and hard to find in India), toilet paper, moist towelettes, hand sanitizer, handkerchiefs (for drying off after washing your hands), insect repellent, and a flashlight.

Hiring a Guide

Guides can help you get more out of your sightseeing. Some are long-winded, so don't be afraid to gently turn the discussion to what interests you. And don't fall for the hard sell: you don't have to hire the first one you see—you can always go back and find that first one after you've had a chance to look around a bit. The guides at some sites, such as the Taj Mahal, are accredited by the local or national government, and in such places rates are fixed. Avoid going shopping with guides, because they will inevitably get a cut of the inflated prices you pay the stores.

Tours

Tours can be useful if you're not inclined to figure out the logistics of planes, trains, and hiring drivers. Make sure you shop around and know what you're paying for, though. Ask questions: How much can the tour be personalized? Will it be a group tour, or will it just be the people in your party? Finally, don't limit your research to just North American or European tour groups; many Indian tour companies put together well-regarded tours for foreign nationals, and their rates are often cheaper than their foreign competitors. ⇨ *See the Travel Smart chapter for some specifics.*

Money

India's main unit of currency, the rupee, is worth roughly 1/60 of a U.S. dollar. In 2010 the government adopted a new symbol for the rupee, but "Rs.," "Re.," and "INR" remain common abbreviations. Because of governmental regulations, it's against the law to take rupees in or out of India, so you must obtain your rupees from an ATM after you land. When traveling, always carry some rupee bills, because charge cards are far from universally accepted. When paying for small items, keep in mind that many shopkeepers will have difficulty breaking large bills.

INDIA TODAY

Economy

India's independence from British rule in 1947 had huge repercussions throughout the country, which was then divided into India and Pakistan. The Indian National Congress party took control of India, and its socialist economy that ensued was characterized by government-controlled industry and limited international trade. While many beneficial policies were put into action, especially in respect of increased food production, the economy lagged, and in 1991 the International Monetary Fund bailed out the nearly bankrupt nation. Realizing the need for a new approach, the country opened its doors to economic reforms and began to embrace capitalism; significant economic changes were enacted, such as relaxed rules on foreign investment in trade, tax reforms, and inflation-curbing measures. Since then, the economy has been growing at an average pace of about 7% per annum, although growth has begun to slow down significantly over the past few years.

Although agriculture is still the predominant occupation in India, employing about half of the work force, the country's economy has diversified a great deal since independence in 1947: manufacturing, tourism, the hospitality industry, and the service sector have become major sources of economic growth.

For the most part, the Indian economy managed to dodge the economic slowdown that sent world economies into a downward spiral starting in 2008. However, India's growth rate began to plummet in 2013 to less than 5%, the lowest it had been in a decade, with manufacturing being the hardest hit industry. And while India continues to develop, with a population of more than a billion people and counting, issues like widespread poverty and inequality of resources continue to be a major concern. Maintaining and building new roads, creating equitable housing, countering sanitation issues, empowering women, and battling widespread corruption continue to be major challenges for the government.

Politics

India is a constitutional republic with a system of governance largely based on the British Parliamentary system. It's the largest democracy in the world, and power is divided between the federal and state governments, with district-level issues dealt with by local governing assemblies known as *panchayats*.

In 2014, the Bharatiya Janata Party (BJP), India's major conservative party, won the outright majority of seats in the Lok Sabha, the lower house of the Indian Parliament. The party's leader, Narendrea Modi, was sworn in as prime minister in late May 2014. Prior to the election, India had been led by Dr. Manmohan Singh of the Congress Party, the largest constituent party of the United Progressive Alliance (UPA), a coalition of left-leaning national and regional parties.

Bilateral ties between India and Pakistan are a major focus of India's foreign policy. Peace talks were halted after terrorist attacks in Mumbai in 2008, carried out by suspected Islamic terrorists from Pakistan, but resumed in 2011.

Technology and Science

Science and technology research and development have been heavily funded in India since Independence, when Jawaral Nehru, the nation's first Prime Minister, launched initiatives to help further the sciences in the country. The Indian Institutes of Technology (IITs) are among the world's top schools for engineering, and many young Indians with a scientific bent see admission into one of these exclusive schools as a golden ticket to a lifetime of good jobs. In recent years India has made large advances in biotechnology, IT, and software services, and thanks to a large, English-speaking workforce, the country has also emerged as a major hub for the outsourcing industry in general. Indeed, the country's software companies alone earn up to 90% of their revenue by providing technical support to companies from Europe and the United States. Although the global economic slowdown marginally affected the galloping growth of the software sector, the industry continues to drive India's economic growth.

Religion

India is a secular country, as laid down by the Indian Constitution, but the vast majority of the population is religiously observant. Just over 80% are practicing Hindus, and the remaining 20% is made up of various religions, including Islam, Christianity, Sikhism, Jainism, and Buddhism. In Mumbai there is a small but vibrant community of Parsis, as the Zoroastrians who settled in India several centuries ago are called. India also has as many as five native Jewish communities, who immigrated thousands of years ago and have their own unique customs. Religious festivals of many persuasions, such as Diwali (the Hindu Festival of Lights), the Muslim festival of Eid-ul-Fitr (which takes place at the end of Ramadan), and Christmas, are all celebrated with fervor.

The Arts

India has a rich cultural heritage dating back several thousand years. Classical music and dance have always been an important part of the social fabric, and each state has its own distinct folk styles as well, such as the Punjabi folk dance form of bhangra. The most popular of the modern-day performing arts, however, are the high-budget, song-and-dance extravaganzas that come out of Bollywood, as the Hindi film industry is popularly known. It is not unusual for India to produce nearly 3,000 movies a year, of which around a third would be feature films. In addition to Hindi films, many states also have thriving regional cinema industries. For instance, Chennai is home to the Tamil film industry, and Tamil superstar Rajnikanth is widely considered the highest-paid actor in the country.

India has had a rich legacy of literature, both in English and in regional languages. Since the early 1900s, when Bengali author Rabindranath Tagore won the Nobel Prize for Literature for the English translation of his collection of Bengali poems, *Gitanjali,* Indian writing has evolved and acquired a distinct voice of its own. British-Indian author Salman Rushdie's *Midnight's Children* (1981), which dealt with the coming of age of the country following independence, also marked the coming of age of contemporary Indian writing in English. His narrative style, which combines historical fiction with magic realism, has had a major influence on postcolonial Indian literature. Authors like Vikram Seth, Arundhati Roy, Amitav Ghosh, Jhumpa Lahiri, and Kiran Desai have powerfully conveyed the idea of a dynamic, ever-changing nation through their writing.

WHAT'S NEW

The 2014 General Elections

General elections were held across India in 2014 to form the 16th Lok Sabha, the lower house of India's Parliament. The Bharatiya Janata Party (BJP), India's primary conservative party, won the outright majority and installed their leader, Narendra Modi, as prime minister on May 26. The election had the highest turnout of any general election in India's history, with more than 66% of India's 814 million eligible voters coming out to vote. It was also the world's largest election of all time.

In the months leading up to his inauguration, Modi campaigned on promises of economic reform and corruption reduction, and was heralded by supporters as a man of the people (Modi comes from a humble background, which is unusual for a prime minister). Opponents feared that the BJP has a pro-Hindu agenda that poses a threat to India's minority groups—notably Muslims—pointing out Modi's alleged provocation of the 2002 Gujarat Riots that resulted in the death of hundreds of Hindus and Muslims.

The Formation of Telangana

Soon after Independence, much of India was divided and merged along linguistic lines, including the princely Hyderabad State, which once occupied a vast swath of territory across South India. The Telugu-speaking parts of the state, known as Telangana, were merged with the newly formed Andhra State to form Andhra Pradesh, and certain safeguards were put into place to protect the people of Telangana from discrimination and unfair distribution of resources. Many locals felt that the protection they had been promised was not upheld; this spurred a series of independence movements that started

in the 1960s and gained momentum in the early 2000s. In June 2014, the South Indian state of Andhra Pradesh was officially bifurcated under the Andhra Pradesh Reorganisation Act of 2014. The state was split into a new state of Telangana in the northwest, which comprises what was once Hyderabad State, leaving the remaining areas to the south and east as part of Andhra Pradesh.

The Symbol of the Rupee

In 2010, the Indian government sent out a message about the growing strength of the Indian rupee against global currencies like the dollar and the euro by unveiling a new symbol for the rupee. With the symbol, a unique blend of the Roman "R" and the Devanagri (or Hindi) script "Ra," the Indian rupee joins the U.S. dollar, the euro, the British pound, and the Japanese yen in having a distinct identity.

As part of the process, in 2009 the Indian government announced a public competition to create the symbol, and more than 3,000 people sent in their suggestions. D. Udaya Kumar, a professor at the elite Indian Institute of Technology, sent in the winning entry; he explained that his symbol "is a perfect blend of Indian and Roman letters" and that the design was inspired by the Indian tricolors "with two lines at the top and white space between." Although the new symbol will not be incorporated into currency notes for the time being, it has been added to major scripts and used in all official communication.

Interplanetary Travel

Despite some failures, such as the loss of India's first unmanned moon orbiter in 2009, India is pursuing significant milestones in space technology, including a second lunar exploration mission in 2016–17. In 2013, India began its first interplanetary mission with the launch of the Mars Orbiter Mission (MOM), known locally as the *Mangalyaan* (Sanskrit for Mars craft), carrying five scientific instruments designed to gather and analyze data pertaining to the planet's surface, atmosphere, and exosphere. The craft entered the orbit of Mars in late September 2014, making the Indian Space Research Organisation the fourth space agency to reach to Mars.

Continued Globalization

International fast-food chain McDonald's was among the first global brands to set up base in India, way back in 1996. Over the ensuing years, they've tweaked their trademark products to better suit the Indian palate, and you won't find items like the McAloo Tikki (it has a potato cutlet in place of a meat patty), the Chicken Maharaja Mac (the Indian version of a Big Mac, with two grilled chicken patties, tomatoes, cheese, and spicy mayonnaise), or the Paneer Salsa Wrap anywhere else in the world.

A host of other international brands have since climbed on to the India bandwagon, including fast-food outlets like Domino's and Subway. International apparel brands such as Levi's and United Colors of Benetton have long been a feature of many an Indian shopping malls, recent years have seen newer players such as Zara, Diesel, and Forever 21 set up shop across the country. In 2012, Starbucks' launched its brand in India through a joint venture with India's Tata Global Beverages, a division of the behemoth Tata Group. By 2014, they had more than 40 outlets across major Indian cities, all serving locally sourced coffee.

Indian Art Booms

Indian art is becoming better known in the international art market, and the works of modern Indian masters have been fetching record prices at art auctions. In 2010, for instance, veteran artist S.H. Raza's *Saurashtra*, a large acrylic on canvas work, was snapped up by a buyer for a staggering $3.5 million at a Christie's auction in London. The sale set a new record for the amount paid for a work of modern Indian art at auction. Other artists, including M.F. Hussain—called the "Indian Picasso" by *Forbes* magazine—have found favor with international collectors, and the Indian art market is expected to continue gaining recognition and renown.

Recycling

Recycling isn't new to India, by any means. Indeed, recycling has been going for many decades, with ragpickers collecting paper, plastic, and metal waste that's then sold and resold up the chain of industry. Bottles and tins have always been reused until they break; newspapers are saved and resold, or used as insulation. The recycling of cow dung for fuel, building material, and many other uses has been going on for centuries. More recently India has become a center for recycling electronic waste. The country's own rapidly growing economy generates more than 50,000 tons of e-waste, and other countries have been sending their electronic waste to India as well—despite bans that prohibit the export of hazardous waste from rich countries to poor ones. In India most e-waste is dismantled and reprocessed by hand, without protective gear to guard against toxins such as lead and mercury that are known to be harmful. Something to think about.

INDIA
TOP ATTRACTIONS

The Taj Mahal, Agra

(A) Despite the plethora of postcards and calendar images, nothing can prepare you for the architectural and awe-inspiring beauty of the Taj Mahal in Agra. An "elegy in marble" as some call it, the mausoleum immortalizes the love between Mughal king Shah Jahan and his wife, Mumtaz, for whom it was built.

Fatehpur Sikri, Agra

This former capital of the Mughal Empire was built by Emperor Akbar during the second half of the 16th century, though Akbar only lived here for about a decade. The red sandstone complex has elaborate palaces, beautiful courtyards, and a large mosque and is noted for its forward-thinking urban planning and blending of Indo-Islamic architecture.

Jama Masjid, Delhi

(B) India's largest mosque is built of deep red sandstone and still manages to retain an aura of calm and beauty, despite the crowds covering it and the timeworn streets surrounding it.

Humayun's Tomb, Delhi

(C) Ornate and yet calming, this complex of tombs in southern Delhi was a precursor to the Taj Mahal and is a stunning Mughal artifact in its own right.

Gateway of India, Mumbai

It might not be the most visually stunning monument you see in India, but the Gateway arch on Mumbai's waterfront is an undeniable focal point of the city: built to commemorate the visit of King George V and Queen Mary in 1911, it has seen the coming and going of important personages and ordinary folk and continues to be a site of vibrant city life.

Ajanta and Ellora, Mumbai Side Trip
(D) Dating back to 200 BC, the cave temples at Ajanta and Ellora are astounding for their intricate paintings and carvings. The Ajanta caves depict the life story of the Buddha, while the nearby Ellora caves feature Buddhist, Hindu, and Jain carvings. Both Ajanta and Ellora are UNESCO World Heritage sites.

Taj Lake Palace (Jag Niwas), Udaipur
(E) Rising out of Lake Pichola like a mirage, the Lake Palace is a real-life wonder. Now that it's a hotel, you'll need to get a room here to inspect the courts and fountains up close, but even if you admire it from afar, you'll still find it a memorable part of the scenery. Some of the best views are from the sprawling, equally stunning City Palace.

Fort, Jaisalmer
More than 5,000 people still live in this spectacular 12th-century citadel, which ascends strikingly out of Rajastan's Thar Desert. Inside is a network of temples, palaces, mansions, and tiny winding lanes.

Ghats (stairs), Varanasi
(F) Varanasi is one of the world's holiest cities, but it's the mighty Ganges that draws so many Hindus (roughly 1 million annually) and other visitors and pilgrims. Spend time along the waterfront *ghats (*stairs) where pilgrims pray, chant, and bathe, and you will get a sense of the city's spirituality and sanctity.

Churches of Old Goa
(G) The ultrabaroque 16th- and 17th-century churches of this Portuguese colony contain the final resting place of St. Francis Xavier, Goa's patron saint, and intricate chapels and carvings.

TOP EXPERIENCES

A Camel Ride in the Desert

What could be more spectacular than a windswept camel ride in Rajasthan's Thar Desert? The calm of the undulating dunes, the quiet of the landscape, perhaps the sun is just coming up over the horizon—it all contrasts so sharply with the commotion of urban India. The western desert town of Jaisalmer is a good place from which to venture out, but many other cities in Rajasthan, including Jaipur and Jodhpur, offer camel safaris. The town of Pushkar hosts a bustling and frenetic camel and livestock fair every November, which coincides with the peak travel season to northern India, and is another way to get up close to a camel.

Join in a Festival

There may be as many festivals in India as there are languages or gods (and that's a lot!), a concept that proves to what extent life in this huge country revolves around family, community, and devotion. Whether it's Diwali, the festival of lights, or the springtime holiday of Holi, where participants toss vibrantly colored powders and water balloons at one another, communities love to gather together and celebrate. Kolkata's Durga Puja is perhaps the most extravagant, when every neighborhood sets up its own larger-than-life installation of the goddess (known as *pandals*). During Ganesh Chaturthi in Mumbai, floatlike statues of the god are submerged into the water at Chowpatty Beach. Joining in on festivities that occur while you're in India is a great way to meet people and get a real feel for the country.

A Boat Ride along the Ganges

To sense the role the Ganges River plays in the lives of devout Hindus, take a dawn or dusk boat trip. Start from the sacred Dashashvamedha Ghat and head upstream or toward the southern end, near Assi Ghat. At sunrise, bathers flock to these 90 or so *ghats*, preparing for a purifying dip into the holy water. And at sunset, hundreds of *diyas* (clay lamps) are lit and floated across the river.

Splurge on a Few Nights at a Taj Hotel

For luxury that surpasses all standards, check into one of the Taj properties around the country, among the grandest in the land. A few of the brand's hotels, such as the landmark Taj Mahal Palace & Tower, Mumbai, or iconic Taj Lake Palace, Udaipur, are particularly splendid. If you're not quite up for the splurge for an overnight, stop for a cocktail or high tea.

Shopping Spree in Jaipur

Fashionistas and designers from across the country flock to the Pink City for semi-precious baubles and block-printed textiles. In Johari Bazaar, a central strip of pedestrian-friendly stalls, jewelers will string stones such as carnelian, turquoise, and pink quartz into necklaces on the spot. Even if you're not looking to buy, it's worth dropping by the Gem Palace, Jaipur's equivalent of Tiffany's, where you can ogle sparkling diamonds, emeralds, and rubies in stunning settings. And at cult-favorite textile shops like Anokhi and Cottons, choose from block-printed tunics and home accessories in bright hues and myriad patterns.

Mumbai Street Food off the Curb, or in a Restaurant

No other Indian city does savory street snacks quite like Mumbai, where stalls selling *pani puri* (canapés dipped into a chilled mint soup) and *pav bhaji* (a spicy mash of potatoes, onions, and tomatoes eaten with buttered bread) are around every corner. You can also try these local favorites at authentic restaurants like Elco or Swati Snacks if you want a cleaner environment.

Watch a Bollywood Movie

Indians easily rival—and probably surpass—Americans with their degree of movie-mania. The Indian film industry, better known as Bollywood (for the "B" in Bombay), churns out around 1,000 of these movies a year. They're hugely popular all across the country, with actors like Shah Rukh Khan and starlets such as Aishwarya Rai holding demigod status among the public. Plots tend to be simple but melodramatic, and there are usually plenty of musical interludes, so even though most films are in Hindi, it's pretty easy to get the gist of the story and be entertained by the song and dance.

Pay Homage at a Temple or Mosque

With faith such an integral part of life, weekly or even daily visits to a place of worship are not uncommon for locals. Many places of worship are open to non-believers (some are not; specifics are noted in our reviews); and a visit to a temple, mosque, or church gives some insight into the devotion of so many. Sites like the Jama Masjid in Delhi, the Kalighat Kali Temple in Kolkata, and the Siddhivanayak Temple in Mumbai are among the more famous and can be quite busy, but smaller neighborhood places of worship are usually more tranquil. If you go, be respectful.

Experience the New India: Nightlife and Art Galleries

Tradition and ritual factor heavily in India's appeal to a first-time traveler, but the country is moving forward—fast—and there are plenty of modern cultural diversions. In urban centers, trendy bars and avant-garde art galleries are popping up almost overnight. For a firsthand glimpse, visit the hip bars and clubs that are becoming more and more prevalent in Delhi and Mumbai. An ambitious space with promising artwork, the two-story Devi Art Foundation, a privately owned space just outside Delhi, is essentially the country's first contemporary art museum. The smaller galleries that are proliferating in districts like Kala Ghoda in Mumbai are also good places to get a look at India's vibrant new art scene.

Ride the Rails

A relic of the British Raj, the train network that connects all of India is surprisingly efficient and extensive. Try to include a train journey in your itinerary if possible, as it is the best way to see the countryside and the smaller villages that are in many ways the heart of India today, even though the big cities may be the focus of travel. Be mindful, however, that the trip can entail rowdy neighbors and less than hygienic corridors. Lines like the Konkan Railway, running from Mumbai to Goa, are known for better service and cleaner quarters.

Eat Dessert

The spicier the meal, the sweeter the dessert: that seems to be the culinary rule of thumb in India. If the milky, syrupy desserts like *gulab jamun* (like a deep-fried donut, soaked in syrup) and *jalebi* (deep-fried swirls of sugar-water paste, often soaked in syrup) prove too sweet for your palate, try the delicious pistachio ice cream known as *kulfi* instead. For a healthier alternative, sample tropical and seasonal fruits like the Alphonso mango, the *sitaphal* (custard apple), or the *chikoo* (a grainy, fleshy caramel-color fruit).

QUINTESSENTIAL INDIA

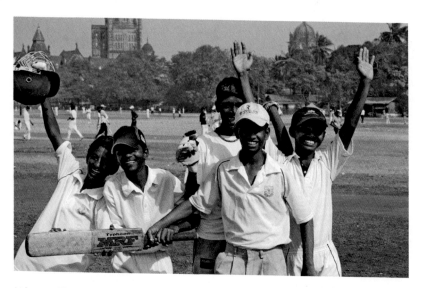

(Almost Always) Time for Tea

Drunk throughout the day, tea (called *chai*) is strong and formidably sweet: it's brewed with lots of milk and spices like ginger, cinnamon, and cardamom. Everyone in India makes time for tea—housewives take their tea breaks, office workers are served at their desk, and rickshaw drivers pull over for a roadside break—and so should you. And don't worry about standing on ceremony; it's not usually a drawn out affair: the tea, served in thick glasses, disappears as soon as it's cool enough to drink, and then it's time to get on with the day.

And Time for Tiffin

Indians want variety and big flavor in their food, and the tiniest towns as well as the biggest megapolises always have their share of tiny restaurants and stalls for buying *tiffin* (small meals or snacks) throughout the day. In the late afternoon, *chaat* (Indian street snacks) stalls set up to sell offerings that are tangy, sour, sweet, crunchy, and delicious all at once. Along the road are *dhabas* (roadside eateries) that are so popular that even big-city restaurants attempt to imitate their culinary skills.

"Is That Your Final Price?"

The uninitiated can find bargaining an intimidating process, at least at first, but try it once or twice and you'll see how much fun it can be. Waiting for an offer, reacting with polite surprise, countering with a much lower offer, and repeating the process until someone either gives up or gives in—the mini-drama of bargaining is still the way most of India buys and sells. To bargain well, keep in mind that the best ammunition to have is knowing what something *ought* to cost, so it can be worth your time to visit some shops with fixed prices to get an idea. When you're ready to haggle, don't volunteer a price—you'll be too high. Wait for an offer, then

If you want to get a sense of India's culture and indulge in some of its pleasures, start by familiarizing yourself with the rituals of daily life. These are a few highlights—things you can take part in with relative ease.

counter with something more reasonable: we usually recommend starting at about half the asking price. And don't be afraid to walk away and come back later—it's all part of the game.

A Sport and a Pastime

Cricket holds the highest place in Indian sports-lovers' hearts. Major games are headline news, and losses can be very deeply felt. Going to a professional game might not be the best way to go, though, because cricket matches tend to be quite long—instead, check out a televised game, and keep your eyes peeled for open spaces in cities and towns: chances are good that when the weather's fine (or even if it isn't) you'll catch some boys working on their game. You'll probably want to familiarize yourself with terms like "sticky wicket" (the wicket is the playing surface and a sticky wicket is a difficult situation) and "century" (when a batter scores 100 or more runs in a single inning).

Cinema Masala

India's mad love for movies is legendary: the country has been the world's leading producer (and consumer) of cinema for decades. Other regions in India have their own industries, but Bollywood (Mumbai's film biz) is king. Whether it's a comedy or a hard-boiled crime story, audiences demand spectacle: high emotions, gorgeous actors and clothes, and (most important) catchy song-and-dance numbers. Getting all that into the spicy mix (the *masala*) takes time: most movies last more than three hours, so let it all wash over you, take advantage of the intermission, and spring for a *chaat* (snack) or two.

FAQ

Planning a trip to India can seem like a bigger undertaking than a trip to a more familiar destination, and lots of questions arise. We've addressed some of the bigger issues here, *and there is more information in the Travel Smart chapter.* For additional advice, check out the travel forums on ⊕ *www.fodors.com.*

Before You Go

Do I need a visa to visit India? How far in advance do I need to apply?

You do need a tourist visa to travel to India. Recently, the entire visa application process was outsourced to Cox & Kings Global Services, a private visa processing company that you can access online. Though Cox & Kings claim to process applications in 3–5 business days, give yourself at least two weeks *(⇨ See Travel Smart for contact info).*

Do I need to get shots before I go to India?

Do discuss inoculations with your doctor as far in advance of your trip as possible. Some travelers to India take a prescription antimalarial drug (especially if you're visiting in summer, when mosquitoes are at their worst) and get inoculated against hepatitis and typhoid.

General Questions

Is the climate in India always hot? Do I need to pack any cold-weather clothes?

Although much of India is quite warm year-round, the subcontinent does experience varying climates from one region to another. Northern India, including Delhi and Rajasthan, tends to have a more desertlike climate, with warm, dry days and cool nights, and it can get pretty chilly November through March. Mumbai, Goa, and Kerala have a much more humid and temperate climate throughout the year. In general, during the peak travel season of November to March, it's cooler in the north and comfortable along the coast.

With all the religions and religious sites in India, do I need to dress extra conservatively?

Though times and social attitudes are changing, Indian culture is still quite conservative. Deter curious stares and unwanted attention by wearing loose-fitting and comfortable (preferably cotton) clothing that's not too revealing, women especially. That said, Mumbai and Delhi both have a pretty hip nightlife scene, so if you're planning to hit the bars and clubs, bring appropriate clothes.

Will I have problems communicating with others if I only speak English?

Although there are more than 400 languages and dialects spoken in India, English is one of the 22 official languages: it's widely spoken in all the big cities, so communicating with locals, hotel staff, and tour operators should pose no problem. If you're traveling in more rural areas, where the language barrier might be challenging, it can't hurt to keep a Hindi phrase book handy.

What can I do to make sure I'm respectful of local customs?

As warm as Indian hospitality is, spending time in the midst of a different culture is not always easy or comfortable. Being polite and thankful goes a long way; accepting that you might get frustrated with inefficiency or lack of personal space at times will also make for fewer trying moments in the long run—realizing that not much happens in a hurry in India is definitely a step in the right direction.

Should I book all my lodgings beforehand, or will I be able to do so once I'm there?

Although most cities along a traveler's route have ample accommodations, it's always a good idea to make reservations, especially for high-season travel (i.e., October to March). If you book with hotels that have a fair cancellation policy, you can often make alternate plans on arrival and cancel your original ones with a few days' notice.

Will all the food be very spicy and/or vegetarian? Will there be alcohol?

Most chefs and restaurants will happily adjust the spice level in dishes if told beforehand; you can also ask your waiter for nonspicy suggestions (*dal*, or stewed lentils, is usually a safe bet). Although a large percentage of the Indian population eats a strictly vegetarian diet, it's more common in the south, *and most cities covered in this guide have a variety of restaurant options*. Most vegetarian-only restaurants will have prominent signage to alert you. Alcohol is served at many hotels, restaurants, and bars, but note that some festivals and holidays are government-mandated dry days.

Can I drink tap water?

Do not drink Indian tap water. Stick with bottled water, and check the seal and date; empty water bottles are sometimes refilled with regular water and resold. You might also want to avoid fresh fruits and vegetables that you haven't washed or peeled yourself.

How should I deal with beggars and hawkers that approach me?

Unfortunately, while you might want to help, it's generally best to roll up car windows or walk away from beggars. Sometimes if you offer alms to one, several more quickly ambush you. With aggressive hawkers peddling their wares, walk away, say a firm "No," and avoid eye contact.

Is it safe to bring my valuables (i.e., jewelry) on my trip?

As with any travel, if you're afraid of losing it, we'd suggest you don't bring it—better safe than sorry. If you must bring valuables, keep them with you at all times, and this also applies to your passport and cash. Use basic street smarts by keeping your wallet in your front pocket and being alert.

What's the best way to bargain with vendors?

Compared to the West, bargaining is almost always expected in India, especially with street vendors and at smaller stalls. Once a price has been quoted, start your bargaining at about half of that. Don't be afraid to walk away either; it's not uncommon for a vendor to run down the street after a buyer—but don't waste your time, or the seller's time, if you have absolutely no intention of making a purchase.

Is India safe for solo female travelers?

Women frequently travel alone in India, usually without too much hassle, and the country is safer for women than many people realize. Mumbai and Delhi have special "ladies carriages" on their commuter trains, and some high-end hotels have begun introducing women-only floors, reserved for women and accompanying small children. That said, sexual harassment (known locally as "Eve teasing") and rape are not uncommon in India, and women should avoid being out alone after dark.

INDIA WITH KIDS

India might not be the typical family destination—there's no getting around the fact that it's dirty, and the unfamiliar can be a bit scary at times—but it's the kind of trip no child (or adult) will ever forget. Here are some ideas to help you plan.

Wildlife Safaris and Animal Rides

India abounds with national parks and reserves: the real-life setting and inspiration for Rudyard Kipling's *The Jungle Book*. An excursion to one of these parks, like **Ranthambhore** or **Keoladeo**, both in Rajasthan, can be a wonderful way for kids to learn about local flora and fauna. Also in Rajasthan, kids and grown-ups will almost undoubtedly get a thrill out of a camel safari in the desert. The **Chokhi Dhani** resort outside Jaipur has a nightly, carnival-like village fair on the resort grounds, complete with magic stalls and elephant rides that will captivate most kids—you can stay at the resort or just visit the village for an afternoon or evening (nighttime is livelier).

Kid-Friendly Museums and Sites

You could argue that all of India is a cultural museum for kids used to life in North America, but there are also specific sites and museums that appeal to the younger generation. The **National Rail Museum** in Delhi, for example, has old steam engines parked outside, and a toy train that kids can ride. For those interested in astronomy and observatories, the **Jantar Mantar collections** of outdoor solar instruments, including things like 90-foot-long sundials, in Jaipur and Delhi can be fascinating (the one in Jaipur is the best preserved). A good guide is crucial if you want to understand how these huge stone-and-marble instruments can tell time, track the position of stars, and predict eclipses, all without a single computer—but even the small

children will have fun climbing around these outdoor "sculptures." **Parks and beaches** are almost always good places to take children, and Kerala's beaches are legendary. In Mumbai you can escape the city congestion at the Hanging Gardens, a park in Malabar Hill overlooking the South Mumbai skyline and Arabian Sea, or head to Chowpatty or Juhu Beach—but don't go in the water.

Festivals

India's festivals are especially fun for younger audiences. From the kite-flying festival of **Makar Sankranti** to the throwing of colors and water balloons during **Holi** to the elaborate parade-and-float-driven **Ganesh Chaturthi in Mumbai,** participating in and viewing these festivals can be cultural immersion for kids without their even knowing it. They'll almost certainly come home with amazing stories to tell their friends.

Kids and Indian Food

Indian food might be different, but it doesn't have to be scary. If your kids are giving it a try for the first time, order less spicy versions and ask your waiter for suggestions that might appeal to picky eaters. In Mumbai, **Cream Centre** along Marine Drive is a classic crowd pleaser that caters to little clients, too. Dishes served here include the famed *chole bathure,* curried chickpeas (ask for the mild version) with a giant puffed bread—what child can resist a piece of bread larger than his or her own head? And for those times when you or your kids want some good old American comfort food, there are usually decent places to find the familiar: Italian restaurants serving pasta and pizza, for instance, are plentiful in tourist destinations.

INDIA LODGING PRIMER

Although Western travelers might expect to get more bang for their buck when it comes to lodgings in India, accommodations and facilities vary widely throughout the country. Luxury hotels may seem especially costly for this part of the world, but the facilities and service are nothing short of the royal treatment in most cases. At the same time, mid-tier hotels aren't always as consistent in service or facilities when compared with their Western counterparts, so adjusting your expectations before you arrive will make for a smoother stay. Prices peak sharply during the November to March high season—and even more so during the Christmas to New Year's week—so it's best to book in advance.

The following is an overview of the different types of lodging options you can expect to find in India. As anywhere else, to avoid any confusion on the ground, make sure to confirm your reservations and arrive as early as possible to check in, or let them know you'll be getting in late.

The lodgings we list in this book are ones we consider the best in their price range. Mid-range hotels will often have only a shower rather than a bathtub. Keep in mind that rates across the board have dipped a great deal from their highs earlier in the decade, so don't be afraid to bargain.

Luxury Hotels

The cream-of-the-crop luxury hotels in India often surpass their counterparts in the United States and Europe when it comes to service and general splendor—often in sumptuously converted palaces or *havelis* (mansions), or properties built using traditional architectural styles (like the intricate stonework and turreted balconies at several Rajasthan properties)

and decorated with local artisanal crafts. Although you might feel like you're shelling out quite a bit to stay at a Taj or an Oberoi, the price usually translates to the best location in town, a generous and delicious buffet breakfast, plush beds, marble baths, and wonderful service. Also look for heritage hotel chains like Neemrana, which has lovely properties. You'll see more and more familiar high-end names like Aman Resorts, the Four Seasons, and JW Marriott, but these tend to have a more contemporary look compared with the heritage properties.

Midrange Accommodations

While the mid-tier is where you might expect most properties to fall, India actually suffers from a dearth of mid-range lodgings, though the situation improves with each passing year. Recognizable chains like Marriott, Holiday Inn, Hilton, Sheraton, and Westin do have quite a few properties across the country, but the branding doesn't always guarantee a stay on par with a Holiday Inn in California or a Westin in Washington, DC. Their Indian counterparts might have rooms that look a bit worn, and service can be spottier than you'd expect.

Guesthouses and Budget Lodgings

Small budget lodges, known as guesthouses in India, are plentiful across the country, especially in remote areas or smaller towns. They can vary widely in cleanliness, service, and even safety. Amenities will be limited, not all will have a restaurant or food available on the premises. Although most rooms in guesthouses come with en suite bathrooms, some of the cheaper digs only offer shared facilities.

GREAT ITINERARIES

India is huge, and it would take months, or even years, to do a full-fledged tour of the country. We've narrowed this book down to what we consider the *essential* India, but even still, unless you have a *really* long vacation, you won't have time to see all the highlights. Keep in mind, too, that the best way to appreciate India is not to rush—in fact, the country tends to run in such a fashion that it's next to impossible to rush while you're here.

To further help you make the most of your time, India's Golden Triangle, spanning roughly 240 km (150 miles) on each of its three sides, links Mughal and Rajput sites in Delhi, Jaipur, and Agra. It's the most well-traveled route in India, and for good reason: for many tourists, the sites here *are* India. What you see—the Taj Mahal, the impressive palace-fort and Islamic monuments in Old Delhi, and the timeless Pink City fairy tale that is Jaipur—are some of the most splendid edifices that India has to offer. Although you could visit most of these sights in a week, or even less, try not to make it a hurried affair if you can. Between the heat and the sometimes tricky dealings of getting around, traveling in India is often more exhausting than elsewhere, and an overpacked day rarely makes for a satisfying visit. We've outlined the basics of the Golden Triangle *below*, with some options and add-ons.

THE GOLDEN TRIANGLE, 11 DAYS

Delhi
3–4 days

Fly into Delhi to explore the old and new capitals. Hit the ground running with some light touring on the first day,

perhaps doing some shopping or taking in the lovely, pre-Mughal Lodi Gardens. Over the next two days, visit Old Delhi's major Mughal sites, including the Red Fort, Jama Masjid, and Chandni Chowk, now a hodgepodge market. Also highly worth a visit: the Mughal Humayun's tomb and the imperial buildings of the Raj-era. Pay a visit to the excellent collections at the National Museum as well, but make sure to also save time for just getting acquainted with Delhi weather, crowds, and food—the higher-end restaurants and shops in South Delhi are worth the trip. ⇨ *Delhi, Chapter 3.*

Option: If you prefer, head right out to Agra on your second day, leaving time to explore Delhi a little more afterward.

Jaipur
2–4 days

Set out early for Jaipur (it's about six hours by train or car; the flight is an hour, but factor in airport time). Alternatively, take an extra day and make an overnight stop at the Neemrama Fort Palace, built in the 15th century and now a luxury hotel about midway between Delhi and Jaipur. Once in Jaipur, head out to explore the city's unforgettable bazaars and monuments to see why it's called the Pink City. Set aside a half day to explore the Amber (Amer) Fort and Palace, just north of the city limits. ⇨ *Rajasthan, Chapter 5.* Then head back to Delhi.

Side Trips: If you drive to Jaipur and have the time and desire, add in a few days for a side trip or two. About 160 km (100 miles) south of Jaipur is Ranthambhore National Park, the most likely place in India to see a tiger or other large cat outside of captivity. If you're inclined to explore more of Rajasthan, the "Land of Princes," head farther afield to either Udaipur, where the sprawling City Palace and Lake Palace seem taken from a fairy-tale book, or the "Blue City" of Jodhpur, the site of the magnificent eight-gated Mehrangarh Fort, built in the 15th century.

Option: Skip Jaipur and go straight to Udaipur: there is more than enough in this magical city to keep you occupied for several days, and there are several spectacular side trips to places like the Jain Temple at Ranakpur.

The Taj Mahal (Agra) and Fatehpur Sikri
2–3 days

From Delhi, travel by road or take the train to Agra. If you're driving, make a stop during the two- to three-hour trip to visit the splendid royal remnants of the ancient Mughal capital Fatehpur Sikri (if you take the train to Agra, rent a car and driver and backtrack to Fatehpur Sikri). The fast train takes about three hours, but isn't at the most convenient times. Plan to stay overnight in Agra so you can fully appreciate the Taj Mahal and Agra's other sites, the impressive Agra Fort and the tomb of Etmad-ud-Daulah (the so-called "Baby Taj"). Then make your way back to Delhi. ⇨ *Chapter 4, Side Trips from Delhi.*

■TIP→ **If this is your first time in India, it may seem like a good idea to rent a car and drive it yourself, but it isn't.** India's traffic is fierce and should only be tackled by seasoned drivers familiar with Indian roads and traffic conditions. Hire a car and driver, which costs only a little more than renting a car by itself.

Delhi is one of the most expensive places to stay in India. In the high season, Agra and Jaipur are a close second. These destinations are among the most popular tourist spots in India, so hotels book up quickly. If you have your heart set on a specific hotel, book early. Northern India is also a popular circuit for guided tours. If you like the comfort of a knowledgeable guide and the structure of a set plan, consider a package tour. ⇨ *See the Travel Smart chapter in the back of this book for recommendations.*

Transportation: If getting there is half the fun in your mind, take a train. Although you give up some flexibility with a train, the countryside views are at least partial compensation, as is being able to avoid the loud, manic Indian driving style. If time is limited and you want to have as much freedom as possible with your route, then a car and driver is the better option.

ADD-ONS FROM DELHI: MUMBAI, GOA, AND KERALA

Mumbai
3–4 days

Fly to Mumbai from Delhi. To get your bearings in Mumbai, start with a visit to the city's most recognizable landmark, the Gateway of India (the nearby Taj Mahal Palace and Tower hotel is a close second in fame). Then visit the Prince of Wales Museum, the Crawford Market, and other signature sights of Raj-era Bombay, ending your day with a visit to Chowpatty Beach, where food stalls and amusement rides line a stretch of sand that comes most alive on Saturday. Another thing that should not to be missed is some time for serious shopping in markets and for experiencing Mumbai's restaurants—two areas in which this often flashy city excels. On one morning, head to Elephanta Island, reached by boat from the Gateway of India; the Hindu and Buddhist cave sculptures there are masterful and mysterious. ⇨ *Mumbai, Chapter 6.*

Side Trip: Ajanta and Ellora Caves, 3 days

The Ajanta and Ellora Caves were built over a period of 700 years starting in the 2nd century BC. To get here, you first must go 400 km (250 miles) east of Mumbai to the city of Aurangabad. Plan on spending the good part of a day at each site (for a total of two days) to avoid getting sculpture fatigue. Aurangabad's impressive Daulatabad Fort, nearly a millennium old, is also worth a visit. ⇨ *Mumbai, Chapter 6.*

Transportation Tips: The number of trains making the seven-hour train ride from Mumbai to Aurangabad is limited, so it probably makes the most sense to fly there and back—it's a 45-minute trip each way. The Ajanta Caves can take up to three hours to reach from Aurangabad, and Ellora is about 30 minutes away. To use your time most efficiently, you will probably want to hire a car and driver to take you to the caves, rather than relying on tour buses.

Goa
4 days

If you're craving some beach time and a look at a totally different part of India, head south to the former Portuguese colony of Goa on the Arabian Sea. You can fly from Mumbai, or take the Konkan Railway, a gorgeous 12-hour trip that tracks the coastline and passes over nearly 150 major bridges on its complete route (book ahead for this popular train). In Goa you'll want to spend time eating seafood and sipping Kingfishers at a beach shack, but make sure to set aside time for a day trip to visit Old Goa's monumental 17-century cathedrals as well as the atmospheric Portuguese-influenced streets of Panjim. When you've had your fill of Goa's many charms, either fly or take the train back to Mumbai. ⇨ *Goa, Chapter 7.*

Kerala
4 days

Remote and serene, Kerala is on the southern coast of the Arabian Sea; you can get there by train or fly into Kochi, Trivandrum, or Calicut. Either way, you'll undoubtedly want to experience nature here. Rent a quaint houseboat for three days to just meander through the majestic backwaters that curve through green hills and the rice paddies of small villages—easily accessible via Kollam. A bit farther inland, the Western Ghats contain vast tea and spice plantations as well as beautiful wildlife. If you want to experience Kerala civilization, the old port city of Kochi is an enchanting mix of traditional South Indian culture and influences from the Portuguese, Jews, Syrian Christians, and Muslims who came this way in the past. ⇨ *Kerala, Chapter 8.*

ADD-ONS FROM DELHI: KOLKATA, KHAJURAHO AND VARANASI.

Kolkata
2–3 days

While there are direct overnight trains linking Delhi to Kolkata, the fastest one takes at least 17 hours, and it makes more sense for most people just to fly. When in Kolkata, be sure to take a stroll along Park Street, a colonial era street with excellent restaurants, hotels, and bookshops, and set aside some time to explore the excellent museum housed inside the white marble Victoria Memorial. Other popular attractions include the Mother House, the headquarters of the Missionaries of Charity, which houses a museum and Mother Teresa's tomb, and the Kalighat Kali Temple.

Khajuraho
2 days

Fly to Khajuraho on your way to Varanasi and spend two days absorbing the exuberant, often erotic bas-reliefs that adorn the town's 10th- and 11th-century Hindu temples. The temples at Khajuraho are fascinating, but not easy to get to. If you plan to go, visit on the way to Varanasi; at the time of writing, there are no direct air links between Delhi or Kolkata and Khajuraho. While there are direct flights from Khajuraho to Varanasi, stopovers

are required when traveling the opposite direction. ⇨ *Chapter 4, Side Trips from Delhi.*

Varanasi
2–3 days

Varanasi, on the holy Ganges River, is the most sacred city for Hindus—and it may also be the oldest continuously populated city in the world. You can visit as a side trip from Delhi if you don't have enough time to do a thorough exploration of Uttar Pradesh. If you can, fly to Varanasi—traveling by train or car eats up a lot of time, and the roads in Uttar Pradesh are not the greatest. Spend your first day getting acquainted with the manic pace of the city's Old Town. Then make it an early night so that you can get up before dawn to take an early morning boat ride on the Ganges and witness morning ablutions along the river. After setting aside some time to wander and take in the Old Town's sights, sounds, and (yes) smells, take an auto-rickshaw south to the Bharat Kala Bhavan Museum, a college institution with some superb examples of local sculpture. ⇨ *Chapter 4, Side Trips from Delhi.*

Side Trip: Sarnath, 1 day

After an early breakfast, head to Sarnath, just 11 km (7 miles) north of Varanasi, where the Buddha preached his first sermon. Take an auto-rickshaw or a taxi—you may want to hire the same driver to take you back at the end of the day. Sarnath's Deer Park contains a Buddhist temple, several 5th- and 6th-century monuments, and an outstanding archaeological museum. Have lunch at one of the nearby cafés, then return to Varanasi to see any last-minute sights and get ready for your return to Delhi.

BY HUMP AND BY TRUNK

In some regions, you may have the chance to take forms of transport that are a lot more unusual than a bus or car. Traveling on the back of an elephant, for instance, makes the steep approach to Amber Fort outside of Jaipur a breeze. As for camels, they're a common sight in Rajasthan, usually carrying cargo in the cities, but often transporting people out in the desert.

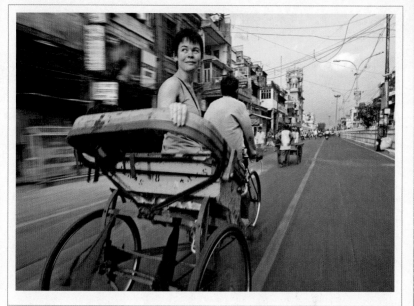

GETTING AROUND INDIA

India is huge country and getting around can be a challenge, so it pays (in time, money, and sanity) to be prepared. Knowing your travel options and the potential for delays will help you get the most out of your trip. With a little planning, getting there can be more than half the fun.

This is a country with a diverse geography and a still-developing infrastructure—which means there are plenty of potholes, lots of aggressive driving, and mysterious plane and train delays. It's important not to try to do too much, or there's a good chance you'll end up frustrated. "Expect the unexpected" are excellent words to live by when you're traveling in India.

If the places you'll be visiting are far apart and you're pressed for time, flying is without question the best option. Trains can be almost as good as flying, especially if you take an overnight train. A car and driver gives you the most freedom, and is often the most comfortable way to go, but not necessarily the fastest since Indian roads are often beset with intense traffic and lots of traffic jams. Buses are typically the worst option. When it comes to travel within a city, taxis and auto-rickshaws are best if you don't have a car and driver.

AIR TRAVEL

The domestic terminal of Chhatrapati Shivaji Airport in Mumbai

INTERCITY TRAVEL

Thanks to domestic carriers like Jet Airways and SpiceJet, flying between cities in India is a practical and relatively affordable option that can save you a lot of time—especially if you have multiple destinations around Rajasthan.

ON TIME?

Flights usually run on or close to schedule, although the fog that descends on Delhi in December or January can bring the city and its airport to a standstill for hours. If you do plan on flying, keep in mind that Indian airports can often be a significant distance from your final destination, and that you'll need to factor in that transfer time.

DELHI'S AIRPORT

Delhi's huge T3 terminal, built in 2010 in part to accommodate tourists for the Commonwealth Games, handles all international flights as well as the domestic flights of Air India, Jet Airways, and Kingfisher. Other domestic flights leave from Terminal 1; there is a shuttle bus between the terminals. In early 2011, the Delhi Airport Metro Express opened operations connecting T3 with the New Delhi Railway station.

MUMBAI'S AIRPORT

Mumbai's airport is north of the city—as in Delhi, travel between the international and domestic terminals requires taking a shuttle. Currently, Mumbai's metro line does not reach the airport, though such a connection is expected to begin operation at some point between 2016 and 2021. Until then, it can take two hours or more to reach South Mumbai during rush hour.

⇨ *For more about transfers into either city from the airport, see the Getting Here and Around sections of the specific chapters. For airline contact info, see the Travel Smart chapter.*

TRAIN TRAVEL

Taking the train

AIR & RAIL ROUTES
PAKISTAN
Chandigarh
Delhi
Ganges R.
Jaisalmer
Jodhpur
Jaipur
Agra
Yamuna R.
Udaipur
Khajuraho
TO →
VARANASI
Ahmedabad
Bhopal
Narmada R.
Gulf of
Khambat
Mumbai
(Bombay)
Godavari R.
Arabian Sea
Goa

TAKE THE TRAIN

A train ride in India remains one of the country's signature events; try to fit at least a short one into your India itinerary. Don't expect your trip to have much to do with the fabled luxury of an Orient Express, though, unless you've booked passage on the opulent Palace on Wheels *(see the next page)*.

PLAN AHEAD

To get the most out of any train ride, plan ahead; otherwise you might end up jammed into a hot compartment with far too many of your fellow passengers and their belongings, or—worse—stranded at a tiny station in the middle of nowhere because of a mix-up. Be aware, too, that train delays are far from uncommon, so pad your schedule, just in case.

Inside Mumbai's train station, Victoria Terminus, also called Chhatrapati Shivaji Terminus

ON THE TRAIN

In a country pretty well obsessed with hierarchies, it may not surprising that there are a full nine classes of train travel. Any class above sleeper is good.

Even first class on an Indian train might seem a bit down-at-the-heels to westerners, but in many ways that's part of the charm. First and foremost, after all, India's trains are a way to get from point A to B, and most of the passengers are Indians rather than tourists. In first class you're likely to find businessmen, politicians, and a smattering of families, perhaps with servants in tow. In the various second classes and the "chair cars" (with individual chairs as opposed to benches) are many more middle-class families. Chair classes, used for relatively short distances, also attract a range of middle-class travelers. The sleeper and unreserved classes have the broadest range and number of people, many of whom cram into narrow seats or just stand.

(top) Outside Victoria Terminus in Mumbai
(bottom) Delhi's Safdarjung train station

TRAIN CLASSES

Inside a second-class train compartment

CLASSES	ABBREVIATION	DESCRIPTION
1st a/c	1A	Your seat is in a lockable air-conditioned compartment with two or four benches that convert to sleeping berths at night. Not the best option for single women travelers, since your fellow travelers are likely to be male. Your compartment will have a small sink and light. Bedding is included.
2nd a/c	2A	Two or four berths that convert to two-tier, bunkbed-like sleepers, but with no lockable compartments. Bedding is included.
3rd a/c	3A	Similar to 2nd a/c, but with six berths in each seating bay (hence the "3," for three tiers). Good for families, but if you're not used to tight quarters, you might get claustrophobic.
3rd a/c economy	3E	This new train class is similar to 3rd a/c, but the berths are along the side of the train and have a little less space. Rare.
1st	FC	No a/c (the windows open instead), but otherwise similar to 1st a/c. Because this class is on its way out, the compartments are usually more dated than those in 1st a/c. Good for relatively short distances when it's not too hot.
A/C executive chair class	EC	Laid out like a standard train in the U.S.: rows of two or three seats on each side.
A/C chair class	CC	Similar in layout to executive chair class but less deluxe.
Sleeper	SL	Similar to 3rd a/c, but with no air-conditioning or reserved seats. Bring your own bedding. Unless you're traveling very light and are feeling adventurous, these cars are probably not for you.
2nd seating	2S	No reservations available. The cars have an open-air plan, with rows of padded or plain wood benches. This class gets crowded—avoid it for any trip longer than a couple of hours.

The toy train to Matheran

TOY TRAINS

The so-called "toy trains" of India, much beloved by tourists, were built to transport goods and overheated members of the Raj to the hill stations—towns up in the hills, to which

An aerial view of the Matheran toy train

members of the British empire would escape when the astonishing heat of summer got to be too much at the lower elevations. Although trucks and buses have made these narrow-gauge trains an anachronism, they remain a charming part of the transportation landscape. The final leg of the train trip to Matheran, a small hill station less than 60 miles east of Mumbai, is via the Matheran Hill Railway, which had its first run in 1907. To reach it, you'll first take a regular train from Mumbai Central (BCT) to Neral Junction (NRL), a 90-minute to two-hour trip. From there, a diesel toy train makes the two-hour trip on the railway six times daily, chugging into the forests and mists beneath Matheran on a two-foot-wide track with hundreds of curves. (*See the Mumbai chapter for more information.*)

Restaurant staff on the Palace on Wheels

LUXURY TRAINS

If you're looking for a luxe rail travel experience, there are several train lines in India that cater to just this desire. The Palace on Wheels travels to the Taj Mahal and other major sights in

Inside the Palace on Wheels

the Golden Triangle, while the Deccan Odyssey has stops in Mumbai, at the Ajanta and Ellora Caves, Goa, and several others destinations. Because these trains are all-inclusive, and because you travel from "port" to "port" while you sleep, it's sort of like being on a high-end cruise ship. Whether this is for you depends on how much the trains' opulent surroundings jibe with what you want from a trip. Among other issues, most meals are on the train and you may find yourself wishing that you could just find your own places to eat from time to time. In addition, luxury trains aren't immune from delays—and a hitch can trim off some time from sightseeing. Still, the comfort of such tours is hard to beat, and if money is no object, they're a tempting option. (*See the Rajasthan and Travel Smart chapters for more information.*)

CARS AND DRIVERS

Auto-rickshaws in Delhi

DRIVING ROUTES

Pamhagen · Churu · Delhi
Bikaner · Jhunjhunu
THAR DESERT · Fatehpur · Alwar
Nagaur · Sikar · Bharatpur
Jaisalmer · Khimsar · NH8 · NH11 · Agra
Osian · Ajmer · Jaipur
PAKISTAN · Jodhpur · Beawar
Pali · Bhilwara
Udaipur · Chittaurgarh

A CAR WITH A DRIVER

Even if there were a good supply of cars for rent in India, it wouldn't be a good idea to rent one and drive on your own. The traffic here often proceeds at a manic pace, it's not uncommon for drivers to disregard lanes markers (even the ones that separate different directions of travel), and sharing the road with trucks, scooters, auto-rickshaws, camels, bullocks, horses, and the occasional elephant is not something that anyone should try when they're also trying to have a vacation. Indeed, even being a passenger in a car can be disconcerting.

Instead, car rentals in India come with drivers, who are generally knowledgable and friendly and who can help make a day of sightseeing a true pleasure rather than the tiring slog it might otherwise be. In general, the drivers they choose will speak at least some English (make sure to ask)—in some cases, you may even want to ask your

Traffic in Mumbai

actual guide in addition to your driver, for any portion of your trip, you can arrange this at your destination or in advance through a tour operator (*see specific chapters for advice on this*). It's worth remembering that guides as well as drivers may sometimes have a financial interest in taking you to visit certain shops, restaurants, and other establishments.

WHAT KIND OF CAR?

The Ambassador, the classic Indian family car, is built like a tank to handle Indian road bumps and potholes; its design hasn't changed much since it was first built in 1958. Rent one if you can, at least for short trips—they are on their way out. Other more modern options, such as a Toyota Qualis or Innova or a Mahindra Scorpio, are roomier but lack the distinction of an "Amby."

driver (nicely, of course) to stop talking so much.

PRACTICALITIES

If your plans are likely to involve having a car and driver for more than half a day, it's a good idea to reserve ahead of time through a travel agent or tour company. The more information you have about your itinerary, the better a company can estimate the total fees. For long trips in most parts of the country air-conditioning is just about essential. In general, when you hire, a fee for the driver's meals and lodging is included in the price, as is gasoline. (Few drivers will drive at night and, given the perilous condition of the roads and the often-heavy truck traffic, you should steer clear of night travel by car.)

DRIVER VS. GUIDE

To a certain extent your driver might also act as a guide—he won't get out of the car at each stop and tell you interesting facts (although he might), but he can often suggest places to visit, or where to eat. If you want an

DHABAS: YOUR FRIEND ON THE ROAD

Dhabas are roadside truck stops that are especially prevalent in the Punjab regions of Pakistan and India, and if you're doing much driving in India, it's likely that you'll stop at one, if only to use the facilities and fill up on gas. If you're ready for a *tiffin* (snack), keep in mind that it's always best to eat at a dhaba that's doing lots of business. And since you're likely to be at least several hours from your hotel when you see one, it pays to be a little conservative about what you eat. If the place seems a little less than sanitary, there's nothing wrong with opting for some plain naan or a bag of wrapped potato chips and a soft drink rather than an order of tandoori chicken or saag paneer, tempting though the latter two may be. Dhabas have had such an influence on Indian cuisine that even upscale restaurants mimic their style and rich, rough-and-ready cuisine. These days you'll find dhabas popping up far from the dusty, busy highways that are their natural home.

TAXIS, AUTO-RICKSHAWS, AND BUSES

(left) A line of Ambassadors (right) A bus in front of the Hawa Mahal in Jaipur

TAXIS

For shorter trips within a city, taxis are available at airports, luxury hotels, and similar destinations, but they can't always be easily located if you're just out and about. One exception is in Mumbai: because auto-rickshaws are only allowed in the suburbs, taxis are much more common than they are in other cities. Taxis generally have meters, but that doesn't necessarily mean that the driver will use them: make sure to agree on a price if you can't reach agreement on using the meter.

AUTO-RICKSHAWS

Along with motor scooters, the iconic three-wheeled, yellow-and-black or yellow-and-green auto-rickshaws of India are the way a large proportion of the country gets from point A to B within cities and towns. Running on compressed gas or gasoline, their small engines can't handle steep hills or long distances, and their sides, open to the dust and fumes of the street, can be hard to take for too long. That said, their maneuverability in traffic means they're invaluable for short trips.

What you'll pay to zip along depends on your location, the time of day, and, often, your bargaining skills. In some places, auto-rickshaw drivers are fairly careful about using the meter, but it's much more common for them to quote a set fare instead. Make sure to work out a price before you get into a rickshaw—if you have the chance, ask a local to tell you how much a particular trip should cost. It's the rare ride that should cost more than 100 rupees, and most short trips are much less.

FINDING YOUR DESTINATION

Many drivers of auto-rickshaws, taxis, and hired cars know the city like the back of their hand, but it's also possible that your driver may have arrived in the big city just a few weeks before you showed up. To avoid problems, it's good to know the name of the neighborhood where you're headed, and preferably a nearby landmark, too, as well as the street address, which may not be used that often (phone numbers are also handy, since just about every driver will have a cell phone). You can probably assume that most drivers will know major hotels and tourist attractions, but for anything else, make sure that your address comes with a little context.

BUS TRAVEL

Buses are not the most comfortable option, but they do generally make good time, and their large number of departures is also handy.

TRAVEL TIMES

	DISTANCE	BY AIR	BY TRAIN
Delhi to Agra	203 km (126 mi)	1 hour	2.5 to 4.5 hours
Delhi to Jaipur	258 km (160 mi)	45 minutes	4.5 to 6 hours
Delhi to Mumbai	1,407 km (874 mi)	2 hours	16 to 22 hours
Delhi to Goa	1,912 km (1,188 mi)	2 hours	35 hours
Delhi to Varanasi	808 km (502 mi)	1.25 hours	9 to 13 hours
Delhi to Udaipur	663 km (412 mi)	1.25 hours	12 hours
Jaipur to Jaisalmer	614 km (382 mi)	no service	12 hours
Jaipur to Jodhpur	332 km (206 mi)	4.5 hours (indirect)	5.5 to 12 hours
Jodhpur to Jaisalmer	285 km (177 mi)	no service	5.5 to 7 hours
Mumbai to Jodhpur	966 km (600 mi)	about 2 hours	17 to 20 hours
Mumbai to Goa	540 km (336 mi)	1 hour	7.52 to 12 hours
Mumbai to Aurangabad	388 km (241 mi)	45 minutes	6.5 to 7 hours
Delhi to Aurangabad	1,209 km (751 mi)	3.5 hours	about 30 hours
Varanasi to Goa	1,803 km (1,290 mi)	6 hours	39 hours
Jaipur to Udaipur	405 km (251 mi)	1 hour	8 to 10 hours

HONK HONK!

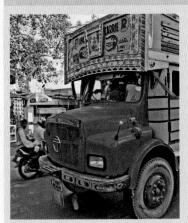

A colorful truck in Agra

Whether you're stuck in traffic in South Mumbai or barreling down the NH-8 highway to Jaipur, honking is always part of the ambient music accompanying a drive in India. But why? In India, it's standard practice to honk as you prepare to pass, to let people know what you're doing so that, hopefully, they'll cede more of the road to you (as you'll find out, lane designations are often completely disregarded). Other drivers honk to alert other drivers of their presence—and their impatience. Because a virile horn is such an important part of a car or truck, it's common for drivers to have after-market extra-loud versions installed.

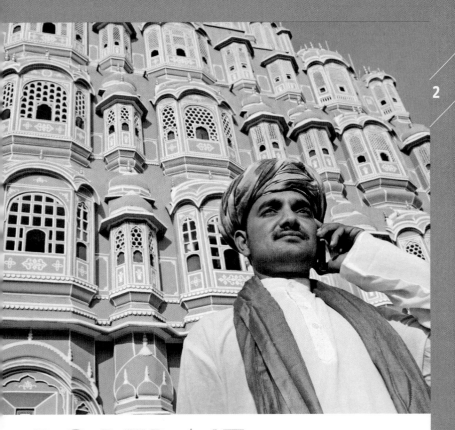

PORTRAIT
OF INDIA

Updated by
Margot Bigg

Like the fragrance from the ubiquitous flower garlands, India is difficult to describe in exact terms. We can't completely prepare you for what you'll find, so instead, we will attempt to give a sense of the country through its different elements. From there, it's yours to experience.

From the desert of Rajasthan to the palm-fringed beaches of Goa, India is a study in contrasts. So how does the casual visitor get beyond the extremes of the sparkle of tourism's "Incredible India" and the squalor of the country's in-your-face poverty? A good place to start is with the subcontinent's lively **History,** marked by periods of unification and fragmentation, and sparked by associations with foreign traders and invaders—from the Portuguese and the English to Turkic and Mongol tribes. Indeed, the six decades or so of India as a modern nation is short compared to the region's past. An understanding of history will also give context to the morals and mores of **Modern Indian Society.**

Variety and contradiction are central themes in India. From the austerity of some types of vegetarianism to the excesses of spice-infused meats found in Indian **Cuisine,** and from the ascetic philosophies to extravagant rituals in its **Religions,** India is probably defined better by its deviations than by its norms. This makes for a densely populated portrait: from the panoply of **Hindu Gods and Goddesses** to the vibrant forms of **Indian Dance, Music, and the Performing Arts** and the packed calendar of **Holidays and Festivals**—every inch of India is alive with kaleidoscopic sight, sound, and color. Even in matters of economic consumption, contradiction is king, and **Shopping** options range from crafts and kitschy cultural artifacts to exquisite designer ware, all found at megamalls, high-end boutiques, traditional bazaars, and street-side stalls.

We've tried to distill India's head-spinning inconsistencies and rich traditions into the thematic pages that follow, starting points for an understanding of India, with an emphasis on the regions covered in this book. This background will help explain the nuances of even the most packaged of tours and—because the unexpected is inevitable in India—help you navigate situations that weren't part of your itinerary.

MODERN INDIAN SOCIETY

At once a stable society, comfortably couched in time-worn traditions, and a chaotic crucible of new ideas, modern India is distinguished by diversity and united by patriotism.

(top left) An information technology center outside of Delhi; (top right) A traditional Indian wedding; (bottom right) Dhobi ghat in Mumbai, where thousands of workers wash clothes by hand

There are countless issues that divide the country, including socioeconomic factors such as caste, class, and access to basic needs and education; regional variations like the dozens of official languages and various different cuisines; religious differences that divide communities and often result in distinct neighborhoods; and the deep gender inequality that transcends even the division between urban and rural populations. And yet many factors unite India. Even in terms of language, English and Hindi are common to most of urbanized India, at least at a basic level. And although major urban areas have been joined by roads (no matter the quality of these roads), the democratizing power of the Indian rail system is not to be underestimated. A shared history of colonialism, active media, a sprawling government bureaucracy, and an engaged political body help create a relatively cohesive Indian society. And, of course, there is the fact that Indian people are, by and large, incredibly warm and welcoming.

ASTROLOGY

Modern India may be known for technology, but this doesn't negate the prevalence of tradition. Many Indians won't make decisions about business, love, or family without consulting the stars. Marriages, if not made in heaven, should at least be consecrated on an auspicious date—on days deemed extra-auspicious for weddings, huge numbers of concurrent ceremonies occur.

URBAN VERSUS RURAL SOCIETY

Possibly the biggest difference in India is one that tourists rarely experience: the division between rural and urban life. India's cities are fueled by labor and resources from India's villages—the majority of the country's population still subsists on an agrarian lifestyle and economy—yet city and small-town life is worlds apart from the fields and dirt roads of the rest of India. While in the cities, access to electricity is frustrated by unannounced power outages, only about half of rural Indian households have any access to power at all. Education and potable water are often elusive commodities outside of India's cities and towns. Idyllic glimpses of rural life are visible from the road or train—yellow-blossomed mustard fields in north India, coconut plantations along the coast, tractors loaded impossibly high with bales of cotton or other goods—but the realities of rural life are something a traveler will rarely get the chance to see. Interestingly, socioeconomic divisions of caste or occupation—though certainly still present—are sometimes less stark in rural areas than in urban ones.

RICH, MIDDLE CLASS, POOR

India's cities are microcosms and melting pots. A small, privileged elite drives (or is chauffeured) between the air-conditioned high-rises of south Mumbai, the gated colonies of south Delhi, the exclusive resorts of Goa, and similar

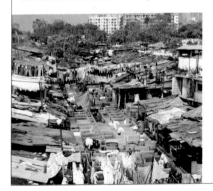

areas. The denizens of this privileged group frequent five-star restaurants, luxury boutiques, and private clubs. But this is just a tiny segment of society.

A large and rapidly growing middle class fuels the urban economy, powering the country's information-technology hubs. More professionalized and better educated than their parents, members of the urban middle class also feed a mushrooming consumer-goods-and-services sector. Spending money is proof of success, and lavish weddings replete with yards of brocade, miles of fairy lights, kilos of gold jewelry, and bushels of fresh-cut flowers are not uncommon. Coffee shops and fast-food outlets cater to and are staffed by members of the upwardly mobile society.

In stark contrast to the rich and the middle-class, India's populated areas are also home to millions of urban poor—from migrants who set up house in tarpaulin shelters while employed in construction and infrastructure projects to low-income families living in slum colonies with open sewers. Many urban migrants live a double life—catering to the wealthy and middle class so they can send money to their families back in their home villages. Besides domestic help, low-income jobs include a wide range of workers—including porters, cycle-rickshaw drivers, and salesmen of cheap goods.

Lunch-wallahs transporting tiffin boxes

GENDER ROLES

Across all walks of life, women and men lead very different, often divergent, lives. While women work the fields and provide manual labor on construction sites right alongside men, these are roles born out of economic necessity. Middle-class and even elite women have less occasion to work outside of the home; although wealthier families may educate daughters as much as sons, the focus for women is squarely on marriage and raising children. Cutting across economic distinctions is a preference for boys—in some states female infanticide is still a serious problem, and it is illegal for doctors to disclose the sex of fetuses. Some villages have such a shortage of marriageable women that they have had to bring in brides from other regions of India—a practice that rubs against the older tradition of marrying within one's caste and culture.

MARRIAGE

Arranged marriages take place all across Indian society. Although the government prohibits child marriage, betrothals and weddings at a very young age

still do take place in remote areas. These days, however, the culture of dating also thrives in India's big cities. Couples can be seen everywhere in Delhi and Mumbai, flaunting their sexual freedom on the dance floors of clubs, sharing coffee and moony looks across a café table, or surreptitiously canoodling under a tree in a public park—often the most convenient meeting ground for poorer youngsters from more conservative families. Online dating is less of a casual affair than in the west, and dating sites are used predominately by middle-class families looking to set up marriages.

CASTE

Marriage classifieds (listings of eligible men and women, living in India or abroad, searchable by caste, religion, profession, and education, etc.) are only one of the many societal phenomena in which caste figures prominently. Caste in India can be as innocuous as a shared community history, signified by a particular last name, or as insidious as a derogatory slur. Although technically abolished, in practical terms caste identity still plays an important role in modern Indian society, particularly in politics. There is still raging debate—akin to but far more polarizing than the American debate over affirmative action—over quotas for historically disadvantaged castes in government jobs and school admissions.

POLITICS

India's parliamentary democracy is rife with corruption and strange liaisons, and the average Indian is either actively cynical or openly engaged with politics—and sometimes both. A multiparty system means that there are significant blocs of special-interest parties besides the dominant Congress Party and BJP (Bharatiya Janata Party). Unfortunately, some parties mine religion to garner support, which can turn whole communities against each other.

RELIGION

Religion plays a large part in modern Indian society, and worship is an important component: people often pray regularly in temples, mosques, gurdwaras, and churches, but may also have family shrines at home, composed of icons, portraits, and statues. Ritual fasting is a regular occurrence in many religions, whether weekly for some very pious Hindus or yearly during Ramadan for devout Muslims. Religious conventions can often bleed into cultural ones, influencing diet, neighborhood, occupation, and clothing choice.

CLOTHING

Clothing in modern Indian society is a signifier of many things—gender, region, wealth, profession, and, often, religion. In general, men usually wear trousers or jeans with collared shirts or T-shirts. In south India and in rural areas, native forms of dress—long pieces of cloth called *lungis* or *dhotis*—are wrapped around the waist and legs, but loose-fitting pajama-type outfits are more common. These are topped with an undershirt, called a *banyan*, and perhaps a tunic or kurta. Headgear can also be an indicator of religion or region. Rajasthani men are known for their bright, coiled turbans (and grandiose mustaches), Sikh men sweep their long hair into streamlined turbans, and Muslim men usually wear skull caps when praying. Poorer or rural women of all religions tend to cover their heads with thin scarves, and urban Muslim women may keep their heads covered and wear body-covering robes as well. Traditional wear for women includes the more typically north Indian tunic or shirt, called a kurta or *kameez*. This is paired with loose pants, or *salwar*, gathered at the ankle or tighter *churidar*, long leggings bunched up at the ankle. Skirts (*lehengas*) with blouses (*cholis*) are also popular, particularly as wedding wear. Saris, yards of cloth that can be tied many different ways around a petticoat and blouse, are worn all over India and come in many regionally and seasonally specific textiles and patterns.

A traditional family in a small village in Rajasthan

HISTORY YOU CAN SEE

India's history is marked by periods of cultural and economic exchange and lively empire building. Among the obvious results are the ruins of ancient planned cities and the chaos of modern India's skyrocketing growth.

(top left) Rashtrapati Bhavan, in Delhi, where the president lives; (top right) A carving at Khajuraho; (bottom right) Stone chariot shrine at Hampi

Blessed with an abundance of natural resources, geographical diversity, and many access points along its coasts, India has historically been an attractive place for settlers and conquerors. Part of the reason for the subcontinent's continued diversity of culture and people is that residents have always been influenced by different forces at each of the area's different boundaries, which themselves have been rather fluid over the centuries. At various points, Indian empires have been some of the richest and most cultured in the world. Though its history is marked by cycles of destruction and construction, and despite a tendency to neglect all things old, India's past is very much alive in fabulous myths, recorded documents, and phenomenal physical artifacts and archaeological sites.

AGES OF ARCHITECTURE

Mughal architecture is a mélange of influences—vaulted spaces recalling Central Asian campaign tents, Persian domes topped with Hindu lotus finials, and Rajput-style pavilions with umbrella-like overhangs. The British adopted what they saw, adding Gothic and art deco touches to create the Indo-Saracenic style of the Victoria Terminus and the Rashtrapati Bhavan.

PREHISTORY

The subcontinent's oldest significant archaeological finds are from the planned cities of the Indus Valley Civilization, which peaked in western India, Pakistan, and points north in the period around 2600–1800 BC. Delhi's **National Museum** has a large collection of artifacts (pottery, toys, copper tools) from this era. Around 1500 BC, Indo-Europeans from Central Asia began to migrate to the region; their Indo-Aryan language was likely influenced by the subcontinent's indigenous Dravidian dialects to form Sanskrit. This gave rise to the Vedic Iron Age, characterized by the oral composition of Sanskrit texts—the underpinnings of Hinduism. Urban centers such as Kashi (modern-day **Varanasi**, the oldest continuously inhabited city in the world) emerged, and India began to split off into various monarchies and republics.

ANCIENT EMPIRES

Succeeding a handful of ancient kingdoms and forays by Macedonian conqueror Alexander the Great, the Hindu Maurya Empire (India's first) was founded in 321 BC. At its peak, under the Buddhist convert Emperor Ashoka, the kingdom encompassed most of the subcontinent. Ashoka built Buddhist shrines and temples at **Sarnath** (where the Buddha preached his first sermon) and at Sanchi. He also furthered the religion through edicts, often inscribed on

pillars. The **Ashokan pillar at Sarnath**, with four lions at the top, later provided the inspiration for modern India's state emblem.

Farther south lay the Dravidian kingdoms of the Cholas, Cheras, and Pandyas. These eventually gave way to other dynasties, while the decline of the Maurya Empire in the north led to smaller kingdoms with ever-shifting boundaries and incursions from the northwest. Most of the north was again united by the Gupta Empire during India's "Golden Age" from the 4th to 6th centuries. Under the tolerant administration of the Guptas, the arts and sciences flourished: the concept of zero, the heliocentric model, and the game of chess are all said to have been invented during this period. Meanwhile, the grandeur of the Vijayanagar Empire in the south, which was strong until the 17th century, is evident in the ruins at Hampi. The rest of India was ruled by other "Middle Kingdoms," like the Vakatakas in central India, who created the Buddhist cave paintings at Ajanta. By the 8th century, martial Rajput clans were a dominant ruling force in north India. Rajput factions built Gwalior's clifftop fort and **Khajuraho**'s erotically embellished temples; their descendents would go on to build forts and palaces in **Jaipur, Udaipur, Jaisalmer,** and other centers of power in **Rajasthan.**

Humayun's tomb, Delhi;.

MUSLIM RULERS

India's early Islamic states were several Turkic and Afghan territories, collectively called the Delhi Sultanate. The first, the Mamluk (Slave) Dynasty, was founded by Qutb-ud-din Aibak in the early 13th century. A slave-soldier whose leader had made incursions into north India, Aibak and his successors built Delhi's **Qutub Minar**. Next, the Turkic-Afghan Khilji rulers took over, expanding their territory west from the Ganges River and building Delhi's **Siri Fort**. Around the same time, the breakaway Bahmani Sultanate, which eventually fragmented into smaller kingdoms, carved out parts of the south's Vijayanagara Empire. In 1321, the Tughlaqs sultans came to power, ruling from Tughlaqabad (now in Delhi). Their rule was weakened in 1398, when Timur (Timurlane), a descendent of Genghis Khan, sacked the city. The Sayyid Dynasty ruled briefly, followed by the Afghan Lodhi sultans, some of whom are buried in the tombs in Delhi's **Lodhi Gardens**.

Relative stability came to north India with the first Mughal Emperor, Babur, who hailed from Central Asia and had Persian, Turkic, and Mongol ancestry. He established his rule in 1526, having defeated the Lodis and neighboring Rajputs. Babur's son was **Humayun**, whose **tomb** in Delhi is an example of the mixing of Islamic and Hindu cultures under the Mughals; it's considered a precursor to the Taj Mahal. Humayun's son, Akbar, reigned for half a century, starting in 1556. Based in **Agra** and nearby **Fatehpur Sikri**, Akbar expanded and consolidated Mughal power through marriage, conquest, and feudal ties. Greatly influenced by Sufi saints, Akbar was curious about and tolerant of other religions. The syncretic Mughal arts and architecture blossomed under his grandson, Shah Jahan, who built his city, **Shahjahanabad (Old Delhi)**, including the **Lal Qila (Red Fort)** and the **Jama Masjid**, as well as **Agra Fort** and, of course, the **Taj Mahal**.

COLONIALISM

Following the expansionist policies of the puritanical Emperor Aurangzeb (1658–1707), Mughal power was compromised by war, especially against the strong Maratha Empire, which had its center in Raigad, south of Mumbai.

Meanwhile, Queen Elizabeth I chartered the British East India Company, arguably the world's first corporation, in 1600. Competing with the Dutch, Portuguese, and French for mercantile control, the British East India Company opened trading posts and spread out, building India's **railroads**, from its **forts** in Madras, Calcutta, and Bombay (now Chennai, Kolkata, and Mumbai). The company steadily gained control over the subcontinent by pitting princely states against each other, leveraging economic power, installing governing and educational institutions, and through outright battle. In 1857, the company's Indian troops revolted. Variously called the Sepoy Mutiny or the First War of Independence, the rebellion's ripple effect gave the British government an excuse to clamp down. Raj-era architecture persists in **Delhi**, especially in the **India Gate** area. South Mumbai, too, is littered with Raj reminders; must-sees are the **Prince of Wales Museum** and **Crawford Market**.

INDEPENDENCE AND STATEHOOD

In 1947, after nearly a century of British Raj, India gained independence in the aftermath of World War II. Leading the push for independence through nonviolent resistance was Mohandas K. Gandhi, known as Mahatma (Great Soul). Gandhi and other leaders are honored at museums and memorials across the country, including Delhi's **National Gandhi Museum**, the **Gandhi Smriti** (where he was assassinated), and the **Nehru Memorial Museum**.

Independence came at a price, however. Before their soldiers sailed out from Mumbai's **Gateway of India**, the British partitioned the country, carving out West and East Pakistan (the latter now Bangladesh) as Muslim nations. The violence of Partition (the largest human migration in history, with a population exchange of millions), an early India-Pakistan war, and the problem of incorporating hundreds of princely states were huge challenges. The first prime minister, Jawaharlal Nehru, set about building a socialist nation—creating infrastructure, universities, and nationalized industries, and taking an active part in the fledgling Non-aligned Movement. In its first few decades, India also saw an agricultural revolution, war with China over disputed territory, and more conflicts with Pakistan. In the 1990s, economic reforms and the privatization of government-run corporations led to a booming economy and increased participation in global trade. Although its economy is still largely agrarian, India has become an offshore provider of skilled services with a large middle class, evident in the proliferation of call centers and glittering malls.

Photo of Jawaharlal Nehru, on the left, with Mahatma Gandhi, on the right

RELIGIONS OF INDIA

India may be a secular country constitutionally, but religion has a central and vital place in the daily lives of most of its citizens.

(top left) An illustration from the Ramayana; (top right) At a Hindu ceremony; (bottom right) Muslim woman praying at Jama Masjid

To just say that India is 80% Hindu oversimplifies the country's complex web of histories, identities, and institutions, many of which were codified in modern terms as "religions" only in the last few centuries. Leaving aside the fact that the population is more than 13% Muslim, with significant Christian, Sikh, and other minorities, even the majority Hindu community is extremely diverse. Regional identities often cut deeper than religion (thus some Kashmiri Hindus eat meat while many Hindus in Gujarat will not). On top of that, each of India's religions encompass age-old traditions that have survived modernity, new-age movements that focus on spirituality, and politically driven ideologies that justify themselves through mythology. But despite the fact that there are, occasionally, the kind of ugly conflicts that flare up in any pluralistic society, for the most part India is a place where you will find an amazing, often touching, degree of compassion—tolerance that extends to curiosity, and secularism that is expressed as humanity.

JUDAISM

The Jews have a long history in India, starting with the Cochin Jews arriving in Kerala around 500 BC. The Bene Israel came a few centuries later, followed by Middle Eastern and Central Asian Jews. More recently, the Bnei Menashe claimed to be a lost tribe of Israel and were recognized by Israeli rabbis. Some Ben Ephraim Jews, who were converted to Christianity in the 1800s, decided to re-embrace Judaism in the 1980s.

2

HINDUISM

About 80% of India's population is Hindu. The world's third-largest religion, Hinduism is also often regarded as the oldest, with roots that stretch back 5,000 years. It may also be the most varied, as this millennia-old tradition is actually an amalgam of texts, schools, civilizations, and beliefs with a host of leaders and no single founder. Though Hindus generally believe in reincarnation, divinity itself may be multiple or monistic, and practice may involve *dharma* (moral duty), ascetic rigor (as in yoga), devotion through prayer, and many other forms of expression. Modern Hinduism draws from four major Vedic "texts"—Sanskrit ritual verses that were recorded orally beginning with the Iron Age Indus Valley civilization and later written down—as well as corollary philosophical and mystical discourses, treatises on the arts, and the epic poems the *Mahabharata* and the *Ramayana*.

Hinduism today is just as multifaceted as its history. Visitors to India may witness or participate in many aspects of observance including ritual ceremonies, some with fire, ghee, milk, and offerings of flowers and sweets; temple worship, with offerings to deities represented by *murthis* (statues); or physical practices: ascetics who deny material comfort as an expression of devotion, yogis who push their bodies to the physical limit

in order to approach the divine, and ayurvedic doctors who prescribe herbal remedies and offer nutritional advice.

ISLAM

The country's largest minority, India's Muslim population is second only to Indonesia's in numbers. As with Hinduism, Islam in India also encompasses many different schools and practices. Although India's earliest encounter with Islam was through Arab traders along the southwest coast, the religion's first real movement was through the north and west of the subcontinent in the 8th century, and it expanded from the 12th century onward, first under the Delhi Sultanate and then the Mughal Empire. Besides the strength of the Mughal seat of power around Delhi, Muslim communities grew around Islamic rulers around the country.

Like Muslims everywhere, Indian Muslims follow the Koran as the word of Allah revealed to Mohammad in the 7th century. Most Muslims in India belong to the majority Sunni sect, but there are significant portions of Shi'a Muslims as well, who believe in the importance of the Imams and of Mohammad's nephew, Ali. The spread of Islam in India also owes a great deal to mystical Sufi sects, whose founders created centers of learning, music, and charity.

Se (Cathedral), in Old Goa

CHRISTIANITY

India's third-largest religion (about 2% of the population), Christianity is most visible in south and southwest India and in the northeastern states. The earliest whispers of Christianity in India are accounts of the arrival of ("Doubting") Thomas the Apostle in Kerala in the 1st century and the establishment of Syrian Christian churches, which likely grew out of extant Indian Jewish communities and populations of Syrian immigrants. Later, European missionaries (like St. Francis Xavier, a Portuguese Jesuit) arrived to proselytize. Most Indian Christians follow Catholic or Orthodox practices, but some Protestant churches were also established.

SIKHISM

Sikhism grew from the teachings of its founder, Guru Nanak Dev, in the early 1500s. Nanak, a Hindu, broke from that religion's rituals and began to preach a monotheistic faith based on meditation and charity. Nine more *gurus,* or teachers, followed in his footsteps, consolidating and spreading the religion over the next few centuries.

Partially as a response to persecution under the later Mughals, Sikhism also acquired a martial flavor, and followers combined elements of both the soldier and the saint. The 11th guru and the spiritual authority for modern Sikhs is the *Guru Granth Sahib Ji*, a sacred text composed of the teachings of previous gurus and other Hindu and Muslim saints. With a majority of its population in Delhi and the northwestern state of Punjab (the Golden Temple in Amritsar is the most important holy site), the Sikh community was directly affected by the violence of India's Partition, as well as suffering later injustices under the Indira Gandhi administration in 1984.

Often identifiable by their uncut hair (which the men tie up under turbans), practicing Sikhs also engage in the singing and chanting of passages of scripture (this can continue over days) and the serving of free daily meals at *gurdwaras* (temples).

BUDDHISM

Although Siddhartha Gautama attained Buddhahood through meditation and became the Buddha in 500 BC in what is now the Indian state of Bihar, India is home to a surprisingly low percentage of the world's Buddhists. In spite of a relatively low number of adherents, Buddhism has had a profound impact on Indian society. With its focus on moderation and individual duty over divisions of caste or divinity, Buddhism peaked in India with the conversion of the Maurya emperor Ashoka around 260 BC. The following centuries saw Buddhist rituals and institutions taking root outside of India, but within the country it was largely subsumed by other systems of faith. Today Buddhists in India include monks (mostly living along India's border with Tibet), low-caste Hindus who converted in large numbers over the last century to improve their social situation, and Tibetan refugees—including the Dalai Lama and the Tibetan government-in-exile in Dharamshala.

JAINISM

While Jainism appears in practice to be a more stringently ascetic, fiercely nonviolent cousin of Buddhism, the religion has most likely existed as a complement to and influence on Hinduism for thousands of years. Jains believe in reincarnation and do not believe in an all-powerful creator. However, Jains do follow 24 *tirthankaras* (teachers), the last of whom, Mahavir, was a contemporary of the Buddha. Jain temples house idols of these *tirthankaras*; these temples are also where you might see devout Jain monks or nuns who wear white and cover their mouths to avoid inadvertently swallowing and killing insects and microbes. Jain sects vary in degrees of asceticism (some even eschew clothing), but strict Jains do not eat meat, garlic, or onions. Jain practices have been important to India's cultural identity, and while they represent just a small portion of the population, Jains are highly influential in political and economic spheres.

BAHÁ'Í FAITH

With the world's largest number of followers living in India, and the landmark House of Worship (Lotus Temple) in Delhi, the syncretic Bahá'í Faith is a significant part of India's spiritual landscape. Founded in Persia in 1863, this faith seeks to unite the world's major religions and claims that Krishna, the Buddha, Abraham, Jesus, Mohammad, the Báb (a 19th-century holy man), and the religion's founder Bahá'u'llah were all divine messengers.

ZOROASTRIANISM

Though Zoroastrianism was once a major monotheistic world religion (founded in Persia by the prophet Zarathustra around 1200 BC), India now has the world's largest contingent of its followers, known as Parsis, a small but well-educated and influential group of Persians who settled in medieval western India. Though many have moved on, Mumbai has a sizeable group, including some prominent industrialists. Mumbai is also home to the Irani community—19th- and 20th-century immigrants who fled persecution in Iran.

Devotees inside Sis Ganj Gurdwara, a Sikh temple

HOLIDAYS AND FESTIVALS OF INDIA

With silk-garbed deities paraded through the streets, and special foods, dancing, and the ritual gifting of everything from saucepans to Swarovski, festivals and holidays bring together the most excessive and ascetic aspects of Indian culture.

(top left) At a Holi festival; (top right) An elaborate tableau for Durga Puja; (bottom right) Republic Day Parade

Holidays in India range from religious days of reflection to patriotic celebrations of nationalism, and festivals can mark time-honored trade fairs or harvest celebrations. Because this is a country of so many regions and religions—with different harvest seasons and different calendars based on the sun, the moon, or both—there are numerous new year's celebrations (sometimes overlapping), different commemorative days for religious or local founders, and any number of minor holidays. There's almost always something going on, and it's worth timing your visit to coincide with a festival. Seeing the elaborate tableaux and dancing; witnessing the masses of people at temples, mosques, and churches; and joining the crowds eating at specially built food stalls is a highlight of many visitors' trips to India.

MAHA NAVRATI

Literally translated as "nine nights," this celebration, which takes place in October and November, marks the beginning of winter. It generally includes worshipping Shakti, the divine Hindu mother goddess. Bengalis honor Shakti in Durga Puja by creating thematic pandals or installations—three-dimensional representations that include a statue of Durga—which are then submerged in the river.

2

MAKAR SANKRANTI

This January 14 festival marks the end of winter and the beginning of the harvest season, depending on the region. In many places it's celebrated by flying brightly colored paper kites (often "fighting kites," on glass-encrusted string used to strike down other kites).

REPUBLIC DAY

January 26 marks the day that the Constitution came into being in 1950; celebrations include a parade in Delhi, with kitschy floats from every region.

HOLI

The Hindu and Sikh equivalent of Carnival, the northern spring festival of Holi is India's most colorful celebration. All social and religious groups get involved on the last and wildest day (in February or March) by throwing colored powder on each other.

INDEPENDENCE DAY

The celebration of India's independence on August 15 is a dignified affair, with flag-hoisting and public speeches.

EID-UL-FITR

The end of the fasting month of Ramadan consists of three days of feasting on special desserts, buying new clothes, visiting family, and distributing alms.

GANESH CHATHURTHI

Mumbai is the epicenter of this August/September celebration of the elephant-headed god, Ganesh, which involves

submerging Ganesh idols of all sizes and types in the sea.

DIWALI

Diwali is the Hindu New Year and the end of the harvest season. Often called the "festival of lights" because people line their homes with twinkling clay lamps, Diwali is celebrated over five days with firecrackers and gift-giving. On the third day people invite Lakshmi, the goddess of wealth, into their homes. The date varies each year, but is usually between September and November.

EID-UL-ADHA

Also called "Bakr-Id," Eid-ul-Adha marks the end of the Hajj (the Muslim pilgrimage to Mecca). It's celebrated by sacrificing a goat, echoing Abraham's willingness to sacrifice his son, and by distributing food to the poor. The date, based on the Islamic calendar, changes every year.

GURU NANAK JAYANTI

The most important Sikh holiday, also known as Gurpurab, marks the birth of Guru Nanak, the founder of the Sikh religion. It's celebrated with all-night chanting, singing hymns, and cooking meals for the poor. Based on the lunar calendar, it falls either in October or November.

HINDU GODS AND GODDESSES

The vast pantheon of Hindu gods and goddesses originates in ancient Hindu mythology but plays an important role in modern life.

(top left) Durga Puja; (top right) Statue of Krishna; (bottom right) Statue of Vishnu

Most of the Hindu deities are represented in the two great Indian epics, the *Ramayana* and the *Mahabharata*, and in the ancient books of Hindu philosophy known as the Vedas. The stories surrounding the various gods and goddesses are steeped with lore of demons vanquished in the ongoing battle of good versus evil. The deities are richly portrayed, and each of their physical features is deeply symbolic. Many gods and goddesses are also characterized by their *vahana*, or vehicle, the traditional animal mount they ride.

A central concept is that of the Trimurti, which encapsulates the three basic cosmic actions: creation, maintenance, and destruction. These are, in turn, personified by Brahma the creator, Vishnu the maintainer or preserver, and Shiva the destroyer or transformer.

One of the key things to look for when you visit a Hindu temple is the intricate carvings and sculptures, which illustrate the gods and goddesses and provide interpretations of Hindu mythology.

PUJA

The tradition of daily *puja*, or prayer, is a central part of Hindu life. Paintings and sculptures of various deities are found in temples and home shrines, where lamps are lit and offerings of food are made to invoke the blessings of the gods. Specific gods or goddesses are often worshipped to deal with specific situations—anything from healing an ailment to doing well on a test or having success in a business venture.

BRAHMA

The God of Creation, Brahma is the first god in the Hindu triumvirate, or Trimurti, and is associated with the daily coming and going of light and dark. He is said to have grown out of the navel of the sleeping Vishnu. Brahma is traditionally depicted with four heads (representing the four Vedas, the four holy books of the Hindu religion), sitting on a lotus. The legends tell that he once had a fifth head but it was lost after he lied to Vishnu and made Shiva angry. In his four arms he holds the Vedas, a *kamandalam* (water pot), a *suruva* (sacrificial spoon), and an *akshamala* (string of beads), which he uses to count time. Brahma has a swan as his *vahana*. Although Brahma is one of the three major gods in Hinduism, there are few temples dedicated to him, the most famous being the Brahma temple at Pushkar in Rajasthan.

VISHNU

Vishnu is the god of preservation, and the second entity in the Trimurti. He is commonly recognized by the blue color of his skin (the color of water) and with four arms that hold the *chakra* (a sharp spinning-discus-like weapon), a conch that produces the mantric Om representing the sound of creation, a lotus representing spiritual liberation, and a *gadha*, or mace. Vishnu is often shown reclining on the ocean, atop Adisesha (a serpent with 1,000 heads) and alongside

his consort Lakshmi, the goddess of wealth. As the divine protector, he is believed to have assumed avatars and descended to Earth to rescue populations from evil rulers and forces, or to restore the balance between good and evil in the world. He is believed to have come to Earth in nine different avatars so far, including one as Krishna, and Hindus believe that he will be reincarnated one last time, right before the end of this world.

KRISHNA

Krishna is an avatar, or incarnation, of Vishnu and is often depicted as a young boy or prince, usually with blue skin. He is said to be the embodiment of love and divine joy that destroys all pain and sin. He takes on many different personas, including prankster, lover, divine hero, and Supreme Being. Common representations show him lying back in a relaxed pose, playing the flute, though he is also represented as the divine herdsman, accompanied by cows or *gopis* (milkmaids). Some paintings show him with Radha, his *gopi* consort.

A Ganesh idol at the Ganesh Chaturthi festival.

SHIVA

Shiva, the third of the Trimurti, is the god of destruction, and is oftentimes worshipped in the form of the phallus (lingam) fixed on a pedestal. He is vested with the power to destroy the universe in order to re-create it His abilities to both create and destroy give an intimidating aura to his austere, meditative demeanor. He is usually portrayed residing in the Himalayas with an ash-smeared forehead, his body clothed in animal skin, and a king cobra draped around his neck. He has a third eye, believed to be his source of knowledge and wisdom and also the source of his untamed energy, when it is unleashed. He is also often depicted as Nataraj, the Lord of Dance, a metaphor for his ability to masterfully maintain the balance in the universe.

LAKSHMI

The goddess of wealth and prosperity and the consort of Vishnu, Lakshmi is commonly depicted as a beautiful woman standing or sitting on a lotus. She has four arms representing the four ends of human life: *dharma* or righteousness, *kama* or desires, *artha* or wealth, and *moksha* or liberation from the cycle of birth and death. Her portrayal as the goddess of wealth is evident from the cascades of gold coins flowing from her hands. A representation of her can be found in nearly every business because of her power to bestow prosperity, and she is celebrated with much veneration during the festival of Diwali.

GANESH

Perhaps the most easily recognized of the Hindu gods, and certainly among the most endearing, Ganesh has an elephant head, large belly, and four arms, one of which holds a *laddu*, a ball-shape popular Indian sweet. He is worshipped at the start of any new venture, and before exams, because he is considered to be the god who removes obstacles (*vignam*). He is variously depicted in seated, standing, and dancing postures, and is most often worshipped in people's homes for removing day-to-day challenges. His *vahana* is a tiny mouse, and he has several other names, including Ganapati, Gajanana, Vigneshwara, Pilliar, and Vinayagar.

MURUGAN
Also known as Subramanya or Kartikeya, Murugan is the second son of Shiva and Parvati. He is widely worshipped in South India, especially in the state of Tamil Nadu. He is the God of War. Legend has it that he was so upset with his father, Lord Shiva, whom he believed showed preferential treatment to Ganesh, Shiva's other son, that Murugan left the Himalayas for a hill in Tamil Nadu. It's there that the six most important shrines devoted to him are found; collectively they are known as Arupadai Veedu (literally "six battle camps"), and each is connected to one of the six stages of his life.

HANUMAN
The monkey god, Hanuman, is an ardent devotee of Lord Rama (one of the avatars of Vishnu) and he is among the key characters in the beloved Hindu epic, the *Ramayana*. The story goes that Lord Rama was banished from his father's kingdom for 14 years, during which time his wife Sita is abducted by the evil king Ravana and taken across the seas to Lanka. Hanuman, who belongs to the varanas, an apelike race of forest dwellers, joins Lord Rama in his mission to rescue Sita. Hanuman is revered and worshipped for his courage and valor in inspiring and leading Rama's army and for being steadfast in his devotion and loyalty to Rama. He is often depicted in temples with a mace in his right hand or kneeling before Lord Rama and Sita.

SARASWATI
As the goddess of knowledge, literature, music, and the arts, Saraswati is said to be the mother of the Vedas, the four holy books of Hinduism. She is also associated with intelligence, creativity, education, and enlightenment. Saraswati is usually pictured dressed in white, sometimes holding a palm-leaf scroll.

Her *vahana* is a swan or a peacock. She is the consort of Brahma.

SHAKTI
Shakti is the divine, formless Hindu mother goddess, a creative feminine force. The goddess Durga is the embodiment of her warrior side. Durga is often shown as the mother of Ganesha, Kartikeya, Lakshmi, and Saraswati. The female equivalent of the Trimurti concept is Tridevi (*devi* means goddess in Sanskrit), and can be represented as the conjoined forms of Lakshmi, Parvati, and Saraswati—essentially, the Shaktis of the Trimurti—Vishnu, Shiva, and Brahma, respectively.

KALI
Kali is the goddess of time and change, which come together as death. She has a dual nature of fierceness and motherliness. Although she represents death, she is also seen as a positive force because she is a destroyer of ego and therefore a granter of liberation and freedom of the soul. Kali is often depicted wearing a garland of severed heads while sticking her tongue out. She is the fierce form of Durga, the consort of Shiva, whose body she is often seen standing upon. Her *vahana* is a jackal.

An enormous Shiva statue

INDIAN CUISINE

Eating in India is an adventure, from the East-meets-West artistry of tandoori-style foie gras to the tangy jumble of flavors in a street snack.

(top left) An assortment of curries and rice dishes; (top right) A dosa with some aloo masala; (bottom right) A bowl of kheer with pistachios

This is a country united by its obsession with food, even as it is divided into countless variations by region, religion, and economics. At the local level, friendships can be jeopardized over diverging loyalties to competing chai-sellers.

Still, visitors expecting a rigid, prohibitive food culture are often more surprised by the inclusive, evolving nature of Indian cuisines, which absorb and adapt ingredients and cooking techniques from all over the world. Despite many traditional taboos surrounding eating, there's a healthy amount of curiosity and sharing as well. In most cities you'll find diverse fare, from South India's famed breakfast dishes (*dosas, uttapams, idlis*) to North India's mouthwatering nonvegetarian dishes.

A growing respect for regional cuisines means that visitors are no longer subject to the sanitized menus of yore. Pay a little attention to the changing flavors around you and you'll never again think of Indian food as limited to kebab and curry.

STREET FOOD

In the busy by-lanes of India's urban centers as much as in its truck-stop towns, stalls, and carts are a constant feature and the fuel of street life. For the faint of stomach, watching locals eat at these venues can be a vicarious pleasure—but in the big cities some vendors are sensitive to hygiene (look for signs indicating the use of bottled water), and some sit-down restaurants offer their own clean versions of street dishes.

UBIQUITOUS INDIAN DISHES

Daal, which in India refers to split pulses (lentils, beans, or split peas), is the country's most basic dish, generally boiled, spiced, and tempered with fried cumin seeds, bay leaves, garlic, and onion. Variations in thickness and hue range from pale yellow (*moong daal*) to smoky black (*urad daal*).

Thanks to the inexorable force of Punjabi culture, **chicken tikka** is a widespread dish. Chicken pieces—usually boneless—are marinated in yogurt, lemon, ginger, garlic and spices, then skewered and baked in a clay oven (tandoor) or grilled over coals. Chicken tikkas are found in this simplest form or covered in various spiced gravies.

Though it consists of rice and sweetened, thickened milk, rice pudding is far too prosaic a translation of **kheer.** Ranging from Kashmir's fruit-flavored *phirnis* to coconut milk-based *payasams* in the south, kheer can also be made of broken wheat or vermicelli noodles. Often served in a shallow clay bowl, it can be garnished with nuts or topped with silver leaf.

Definitely a candidate for most ubiquitous dish, the **"Manchurian"** purports to be a Chinese specialty but is as Indian as *saag paneer*. Supposedly invented by Kolkata Chinese chef Nelson Wang in Mumbai in 1975, it consists of strips of battered and deep-fried poultry, doused

in a thickened soy-based sauce. Both chicken and veggie Manchurians are now found on every Indian Chinese menu in the country.

For many North Indians, South Indian food begins and ends with the **dosa.** Popular as a breakfast food, these crisp crepes are made of fermented ground-rice-and-lentil batter. They can be as big as small boats and are served with a thin lentil soup called *sambar*.

Only a small percentage of desserts in any place are regional—the vast majority of Indian confectioners sell the brightly colored **Bengali sweets,** available in an astonishing variety of flavors and pretty, molded shapes. The catalyst for the invention of these candies—by one Nobin Chandra Das in 1860 Bengal—was the Portuguese introduction of intentionally curdling milk to make cheese; the sweets, too, are based on curdled milk.

Whether it's called *puchka, gol-guppa,* **panipuri,** or *gup-chup,* this delightful snack or "chaat" is found all over eastern, northern, and western India. Street vendors crack open hollow puffed crisps, stuff them with bits of boiled vegetable (usually potato and chickpea), dunk them in tamarind sauce and lethally spiced mint-coriander water, and deliver them to salivating customers. Pop each panipuri into your mouth whole and wait for the fireworks.

A variety of spices, including coriander, cardamom pods, turmeric, cinnamon, bay leaves, black pepper, cloves, saffron, and red pepper.

EATING PHILOSOPHIES

Indian cuisines have evolved in anything but a vacuum. As part of a subcontinent with landlocked borders along the silk route, India has always been at the crossroads of commerce between East and West, and its culinary traditions have benefited from centuries of cross-pollination.

When it comes to **eating meat,** scholars believe that even during Vedic times, meat was a regular fixture of the Indian diet. This included cattle, which are now considered strictly off-limits to most observant Hindus. In fact, nearly all items that are labeled "beef," "steak," or "burger" in India are actually buffalo meat. Only rarely is cow meat encountered in the country. Although the Hindu Vedas discuss meat-eating and animal sacrifice quite openly, these texts also mention the benefits of vegetarianism and allude to the later prohibition against killing cows.

The system of **ayurveda,** which focuses on six flavors (sweet, sour, salty, spicy, bitter, and astringent) and catalogs the benefits and ill effects of various spices, vegetables, fruits, and grains, is also rooted in these texts. Indians are hyperconscious of the consequences of eating certain foods and are quite fond of imparting advice on the subject—this is perhaps best exemplified in the obsessive attention paid to diet in Gandhi's autobiography.

Many historians believe that the protected status of cattle arose first as an economically practical phenomenon and later became codified as religious practice. In general, **vegetarianism** is considered to have spread from North to South India, starting in the 4th century, propelled largely by the rise of Buddhism and Jainism. Contrary to popular belief, about a third of India's population is vegetarian. Still, a third of a population as big as India's is substantial, and the country's vegetarian options are arguably the most diverse, creative, and accessible in the world. Regions with high numbers of Jains (whose dietary restrictions surpass kosher laws in their complexity) have rich vegetarian traditions, making do even without onions, garlic, and other tubers.

2

INTERNATIONAL INFLUENCES

While everyday spices such as black pepper, cardamom, turmeric, and bay and curry leaf originated in India, many others that are just as commonly used were brought from the Mediterranean, Middle East, and Central Asia.

The Spice Traders. Fennel, coriander, cumin, fenugreek, saffron, and asafetida all came to India either over land, following Alexander the Great's route, or by sea, with Arab pepper merchants who plied the eastern coast. Syrian Christians also made their mark, particularly enriching the nonvegetarian traditions of the Malabar region. Later, the Portuguese likely brought chillies and other New World plants to India. Also along eastern and western maritime trade routes, India absorbed tamarind from East Africa, cinnamon from Sri Lanka, and cloves from Southeast Asia.

The Mughal Empire. The Central Asian influence of the Mughals is the best-documented exchange in Indian culinary history. In his autobiography, Babur, the first Mughal king, pines for the grapes and melons of his Central Asian homeland and describes experimenting with planting these fruits in his new kingdom. Muslim rulers—both the Mughals in the north and the Nawabs of Lucknow and Bengal in the east and Hyderabad in the south—introduced elaborate courtly eating rituals to India, as well as the use of raisins, nuts, dried fruit, fragrant essences, and rich, ghee-soaked gravies. They brought their own technique of animal slaughter (halal) and introduced new ways to cook meat, including fine-ground mince dishes like *haleem*.

Colonizers. Indian cuisine adopted many imported plants introduced by the Portuguese, Dutch, and British traders and colonizers. Such integral ingredients as chillies, potatoes, tomatoes, maize, peanuts, and peanut oil are all New World additions; tea and soybeans are China's major contributions. Besides their role as traders, the British also brought their own culinary traditions to India. Anglo-Indian cuisine, which takes its cues from the chops, bakes, and puddings of Britain, has endured in the country-club culture of urban elites but has also influenced street snacks that are a twist on, for example, teatime sandwiches. The Portuguese introduced cottage cheese to east India, giving rise to the now omnipresent world of Bengali sweets.

Settler Groups. Smaller populations with their own distinct traditions (some of them nearly extinct in modern India) include various Jewish groups and Zoroastrians—both the Parsis who settled in Gujarat around the 10th century and the Iranis, who arrived later. Finally, the influence of India's Chinese population—descendants of settlers from the 19th century onward, and later Tibetan refugees—is formidable. Just as chicken tikka masala has become a national dish in Britain, dishes such as chilli chicken, "Manchurian," and chow mein are an undeniable part of India's culinary landscape.

Tandoor prawns

A thali combination plate with a side of rice.

THE INDIAN MEAL

Eating out in India could generally be divided into three categories: proper restaurants, holes-in-the-wall or open-air *dhabas* (cheap cafeteria-style eateries), and street food sold out of small stalls or carts. In someone's home or in a sit-down restaurant, a traditional, full meal follows certain general rules. Food is served in a *thali*—a stainless steel plate (silver on special occasions) with raised edges—and in small bowls. The thali contains condiments (a wedge of lime, salt, raw onions, pickles, or chutneys), possibly some fried items, and either rice or bread. The bowls contain servings of vegetable or meat dishes. There's a great deal of regional variation, but a sweet might be included with the savory food. In South India, a banana leaf might substitute for tableware, and in North India, street food or religious offerings are often served on plates made of stitched-together Banyan leaves. It's traditional to scoop up food with the tips of your fingers: curries are generally mixed with rice while torn-off bits of bread are used to pinch food between the fingers. Most places do offer Western cutlery as well. Traditionally, a group of diners shares several dishes, and in *dhabas* you'd usually order a few things for the table. However, some upscale Indian restaurants have started experimenting with single-portion plating; their nouvelle-inspired dishes are well worth a taste.

COMMON SPICES

The word "masala," which loosely translates to "mixture of spices," has become a default adjective for all things Indian—and it's no wonder, given the infinite permutations of seasonings available to the Indian cook. Some of the most commonly used include cumin (*jeera*), turmeric (*haldi*), asafetida (*hing*), powdered and fresh coriander (*dhania*), cloves (*laung*), pepper (*kalimirch*), dried or powdered red chillies (*lalmirch*), fennel seed (*saunf*), mustard seeds (*rai*), ginger (*adhrak*), garlic (*lasson*), cardamom (*elaichi*), cinnamon (*dalchini*), and bay (*tej patta*). A popular premixed powder called garam (hot) masala includes cumin, coriander, cinnamon, cardamom, and cloves.

COOKING METHODS

In general, special dishes tend toward lower heat and slower processes, while street food is generally quickly fried. But India's vast array of cooking processes includes sun-drying, parboiling, braising, steaming, dry-roasting, grilling, baking, and shallow and deep frying.

The use of the **tandoor**, a clay cylindrical oven, lit from the inside to bake flatbreads and meats, is widespread in North India. In this process, skewers of marinated meat are basted with ghee and suspended in the oven. The tandoor has been made famous by Punjabi restaurants, but it is used right across Central Asia and is an important component in both Mughal and Kashmiri cooking.

Frying is an essential part of street food, which includes a wide variety of fried snacks, from harder, storable munchies like plantain chips to savories and sweets that are meant to be eaten on the spot. The latter include *pakoras* (tempura-like vegetables dipped in gram flour batter), *samosas* (crispy pyramids stuffed with potatoes and peas), and much more. Several kinds of deep-fried wafers or hollow puffs also get incorporated into other snacks, like *paapdi chaat* or *golguppa*.

Most main dishes involve a combination of spices, either powdered or in a paste, fried and added to meat, vegetables, or lentils. **Slow-cooked** dishes are a special treat, and traditional methods include *dhum* cooking, which involves sealing the cooking pots with dough and burying them to cook their contents.

CONDIMENTS

Then there's the wonderful, colorful, and unending array of condiments that spice up every Indian meal. These might be freshly ground, spiced ingredients like mint, coconut, or peanuts. Or they might be sweet, vinegary, or acetic preservelike chutneys with slivers of mango or dates, or the syrupy, candied *murrabbas* made of fruit and vegetables like carrots or the medicinal Indian gooseberry (*amla*). Then there are *achhars*, spicy, oily pickles composed of everything from dried prawns to fiddlehead ferns, whose name describes their shape.

BREADS

Indian "bread" encompasses an assortment of flat or puffed, pale or golden, griddle-toasted, deep-fried or baked disks, triangles, and ellipses. Unleavened bread is generically called *roti*, and can be of varying thickness and made from refined, unrefined, and other types of flour. *Chapati* or *phulka* is a tortilla-like version made of wheat, cooked on a griddle, and finished on the flame. *Parathas*, rolled with oil to make layers, can be stuffed with all sorts of fillings and are almost a meal in themselves. Leavened breads, like *naan*, can be cooked in a tandoor, while the perfectly round *puri* and its giant cousin, the *bhatura*, are deep-fried so they puff up like crispy-soft balloons.

Frying up some street food delicacies

TEXTILES AND SHOPPING

Vibrantly colored shawls, necklaces strung together on the spot, copper pitchers and serving bowls ... these are a few of our favorite Indian things.

(top left) Dolls for sale at the flea market at Anjuna Beach in Goa; (top right) An embroidered pashmina; (bottom right) Painted pottery

With centuries-old crafts and textile traditions preserved from province to province, it's no wonder that shopping factors heavily in many travelers' itineraries on the Indian subcontinent. And these days, knowing where to shop is as important as knowing what to buy. In many cities you'll encounter bazaars and markets lined with street hawkers; in heavily touristed areas you'll mostly find trinkets like miniature Taj Mahal replicas and carved-wood coasters—and at all of these you can bargain down the prices.

As an alternative, government-run emporiums source good-quality handicrafts from various regions and sell them at fair but nonnegotiable prices. These emporiums (there's one in most big cities) carry a great variety of goods, making them great for one-stop shopping or for getting an idea of what you should be paying at a market.

BARGAINING

Bargaining is customary at most markets and bazaars. Keeping a poker face while browsing will help so the seller won't see whether you're really attached to a particular item. Once you're ready to bargain, start below half the asking price: the salesperson will undoubtedly work you back up. If you don't intend to buy, it's best to just voice a firm *no* to any coaxing and move along.

PASHMINA SHAWLS

Pashmina refers to the cashmerelike wool from the goats that are indigenous to the Himalayas; these days, however, not all shawls labeled pashmina are made from this special wool. Many are silk-wool blends, or man-made viscose, making it important to really understand the fabric before buying. When possible, buy pashminas from government-run emporiums or reputable stores where you can ask questions about the fabric. Many shawls or wraps will also have some embroidery along the borders—look for neatly done threadwork, which gives a good clue about the shawl's quality.

SILVER AND STONE JEWELRY

From eye-catching stones to shimmering silver and gold, from traditional ethnic and tribal designs to chic contemporary pieces, jewelry shopping in India runs the gamut. Jaipur, India's gem-cutting capital, sees thousands of semiprecious stones passing through its gates to markets in Europe and North America. It does pay to carefully examine stones like amazonite, smoky topaz, and chalcedony, as glass beads are sometimes passed off as more precious baubles. If you find a wholesaler who will sell retail to individuals who walk in, these merchants are generally more legitimate because they're not looking to take advantage of retail customers. If you're shopping for silver pieces, look on the back for a

stamp that says 92.5% sterling silver to be assured it's the genuine article.

STONEWARE AND POTTERY

From coasters to jewelry boxes, stoneware, usually featuring floral inlay, is a popular souvenir. Merchants might try to convince you that the stone is marble, but it's more likely soapstone. Also look for terra-cotta and blue pottery, the making of which are traditions dating back hundreds of years. Many blue pottery showrooms in Jaipur sell colorful, antique-style doorknobs, tiles, and platters.

COPPER AND BRASSWARE

Copper-bottom pots and pans might be all the rage at the moment, but copper kitchenware has been a long-standing tradition in India. Ask for *handi*-style pots (similar to a wok) and serving bowls. As for brassware, you'll find stunning Ganesh statues, incense-stick holders, and other household items. Many of these can be quite hefty, so be sure to keep your airline's suitcase weight limits in mind. With locations in many big cities, the popular Fabindia brand and the slightly more upscale Good Earth carry quality household products ranging from pottery and brass to linens and beauty products.

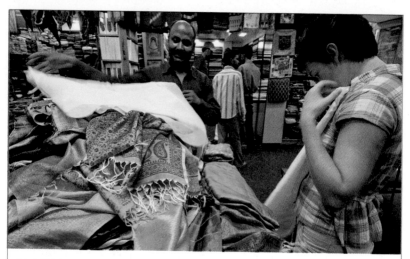

Colorful fabrics

TEXTILES

Whether you're shopping for yourself or for convenient presents to take home, Indian textiles are a good way to go: perhaps block-printed tunics in bold hues, embroidered pillow covers, or quilted bedspreads. Established stores like Fabindia, Anokhi, and Cottons, which have locations in many cities, specialize in these types of textiles, as well as hand-woven table linens, rugs, and more, but you'll also find similar goods at markets all over the country. Look for a type of highly durable cotton called *khadi* (popularized by Gandhi himself during the independence movement); it's coarse but softens with each wash. Although textile traditions do vary from state to state, the most dramatic regional differences are visible in the sari, India's most iconic garment.

SPICES

From cardamom to cloves, aromatic spices seem to fill the air wherever you are in India. Head to a local spice market to stock up on turmeric or cumin seeds at a fraction of the price of grocery stores back home—most merchants will even grind the spices for you on the spot. Be sure to bring back some garam masala, as well, a basic blend of ground spices used in many Indian dishes. The ingredients can vary slightly but usually include cloves, peppercorns, cumin, cardamom, star anise, and coriander seeds. A *masala dabba* is a traditional, round spice holder that has two lids and fits several smaller tins of spices inside, along with one or more spice spoons. These are good souvenirs, too, with or without spices included.

SOAPS AND BEAUTY PRODUCTS

With its history of ayurveda, or holistic medicine, that dates back thousands of years, India has always espoused the use of natural beauty products. Look for specialty brands like Forest Essentials, Kama Ayurveda, and Himalaya Herbals (found at local pharmacies and chemists shops). Popular ingredients and herbs include rose, sandalwood, neem (the leaves and bark from a tropical evergreen-like tree), and *khus-khus* (an Indian grass used as an exfoliant).

MINIATURE PAINTINGS

Scenes of courtship, palace living, and the pursuit of the arts are often portrayed in the miniature watercolor and oil paintings available throughout the country. You'll undoubtedly find framed miniatures like these in New Delhi and Mumbai, but the art of miniature painting originated in Udaipur, making it worthwhile to look for these paintings in Rajasthan.

BOOKS AND CDS

Whether you're in search of a copy of the Bhagavad Gita or just the latest mystery novel, English-language bookstores are ubiquitous in India's big cities. Many have generous selections of Indian fiction, so it's easy to pick up works by authors like Vikram Seth, William Dalrymple, Rohinton Mistry, and others for a fraction of the price you'd pay Stateside. For Bollywood CDs or Indian instrumentals, you might not need to look farther than the bookstores as well, since many of them have extensive audiovisual sections.

ANTIQUES AND CARPETS

From rosewood furniture to ornate carpets, some people come to India specifically to search for top-notch furnishings at deep discounts. Since stores and dealers vary so greatly, though, it's best to employ a degree of caution when making big-ticket purchases. Getting an unbiased expert to come with you, or asking for recommendations from a concierge, can help.

SHOES AND LEATHER GOODS

In general, you'll find more variety than you can choose from when it comes to sandals and shoes. From the classic Kohlapuri *chappal,* a thonglike flat sandal with a toe strap, to more modern wedge-heel and peep-toe sandals and shoes, Indians just love their footwear! Compared to street stalls, shoe chains like Metro and Catwalk in Mumbai and Delhi stock products of better quality and durability at reasonable rates. For other leather goods, such as wallets and purses, start by exploring the government-run emporiums or consider department stores like Shoppers Stop, which has more than a dozen locations across the country.

CONTEMPORARY CLOTHING

Although India's textile traditions continue to be preserved in provinces across the country, its modern fashion industry continues to grow. Designers are moving forward to bring an Indian eye and aesthetic to modern-day silhouettes and garments. Several of them, including Manish Arora, Ashish N Soni, and Sabyasachi Mukherjee, have shown at international fashion weeks in Milan and New York. Whether at shopping complexes like Santushti in New Delhi or the Courtyard in Mumbai, you can find chic boutiques stocking chiffon and organza dresses, A-line skirts with delicate touches of embroidery, and accessories adorned with Indian fabrics or trimmings. Increasingly, many of these designers are also drawing on endangered traditional techniques and more eco-friendly weaving methods and incorporating them into their modern aesthetic.

A miniature painting

INDIAN DANCE, MUSIC, AND PERFORMING ARTS

The appreciation of beauty, combined with a love of celebration and worship, is evident throughout India, especially in the realm of the performing arts.

(top left) Young girls practicing a traditional dance; (top right) A music performance at Mumbai's National Centre for the Performing Arts; (bottom right) An Indian music and dance performance

Centuries of different cultural influences and religious traditions make for a rich array of delights when it comes to the performing and visual arts. Ancient styles and themes continue to flourish alongside growing contemporary movements, and there are also varieties of performing arts that bring together features from throughout the ages.

Whether you choose to attend a formal dance or music performance, go to a Bollywood film, happen upon a street musician, or find yourself in the midst of a religious celebration, experiencing the various manifestations of Indian culture will bring you closer to understanding the Indian way of life.

Mumbai's National Centre for the Performing Arts is a particularly good place to see live performances, although there are all sorts of formal and informal venues throughout the country.

RAMLILA

If you're in North India during the Navratri festival (*see Holidays*), try to see part of a *Ramlila* (literally, "Ram's play"). Actors—traditionally men and boys—wearing gaudy costumes and fake mustaches, dramatize the story of Ram, Prince of Ayodhya, who must fight the demon Ravana to rescue his kidnapped wife Sita. Some performances are makeshift, but others are hundred-year-old institutions.

MUSIC

Music is fundamental to Indian life, and it's almost impossible to walk from one end of a street to another without hearing an old Hindi film song crackling from a radio or the thumping bass of a gangster rap Bhangra mash-up from a passing car. Beyond this, however, there is a rich tradition of classical Indian music. Classical music is divided into Hindustani (predominately from North and Central India and heavily influenced by Persian traditions), and Carnatic (the melodic, formal tradition of the south). There is also a lively tradition of folk music, ranging from classical deviations to lusty rural songs about everything from the monsoons to migrant life. Nonclassical music can be boisterous—like Punjabi Bhangra—or steeped in refined sentimentality—like Bengali Rabindrasangeet (based on Rabindranath Tagore's lyrical works). Contemporary music ranges from Bollywood film music to Hindi (and other language) pop, rap, and hip-hop. In bars and clubs in the cities, it's not uncommon to find electronic music DJs, heavy-metal bands, and classically trained fusion artists.

DANCE

Hand in hand with music is classical dance, of which there are a number of schools. Performances are enhanced by unusual and colorful costumes. Among dance performances to look for are the

silk-clad and jewel-ornamented dancers of the Bharatnatyam, Kuchipudi, and Mohiniyattam styles, which were once performed in temples; the exacting beat-driven Kathak, which evolved in royal courts; the grotesque and gorgeous makeup and wide skirts of Kathakali from Kerala; and gracefully delicate Manipuri from the northeast.

FILM

With such strong traditions of music and movement in Indian culture, it's not surprising that song and dance come together in Indian cinema. From the early days of sugar-sweet love songs and jaunty, jazzy numbers, Hindi films have absorbed and transformed many influences over the years, and these days the cinema produces endless pop and R&B-flavored film music. Independent cinema, once influenced by the New Wave movement of the 1950s and 1960s, continues to exist in the shadow of Bollywood but has also seen recent growth in experimental efforts and documentaries.

THEATER

Theater is also important, and you might see troupes who perform special street plays on religious occasions or public service plays on issues like child labor or female infanticide. Folktales told through puppetry.

DELHI

WELCOME TO DELHI

TOP REASONS TO GO

★ **The Mughal Capital:** Delhi has a wealth of Mughal architecture— including Lal Qila (The Red Fort), Humanyun's Tomb, and Jama Masjid—that's survived for 450 years.

★ **Remnants of the Raj:** The British may have left in 1947, but colonial architecture still dominates Central Delhi, popularly known as Lutyens' Delhi: beautiful villas and large avenues lined with trees make this one of the most peaceful areas in the city.

★ **Shopping Nirvana:** From Western designer duds to beautiful silk Indian saris, there's an incredible selection of ready-to-wear and custom-made clothing in Delhi's variety of malls, shopping centers, and street markets.

★ **Taste of India:** Delhi is known as the unofficial food capital of India. From the best Mughlai cuisine (tandoori chicken done right) to tantalizing street food and international fare, you'll find kebabs and more around every corner.

1 **Old Delhi.** Anchored by Lal Qila (the Red Fort) and Jama Masjid, India's largest mosque, the walled Old City (originally called Shahjahanabad) provides the best glimpse into the city's treasured Mughal past, with a chaotic mix of colors and scents that stir the senses. Narrow, winding lanes branch off the main avenue, Chandni Chowk, crowded with wholesale markets, ancient shops, hidden monuments, and crumbling *havelis* (mansions).

2 **Central Delhi.** With the India Gate memorial at its heart, the capital built in interlocking circles by the British is now home to government buildings, parks, upscale markets, and the low-lying bungalows of the country's most powerful citizens.

3 **South Delhi.** The suburbs to the south of Central Delhi include semi-gated residential colonies, markets, and commercial districts. Here, too, are some of the oldest monuments in the capital, lovely parks, and charming locales such as Hauz Khas Village. It also has many of Delhi's can't-miss sites, including Humayun's Tomb and the Qutub Minar.

GETTING ORIENTED

India's wildly colorful, loud capital radiates from the broad avenues of its British-built center, its sprawl circumscribed by several concentric roads. The suburbs to the south are the most relevant for the first-time visitor. And just north of Central Delhi, the compact, dense Old City has its own internal warren of neighborhoods. Lodhi Road is a good demarcation between Central and South Delhi. Delhi is part of the 12,965-square-mile (33,579-square-km) National Capital Region, which packs in more than 22 million people as well as satellite cities (like the outsourcing hub Gurgaon) dotted with luxury high-rises and malls, in neighboring states.

EATING WELL IN DELHI

As a city of migrants, Delhi gives you the chance to sample the sweeping range of Indian cuisine without having go anywhere else. There are, however, several key groups that dominate the city's food culture.

(top left) Mango kulfi; (top right) Aloo paratha (bread with potatoes in it); (bottom right) A bowl of nihari stew

Delhi's oldest food traditions are found in the chaotic lanes of the Old City. There are Muslim kebab sellers who claim to have cooked for the royal courts; the Hindu merchant class's lip-smacking street food, sold off carts and corner shops; and the simple vegetarian fare of the Old City's Jains. Since India's independence in 1947, an influx of Punjabi migrants has brought that region's earthy flavor to the city. Cooked greens, creamy dals, thick lassis, and hearty breads feature prominently. Local spots that cater to specific migrant communities are tucked away in markets and colonies, and you can find anything from South Indian vegetarian diners to northeastern spots specializing in spicy pork dishes, as well as a range of Afghani, Korean, and Japanese eateries. Delhi also has a couple of "nouvelle" Indian restaurants, where Indian flavors meet Western gastronomic techniques with striking results.

OLD DELHI

The walled Old City is a maze of edible treasures. Khari Baoli, the spice market at the end of Chandni Chowk, is a must-visit. Piles of twisted roots and dried fruit sit between sacks of red chilli powder, yellow turmeric, and other spices. Nearby, the wholesale paan market at Naya Bans carries everything necessary for the preparation of the betel-based digestive.

DAAL MAKHANI

A Punjabi staple, **daal makhani** (also known as *kaali daal*, or *maa ki daal*) is a nearly ubiquitous lentil stew, served by humble villagers and in superluxe hotel restaurants. Black urad beans and red kidney beans are tempered with a fry-up of garlic, ginger, tomato, and spices and ideally slow-cooked overnight on a coal fire. The *daal* is often finished with generous amounts of butter or cream.

PARATHA

Served with spicy achhaar pickles and yogurt, and topped with a dollop of butter, a **paratha** is a meal in itself. Whole wheat flour dough is rolled with oil before being panfried to create a flaky flatbread. The dough can be stuffed with anything; some fillings include radish, cauliflower, and sweet milk solids. "Mughlai" parathas include egg and are thicker. In Old Delhi, Gali Paranthe Wali, a lane dedicated to this originally Punjabi bread, has hosted prime ministers—who now peer down at diners from black-and-white photos.

KULFI

As early as the 16th century, Mughal emporers enjoyed the frozen dessert called **kulfi**. The Indian version of ice cream, standard *kulfi* is a mixture of milk solids (*khoya*) or cream, sugar, and pistachios—which are frozen in a conical metal or clay container sealed with dough. *Kulfi* is eaten as is, or with

starch vermicelli noodles (*faloodeh*). Besides flavors like pistachio and rose, Old Delhi *kulfiwallas* make fruit-flavored *kulfis*, sometimes frozen inside hollowed-out fruit, like mangoes.

NAGORI HALWA

Not well known but quintessentially Delhi, the **nagori halwa** breakfast is found almost exclusively in the Old City. It's a combination of three elements: small crisp breads made of deep-fried wheat and semolina flour; a mushy potato curry packed with fiery and warming spices; and a bit of *halwa*—a sweet preparation of semolina roasted in ghee and mixed with water. It's best eaten mixed all together for a delicious hot, sweet, and spicy combination.

NIHARI

Easily the most coveted dish from Old Delhi, **nihari** is a buffalo (since beef is not eaten) or goat stew cooked overnight in a virtual swimming pool of ghee. More scorching than the city's summer sun, *nihari* is usually eaten in the morning, especially in the foggy winter months. Legend has it that when Shah Jahan settled Delhi his doctor deemed the Yamuna River's water unfit for consumption; this firecracker of a dish, however, was believed to kill the germs.

DELHI'S HOLY SITES

Brash, corrupt, political—the capital of India doesn't have a particularly spiritual reputation, yet Delhi, as the recurring seat of empires with vested religious and cultural interests, is a veritable melting pot of religiously significant sites.

(top left) At Hazrat Nizamuddin Dargah; (top right) The Akshardham Temple; (bottom right) The Bahá'í House of Worship (Lotus Temple)

Because the walled city of Old Delhi was divided into religious ghettos when it was first built by the Emperor Shah Jahan, it is home to a great variety of religious sites: the area is dotted with domes and spires of mosques, dozens of Hindu shrines to Shiva, the bustling Sisganj Gurdwara (an important Sikh site), and peaceful, marble-clad Jain temples.

Beyond Old Delhi, Sufi saints still draw thousands of visitors to their graves. Churches and cemeteries testify not only to the continued presence of South Indian Christians in Delhi, but also to the city as a place where scores of British lived and died. Among other things you can also find Buddhist monasteries and Bengali temples in this city.

HANUMAN MANDIR

In the thick of things near Connaught Place is **Hanuman Mandir**. Said to have mythic origins, the temple was constructed over the 16th and 17th centuries. Note the crescent-moon finial, typically associated with Islam. The surrounding area can be overwhelming, with beggars dressed as the monkey god worshipped here, women painting henna tattoos, and Delhi's best bangle market.

AKSHARDHAM TEMPLE

One of the newest additions to Delhi's spiritual scene is **Akshardham temple**: a theme park of polytheistic Hinduism. Despite criticism over its environmentally dubious location (a sprawling 90 acres on the Yamuna riverbank), this bulwark of pink sandstone and Italian marble—possibly the largest Hindu temple in the world—is undeniably dramatic. Set in landscaped gardens with a musical fountain, the temple incorporates traditional hand-carving and craftsmanship as well as a peacock-boat ride through dioramas of Indian history and mythology, and an IMAX film about the sect's founder.

HAZRAT NIZAMUDDIN DARGAH

In many ways the still-beating heart of spirituality in central Delhi is the mausoleum of saint Nizamuddin Auliya of the Sufi Chishti order. At **Hazrat Nizamuddin Dargah** Thursday evenings are enlivened by a troupe of qawwals (who sing Sufi devotional music) and the distribution of food. You'll have to leave your shoes outside (tip a rose-petal seller a few rupees to keep them safe).

JAMA MASJID

India's largest mosque, **Masjid-i-Jahan-Numa** ("world-showing mosque") as it is properly named, is a welcoming space with a well-loved, worn-in feel. Visitors are welcome any time except during prayers, and it is advisable to cover your head as a sign of respect. Climb the minaret for an incredible view of the city and note the north gate's reliquary, which houses a beard hair and footprint of the Prophet Muhammad and an antique Koran.

SIS GANJ SAHIB GURDWARA

Right on Chandni Chowk itself is the Sikh **Sis Ganj Sahib Gurdwara**. It was on the site of this bustling *gurdwara* (temple) that the ninth Sikh leader, Guru Tegh Bahadur, was beheaded on order of the Mughal Emporer Aurangzeb in 1675. To learn more about Sikh martyrs, visit the gloriously kitsch Bhai Mati Das Bhai Sati Das Bhai Dyala Museum of Sikh history across the street. Delhi's grandest *gurdwara*, Bangla Sahib near Connaught Place, has gleaming golden domes that reflect in its large pond of holy water.

BAHA'I HOUSE OF WORSHIP

The Lotus Temple, as the **Baha'i House of Worship** is also known, is probably Delhi's most iconic modern holy site and one of the most visited places in the world—designed by the Canadian architect Fariborz Sahba, it was built in 1986. The crowds can be thick on the approach to the building but it's surprisingly peaceful inside. Eminently egalitarian, the building has no point of focus for preaching and no obvious religious trappings.

Updated
by Snigdha
Poonam

Delhi is the best place to experience all that brings people to India: history, culture, food, spirituality, madness, mystery. Spend a day amid its lived-in splendor, and you'll realize why so many battles have been fought over it. Here are the extremes that make India so compelling. Old Delhi's Mughul glory, Central Delhi's European grandeur, West Delhi's Punjabi opulence, and South Delhi's bars, boutiques, and massive houses—all come together with the poor, the pollution, and overpopulation.

Modern Delhi has its foundation on a city base that has been around for centuries. Various monuments lie scattered across the region, revealing the numerous empires that have invaded Delhi and made it their home. Of these, the Mughals and British have left the deepest mark.

The city has grown exponentially over the years and continues to do so to accommodate the expanding population, currently estimated at more than 16 million, within a little less than 1,554 square km (600 square miles). It's part of the larger National Capital Region (NCR), which includes neighboring state suburbs like Ghaziabad, Faridabad, Noida, Greater Noida (all across the border in Uttar Pradesh), and Gurgaon (in Haryana). The latter is known in particular for its call centers and gleaming malls, which feed the consumer craze of India's rapidly expanding middle class.

In Delhi the different versions of modern India all coexist, and its contradictions quickly become abundantly clear to visitors. Newly minted junior executives ride in chauffeured, air-conditioned comfort as scores of children beg and hawk magazines in the streets.

PLANNING

MAKING THE MOST OF YOUR TIME

If you'll only be in Delhi a few days, note that the Red Fort and most museums are closed on Monday, and the Jama Masjid is closed to non-Muslims on Friday.

The best way to cover a lot of ground in Delhi is to hire a car, especially if you're on a limited schedule. Avoid tackling Old Delhi on your first day if you've never been to India before—its startling chaos can be overwhelming. Starting with New Delhi will also give you a better idea of the aesthetic and cultural dichotomy between the two areas. A drive through the graceful avenues of the British capital will ease you gently into the capital, but don't let it lull you into a state of pleasant, orderly inertia. The rest of the city requires that all your senses be in working order. Depending on your interests, visit South and Central Delhi's monuments (Humayun's and Safdarjang's tombs, the Qutub Minar, Lodhi Gardens, Hazrat Nizamuddin Dargah), some sites commemorating the leaders of India's independence movement (the Nehru Museum or Gandhi Smriti), a museum, or a temple or *gurdwara* (Sikh temple). When you're ready, plunge into Old Delhi—explore the Lal Qila (Red Fort) and the stunning Jama Masjid, then venture into Chandni Chowk. Make sure to eat at the famous Gali Paranthe Wali and the restaurant Karim's.

WHEN TO GO

HIGH SEASON: MID-NOVEMBER–MARCH

The most popular time to visit is during peak festive season, when cool temperatures (near-freezing at times) get people out of their homes, wrapped in shawls on the street, huddled around charcoal braziers at lawn parties, clutching hot kebab rolls in their hands. This is also peak cultural season; calendars are packed with music, dance, theater, and more. It does get cold though, and Delhi is especially foggy around New Year's, so try not to schedule any night-driving around then. Delhi's February sun has its own charming character, and seasonal trees turn the city into a riot of colors in the late winter.

LOW SEASON: MAY TO MID–AUGUST

The heat is intense from April until the monsoons arrive in July, after which rain and intense humidity add to the misery. Air-conditioning is a staple, and there's plenty to do indoors, from museums to malls, so don't let the outside stickiness deter you. Unfortunately, the rains shut the city down because of improper drainage, and the already intense traffic takes a turn for the worse, with people stuck on roads for hours on end.

SHOULDER SEASON: SEPTEMBER AND OCTOBER AND MARCH AND APRIL

Autumn and early spring bring mild, sunny days and the tourist crowds are thinner than in winter. Temperatures are comfortable, though a light sweater may come in handy in the evenings closer to the cold months.

GETTING HERE AND AROUND
AIR TRAVEL
All flights arrive and depart from Delhi's Indira Gandhi International Airport, along the southwestern edge of the city. It has separate domestic and international terminals that are quite a few miles apart, though connected by a free hourly shuttle bus.

AIRPORT TRANSFERS The airport is about a 45-minute drive from Delhi's center in light to moderate traffic (i.e., before 9 am or after 8 pm).

Major hotels provide airport transfers, otherwise taking a cab is your best bet. To avoid being overcharged, use the prepaid taxi service from a counter near the exit. Unfortunately, hucksters have set up similar services; ignore them. Your destination determines the fare, to which a small fee for each piece of luggage is added. Pay in advance at the counter, then take the receipt and exit. When you get outside, people might try to help you with your luggage; ignore them also, and make sure they do not touch your things. Wheel your luggage down the ramp toward the black taxis with yellow tops, at which point the drivers will appear. If your receipt contains a taxi number, use that cab; if not, the drivers will decide among themselves who should take you. Tell the driver where you're going, and hold on to the receipt until you arrive. Tips are not expected unless they help with your luggage.

BUS TRAVEL
You're best off avoiding bus travel in Delhi: public buses are generally dirty, crowded, and unpleasant.

CAR TRAVEL
Hiring a car and driver is the best way to see the most of this sprawling city, especially for those with a limited amount of time. Most hotels can arrange a car, but they will also charge a premium for the service. Reputable travel agents do the same for less money (budget Rs. 1,000 or more per day for a basic car with air-conditioning and an English-speaking driver, for travel in Delhi only). Tip in advance if you want some extra-deferential, but exceedingly helpful service.

METRO TRAVEL
The city's metro service, which came into service in 2002, is air-conditioned, reliable, and state-of-the-art. With new stations and lines opening for service every few months, subway service is rapidly changing the face of the city. It's an inexpensive (starting at Rs. 8 per one-way trip) and convenient way to move between Connaught Place (Rajiv Chowk station), Lutyens' Delhi (Central Secretariat station), and Old Delhi (Chandni Chowk and Chawri Bazaar stations). For example, getting to Old Delhi from CP is three stops and takes about 15 minutes. There are currently six lines—red, yellow, blue, green, violet, and the airport express, which links the airport with the centrally located New Delhi stop, which is close to the New Delhi railway stop. The fare for the airport express is Rs. 150. Maps are available at the official tourist office and often at your hotel concierge desk. The Rajiv Chowk station is massive; ask for directions as you go.

TAXI AND AUTO-RICKSHAW TRAVEL

Apart from a hired car, the best way to get around New Delhi is by black-and-yellow taxi or radio cab service, which includes the use of Uber. Most hotels and restaurants will gladly call you a cab, and major markets and tourist attractions usually have a taxi stand. Most drivers speak a little English. ■**TIP**➔ **Tell the driver where you want to go and make sure he turns on the meter before you set off.** If he insists the meter is broken, get out of the car and find another cab. Most taxi drivers are honest, so it's not worth dealing with one who isn't.

The ubiquitous green-and-yellow auto-rickshaws are a good way to see the city from a different angle. But they aren't for the faint of heart, as the drivers zip through traffic at breakneck speed. The three-wheeled auto-rickshaws, often just called "autos" in India, are half the price of taxis and roughly half as comfortable—except in summer, when the open-air breeze keeps you cool while taxis trap the heat horrendously. The problem is that auto-rickshaw drivers refuse to use their meters (here they really often are broken, as the drivers deliberately break them), and if you look even remotely new to Delhi they will quote absurdly high fares. A trip around the corner should cost about Rs. 30, and a trip across the city should never cost more than Rs. 200. Government-run booths for prepaid auto-rickshaws can be found at Connaught Place, Basant Lok, Dilli Haat, and the Community Centre in Saket, among other places. Try to have exact change, as many drivers will claim to have none, and discussion is difficult, as most do not speak English.

In Old Delhi and a few other neighborhoods you can still hire a cycle-rickshaw. It's a great way to cruise Chandni Chowk, explore the maze of narrow lanes, and get from one sight to the next. A short one-way trip costs Rs. 30; work out a higher fare, up to Rs. 200, if you want to ride around for longer.

TRAIN TRAVEL

Delhi is the major hub for India's northern rail system, with five train stations. Most arrive at New Delhi Station, within walking distance of Connaught Place; Hazrat Nizamuddin, from which trains leave for Agra and points south; or Old Delhi Station. With luggage in tow and crowded streets, consider taking a taxi or auto-rickshaw to your hotel. Note that traveling by train in India is much different than in the United States or in Europe, in part due to the sheer number of travelers. Terminals are chaotic, and it can be unclear and confusing to determine when and from where your train is scheduled to leave. Trains are often also crowded and delayed. Your best bet, if you choose this means of travel, is to factor in plenty of extra time and a lot of patience. All stations have prepaid taxi and auto-rickshaw stands, though these can get quite busy.

EMERGENCIES

Most hotels have physicians on call. For emergencies, go to Indraprastha Apollo Hospital, Delhi's premier private hospital, southeast of town, or ask at your hotel. From there you can call Meera Rescue if international evacuation is necessary; *do not* go to a government hospital. In a grave emergency, contact your embassy.

Although not equipped for trauma, the Max Medcentre—in conjunction with Harvard Medical International, one of India's major pharmaceutical companies—runs a first-rate clinic open daily from 8 am to 8 pm. Its hospital in Saket can treat complicated ailments and has many specialists. Many of the physicians are American-trained, and there's a 24-hour pharmacy on-site. The East–West Medical Centre is also a great resource for travelers, with ambulance service and regional evacuation, though it has no pharmacy.

Contacts East–West Medical Centre ⊠ *B-28 Greater Kailash I, South Delhi* ☎ *11/2469–9229, 11/2469–8865* ⊕ *www.eastwestrescue.com.* **Indraprastha Apollo Hospital** ⊠ *Mathura Rd., Sarita Vihar, South Delhi* ☎ *11/2692–5801, 11/2692–5858* ⊕ *www.apollohospdelhi.com.* **Max Medcentre** ⊠ *N-110 Panchsheel Park, South Delhi* ☎ *11/4609–7200* ⊕ *www.maxhealthcare.in.* **Meera Rescue** ⊠ *112 Jor Bagh, Central Delhi* ☎ *11/2465–8075, 11/2465–3170* ⊕ *www.meera-rescue.com.*

24-Hour Pharmacies Max Super Specialty Hospital ⊠ *2 Press Enclave Rd., Saket, South Delhi* ☎ *11/2651–5050* ⊕ *www.maxhealthcare.in.* **New Delhi Medicos** ⊠ *12 Old RK Ashram Marg, Gate 6, Dr RML Hospital, near Connaught Place, Central Delhi* ☎ *11/2334–7151.*

RESTAURANTS

Restaurants are generally open daily 12:30 to 3 for lunch and 7:30 to 11 for dinner. You can assume that all restaurants serve alcohol unless we indicate otherwise. However, imported liquor is extremely expensive—inquire before you imbibe. Expect a 20% tax on your food and beverage bill.

HOTELS

Unless otherwise specified, you can expect private bath, phone, and TV in your room. Be sure to reserve in advance for stays between October and February, as even the largest hotels fill up.

Hotel reviews have been shortened. For full information, visit Fodors. com.

WHAT IT COSTS IN RUPEES			
	$	$$	$$$	$$$$
Restaurants	under Rs. 500	Rs. 500–Rs. 1,000	Rs. 1,001–Rs. 1,400	over Rs. 1,400
Hotels	under Rs. 6,000	Rs. 6,000–Rs. 9,000	Rs. 9,001–Rs. 13,000	over Rs. 10,000

Restaurant prices are the average cost of a main course at dinner or, if dinner is not served, at lunch. Hotel prices are the lowest cost of a standard double room in high season.

INTERNET, MAIL, AND SHIPPING

Internet facilities can be found in most major markets, but are often holes-in-the-wall with a handful of grimy, outdated terminals. Coffee-shop chains and some larger bookstores often have Wi-Fi hot spots available.

One centrally located post office is on the roundabout just southwest of Connaught Place. Hotels usually have mailing facilities, too. DHL outlets are available around the city, but you'll pay a premium—possibly as much as your own plane ticket—to ship anything heavy to the West (just sending documents will cost you at least $60). Use Speed Post at the main post office, which is a fraction of the price and usually reliable. Be prepared to wait (and then wait some more).

Post Offices Main Post Office ⊠ *Baba Kharak Singh Marg, at Ashoka Rd., Connaught Pl., Central Delhi* ⊕ *www.indiapost.gov.in.*

VISITOR INFORMATION

The Government of India Tourist Office south of Connaught Place is open weekdays 9 to 6 and Saturday 9 to 2, but it doesn't have anything a decent hotel can't offer. Its airport counters are open for major flight arrivals, and its train-station counters are open 24 hours.

Contacts Government of India Tourist Office ⊠ *88 Janpath, Connaught Pl., Central Delhi* ☏ *11/2332–0005.*

EXPLORING DELHI

Most of sprawling Delhi is best navigated on wheels—hire a car, taxi, or auto-rickshaw to get around. In contrast, the narrow lanes of Old Delhi are a walker's delight, though you can hop on a cycle rickshaw if you get tired. Most people speak workable English, so don't assume there will be an insurmountable language barrier.

The challenge Delhi presents is to find areas—beyond the Old City—in which walking is a viable mode of exploration. One of these areas is the central British-built commercial hub, Connaught Place. "CP" is a tourist magnet for its travel agent bucket shops, restaurants, and shops, as well as proximity to a number of mid-range and budget hotels. It's also the location of Delhi's main Metro station and can be a pleasant area to meander along colonnaded circles, or people-watch in the central park. There are plenty of shopping options nearby, including the street market, Janpath, where everything from brightly colored *kolhapuri* slippers to designer overstock to incense and natural soaps can be found. Keep in mind that even though it's commonly referred to as Connaught Place, the name was officially changed to Rajiv Chowk, which is what you'll see on metro stops and maps.

Around the hubs of Connaught Place and India Gate is the British-built city. This is the seat of the Indian government, with Rashtrapati Bhavan (the Presidential Palace), the North and South Secretariats, Sansad Bhavan (Parliament House), and India Gate (a monument to British Indian Army soldiers killed in World War I and the Afghan wars) within a tight radius. Getting ice cream at India Gate's huge lawns or boating in the ornamental canals here are "very Delhi" things to do. Many museums are nearby, including the National Gallery of Modern Art and the National Museum.

Also here are the palatial residences of the affluent and lavish government bungalows. Khan Market, one of Asia's most expensive retail locations, is perfectly at home in this setting. It's also the place where Delhi's expats feel most at home, with its coffee shops and multiple ATMs. Down the road is Delhi's green lung, Lodhi Gardens, and several cultural centers, including the elite's mainstays the India International Centre and the India Habitat Centre (performances are pretty much on tap, especially in winter).

The mostly residential areas of South Delhi, West Delhi, North Delhi, and East Delhi (across the Yamuna) all have their own flavor, but visitors are most likely to venture into the neighborhoods, markets, and monuments of the first, roughly defined as south of Lodhi Road. In between semi-gated colonies are a good mix of urban villages, hectic alleyways, posh markets, and office complexes. Some of the city's oldest monuments can be found here, as well as some of its newest monuments to modernity: the massive malls squatting southward, en route to mega-suburb Gurgaon. The hippest of Delhi's hot spots though, is not a mall, but a gentrified urban village—Hauz Khas Village—with boutiques and trendy restaurants nestled atop each other along narrow alleys, next to a 13th-century reservoir and several Sultanate ruins.

OLD DELHI AND NEARBY

Old Delhi (6 km [4 miles] north of Connaught Place), or Purani Dilli, is also called by its original name of Shahjahanabad, for the emperor, Shah Jahan, who built it. The havelis that line the gullies are architecturally stunning but irreversibly crumbling. Old Delhi's monuments—the Jama Masjid and the Red Fort that anchors the Old City—are magnificent, and the main artery, Chandni Chowk, should not be missed. It's a convenient metro ride to the Old City from Connaught Place.

Old Delhi is crowded and hectic, and the roads and footways are poorly maintained. It's best to chalk up all the bustle to added charm and just immerse yourself in the experience. It's one of the most incredible places to shop and eat, with lots of specialty markets crowding the area on both sides of Chandni Chowk (literally the "silver crossroad" but also meaning moonlit market or square). Kinari Bazaar and Katra Neel are two others, and are a tight squeeze with their maze of alleys. Gorgeous, intricately embroidered fabrics and appliqué materials, lace, bangles, spices, herbs, and Indian sweets can be found in all of them. Watch out for Khari Baoli, Asia's largest spice market, toward the western end of Chandni Chowk (after Fatehpuri Masjid). You'll smell it before you see it.

Jama Masjid is the principle mosque in Old Delhi, and was built by Shah Jahan as well. It's the largest mosque in India, a colossal structure beautifully constructed out of red sandstone. The courtyard of the mosque can be reached from the east, north, and south gates by three flights of steps, all of which have religious significance. The northern gate has 39 steps, the southern side has 33 steps, and the eastern gate, which was once the royal entrance that Shah Jahan and his entourage used, has 35 steps. Arched colonnades and minarets surround the mosque itself, which rests on a platform. Apparently, the courtyard can hold up to 25,000 devotees.

The view down broad Rajpath Avenue from Rashtrapati Bhavan to India Gate is similar to the view up the Champs-Élysées in Paris, to the Arc de Triomphe.

The Red Fort, or Lal Qila, is another Old Delhi institution, and was also built by Shah Jahan as the main residence of the royal family. It's an important top attraction, and combines Indo-Persian architecture to perfection.

If you find yourself daunted by the throngs of people or just need a break after a few hours, try a cycle-rickshaw tour: for about Rs. 100 you can be carted around in a cycle-rickshaw (which seats two slim people) for about an hour. The rickshaw-*wallahs* (drivers) in front of the Red Fort are serious bargainers, but they know the city well, and many can show you places you wouldn't discover on your own.

The variety of traditional Indian food that can be found in Old Delhi is heavenly. Try the *kulfi* (a flavored frozen milk dessert) at places like Lala Dulichand, which serves the treat inside fruit. The *aam* (mango) and *anjeer* (fig) versions are to die for. Karim's, a restaurant right around the Jama Masjid, is another stop. Make sure you have cash on hand, because many of the smaller shops and stalls don't have credit card machines.

TOP ATTRACTIONS

Fodor'sChoice ★ **Chandni Chowk.** This was Delhi's former imperial avenue, where the Mughal emperor Shah Jahan rode at the head of his lavish cavalcade. That scene is hard to picture today, as bullock carts, bicycles, shuttle buses (cars are technically banned), freight carts, cows, auto-rickshaws, horse-drawn tongas (two-wheeled carts), and pedestrians create a constant, breathtaking bazaar. It runs from the Red Fort into the walled city, functioning as a major, if congested, artery. As in the days of the Mughals, commerce is everywhere: astrologers set up their charts on

Some Delhi History

The ancient epic *Mahabharata* places the great town of Indraprastha on the banks of the Yamuna River, perhaps in what is now Delhi's Old Fort. Late in the first millennium AD, Delhi became an outpost of the Hindu Rajputs, warrior kings who ruled what's now Rajasthan. It was after 1191, when Mohammad Ghori of Central Asia invaded and conquered, that the city first acquired its Islamic flavor. Other Afghan and Uzbek sultanates handed Delhi back and forth over the next 300 years, until the mighty Mughals settled in. Beginning with the invasion of Babur in 1526, the Mughals shifted their capital between Delhi and Agra until 1858, leaving stunning architecture at both sites, including the buildings at what's now known as Old Delhi.

THE BRITISH ARRIVE

The fall of the Mughal Empire coincided with the rise of the British East India Company, first in Madras (modern-day Chennai) and Calcutta and eventually throughout the country. When several of Delhi's Indian garrisons rose up against their Company employers in 1857, the British suppressed them, moved into the Red Fort, and ousted the aging Mughal emperor. In 1911, with anti-British sentiment growing in Calcutta, they moved their capital from Calcutta to Delhi—the ultimate prize, a place where they could build a truly imperial city that would dwarf the older ones around it. Architect Sir Edwin Lutyens was hired to create New Delhi, a majestic sandstone government complex surrounded by wide, leafy avenues and traffic circles, in contrast to Old Delhi's hectic lanes.

INDEPENDENCE AND UPHEAVAL

When India gained independence on August 15, 1947, with Jawaharlal Nehru the first prime minister, the subcontinent was partitioned into the secular republic of India and the Muslim nation of Pakistan, which was further divided into West Pakistan (now Pakistan) and East Pakistan (now Bangladesh). Trapped in potentially hostile new countries, thousands of Muslims left Delhi for Pakistan while millions of Hindu and Sikh refugees streamed in—changing Delhi's cultural overtone almost overnight from Persian to Punjabi.

LIBERALIZATION AND FLUX

Since Prime Minister Rajiv Gandhi (grandson of Nehru) and his successor, Narasimha Rao, began to liberalize India's planned economy in the late 1980s and early 1990s, Delhi has experienced tremendous change. Foreign companies have arrived and hired locals for white-collar jobs, residential enclaves and shopping strips have sprouted in every crevice, and land prices have skyrocketed. Professionals seeking affordable living space now move to the suburbs and drive into town, aggravating the already substantial pollution problem. At the same time, North Indian villagers still come here in search of work and build shanties wherever they can, sometimes in the shadows of forgotten monuments. It is they—Rajasthani women in colorful saris digging holes with pickaxes, men climbing rickety scaffolds in saronglike lungis—who build new homes for the affluent. Many Delhiites say, with a sigh, that their city is in a perpetual state of flux.

the pavement; shoemakers squat and repair sandals; sidewalk photographers with old box cameras take pictures for a small fee; medicine booths conceal doctors attending to patients; and oversize teeth grin from the windows of dentists' offices. Peer through a portico, and you might see men getting shaved, silver being hammered into paper-thin edible sheets, or any other conceivable form of commerce. While the scenes may seem archaic, the shopping is exactly where it's supposed to be, so make sure you carry cash (safely tucked about your person). The stores in tinsel-filled Kinari Bazaar and Dariba Kalan, with its jewelry and gemstones, may make you want to empty your wallet. Also, lining just about every alley are the famous *halwais*, a group of sweets-makers. Everything from staples such as fried orange jalebis to even more exotic confections is sold. Vendors can be found Monday to Saturday from 9 am to 7 pm at Dariba Kalan. ⊠ *East–west artery from Red Fort 1.5 km (1 mile) west to Fatehpuri Masjid* ⊙ *Most shops closed Sun.* Ⓜ *Chandni Chowk.*

Gali Paranthe Wali. This narrow, festive lane is filled with shopkeepers selling fabric and saris, including the well-known Ram Chandra Krishan Chandra's, where young brides choose their red-and-gold finery. The lane is named for its other industry: the fabulous *paranthas* (fried flatbreads) that are sold here in no-frills open-air eateries. Stuffed or served with a variety of fixings, such as radishes, soft cheese, and seasonal vegetables, paranthas are delicious. The parantha makers moved into this lane in the 1870s, even though a couple of its original sari and jewelry shops still dot the lane. The three oldest and most famous of these parantha makers are Pundit Kanhaiyalal Durgaprasad (established in 1875), Pundit Dayanand Shivcharan (1882), and Pundit Baburam Devidayal Paranthe Wali (1886). A few kitchens have seating, making them excellent places to refuel while looking at photos of famous statesmen doing the same. ⊠ *South off Chandni Chowk, en route to Kinari Bazaar* Ⓜ *Chandni Chowk.*

Fodor'sChoice
★ **Jama Masjid.** An exquisite statement in red sandstone and marble, India's largest mosque was the last monument commissioned by Shah Jahan. Completed in 1656 after six years of work by 5,000 laborers, it's arguably one of the loveliest houses of worship in the world. Three sets of broad steps lead to two-story gateways and a magnificent courtyard with a square ablution tank in the center. The entire space is enclosed by pillared corridors, with domed pavilions in each corner. Thousands gather to pray here, especially on Friday.

With its onion-shape dome and tapering minarets, the mosque is characteristically Mughal, but Shah Jahan added an innovation: the stripes running up and down the marble domes and minarets. The whole structure exudes peace and harmony—climb the south minaret to see the domes up close, complete with swarms of pigeons, and to see how finely the mosque contrasts with the commercial streets around it. (Women cannot enter the minaret without a man; if you're a woman traveling solo, enlist a man to help you, as the beauty of the architecture is best appreciated from above.) Look into the prayer hall (you can only enter after a ritual purification at the ablution tank) for the pulpit carved from a single slab of marble. In one corner is a room where Shah Jahan

Commerce is everywhere along Chandni Chowk; it's a great place to stroll, but keep a firm hold on your purse, wallet, and mobile phone.

installed the marble footprints of the Prophet Mohammed. Each of the arched colonnades has black-marble inscriptions inlaid in white marble that relate the history of the building and extol the virtues of Shah Jahan's reign.

If you're feeling hungry, the restaurant Karim's *(⇨ See Where to Eat)* is in the shadow of the Jama Masjid. ⊠ *4.5 km (3 miles) north of Connaught Pl., across from Red Fort* ☎ *11/2326–8344* ✉ *Free; Rs. 50 to climb minaret; camera or video camera fee Rs. 200* ☉ *Non-Muslims: winter, daily 8:30–12:15 and 1:45–½ hr before sunset; summer, daily 7–12:15 and 1:45–½ hr before sunset. Closed for prayer ½ hr each afternoon. Muslims: daily 5 am–8 pm* Ⓜ *Chawri Bazaar, Chandni Chowk.*

Lal Qila (Red Fort). Named for its red-sandstone walls, the Red Fort, near the Yamuna River in Old Delhi, is the greatest of Delhi's palace cities. Built by Shah Jahan in the 17th century, Lal Qila recalls the era of Mughal power and magnificence—imperial elephants swaying by with their mahouts (elephant drivers), a royal army of eunuchs, court ladies carried in palanquins, and other vestiges of Shah Jahan's pomp. At its peak, the fort housed about 3,000 people. After the Indian Mutiny of 1857, the British moved into the fort, built barracks, and ended the grand Mughal era; eventually the Yamuna River changed course, so the view from the eastern ramparts is now a busy road. Still, if you use your imagination, a visit to the Red Fort gives an excellent idea of what a fantastic city Shahjahanabad was.

The view of the main entrance, called **Lahore Gate,** flanked with towers facing Chandni Chowk, is unfortunately blocked by a barbican (gatehouse), which the paranoid Aurangzeb added for his personal

A Good Walk in Old Delhi

Start in Old Delhi with a morning tour of the **Lal Qila** (Red Fort), Emperor Shah Jahan's sprawling 17th-century capital. Exit the Red Fort onto **Chandni Chowk**. Chaos reigns supreme here, so gather your wits and watch your feet lest they be flattened by a cart or cycle-rickshaw. You'll pass a short but fragrant row of flower-sellers. About four blocks down the street on the left, identifiable by its small gold dome, is the marble **Sis Ganj Sahib Gurdwara**, a Sikh shrine. After a look around, continue down Chandni Chowk and cross three more lanes (*galis*); then, at Kanwarji's sweet shop (opposite the Central Bank of India), turn left on **Gali Paranthe Wali**. Continue down the lane, following its jogs to the right, until the T at the Sant Lal Sanskriti sari shop. Turn left into Kinari Bazaar, a sparkling bridal-trimming market where Hindu families can buy every item required, and then some, for their wedding festivities.

At 2130 Kinari Bazaar (a bric-a-brac shop called Krishna & Co.), turn right into one of Chandni Chowk's most beautiful lanes, Naughara Gali, where a community of Jains lives in some colorful old havelis. At the end of this peaceful alley is the **Svetamber Jain Temple**. Even if the temple is closed (as it is between 12:30 and 6:30 every afternoon), Naughara Gali offers a respite from the bustle of the bazaar.

Return to Kinari Bazaar and turn right, continuing until Kinari Bazaar intersects with **Dariba Kalan,** or "Silver Street." If you're in the market for jewelry or curios, check out the shops to the left; if not, turn right and head down Dariba Kalan to its end. Turn right again and you'll find yourself on a broad street in the brass and copper

district. Take the next right, then an immediate left under a stone arch. Now head up Chah Rahat, a typical narrow lane with old wooden balconies and verandas.

When Chah Rahat opens into a courtyard, take the hairpin turn to the left and follow the arrow on the sign for "Singh Copper and Brass Palace." After about 30 feet, a second sign directs you down an alley on the right. Singh's emporium is filthy but has an interesting collection of miscellany.

From Singh's, return to the courtyard on Chah Rahat and take the short, narrow lane to the left. You'll emerge to see the splendid **Jama Masjid,** preceded by a somewhat incongruous tool bazaar. To reach the mosque's entrance, head right, then follow the bazaar to the left.

At the end of this long tour, you'll probably be ready for a proper Muslim meal. Make for Karim's, on the colorful lane heading away from the mosque's entrance, or take a cycle-rickshaw to Chor Bizarre. Another option, a bit farther afield, is to take a taxi or rickshaw to **Raj Ghat** and the **National Gandhi Museum.**

TIMING

Allow a full day—but not a hot one. Avoid Friday, when the mosque is closed to non-Muslims; Sunday, when most shops in Old Delhi are closed; and Monday, when the Red Fort is closed. (If Sunday and Monday are the only options, go for Monday. The bazaars are crucial to Old Delhi's flavor.) Note, too, that the Svetamber Jain temple is closed to visitors for most of each afternoon, so if art and architecture make your heart sing, try to start very early *or* right after lunch.

security—to the dismay of Shah Jahan, his father. From his prison, where he was held captive by his power-hungry son, Shah Jahan wrote, "You have made a bride of the palace and thrown a veil over her face."

Once you pass through Lahore Gate, continue down the **Chhatta Chowk** (Vaulted Arcade), originally the shopping district for the royal harem and now a bazaar selling rather less regal goods. From the end of the arcade you'll see the **Naubat Khana** (Welcome Room), a red-sandstone gateway where music was played five times daily. Beyond this point, everyone but the emperor and princes had to proceed on foot. Upstairs, literally inside the gateway, is the Indian War Memorial Museum (☉ Tuesday–Sunday 10–5 ▦ No extra charge), with arms and military regalia from several periods.

An expansive lawn leads to the great **Diwan-i-Am** (Hall of Public Audience)—you have now entered the Delhi of Shah Jahan. Raised on a platform and open on three sides, the hall is studded with some of the most emblematic arches in the Mughal world. In the center is Shah Jahan's royal throne, once surrounded by decorative panels that sparkled with inlaid gems. (It was stolen by British soldiers after the Indian Mutiny, but some of the panels were restored 50 years later by Lord Curzon.) Watched by throngs of people from the courtyard below, the emperor heard the pleas of his subjects; the rest of the hall was reserved for rajas and foreign envoys, all standing with "their eyes bent downward and their hands crossed." High above them, wrote the 17th-century French traveler François Bernier, under a pearl-fringed canopy resting on golden shafts, "glittered the dazzling figure of the Grand Mughal, a figure to strike terror, for a frown meant death."

Behind the Diwan-i-Am, a row of palaces overlooks the now-distant river. To the extreme right is the Mumtaz Mahal, now the **Red Fort Museum** (⊙ Tuesday–Sunday 10–5 ✉ No extra charge), with numerous paintings and relics from the Mughal period, some in better lighting than others.

Heading back north, you'll come next to the **Rang Mahal** (Painted Palace), once richly decorated with a mirrored ceiling that was dismantled to pay the bills when the treasury ran low. Home of the royal ladies, the Rang Mahal contains a cooling water channel—called the Canal of Paradise—that runs from the marble basin in the center of the floor to the rest of the palace and to several of the others. You can't enter this or any of the palaces ahead, so you must peer creatively from the side.

The emperor's private **Khas Mahal** has three sections: the sitting room, the "dream chamber" (for sleeping), and the prayer chamber, all with lavishly carved walls and painted ceilings still intact. The lovely marble screen is carved with the Scale of Justice—two swords and a scale that symbolize punishment and justice. From the attached octagonal tower the emperor Muthamman Burj would appear before his subjects each morning or watch elephant fights in the nearby fields.

The **Diwan-i-Khas** (Hall of Private Audience) was the most exclusive pavilion of all. Here Shah Jahan would sit on his Peacock Throne, made of solid gold and inlaid with hundreds of precious and semiprecious stones. (When Nadir Shah sacked Delhi in 1739, he hauled the famous throne back to Persia. It was destroyed a few years later after Nadir Shah's assassination.) A Persian couplet written in gold above a corner arch sums up Shah Jahan's sentiments about his city: "If there be a paradise on Earth—It is this! It is this! It is this!"

The **Royal Hammam** was a luxurious three-chamber Mughal bath with inlaid-marble floors. The fountain in the center supposedly had rose-scented water. Sometimes called a Turkish bath, the *hammam* is still used in many Muslim cultures. Peek through the windows for a look.

Next door to the hammam is the **Moti Masjid** (Pearl Mosque), designed by Aurangzeb for his personal use and that of his harem. The building is now closed, but the prayer hall is inlaid with *musalla* (prayer rugs) outlined in black marble. Though the mosque has the purity of white marble, some critics say its excessively ornate style reflects the decadence that set in late in Shah Jahan's reign.

Beyond the mosque is a typical Mughal *charbagh*, or four-section garden. Stroll through this quieter part of the fort to see some small pleasure palaces including the Zafar Mahal, decked out with carved sandstone *jalis* (screens) and once surrounded by water. ✉ *Netaji Subhash Marg, eastern end of Chandni Chowk* 🎟 *Rs. 250; sound-and-light show, Rs. 60, purchase tickets 30 mins in advance* ⊙ *Tues.–Sun. sunrise–sunset. Sound-and-light show times, weather permitting: Nov.–Jan., daily 7:30 pm–8:30 pm; Feb.–Apr., Sept., and Oct., daily 8:30 pm–9:30 pm; May–Aug., daily 9 pm–10 pm* Ⓜ *Chandni Chowk.*

Svetamber Jain Temple. Properly called the Indraprastha Tirth Sumatinatha Jain Svetamber Temple, this splendid house of worship is painted head to toe with finely rendered murals and decorations covering the walls, arches, and ceilings. Reflecting the building's surroundings, some of the artwork shows Mughal influence. Look inside the silver doors of the shrine to Sumatinatha—the fifth of Jainism's 24 *Tirthankaras* (perfect souls)—to see some incredible original painting finished with gold leaf.

As interesting as the temple itself is the street it's located on. It's called Naughara Gali, which directly translates into Nine Houses Street (they date back to the late 18th century). Owned mainly by jewelers, this gated cul-de-sac somehow shuts out all the noise and chaos of the Old City. It's peaceful and charming and each of the houses is brightly painted in shades of pink and blue with floral motifs drawn intricately over the doorways. ✉ *Naughara Gali, Kinari Bazaar* ☎ *11/2327–0489* ⊙ *Visitor hrs 5 am–1 pm and 6 pm–8 pm.*

WORTH NOTING

National Gandhi Museum. Run by a private foundation, this museum across Mahatma Gandhi Road from Raj Ghat houses a great many photographs, a display of spinning wheels with some information on Gandhi's *khadi* (homespun cotton) crusade, and some of the Mahatma's personal effects, including the blood-stained dhoti he was wearing at the time of his murder. The tiny art gallery has a poignant wooden sculpture, made by a South African, of Gandhi in a pose suggesting Jesus's Crucifixion. A film on Gandhi's life is shown on weekends at 4. ✉ *Mahatma Gandhi (M. G.) Marg, Ring Rd.* ⊕ *www.gandhimuseum. org* 🎫 *Free* ⊙ *Tues.–Sun. 9:30–5:30.*

Raj Ghat. After Mahatma Gandhi was shot and killed by a Hindu fanatic on January 30, 1948, his body was cremated on the banks of the Yamuna River; the site is now a national shrine called Raj Ghat, where tourists and pilgrims stream across the peaceful lawn to pay their respects to the saintlike "Father of the Nation." At the center of a large courtyard is a raised slab of black marble adorned with flowers and inscribed with Gandhi's final words, "Hai Ram!" (Oh, God!). An eternal flame burns at its head. The sandstone walls enclosing the shrine are inscribed with passages written by Gandhi, translated into several tongues including Tamil, Malayalam, Nepali, Urdu, Spanish, Arabic, and Chinese. Near Raj Ghat are the cremation sites of two other assassinated heads of state, Indira Gandhi and her son Rajiv (no relation to Mohandas). ✉ *Mahatma Gandhi Marg, Ring Rd.* 🎫 *Free* ⊙ *Daily sunrise–sunset.*

Sis Ganj Sahib Gurdwara. Old Delhi's most famous Sikh shrine is a restful place to see one of North India's emblematic faiths in practice. Built at various times between 1784 (when the Sikhs conquered Delhi) and the 20th century, it marks the site where the Mughal emperor Aurangzeb beheaded Guru Teg Bahadur in 1675, when the guru refused to convert to Islam. It's a gory story, but before his body could be quartered and

Outside the Jama Masjid

displayed to the public as an example, it was stolen by disciples. He was cremated by his son, Guru Gobind Singh, the tenth and last great Sikh Guru. As in any *gurdwara* (Sikh temple), sections of the *Guru Granth Sahib* scripture are chanted continuously; depending on the season, you might also find decorations of tinsel, colored foil, and blinking lights. Leave your shoes at the opening about 30 feet to the right of the entrance, and cover your head before entering. Women: if you don't have a head covering, climb the stairs and ask the man on the left to lend you one (it's free). If you have any questions about Sikhism or the shrine after your visit, stop into the friendly information office to the left of the entrance to hear legends and symbols unfold. ⊠ *Chandni Chowk* ☉ *Daily 24 hrs* Ⓜ *Chandni Chowk.*

CENTRAL DELHI

Sometimes also called Lutyens' Delhi after the British urban planner and architect who was largely responsible for its design, Central Delhi houses the government center and the broad, imperial streets of power. Also sometimes referred to as "New Delhi" (as opposed to Old Delhi, Shah Jahan's pre-British city), it begins around Connaught Place and extends about 6 km (4 miles) south. Most sights are south of Connaught Place.

TOP ATTRACTIONS

Akshardham Temple Complex. Rising over the traffic jams of National Highway 24 on the way to the eastern suburb of Noida lies a massive, 100-acre temple complex. Completed in November 2005, the pink-stone religious emporium pays tribute to Bhagwan Swami Narayan

The Raj Ghat memorial to Mahatma Gandhi

(1781–1830), the founder of a worldwide spiritual movement that claims a million devotees. An architectural marvel built over five years and without using steel, the elaborate main temple and its soaring domes and 20,000 carved figures only appear ancient. This gleaming complex includes a giant movie theater and a 14-minute boat ride that is quite an experience. Whisking the visitor through 10,000 years of Indian culture, the ride could be mistaken for something straight out of Disney World—Indian style! Just viewing the exhibits takes at least two hours. Admission lines can be lengthy, so allow plenty of time. Security is airtight. ⚠ All bags and purses, electronics (including mobile phones and cameras), and tobacco products are banned, so check them in or leave them at the hotel or in the car before you get in line. But don't forget your wallet. While donations are voluntary, marketing is persistent. Exhibitions tend to shut an hour before the complex itself; the food court provides decent, cheap vegetarian meals and snacks for those who opt to spend the day. ⊠ *Nizamuddin Bridge, National Hwy. 24* ☏ *11/2202–6688* ⊕ *www.akshardham.com* ☞ *Free; exhibitions Rs. 170* ☼ *Tues.–Sun. 9:30–6:30* Ⓜ *Akshardham.*

Jantar Mantar. This odd grouping of what might seem like random modern sculptures is actually a huge sundial and open-air observatory. One of five such installations built by the Maharaja Sawai Jai Singh II of Jaipur in the early 18th century (the one in Jaipur is the best preserved), it's an interesting place to wander, though better understood with a good guide. The Samrat Jantar, the sundial, is the largest structure here, at 90 feet. The Hindu Chhatri, a small domed building, can tell when the monsoons are coming in and whether the weather will change. The Jai

Prakash shows the sun's position at the time of the equinox. The Ram Yantra consists of two large buildings, both with open tops: they're used, together, to measure the altitude of stars. The Mishra Yantra consists of five instruments, which are used to measure the shortest and longest days of the year. ✉ *Sansad Marg, Connaught Pl.* ☎ *11/2336–5358* 🖼 *Rs. 100* 🕐 *Daily sunrise–sunset* Ⓜ *Patel Chowk.*

Lutyens' Delhi. Rajpath—the broadest avenue in the city—leads to Delhi's British capital: Sir Edwin Lutyens' imperial city, built between 1914 and 1931 in a symbolically heavy-handed design after the British moved their capital from Calcutta to Delhi in 1911. (During construction, they hit marshy land prone to floods, so they reversed direction and put the bulk of their capital a few miles to the south.)

Starting from India Gate, at the lowest and eastern end of Rajpath, nearby land was allocated to numerous princely states, each of which built small palaces, such as the **Bikaner House** (now the Rajasthan tourism office) and **Jaipur House** (now the National Gallery of Modern Art). It might be said that this placement mirrored the British sentiments toward the princes, who lost much of their former power and status during the British Raj. Here, too, are the state Bhavans (houses), where you can taste the cuisine of each state.

Moving up the slowly inclining hill at the western end of the avenue, you also move up the British ladder of power, a concept inherent in the original design. First you come to the enormous **North and South Secretariats,** facing each other on Rajpath and reflecting the importance of the bureaucracy, a fixture of Indian society since the time of British rule. Identical in design, the two buildings have 1,000 rooms and miles of corridors.

Directly behind the North Secretariat is the Indian parliament house, **Sansad Bhavan,** a circular building in red and gray sandstone, encompassed by an open colonnade. Architecturally, the Indian design is meant to mirror the spinning wheel that was the symbol of Mahatma Gandhi, but the building's secondary placement, off the main avenue, may suggest the attitude of the British toward the Indian legislative assembly.

At the top of the hill is the former Viceroy's House, now called **Rashtrapati Bhavan,** where the President of India (not the prime minister) resides. It was built in the 20th century, but the building's daunting proportions seem to reflect an earlier, more lavish time of British supremacy. The Bhavan contains 340 rooms, and its grounds cover 330 acres. The shape of the central brass dome, the palace's main architectural feature, reflects that of a Buddhist *stupa* (shrine). The execution of Lutyens' design has a flaw: the entire palace was supposed to fill the vista as you approach the top of the hill, but the gradient is too steep, so only the dome dominates the horizon. Just a few years after the imperial city was completed, the British packed up and went home, and this lavish architectural complex became the grand capital of newly independent India.

Permission to enter Rashtrapati and Sansad Bhavan is almost impossible to obtain; unless you have contacts in high places, you'll have to satisfy yourself with a look at the poshest address in town from outside. ■ TIP→ The extensive Rashtrapati gardens are open to the public in February and March (Tuesday–Sunday 9:30–2:30; www.presidentofindia.nic.in). Heavy security is in place (no bags or cell phones, for instance), but a rare view of the impressive gardens is worth the hassle.

For an experience of imperial Delhi, stop for tea at the Imperial Hotel on Janpath; for a glimpse of Delhi's contemporary elite, browse at Khan Market. A stroll through Lodhi Gardens *(⇨ See South Delhi listings)* is a relaxing break and Habitat World or the India International Centre are good bets if you have a taste for culture. ⊠ *Central Delhi* Ⓜ *Central Secretariat.*

National Crafts Museum. Designed by the Indian architect Charles Correa, this charming museum near the Purana Qila houses thousands of artifacts and handicrafts. You're greeted outside by playful terra-cotta sculptures from Tamil Nadu. Inside, the annotations are sketchy, but the collection is fascinating. Items in the Folk and Tribal Art Gallery, including some charming toys, illustrate village life throughout India. In one courtyard you'll see a giant wooden temple car (cart), built to carry deities in festive processions; one of the adjacent buildings contains a lavishly decorated Gujarati haveli. The Courtly Crafts section suggests the luxurious lives of India's former royalty, and the entire upper floor is a spectacular showcase of saris and textiles. In the village complex out back, craftspeople demonstrate their skills and sell their creations in replicas of village homes. The museum shop is one of the best in Delhi, with high-quality art books and crafts. ■ TIP→ The in-house restaurant, Café Lota, serves regional highlights from all over the country. ⊠ *Bhairon Rd., off Mathura Rd., opposite Pragati Maidan* ☎ *11/2337–1641* ⊕ *nationalcraftsmuseum.nic.in* ⊑ *Rs. 150* ☉ *Tues.–Sun. 10–5* Ⓜ *Pragati Maidan.*

National Museum. The facade of this grand building imitates Lutyens' Presidential Palace: a sandstone dome is supported by classical columns of brown sandstone on a red-sandstone base. When you enter, you'll see a 13th-century idol—from the Konark Sun Temple in Bhubaneswar—of Surya, the sun god, standing beneath the dome. Such a statue is emblematic of the National Museum's strength—it showcases ancient, mainly Hindu, sculptures. An entire room is dedicated to artifacts from the Indus Valley Civilization, circa 2,700 BC; others display works from the Gandharan, Chandela, and Chola periods. Besides sculpture, also on exhibit are jewelry, painting, musical instruments, coins, carpets, and weapons, including Shah Jahan's sword. Be sure to pick up a brochure to help you navigate, and get the audio guide, included in ticket rates, which is also worth a listen. ⊠ *Janpath and Rajpath, India Gate* ☎ *11/2379–2775* ⊕ *www.nationalmuseumindia.gov.in* ⊑ *Rs. 300; camera fee Rs. 300* ☉ *Tues.–Sun. 10–5* Ⓜ *Central Secretariat.*

Nehru Memorial Museum. This colonial mansion, also known as Teen Murti Bhavan, was originally built for the commander of the British Indian Army. When the Viceroy's residence, Rashtrapati Bhavan (at the other end of South Avenue), became the home of India's president, India's first prime minister, Jawaharlal Nehru, took up residence here. Those interested in the Independence movement should not miss

The astronomical instruments at Delhi's Jantar Mantar resemble modern sculpture.

this landmark or the nearby Gandhi Smriti. Nehru's yellow mansion is fronted by a long, oval-shape lawn; out back there's a tranquil flower garden. Inside, several rooms remain as Nehru left them, and extensive displays chronicle Nehru's life and the Independence movement. Move through the rooms in order: one by one, photographs, newspaper clippings, and personal letters tell the breathtaking story of the birth of the world's largest democracy. On your way out, stop and see the 14th-century hunting lodge next to the Nehru Planetarium. (The latter, good for children, has shows in English at 11:30 am and 3 pm.) ✉ *Teen Murti Marg* ☎ *11/2301–7587* 🖃 *Free; planetarium Rs. 50* ☉ *Tues.–Sun. 9–5:30* Ⓜ *Race Course.*

WORTH NOTING

Bangla Sahib Gurdwara. This massive *gurdwara* (Sikh temple) is always full of activity—no surprise, given Delhi's huge Sikh population, most of whom came here as refugees from Pakistan in 1947. If you can't make it to Amritsar to see the Golden Temple, come here to admire the distinctively ostentatious style of their temples. Sikh gurdwaras reflect both the symmetry of Mughal mosques and the chaos of Hindu temples. Bangla Sahib is built of white marble and topped with a shiny, gold onion dome.

The gurdwara stands on the site where Guru Hari Krishan, the eighth of 10 Sikh gurus who lived between 1469 and 1708, performed a small miracle. Before entering, remove your shoes and socks (check them at the counter on the left), get rid of cigarettes, and cover your head with a piece of cloth. As you walk up the stairs and enter the sanctum, you'll see people filling jugs of water from enclosed cisterns. Guru Hari

3

Mahatma Gandhi Marg

Greens Colony Road

Vikas Marg

Vikas Marg

Vikas Marg

Mahatma Gandhi Marg

Yamuna

National Hwy. 24 Bypass

0   1/2 mi

0   1/2 km

National Zoological Park

9

Mahatma Gandhi Marg

NIZAMUDDIN EAST

◆ Hazrat Nizamuddin Railway Station

JANGPURA EXTENSION

NH2

Mahatma Gandhi Marg

KEY
𝑖 *Tourist information*

A view of the government buildings at Lutyens' Delhi

Krishan used to distribute sanctified water to the sick, believing it had a miraculous healing effect on their mind, body, and soul, and people still treat the contents of these pools as holy water. Inside, devotees sit facing a small pavilion in the center that holds the *Granth Sahib* (Sikh scriptures). Hymns from the holy book are sung continuously from well before sunrise until approximately 9 pm, and you're welcome to sit and listen; if you fancy something cultural in the evening, come at about 9 to see the ceremony by which the book is stored away for the night. As you walk around inside, be careful to proceed in a clockwise direction, and exit on the right side in back. Out the door to the right a priest distributes *prasad*, a ritual that Sikhs share with Hindus and that resembles the Christian sacrament of Communion: take a lump of this sugar, flour, and *ghee* (clarified butter) concoction with both hands, pop it into your mouth with your right hand, then rub the remaining ghee into your hands. ✉ *Bangla Sahib La., off Baba Kharak Singh Marg, near Connaught Pl.* ✉ *Free* ⊙ *Daily 4 am–9 pm* Ⓜ *Rajiv Chowk, Patel Chowk.*

Gandhi Smriti. Mohandas K. Gandhi, better known as the Mahatma (Great Soul), lived a life of voluntary poverty, but he did it in some attractive places. It was in this huge colonial bungalow, designed by a French architect for Indian industrialist G. D. R. Birla, that Gandhi was staying as a guest when he was assassinated in the back garden on his way to a prayer meeting. Gandhi's bedroom is just as he left it, with his "worldly remains" (only 11 items, including his glasses and a walking stick) mounted on the wall. Pictures and text tell the story of Gandhi's life and the Independence movement; there's also a collection of dioramas depicting events in Gandhi's life. In the theater, 10 different documentaries are available for viewing on request. Take off your shoes before entering the somber prayer ground in back; an eternal flame marks the very spot where Gandhi expired. This, not the National Gandhi Museum at Raj Ghat, is the government's official museum dedicated to the Mahatma. ⊠ *5 Tees January Marg* ☎ *11/3095–7269* 🖃 *Free* ⊙ *Tues.–Sun., 10–5; museum closed 2nd Sat. in month* Ⓜ *Race Course.*

India Gate. Anchoring a traffic circle near the far end of Rajpath from the Indian government, this massive sandstone arch was designed by Lutyens in 1931, in memory of the 90,000 soldiers of the British Indian Army who fell in World War I and the Third Afghan War of the late 19th century. In the 1970s the government of India added a memorial to India's unknown soldier, the Amar Jawan Jyoti, beneath the arch. It has huge sentimental value to Indians. The Indira Gandhi Canal runs through the circle; if it's not dry, go boating! While traffic speeds neatly around the outer circle, vendors occupy the inner circle, and people amble and socialize on the lawns. Come in early evening and you'll find all sorts of activity, from men offering to make monkeys "dance" (for a fee) to impromptu cricket matches to youngsters splashing in the ornamental fountains. *The* thing to do is get an ice cream—Mother Dairy is one of the better brands. ⊠ *Rajpath, east end.*

Indira Gandhi Memorial Museum. On October 31, 1984, Prime Minister Indira Gandhi was shot outside her home by two of her Sikh bodyguards in retaliation for her violent suppression of a violent Sikh independence movement in Punjab, which included a military operation that entered Amritsar's Golden Temple. The murder sparked gruesome anti-Sikh riots in Delhi, and political turmoil ensued. The simple white bungalow in which Mrs. Gandhi lived from the 1960s to 1980s is now a small museum with endless photographs, quotations, and newspaper articles, plus a few rooms preserved as they were used. The photos get more interesting as you progress, and the museum ends with displays on Indira's son, Rajiv, himself prime minister from 1984 to 1991 before he, too, was assassinated. Displays include the sari, handbag, and shoes Mrs. Gandhi was wearing when she was killed, and the sneakers Rajiv was wearing during his even more grisly demise at the hands of a female suicide bomber who killed him and 14 others bcause of India's support of the Sri Lankan government during a civil war. Outside, the spot where Indira fell is marked and preserved. Popular with Indian tourists, the museum can get very crowded; allow extra time if you want to peruse things carefully. ⊠ *1 Safdarjung Rd.* ☎ *11/2301–0094* 🖃 *Free* ⊙ *Tues.–Sun. 9:30–4:45* Ⓜ *Race Course.*

National Gallery of Modern Art. Facing India Gate, this neoclassical building was built by the British in the early 20th century as a palace for the Maharaja of Jaipur. With its small dome and large, open rooms, the structure makes a fine space for this art museum, established in 1954 to preserve Indian art forms (mainly painting) that developed after 1850. A large new wing was added in 2008 so that more of the extensive collection could be displayed. The displays are attractive by local standards but are unfortunately uneven and not always well explained. Highlights are the colorful paintings of Amrita Sher-Gil (the Frida Kahlo of India) and, upstairs, the myth-inspired works of Raja Ravi Varma and the Bengali Renaissance oils and watercolors of the Tagore family, Jamini Roy, and Nandalal Bose. There are a few representative works by contemporary masters, including M. F. Husain and Ganesh Pyne. Documentaries, shown daily at 11 and 3, explain Indian art. The old wing often hosts interesting temporary or traveling exhibitions. ⊠ *Jaipur House, India Gate* ☎ *11/2338–4640* ⊕ *www.ngmaindia.gov. in* ⊠ *Rs. 150* ⊗ *Tues.–Sun. 10–5, Thurs. 10–8.*

SOUTH DELHI

South Delhi, the older suburbs and colonies of the new city, has monuments even older than those in Old Delhi, including the Qutub Minar, Kauz Khas, and numerous pre-Mughal tombs, some of which lie abandoned in the midst of contemporary houses and apartments.

Along with a mix of government-built apartments, posh mansions and "farmhouses" of the elite, and refugee colonies from the 1950s, South Delhi also has the more recent addition of malls, particularly in Saket and Vasant Kunj. There is also plenty of soul and tradition. Getting in some quiet meditation at the Lotus Temple is a must. The incredible urbanized villages of Hauz Khas and Shahpur Jat may turn up anything from vintage Bollywood posters to beautifully beaded slippers. Visit Nizamuddin East for a sufi music performance that may transport you to a spiritual plane. Most destinations in South Delhi are now accessible by the Delhi Metro, including its wealth of restaurant and bars, many of which are packed on weekends.

TOP ATTRACTIONS

Baha'i House of Worship (The Lotus Temple). The lotus flower is a symbol of purity and spirituality throughout India, and Delhi's Baha'i Temple celebrates this in a unique architectural way. Designed by Fariborz Sahba, an Iranian-born Canadian architect, and completed in 1986, the building incorporates the number nine—the highest digit and, in the Baha'i faith, a symbol of unity. The sleek structure has two layers: nine white marble-covered petals that point to heaven, and nine petals that conceal the portals. From a short distance it looks like a fantastic work of origami. The nine pools outside signify the green leaves of the lotus and cool the starkly elegant, usually silent marble interior. The interior conforms to that of all Baha'i houses of worship: there are no religious icons, just copies of the Holy Scriptures and wooden pews. The road to the temple passes through a colorful temple bazaar connected to the nearby Kalkaji Mandir. ⊠ *Near Nehru Pl.* ☎ *11/2644–4029* ⊕ *www. bahaihouseofworship.in* ⊠ *Free* ⊗ *Apr.–Sept., Tues.–Sun. 9–7; Oct.–Mar., Tues.–Sun. 9:30–5:30* Ⓜ *Kalkaji Mandir.*

Hauz Khas Village. The road south to the urban village of Hauz Khas is lined on both sides by ancient stone monuments, and the entire village is dotted with domed structures—the tombs of minor Muslim royalty from the 14th to the 16th centuries. At the end of the road is the tomb of Firoz Shah Tughlaq, who ruled Delhi in the 14th century. Hauz Khas means "Royal Tank," referring to the artificial lake visible from Firoz Shah's pillared tomb. The tank was actually built a century earlier by

The gardens leading up to the Lotus Temple, also known as the Baha'i House of Worship

Allauddin Khilji as a water source for his nearby fort, then called Siri (the second city of Delhi). Back in the village, wander through the narrow lanes to experience a medley of old and new structures—expensive shops and art galleries in a medieval warren. ■ TIP➜ **Find your way to the gardens near the ruin of a madrassa at the back of the village. The kindly old gentleman often playing cards can sometimes be coaxed into an impromptu Urdu lesson.** In the 1980s Hauz Khas was designated an upscale tourist destination, but of late it more accurately aspires to emulate Manhattan's West Village. After exploring, stop for a meal at one of the village's restaurants *(⇨ See Where to Eat listings)*, particularly Park Balluchi (in the Deer Park), Naivedyam, or Yeti. The Toddy Shop and the Coast Café, serves some of the best South Indian food this side of the country. "HKV" also has the popular TLR Café, which hosts live and DJ performances over the weekends—from reggae to rock bands and retro nights—and a new host of rooftop bars. There are a fair number of young, funky upcoming designers that have opened their stores here. The biggest store to look out for is White: a minimal, very cool multidesigner outlet, in the same building as the TLR. ⊠ *Off Aurobindo Marg, Hauz Khas Village.*

Hazrat Nizamuddin Dargah. One of Delhi's greatest treats is hearing devout Sufis sing *qawwalis*, ecstatic devotional Muslim songs with a decidedly toe-tapping quality. Evenings from around 5 to 7, especially Thursday, the followers of the Sufi saint Hazrat Nizamuddin Aulia often gather to sing in front of his *dargah* (tomb); this is one of the best places to catch a performance. To get here, follow the twisting lanes in the bazaar section of Nizamuddin West—you'll pass open-air

South Delhi

Talkatora Garden

NEW DELHI

CENTRAL DELHI

Mughal Gardens

Jaipur to Delhi Expressway

Mother Teresa Crescent

Raisina Rd
Feroz Shah Rd
Rajendra Prasad Rd
Rajpath
Maulana Azad Rd
Akbar Rd

Dalhousie Rd

Bhairon Marg

NH2

SUNDAR NAGAR

National Zoological Park

11

12

Yamuna

NH8

Sardar Patel Marg

Feroz Shah Rd
Kushak
Menon

Panchsheel M

Aurangzeb Rd

Prithviraj Rd

Amrita Shergill Marg

Lodi Gardens

Subramanium Bharti Marg

Lodhi Rd

CHANAKYAPURI

Nehru Park

9

10

JOR BAGH

LODHI COLONY

Jor Bagh Rd

NIZAMUDDIN WEST

Lodhi Rd

2

1

NIZAMUDDIN EAST

JANGPURA EXTENSION

8

Brigadier Hoshiar Singh Marg

Najafkhan Rd

Barapullah Rd

Barapullah Rd

NH2

SAROJINI NAGAR

SOUTH DELHI

DEFENCE COLONY

Marg

SOUTH EXTENSION I

Mahatma Gandhi Marg (Ring Road)

Ring Road

BHIKAJI CAMA PLACE

SAFDARJUNG ENCLAVE

SOUTH EXTENSION II

Africa Avenue

Aurobindo Marg

August Kranti Marg

GREATER KAILASH I

4
Lotus Temple

3

NEHRU PLACE

7

GREEN PARK

HAUZ KHAS

Hauz Khas Deer Park

Siri Fort Model Park

Hans Raj Gupta Marg

0   1 mi

0   1 km

Outer Ring Road

Outer Ring Road

Press Enclave

GREATER KAILASH II

5 6

Shaheed Jeet Singh Marg

restaurants serving simple meat-based meals, tiny shops selling Urdu-language books and CDs (some by famous qawwali singers), and probably a number of beggars appealing to the Muslim tradition of alms for the poor. When you see vendors selling flowers and garlands, you're getting close to the dargah. Nizamuddin, who was born in Bukhara (now in Uzbekistan) in 1238, later fled with his family to Delhi, where he became an important Sufi mystic and attracted a dedicated following. He died in 1325.

The tomb, built in 1562 in the center of a courtyard, is topped with an onion-shaped dome. It's also covered with intricate painting and inlay work, best viewed on the carved parapet above the verandas. Men can enter the shrine to pay their respects; women must peer in from outside. The tomb is flanked by a mosque and the graves of other important Muslims, including the great Sufi poet Amir Khusro and Jahanara, a daughter of the Mughal emperor Shah Jahan. △ Crowds can be dense, and it's easy to have your wallet or purse stolen before you notice. Keep money and valuables secured when you're in and around the dargah. ✉ *Nizamuddin Basti, enter bazaar from Mathura Rd., Nizamuddin West* ✉ *Free, donations to shrine and musicians accepted* ⊙ *Daily 24 hrs.*

Fodor's Choice ★ **Humayun's Tomb.** Freshly restored in 2013 after six years of painstaking conservation work, this moument is a sight to behold. Built in the middle of the 16th century by the widow of the Mughal emperor Humayun, this tomb launched a new architectural era of Persian influence, culminating in the Taj Mahal and Fatehpur Sikri. The Mughals brought to India their love of gardens and fountains and left a legacy of harmonious structures, including this mausoleum, that fuse symmetry with decorative splendor.

Resting on an immense two-story platform, the tomb structure of red sandstone and white marble is surrounded by gardens intersected by water channels in the Mughals' beloved *charbagh* design: gardens divided into four (*char*) perfectly square parts. The marble dome covering the actual tomb is another first: a dome within a dome (the interior dome is set inside the soaring dome seen from outside), a style later used in the Taj Mahal. As you enter or leave the tomb area, stand a moment before the beveled gateway to enjoy the view of the monument framed in the arch.

Besides Humayun, several other important Mughals are buried here, along with Isa Khan Niyazi, a noble in the court of Sher Shah—who lies in the fetching octagonal shrine that precedes the tomb itself. The site's serenity belies the fact that many of the dead buried inside were murdered princes, victims of foul play. To see where Humayun actually died, combine this visit with a trip to the Purana Qila. ✉ *Off Mathura Rd., Nizamuddin East* ☎ *11/2435–5275* ✉ *Rs. 250* ⊙ *Daily sunrise–sunset.*

Lodhi Gardens. After the Mughal warrior Timur (aka Tamerlane) ransacked Delhi at the end of the 14th century, he ordered the massacre of the entire population—acceptable retribution, he thought, for the murder of some of his soldiers. As if in unconscious response to this horrific act, the subsequent Lodhi and Sayyid dynasties built no city, only a few mosques and some mausoleums and tombs, the latter of which stand in what is now a delightful urban park. Winding walks cut through landscaped lawns with trees and small flowers, past schoolboys playing cricket, politicians taking in some air, friends and lovers relaxing in the greenery, and parrots squawking. Lodi—the Garden Restaurant is a good place to get a meal after an evening walk. Made of wood and glass, it's as verdant as the garden itself. Near the southern entrance on Lodhi Road is the dignified mausoleum of Mohammed Shah, third ruler of the Sayyid dynasty, and some members of his family. This octagon, with a central chamber surrounded by verandas carved with arches, is a good example of the architecture of this period. Near the road is the open-air National Bonsai Park, with some nice specimens of the trees. The smaller, equally lovely octagonal tomb of Sikandar Lodhi, surrounded by a garden in the park's northwestern corner, has an unusual double dome. ⊠ *Lodhi Rd., southeast of Khan Market* 🖾 *Free* ☉ *Daily sunrise–sunset* Ⓜ *Jor Bagh.*

Purana Qila (*Old Fort*). India's sixth capital was the scene of a fierce power struggle between the Afghan Sher Shah and Humayun, son of the first Mughal emperor, Babur, in the 16th century. When Humayun started to build his own capital, Dinpanah, on these grounds in the 1530s, Sher Shah forced the emperor to flee for his life to Persia. Sher Shah destroyed what existed of Dinpanah to create his own capital, Shergarh. Fifteen years later, in 1555, Humayun returned and seized control, but he died the following year, leaving Sher Shah's city for others to destroy.

Unfortunately, once you enter the massive Bara Darwaza (Main Gate), only two buildings are intact. The **Qila-i-Kuhna Masjid,** Sher Shah's private mosque, is an excellent example of Indo-Afghan architecture in red sandstone with decorative marble touches—walk around to the "back" to see the beautiful front of the building. The nearby **Sher Mandal,** a two-story octagonal tower of red sandstone and white marble, became Humayun's library and ultimately his death trap: hearing the call to prayer, Humayun started down the steep steps, slipped, and fell to his death. On pleasant afternoons, seemingly every bush on these grounds hides a pair of young lovers in search of a little privacy. ⊠ *Delhi Zoo, off Mathura Rd., near Pragati Maidan* 🖾 *Rs. 100* ☉ *Daily sunrise–sunset* Ⓜ *Pragati Maidan.*

Qutub Minar. Named for the Muslim sultan Qutab-ud-din Aibak, this striking tower is 238 feet high, with 376 steps, and the tallest stone tower in India. Qutub-ud-din Aibak began construction in 1193; his son-in-law and successor, Iltutmish, added the top four stories. The result is a handsome sandstone example of Indo-Islamic architecture, with terra-cotta frills and balconies. At its foot lies the **Quwwat-ul-Islam Masjid,** the first mosque in India. The Muslims erected the mosque in the 12th century after they defeated the Hindu Chauhan dynasty—they built it on the site of a Hindu temple and used pillars and other materials from 27 demolished Hindu and Jain shrines. (Which explains why you see Hindu and Jain sculptures in the mosque.) The mosque is also famous for a 24-foot-high, 5th-century iron pillar, inscribed with six lines of Sanskrit. According to legend, if you stand with your back to the pillar and can reach around and touch your fingers, any wish you make

will come true. (Unfortunately, it's now fenced off.) ⊠ *Aurobindo Marg, near Mehrauli* ⬛ *Rs. 250* ⊙ *Daily sunrise–sunset* Ⓜ *Qutub Minar.*

Safdarjang's Tomb. Delhi's last great garden tomb, built in 1754 for the prime minister of the emperor Mohammad Shah, is pleasantly located in the center of town. With its marble oversize dome and minarets, it can't compete with Humayun's resting place, but the finials and other details have a distinctly Mughul fineness, and the charbagh (four-section garden, which is a typical Mughal style) is a peaceful place to listen to the birds chirp. The site would be lovelier if water still ran through the four large channels in the gardens, but you have to imagine that part to complete the 18th-century scene. ⊠ *Aurobindo Marg at Lodhi Rd., Jor Bagh* ⬛ *Rs. 100* ⊙ *Daily sunrise–sunset* Ⓜ *Jor Bagh.*

WORTH NOTING

Chhattarpur Temples. If you're on your way south to Agra or Jaipur, drive a few miles beyond the Qutub Minar on Mehrauli Road and check out this massive Hindu temple complex. It's a mishmash of styles, but the unifying factor—from the huge dome over the Shiva lingam to the 92-foot statue of the monkey god Hanuman—is its flashy and elaborate architecture, done in so-called Punjabi Baroque. It's quite a sight to take in: these huge temples looming on either side of the road. Enter through the sanctum with the devotees, stop at the idols to pay respects, and take some prasad on the way out. Many gods and goddesses are represented, but the inner sanctum is dedicated to Adhya Ma Katyan, a mother goddess. Hymns are sung all night during full moons. Make sure you're dressed respectfully, and be ready to take off your shoes. ⊠ *Chhattarpur Rd., Chhattarpur* ⬛ *Free* ⊙ *Daily sunrise–sunset* Ⓜ *Chhattarpur.*

ISKCON Temple. The International Society for Krishna Consciousness is better known as the Hare Krishna sect, and despite the 1960s association they are very much alive and kicking. In the 1990s ISKCON erected enormous, gleaming Krishna temples in several Indian cities, and these offer a unique glimpse into the remaining pockets of international Hinduism, with shaven-headed foreigners in saffron robes mingling with Indian colleagues, devotees, and tourists. Built impressively on a rock outcropping near a residential market, Delhi's temple is an amalgam of architectural styles: Mughal, Gupta, and the flashy Delhi style jokingly called Punjabi Baroque. The sanctum contains three idols—Balram Krishna, Radha-Krishna, and Laksman (along with Rama and Sita)—each representing a different incarnation of Lord Krishna. The art gallery behind the idols must be viewed in a clockwise direction, as this *parikrama* (revolution) is the only appropriate way to move around the gods. To learn more about Krishna, pop into the "Vedic Expo," where an upstairs collection of dioramas illustrate his life in the incarnation of Lord Chaitanya, and various sound-and-light shows (even a robotics display) enact the *Bhagavad Gita* scriptures and the ancient epic, the *Mahabharata*, from which the scriptures come. It's all a bit Southern California, but ISKCON's temples are by far the cleanest in India, and very welcoming to visitors. Finish with a meal at Govinda's, the on-site restaurant, where a delicious vegetarian buffet goes for Rs.

380. ✉ *Sant Nagar Main Rd., east of Kailash* ☎ *11/2623–5133* 💳 *Free* 🕐 *Daily 4:30 am–12:45 pm and 4 pm–8:45 pm.*

FAMILY **National Rail Museum.** This large, mostly outdoor museum is a glimpse into the largest railroad system in the world. The 10-acre grounds are home to 75 authentic locomotives, bogies (railway cars), and even a working roundabout (a device that turns rail cars). Parked behind glass is the *Fairy Queen*; built in 1855, it's the oldest running steam engine in the world. It still takes nine trips a year to Sariska National Park and back for a weekend trip (contact the director of the museum if you're interested, but it's not worth the outrageous price). Inside the museum are displays that discuss the history of India's rail system. The museum is good not only for train buffs but also children, who love riding the tiny train that circles the grounds. ✉ *Nyaya Marg, off Shanti Path, Chanakyapuri* ☎ *11/2688–1816, 11/2688–0939* ⊕ *www. nrm.indianrailways.gov.in* 💳 *Rs. 10* 🕐 *Oct.–Mar., Tues.–Sun. 9:30–5; Apr.–Sept., Tues.–Sun. 9:30–7:30.*

FAMILY **National Zoological Park.** White tigers are the draw at Delhi's zoo, which was designed in the late 1950s by the German designer Carl Hagenbeck. There are many other noteworthy animals roaming about, such as emus, gazelles, Indian rhinos, and a great many deer, not to mention some smart-looking waterbirds. Animals in cages, including the famous white tigers and Asiatic lions, are part of the national collection. The zoo is spacious and leafy, a virtual botanical garden for peaceful walks, and the central lake hosts numerous Central Asian migratory aquatic birds (pelicans, storks, and cranes) pausing on their way to Keoladeo National Park in Bharatpur, Rajasthan, for the winter. If you don't have time to make it to Bharatpur or a tiger reserve, this is a pretty good alternative. ✉ *Mathura Rd., behind Sundar Nagar* ☎ *11/2435–9825, 11/2435–8500* ⊕ *www.nzpnewdelhi.gov.in* 💳 *Rs. 50* 🕐 *Mid-Oct.–Mar., Sat.–Thurs. 9:30–4; Apr.–mid-Oct., Sat.–Thurs. 9–4:30.*

WHERE TO EAT

OLD DELHI

$ ✕ **Chor Bizarre.** Delhi's best-known Kashmiri restaurant is also one of
NORTH INDIAN   its most beautiful, an art deco enclave with a tile floor, a spiral staircase
Fodor's Choice   leading nowhere, and antique furniture and mirrors from various *chor*
★   ("thieves'") bazaars. The bar is all dark wood and stained glass, and the salad bar is a 1927 Fiat roadster. Kashmiri food, which is milder than many Indian regional cuisines, is exemplified by mutton *yakhni* (in a sauce of yogurt, cardamom, and aniseed) and mutton *mirchi korma* (in cardamom and clove gravy). Try a *tarami* platter to sample several dishes, and drink *kahwah*, fragrant Kashmiri tea. 💲 *Average main: Rs. 425* ✉ *Hotel Broadway, 4/15A Asaf Ali Rd., just outside Old Delhi, near Delhi Gate* ☎ *11/4366–3600* ✛ *F1.*

$ ✕ **Karim's.** This is an Old Delhi institution where mutton (which generally
NORTH INDIAN   means goat in India) is king, especially in thick, rich gravies. Try *mutton Mughlai* or *badaam pasanda* ("almond delight," mutton in a slightly sweet gravy) for the full experience. Open from 7 am to midnight, it's

BEST BETS FOR DELHI DINING

With so many restaurants to choose from, how to decide? Fodor's writers and editors have chosen their favorites, by price, cuisine, and experience, in the lists below.

Fodor's Choice ★

Basil & Thyme, p. 122
Chor Bizarre, p. 118
Diva, p. 126
Dum Pukht, p. 123
Indian Accent, p. 126
Kainoosh, p. 127
Khan Chacha, p. 124

By Price

$

Chor Bizarre, p. 118
Karim's, p. 118
Khan Chacha, p. 124
Lala Duli Chand
Naresh Gupta, p. 122
Mamagoto, p. 124
Swagath, p. 128

$$

Diva, p. 126
Dum Pukht, p. 123
Kainoosh, p. 127
Latitude 28, p. 124
San Gimignano, p. 125
The Yum Yum Tree, p. 129

$$$

Indian Accent, p. 126

By Cuisine

AMERICAN

The All American
Diner, p. 122

ASIAN

Gung the Palace, p. 126
The Yum Yum Tree, p. 129

DESSERTS AND
SNACKS

Bikanervala, p. 123
Lala Duli Chand
Naresh Gupta, p. 122

INDIAN

Chor Bizarre, p. 118
Dum Pukht, p. 123
Indian Accent, p. 126

ITALIAN

Diva, p. 126
San Gimignano, p. 125

NORTH INDIAN

Bukhara, p. 123
Karim's, p. 118
Khan Chacha, p. 124
Moti Mahal Delux, p. 127

SEAFOOD

Coast Cafe, p. 125
Swagath, p. 128

SOUTH INDIAN

Coast Cafe, p. 125
Naivedyam, p. 127
Swagath, p. 128

By Experience

BEST BRUNCH

The All American
Diner, p. 122
Chez Nini, p. 123

BEST HOTEL DINING

Bukhara, p. 123
Dum Pukht, p. 123
Indian Accent, p. 126

BEST
PEOPLE-WATCHING

Khan Chacha, p. 124
Moti Mahal Delux, p. 127
Olive Bar & Kitchen, p. 127

BEST VEGETARIAN

Naivendyam, p. 127
Sagar, p. 128

BEST WITH KIDS

Bengali Sweet House, p. 122
Sagar, p. 128

HOT SPOT

Latitude 28, p. 124
Olive Bar & Kitchen, p. 127

MOST ROMANTIC

Kainoosh, p. 127
Park Balluchi, p. 128

3

off the street that runs out from the mosque's main entrance, Gate 1; about four shops down on the left, take the passageway into a small courtyard—you'll see large cauldrons of meaty concoctions, smoking kebabs on spits, and several indoor seating areas. The newer Karim's, **Dastar Khwan-e-Karim,** near Hazrat Nizamuddin Darga, is more restaurant-like. Alcohol is not served. $ *Average main: Rs. 300* ⊠ *Gali Kababian, near Jama Masjid* ☎ *11/2326–9880, 11/2326–4981* ⊕ *www. karimhoteldelhi.com* ⊟ *No credit cards* ☉ *Closed daylight hrs during Ramadan* Ⓜ *Chawri Bazaar* ✚ *E1* $ *Average main: Rs. 300* ⊠ *168/2 Jha House Basti, Nizamuddin West, South Delhi* ☎ *11/4182–7871* ⊕ *www.karimhoteldelhi.com* ✚ *E1.*

$ ✕ **Lala Duli Chand Naresh Gupta.** A Delhi summer isn't complete without
INDIAN one of these famous *kulfis*—the frozen milk–based treats similar to
Fodor'sChoice ice cream. What makes this spot so unique is that you'll get your kulfi
★ served in the fruit that it's flavored with: order apple, for instance, and you'll get an apple (it looks like a frozen candy apple) that splits open to reveal the delicious kulfi inside. They'll kulfi up just about any fruit, from mangoes to figs to kiwis. $ *Average main: Rs. 100* ⊠ *Bazaar Sita Ram, 934 Kucha Pati Ram* ☎ *11/2323–7085* Ⓜ *Chawri Bazaar* ✚ *E1.*

CENTRAL DELHI

$ ✕ **The All American Diner.** It's the city's best-known faux-1950s diner,
DINER complete with old advertisements on the wall and Elvis music on the hi-fi. For those eating alone, there's a comfortable and long meal counter. Otherwise, take one of the booths, get ready for standard, but high-quality, diner fare. Most people go for the breakfast options, served all day. The waffles and pancakes are among the best in Delhi—the pancakes taste freshly made, and the waffles don't feel reheated. Most of the egg dishes come with perfectly made hash browns, and the French toast platter is justly famous. Top it off with specialty coffees, including those spiked with alcohol of various kinds. There's also very pleasant outdoor seating. $ *Average main: Rs. 350* ⊠ *India Habitat Centre, Lodhi Rd.* ☎ *11/4122–0000* ⊕ *www.habitatworld.com* ✚ *E4.*

$$ ✕ **Basil & Thyme.** This is one of Delhi's oldest and most beloved continen-
MODERN tal restaurants; the family-run enterprise is holding up after the demise
EUROPEAN of its matriarch and legendary chef, Bhicoo Manekshaw, in 2013. You
Fodor'sChoice can bank on fresh flavors, such as carrot-and-orange soup, pita triangles
★ with garlic butter, roast chicken stuffed with black mushrooms, or a "filo parcel" stuffed with vegetables and glazed with a coriander hollandaise. The room is a minimalist warm white, with stone floors and large windows overlooking the greenery of Santushti Shopping Complex. This lunch spot is a favorite of Delhi's upper crust and the embassy crowd. Alcohol is not served. $ *Average main: Rs. 500* ⊠ *11 Santushti Shopping Complex, Chanakyapuri* ☎ *11/3303–6627* ⌲ *Reservations essential* ☉ *Closed Sun. No dinner* ✚ *D4.*

$ ✕ **Bengali Sweet House.** This is a classic spot for evening golgappa outings.
INDIAN Also on offer are other Delhi snack staples: *chhole bhature* (also known
FAMILY as *chana bhatura*—spicy chickpeas with fried, airy puri bread), stuffed parathas, paneer fritters, *raj kachori* (spicy chaat bowl with assorted fillings). A snack is supposed to be finished with sweets: *gulab jamun* (milk-and-dough dumpling soaked with sugar syrup), *gajar ka halwa* (a

fudgelike, carrot-based dessert), and *rasmalai*, made of cottage cheese and cream. $ *Average main: Rs. 120* ✉ *27–33 Bengali Market, near Connaught Pl.* ☎ *11/2331–9224* ▬ *No credit cards* Ⓜ *Mandi House* ✛ *E2.*

$ ✕ **Bikanervala.** A reliable place for Gujarati snacks—ask for *khandvi*
INDIAN (a delicious pan-fried snack made from a seasoned batter of chickpea flour and buttermilk, then cut into rolls and sprinkled with coconut and coriander) or *dhokla* (a savory, fluffy, steamed cake made with chickpea flour, mustard seeds, and a pinch of sugar and topped with coriander leaves). $ *Average main: Rs. 120* ✉ *Rajiv Gandhi Handicraft Bhavan, Baba Kharag Singh Marg, 1st fl., near Connaught Pl.* ☎ *11/2336–7742* ⊕ *www.bikanervala.com* Ⓜ *Rajiv Chowk* ✛ *B2.*

$$ ✕ **Blue Ginger.** Classy and expensive, with a tantalizing menu full of
VIETNAMESE excellent choices, this is Delhi's only Vietnamese restaurant. Not sure whether to start with taro prawns or the fresh summer rolls with chicken, shrimp, and chives? We'd say order both; you won't be disappointed with the presentation or the flavor. It's equally hard to narrow down the main courses, but the stir-fried prawns with tamarind sauce is an excellent bet, as are lamb shanks in oyster sauce. The adjacent Blue Bar has one of the most innovative cocktail lists in town, so stop in before or after dinner. $ *Average main: Rs. 1000* ✉ *Taj Palace Hotel, Sardar Patel Marg, Diplomatic Enclave, Chanakyapuri* ☎ *11/6650–3665* ⊕ *www.tajhotels.com* Ⓜ *Dhaula Kuan* ✛ *B4.*

$$$$ ✕ **Bukhara.** Served amid stone walls, rough-hewn dark-wood beams,
NORTH INDIAN copper urns, and blood-red rugs, Bukhara's menu hasn't changed in years, and its loyal clientele wouldn't have it any other way. The cuisine of the Northwest Frontier, now the Pakistan–Afghanistan border, is heavy on meats, marinated and grilled in a *tandoor* (clay oven). The *murgh malai kebab* (boneless chicken marinated with cream cheese, malt vinegar, and green coriander) is very good. Bukhara's famous *dal* (black lentils with tomatoes, ginger, and garlic) is now sold in grocery stores. Vegetarians choices are limited. Service can sometimes be perfunctory, especially for smaller groups. $ *Average main: Rs. 1550* ✉ *ITC Maurya Hotel, Sardar Patel Marg, Diplomatic Enclave, Chanakyapuri* ☎ *11/3303–6086* ⊕ *www.itcwelcomgroup.in* ✛ *B4.*

$$ ✕ **Chez Nini.** The French-Canadian brasserie, run by a Quebecoise with
FRENCH Punjabi ancestry, sits at the center of a collection of excellent little cafés and restaurants—but it's still the best. They're known for their pork belly, cured and roasted over seven days—order it only if you're hungry, because it's quite filling. Another special is the chicken in a pot, with perfectly baked flaky pastry, and the perfect mix of herbs flavoring the chicken. Always ask about the day's specials; the beef in a pot, when available, is the best dish here. Chez Nini is also one of the best places to eat brunch, with a fixed-rice menu with all the usual suspects, as well as smoked mackerel rillettes and an open-face ratatouille sandwich on challah bread. $ *Average main: Rs. 600* ✉ *79–80 5th Ave. Rd., Meher Chand Market, Lodhi Colony* ☎ *11/4905–0665* ✛ *E4.*

$$ ✕ **Dum Pukht.** Like the *nawabi* (princely) culture from which it's drawn,
NORTH INDIAN the food and style at this restaurant are subtle and refined. Chef Imtiaz
Fodor'sChoice Qureshi, descended from court cooks in Avadh (Lucknow), creates
★ delicately spiced meals packed with flavor: *dum ki khumb* (button

mushrooms in gravy, fennel, and dried ginger), *kakori kabab* (finely minced mutton, cloves, and cinnamon, drizzled with saffron), and the special *raan-e-dumpukht* (a leg of mutton marinated in dark rum and stuffed with onions, cheese, and mint). The formal room is white, blue, and hushed. $ *Average main: Rs. 900* ⊠ *ITC Maurya Hotel, Sardar Patel Marg, Diplomatic Enclave, Chanakyapuri* ☎ *11/2611–2233* ⊕ *www.itcwelcomgroup.in* ⌂ *Reservations essential* ✛ *B4.*

$$ ✕ **Fire.** Seasonal ingredients and unexpected flavor combinations update
INDIAN and transform Indian classics, making the Park Hotel's flagship restaurant a real standout. Recent stunners included a savory banana stem salad (it uses all parts of the fruit) and a surprisingly light, tomato-infused *dal* (stewed lentils). Regional classics with a twist, such as the fiery chicken chettinad from Tamil Nadu, are consistently delicious menu mainstays. Taster menus offer a sample of the season's goods, and the carefully chosen wine list is presented by staff knowledgeable enough to make informed recommendations, a rarity in Delhi. Service can be haughty. $ *Average main: Rs. 800* ⊠ *The Park New Delhi, 15 Parliament St., Connaught Pl.* ☎ *11/2374–3000* ⊕ *www.theparkhotels. com* ⌂ *Reservations essential* ✛ *D2.*

$ ✕ **Khan Chacha.** You'll recognize this spot by the crowd of people clam-
NORTH INDIAN oring for the kebabs hot off the grill. You won't notice the crowds
Fodor's Choice though once you bite into your first chicken *tikka* or *paneer tikka*
★ *roomali* roll (spiced chicken or soft cheese grilled and wrapped in a thin, flatbread). Eat the succulent *seekh kebabs* (minced mutton rolls) before they get cold. $ *Average main: Rs. 120* ⊠ *50 Khan Market, Middle La.* ☎ *98/1080–4114, 98/1115–2722* ▭ *No credit cards* Ⓜ *Khan Market* ✛ *E4.*

$$ ✕ **Latitude 28.** One of Delhi's prettiest, hippest cafés, Latitude 28 is the
ECLECTIC place to go if you want to relax over a thoughtful meal. Celebrity
Fodor's Choice chef Ritu Dalmia has put together a playful mix of comfort food from
★ around the world—chicken skewers, "old-fashioned chow mein," pasta with bacon and cheese, a mezze platter—and quirky takes on regional staples from around India: a Kolkata-style crispy chicken cutlet paired with *baingan bhaja* (sliced and toasted eggplant) and a apricot-tamarind-chilli salsa, or lamb cooked in yogurt and fenugreek curry and served with Malabar *parotta,* the flaky flat bread native to Kerala. The café is a part of Good Earth, Delhi's classiest home store, and it looks the part, with stenciled walls, delicate chandeliers and a patio section with the best view in the market. $ *Average main: Rs. 560* ⊠ *9 Khan Market* ☎ *11/2462–1013* ⊕ *divarestaurants.com/latitide.php* ✛ *E4.*

$ ✕ **Mamagoto.** "Mamagato" is Japanese for "play with your food," and
ASIAN this cheery restaurant, hidden behind a yellow door in the middle lane of Khan Market, is indeed a fun place for a low-key meal. This is a great spot to have a couple of cocktails and share several dishes. Choose items like the addictive crispy chilli potato from the "small plates" menu to pair with larger dishes like the "signature" Street Vendor's Panang Curry or crispy lamb with onions and peppers. $ *Average main: Rs. 300* ⊠ *53 Khan Market, 1st fl., Middle La.* ☎ *11/4516–6060* ⊕ *www. mamagoto.in* Ⓜ *Khan Market* ✛ *E3.*

$ ✕**Nathu's.** There's a very wide selection of breads and sweets here—
INDIAN there are more than a dozen options in parattas alone; go for the ones
filled with mint or cauliflower. Sweets are all on the richer side, but it
would be a pity to leave Delhi without trying a doughnut-like *balushahi*
(deep fried and sticky, but delicious nevertheless) or *sohan halwa*, a delicacy of Persian origins made of long-cooked sugar and corn flour that's
stuffed with almonds and pistachios. $ *Average main: Rs. 110* ⊠ *2 Sun-*
dar Nagar Market ☎ *11/3303–6428* ⊕ *www.nathusweets.com* ✢ *F3*.

$$ ✕**San Gimignano.** Delhi's most rarefied Italian restaurant is known for its
ITALIAN playful, sensuous dishes. The three-course regional menu changes peri-
odically, but you might find such fancies as a "flan" of spinach, black
olives, and risotto with a fresh basil-and-tomato sauce; tagliatelle with
a fresh herb sauce of minced duck and Parmesan cheese; sliced grilled
tenderloin with grilled polenta and marsala sauce; or a grilled baby
lamb chop with grilled balsamic vegetables. The small wood-paneled
rooms are inviting, and in winter you can dine on a terra-cotta patio
in the fabulous garden. Service is excellent. $ *Average main: Rs. 950*
⊠ *Imperial Hotel, Janpath, Connaught Pl.* ☎ *11/4111–6608* ⊕ *www.*
theimperialindia.com/san_gimignano ⌕ *Reservations essential* ✢ *E2*.

$$ ✕**Taipan.** The formal Taipan is one of the finest Chinese restaurants in
CHINESE Delhi. The food is authentic, luscious, and artfully presented, and the
view from the top of the Oberoi—over the Delhi Golf Course toward the
high-rise buildings of Connaught Place—is grand. The menu highlights
Cantonese and Szechuan cooking, including salt-and-pepper prawns,
minced prawns with asparagus, Calcutta beckti fish in a *nonya* (spicy
lemon) chilli sauce, and various duck dishes. The best-loved house specialty is dim sum, available in a daily fixed-price lunch—reserve in
advance for this feast. $ *Average main: Rs. 900* ⊠ *The Oberoi Hotel,*
Dr. Zakir Hussain Rd., next to Delhi Golf Club ☎ *11/2436–3030*
⊕ *www.oberoihotels.com* ✢ *F4*.

$$ ✕**Yellow Brick Road.** Delhi's insomniacs love this super-bright, tiny
INTERNATIONAL 24-hour coffee shop. The blinding-yellow striped wallpaper, vintage
French-colonial posters, and distressed-yellow tables are a perfect cure
for jet lag. The menu wears several hats, mainly North Indian and Euro-
pean, and everything is cheerfully presented. Vegetarian options are
many, including tasty paneer dishes, mushroom crepes, and sweet corn
soup. The *chote miya biryani* (lamb in seasoned rice) is rich and filling
and the risotto with chicken and asparagus is very good, too. $ *Average*
main: Rs. 500 ⊠ *Vivanta by Taj Ambassador Hotel, Subramani Bharti*
Marg, near Khan Market, Sujan Singh Park ☎ *11/2463–2600* ⊕ *www.*
tajhotels.com Ⓜ *Khan Market* ✢ *E3*.

SOUTH DELHI

$ ✕**Coast Cafe.** One of the few places in Delhi where you could sample
SOUTH INDIAN the cuisine of India's west coast, famous for its lush and bold flavors.
Their celebrated items include the prawn *moily*, sweet and spicy and
rich with coconut milk, and lamb with garam masala, a heady blend of
ground spices. Vegetarians might want to try the home-style eggplant
curry flavored with *kokum*, a sour fruit native to the west coast, or the
safer but equally delicious vegetable stew. The mains are served with
appams (rice pancakes) or *parottas* (layered flat breads). The place

is well-lit and spacious, and designed for a laid-back evening, with wicker chairs, winding staircase, arches, balconies, and terrace windows. $ *Average main: Rs. 440* ⊠ *OGAAN, H2 Hauz Khas Village* ☎ *11/4160–1717* ✛ *C6.*

$$
ITALIAN
Fodor'sChoice
★

✕ **Diva.** Count on this popular, classy joint for delicious pizza and pasta—most of Delhi does—but if you're looking for something more substantial, mains like pan-seared lamb chops are also excellent, so make sure to ask about the daily specials. The excellent wine list is a draw here, too, as are top-quality desserts like the apple pie with hazelnuts. $ *Average main: Rs. 800* ⊠ *M-84 M Block Market, Greater Kailash 2* ☎ *11/2921–5673* ⊕ *www.divarestaurant.com* ⌆ *Reservations essential* ✛ *E6.*

$
INDIAN

✕ **Evergreen Sweet House.** A well-known stop in south Delhi for *chole bhatura* (spicy chickpeas and puffy fried bread) and vegetarian *thalis* (combination platters). Under a charming tin ceiling, a large crowd gathers every evening to unwind over its soothing array of fast food, desserts, cookies, and confections. $ *Average main: Rs. 120* ⊠ *Green Park Market, S-29 and 30* ☎ *11/2651–4646* ⊕ *www.evergreensweethouse.com* Ⓜ *Green Park* ✛ *D6.*

$$
ITALIAN

✕ **Flavors of Italy.** Nestled in the heart of South Delhi, what started as a tiny ice-cream parlor has morphed into a large space with plenty of seating, both indoors and out. This is a staple for Delhi families, who come for basic, if overpriced, Italian dishes including fresh home-made pastas, a selection of thin-crust pizzas and calzones, bounteous salads, and main courses. Proprietor Tarsillo Nataloni is often on hand to make suggestions, and the beer is always super-chilled. $ *Average main: Rs. 550* ⊠ *49–54C, Moolchand Flyover Complex, Ring Rd., Defence Colony* ☎ *11/2464–5644* Ⓜ *Lajpat Nagar* ✛ *F5.*

$$$
KOREAN

✕ **Gung the Palace.** Set over three floors and a basement, the main gathering place for New Delhi's large population of Korean expats is mostly furnished with a combination of sunken tables and little booths, though there are several stand-alone tables for those uncomfortable or unable to use traditional Korean seating. If you're with a large group, the friendly Korean waitstaff will fire up the barbeque embedded in the sunken tables; otherwise, a grill is wheeled up to the table. The *bulgogi*—made with marinated beef—is fine, but the real specialties are the *so galbi* (barbecued beef ribs) and the *wang galbi* (pork ribs). The whole sweet-and-sour fried cod is pretty spectacular, and an excellent value for a large party. Wash it down with some sweet plum wine. $ *Average main: Rs. 800* ⊠ *D 1-B, Green Park* ☎ *11/4608–2663* ⊕ *www.gung.in* ✛ *D6.*

$$$
MODERN INDIAN
Fodor'sChoice
★

✕ **Indian Accent.** No restaurant in India is better suited as an introduction to Indian flavors than Indian Accent. It's inside a delightful boutique hotel in one of Delhi's quietest—and wealthiest—neighborhoods; the quiet decor has been chosen to ensure that nothing distracts you from your food. Not that anything is likely to; the chef, Manish Mehrotra, is among India's most celebrated, and he has been working to redefine "fusion" cuisine in Delhi since Indian Accent opened in 2009. The food combines Indian flavors and preparation methods with Western or Asian ingredients, or vice versa. Some dishes, such as the foie gras–stuffed *galawati* kebab, the mango pickle–rubbed Chilean spare-ribs, and the bacon-and-apple *kulcha* bread, have achieved considerable fame. These dishes are usually part of the 11-course tasting menu, which is paired with five glasses of wine. Not all the experiments work perfectly, but most do. Leave room for dessert, in particular the cheese-cake. ⑤ *Average main: Rs. 1010* ✉ *Manor, 77 Friends Colony (West)* ☎ *11/4323–5151* ⊕ *www.indianaccent.com* ✛ *G5.*

$$
MODERN INDIAN
Fodor'sChoice
★

✕ **Kainoosh.** Low-hanging lamps and delicate latticed screens set the refined mood at this upscale Indian restaurant where the extensive menu, with an "India through the ages" theme, covers the whole country. The *lal maas*, lamb cubes slow-cooked with the fiery Rajasthani chilli, is as exciting as it looks; the yam and zucchini kebabs stand out among the vegetarian appetizers. Their version of create-your-own *thali* (many dishes on one plate) is several steps above the usual: all the lamb options are excellent, as are the prawns, the okra, and anything with lentils. This is Indian food like you've never seen or tasted before. ⑤ *Average main: Rs. 925* ✉ *DLF Promenade Mall, Nelson Mandela Marg, ground fl., Vasant Kunj* ☎ *11/3303–6021* ⊕ *www.keya-kainoosh.com* ✍ *Reservations essential* ✛ *B6.*

$$
NORTH INDIAN

✕ **Moti Mahal Delux.** This old-fashioned family restaurant serves North Indian comfort food. It's an update of an Old Delhi classic, Moti Mahal (now under separate management). The meal of choice is butter chicken, otherwise known as chicken *makhni*, a tomato-based Punjabi classic that sticks to your ribs. The basic chicken curry is also good. There's no plain rice here; the so-called "plain *pulao*," zesty rice made with cumin, has a kick of its own. All meals are served with spicy little pickled onions. There are many other locations. ⑤ *Average main: Rs. 625* ✉ *M-30 Greater Kailash I* ☎ *11/2923–2467* ⊕ *www.motimahal. in* ◷ *Closed Tues.* ✛ *F6.*

$
SOUTH INDIAN
FAMILY

✕ **Naivedyam.** This dark, soothing restaurant with gold-embossed paintings was designed by artisans from the Tamil Nadu town of Thanjavur. The food is Udupi, a vegetarian cuisine from a town near Mangalore. All meals begin with a *rasam* (peppery soup) that must be the best in Delhi, and the rice dishes are a great introduction to South Indian home cooking. Try a *dosa*—a giant semolina or lentil-flour crêpe filled with spicy potatoes—particularly the *maharaja sajjigemasala dosa*, which also includes vegetables. At night, look for the stained-glass entrance; by day, follow signs for the "South Indian Eating Panorama." Alcohol is not served. ⑤ *Average main: Rs. 120* ✉ *1 Hauz Khas Village* ☎ *11/2696–0426* ✛ *C6.*

$$
MEDITERRANEAN

✕ **Olive Bar & Kitchen.** Though it's in the shadow of the Qutub Minar, this sprawling restaurant just might make you believe you're in Santorini, or on the Italian Riviera. White on white is the color scheme, from the stucco walls to the pebbles in the courtyard to the cluster of white carnations on each table. The world cuisine has an emphasis on the Mediterranean, so you'll find options like a light-as-air goat-cheese soufflé, several pizza options, and pastas like the lasagna *verdure* or blue-cheese gnocchi, as well as Cajun spiced fish, Australian lamb chops, and Spanish-style chicken *a la plancha*. Because it's a little clubby, Olive's probably not the best place to taken children under 12. ⑤ *Average main: Rs.*

3

600 ⊠ Haveli 6/8, One Style Mile, Kalkadass Marg, near Qutub Minar, Mehrauli ☎ 11/2957–4444 ⊕ www.olivebarandkitchen.com ✣ D6.

$ ✕ **Park Balluchi.** No, it's not Italian; it's Baluchistan, now in Pakistan.

NORTH INDIAN With glass on three sides to better enjoy the surrounding park, this kebab house serves amazing barbecue dishes: *nawabi kesri kabab* (chicken marinated in a saffron mixture, stuffed with chopped chicken, and grilled), *murg potli* (marinated chicken breast wrapped around minced mutton and flambéed), and *mewa paneer tukra* (soft cheese stuffed with nuts, currants, and mushrooms, marinated in cream and grilled). Kebabs are served all day; other dishes are not served between 3:30 and 6. Service can be extraordinarily slow and poorly informed. Reservations are essential for dinner. ⑤ *Average main: Rs. 480 ⊠ Deer Park, Hauz Khas Village ☎ 11/2685–9369 ⊕ www.parkballuchihauzkhas. com ✣ C6.*

$ ✕ **Prince Paan Box.** One of Delhi's most popular *chaatwallahs* (snack-sell-

NORTH INDIAN ers) is here, with a crowd at all hours. Among its most popular offerings are the fried spinach chaat and the *raj kachori* (spicy chaat bowl stuffed with assorted fillings). They're also known, of course, for their paan (betel-nut leaves that include various ingredients, including tobacco in some cases). There's no seating. ⑤ *Average main: Rs. 100 ⊠ M Block Market, Greater Kailash I 29/5, eastern corner ☎ 11/2923–0434 ✣ F6.*

$$ ✕ **Punjabi by Nature.** It may no longer be the go-to place for Punjabi

NORTH INDIAN food it once was, but its versions of hearty classics like *murgh Punjabi masala* (the house chicken curry), *dal makhni* (black lentils with butter and cream), and *raan-e-Punjab* (a tender whole leg of lamb grilled just so) make up for it. It's now inside one of Delhi's swishiest shopping malls, which means a visit can also double as a chance to check out Delhi's high-end fashion scene. The mall is huge, so expect a fair amount of walking to get to the restaurant. ⑤ *Average main: Rs. 595 ⊠ Ambience Mall, T 305, 3rd fl., Nelson Mandela Rd., Vasant Kunj ☎ 11/4087–0001 ⊕ www.punjabibynature.in ✣ B6.*

$ ✕ **Sagar.** This no-frills, three-story vegetarian family joint bustles non-

SOUTH INDIAN stop from 8 am to 11 pm. The dosa is king, and you can choose from 20 varieties, including some made with *rava* (semolina) rather than lentil flour. The vegetable *uttapam* (rice-flour pancake) is also good, and there's a North Indian menu with delicious *bhindi masala* (spicy okra). The wonderful *thalis*, or combination platters, are served from 11 to 3 and 7 to 11. ⑤ *Average main: Rs. 130 ⊠ 18 Defence Colony Market ☎ 11/2433–3110 ⊕ sagarratna.in ⓜ Lajpat Nagar ✣ E5.*

$ ✕ **Swagath.** Delhi's original Mangalorean restaurant—specializing in

SOUTH INDIAN seafood from the western coast between Goa and Kerala—is outstanding. Choose your sauce, then decide between fish, prawns, or crab. Anything served *sawantwadi* (in spicy mint-and-coriander sauce) is unforgettable, as is *gassi*, a mild coconut-flavored gravy, and the butter-pepper-garlic sauce. Another specialty is Chettinad food from Tamil Nadu, cooked in a very spicy black-pepper sauce (there's also decent Chinese and North Indian food). Mop up your food with *appam* or *neer dosa*, soft South Indian rice breads. The prim dining rooms are softly lit, and service is excellent. Doors are open all day. ⑤ *Average main: Rs. 475 ✉ 14 Defence Colony Market ☎ 11/2433–0930 ⊕ www. swagath.in* Ⓜ *Lajpat Nagar* ✛ *E5.*

$$
ASIAN
Fodor's Choice
★

✕ **The Yum Yum Tree.** "Yum" is the key word at this large but tastefully decorated Pan-Asian spot. The sushi attracts high praise, and selections from the extensive list of hot foods are also top-notch. For starters, try the crispy duck spring rolls with gooseberry sauce, barbecue pork buns (*bao*), or prawn and water-chestnut dumplings (*har gao*). Mains like sweet and crispy pork with pineapple, chilli roasted eggplant, and duck pancakes should be next. There are great desserts, too, from the simple chocolate-dipped fresh figs to something more elaborate, like cream-cheese-and-walnut-stuffed deep-fried wontons drizzled with strawberry coulis. Ⓢ *Average main: Rs. 585* ✉ *Community Centre Market, 1st fl., New Friends Colony* ☎ 11/4260–2020 ⊕ *www.theyumyumtree.in* ✛ *G6.*

$
NORTH INDIAN

✕ **Zaffran.** Simple presentations of classic Punjabi and Mughlai fare such as *raan* (leg of mutton), tandoori naan, and *dal makhani* (lentils with tomatoes, ginger, garlic, and cream) draw top marks here thanks to fresh ingredients and a light hand with the oil and ghee (not the case at many North Indian joints). Zaffran also serves excellent spicy biryani (rice and meat, cooked together) and imports Parsi *kulfi* (ice cream) from a dairy in Mumbai. Despite its popularity with families and the busy open kitchen, the minimalist blond-wood dining room is refreshingly calm, thanks largely to efficient, friendly, and knowledgeable staff. Ⓢ *Average main: Rs. 485* ✉ *N-2 Kasbah restaurant complex, N-Block Market, Greater Kailash I* ☎ 11/4163–5000 ⊕ *www.kasbahrestaurants. com* ✛ *F6.*

WHERE TO STAY

OLD DELHI

$
HOTEL

🏨 **Maidens.** Opened in 1903, before New Delhi even existed, this is one of the city's oldest hotels, and with a Metro station adjacent, it's a speedy, air-conditioned ride from both Old Delhi and Connaught Place. **Pros:** coffee shop has a nice patio and an English feel, especially when British tour groups are in residence; renovations have brightened up the rooms. **Cons:** even with the metro, you are removed from the rest of the city; food and beverage options are limited. Ⓢ *Rooms from: Rs. 5500* ✉ *7 Sham Nath Marg, Civil Lines* ☎ 11/2397–5464 ⊕ *www. maidenshotel.com* ⤳ *53 rooms, 3 suites* ⊘ *No meals* Ⓜ *Civil Lines* ✛ *G1.*

CENTRAL DELHI

$$$$
HOTEL

🏨 **The Claridges, Delhi.** In 1950, three years after Independence, an Indian family was talked into building a hotel with a British aesthetic, and the result was a winner: tasteful yet unpretentious, in a central yet quiet location. **Pros:** Sevilla, the Mediterranean eatery, gets high marks; excellent pool. **Cons:** rooms near the nightclub can be noisy. Ⓢ *Rooms from: Rs. 17000* ✉ *12 Aurangzeb Rd.* ☎ 11/3955–5000 ⊕ *www.claridges.com* ⤳ *128 rooms, 12 suites* ⊘ *Breakfast* Ⓜ *Race Course* ✛ *E4.*

BEST BETS FOR DELHI LODGING

Fodor's Choice ★	$$$$	BEST LOCAL FLAVOR
Ahuja Residency, p. 131	Lodhi Hotel, p. 131	Amarya Haveli, p. 131
Amarya Haveli, p. 131	The Oberoi, p. 132	The Claridges, p. 129
The Imperial, p. 130		The Imperial, p. 130
Jor Bagh 27, p. 131	**By Experience**	
Lodhi Hotel, p. 131		BEST LOCATION
The Oberoi, p. 132	BEST FOR KIDS	Jor Bagh 27, p. 131
	Lodhi Hotel, p. 131	Vivanta By Taj Ambas-
By Price	The Manor, p. 132	sador, p. 132
	Maidens, p. 129	
$		BEST SPA
Ahuja Residency, p. 131	BEST HOTEL BAR	The Oberoi, p. 132
Jor Bagh 27, p. 131	Vivanta By Taj Ambas-	
	sador, p. 132	BEST VIEWS
$$	Taj Mahal, p. 130	Ahuja Residency, p. 131
Amarya Haveli, p. 131	BEST INTERIOR	GRANDEST
Shervani, p. 130	DESIGN	The Imperial, p. 130
$$$	The Imperial, p. 130	The Oberoi, p. 132
The Imperial, p. 130	ITC Maurya, p. 131	Taj Mahal, p. 130
The Manor, p. 132		

$$$ **The Imperial.** Easily the most appealing hotel in Delhi, with a driveway
HOTEL   lined by soaring king palms, the luxurious Imperial offers unparalleled
Fodor's Choice   service and location. **Pros:** top-notch restaurants and bar. **Cons:** expen-
★   sive; standard rooms on the small side. *$ Rooms from: Rs. 10500 ☒ Jan-
path, south of Tolstoy Marg, Connaught Pl. ☎ 11/2334–1234 ⊕ www.
theimperialindia.com ↝ 180 rooms, 43 suites ⦿ No meals ✢ E2.*

$$ **Shervani New Delhi.** In a central yet quiet location, the Shervani has
B&B/INN   understated and elegant guest rooms, with clean white cotton duvets,
silk accents in muted colors, and gleaming white marble bathrooms.
Pros: staff is efficient, friendly, and willing to go out of its way for
guests. **Cons:** in-house food options are limited; taxis at the neighborhood stand can be slow to arrive. *$ Rooms from: Rs. 6000 ☒ 11 Sun-
der Nagar ☎ 11/4250–1000 ⊕ www.shervanihotels.com ↝ 19 rooms,
2 suites ⦿ Breakfast ✢ F3.*

$$$$ **Taj Mahal.** The Taj Mansingh, as it's locally known, is Delhi's premier
HOTEL   social hotel, with nightly cocktail affairs, cultural events, and occasional society weddings drawing the glitterati. **Pros:** centrally located
in Lutyens' Delhi; popular with business travelers and celebrities, and
the service is correspondingly slick; excellent dining options, including
Varq and Wasabi by Marimoto. **Cons:** rooms on the small side; very

expensive. $ *Rooms from: Rs. 23000* ✉ *1 Mansingh Rd.* ☎ *11/2302–6162* ⊕ *www.tajhotels.com* ↩ *267 rooms, 27 suites* ⦿ *No meals* Ⓜ *Khan Market* ✛ *E3.*

SOUTH DELHI

$
B&B/INN
Fodor's Choice
★

⛌ **Ahuja Residency.** This little-known guesthouse is a jewel, Delhi's only combination of style and affordability, where hospitality and attention to detail are second to none. **Pros:** immaculately clean; fresh-squeezed juice at breakfast; organic bath products. **Cons:** reservations difficult to get; bathrooms have showers only. $ *Rooms from: Rs. 5500* ✉ *193 Golf Links, Central Delhi* ☎ *11/2462–2255* ⊕ *www.ahujaresidency. com* ↩ *12 rooms* ⦿ *Breakfast* Ⓜ *Khan Market* ✛ *E4.*

$$
B&B/INN
Fodor's Choice
★

⛌ **Amarya Haveli.** Run by two charming Frenchmen, Amarya Haveli, in the residential Safdarjung enclave, is comfortably kitschy, with themed rooms and friendly staff. **Pros:** chic, well-designed space; great en suite bathrooms. **Cons:** room service can be slow. $ *Rooms from: Rs. 6900* ✉ *A2/20 Safdarjung Enclave* ☎ *11/4175–9268, 11/4103–6184* ⊕ *www. amaryagroup.com/amarya-haveli* ↩ *9 rooms* ⦿ *Breakfast* ✛ *D6.*

$$
HOTEL

⛌ **Hyatt Regency.** For its size and range of amenities, the Hyatt has a surprisingly homey feel. **Pros:** the shopping arcade is easily the best in Delhi, with dozens of shops selling jewelry, handicrafts, Kashmiri carpets and more; the pool may take top honors, too. **Cons:** service can be impersonal. $ *Rooms from: Rs. 8000* ✉ *Ring Rd., Bhikaji Cama Pl.* ☎ *11/2679–1234* ⊕ *www.delhi.hyatt.com* ↩ *507 rooms, 51 suites* ⦿ *Breakfast* ✛ *C5.*

$$$$
HOTEL

⛌ **ITC Maurya.** A favorite with executives and dignitaries, the Maurya works hard to style itself as the swankiest hotel in Delhi, and the whole place buzzes with importance. **Pros:** knockout restaurants draw as many locals as travelers, especially the famous Bukhara and Dum Pukht; pool and gym are best-in-class; business services get top marks. **Cons:** expensive; far from most major sites; chattering tour groups can dominate the atmosphere. $ *Rooms from: Rs. 19500* ✉ *Sardar Patel Marg, Diplomatic Enclave, Chanakyapuri* ☎ *11/2611–2233* ⊕ *www. itchotels.in* ↩ *411 rooms, 29 suites* ⦿ *Breakfast* ✛ *B4.*

$
B&B/INN
Fodor's Choice
★

⛌ **Jor Bagh 27.** Peace, proximity, and price are the benefits at this white-washed guesthouse—popular with visiting UN and World Bank staffers—opposite Lodhi Garden. **Pros:** five minutes from Khan Market; serene neighborhood. **Cons:** some rooms are shabby—look at what's available before you settle in; breakfast is the only meal served here; generator cannot run all air-conditioners for very long, so this isn't your best bet in summer. $ *Rooms from: Rs. 4500* ✉ *27 Jor Bagh* ☎ *11/2469–4430* ⊕ *www.jorbagh27.com* ↩ *18 rooms* ⦿ *No meals* Ⓜ *Jor Bagh* ✛ *E4.*

$$$$
HOTEL
Fodor's Choice
★

⛌ **Lodhi Hotel.** An exclusive hotel at an exclusive address, the Lodhi Hotel is over-the-top luxury all the way, starting with the private pool nestled on the balcony of each of the rooms. **Pros:** luxurious to the hilt; next door to Khan Market and close to Lodhi Garden; excellent restaurants; great spa. **Cons:** staff can be hard to find when you need them. $ *Rooms from: Rs. 18500* ✉ *Lodhi Rd., Central Delhi* ☎ *11/4363–3333* ⊕ *www.thelodhi.com* ↩ *40 rooms, 28 service apt.* ⦿ *No meals* ✛ *F4.*

$$$
HOTEL

The Manor. In one of Delhi's wealthiest residential neighborhoods, this is Delhi's premier boutique hotel, with a stylish ultramodern interior, a nouvelle-Indian restaurant, and stunning, ultraprivate grounds. **Pros:** romantic, candlelighted restaurant. **Cons:** slightly off the beaten path and extremely difficult for drivers to locate; far from most sites and restaurants. $ *Rooms from: Rs. 10500* ✉ *77 Friends Colony W* ☎ *11/4323–5151* ⊕ *www.themanordelhi.com* ➔ *14 rooms* ❍*Breakfast* ✛ *G5.*

$$$$
HOTEL
Fodor's Choice
★

The Oberoi. A beloved destination for those who visit Delhi often, the city's first modern luxury hotel, built in 1965, is distinguished by its calm—even when it's packed, the sleek, black-marble lobby is peaceful. **Pros:** restaurants are among Delhi's finest; top-flight spa. **Cons:** extremely expensive. $ *Rooms from: Rs. 21500* ✉ *Dr. Zakir Hussain Rd., next to Delhi Golf Club* ☎ *11/2436–3030* ⊕ *www.oberoihotels. com* ➔ *252 rooms, 31 suites* ❍*No meals* ✛ *F4.*

$$$$
HOTEL

Taj Palace. Facilities are top-notch in this giant, boomerang-shaped hotel with first-rate business services and good leisure amenities. **Pros:** business services are best-in-class; has one of India's finest European restaurants. **Cons:** far from some tourist sites; in high season you'll battle package-tour crowds. $ *Rooms from: Rs. 23000* ✉ *Sardar Patel Marg, Diplomatic Enclave, Chanakyapuri* ☎ *11/2611–0202* ⊕ *www.tajhotels. com* ➔ *362 rooms, 40 suites* ❍*Breakfast* Ⓜ *Dhaula Kuan* ✛ *B4.*

$$$$
HOTEL

Vivanta by Taj Ambassador Hotel. In an exclusive 1930s neighborhood dripping with late-Raj charm, this quiet Taj Group hotel's service is heart-warmingly friendly, and it may cost a bit less than its glamorous siblings. **Pros:** excellent value for money; next door to Khan Market and close to Lodhi Garden. **Cons:** not as up-to-date as other, similarly priced properties. $ *Rooms from: Rs. 18000* ✉ *Subramania Bharti Marg, near Khan Market, Sujan Singh Park* ☎ *11/2463–2600* ⊕ *www.tajhotels.com* ➔ *76 rooms, 12 suites* ❍*No meals* Ⓜ *Khan Market* ✛ *E3.*

NIGHTLIFE AND PERFORMING ARTS

NIGHTLIFE

Delhi's nightlife is in a constant state of flux, and among the growing set of young people who can afford it, the scene is intense. Various kinds of watering hole are on offer, with the lounge bar emerging as the most successful formula. Though Delhi doesn't rival the cosmopolitan feel of Mumbai, it seems as if a new lounge opens here every week. That said, the city's somewhat stodgy reputation is still partly deserved: All the major hotels have bars, but most are better suited for a collective nap with a few tired foreigners than a night of Indian camaraderie; they still shut by midnight and many nightclubs close not much later, though there are a few all-night venues.

Hotel bars come in two stripes: those that aim for a British Raj look and an older, quieter clientele, or raucous, late-night dance clubs. Due to high taxes on alcohol, especially imported brands, drinks prices come close to those in London and New York. Those in search of late-night dancing and drinking sometimes head for the suburbs or five-star hotels, which can stay open later.

The disco scene has undergone a transformation in recent years. Select places attract top international DJs and charge cover prices to match. Slowly electronic dance music is overtaking drunk renditions of classic rock and Bollywood favorites at most places. Overly casual attire (shorts, T-shirts, sandals on men) is typically frowned on, and closing times tend to vary with the mood of the city government that month.

CENTRAL DELHI
BARS AND PUBS

Baci. Baci is a charming Italian-style bistro that serenades with soft jazz. The sophisticated cocktail list has some delicious creamy drinks. Make sure you order the tiramisu with whatever you're drinking; it goes particularly well with the Irish coffee. ⊠ *23 Sunder Nagar Market* ☎ *11/4150–7445.*

Q'BA. A cavernous space, a pleasant terrace with wonderful views, and well-mixed drinks that all add up to a pleasant nightspot. ⊠ *E-42/43 Connaught Pl., Inner Circle* ☎ *11/4151–2888* ⊕ *www.qba.co.in* Ⓜ *Rajiv Chowk.*

Rick's. A magnet for Delhi's beautiful people, with as many voices yelling into their cell phones as talking to each other. The booze selection is hard to beat, and the snacks are Southeast Asian. Go before 9 pm if you want a seat. ⊠ *Taj Mahal Hotel, 1 Mansingh Rd.* ☎ *11/2302–6162* ⊕ *www.tajhotels.com* Ⓜ *Khan Market.*

HOTEL BARS AND LOUNGES

1911. The large bar here is a classic watering hole decked out the way it looked in the years leading up to the end of the Raj. The drink menu is massive, and lounge music keeps the vibe contemporary. ⊠ *Imperial Hotel, Janpath, Connaught Pl.* ☎ *11/2334–1234, 11/4150–1234* ⊕ *www.theimperialindia.com.*

Agni. Named for the Vedic fire god, the swanky Agni, in the lobby of the Park Hotel, attracts Delhi's party crowd, playing electronic interspersed with pop, hip-hop, and Bollywood hits. The door staff can be selective. ⊠ *The Park Hotel, 15 Parliament St., near Connaught Pl.* ☎ *11/4663–8809* ⊕ *www.theparkhotels.com.*

Aqua. As the name suggests, Aqua is a giant outdoor space focused on a large swimming pool surrounded with lovely cabanas. It's got a well-heeled, more sedate crowd, especially when compared to its crazy next-door neighbor, Agni. ⊠ *The Park Hotel, 15 Parliament St., Connaught Pl.* ☎ *11/6657–5732* ⊕ *www.theparkhotels.com.*

SOUTH DELHI
BARS AND PUBS

Blue Frog. Blue Frog promises interesting live music from all over the country and internationally almost every night, delivered via a state-of-the-art sound system and accompanied by classy cocktails and snacks. Entry is free before 9 pm on most evenings, except for ticketed events. ⊠ *The Kila, 4-A Seven Style Mile, Kalkadass Marg, opp.*

Qutab Minar ☎ *011/3080–0300* ⊕ *www.bluefrog.co.in/club-info-delhi* ⊙ *Closed Mon.*

Keya. Chic, chic, chic, and the cocktails are innovative and delicious: street-food-inspired concoctions include the betel-leaf martini and the sour mango mojito. It's one of the new classics in town, with a loyal following. ⊠ *DLF Promenade Mall, Nelson Mandela Marg., Vasant Kunj* ☎ *95607–15533* ⊕ *www.keya-kainoosh.com.*

Stone. This laid-back lounge with plenty of low-slung couches is where expats head for quiet drinks and conversation over wood-fired pizza. ⊠ *Moets Restaurant Complex, 50 Defence Colony Market, Defence Colony* ☎ *11/4655–5777* ⊕ *www.moets.com* Ⓜ *Lajpat Nagar.*

PERFORMING ARTS

Delhi is India's cultural hub, with performers from all over the country heading to the capital to cultivate their national audience. Painting, music, dance, theater, and, of course, film are all well represented. The large and modern India Habitat Centre has the best combination of all of the above; on any given evening, it hosts several good programs. The only problem is that publicity is nonexistent, so you must be persistent to find out what's happening— ⊕ *www.delhievents.com* is a reliable source of information on cultural events. Failing that, the daily newspapers, especially the *Times of India* and the *Hindustan Times,* are also good sources. The staff at your hotel may be able to help, too.

ART GALLERIES

Delhi's art scene is extremely dynamic. Contemporary Indian painting—which often blends traditional Indian motifs with Western techniques—is blossoming, but if you're looking to buy, bargains are hard to come by. Private galleries have mushroomed, and art prices have skyrocketed. Most galleries are quite small, so if you want a broad view of what's happening, hire a car or taxi for an afternoon of gallery-hopping. Authenticating any major purchases is advisable. Visit ⊕ *in.blouinartinfo.com* for exhibit details and artist profiles. Many galleries are closed on Sunday. Hauz Khas Village has a cluster of galleries.

Art Heritage. Part of a cultural institute with several galleries and performing spaces, Art Heritage has some of the finest exhibits in town. ⊠ *Triveni Kala, Sangam, 205 Tansen Marg, Mandi House, near Connaught Pl.Central Delhi* ☎ *11/2371–9470* ⊕ *www.artheritagegallery.com* Ⓜ *Mandi House.*

Delhi Art Gallery. A substantial collection of paintings by old masters and contemporary artists can be seen here; it often hosts comprehensive historical art exhibitions. ⊠ *11 Hauz Khas VillageSouth Delhi* ☎ *11/4600–5300* ⊕ *www.delhiartgallery.com* ⊙ *Closed Sun.*

Devi Art Foundation. The Devi Art Foundation, with its sprawling exhibition area, is out of the way for the typical visitor—and the walk from the Metro station is unpleasant—but it's worth a visit for art enthusiasts. Shows on various themes are usually curated out of the permanent collection, which consists of long-time collector Lekha Poddar's folk art and historically significant acquisitions, as well as her son

Anupam's trove of more cutting-edge contemporary works (he's a high-end hotelier). ⊠ *Sirpur House, Plot 39, Sector 44, Gurgaon, South Delhi* ☎ *0124/488–8177* ⊕ *www.deviartfoundation.org* ⊞ *Free* ☽ *Tues.–Sun. 11–7* Ⓜ *HUDA City Centre.*

Dhoomimal Gallery. It's a bit chaotic but this gallery that focuses on older contemporary artists is centrally located and large. ⊠ *G-42 and A-8 Connaught Pl., Central Delhi* ☎ *11/4151–6056* ⊕ *www. dhoomimalgallery.com* Ⓜ *Rajiv Chowk.*

Gallery Espace. A small but remarkable space featuring both new and canonical artists, sometimes mixed together in edgy theme shows. ⊠ *16 Community Centre, New Friends Colony, South Delhi* ☎ *11/2362– 6267* ⊕ *www.galleryespace.com.*

Habitat World. The various exhibition spaces here showcase painting, sculpture, Indian craft, and creativity of every kind. The main Visual Arts Gallery is just inside Gate 2. ⊠ *India Habitat Centre, Lodhi Rd., South Delhi* ☎ *11/2468–2222* ⊕ *www.indiahabitat.org* Ⓜ *Khan Market.*

Lalit Kala Akademi. This government-run gallery in a large 1950s building shows several exhibits at once, usually of varying quality. ⊠ *Rabindra Bhavan, 35 Ferozeshah Rd., near Connaught Pl., Central Delhi* ☎ *11/2300–9239* ⊕ *lalitkala.gov.in* Ⓜ *Mandi House.*

Nature Morte. This is one of the most cutting-edge art and photography galleries in town. ⊠ *A-1 Neeti Bagh, opposite Kamla Nehru College, Neeti Bagh, South Delhi* ☎ *11/4174–0215* ⊕ *www.naturemorte.com.*

The Stainless. One of the more experimental galleries in Delhi, this space welcomes designers, architects, artists, and sculptors to display their work, and there is a permanent collection of stainless-steel installations. ⊠ *Mira Suites Complex, 1–2 Old Ishwar Nagar, Mathura Rd., Okhla Crossing, South Delhi* ☎ *11/4260–3167* ⊕ *www.thestainless.com.*

Vadehra Art Gallery. Respected for its permanent collection of 20th-century masters, this is also one of Delhi's best galleries for contemporary, established artists. There are several locations. ⊠ *D-40 Defence Colony, South Delhi* ☎ *11/2462–2545* ⊕ *www.vadehraart.com* Ⓜ *Lajpat Nagar.*

FILM

Popular films are easily the biggest influence on contemporary Indian culture, and understanding the country and its eccentricities can be much easier if you've watched a few of the standard stars. India's Mumbai-based film industry, known as Bollywood, produces more films annually than any other country in the world. Most Bollywood films last longer than three hours and are in Hindi, but anyone can get the gist—most are romantic musicals, with dollops of family drama and occasionally a violent villain. Delhi cinemas show all the latest Hindi movies plus a few current Hollywood films, the latter tending toward action, comic-book adaptations, and young romantic comedy.

Art films from all over the world are shown at various cultural institutes; events websites, such as ⊕ *www.delhievents.com* and ⊕ *bpbweekend.com*, carry schedules for local film festivals and other screenings.

PVR Plaza ⊠ *H Block, Connaught Pl., Central Delhi* ⊕ *www.pvrcinemas. com* Ⓜ *Rajiv Chowk.*

PVR Saket ✉ *Community Centre, Saket, South Delhi* ⊕ *www.pvrcinemas. com* Ⓜ *Malviya Nagar.*

MUSIC, DANCE, AND THEATER

India has an ancient dramatic tradition, and *nautanki* plays, which combine drama, comedy, and song, are still held in many villages. Delhi has an active theater scene in both English and Hindi, with many shows locally written, produced, and performed. Most run only for one weekend and don't travel afterward, so they can seem a bit unpolished even when they're fundamentally good.

And great musicians and dancers are always passing through Delhi. Most performances are free, but tickets ("passes") are sometimes required for high-demand performers. For many of them, however, it's enough to show up at the venue an hour or so in advance to get free tickets from the organizers. You can also visit Bookmyshow.com to book tickets for many cultural events.

India Habitat Centre. Several cultural events, from classical Indian dance performances to local stand-up comedy acts, take place here every evening. It's also a regular venue for local theater troupes. ✉ *Lodhi Rd., Lodhi Institutional Area, South Delhi* ☎ *11/2468–2222* ⊕ *www. indiahabitat.org.*

India International Centre. This is an established performance space near the Habitat Centre. From poetry readings to documentary film festivals, this is the place to witness the capital's famed love of high art. ✉ *40 Max Mueller Marg., Lodhi Estate, South Delhi* ☎ *11/2461–9431.*

Kamani Auditorium. This is a long-standing venue for Indian classical music and dance. It's also a good place to sample Delhi's vibrant student-theater scene. ✉ *1 Copernicus Marg, Mandi House, Central Delhi* ☎ *11/4350–3351* ⊕ *www.kamaniauditorium.org* Ⓜ *Mandi House.*

Shri Ram Centre. A constant stream of plays are staged here, some for one day only. The institute's famous for its annual Ramlila production, an enactment of the life of Rama, which is staged during the Dussehra festival, usually in October. ✉ *4 Safdar Hashmi Marg, near Connaught Pl., Central Delhi* ☎ *11/2371–4307* ⊕ *www.shriramcentre. org* Ⓜ *Mandi House.*

Triveni Kala Sangam. In addition to the galleries at Art Heritage, regular dance performances and classes take place here. There's also a cozy cafeteria where you can retire afterward for a relaxed tea and paranthas amid lush greenery. ✉ *205 Tansen Marg, near Connaught Pl., Central Delhi* ☎ *11/2371–8833* Ⓜ *Mandi House.*

SHOPPING

Delhi is a shopping center for goods from all over India, making it the best place to stock up on gifts and souvenirs. Bargaining is often appropriate—and almost mandatory. A good rule of thumb: When the price is written down, it's probably fixed; when you have to inquire about the price, it's negotiable.

NAVJOT ALTAF
Touch – 2008
Duco paint on fiber glass
83.5 x 55 x 64 in. / 212.1 x 162.6...

Inside the Delhi Art Gallery

Old Delhi is an endlessly interesting place to shop, admittedly more for the experience than for what you'll take away. The sidewalks of Chandni Chowk are lined with clocks, baby clothes, tacky toys, blankets, and much more; the shops on Dariba Kalan are filled with silver and gold jewelry. Stalls behind the Jama Masjid sell metalware and utensils, and one street specializes in stationery, especially Indian wedding invitations. Kinari Bazaar glistens with Hindu wedding paraphernalia. Khari Baoli, west of Chandni Chowk toward Lahori Gate, is renowned for its wholesale nuts, spices, and Indian pickles and chutneys.

India has one of the world's foremost **Oriental-rug** industries, and there are carpet vendors all over Delhi. Unfortunately, carpet sellers are a notoriously dishonest crowd. In addition to being obnoxiously pushy, they are likely to sell you inauthentic merchandise at colossally inflated prices and then deny it later. There are some exceptions to this rule, but they tend to sell out of their homes rather than upscale showrooms—so call before you go.

Clothes shopping is one of Delhi's great pleasures. *Khadi*, the hand-spun, hand-woven cotton that Gandhi turned into a nationalist symbol during the Independence movement, has made a roaring comeback and is now worn by many Delhi women during the long, hot summer. You can experience khadi in a salwar-kameez—the classic North Indian ensemble of long tunic and loose pants, also popular in a variation called the kurta-churidar—and in Western-style tops and skirts. Some Indian fabrics can fade or bleed easily, so it's always a good idea to wash clothes first before wearing.

If you find yourself shopping for a sari, savor the experience of learning about this amazing handicraft. Silks and attractive cotton saris are sometimes sold at Dilli Haat market, depending on which vendors have set up shop that week. Silks are sold en masse at upscale stores in South Extension, Greater Kailash I, and Connaught Place, but the highest thumbs-up go to Kalpana and Padakkam.

For **crafts and curios**, Delhi's fixed-price government emporiums near Connaught Place offer good values to travelers with limited time. They're also conveniently open seven days a week. The best market for fine curios and antiques is in the exclusive leafy neighborhood of Sundar Nagar. In addition to the shops listed here, a few shops on the southern (right-hand) side of the market have collections of old optical instruments.

Jewelry is another popular item on visitors' shopping lists. India consumes more gold annually than any other country in the world, mainly because gold is an essential part of a bride's trousseau. With Delhi's upper middle class spending ever more money, and now chasing such Western fancies as diamonds and platinum, jewelry is big business here. The flashiest jewelry stores are clustered in South Extension, Greater Kailash I, and Connaught Place, offset by a handful of older shops in Sundar Nagar. Indian gold is 22-karat, and some Westerners tend to find its bright-yellow tone a bit too flashy. For a gold Indian piece in a subtler antique style, stroll through the market in Sundar Nagar. Hit the glitzier stores for the princess look. Indian jewelers as a group have been accused of adulterating their gold, but alas, you as a consumer will have no way to determine the content of each piece. Old Delhi is packed with jewelry and curio shops, though you have to search harder for fine designs. Stroll Dariba Kalan for the best selection of silver and gold.

As the center of India's English-language publishing industry, and, arguably, India's intellectual capital, Delhi has something of a literary scene. For those with hard currency, Indian **books** are great bargains, including lower-price local editions of titles published abroad. If you'll be in Delhi for a while, hunt down the elusive but excellent *Old Delhi: 10 Easy Walks,* by Gaynor Barton and Laurraine Malone (New Delhi: Rupa, 1997)—these painstakingly detailed routes are fascinating and manageable. The top hotels have small bookshops, but Khan Market has several of the capital's best.

South Delhi is best for discriminating **music** lovers.

OLD DELHI
CLOTHING
Ram Chandra Krishan Chandra. This venerable shop has several rooms full of traditional silks. ⊠ *1976–1978 Chandni Chowk, Gali Parathe Wali* ☎ *11/2327–7869* Ⓜ *Chandni Chowk.*

CRAFTS AND CURIOS
Shivam Zari Palace. In Old Delhi, Shivam Zari Palace and its neighbors sell inexpensive Hindu wedding paraphernalia such as turbans, fabric-covered boxes, *torans* (auspicious door hangings), tiny brass gods, and shiny bric-a-brac. ⊠ *2178 Kinari Bazaar* ☎ *11/2327–7617* Ⓜ *Chandni Chowk.*

CLOSE UP

Dressing the Part

Many traveling women (and a few traveling men) are inspired to buy an Indian outfit to wear for all or part of their trip. Here's a primer:

TRADITIONAL WEAR

The traditional North Indian women's ensemble of a long tunic over loose pants is known as a salwar-kameez. Today it is equally common in a variation called the kurta-churidar. The word *kameez* is a general term meaning "shirt," whereas *kurta/kurti* specifies a traditional Indian tunic worn by men or women, respectively. The pants worn beneath women's kurtas take two forms: the *salwar*, which is very loose, with only a slight tapering at the ankle, and the *churidar*, which is loose in the thigh but tight along the calf, bunched up near the ankle like leggings. Presently the churidar is in greater vogue than the salwar, and true fashionistas now wear very short (above the knee) kurtas over thigh-tight churidars, a look with a Western element: it favors skinny women. Most women opt for knee- or calf-length kurtas.

The outfit is usually finished with a matching *dupatta* or *chunni*, a long scarf draped over the chest with the ends dangling in back, traditionally 6 feet long and 3 feet wide. These days you're free to drape the dupatta however you like; slinging it back from the neck, or even forward from the neck (Western-style), gives the outfit a modern twist. Just beware of dupattas made of stiff or starchy fabric—no matter how beautiful they look, you will probably find them unwieldy. A dupatta is particularly useful in places like Old Delhi and Nizamuddin, where you can pull it over your head as a kerchief if you feel too conspicuous.

WHERE TO BUY IT

You won't have to invest much in any of these items; at Fabindia or Dilli Haat you can buy a smart trio of kurta, churidar or salwar, and dupatta for US$25–US$50. Another option at Dilli Haat and some fabric stores is to buy uncut "suit fabric," a smartly matched set of three pieces of fabric meant to be sewn into the full regalia. If you buy suit fabric, simply take it all to a tailor (ask any market merchant to suggest one; most are holes-in-the-wall), allow him to measure you, tell him what kind of neckline you fancy and whether you want a churidar or salwar, and come back for your custom-made "suit." This can take a few days, but the tailoring costs about US$10 and these ensembles are very attractive.

MUTED OR JEWEL TONES?

Men's kurtas are traditionally paired with a churidar or with loose, straight-legged "pyjamas." Most urban Indian men wear Western shirts and trousers, but Delhi's politicians keep the white cotton kurta-pyjama and the more formal *dhoti* (a bunchy wrap skirt) alive and kicking. Formal silk kurta-churidars are trotted out only for weddings.

Many Western women who buy salwar-kameez choose muted colors, perhaps on the premise that light skin tones need light fabric tones. Unfortunately, muted colors often make Westerners look washed-out and even more "foreign." Be bold! Women of all complexions are flattered by the jewel tones of many Indian clothes.

3

Singh Copper & Brass Palace. Several dusty floors here are filled with brass, copper, and wood artifacts. ✉ *1167 Chah Rahat Gali, near Jama Masjid* ☎ *11/2326–6717* Ⓜ *Chandni Chowk.*

JEWELRY

Multan Enamel Mart. Along with other stores in the area, Multan Enamel Mart sells old and new silver jewelry and curios by weight. ✉ *No. 246–247 Dariba Kalan* ☎ *11/2326–4012, 11/2324–2725* Ⓜ *Chandni Chowk.*

CENTRAL DELHI

BAZAARS AND MARKETS

Connaught Place. Open every day but Sunday from about 10 to 7:30, this is the former commercial district of the British Raj. Pillared arcades and a wheel-shaped layout make it a pleasant place to stroll, especially the inner circle, though you have to get used to the intermittent entreaties of hawkers and beggars. Shops run the gamut from scruffy to upscale. Beneath the green park at the center of Connaught Place is **Palika Bazaar,** a cheap underground market with all the charm of a Times Square subway station. Avoid it: it's a favorite haunt of pickpockets, and many shopkeepers are dishonest. ✉ *Central Delhi.*

Khan Market. This is one of the capital's most pleasant and popular markets—though it's not cheap—with dozens of fine shops selling books, CDs, cameras and film processing, drugs, ayurvedic cosmetics, clothing, home decorations, imported magazines, and imported foods. The shops are open roughly 10 to 7 every day but Sunday; some of the cafés and restaurants stay open for dinner. The crowd is thick with expats and Delhi intelligentsia, bureaucrats, and politicians. ✉ *Sujan Sing Park N* Ⓜ *Khan Market.*

Santushti Shopping Complex. Open every day but Sunday from 10 to 6 or 7, this collection of posh and arty boutiques is scattered around a small, quiet garden across from the Ashok Hotel in the Diplomatic Enclave. Prices can approach those in the West, but this is a relaxing place to stroll and browse. Clothing is the main draw, followed by home furnishings, jewelry, leather, and ayurvedic beauty products. The restaurant Basil & Thyme serves excellent contemporary Euro-American food. ✉ *Chanakyapuri* Ⓜ *Race Course.*

BOOKS

Bahri Sons. This place is stuffed to the ceiling with dusty nonfiction, particularly academic history, politics, and Indian heritage, as well as a good amount of fiction titles. ✉ *Subramaniam Bharti Marg, opposite main gate, Khan Market* ☎ *11/2469–4610* ⊕ *www.booksatbahri.com* Ⓜ *Khan Market.*

The Bookshop. Strong on literary fiction, including hot new titles from abroad. ✉ *13/7 Jor Bagh, Main Market* ☎ *11/2469–7102* Ⓜ *Jor Bagh.*

CMYK. Come here for art and design books, and perhaps one of the occasional movie screenings (check the website or drop in for a schedule). ✉ *15–16 Meher Chand Market, Lodhi Rd.* ☎ *11/2464–1881* ⊕ *www. cmykbookstore.com.*

Full Circle. Spirituality, self-help, and coffee-table books are the specialty here. ✉ *23 Khan Market* ☎ *11/2465–5641* ⊕ *fullcirclebooks.in* Ⓜ *Khan Market.*

Café Turtle. Two flights up, in the Full Circle bookshop, Café Turtle serves light bistro food, exotic fruit juices, and excellent Western desserts in a smart contemporary setting, with music from the record shop below. The terrace is very pleasant in winter. ✉ *23 Khan Market* ☎ *11/2465–5641* ⊕ *www.cafeturtle.com* Ⓜ *Khan Market.*

CLOTHING

MEN'S FABRIC AND TAILORS

Fodor's Choice ★

Anokhi. Stylish Delhiites, expats, and tourists rub shoulders at Anokhi for chic kurtas, dupattas, and Western separates in boldly colored block-printed cottons. It's also loved for its block-print cotton home furnishings and gifts, including tablecloths, bedcovers, makeup bags, bathrobes, and clothbound journals. ✉ *32 Khan Market* ☎ *11/2460–3423* ⊕ *www.anokhi.com* Ⓜ *Khan Market* ✉ *Santushti Shopping Complex, Chanakyapuri* ☎ *11/2688–3076* ⊕ *anokhi.com* Ⓜ *Race Course* ✉ *Santushti Shopping Complex, Chanakyapuri* ☎ *11/2688–3076.*

D. Vaish & Sons. Some of the oldest and finest men's tailors are in Connaught Place. D. Vaish & Sons has a huge selection of fabric and can tailor both men's and women's Western suits, not to mention Indian outfits, for about US$80 plus fabric. ✉ *17 Regal Bldg., Connaught Pl.* ☎ *11/4150–0850* ⊕ *www.dvaish.com* Ⓜ *Rajiv Chowk.*

Mohanlal & Sons. This tailors shop whips up men's Western and Indian suits at very low prices. ✉ *B-21 Connaught Pl.* ☎ *11/4151–3893* ⊕ *www.mohanlalsons.com* Ⓜ *Rajiv Chowk.*

SARIS

Banaras House. This store sells the rich brocaded silks of Varanasi. ✉ *N-13 Connaught Pl.* ☎ *11/2331–4751* Ⓜ *Rajiv Chowk.*

Kalpana. Like an upscale version of the Dilli Haat market, Kalpana has exquisite traditional saris from all over India plus gorgeous Kashmiri shawls. ✉ *F-5 Connaught Pl.* ☎ *11/4362–3738, 11/6472–3772* Ⓜ *Rajiv Chowk.*

Padakkam. An incredible collection of one-of-a-kind saris—mostly South Indian silks, but also interesting cottons—and Kashmiri shawls. ✉ *17 Santushti Shopping Complex, Chanakyapuri* ☎ *11/2467–1417* Ⓜ *Race Course.*

WOMEN'S FABRIC AND SALWAR-KAMEEZ SETS

Fabindia. An India institution, this emporium is stuffed with block-printed kurtas, salwars, churidars, dupattas, Western tops, and skirts in subtle colors for trendy Delhiites, their moms and dads, expats, and tourists. Quality can vary. Avoid Saturday, when the place is a madhouse and it's difficult to get your hands on the stock. There are also branches in Khan Market, the Delhi airport, Green Park, a mall in Vasant Kunj and elsewhere. ✉ *Hamilton House, A 1, Connaught Pl.* ☎ *11/4304–8295* ⊕ *www.fabindia.com* ☉ *Closed Sun.* Ⓜ *Rajiv Chowk.*

Kanika. Beautiful, if somewhat pricey, salwar-kameez sets in contemporary cuts of traditional fabrics are sold here. ✉ *M-53 Connaught Pl.* ☎ *11/2341–6515* Ⓜ *Rajiv Chowk.*

Khanna Creations. This is a good place for handsome salwar-kameez, some hand-embroidered, and raw fabric sets in great colors and patterns at good prices. Their in-house tailor can create a salwar-kameez in as little as four hours for Rs. 300. ⊠ *D-6 Connaught Pl.* ☎ *11/2341–1929* Ⓜ *Rajiv Chowk.*

Tulsi. The supple garments and home furnishings here are made of handwoven silk, linen, and cotton. ⊠ *19 Santushti Shopping Complex, Chanakyapuri* ☎ *11/2687–0339* ⊕ *www.neerukumar.com* Ⓜ *Race Course.*

CRAFTS AND CURIOS

Bharany's. Specializing in jewelry, this store also sells rare old shawls and wall hangings from all over India. ⊠ *14 Sundar Nagar Market* ☎ *11/2435–8528* ⊕ *www.bharanys.com.*

Central Cottage Industries Emporium. Purchase crafts from all over the country at this fixed-price, government-run shop; they will ship items abroad, too. Even if you don't buy anything, it's a good place for getting an idea of the upper bounds of prices before you go bargaining elsewhere. ⊠ *Jawahar Vyapar Bhavan, Janpath, opposite Imperial Hotel, near Connaught Pl.* ☎ *11/2332–3825* ⊕ *www.cottageemporium. in* Ⓜ *Rajiv Chowk.*

Curio Palace. There's an overwhelming array of silver and brass curios here, with much of the brass oxidized for an antique look. ⊠ *17 Sundar Nagar Market* ☎ *11/2435–8929.*

Friends Oriental Arts. Among the bizarre, kitschy miscellany at Friends Oriental Arts are Kashmiri lacquerware, antique glassware, and old optical instruments. ⊠ *15 Sundar Nagar Market* ☎ *11/2435–8841.*

Happily Unmarried. This light-hearted store carries products like an ashtray shaped like a *sandaas,* or Indian-style squat toilet. Also fun are wine-bottle stoppers shaped like old-fashioned water pumps and CD stackers in cylindrical tiffin carriers. ⊠ *Bombay Life Bldg., N35-A Connaught Pl., Outer Circle* ☎ *11/2331–3326* ⊕ *www.happilyunmarried. com.*

Ladakh Art Gallery. Distinctive silver items and small Hindu icons are offered by this gallery. ⊠ *10 Sundar Nagar Market* ☎ *11/2435–5424* ⊕ *www.snsvo4.seekandsource.com/ladakh.*

State Emporiums. The many state emporiums, strung out over three blocks, can keep you busy for hours: the Kashmir store specializes in carpets, Karnataka in sandalwood, Tripura in bamboo, and so on. The prices are all fixed. ⊠ *Baba Kharak Singh Marg, near Connaught Pl.* Ⓜ *Rajiv Chowk.*

HOME FURNISHINGS

Good Earth. Geared to the sophisticated shopper, Good Earth sells items like jewel-toned, pop-art cushion covers and other high-end home accessories, including linens, pottery, and brass. There's a store in the Santushti Shopping Complex and one in the Select Citywalk Mall in Saket as well. ⊠ *Khan Market, 9 ABC,* ☎ *11/2464–7175* ⊕ *www.goodearth. in* Ⓜ *Khan Market* ⊠ *18 Santushti Shopping Complex, Chanakyapuri* ☎ *11/2410–0108* ⊕ *www.goodearth.in.*

Shopping at Dilli Haat

Neemrana Shop. This upscale shop has some beautiful India-inspired women's clothing, men's kurtas, and household gifts at nearly Western prices. ✉ *23B Khan Market* ☏ *11/4358–7185* ⊕ *neemranahotels.com/neemrana-shop* Ⓜ *Khan Market.*

Play Clan. The design collective (also in Mumbai and Goa) has collaborated with the likes of Paul Smith. Popular items are cushion covers and totes with maps of Indian locales, Mughal-ruler playing cards, T-shirts, and more (they even add custom kitsch to Converse shoes). ✉ *17 Meher Chand Market, Lodhi Rd., Saket* ☏ *11/2464–4393* ⊕ *www.theplayclan.com.*

JEWELRY

Ivory Mart. There's a huge selection of lovely necklaces in updated traditional styles. Reproductions of antique *kundan* jewelry, in which several gems are set in a gold-outlined design, are a specialty. ✉ *F-22 Connaught Pl.* ☏ *11/2331–0197* ⊕ *www.ivorymartjewellers.com* Ⓜ *Rajiv Chowk.*

Meyer Jewellers. Beautiful silver and gold jewelry, especially necklaces, is in tasteful traditional styles, including gemstone wedding sets. ✉ *4 Sundar Nagar Market* ☏ *11/2435–8664.*

Roopchand. Some eye-popping regal pieces in antique styles are among the offerings here. ✉ *C-13 Connaught Pl.* ☏ *11/2341–1709* Ⓜ *Rajiv Chowk.*

MUSIC

Mercury. It looks ordinary, but Mercury is a good place to pick up Indian classical music and *ghazels* (Urdu-language love songs). ✉ *20 Khan Market* ☏ *11/2469–0134* ⊕ *www.atmercury.in* Ⓜ *Khan Market.*

Classic Chaats

No trip to India is complete without some Indian snack food. The most popular street foods are *papri chaat* (fried wafers piled high with potatoes, chickpeas, yogurt, and chilli powder), *chole bhatura* (also known as chana bhatura—spicy chickpeas with fried, airy *puri* bread), and *golgappas* (fried dough in a hollow golf-ball shape, which you fill with a spicy mixture of potatoes, chickpeas, tamarind, and coriander sauce), *pakoras* (battered and fried vegetables, cheese, or chicken), and the Mumbai delicacy known as *bhel puri* (spicy rice with bits of onion). The best places to nosh on these snacks, other than in the by-lanes of Old Delhi, are in neighborhood markets. Here are a few recommendations in Central and South Delhi.

The **Bengali Sweet House** (⊠ *27–37 Bengali Market, near Connaught Pl., Central Delhi* Ⓜ *Mandi House*) is a classic spot for evening golgappa outings.

At **Bikanervala** (⊠ *Rajiv Gandhi Handicraft Bhavan, Baba Kharak Singh Marg, 1st fl., near Connaught Pl., Central Delhi*) you can sample Gujarati snacks: *khandvi* is a delicious

pan-fried snack made from a seasoned batter of chickpea flour and buttermilk, then cut into rolls and sprinkled with coconut and coriander; *dhokla* is a savory, fluffy, steamed cake made with chickpea flour, mustard seeds, and an inch of sugar and topped with coriander leaves.

Nathu's (⊠ *2 Sundar Nagar Market, Central Delhi* ⊕ *www.nathusweets. com*) is the perfect place to kick back after shopping for high-end souvenirs, with its robust Indian sweets and pleasant seating area. The nearby **Sweets Corner** supplies the fried stuff outdoors.

Under a charming tin ceiling at the **Evergreen Sweet House** (⊠ *S-30 Green Park Market, South Delhi* Ⓜ *Green Park*), a large crowd stuffs itself with chole bhatura and vegetarian *thalis* (combination platters).

Prince Paan Box (⊠ *M-Block Market, eastern corner, Greater Kailash-1, South Delhi*) is where you will find one of Delhi's most popular *paanwallahs* (paan sellers), attracting a crowd at all hours. They're also known, of course, for their paan, betel-nut leaves wrapped around various ingredients. There's no seating here.

TEA AND COFFEE

Asia Tea House. Next door to Mittal, Asia Tea House sells fine teas and tea paraphernalia. ⊠ *12 Sundar Nagar Market* ☏ *11/2435–0115.*

Fodor's Choice ★ **Mittal Tea House.** Stuffed to the ceiling with Indian teas, herbs, and spices, this tea house has a charming owner, Vikram Mittal, who will tell you everything you ever wanted to know about tea. Another branch is at 8A Lodhi Colony Market, in South Delhi. ⊠ *12 Sundar Nagar Market* ☏ *11/2435–8588* ⊕ *www.mittalteas.com.*

SOUTH DELHI

BAZAARS AND MARKETS

Fodor's Choice ★ **Dilli Haat.** This government-run food and crafts bazaar invites artisans from all over the country to sell their wares directly. More than 60 do so at any given time; the vendors rotate every two weeks according to changing themes such as handicrafts, textiles, or Rajasthani goods. Constants include Kashmiri shawls, Lucknavi *chikan* (white embroidery on pastel cotton), woodwork, pottery, cotton dhurries, and simple children's toys from around the country. At the back of the bazaar 25 stalls serve regional food from around the country, a rare opportunity to sample Goan fish curry, Bengali fish in mustard sauce, and Kerala chicken stew outside their states of origin. Best of all, doors are open daily from 10 to 9 (10 to 10 in summer). Admission is Rs. 20. ✉ *Aurobindo Marg* ☎ *11/2611–9055, 11/2467–8817* ⊕ *www.dillihaat.net. in* Ⓜ *INA Market.*

Hauz Khas Village. In the narrow medieval alleys of South Delhi's Hauz Khas Village, boutiques and shops in converted old homes sell crafts, curios, jewelry, artisanal furniture, and clothing (mostly glitzy Indian wear). Newer design stores include places like White and Shrivan Narresh. The back alley also has fun vintage stores where you can find movie posters from Hollywood and Bollywood films. Most stores are open every day but Sunday from 10:30 to 6 or 7. The village is also dotted with bars and restaurants. ✉ *South Delhi.*

INA Market. Across the street from Dilli Haat, this colorful market is open every day but Monday. This is one of Delhi's most exciting food bazaars, with shops full of imported packaged foods giving way to a covered fruit-and-vegetable market complete with coolies (porters) ready to carry your choices in a basket while you shop. Dry-goods merchants sell spices, nuts, and Indian salty snacks, and meat is prepared and sold on a muddy lane in back. This is the place to find the best incense. ✉ *Aurobindo Marg* Ⓜ *INA Metro Station.*

Lajpat Nagar Market. Middle-class locals stock their households at this lively market. Several Western brand names have outlets here, but Lajpat is best known for cheap kitchenware, curtains, Indian clothing, raw fabric, and shoes. A good place to take in the chaos and sample some street food, it's open every day but Monday from about 10:30 to 8. Try to time things so that you are able to try one of the many Afghan restaurants in the market. ✉ *South Delhi* Ⓜ *Lajpat Nagar.*

BOOKS

Fact and Fiction. Open since 1984, this store caters to the diplomatic community with books on international affairs, history, science, and language study. ✉ *39 Basant Lok, Vasant Vihar,* ☎ *11/98107–23753.*

CARPETS

Carpet Cellar. This store has a vast selection; there's also a shop in Santushti. ✉ *1 Anand Lok, Khel Gaon Marg, Siri Fort Rd.* ☎ *11/4164–1777.*

Janson's Carpets. Jasim Jan, of Janson's Carpets, delivers exactly what he describes—carpets old and new, silk and wool, Persian and tribal— and at fair (not cheap) prices. ✉ *A-14 Nizamuddin E* ☎ *11/2435–5615, 98111–29095 cell phone.*

Novel Exports. The family that runs Novel Exports comes from Kashmir, and they have stunning Kashmiri carpets, shawls, jewelry, and lacquered papier-mâché items. ✉ *D-23 Jangpura Extension* ☎ *11/2431–2226.*

CLOTHING

SARIS **L'Affaire.** Flamboyant party wear at prices to match. ✉ *M-59 M Block Market, Greater Kailash I* ☎ *11/2923–9974* ⊕ *www.laffaire.net.*

Nalli. This is a Chennai-based chain specializing in gold-trimmed silks from the Tamil town of Kanchipuram. The South Extension location is larger than the Connaught Place one. ✉ *F-44 South Extension I* ☎ *11/2462–9926* ⊕ *www.nalli.com* ✉ *P-7/90 Connaught Pl., Central Delhi* ☎ *11/2374–7154* Ⓜ *Rajiv Chowk* ✉ *P-7/90 Connaught Pl.* ☎ *11/2336–7334.*

WOMEN'S
FABRIC AND
SALWAR-
KAMEEZ SETS

Cottons. You guessed it—this store sells a variety of ethnic and Western-style cotton casuals. It's closed on Tuesday. ✉ *11 N Block Market, Greater Kailash I* ☎ *11/4163–5108.*

Daman Choli. Bright, tastefully decorated cotton salwar-kameez are sold here, and they have a convenient while-you-wait alteration service. ✉ *V-1 Green Park* ☎ *11/2656–2265* Ⓜ *Green Park.*

Kilol. Some of the most stunning salwar-kameez fabric sets in India are available here, with color-drenched crepe dupattas topping off soft, block-printed cottons. They're stacked on shelves upstairs. ✉ *N-6 N Block Market, Greater Kailash I* ☎ *11/2924–3388* ⊕ *www.kilol.com.*

**NEED A
BREAK?**

Market Café. In Khan Market, this café serves light Western salads, pastas, and desserts and refreshing cold drinks in an airy contemporary setting. ✉ *8 Khan Market, Central Delhi* ☎ *11/4175–7703* ⊕ *www.marketcafe.in* ⊙ *Daily 10–10:30* Ⓜ *Khan Market.*

CRAFTS AND CURIOS

India Arts Palace. This is an absolute hurricane of Indian ephemera, with dangling colored lanterns, Hindu icons, cute animal curios, drawer pulls, and so forth. ✉ *33 Sundar Nagar Market* ☎ *11/2435–7501* ⊕ *www.indiaartspalace.net.*

La Boutique. This shop pleases the eye with painted wooden items from Rajasthan, plus Hindu and Buddhist icons and other curiosities. ✉ *20 Sundar Nagar Market* ☎ *11/2435–0066* ⊕ *www.laboutiqueindia.com.*

HOME FURNISHINGS

Purple Jungle. This shop is a riot of color wrangled into kaleidoscopic order by two French expats. Packed into the ground floor are bags, cushions and home accessories—many using recycled products. Upstairs are pricier items like trays and hand-painted trunks. ✉ *16 Hauz Khas Village* ☎ *96509–73039, 11/2653–8182* ⊕ *www.purple-jungle.com.*

JEWELRY

Bharany's. Traditional gold earrings and beaded necklaces in muted colors and styles are the specialty of this shop. ✉ *14 Sundar Nagar Market* ☎ *11/2435–3957* ⊕ *www.bharanys.com.*

Ethnic Silver. Supremely elegant pieces, especially earrings, will tempt buyers here. The store is open daily until 9 pm. ✉ *9A Hauz Khas Village* ☎ *11/2696–9637.*

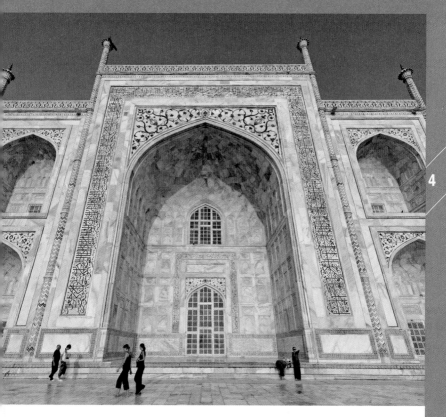

SIDE TRIPS FROM DELHI

Agra and the Taj Mahal, Fatephur
Sikri, Khajuraho, and Varanasi

WELCOME TO SIDE TRIPS FROM DELHI

TOP REASONS TO GO

★ **Fatehpur Sikri:** Easily visited in conjunction with the Taj Mahal, this UNESCO World Heritage Site, the former Mughal capital, is astounding for its prescient urban planning and architecture.

★ **Khajuraho:** The temples of Khajuraho, built between the 9th and 10th centuries, are famous for their exquisite sculptures, especially the erotic ones; it is also a UNESCO World Heritage Site.

★ **The Taj Mahal:** One of the most iconic sites in the world, the Taj is even more enchanting in real life; the minute detail is awe-inspiring.

★ **Varanasi:** One of the oldest and holiest cities in the world, Varanasi is unlike anywhere else you'll go; it can be quite a culture shock, but it's a truly awesome, unforgettable experience. Nearby Sarnath is the site of the Buddha's first teachings.

1 Agra and Fatehpur Sikri. Full of squalor and magnificence alike, this is the architectural heart of North-Central India, with over-the-top creations left by the Mughuls, including the Taj Mahal and the abandoned fortress-city of Fatehpur Sikri.

2 Khajuraho. In contrast to Agra's chaos, Khajuraho projects extreme calm amid equally impressive temples built by the Chandelas.

NEPAL

Basti   Gorakhpur   Motihari
         Gopalganj
Azamgarh   Muzaffarpur   Darbhanga   Purnia
Jaunpur   Chhapra   Samastipur
Ghazipur   Patna   Baruni
Sarnath   Dumraon   Jamalpur
Varanasi   **BIHAR**   Bhagalpur
Sasaram   Jamui
         Nawada
Gaya   Jamui
Bodhgaya

JHARKHAND

CHHATTISGARH

0   100 mi
0   100 km

GETTING ORIENTED

The places covered here may be the most awe-inspiring region of this tremendous country, and if you plan to visit India only once in your lifetime, this is the place to go, tourist traps and all. With a sprawling popula-tion, North-Central India is composed of the states of Uttar Pradesh (Northern Province in English) and Madhya Pradesh (the "Middle" Province). It's fairly easy to move from one place to another as the area is well connected, mainly by plenty of trains.

4

3 **Varanasi and Sarnath.**
These two cities are, respec-tively, central to Hinduism and Buddhism. Varanasi is a maze of nameless lanes and corridors, making it well suited to getting blissfully lost amid its constant din. The Ganges flows through this sacred city, which is

one reason why thousands of *sadhus* (holy men) and others flock to it all year round.

EATING WELL ON DELHI SIDE TRIPS

The Awadh region, with Lucknow as its traditional center, has a vibrant culinary history that arose from the royal courts of the Muslim Nawabs who ruled the area.

(top left) Paan ingredients in a betel leaf; (top right) Barbecued kakori kebabs of spicy minced lamb; (bottom right) Dumpukht biryani in a clay pot

The often quite refined dishes that make up Awadhi cuisine are reminiscent of the Mughal traditions of Delhi, Agra, and Kashmir and the Nawabi cuisine of Hyderabad, but they remain distinct. Awadhi *bawarchis* and *rakabdars* (cooks and specialty cooks) are most-often credited with inventing the "dumpukht" style of sealing ingredients like rice, spices, and meat in an earthen pot and slow-cooking them.

Agra's better hotels offer a taste of nonvegetarian Awadhi food, but in the part of Varanasi near the Ganges you'll mostly find just simple vegetarian restaurants and international backpacker-friendly cafés. The city's importance as a Hindu holy site has led to the popularization of bland, "sattvik" food, made by using vegetarian ingredients deemed conducive to meditation and avoiding others, such as onions and garlic, deemed too stimulating.

DIGESTIVE AID

Chewed as a digestive all over India, **paan** is a slightly intoxicating slug of areca nut and other ingredients wrapped in a betel leaf. It often includes varieties of tobacco, which can be left out on request. *Paan* can also include chutneys, spices, and sweets. Every *paanwallah* (paan vendor) has his own way of doing things. Beginners should ask for a sweet or "mitha" *paan*, "no tambacu."

PETHA

Resembling blocks or cylinders of marble cut from the Taj Mahal itself, **petha** is Agra's most famous sweet. Usually white and slightly translucent, this somewhat gelatinous confection is made, improbably, from boiled and sweetened winter melon. There's also a yellow version called *angoori petha*. The sweet varies in consistency from soft and syrup-filled to crunchy and nearly crystalline. *Petha* is sold by weight in cardboard boxes at the train station and all over Agra, and comes in many flavors like rosewater, *paan* (betel), and coconut.

LITTI CHOKHA

A laborer's staple, the dish called **litti chokha** is especially common in eastern Uttar Pradesh and in the neighboring state of Bihar. Similar to Rajasthan's *batti* (and sometimes referred to by that name), the *litti* is a tough ball of baked dough made of *sattu*, a roasted flour particular to the region that's made from chickpeas. Around Varanasi and farther afield, you may see stalls serving *litti* with *chokha*—a vegetable accompaniment of eggplant, potato, or tomato.

MALLAIYO

One of the more fussy foods you may find in Varanasi is a yellow dairy dessert called **mallaiyo**. Like the version of the dish found in Delhi (where it's called *daulat ki chaat*), *mallaiyo* is an airy, saffron-scented concoction that magically melts away on your tongue. Traditionally, this is a winter morning sweet: to prepare it, milk has to be thickened and allowed to foam, then set overnight. The foam is then skimmed off and sold as *mallaiyo*.

KAKORI KEBABS

Tender, melting morsels of meat called **kakori kebabs** are a common menu item in Uttar Pradesh. You can try these kebabs at the better restaurants in Agra, especially those that serve Awadhi food. Minced twice and tenderized with *papain* (from raw papaya), this delicately spiced dish is typically eaten with a large, very thin and soft *roomali roti* ("handkerchief" bread). Various theories as to the origin of the kebab include its provenance as a dish for a toothless Nawab and as a dish cooked to impress a British officer.

DUMPUKHT BIRYANI

An elaborate dish that originated in the royal Awadhi court, **dumpukht biryani** consists of rice and meat suffused with aromatic spices. The spices are tied up in a muslin cloth, so as not to disintegrate in the dish. Half-cooked lamb (or other meat) and rice are layered in a clay pot, which is then sealed with dough and slow-cooked over low heat. Although you won't find *dumpukht biryani* in vegetarian Varanasi, it's well worth sampling at one of Agra's better restaurants.

Updated by
Malavika
Bhattacharya

Grand tales of love and loss, and myth and legend, come to life in this section of the Hindi heartland, anchored by Agra, home of the stunning Taj Mahal; Varanasi, one of the world's oldest and holiest (and most chaotic) cities; and Khajuraho—a sleepy, unforgettable temple town dating back around a thousand years. In this spiritually rich, highly diverse, and deeply historical part of North India, surrounded by Mughal magnificence and houses of worship, it's quite possible to believe you're in the home of the Gods.

Agra was a seat of the Mughals' power, and their legacy remains (partially intact) for us to marvel at. Dominated by Muslim influences in culture, art, architecture, and cuisine, the city is a testament to the beauty and grandeur of Mughal aesthetics, most notably in the form of the Taj Mahal and Fatehpur Sikri.

Some 440 km (273 miles) southeast of Agra, in the northern part of Madhya Pradesh, the sleepy village of Khajuraho predates the Mughals. Khajuraho was founded at the end of the classical age of Hindu civilization, and is home to stunning Hindu and Jain temples that are famous for their erotic, often explicit sculpture. Excavations here have also uncovered a long-forgotten complex of Buddhist temples.

According to legend, Varanasi was founded by the Hindu god Shiva, and it's said to be one of the oldest populated cities in the world—about 3,000 years old. In many ways, the city (still sometimes called by its Raj-era name, Benares), in southwestern Uttar Pradesh, is the antithesis of Khajuraho. Varanasi teems with pilgrims, hospice patients, mourners, ascetics, priests, Hindu pundits, and international citizens of many religions. Its famous *ghats* (wide stone stairways leading down to the Ganges) are both key religious sites and secular promenades. Writer Mark Twain explained its charm perfectly. He said it is "older than history, older than tradition, older even than legend and looks twice as old as all of them put together." Hindus believe that a person who dies here will gain *moksha* (salvation and freedom from the cycle of birth and rebirth). Sarnath, on the outskirts of Varanasi, is where the Buddha is said to have preached his first sermon after his enlightenment. The ruins and temples here draw Buddhist pilgrims from all over the world.

PLANNING

WHEN TO GO

HIGH SEASON: MID-OCTOBER TO MARCH

The weather during these months is cool and nice, but hotels tend to charge premium rates. December and January are the best times to visit, but it can get relatively cold, with temperatures dropping to 40 degrees Fahrenheit. Remember to pack some warm clothes. While it's the best time of year for outdoor sightseeing, you're trading the sun for much higher prices and unbelievable amounts of foot traffic. The weather from early February to mid-March is wonderfully temperate.

LOW SEASON: APRIL TO AUGUST

If you decide to go to Agra from April to early July, even Indians might look at you as if you're crazy. There's no denying that this region is at its hottest then, making sightseeing in Agra and Khajuraho, which involves hours in the sun, borderline unbearable, especially while looking at the red sandstone monuments, which radiate heat. Temperatures will be well above 100 degrees Fahrenheit, with monsoon showers picking up toward the end of July and continuing through August. Temperatures during this period will be in the 80s, rain is intermittent, and hotel rates go down, so this is a good time to get a deal.

SHOULDER SEASON: SEPTEMBER TO MID-OCTOBER

During this period the weather just begins to cool, and while you might still be unlucky enough to catch a shower or two, is a great time to visit. Some hotels still give discounts for off-peak season.

PLANNING YOUR TIME

It's a good idea to take an express train to Agra to avoid Delhi traffic. To see the Taj and related sights without being completely rushed, plan on spending at least one night in Agra.

Most people visit Khajuraho in conjunction with Varanasi: the best idea is to fly here either on your way to or from Varanasi. Plan to spend two days exploring the Chandela temples.

Varanasi requires at least two days, including half a day for Sarnath. Again, the best option is to fly from Delhi, perhaps stopping in Khajuraho.

GETTING HERE AND AROUND

The Yamuna Expressway has reduced driving time from Delhi to Agra to 2½ hours, making driving a convenient but somewhat pricey option. Taking the train—just a three-hour commute—is a good alternative.

4

AIR TRAVEL

Air India operates direct flights from Varanasi to Agra. From Agra, there's an Air India flight to Khajuraho. The Varanasi airport is connected by air from Delhi, with flights by Air India, Jet, SpiceJet and Indigo.

AIRPORT
TRANSFERS
Khajuraho Airport is 7 km (4 miles) from town; the taxi ride costs about Rs. 500.

Bhabatpur, the nearest airport to Varanasi, is 22 km (14 miles), or a 45-minute drive, from most hotels. A taxi costs about Rs. 800 (air-conditioned) to the Cantonment area, or about Rs. 1,000 into the city proper.

AUTO-RICKSHAW AND TAXI TRAVEL

Auto-rickshaws and taxis are a cheap, convenient option for getting around in all the big cities, and can also be hired for an entire day of sightseeing. Be prepared to bargain, though.

Fares for an auto-rickshaw ride, especially one in Agra, depend on several factors, including how wealthy you look, how far you want to go, how many times you want to stop, the time of day, and whether it's raining. You can generally expect to pay about Rs. 600 for a half day, and Rs. 800 for a full day. If you're not comfortable with the price you're given, look for another auto-rickshaw, and if you don't want to haggle, take a metered taxi or book a car.

Auto-rickshaws are a fast way to scoot through crowded city streets, but the fumes from other automobiles can be horrendous at busy times. In Varanasi, an auto-rickshaw from the Cantonment area to the ghats costs around Rs. 200. When traffic is heavy, take an air-conditioned taxi with the windows closed, especially if you're coming from one of the hotels far from the ghats. Ask your hotel or the tourist office for the going rate, and agree on a fare in advance.

BUS TRAVEL

Traveling to these cities via bus is the cheapest option, but it's only for the truly adventurous, because local schedules are difficult to come by and service is spotty. If you're taking off from Delhi, the bus stations are large and can be chaotic and hard to deal with. You can book a seat on a private, air-conditioned bus for travel between the cities through any local travel agent.

Within cities, local bus lines are the only form of public transportation. In general, they are too crowded and difficult to use for the average foreign visitor.

CAR TRAVEL

Hire a car and driver only through your hotel or tour operator; UP Tours, the government of Uttar Pradesh's tour arm (⇨ *Tours*); the Madhya Pradesh State Tourism Development Corporation (⇨ *Visitor Information*); or a recommended local travel agent.

For trips to Agra from Delhi, contact Dhanoa Tours and Travels. Rates start around Rs. 9,000 and go up to Rs. 10,000 for a day trip, depending on the size of the vehicle. The price includes tax, a driver, and a guide. Expect to pay about Rs. 500 extra for a worthwhile detour to Fatehpur Sikri.

Prices in Agra are generally Rs. 8–Rs. 10 per kilometer. A non-air-conditioned car for four hours or 40 km (25 miles) should cost about Rs. 1,200–Rs. 1,400—the minimum charge. For overnight excursions, add a halt charge of Rs. 600. The standard charge for a trip to Fatehpur Sikri is Rs. 1,800, but prices are always negotiable. You can hire a taxi at the train station under a fixed-rate system. If you'd prefer not to be taken to the driver's choice of stores, restaurants, or hotels (where he gets a commission), say so firmly up front.

In Khajuraho, a hired car can be convenient if you want to wander outside town or can't walk the 3 km (2 miles) to the most distant temples. An air-conditioned car should cost about Rs. 800 for four hours or 40 km (25 miles). You can hire a taxi for about Rs.7–Rs. 9 per km.

Contacts Dhanoa Tours and Travels ✉ *Dharam Marg, near Malcha Marg Market, Chanakyapuri, Central Delhi* ☏ *011/26886051, 981/0058913.* **Touraids Travel Service.** One of the largest travel agencies in Northern India, Touraids Travel provides hotel bookings, train and bus tickets, and travel advice. ✉ *Behind Hotel Trident, Agra, Uttar Pradesh* ☏ *0562/2230741, 931/9100644* ⊕ *www.touraidsi.com* ✉ *Moti Mahal, Moti Palace, Gwalior* ☏ *751/232–4354, 751/232–0758* ✉ *touraidsi@yahoo.com* ✉ *Jai Complex, Civil Lines, Jhansi* ☏ *517/233–1760* ✉ *tourjhs@sancharnet.in.*

CYCLE-RICKSHAW TRAVEL

You can get the latest rate estimates for cycle-rickshaws from the local India Tourism office. Cycle-rickshaws should cost no more than Rs. 100 per hour in Agra or Khajuraho. They're a particularly pleasant way to get around Khajuraho, especially to the outlying temples. Distances are long in Varanasi, so a cycle-rickshaw is better for a leisurely roll through the Old City (it frees you from fighting the crowds) than for cross-town transportation. A trip from the Cantonment to the ghats should cost about Rs. 100. If you hire a cycle-rickshaw for the day, agree on the price in advance and expect to pay about Rs. 400.

TRAIN TRAVEL

Train service is superb, as the region is connected by several local and express trains originating in Delhi and other major cities, and taking the train to Agra is a good option. Otherwise, if your time is limited, you're probably better off flying. *For more info about train travel, see the Travel Smart chapter.*

TOURS

UP Tours (Uttar Pradesh's tour agency) has a vast offering of tours, including Buddhist circuit tours and a daily guided bus tour (except Friday) of Fatehpur Sikri, Agra Fort, and the Taj Mahal for Rs. 1,700–Rs. 2,000 per person (this covers transportation, a guide, and admission fees, including the Rs. 750 admission to the Taj); a half-day tour of Fatehpur Sikri alone is Rs.700–Rs. 550. For a personal guide, ask your hotel or contact the nearest India Tourism office.

Contacts Kamalan Travels. Kamalan Travels can organize tour in Varanasi that includes a visit to traditional silk weavers or a visit to a *gharana*, an organization of musicians studying and playing Hindustani classical music. ✉ 508, Hemkunt House, 6 Rajendra Pl., Delhi ☎ 11/258-10256 ⊕ www.kamalan-travels.com. **Outbound Travels.** This agency can arrange flights and coordinate flights with train or car travel to help you make the most of limited travel time. ✉ 216A/11 Gautam Nagar, 3rd fl., South Delhi ☎ 011/4164-0565, 981/004-9620 ⊕ www.outboundtravels.com. **UP Tours** ✉ Urban Haat Sanskritik Sankul, Maqbool Alam Rd., UP Tourism Office, Varanasi, Uttar Pradesh ☎ 0542/222-6431 ⊕ www.up-tourism.com.

> **A VERY GOOD GUIDE**
>
> **Ashok Sharma.** Associated with the Pradeep Hotel, this guide presents Varanasi with fascinating details, as only a local can. All the boat operators know him, and he'll negotiate a reasonable price for boat rides, too. Contact him directly or through the hotel to book a tour with him. ☎ 542/220-4963 Pradeep Hotel, 933/691-4387 cell phone, 979/212-4190 cell phone.

VISITOR INFORMATION

If you are planning your trip from New Delhi, the India Ministry of Tourism's office on Janpath is worth a visit.

You can pick up maps and information about approved guides at the India Ministry of Tourism offices in Agra, Khajuraho, and Varanasi's Cantonment, and at an information desk at Varanasi's airport. The Madhya Pradesh State Tourism Development Corporation, one of India's better state tourist offices, has friendly staff and information on Khajuraho.

The Uttar Pradesh State Tourism Development Corporation arranges tours and cars in Agra. The New Delhi office (centrally located near the Imperial Hotel) has maps, brochures, and information on approved guides. The best information at Varanasi's Uttar Pradesh State Tourism office is in Hindi, but the staff can still help you, and there's a satellite desk at the train station.

Tourist Offices India Ministry of Tourism ✉ 88 Janpath, Connaught Pl., Delhi ☎ 011/23320005 ⊕ www.incredibleindia.org. . ✉ Sudama Palace, Kankar Bagh Rd., Patna ☎ 612/234-5776 **Madhya Pradesh State Tourism Corporation.** The tourism office can help organize a car and provide maps and information. ✉ Near Circuit House, Khajuraho, Madhya Pradesh ☎ 768/627-4051 ✉ At airport, Khajuraho, Madhya Pradesh ⊕ www.mptourism.com. **Uttar Pradesh Tourist Office** ✉ Chandralok Bldg., 36 Janpath, Central Delhi ☎ 011/2332-2251 ⊕ www.up-tourism.com. ✉ Rahi Tourist Bungalow, Sarnath, Varanasi, Uttar Pradesh ☎ 0542/259-5965 ✉ 10 Station Rd., Lucknow ☎ 522/263-8105

RESTAURANTS

Restaurants on this route generally serve kebabs and other grilled meats, *biryanis* (rice casseroles), and the rich almond-and-saffron-scented concoctions of Mughlai (Mughal-style) cuisine. Most hotels offer a menu of Indian (with choices from various regions), continental, Chinese (adapted for Indian tastes), and sometimes Thai or Japanese dishes; Khajuraho has several Italian restaurants. Small places in villages along the way have simple local vegetarian dishes that are often delicious and cheap. Also keep an eye out for South Indian joints, where a delicious spiced-potato-filled *dosa* (crisp rice crepe) will fill you up for a 70 rupees or less and is tremendously satisfying. Most restaurants are open from 7 to 10 for breakfast, noon to 3 for lunch, and 7:30 to 11 for dinner; hotels often have a 24-hour or all-day coffee shop.

HOTELS

India's main hotel groups are represented in this region, providing increased amenities and efficiency at increasing prices. More and more good, air-conditioned hotels cater to India's upper-middle class and businesspeople, but such places can be generic. Outside the old British cantonment areas, where most top hotels are clustered, and often closer to the center of town, you'll find well-run guest houses and small heritage hotels. Unless otherwise specified, you can expect private bath, phone, and TV in your room. *Hotel reviews have been shortened. For full information, visit Fodors.com.*

WHAT IT COSTS IN RUPEES			
	$	$$	$$$	$$$$
Restaurants	under Rs. 300	Rs. 300–Rs. 499	Rs. 500–Rs. 700	over Rs. 700
Hotels	under Rs. 4,000	Rs. 4,000–Rs. 5,999	Rs. 6,000–Rs. 10,000	over Rs. 10,000

Restaurant prices are the average cost of a main course at dinner or, if dinner is not served, at lunch. Hotel prices are the lowest cost of a standard double room in high season.

EXPLORING AGRA, VARANASI, AND KHAJURAHO

Agra and Varanasi are at opposite ends of Uttar Pradesh. Both lie on the Gangetic plain, also known as the Northern Plain, which stretches across most of Northern India. The countryside in both areas is similar: a dry landscape planted with sugarcane, mustard, and wheat in winter. In Khajuraho, 418 km (260 miles) southeast of Agra—sort of midway, but south, between Agra and Varanasi—you'll get a good sense of the natural environment, because it's an uncongested area. The monsoon hits harder to the east, around Varanasi, so the terrain there is a little more lush.

AGRA AND ENVIRONS

The fastest way to drive to Agra from Delhi is via the Yamuna Expressway, or you can take the other, more historic route, which follows the Grand Trunk Road—a royal route established by India's Mughal emperors in the 16th and 17th centuries, when their capital alternated between Delhi, Agra, and Lahore (now in Pakistan). If you get an early start, you can see Agra's sights in one very tiring day: start at Akbar's Tomb, 10 km (6 miles) north of Agra, then move on to Itimad-ud-Daulah's Tomb, the Taj Mahal, and Agra Fort.

NORTH CENTRAL'S FESTIVALS

Agra's Taj Mahotsav (10 days in February) is a festival celebrating the arts, crafts, and culture of North India. The Khajuraho Festival of Dance (a week between late February and March) is geared primarily to visitors. It's a spectacular event that attracts classically trained dancers from all parts of the country, who perform against a magnificently floodlighted backdrop of the temples.

In Varanasi there's a major religious festival practically every week, but their dates shift every year (check ⊕ www.incredibleindia.org for upcoming dates). Varanasi's great bathing days, when thousands stream down the ghats into the Ganges, include Makar Sankranti (January), the full moon of the Hindu month Kartik (October or November), and Ganga Dussehra (May or June). Durga Puja (September or October) ends with the city's large Bengali community marching to the river at sunset to immerse large mud-daubed images of the goddess Durga. The Bharat Milap festival, held in October or November, occurs the day after the major Hindu festival of Dussehra. It marks Lord Rama's return from exile (from the epic *Ramayana*). It's held in Nati Imli in Varanasi.

Buddhists from Tibet and all over Asia celebrate their festivals in Sarnath. The Buddha Jayanti is celebrated on a full moon day in April or May. It celebrates the Buddha's birth anniversary as well as his day of enlightenment.

A short drive farther, toward Jaipur, is Akbar's deserted dream city at Fatehpur Sikri. Many visitors find this atmospheric place as rewarding as the Taj Mahal.

AGRA

200 km (124 miles) southeast of Delhi.

Agra is synonymous with that monument of love: the stunning Taj Mahal. The city is crowded and congested, but once you lay eyes on the dazzling marble monument, inlaid with precious stones, shrouded in tales of romance and valor, even an arduous journey to get here feels worth it. Imagine walking down an avenue of stores selling tiny replicas of the Taj Mahal, with guides and hawkers vying for your attention, and then passing through a massive doorway and seeing the Taj Mahal in all its splendor. It's a magical moment.

It's safe to say that this sprawling city of nearly 1.5 million inhabitants would not be on many tourists' maps if it weren't for the Taj Mahal, but you'll soon discover that other amazing sights are also near. You can drive to the old fortress city of the Mughals, Fatehpur Sikri, as well as Agra's fort, where the emperor who had the Taj built was imprisoned near the end of his life.

In this Mughal stronghold every successive emperor added something new to prove his cultural sensibilities and his power. Under the Mughal emperor Akbar (1542–1605) and his successors Jahangir (1605–27) and Shah Jahan (1628–58), Agra flourished. However, after the reign of Shah Jahan's son Aurangzeb (1658–1707) and the gradual disintegration of the empire, the city passed from one invader to another before the British took charge early in the 19th century. The British, particularly Governor General Lord Curzon (in office 1898–1905), did much to halt and repair the damage inflicted on Agra's forts and palaces by raiders and vandals.

Much of Agra today may be crowded and dirty, and some of the Mughal buildings are irrevocably scarred. But the government has taken steps to protect the city's most important site from pollution, closing the streets around the Taj Mahal to gas-fueled vehicles (visitors are ferried from a remote parking lot by battery-powered buses) and relocating small factories and fire-burning shops away from the area. Still, Agra's monuments remain strewn like pearls in ashes, evoking that glorious period in Indian history when Agra was the center of the Mughal empire.

4

■ TIP➔ Opening hours change constantly; inquire in advance at your hotel or the Uttar Pradesh State Tourist Office.

GETTING AROUND

It's a good idea to spend a night in Agra and start tackling the sights early in the morning, if only because you'll get a couple of hours in before the hot sun begins to bear down. It's true that the Taj at sunrise is glorious, but if you happen to sleep in, don't worry. Hotels and tour guides tend to make a big deal about the best times of day to see the Taj Mahal, but this legendary mausoleum is spectacular whenever you choose to visit, so you shouldn't feel despondent if you arrive at noon as opposed to sunrise or sunset. (A midday visit, however, *would* be the worst time to forget your sunglasses.) Another thing to remember is that the Taj Mahal is extremely crowded at all hours of the day, so don't assume that an early start will necessarily save you from the relentless foot traffic.

A GOOD TOUR

Assuming you see the Taj Mahal first (and that's certainly not mandatory), it's easy to take leisurely drives to the rest of the sights and be ready to unwind by early evening. Drive 5 km (3 miles) north of the Taj Mahal—about a 20-minute drive on a congested road—to **Itimad-ud-Daulah's Tomb** and then 8 km (5 miles) northwest—about a half-hour drive, with traffic—to **Akbar's Tomb**. (Also known as Sikandra for the town it's in, this monument is often overlooked, but it's an impressive sight that's well worth a stop.) From here it's a 12-km (7-mile), or 45-minute, drive northeast to **Agra Fort**, where it's easy to spend an hour or more. If you have the time and energy, drive southwest for an hour (37 km [23 miles]), to **Fatehpur Sikri.**

If you're day-tripping from Delhi with a car and driver, it's a must to leave it by 5 am to avoid terrible traffic. You can see Akbar's Tomb and Itimad-ud-Daulah's Tomb on the way to the Taj Mahal, at which you'll easily arrive before noon. Spend the afternoon visiting the Agra Fort or Fatehpur Sikri, then hit a good restaurant before heading back to Delhi.

TIMING

Any time between September through March is a good time to visit. Winters here are cool and sometimes quite cold in December and January, so make sure you have some layers packed if you visit at that time.

If you try to pack all of Agra's sights into a day that starts in Delhi, you'll have a long, tiring day; starting fresh in the morning from Agra will make for a full, but fairly easy day. Consider staying a second night at your hotel and dividing your excursions between two days to eliminate that constant hectic feeling that Agra's crowds, congested traffic, and sights often impart.

ESSENTIALS

Government-approved tourist guides can be found through the local tourist offices.

Contacts Uttar Pradesh Tourist Office. This is a good resource for local transportation queries, and they have a list of government-approved drivers and tour guides at market rates so you will not be cheated. Their recommendations for restaurants and hotels, however, are less reliable. ⊠ *64 Taj Rd., UP Tourist Office* ☎ *562/222–6431* ⊕ *www.up-tourism.com* ⊗ *Closed Sun.*

EXPLORING

Fodor's Choice ★ **Agra Fort.** The architecture of this fort reflects the collective creative brilliance of Akbar, his son Jahangir, and grandson Shah Jahan. The structure was built by Akbar on the site of an earlier fort. A succession of Mughal emperors lived here, including Humayun, Akbar, Jehangir, Shah Jahan, and Aurangzeb. It was from here that the country was governed, and the fort contained the largest state treasury and mint. As with similar Mughal facilities in Delhi and Lahore, the word "fort" is misleading: the complex is really a fortified palace, containing royal apartments, mosques, assembly halls, and a dungeon—the entire cityscape of an imperial capital. A massive wall 2½ km (1½ miles) long and 69 feet high surrounds the fort's roughly triangular shape. With the Yamuna River running at its base, the fort was also protected by a moat and another wall, presenting a daunting barrier to anyone hoping to access the treasures within.

This was originally a brick fort, and Ibrahim Lodi held it for nine years until he was defeated and killed in the battle of Panipat in 1526. The Mughals captured the fort along with masses of treasure, which included one of the most famous gems in the world, the Koh-i-Noor diamond. The emperor Babur stayed in the fort in the palace of Ibrahim, while Humayun was crowned here in 1530. Emperor Akbar decided to make it his capital when he arrived in Agra in 1558. He rebuilt it with red sandstone from the Barauli area in Rajasthan, and the whole process took eight years.

The fort's entrance is accessible through the Amar Singh Gate (also called the Lahore Gate, for the city in modern-day Pakistan that it faces). It was named for Amar Singh Rathore, a legendary general who served the Mughals. North of this entrance sits the fort's largest private residence, the **Jahangiri Mahal,** built by Jahangir as a harem, mainly for his Rajput wives. (Akbar's own palace, closer to the entrance, is in ruins.) Measuring 250 feet by 300 feet, the Jahangiri Mahal juxtaposes *jarokhas* (balconies) and other elements of Hindu architecture with pointed arches and other Central Asian influences imported by the Mughals. The palace's central court is lined with two-story facades bearing remnants of the rich, gilded decoration that once covered much of the structure.

After Jahangir's death in 1628, Shah Jahan assumed the throne and started his own buildings inside the fort, often tearing down those built by his father and grandfather and adding marble decorations (it is said that he was partial to the material). The **Anguri Bagh** (Grape Arbor) shows the outlines of a geometric garden built around delicate water channels and chutes. The 1637 **Khas Mahal** (Private Palace) is an early masterpiece of Shah Jahan's craftsmen. The central pavilion, made of white marble, follows the classic Mughal pattern: three arches on each side, five in front, and two turrets rising out of the roof. Of the two flanking pavilions where Shah Jahan's two daughters resided, one is of white marble and was supposedly decorated with gold leaf; the other is made of red stone. The arched roofs of all three pavilions are stone interpretations of the bamboo architecture of Bengal. In one part of the Khas Mahal a staircase leads down to the palace's "air-conditioned" quarters—cool underground rooms that were used in summer. It's famous for its paintings on marble.

Agra's massive fort

The octagonal tower of the **Mussaman Burj** has fine inlay work and a splendid view down the river to the Taj Mahal. This is where Shah Jahan is said to have spent the last seven years of his life, imprisoned by his son Aurangzeb but still able to look out on his greatest monument, the Taj Mahal. He may have built the tower for his wife Mumtaz Mahal (for whom he also built the Taj Mahal). On the northeastern end of the Khas Mahal courtyard stands the **Sheesh Mahal** (Palace of Mirrors), built in 1637 as a bath for the private palace and dressing room for the harem. Each of the two chambers contained a bathing tank fed by marble channels.

The emperor received foreign ambassadors and other dignitaries in the **Diwan-i-Khas** (Hall of Private Audience), built by Shah Jahan in 1636–37. Outside, the marble throne terrace holds a pair of black and white thrones. The black throne, carved from a single block of marble, overlooks the Yamuna and, according to the inscription, was used by Shah Jahan; the white throne is made of several marble blocks and was his father's seat of power. Both thrones face the **Machhi Bhavan,** an enclosure of fountains and shallow pools, and a number of imperial offices.

To the empire's citizens and to the European emissaries who came to see these powerful monarchs, the most impressive part of the fort was the **Diwan-i-Am** (Hall of Public Audience), set within a large quadrangle. This huge, low structure rests on a 4-foot platform, its nine cusped Mughal arches held up by rows of slender supporting pillars. Here the emperor sat and dispensed justice to his subjects, sitting on the legendary Peacock Throne, now lost.

Northeast of the Diwan-i-Khas is the **Nagina Masjid,** a private mosque raised by Shah Jahan for the women of his harem. Made of white marble and walled in on three sides, it has typical cusped arches, a marble courtyard, and three graceful domes. While in the Nagina Masjid, royal ladies could buy beautiful items from tradesmen who set up a temporary bazaar for them in front of its balcony. Nearby is the lovely **Moti Masjid,** a perfectly proportioned pearl mosque (*moti* means pearl) built in white marble by Shah Jahan. The Agra Fort is one of the area's seven World Heritage Sites (and India's 32), along with the Taj Mahal and Fatehpur Sikri. ⊠ *Yamuna Kinara Rd.* ▨ *Rs. 300 (Rs. 250 with ticket to Taj Mahal)* ☉ *Daily sunrise–sunset.*

Akbar's Tomb. Akbar's resting place, in what's now the small town of Sikandra, was begun by the emperor himself in 1602 and completed after his death by Jahangir. Topped with white marble and flanked by graceful minarets, this mausoleum of rough red sandstone sits in a typical Mughal garden called a *charbagh*—four quadrants separated by waterways. The garden, however, is not well tended, and Jat raiders (who invaded Agra after the fall of the Mughul empire) destroyed much of the gold work that once adorned the tomb, though the British partially restored it. In a domed chamber three stories high, the crypt is inscribed with the 99 names of Allah, plus the phrases *Allah-o-Akbar* (God is great) at the head and *Jalla Jalalahu* (Great is His glory) at the foot. It's a charming spot to visit; you'll spot many langurs (long-tailed monkeys) and deer in the gardens. Akbar had originally meant this to be the official resting place for the Mughals, but it didn't turn out that way: only two of his daughters are buried here. ∎ TIP→ You can actually see the tomb's enormous gateway, topped with bright tilework, from the train from Delhi—look out the left window 10 or 15 minutes before the train is due to reach Agra. ⊠ *10 km (6 miles) north of Agra on Grand Trunk Rd. to Delhi, Sikandra, Uttar Pradesh* ▨ *Rs. 110 (Rs. 100 with ticket to Taj Mahal)* ☉ *Daily sunrise–sunset.*

Itimad-ud-Daulah's Tomb. The empress Nur Jahan (Jahangir's favorite wife) built this small, gorgeous tomb for her father, Mirza Ghiyas Beg (pronounced Baig), a Persian nobleman who became Jahangir's chief minister. Beg was also the grandfather of Mumtaz Mahal, the wife of the emperor Shah Jahan. The monument, one of Agra's loveliest, was supposedly built by workers from Persia. The tomb incorporates a great deal of brown and yellow Persian marble and marks the first use of Persian-style marble inlay in India—both features that would later characterize the style of Shah Jahan. Particularly in its use of intricate marble inlay, this building was a precursor of, and very likely an inspiration for, the Taj Mahal (for this reason it has earned the somewhat goofy nickname of the "Baby Taj"). The roof is arched in the style of Bengali terra-cotta temples, and the minarets are octagonal, much broader than the slender cylinders of the Taj Mahal—in its fine proportions this mausoleum almost equals that masterpiece. Inside, where the elegant decoration continues, the central chamber holds the tombs of Itimad-ud-Daulah and his wife; other relations are buried in adjacent rooms. Most travelers to Agra never see this place, but its beauty and tranquillity are extraordinary, and its well-maintained gardens make it a wonderful place to pause and reflect. ⊠ *5 km (3 miles) north of Taj Mahal on left bank of Yamuna River* 🎟 *Rs. 110 (Rs. 100 with ticket to the Taj Mahal)* ☉ *Daily sunrise–sunset.*

Fodor'sChoice   **Taj Mahal.**
  ★   *See the highlighted feature in this chapter.*

WHERE TO EAT

$$$$ ✕ **Bellevue.** You can have breakfast, lunch, and dinner here at this airy
INTERNATIONAL   indoor restaurant, which looks out on the Oberoi's gardens, and has a
Fodor'sChoice   distant view of the Taj. Bellevue is stylishly decorated, with chic brown-
  ★   and-white tile floors, plush turquoise booths and dusky wooden tables
and chairs. Indian food is the specialty–try their *murgh tikka masala* (a chicken dish with a tomato-based gravy) or their *raan*—a whole leg of lamb. The menu also includes continental dishes such as steaks and pastas. ⑤ *Average main: Rs. 1800* ⊠ *Oberoi Amarvilas, Taj East Gate Rd.,* ☎ *0562/223–1515.*

$ ✕ **Dasaprakash.** The light and spicy South Indian vegetarian dishes
SOUTH INDIAN   served at this casual town favorite are a nice change from Agra's usual
rich Mughlai fare. The food is excellent and service is fast. Try the fluffy *idlis* (steamed rice cakes) and *dosas* (rice crepes)—especially the Mysore masala dosa. The *thali* (a combination plate) includes rice, *puri* (deep fried, fluffy bread), *rasam* (thin, spicy lentil soup), *sambar* (thick lentil soup with tamarind and vegetables), vegetables, and sweets. Also available are an unusual selection of fresh juices and a large dessert menu with ice creams and floats. ⑤ *Average main: Rs. 200* ⊠ *9 Bansal Nagar, Fathehabad Rd., behind ManSingh Hotel,* ☎ *0562/223–0089* ⊕ *www.dasaprakash.in.*

$$$$ ✕ **Jhankar.** Occupying an elegant, airy space open to the lobby of the
INDIAN   Taj View Hotel, Jhankar has a menu of excellent Mughlai dishes that
include the house specialty, *aloo dum chutneywale* (potatoes with dried fruits and herbs simmered in a mint and coriander sauce). Also terrific is the Agra delicacy *magazi murgh korma* (chicken in yogurt, cashews, and poppy seeds, garnished with rose petals and melon seeds). Flavors are subtle and distinct; many herbs and vegetables come from the kitchen garden. ⑤ *Average main: Rs. 1200* ⊠ *Taj Gateway Hotel, Fatehabad Rd., Taj Ganj* ☎ *562/223–2400* ☉ *No lunch.*

$$$$ ✕ **Mughal Room.** The panoramic view from a wall of windows takes in
INDIAN   both the Taj Mahal and the Fort, while after dark live *ghazals* (Urdu
love songs) set the mood for Mughlai dishes. A ceiling of faux twinkling stars floats over an interior of rich reds, with brass trays hanging on walls and tables set with silver goblets. Behind a display window, a chef can be seen making such delicious dishes as *murg malai tikka* (chicken marinated in cream, coated with spices, topped with walnuts, and cooked in a clay oven) and *kabuli naan* (bread stuffed with dried fruits and cheese, sprinkled with cumin seeds). ⑤ *Average main: Rs. 900* ⊠ *Clarks Shiraz, 54 Taj Rd., top fl.* ☎ *0562/222–6121 to 6127.*

$$$$ ✕ **Peshawri.** Rustic wood tabletops resting on tree-trunk bases, plush,
INDIAN   bright-orange seat cushions, and hammered copper plates and goblets
Fodor'sChoice   create a dark, romantic mood, complemented by the simple, delicious
  ★   barbecue cuisine of the North West Frontier, parts of which are in

what's now Pakistan. All kinds of meats are freshly prepared over open flames and served with rich, aromatic sauces. The ultrarich *dal bukhara* (a combination of whole black lentils, tomatoes, ginger, and garlic along with plentiful ghee and cream) is slow-roasted for hours and makes a perfect choice for any vegetarians in the group. The *sikanderi* raan is a whole leg of lamb, highly recommended for its tender, falling-off-the-bone meat. Reservations are recommended: it gets packed. ⓢ *Average main: Rs. 1400* ✉ *ITC Mughal Hotel, Taj Ganj* ☎ *562/402–1700.*

$$ ✕ **Pinch of Spice.** One of Agra's choice destinations for Mughal food, this
NORTH INDIAN sleek, modern restaurant is decorated in rich shades of purple, beige, and orange, and lighted by glittering glass chandeliers. The five-page menu includes Chinese and European dishes, but the North Indian cuisine is what makes the restaurant so popular with the locals. Try their signature butter chicken and *dal bukhara* (slow-cooked black lentils) and wash it down with a "paan shot," a creamy liquid breath freshener served after every meal. Massively popular, this restaurant is usually crowded, so it's best to make a reservation for dinner. ⓢ *Average main: Rs. 400* ✉ *23/453 Wazirpura Rd., Sanjay Pl., opposite Sanjay Cinema* ☎ *0562/400–9004* ⊕ *www.pinchofspice.in.*

$$ ✕ **Sai Khandelaa.** The multicuisine menu features Italian, Chinese, and
NORTH INDIAN Lebanese sections, but your best bet would be the North Indian items. The *laal maas* and paneer butter masala are house specialties, while the *murg khajana* (a tandoori chicken combo with biryani, egg, and gravy) is among their most popular dishes. With its grand wooden facade, white walls adorned with paintings of Indian princesses, white linen tablecloths, and royal blue chairs, the restaurant can feel a bit stuffy when it's full. ⓢ *Average main: Rs. 400* ✉ *Sadar Bazar, Taj Rd.* ☎ *562/222–7003* ⊕ *www.saikhandelaa.com.*

$ ✕ **Taste of Maya Restaurant.** One of the loveliest rooftop restaurants in
ECLECTIC Agra, this is a relaxing place to enjoy a coffee or glass of wine in the evening by candlelight, accompanied by live Indian classical music. Shaded from the sun by an enormous pipal tree, the tables, covered with Rajasthani-dyed cloths, are set up on a blue Moroccan tile floor, amid a garden of potted plants. The menu is eclectic, with mostly Chinese and Indian fare. It's a great place for breakfast as well as dinner—one of the few restaurants outside of five-star hotels that serves fresh seasonal fruit juice and organic bread. ⓢ *Average main: Rs. 200* ✉ *18/184 Purani Mandi Circle, Fatehabad Rd., Taj Ganj* ☎ *97191–07691* ⊕ *www.mayainmagic.com* ▭ *No credit cards.*

WHERE TO STAY

$$$$ ⌂ **ITC Mughal.** Done up in tones of pearl and beige, the Kaya Kalp spa
RESORT is the hotel's most winning feature. **Pros:** you'll never be bored; the spa is incredible. **Cons:** so huge you may need a map. ⓢ *Rooms from: Rs. 12500* ✉ *Fatehabad Rd., Taj Ganj* ☎ *562/402–1700* ⊕ *www.itchotels.in* ⤶ *188 rooms, 45 suites* ⍟ *Breakfast.*

$$$ ⌂ **Jaypee Palace Hotel and Convention Centre.** The largest hotel in all of
RESORT Agra, the Jaypee sits on nearly 25 acres of lawns and gardens and, in
FAMILY addition to the usual type of resort amenities, has an in-house bowling alley and theater, with an arcade and playroom to keep children happy. **Pros:** lots of in-house amenities; a good place to bring children. **Cons:**

Continued on page 172

THE TAJ MAHAL

Described as an "elegy in marble," the Taj Mahal is an epic monument to Emperor Shah Jahan's beloved wife. Seeing the magnificent structure in person reveals the minute details of its decoration and its construction, and the incredible symmetry of the elements.

The Taj Mahal is one of the most recognizable, most reproduced images in the world, and the tale of love and loss that sparked its creation is almost as incredible as the monument's beauty. It was built by the fifth Mughal emperor, Shah Jahan, in memory of his third but favorite wife, who was called his Mumtaz Mahal (the Jewel of the Palace). As the legend goes, she asked him to build her a monument so beautiful that the world would never forget their love. She died after giving birth to their thirteenth child, and six months after her death a huge procession brought Mumtaz Mahal's body to Agra, where Shah Jahan began the process of honoring her request with the Taj Mahal. Construction of the monument began in about 1632, and it took 20,000 laborers a period of about 17 years to complete the vast, bejeweled, white marble tomb on the banks of the Yamuna River. The building's perfect proportions, scale, and exquisite detail make it a vision unlike anything else. It was made a UNESCO World Heritage site in 1983.

Up close the intricately crafted and colorful detail of the building is apparent, but from far away, the magnificent structure appears all white—though depending on the sun and the time of day it takes on different hues. At sunrise it takes on a pinkish hue; at sunset it's a lemon yellow, then orange. Once the sun goes down, the marble is pure white against a black sky.

(top) An artist's rendition of Mumtaz Mahal
(right) The reflecting pool leading up to the Taj Mahal is a typical element of Islamic gardens and courtyards

ENTRANCE

You enter the grounds through a huge sandstone gateway boldly emblazoned with an inlaid Koranic inscription.

THE GARDENS

The Taj Mahal stands at the end of a large garden that is divided into four sections by pools of water. Midway between the entrance and

(top left) Emperor Shah Jahan standing on a globe (top middle) Entrance to the Taj Mahal (top right) Interior of the mosque (bottom left) The Taj Mahal in early morning (bottom middle) An artist's drawing of the Taj Mahal (far right top) The lotus pool (far right bottom) Map of the Taj

the Taj is a large pool, called the Lotus pool because of its lotus-shaped water spouts. The water reflects the Taj, and standing in front of the lotus pool makes for a popular photo op.

The garden in front of the Taj is said to symbolize Paradise, because Islamic texts of the period describe Paradise as a garden of abundance with four rivers separating it into four quadrants.

THE TOMB

The 190-square-foot central marble building, the mausoleum or pavilion, is the focus of the structure, and it stands on two bases: sandstone on the

bottom level, and marble on the top (measuring 313 square feet) that has been worked into a chessboard design.

The mausoleum's central archway is deeply recessed, as are the smaller pairs of companion archways along the sides and the beveled corners of the 190-square-foot structure.

Behind the main pavilion, the Yamuna River winds along its broad, sandy bed.

THE DOME

The Taj Mahal's most extraordinary feature is its onion-shaped dome, crowned by a brass finial mounted in a scalloped ornament: an inverted Hindu motif of the lotus. The dome uses the Central Asian technique of placing a central inner dome, in this case 81 feet high, inside an outer shell to attain the extraordinary exterior height of 200 feet; between the two is an area nearly the size of the interior hall itself.

MINARETS
There are four slender, marble minarets—one at each corner of the Taj platform. They blend so well into the general composition that it's hard to believe each one is over 130 feet tall. The minarets were built at a slight tilt away from the tomb so that, in

case of an earthquake, they'd fall away from the building.

MOSQUES
On opposite sides of the Taj Mahal are two majestic sandstone buildings: on the left is a mosque; the one on the right is believed to have been built as a mirror image, for symmetry, but may also have been used as a guesthouse.

MUSEUM
The small Taj Mahal Museum stands near the mosque to the left of the Taj. It contains Mughul memorabilia and provides some historical background to the Taj, as well as paintings of the famous

couple, manuscripts, letters, and a display of precious stones used in the construction of the Taj.

INSIDE THE MAUSOLEUM

The Taj Mahal is a glorious example of the refined aesthetics of the Mughals. In addition to the magnificent architecture of the buildings and the layout of the gardens, the mausoleum itself, likened to a jeweled box, showcases a range of art forms. One of the recurring motifs throughout the Taj are the many flower forms: flowers were believed to symbolize paradise on earth.

Carved marble screen

CARVED MARBLE SCREENS

Directly under the marble dome lie what look like the coffins of Mumtaz Mahal and Shah Jahan (photo at left), surrounded by a screen chiseled from a single block of marble, with latticework as intricate as lace. In fact, however, both are buried in a crypt below, in deference to the Islamic tradition that no one should walk upon their graves.

Crypt

CRYPT

Visitors are no longer allowed to go downstairs to the main crypt area (photo at right), where the bodies of Mumtaz Mahal and Shah Jahan are buried, because of the vandalism that has occurred over the years.

INLAY WORK

Pietra dura, a type of mosaic work, is believed to have originated in Italy and later imported to Asia. It makes use of colorful, cut stones set in marble to create images. The intricate designs in the Taj use semiprecious stones including agate, carnelian, coral, jasper, lapis lazuli, malachite, tiger's eye, and turquoise, set in different shades of marble, sandstone, and slate. Look closely at the tiny flowers and detailed stonework on each petal and leaf in the Taj. The work is so fine that not even a magnifying glass reveals the tiny breaks between stones, yet a single one-inch flower on the queen's tomb has 60 pieces.

Inlay work

CARVED RELIEF WORK

Panels of carved flowers, foliage, and vases decorate the lower parts of the walls inside the mausoleum.

Carved relief work

CALLIGRAPHY

Inlaid calligraphy of black marble ornaments the undecorated surfaces of the mausoleum. The banner-like inscriptions on the arches are passages from the Koran.

Calligraphy

TAJ MAHAL VISTING TIPS

Hours: The Taj is open Saturday to Thursday, from sunrise to sunset. It's closed on Friday. The Taj Mahal museum is open Saturday to Thursday 10 am to 5 pm.

Admission: Rs. 750

Best time to visit: Many people say that sunrise or sunset is the best time to see the Taj Mahal, for the glorious colors. Though the Taj Mahal is glorious any time of day, midday is probably the worst time to visit because of the bright sun reflecting off the white marble (bring your sunglasses). By all means, go early to beat the heat, but don't count on having the place to yourself, as there are almost always crowds at the Taj Mahal.

Night Viewing: The Taj is open for viewing 5 nights per month, on the full moon and two nights before and after, except Friday and during Ramadan. Limited numbers of tickets are sold one day in advance (your hotel might be able to arrange tickets for you), for a half-hour visit between 8:30 pm and 12:30 am. Admission price is the same as during regular hours. It's a romantic way to see the Taj but definitely not a substitute for a day-time visit. ⊠ Taj Ganj, Taj Rd. ⊕ www.tajmahal. gov.in/

To buy night-view tickets: Archaeological Survey of India. ⊠ Agra Circle, 22 The Mall, Agra (10 am to 6 pm). ☎ 562/222–7261 or 562/222–7262

easy to get lost on the grounds; not for those after something cozy. ⑤ *Rooms from: Rs. 10000* ⊠ *Fatehabad Rd.* ☎ *562/233–0800* ⊕ *www. jaypeehotels.com* ⬎ *326 rooms, 15 suites* ⦿| *Breakfast.*

$
B&B/INN

⌂ **N. Homestay.** It would be difficult to find a more warm and inviting hostess than Naghma Haider, who runs this homestay—and offers cooking classes—in the spacious, three-story home she shares with her easygoing family. **Pros:** a great cultural experience; the family is full of local knowledge. **Cons:** you are in someone's house, so you won't necessarily have privacy outside of your room. ⑤ *Rooms from: Rs. 1800* ⊠ *15 Ajanta Colony, Vibhav Nagar* ☎ *0562/404–3726* ⊕ *www. nhomestay.com* ⬎ *6 rooms* ▭ *No credit cards* ⦿| *Breakfast.*

$$$$
RESORT
Fodor's Choice
★

⌂ **Oberoi Amarvilas.** One of India's best resorts emulates the opulent lifestyle of the Mughal emperors—complete with your own butler—and has a breathtaking view of the Taj Mahal. **Pros:** gorgeous views; flawless service; free rides to the Taj Mahal and guide services. **Cons:** extremely expensive. ⑤ *Rooms from: Rs. 48000* ⊠ *Taj East Gate Rd.* ☎ *0562/223–1515* ⊕ *www.oberoihotels.com* ⬎ *102 rooms, 8 suites* ⦿| *No meals.*

$
HOTEL

⌂ **Ray of Maya.** Less than a 10-minute (500 m) walk from the western gate of the Taj Mahal, this clean, cozy, and elegant place is ideal for couples and singles on a budget who don't want to rough it. **Pros:** cozy, intimate, and economical; top of the Taj visible from rooms 6 and 8; good location. **Cons:** while the inside is lovely, the exterior isn't much to look at; lots of stairs; toiletries not provided. ⑤ *Rooms from: Rs. 2000* ⊠ *Purani Mandi, Fatehabad Rd.* ☎ *0562/405–2665, 971/910–7692* ⊕ *www.mayainmagic.com* ⬎ *7 rooms* ⦿| *No meals.*

$$$$ [icon] **Taj Gateway.** A good, though dis-
RESORT tant, view of the Taj Mahal from
FAMILY some rooms and the rooftop make
this hotel a popular choice. **Pros:**
close to the Taj Mahal; a dedicated
yoga channel in every room. **Cons:**
the hotel's popularity, and its small
lobby, can make it seem extremely
crowded. $ *Rooms from: Rs.
11500* ✉ *Fatehabad Rd., Taj
Ganj* ☎ *0562/660–2000* ⊕ *www.
tajhotels.com* ⤴ *95 rooms, 5 suites*
Breakfast.

$$$$ [icon] **Trident Agra.** Built around a large
HOTEL garden courtyard with fountains,
FAMILY water spilling over rocks, a sooth-
Fodor's Choice ing expanse of green lawn, and a pool, this place is a real oasis in
★ Agra. **Pros:** a thoughtful feature—rare in India—is a handicap-accessi-
ble room; kids will love the cozy tent stocked with a PS3, games, and
movies; 81 rooms newly renovated in mid-2014. **Cons:** with only one
restaurant, it tends to get crowded around mealtimes. $ *Rooms from:
Rs. 12500* ✉ *Fatehabad Rd.* ☎ *562/223–5000* ⊕ *www.tridenthotels.
com* ⤴ *133 rooms, 2 suites* *Breakfast.*

$$$$ [icon] **Wyndham Grand Agra.** A night here feels a bit like staying in a
RESORT Mughal palace, with sweeping beige and white marble arches, mani-
FAMILY cured gardens, gurgling fountains, and elaborate rooms. **Pros:** five restaurants offer plenty of dining options. **Cons:** rooms are far from the
lobby. $ *Rooms from: Rs. 14000* ✉ *7th Mile Stone, Fatehabad Rd.*
☎ *562/223–7000* ⊕ *www.wyndhamgrandagra.com* ⤴ *136 rooms, 12
suites* *Breakfast.*

SHOPPING

Tourist shops are generally open daily from 10 to 7:30. Many Agra
shops sell hand-knotted dhurries and other rugs, jewelry made from
precious and semiprecious stones, brass statues, and marble inlays that
continue the form and motifs seen in the city's great monuments. Resist
drivers and touts who want to take you to places offering special "bargains"; they receive big commissions from shopkeepers, which you pay
in the inflated price of the merchandise. Beware, too, of soapstone
masquerading as marble: this softer, cheaper stone is a convincing substitute, but you can test it by scraping the item with your fingernail—
Indian marble won't scrape. Finally, for what it's worth, local lore has
it that miniature replicas of the Taj Mahal bring bad luck.

Agra Marble Emporium. This large, three-room marble shop specializes in marble inlaid tabletops, and also sells knickknacks like plates
and trays. You can often see workers carving marble in the front of
the shop. All marble can be shipped internationally. ✉ *A Block No.
4, Taj Nagri Phase-2, Fatehabad Rd.* ☎ *0562/223–2321* ⊕ *www.
agramarbleemporium.com.*

4

Cottage Industries Exposition. This chain of privately owned stores (not to be confused with the government-run Central Cottage Industries) carries high-quality rugs (mostly Kashmiri), silks, gemstones, and, like everyplace else in Agra, marble inlay. Prices are extremely high—bargain fiercely. ⊠ *39 Fatehabad Rd., opposite Agra Commissionary* ☎ *0562/222–6813* ☉ *Daily 8:30–8:30.*

Ganeshi Lall and Son. This reliable, family-owned jeweler, established in 1845, retails precious and semiprecious gold and silver jewelry. They specialize in older pieces and also create new ones. Past clients have included Prince Charles and Jacqueline Kennedy Onassis. ⊠ *Hotel ITC Mughal, Fatehabad Rd.* ☎ *0562/233–0181.*

Kohinoor. This company has been designing jewelry using cut and uncut emeralds and other precious stones since 1862; a special "connoisseur's room" with unique pieces is open only by appointment. Don't miss the little museum display of fantastic 3-D *zardoji* (embroidered paintings). Some paintings, known as Shams, have been encrusted with gems by the master of the technique, Shamsuddin; some are for sale. ⊠ *Fatehabad Rd.* ☎ *0562/223–0027, 0562/223–0028* ⊕ *www.kohinoorjewellers.com.*

Munshi Ganeshi Lal & Son. This three-room emporium stocks *zardozi* (embroidery), traditional jewelry, and marble inlay work. A large room on the upper floor is dedicated to antique-style gold and silver jewelry inlaid with precious stones. The basement doubles up as a workshop for marble inlay tables, plates, and other items. ⊠ *194 Fatehabad Rd.* ☎ *0562/233–0168* ⊕ *www.mglagra.com* ☉ *Daily 10–8.*

Oswal Exports. Excellent examples of inlaid white, pink, green, and black marble are produced here; you can watch daily demonstrations as artisans work on marble and also learn their techniques. Handicrafts, jewelry, and textiles are also available. ⊠ *30 Munro Rd., Sadar Market* ☎ *562/222–5710, 562/222–5712.*

Subhash Emporium. This was the first store to revive Agra marble work in the 1960s. Ask to see some of the masterpieces in the private gallery to give you a better perspective on quality. ⊠ *18/1 Gwalior Rd.* ☎ *0562/326–0604, 0562/326–0605* ⊕ *www.marbleemporium.com.*

U.P. Handicrafts Palace. Stunning marble-inlaid tabletops in every size, some with latticework, are on display in this massive showroom of marble collectibles. At the demo workshop outdoors, you can watch craftsmen work and paint on marble. Other pieces include vases, decorative elephants, and plates. ⊠ *Fatehabad Rd., next to Munshi Ganeshi Lal & Son* ☎ *0562/400–1601, 0562/223–2661 to 2663* ⊕ *www.upcraftspalace.com* ☉ *Daily 9–7.*

FATEHPUR SIKRI

37 km (23 miles) southwest of Agra.

Fodor's Choice
★

The capital of the Mughal Empire for only 14 years (from 1571 to 1585), the majestic red sandstone buildings of the now uninhabited fortified city of Fatehpur Sikri are remarkably well preserved, and showcase elegant architecture and an inspired sense of planning.

In a sense, Fatehpur Sikri was built on faith: in 1569, so the story goes, the Mughal emperor Akbar was driven to despair because he didn't have a male heir. He made a pilgrimage to visit the Sufi mystic Salim Chisti, who blessed him. The blessing evidently worked, as Akbar had a son within the next year, naming him Salim (the future emperor Jahangir) in honor of the saint. Two years later, Akbar began building a new capital in Chisti's village of Sikri, later renaming it Fatehpur Sikri (City of Victory) after a great triumph in Gujarat. Standing on a rocky ridge overlooking the village, Fatehpur Sikri originally had a circumference of about 11 km (7 miles). Massive walls and seven gates enclosed three sides, and a lake (now dried up) protected the fourth. When the British came to Fatehpur Sikri in 1583 to meet Akbar, they were amazed to see a city that exceeded contemporary London in both population and grandeur—with more rubies, diamonds, and silks than they could count.

> ### THE MARBLE MECCA
>
> The Taj Mahal's marble may have come from the mines of Makrana, a small Rajasthani village 400 km (250 miles) to the west that's renowned for its marble supply. The artisans creating marble inlay in Agra today are likely using Makrana marble, and they're believed to be descendants of those who mined the marble or did the inlay work on the Taj.

4

What remains is a beautiful cluster of royal dwellings on the top of the ridge, landscaped with lawns and flowering borders. The structures elegantly blend architectural styles from Persia as well as Akbar's various Indian holdings, a reflection of the synthesizing impulse that characterized the third and greatest of the Mughal emperors. Also notable is how Akbar synthesized Muslim and Hindu beliefs here. The magnificently carved Brahma pillar is testament to his stand on communal harmony. Akbar ruled here for only 14 years before moving his capital—perhaps in pursuit of water, but more likely for political reasons—to Lahore and then eventually back to Agra. Because it was abandoned and never resettled, the city was not modified by later rulers, and thus is the best reflection of Akbar's aesthetic and design philosophies. Fatehpur Sikri now stands as an intriguing ghost town, reflecting a high point in India's cultural history.

GETTING HERE AND AROUND
To reach Fatehpur Sikri from Agra, hire a car and driver or join a tour. The drive takes about an hour. There are ticket offices at the Jodh Bai Palace entrance, Diwan-i-Aam.

TIMING
Fatehpur Sikri is best visited early in the morning. Set out from Agra by about 6:30 am to avoid traffic. You'll be done well before 11 am, which is when the heat begins to really kick in. Plan to spend at least two or three hours wandering the grounds. Wear good walking shoes; there's a lot of ground to be covered here.

Fatehpur Sikri

Naubat Khana

MINT

Agra Road

Hiran Minar

CARAVANSERAI

Treasury

Diwan-i-Khas

TICKET OFFICES

Astrologer's Seat ◆ Diwan-i-Aam

Elephant Gate

Nojina Masjid

Pachisi Court

Panch Mahal

Turkish Sultana's Pavilion

Birbal's Palace

House of Mariam

Akbar's Chamber

Anup Talao (Peerless Pool)

Jodh Bai Palace

Royal Stables

TICKET OFFICES

FATEHPUR SIKRI

Fatehpur Sikri Road

Salim Chisti's Tomb

JAMA MASJID

Shahi Darwaza

Buland Darwaza (Great Gate)

Buland Gate Rd.

Clock Tower

0 — 100 meters

0 — 100 km

EXPLORING

Buland Darwaza (Great Gate). The usual starting point for exploring Fatehpur Sikri is the Buland Darwaza (Great Gate) of the **Jama Masjid**, near the parking lot, but the cluster of hawkers and guides nearby can be unrelenting. If you arrive by car, you can avoid this minor annoyance by asking to be dropped at the subsidiary entrance at the northeastern end of the city, where the following tour begins. Coming from Agra, bear right just after passing through **Agra Gate**, the main one in Akbar's day. The tour ends at the Great Gate, so have your driver meet you there.

Approaching the Fatehpur Sikri complex, you'll walk through the **Naubat Khana,** a gate that was manned by drummers and musicians during imperial processions. Just ahead on the right is the **Mint,** a workshop that may have minted coins.

A few steps from the museum is the **Diwan-i-Aam** (Hall of Public Audience), a large courtyard 112 meters long and 55 meters wide (366 feet by 181 feet) with colonnades on three sides. Ahead is the balcony where the emperor sat on his throne to meet subjects or observe celebrations and other spectacles. Through chiseled marble screens, the women of the court would watch as Akbar, the empire's chief justice, hand down his decisions: it's said that those condemned to die were impaled, hanged, or trampled under the feet of an elephant. What looks like a square two-story building with domed cupolas at each corner is the **Diwan-i-Khas** (Hall of Private Audience). Inside it's actually one tall room where Akbar sat on an elaborate elevated platform and, it's thought, conducted meetings with his ministers. Supported by a stone column topped with a giant lotus flower intricately carved in stone, it's connected by causeways to four balconies with window seats on which the ministers sat. The throne's position is thought to have symbolized the center of the world or, alternatively, the one god sought by several major religions; it also may have had a practical side, shielding the emperor from would-be assassins.

Across from the hall is the **Treasury**, also known as **Ankh Michali** (Hide and Seek), said to be named for Akbar's playful habit of playing the game with his harem inside the broad rooms and narrow passageways. The deep recesses in the walls, though, suggest that it may have been used as a treasury. Adjacent is the **Astrologer's Seat**, a platform where Akbar's royal astrologer sat. Pass through the courtyard paved with a board on which Akbar played *pachisi* (an early form of parcheesi that used slave girls as pieces), into the pavilion centered by the **Anup Talao** (Peerless Pool), a square pool with a central platform, connected by four bridges. Below the basement of the pavilion is an excavated underground palace whose entrances cleverly concealed it until archaeologists, led by reports from Akbar's day, discovered it. The emperor would come to these rooms, constructed at the center of a water-filled tank, to escape the summer heat. Unearthed within them was the 12-foot-high stone bowl (now displayed on the pavilion) used to store water transported from the Ganges—the only water Akbar would drink. At the edge of the pool is the **Turkish Sultana's Pavilion,** a charming structure covered with elaborate Persian carvings in floral and zigzag patterns. It is said to have been the home of the emperor's Turkish wife, but was more likely a place to relax by the pool and have a quiet conversation. Separated from the sultana's pavilion as well as from the official buildings of the palace by the Anup Talao are Akbar's private chambers.

The Imperial Harem, where the women of Akbar's household resided, consists of several buildings connected by covered passages and screened from view of the more public areas. The **Panch Mahal** is a breeze-catching structure with five (*panch* in Hindi) arcaded stories, each smaller than the one below. Its 176 columns are carved with tiny flowers or other motifs (no two of the first floor's 56 columns have the same design). As Fatehpur Sikri's tallest building, it affords grand views of the city and the surrounding landscape from its upper stories. When the women prayed, they did so behind the screened arches of the **Najina Masjid** (Small or Jewel Mosque), behind the Panch Mahal across a small garden. The largest residence in the complex is the Gujarati-influenced **Jodh Bai Palace,** more properly called Principal Haram Sara, because behind its eunuch-guarded entrance lived a number of the emperor's wives rather than just that of his Hindu wife, Jodh Bai. The **Hawa Mahal** (Palace of the Winds) is a cool vantage point from

One of the red sandstone buildings at Fatehpur Sikri

which women could peek out at the court unseen from beautifully carved stone screens.

The **House of Mariam** (on a diagonal between Jodh Bai's Palace and the Panch Mahal) is the home of either Akbar's Christian wife or, more likely, his mother. Look for the faded paintings of horses and elephants on the exterior walls. Some of the brackets supporting the eaves are carved with scenes from mythology. **Birbal's Palace,** which sits a few yards northwest of Jodh Bai's Palace and the Hawa Mahal, was named for the emperor's playfully irreverent Hindu prime minister. Because it's unlikely that he would have lived inside the harem, the Archaeological Survey of India ascribes it to Akbar's two senior wives. The palace's ornamentation makes use of both Hindu and Islamic motifs.

The big open colonnade behind the harem is known as the **Royal Stables** because the stalls were once thought to have housed elephants and horses; however, it is more likely that it was the quarters of the serving women, and that the open stalls were enclosed by curtains tied to the stone rings once thought to have tethered the animals. At the edge of the city complex, by Sikri Lake, you should be able to see the **Hiran Minar** tower, decorated with six-pointed stars and hexagons, from which elephant tusks protrude (the originals have been replaced with stone tusks). If it's open, there are 53 steps that take you to the top of the tower, from where you have a bird's-eye view of Fatehpur Sikri.

Follow the path down to the east gate of the **Jama Masjid** (Imperial Mosque); built around 1571 and designed to hold 10,000 worshippers, it's still in active use. Note the deliberate incorporation of Hindu elements in the design, especially the pillar decorations. The

Shahi Darwza (Emperor's Gate) is on the eastern side of the mosque; only the Emperor and his courtiers were allowed to pass through this gate. The sandstone gateway is fully carved in geometrical design, and has two arches, one on top of the other; a lotus-bud motif runs through the smaller arch.

In the courtyard of the Jama Masjid (opposite the Buland Darwaza) lies **Salim Chisti's tomb,** surrounded by walls of marble lace, each with a different design. Begun upon the saint's death in 1571 and finished nine years later, the tomb was originally faced with red sandstone, but was refinished in marble by Jahangir, the heir Akbar's wife bore after the saint's blessing. From here you can cross the courtyard and exit through the imposing Buland Darwaza. Tombs of those people lucky enough to be buried by the revered saint are in this area. And here is the **Buland Darwaza** (Great Gate), at the southwestern end of the city. The beautiful inscription etched on it translates to "The world is but a bridge, pass over but build no houses on it." With its beveled walls and inset archways, the southern gate rises 134 feet over a base of steps that raise it another 34 feet, dwarfing everything else in sight. Akbar built it after conquering Gujarat, and it set the style for later gateways, which the Mughals built habitually as symbols of their power.

The various upper stories of Fatehpur Sikri are now closed to visitors because of the proliferation of graffiti. ✉ *Rs. 260* ☽ *Daily sunrise–sunset.*

> **NEED A BOY?**
>
> Many people believed that Salim Chisti, the famous Sufi saint, could perform miracles. Women of all faiths still come to his tomb to cover it with cloth and tie a string on the marble latticework in hopes of giving birth to a son.

NEED A BREAK? **Gulistan Tourist Complex.** The simple Indian restaurant at the Gulistan Tourist Complex, just down the road from Fatehpur Sikri on the way to Agra, is a convenient and welcoming lunch stop. ☎ *561/328–2490.*

KHAJURAHO

395 km (245 miles) southeast of Agra; 379 km (235 miles) southwest of Varanasi.

The UNESCO World Heritage Site temples of Khajuraho are known for their carved erotic images, but they are also examples of the advanced architectural styles of the Chandela kings. The soaring *shikharas* (spires) of the temples are meant to resemble the peaks of the Himalayas, the abode of Lord Shiva. The spire of each temple rises higher than the one before it, as in a range of mountains that seems to draw near the heavens. Designed to inspire the viewer toward the highest human potential, these were also the builders' attempts to reach upward, out of the material world, to moksha, the final release from the cycle of rebirth. It's definitely worth a visit here, though getting to Khajuraho is not easy.

This small rural village in the state of Madhya Pradesh was the religious capital of the Chandelas, one of the most powerful Rajput dynasties of Central India, from the 10th to 12th century. They built 85 temples here, 22 of which remain to give a glimpse of a time when Hindu art and devotion reached its apex. When the dynasty eventually succumbed to invaders, Khajuraho's temples lapsed into obscurity until their rediscovery by the British explorer Captain T.S. Burt in 1838.

During the Chandelas' rule, the temples' royal patrons were rich, the land was fertile, and those at the top lived the good life, trooping off to hunts, feasts, and theater, music, and dance performances. This abundance was the perfect climate for creativity, and temple-building emerged as the major form of expression. There were no strict boundaries between the sacred and the profane, no dictates on acceptable deities: Shiva, Vishnu, Brahma, and the Jain saints were all lavishly honored here. Among other things, Khajuraho represents an incredible testament of the strength of human devotion and faith.

Excavations have also uncovered a complex of Buddhist temples. Despite the interest in heaven, the real focus was Earth, particularly the facts of human life. Here, immortalized in stone, virile men and voluptuous women cavort and copulate in the most intimate, erotic, and sometimes bewildering postures. Khajuraho represents the best of Hindu temple sculpture: sinuous, twisting forms, human and divine, pulsing with life, tension, and conflict. But its Buddhist side is more serene.

A number of sculptural motifs run through the temples. Certain gods, for instance, have directional positions: elephant-headed Ganesh faces north; Yama, the god of death, and his mount, a male buffalo, face south. Other sculptures include the *apsaras* (heavenly maidens), found mainly inside, and the Atlas-like *kichakas*, who support the ceilings on their shoulders. Many sculptures reflect everyday activities, such as a dance class, and there are sultry *nayikas* (mortal women) and plenty of *mithunas* (amorous couples). The scorpion appears as an intriguing theme, running up and down the thighs of many female sculptures as a kind of erotic thermometer.

Of the extant temples, all but two were made from sandstone mined from the banks of the River Ken, 30 km (19 miles) away. The stone blocks were carved separately, then assembled as interlocking pieces. Though each temple is different, all observe precise architectural principles of shape, form, and orientation and contain certain essential elements: a high raised platform, an *ardh mandapam* (entrance porch), a *mandapam* (portico), an *antrala* (vestibule), and a *garbha griha* (inner sanctum). Some of the larger temples also have a walkway around the inner sanctum, a *mahamandapam* (hall), and subsidiary shrines at each corner of the platform, making a complete *panchayatana* (five-shrine complex).

No one knows why erotic sculptures are so important here, though many explanations have been suggested. The female form is often used as an auspicious marker on Hindu gateways and doors, in the form of temple sculptures as well as domestic wall paintings. In the late classical and early medieval periods, this symbol expanded into full-blown erotic art in many places, including the roughly contemporary sun temple at Modhera, in Gujarat, and the slightly later one at Konark, in Odisha. A common folk explanation is that the erotic sculptures protect the temples from lightning; and art historians have pointed out that many of the erotic panels are placed at junctures where some protection or strengthening agent might be structurally necessary. Others say the sculptures reflect the influence of a Tantric cult that believed in reversals of ordinary morality as a religious practice. Still others argue that sex has been used as a metaphor: the carnal and bestial sex generally shown near the bases of the temples represents uncontrolled and baser human appetites. They're metaphors of leaving bodily desires behind, to follow a spiritual path. Conversely, the couples deeply engrossed in each other, oblivious to all else, represent a divine bliss, the closest humans can approach to God.

EVENING ENTERTAINMENT

Sound-and-Light Show. This popular 50-minute extravaganza, narrated in Hindi and English, traces the story of the Chandela kings and the temples from the 10th century to the present. The exact showtime varies based on sunset, so confirm it with your hotel or the tourist office. Buy tickets at the tourism office. ⊠ *Western Group* ⊕ *www.mptourism.com* ✉ *Rs. 400* ⊙ *English-language show: Oct.–Feb., daily 6:30 pm; Mar.–Sept., daily 7:30.*

GETTING HERE AND AROUND

Khajuraho Airport, 7 km (4 miles) from the city, is connected via Air India to Agra. If you're going by train, one good option is to take the UP Sampark Kranti Express, which comes in from Delhi H. Nizamuddin Station to Khajuraho three times a week (Tuesday, Friday, and Sunday). Khajuraho is about a 6-hour drive from Varanasi, 6½ hours from Agra, and more than 9 hours from Delhi.

Khajuraho is so small that bicycles, cycle-rickshaws, and/or walking are the best available options for getting around, rather than taxis or auto-rickshaws. For Rs. 70–Rs. 100 you can **rent a bicycle** for the day from one of the many places across from the bus stand, behind the museum, and from some hotels. It's a great way to get around this relatively traffic-free town and to explore the small streets of Khajuraho village, the old residential area near the Eastern Group of temples that teems with shops, animals, and children. Entrepreneurial boys will gladly guide you around for Rs. 50.

TIMING

Dance Festival. In late February or early March, Khajuraho holds an annual, week-long dance festival, set in part against the backdrop of the temples. This superb event attracts some of the country's best performers. Contact the tourist office for more information. ⊠ *Khajuraho, Madhya Pradesh.*

Kandariya. From October through May, for Rs. 500 you can see folk dances from all over India performed nightly at 7 and 8:40 pm at Kandariya, a theater attached to the **Shilpgram** shop. ⊠ *Bamitha Rd., near Jhankar Hotel* ☎ *07686/274–125.*

ESSENTIALS

Madhya Pradesh Tourism. For maps, information brochures, and seeing about arranging a hired car, contact the MP Tourist Office. ✉ *Near Circuit House* ☎ *768/627–4051* ⊕ *www.mptourism.com.*

WESTERN GROUP OF TEMPLES

Most of the Western Group of temples, the richest and largest group, are inside a formal enclosure whose entrance is on Main Road, opposite the State Bank of India. Although the rest of the town's temples are always accessible and free, these are open daily only from 10 to 6, and have an admission charge of Rs. 350. The first three temples, though considered part of the Western Group, are at a slight distance from the enclosure.

To actually enter the temples, you'll need to leave your shoes outside. The stone steps get really hot on summer afternoons—carry socks if you don't want to burn your feet.

Chausath Yogini Temple. The oldest temple at Khajuraho is set on a granite outcrop southwest of the Shivsagar Tank, a small artificial lake. It may have been built as early as AD 820. It's dedicated to Kali (a form of the Goddess Durga, Slayer of Demons), and its name refers to the 64 (*chausath*) female ascetics (*yogini*) who serve this fierce goddess in the

Hindu pantheon. A little more than half that number have survived. Unlike its counterparts, which are made of pale, warm-hued sandstone, this temple is made of granite. ⊠ *Khajuraho, Madhya Pradesh.*

Lalguan Mahadeva. Lying in ruins, with the original portico missing, this Shiva temple is 600 meters west of Chausath Yogini. It is historically significant because it was built of both granite and sandstone, marking the transition from Chausath Yogini to the later temples. ⊠ *Khajuraho, Madhya Pradesh.*

Matangesvara Temple. Just outside the boundary of the Western Group stands this temple, which has its own gate to the left of the entrance. It's the only one still in use here; worship takes place in the morning and afternoon. The lack of ornamentation, the square construction, and the simple floor plan date this temple to the early 10th century. It has large bay windows, a projecting portico, and a ceiling of overlapping concentric circles. An enormous lingam (a phallic symbol associated with Shiva), nearly 8½ feet tall, is enshrined in the sanctum. ⊠ *Khajuraho, Madhya Pradesh.*

Archaeological Museum. Across the street from Matangesvara Temple, this museum displays exquisite carvings and sculptures that archaeologists have recovered from the temple sites. The three galleries attempt to put the works into context, according to the deities they represent. ⊠ *Main Rd.* ☎ *768/627–2320* ☼ *Mon.–Sat. 10–6.*

Varaha Temple. Just inside the main entrance gate, to your left, next to a small Lakshmi temple, is this beautiful temple dedicated to Vishnu's Varaha avatar (his incarnation as a boar). It was built circa 900–925. Vishnu assumed this form in order to rescue the earth after a demon had hidden it in the slush at the bottom of the sea. In the inner sanctum, all of creation is depicted on the massive and beautifully polished sides of a stone boar, which in turn stands on the serpent Shesha. The ceiling is carved with a lotus relief, which represents the flowering of the crown chakra, the spiritual center. ⊠ *Khajuraho, Madhya Pradesh.*

Fodor's Choice ★ **Lakshmana Temple.** Across from the Varaha Temple stands this temple dedicated to Vishnu. It is the only complete temple remaining. Along with Kandariya Mahadeva and Vishvanath, this edifice represents the peak of achievement in North Indian temple architecture. All three temples were built in the early to mid-10th century, face east, and follow an elaborate plan resembling a double cross, with three tiers of exterior sculpture on high platforms. The ceiling of the portico is carved with shell and floral motifs. The support beam over the entrance to the main

---

DON'T MISS THE DETAILS

It's well worth hiring a guide, for the Western Group at least, who can point out the more quirky aspects. The number of carvings can seem overwhelming, but keep an eye out for work into which the carvers injected their own views of life, often with a sense of humor. In the Western Group's Lakshmana temple, there is an elephant turning his head and laughing at the couple having sex beside him. In another carving a man has covered his face in embarrassment, but he's still peeping through his fingers at what's going on nearby.

4

shrine shows Lakshmi, goddess of wealth and consort of Vishnu, with Brahma, Lord of Creation, on her left and Shiva, Lord of Destruction, on her right. Around the exterior base are some of Khajuraho's most famous sculptures, with gods and goddesses on the protruding corners, erotic couples or groups in the recesses, and apsaras and *sur-sundaris* (apsaras performing everyday activities) in between. Along the sides of the tall platform beneath the temple, carvings depict social life, including battle scenes, festivals, and more X-rated pursuits. According to the inscription on the Lakshmana Temple, it was built by King Yasovarman. The whole temple was built to house an image of Vishnu given him by his Pratihara overlord, Devapala. This image (it can still be seen here) was originally brought over from Tibet. ⊠ *Khajuraho, Madhya Pradesh*.

Fodor'sChoice   **Kandariya Mahadev.** This temple, which lies west of the Lakshmana, is
★   the tallest and most evolved temple in Khajuraho in terms of the blending of architecture and sculpture, and one of the finest in India. Probably built around 1025–50 by King Vidyahara (the greatest of the Chandela kings), it follows the five-shrine design. Its central spire, which towers 102 feet above the platform, is actually made up of 84 subsidiary towers built up in increments. The feeling of ascent is repeated inside, where each succeeding portico rises a step above the previous one, and the inner sanctum is higher still; dedicated to Shiva (Mahadev is another name for Shiva), this inner sanctum houses a marble lingam with a 4-foot circumference. Even the figures on this temple are taller and slimmer than those elsewhere. The rich interior carving includes two beautiful *toranas* (arched doorways). Outside, three bands of sculpture around the sanctum and transept bring to life a whole galaxy of Hindu gods and goddesses, mithunas, celestial handmaidens, and lions. ⊠ *Khajuraho, Madhya Pradesh*.

Devi Jagdamba Temple. This temple was originally dedicated to Vishnu, as indicated by a prominent sculpture over the sanctum's doorway. It now honors Parvati, Shiva's consort, but because her image is black—a color associated with Kali—it's also known as the Kali Temple. From the inside, its three-shrine design makes the temple appear to be shaped like a cross. The third band of sculpture has a series of erotic mithunas, considered some of the finest sculpture of this type in all of Khajuraho. The ceilings are similar to those in the Kandariya Mahadev, and the three-headed, eight-armed statue of Shiva is one of the best cult images in Khajuraho. ⊠ *Khajuraho, Madhya Pradesh*.

Mahadeva Temple. Sharing the platform with the Kandariya Mahadev and the Devi Jagdamba, this small temple is mostly in ruins. Now dedicated to Shiva, it may originally have been a subsidiary temple to the Kandariya, probably dedicated to Shiva's consort. In the portico stands a remarkable statue of a man caressing a mythical horned lion. ⊠ *Khajuraho, Madhya Pradesh*.

Chitragupta Temple. This temple that's just north of the Devi Jagdamba also resembles it in construction. In honor of the presiding deity, the sun god Surya, the temple faces east, and its cell contains a 5-foot-tall image of Surya complete with the chariot and seven horses that carry him across the sky. Surya also appears above the doorway. In the central

Carvings on the Kandariya Mahadev

niche south of the sanctum is an image of Vishnu with 11 heads; his own face is in the center, and the other heads represent his 10 main incarnations. Sculptural scenes of animal combat, royal processions, masons at work, and joyous dances depict the lavish country life of the Chandelas. It also has an ancient three-story stepped tank (water reservoir). ⊠ *Khajuraho, Madhya Pradesh.*

Vishvanath Temple. Two staircases lead up to this temple, the northern one flanked by a pair of lions and the southern by a pair of elephants. The Vishvanath probably preceded the Kandariya, but here only two of the original corner shrines remain. On the outer wall of the corridor surrounding the cells is an impressive image of Brahma, the three-headed Lord of Creation, and his consort, Saraswati. On every wall the female form predominates, portraying some women's 10th-century occupations: writing a letter, holding a baby, applying makeup, or playing music. The nymphs of paradise are voluptuous and provocative, the erotic scenes robust. An inscription states that the temple was built by Chandela King Dhanga in 1002. The temple sits on a terrace to the east of the Chitragupta and Devi Jagdamba temples. ⊠ *Khajuraho, Madhya Pradesh.*

Nandi Temple. This simple temple, which faces Vishvanath, houses a monolithic statue of Shiva's mount, the massive and richly harnessed bull Nandi. ⊠ *Khajuraho, Madhya Pradesh.*

Parvati Temple. The small and heavily rebuilt temple, near Vishvanath, was originally dedicated to Vishnu. The present icon is that of the goddess Ganga (a representation of the river Ganges) standing on her mount, the crocodile. ⊠ *Khajuraho, Madhya Pradesh.*

NEED A BREAK?

Blue Sky. Exit the gate, and across the street from Vishvanath and Nandi temples is Blue Sky, a favorite café that's on the Main Road. Don't miss the view from the second floor and rooftop terraces. ⊠ *Main Rd., near Western Group of Temples* ☎ *91/76862–74120.*

State Museum of Tribal and Folk Arts. There's an excellent collection here, consisting of more than 500 artifacts of terra-cotta, metal, and wood crafts, paintings, jewelry, and masks from all over Madhya Pradesh and the Bastar region (known for tribal crafts) in the neighboring state of Chhattisgarh. ⊠ *Chandela Cultural Complex, Rajnagar Rd.* ☎ *768/627–4051* 🖘 *Free* ⊙ *Tues.–Sun. 10–5.*

EASTERN GROUP OF TEMPLES

Scattered around the edges of the old village of Khajuraho, the Eastern Group of temples includes three Brahma and four Jain temples. Their proximity attests to the religious tolerance of the times in general and the Chandela rulers in particular.

Vamana Temple. The late-11th-century Vamana Temple, the northern-most one in the Eastern Group, is dedicated to Vishnu's dwarf incarnation (though the image in the sanctum looks more like a tall, sly child). The sanctum walls show unusual theological openness, depicting most of the major gods and goddesses; Vishnu appears in many of his forms, including the Buddha, his ninth incarnation. Outside, two tiers of sculpture are concerned mainly with the nymphs of paradise, who strike charming poses under their private awnings. The pretty view from this temple includes barley fields. ⊠ *Khajuraho, Madhya Pradesh.*

Javari Temple. Small and well-proportioned, this temple is just south of the Vamana and roughly contemporary with it. It has a simplified three-shrine design: the two main exterior bands of sculpture bear hosts of heavenly maidens. It's also dedicated to Lord Vishnu. ⊠ *Khajuraho, Madhya Pradesh.*

Brahma Temple. This granite-and-sandstone temple, one of the earliest here (circa 900), is probably misnamed. Although Brahma is a member of the triad of Hinduism's great gods, along with Shiva and Vishnu, he rarely gets a temple to himself. (The only other famous Brahma Temple is at Pushkar, in Rajasthan.) It differs in design from most of the other temples here, particularly in the combination of materials and the shape of its spire. Nearby is Ninora Tal, one of the largest tanks in Khajuraho. ⊠ *Khajuraho, Madhya Pradesh.*

Ghantai Temple. All that's left of the temple here are its pillars, festooned with carvings of pearls and bells. Adorning the entrance are an eight-armed Jain goddess, Chakreshvari, riding the mythical bird Garuda and a relief illustrating the 16 dreams of the mother of Mahavira, the founder and greatest figure in Jainism and a counterpart to the Buddha. The temple sits south of the Vamana, Javari, and Brahma temples, toward the Jain complex. ⊠ *Khajuraho, Madhya Pradesh.*

Adinath Temple. The late-11th-century Adinath Temple, a minor shrine, is set in a small walled compound southeast of the Ghantai temple. Its porch and the statue of the Tirthankara (literally, Ford-Maker, a figure who leads others to liberation) Adinatha are modern additions. Built at the beginning of the Chandelas' decline, this temple is relatively small, but the spire and base are richly carved. ⊠ *Khajuraho, Madhya Pradesh.*

Parsvanath Temple. This temple was built in the mid-10th century during the reign of King Dhangadeva. It is the largest and finest in the Eastern Group's Jain complex and holds some of the best sculpture in Khajuraho, including images of Vishnu. In contrast to the intricate calculations behind the layout of the Western Group, the plan for this temple is a simple rectangle, with a separate spire in the rear. Statues of flying angels and sloe-eyed beauties occupied with children, cosmetics, and flowers adorn the outer walls. The stone conveys even the texture of the women's thin garments. ⊠ *Khajuraho, Madhya Pradesh.*

Shantinath Temple. Set within the walled Jain temple complex alongside the Adinath and Parsvanath temples, the Shantinath Temple is a collection of small, early-11th-century shrines. Though remodeled extensively, it still contains some old Jain sculptures. The main draw is the 12-foot idol of Lord Shantinath in the inner sanctum. ⊠ *Khajuraho, Madhya Pradesh.*

SOUTHERN GROUP OF TEMPLES

The Southern Group, the smallest, includes two impressive temples from the 12th century. They are the Chaturbhuja Temple (which has a massive, carved image of Vishnu) and the Duladeo Temple, one of the last temples of the Chandela era.

Duladeo Temple. Though built in the customary five-shrine style, this 12th-century temple looks flatter and more massive than most Khajuraho shrines. About 900 yards south of the Eastern Group's Ghantai, it stands near the Khudar rivulet. Probably the last temple built in Khajuraho, the Duladeo lacks the usual ambulatory passage and crowning lotus-shaped finials. Here, too, in this temple dedicated to Shiva, eroticism works its way in, though the amorous figures are discreetly placed. ⊠ *Khajuraho, Madhya Pradesh.*

Bijamandala Temple. As part of continuing explorations since 1999, the largest temple yet—4 meters longer than the Kandariya Mahadeva—has been partially unearthed. On the Bijamandala you can see multiple tiers of beautifully carved moldings and a Shiva lingam placed on a marble pedestal. Images of Vishnu and Brahma have been found as well, and it also houses a lovely image of Saraswati. Archaeologists surmise that the temple, begun in the late 10th or early 11th century and between the Duladeo and the Chaturbhuj, may never have been completed, judging by the remains and unfinished statues found on the site. ⊠ *Khajuraho, Madhya Pradesh.*

Chaturbhuj Temple. This small 12th-century temple, nearly 3 km (2 miles) south of Duladeo, is often ignored given its distance from the main complex. It has an attractive colonnade entrance and a feeling of verticality thanks to its single spire. Inside, its impressive four-armed image of Vishnu in a sunken sanctum, may be the single most striking piece

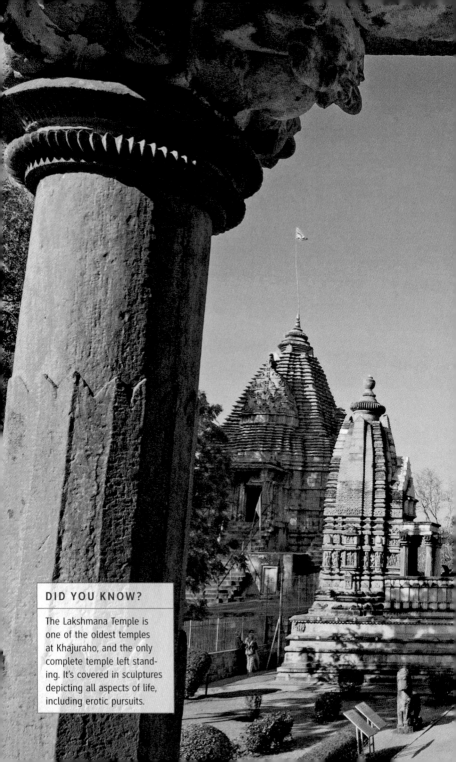

DID YOU KNOW?

The Lakshmana Temple is one of the oldest temples at Khajuraho, and the only complete temple left standing. It's covered in sculptures depicting all aspects of life, including erotic pursuits.

of sculpture in Khajuraho. The exterior sculpture here is not nearly as impressive as other examples in the area, but the temple is definitely the best place in Khajuraho to watch the sun set. In the north corner there is a rare image of the goddess Narsimhi, who has a lion's face and a human body. ⊠ *Khajuraho, Madhya Pradesh.*

WHERE TO EAT

$ ✕ **Bella Italia.** In this simple, no-frills rooftop restaurant, with plastic
ITALIAN   tables and chairs, adorned only by a few potted plants, the main draw is the food. This restaurant specializes in fresh homemade pastas, including lasagna, fettuccini, and ravioli. Thin-crust pizzas are decent, and the crepes—both savory and sweet—are delicious. Try the Nutella crepe topped off with ice cream for a special treat. ⑤ *Average main: Rs. 250* ⊠ *Jain Temple Rd.* ☎ *98934–54795 cell phone* ▭ *No credit cards.*

$ ✕ **Blue Sky Restaurant.** Across from the Vishvanath and Nandi temples,
INTERNATIONAL   Blue Sky is open for all meals. It has a great view of the entire Western Group from its second-floor and rooftop terraces. The view's the thing, but the food's not bad. You can just stop by for a *lassi* (a yogurt-based drink) or tea, breakfast on omelets, porridge (oatmeal), and Indian items; at lunch and dinner there are soups and salads, plus Indian, Chinese, Italian, and Japanese choices. ■TIP→ **At dinner you can watch the sound-and-light show from your table.** ⑤ *Average main: Rs. 200* ⊠ *Main Rd., near Western Group of Temples* ☎ *094/25143803 mobile number* ▭ *No credit cards.*

$ ✕ **Maharaja Cafe.** A spiral staircase leads up to this indoor, air-condi-
INTERNATIONAL   tioned restaurant with cheery bright curtains on a rooftop. The Maharaja Cafe overlooks a *maqbara* (domed memorial) to the left and the Western Temples to the right. When the weather's good, sit outdoors on a wooden platform for a good view of the sights and market below. There are plenty of pizzas, pastas, and Chinese and continental choices, but the curry and tandoori items are most popular. ⑤ *Average main: Rs. 250* ⊠ *Opposite Western Group of Temples* ☎ *834/901–7939 cell phone* ⊕ *www.maharajacafe.com* ▭ *No credit cards.*

$$ ✕ **Mediterraneo.** Eat on the rooftop or in a small dining room at this
ITALIAN   Italian restaurant near the Western Group. Like most of the restaurants in Khajuraho that aren't connected to a hotel, there are few frills here. The pizzas, one of the many pasta dishes (the carbonara has actual bacon), or standbys like eggplant parmigiana or lamb cacciatore may just do the trick when you're tired of the Indian-continental-Chinese options popular in tourist areas throughout India. At breakfast, you can order crepes and omelets. ⑤ *Average main: Rs. 350* ⊠ *Jain Temple Rd., opposite Surya Hotel* ☎ *768/627–2246* ▭ *No credit cards.*

$ ✕ **Raja Café.** This charming, two-story restaurant just across the road
INTERNATIONAL   from the Western Temples has a distinctly European aesthetic, with an
Fodor'sChoice   open courtyard where marble-top tables are shaded by an enormous
★   neem tree and overhanging branches of bougainvillea. The small indoor section is air-conditioned (the summer heat can be quite punishing), and the terrace has a stunning view of the temples. The food is a mix of Indian and continental fare—highlights include Swiss crostinis, freshly

baked pastries, and wood-fire pizzas. $ *Average main: Rs. 250* ✉ *Opposite Western Temples* ☎ *07686/272–307* ⊕ *www.rajacafe.com.*

$ × **Shambala Chill Out Restaurant (The Green View).** With plastic tables set
INTERNATIONAL under billowing strips of brightly colored cloth, this hippyish rooftop restaurant has a good view of the temples. Don't expect anything too posh on the menu, but everything is cooked well and the staff (an Indian-Swedish husband-wife duo) are friendly and can tweak dishes to your specifications. Cuisines include Indian, Chinese, and European, with plenty of vegetarian choices. $ *Average main: Rs. 200* ✉ *In front of Western Group of Temples* ☎ *99932–13301 cell phone* ▭ *No credit cards.*

WHERE TO STAY

4

$$$ 🏨 **Hotel Clarks Khajuraho.** A 10-minute drive from the main group of
HOTEL temples, this is a clean and tastefully decorated hotel, and though it rather much personality, it does have an excellent range of sport and leisure options on-site. **Pros:** good value; plenty to do. **Cons:** somewhat nondescript. $ *Rooms from: Rs. 6500* ✉ *Near Airport Rd., between airport and temples, off main road* ☎ *7686/274–038, 7686/274–056, 7686/274–421* ⊕ *khajuraho.hotelclarks.com* 🛏 *96 rooms, 4 suites* ▯◯▮ *No meals.*

$ 🏨 **Hotel Tourist Village.** Affordable and charming, this hotel, run by the
HOTEL Madhya Pradesh Government, is built in the style of a "traditional vil-
FAMILY lage," and although it's a 10-minute walk from the bustle and noise of the main road, it feels much more remote. **Pros:** quiet, relaxing ambience; economical. **Cons:** white fluorescent lights in the rooms detract from the village charm. $ *Rooms from: Rs. 1990* ✉ *Near Vidhyadhar Colony* ☎ *7686/274–062* ⊕ *www.mptourism.com* 🛏 *11 rooms* ▯◯▮ *Breakfast.*

$ 🏨 **Jhankar.** The government-run Jhankar is ideal for absolutely basic
HOTEL accommodations close to the sights at a great price. **Pros:** small and easy to navigate; economical. **Cons:** some walls are moldy and riddled with chipping paint. $ *Rooms from: Rs. 1990* ✉ *Airport Rd.* ☎ *768/627–4063, 768/627–4194* 🛏 *19 rooms* ▯◯▮ *Breakfast.*

$$$ 🏨 **Ken River Lodge.** Near Panna National Park, about a half hour from
RESORT Khajuraho, this lodge is perfect for nature lovers, with basic mud huts and cottages with hot water and private baths, but no phones, or TVs, and air-conditioning only in the huts. **Pros:** very secluded, with no tourist traps in sight. **Cons:** 30 km (20 miles) from town, making transportation expensive; monkeys regularly (and loudly) run across the roofs. $ *Rooms from: Rs. 8000* ✉ *Near Madla Village, Panna District* ☎ *0124/4222–657 reservations* ⊕ *www.kenriverlodge.com* 🛏 *13 cottages, 6 huts* ▭ *No credit cards* ⊙ *Closed May–Sept.* ▯◯▮ *All meals.*

$$$$ 🏨 **Lalit Temple View Khajuraho.** As the closest hotel to the temples, the
HOTEL Lalit has a great view of them—one you can enjoy while lounging in the manicured garden, sipping cocktails next to the pool. **Pros:** a five-minute walk from the main temples; food available 24 hours; kids' playground on-site. **Cons:** very expensive. $ *Rooms from: Rs. 15000* ✉ *Opposite Circuit House* ☎ *7686/272–111* ⊕ *www.thelalit.com* 🛏 *43 rooms, 4 suites* ▯◯▮ *Breakfast.*

$$$ 🏨 **Radisson Hotel Khajuraho.** Luxurious and modern, this hotel situated
HOTEL   just a kilometer from the Western Temples has a lively restaurant and lovely surroundings—the pool, one of the deepest in Khajuraho at 9 feet, is surrounded by undulating landscaped gardens, so you can always hear birdsong. **Pros:** feels fresh; free Wi-Fi; lovely pool. **Cons:** feels like a big-city hotel, with little local charm. Ⓢ *Rooms from: Rs. 7000* ✉ *Bypass Rd.* ☎ *768/627–2777* ⊕ *www.radisson.com/khajurahoin* ⇄ *86 rooms, 4 suites* ⦿ *Breakfast.*

$$ 🏨 **Ramada Khajuraho.** The expansive lawns of this 14-acre property feature
HOTEL   a lovely walking track, a rose garden, and an organic kitchen gar-
Fodor's Choice   den. **Pros:** a lot of bang for your buck compared with others in town;
★   discounts available; friendly and attentive staff. **Cons:** you might wonder why you need such luxury in a sleepy Indian village. Ⓢ *Rooms from: Rs. 4750* ✉ *Airport Rd.* ☎ *768/627–2302* ⊕ *www.ramadakhajuraho. com* ⇄ *79 rooms, 6 suites* ⦿ *Breakfast.*

$$$ 🏨 **Taj Chandela.** Though it lacks the usual sparkle of many Taj Hotels,
HOTEL   this is a fine property (close to the temples) with lots of amenities and an unusual (for India) attention to safety issues. **Pros:** warm, friendly service; all rooms have smoke detectors and sprinklers. **Cons:** restaurant is small, occupying a windowless area behind the lobby. Ⓢ *Rooms from: Rs. 8000* ✉ *Airport Rd., Chhatarpur District* ☎ *768/627–2355, 768/627–2364* ⊕ *www.tajhotels.com* ⇄ *84 rooms, 5 suites* ⦿ *No meals.*

$$ 🏨 **Usha Bundela.** With friendly staff, large rooms, and great prices, this
HOTEL   nice hotel hits the spot for travelers on a budget without sacrificing on location and style. **Pros:** yoga and meditation classes can be arranged. **Cons:** pool looks very worn and has a green tinge. Ⓢ *Rooms from: Rs. 4000* ✉ *Temple Rd.* ☎ *768/627–2386* ⊕ *www.ushalexushotels.com* ⇄ *66 rooms* ⦿ *Breakfast.*

SHOPPING

Numerous shops around the Western Group of temples sell curios, including humorous takeoff of Khajuraho's erotic sculptures, as well as tribal metalwork.

Chandela Emporium. This expansive stores stocks local handicrafts, miniature wood paintings, brass sculptures, and jewelry. The textiles are particularly impressive: there's a huge collection of scarves, saris, and clothing in silks and cottons, with traditional Indian prints. ✉ *Opposite Pahil Batika* ☎ *768/627–4077.*

Kandaryia Shilpgram. This large crafts shop, with woodwork, handicrafts, jewelry, and silks, is owned by the Agra marble-inlay maker Oswal. It's associated with a government project that hosts craftspeople from all over India for residences during peak travel season; you can watch the artisans at work as you shop. ✉ *Bamitha Rd., near Jhankar Hotel* ☎ *0768/627–4125.*

SIDE TRIPS

If you have time, take an extra day to explore and picnic in the beautiful countryside around Khajuraho.

Gharial Sanctuary. Drive or bike to the Gharial Sanctuary on the Ken River, 28 km (17 miles) away; the park was set up to protect the slender-snouted crocodile and has some lovely waterfalls. The Madhya Pradesh Tourism office has information about renting a jeep, and can provide directions. ⊠ *Gharial Sanctuary.*

Khajuraho Village. Backed by the distant mountains, Khajuraho Village—the old residential part of town near the Eastern Group of temples—is a typical Indian village. Contact the Ministry of Tourism office in Khajuraho for directions, or to request a guide. ⊠ *Khajuraho, Madhya Pradesh.*

Panna National Park. October through June, hire a jeep and driver to take you to Panna National Park to see wildlife that includes antelope, deer, and a lot of monkeys; if you're lucky (and arrive very early in the morning or in late afternoon and hire a guide at the park or come with Ken River Lodge), you'll see one of the 27 elusive tigers in the Panna Tiger Reserve. The best viewing season is January through March. (Sightings are said to be better at Bandhavgarh Park, but that's a five-hour, 237-km [147-mile] drive from Khajuraho.) For Rs. 6,500 you can hire a six-seat jeep for a four-hour safari with a guide. ⊠ *31 km (19 miles) SE of Khajuraho* ⊕ *www.pannanationalpark.net.*

VARANASI

406 km (252 miles) east of Khajuraho; 765 km (474 miles) southeast of Delhi.

A visit to Varanasi, also known as Benaras or Benares, or as Kashi (meaning "resplendent with light"), is an experience unlike any other. This is the epitome of a holy city, inundated with religious pilgrims and sacred cows, yet it is also a city firmly grounded in the commerce and reality of day-to-day existence. A visit here is thrilling but exhausting, and never boring.

Along the left bank of the Ganges, a river believed by Hindus to hold the power of salvation in every drop, Varanasi is one of the most sacred places in the world, considered by many to be the spiritual heart of India. Every year the city welcomes millions of pilgrims for whom the water—physically fouled by the pollution of humans both living and dead—remains spiritually pristine enough to cleanse the soul.

About 90 ghats, or steps, line this 6-km (4-mile) stretch of the Ganges, wedding the holy river to the chaotic city above it—a maze of streets and alleys crammed with derelict palaces, homes, and about 2,000 temples and shrines (most of these holy sites are open only to those of their respective religion, however). Here you'll see funeral processions, cows and goats munching on whatever they can find, and, especially near the Golden Temple (Kashi Vishvanath) and centrally located Dashashvamedh Ghat, assertive hawkers and phony guides.

Varanasi

TO AZAMGAR

TO BABATPUR AIRPORT

Raja Bazar Rd

Varanasi Junction Station

UP Tourist Office

JAITPURA

Station Rd

St Kabir Rd

KOTWALI

ADAMPURA

Rabindranath Tagore Rd

Malaviya Bridge

TO ALLAHABAD

Nai Sarak Rd

CHOWK

Raja Sir Motichand Rd

GODAULIA

Lura Rd

Bhadani Road

Rathyatra Mahmurganj Rd

Thatheri Bazaar

Panchganga Ghat

Scindia Ghat

Manikarnika Ghat

1

2 Man Mandira Ghat

Prayaga Ghat

3 Darabhanga Ghat

Caowki Ghat

Harish Chandra Ghat

Hanuman Ghat

Shivala Ghat

Chet Singh Ghat

Jain Ghat

Anandamayi Ghat

Tulsi Ghat

Assi Ghat

BHELUPURA

Durga Kund Road

Sankat Mochan Road

4

Assi

5

Ravidas Ghat

Ganga (Ganges) River

National Highway

University Rd

NAGWA

Ramnagar Rd

Pontoon Bridge

RAMNAGAR

6

BANARAS HINDU UNIVERSITY

7

0   1 mi

0   1 km

The most essential thing to do in Varanasi is to take a boat ride along the Ganges, preferably at dawn or sunset, to see the ghats and the rituals being performed—it's also a peaceful respite from the chaos of the city.

Sarnath, just a few kilometers north of Varanasi, is a peaceful park and the historic center of the Buddhist world, where the Buddha preached his first sermon, revealing the Eightfold Path that became the central tenets of Buddhism. It is an easy, and fairly peaceful, place to visit.

GETTING ORIENTED

Varanasi is on the west bank of the Ganges, which is intersected by two smaller rivers: the Varana, to the north, which winds by the Cantonment area (often abbreviated as Cantt) and joins the Ganges near Raj Ghat, and the Asi, a small stream in the south. The ghats stretch along the river from Raj Ghat in the north to Assi Ghat in the south; beyond Assi is the university, across the river from Ramnagar Fort and Palace. The city itself spreads out behind the ghats, where there are smaller hotels and restaurants; the larger chain hotels are in the Cantonment area, about 20 minutes from the river by auto-rickshaw.

Traditionally, Varanasi is divided into three sections named after important temples to Shiva. Omkareshvara is the namesake temple in the northern section, which is probably the oldest area but is now impoverished and seldom visited by pilgrims. The central section is named after Kashi Vishvanath, the famous "Golden Temple." Vishvanath itself means "Lord of the Universe," one of Shiva's names, and there are many Vishvanath temples. The southern area, the Kedar Khand, is named for Kedareshvara, a temple easily spotted from the river thanks to the vertical red and white stripes painted on its walls, a custom of the South Indian worshippers who are among the temple's devotees.

GETTING AROUND

Varanasi is a chaotic place, and although you can certainly find your own way around, you might want to hire a guide for your first day to help you get oriented: it will cost you Rs. 1,035 for a half-day, and about Rs. 1,320 for an eight-hour full day. You can book a guide through your hotel, or through the Indian Tourism Office. A guide will also know which temples and mosques are open only to their own sects; he may be able to help get you in.

Out on your own, walking is your best bet within the old city, and if your feet get tired, or you get lost, take an auto- or cycle-rickshaw.

Varanasi's airport is about 23 km (14 miles) from the Cantonment area, or 30 km (19 miles) from the riverfront area.

ESSENTIALS

India Ministry of Tourism. You can also find an official tourist counter at the airport. ✉ *15B The Mall* ☎ *0542/250–1784* ⊕ *www.incredibleindia. org.*

EXPLORING

Bharat Kala Bhavan Museum. No one interested in Indian art should miss this museum on the campus of Banaras Hindu University. The permanent collection includes brocade textiles, excellent Hindu and Buddhist sculptures, and miniature paintings from the courts of the Mughals

Continued on page 202

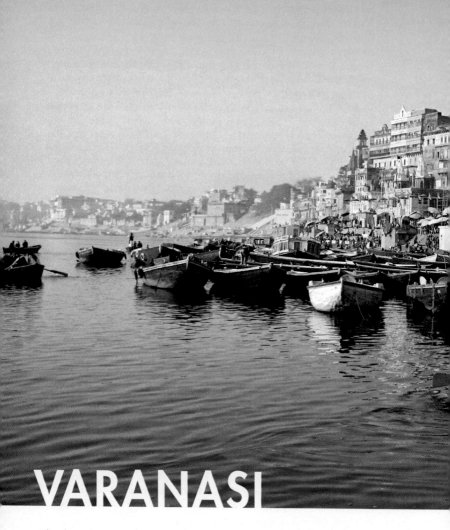

VARANASI

Also known as Kashi (City of Light) or Kashika (Shining One), Varanasi is one of the holiest cities on earth: there are more than 700 temples and countless shrines here—though none of these are more holy than the Ganges River itself.

Each drop of Ganges water is believed to hold the power of salvation: immersing oneself in it is said to cleanse one not just of sins in this life, but of all the sins of past lives, too. As a result, millions of pilgrims come to this city every year to take part in ritual cleansing. Dying here and being cremated is believed to give instant enlightenment and freedom from the cycle of rebirth.

While the water here might be spiritually pure, the Ganges is also one of the dirtiest bodies of water in the world, and drinking it or bathing in it carries the risk of infection. To get the full experience of the river (without actually going in), take a boat ride, preferably as the sun comes up in the morning. From this vantage point you'll see not only the various *ghats* (stairs down to the river) but also the daily rituals and prayers that are a part of this incredible city: everything from elderly men sitting cross-legged in prayer or meditation, to young men exercising, people washing clothes, and various and sundry people and animals bathing.

Above, Dashashvamedh ghat on the banks of the Ganges River, in Varanasi.

ALONG THE GANGES

Roughly 85 ghats line the west bank of the Ganges, stretching out over about 6 km (4 mi); each has a different historical or ritual significance.

Chet Singh Ghat

Dashashvamedh Ghat

Chausath Yogini Temple

Dashashvamedh Ghat

Prayaga Ghat

Darabhanga Ghat

Caowki Ghat

Lali Ghat

Harish Chandra Ghat

Hanuman Ghat

Dashashvamedh is one of the busiest ghats along the Ganges. This is a good place to hire a boat *(see full listing)*.

Shivala Ghat

Chet Singh Ghat

Jain Ghat

Bhadani Rd.

Pandit Manmohan Malviya Rd.

Durga Temple (Monkey Temple)

Anandamayi Ghat

Sankat Mochan Temple

Tulsi Ghat

Assi Ghat

Assi Ghat. This southernmost ghat marks the place where the Assi River and the Ganges meet.

On the eastern side of the river is the **Ramnagar Fort and Palace** *(see full listing)*.

Durga Temple (aka Monkey Temple). Inland and a short walk from Assi Ghat, the monkey temple is recognizable by its mulitiered spire *(see full listing)*.

Tulsi Ghat. This ghat was named for Tulsi Das, the great 16th-century Hindu poet who wrote the epic Ramcharitmnanas while he was in Varanasi; the poet's house and temple are close by as well. Legend has it that the manuscript fell into the water and did not sink, but floated instead, and was saved. Cultural activities often take place at this ghat.

Anandamayi Ghat. This ghat is named after the Bengali (female) saint Anandamayi Ma who died in 1982. The ashram that she founded here attracts thousands of devotees.

Jain (Bachraj) Ghat. Previously part of the adjoining ghat, the Jains made this their own in the early 20th century. The Jain temple here is quite impressive.

Chet Singh Ghat. The reddish color of the fort at Chet Singh ghat stands out, although you won't see many bathers here because it's said that the currents here are dangerous. The ghat is historically notable as being the spot where the maharaja of Varanasi was defeated by the British in the mid 1800s.

Shivala Ghat. Built in 1770 by Chet Singh, the maharaja of Varanasi, the ghat has a large mansion and temple.

Hanuman Ghat. Legend has it that this ghat was built by Lord Ram (the original name was Ra-mesvaram ghat), and that the ghat is dedicated to his favorite disciple: Hanuman. Because Hanuman is a symbol of strength, you can often see local wrestlers and body builders here.

Harish Chandra Ghat. This cremation ghat has been modernized and has an electric crematorium. It's also known as Adi Manikarnika, which means "original creation ground."

Lali (Dhobi) Ghat. *Dhobis* (washer men and women) do early morning laundry here, beating the clothes against the stones in the river.

Caowki Ghat. A huge ficus tree at the top of the steps makes this ghat recognizable. Under

Ganga Ghats

Along the Ganges

Offering to the Gods

KEY

🏚 Ghats

🕌 Mosques

⛩ Temples

⛵ Boats

Man Mandira Ghat

Nepali Ghat

Manikarnika Ghat

Vishvanath Temple

Scindia Ghat

Aurangzeb's Mosque

Panchganga Ghat

Ganga River

4

IN FOCUS VARANASI

Manikarnika Ghat

the tree many stone figures of snakes are arranged.

Darabhanga Ghat. You can recognize this ghat by the Greek-style pillars.

Chausath Yogini Temple. A steep set of stairs leads from the Chausath Yogini ghat to the temple of the same name. Originally devoted to a Tantric cult that is also associated with an important ruined temple at Khajuraho, it's now dedicated to Kali (the goddess most popular with Bengalis), known here simply as "Ma"—Mother. The worshippers are mainly white-sari-clad widows from Varanasi's Bengali quarter; in the early morning you'll see

them coming for the *darshan* (vision) of Kali after bathing in the Ganges.

Prayaga Ghat. This ghat marks the location where the Ganges, the Yamuna, and the invisible Sarasvati rivers all come together. The temple is not often used, however, except by boatmen, who store their boats here.

Man Mandira Ghat. Maharajah Jai Singh, of Jaipur, built his palace here, along with one of his 5 observatories (the most famous is the Jantar Mantar in Jaipur).

Vishvanath (Golden) Temple. With its gold-plated spire, this temple is easy to spot on the skyline. It's the most sacred shrine in Varanasi *(see full listing).*

Nepali Ghat. One of the more prominent ghats, Nepali has a golden lion outside a pagoda-like temple,

built by the royal family of Nepal. Many Nepalese live in the area.

Manikarnika Ghat. Varanasi's main burning ghat is a focal point for most trips along the river, and the traditional funeral pyres burn 24 hours a day. Boats keep a distance, out of respect, but you can still see the fires. At the top of Manikarnika's steps is a small, deep pool, or *kund,* said to have been dug by Vishnu at the dawn of creation and thus to be the first *tirtha*—literally, "ford," and figuratively a place of sacred bathing. Shiva is said to have lost a jeweled earring *(manikarnika)* as he trembled in awe before this place, one of the holiest sites in Varanasi.

Scindia Ghat. This ghat is notable for its ornate temple, which was so heavy that it collapsed into the

river and is now partially submerged.

Aurangzeb's Mosque. The Alamgir Mosque, known as Aurangzeb's Mosque, was built by the Mughul emperor Aurangzeb over the remains of the Hindu temple that had previously stood here. When Aurangzeb conquered Banaras, he had ordered destruction of all temples. The mosque's dramatic vantage point overlooking the Ganges gives it a prominent place in the skyline. The mosque is closed to non-Muslims.

Panchganga Ghat. Below Aurangzeb's Mosque, this is an important bathing point. It's the mythical meeting place of the 5 sacred rivers and images of the river goddesses are displayed here.

Ramnagar Fort

PRACTICAL MATTERS (FAQ)

Where can I hire a boat? The most popular place to hire a boat is at Dashashvamedh Ghat—essentially in the middle of Varanasi, and convenient if you're staying near the water. You can also hire one at Assi Ghat, the southernmost end of the ghats. It's a good idea to arrange your boat trip the afternoon before, then get up and meet your boatman early the next morning so that you can be out on the water as the sun comes up.

How much will it cost? Rates are negotiable, but it should cost about Rs. 100–150 for a one-hour trip.

Where do I want to go? The most popular routes are any that take you past the Manikarnika cremation ghat, the main burning ghat. In general, though, the people and their rituals are more sightworthy than the ghats themselves.

When should I go? The best time to be on the river is as the sun comes up in the morning, when people and pilgrims are getting ready to start the day.

Saris draped on the stairs to dry

At morning prayer

Crowds bathing in the sacred Ganges

A *sadhu* (holy man)

Morning traffic on the Ganges

A painting on a temple wall

Climbing the steep ghat stairs

A *puja* offering to the Gods

Darabhanga Ghat

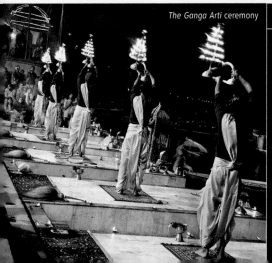
The *Ganga Arti* ceremony

GANGA ARTI

Take a boat ride on the Ganges at sunrise, but come back to the water's edge in the evening, as the sun goes down for *Ganga Arti* (*arti* means prayer), at Dashashvamedh Ghat. The steps fill with people singing Vedic hymns, lighting lamps, and praying along with the priests. It can get very crowded, so you might even want to hire another boat so that you can witness the whole scene from the water, without dealing with the crush on the ghat.

and the Hindu princes of the Punjab hills. One sculpture with particular power is a 4th-century Gupta-dynasty frieze depicting Krishna (an incarnation of Vishnu) holding up Mt. Govardhan to protect his pastoral comrades from the rain. Have your car or rickshaw wait for you, as transportation can be hard to find on the university's sprawling campus. It's a good idea to go with a guide, because the upkeep of the museum is a bit haphazard and you might need someone who knows his way around and can turn the lights on. ⊠ *Banaras Hindu University, Lanka* ☎ *542/230–7621* ⊕ *www.bhu.ac.in* ☙ *Rs. 100* ⊙ *Mon.–Sat. 10–4:30.*

Fodor's Choice   **Dashashvamedh Ghat.** At roughly the midway point of Varanasi's ghats,
★   this is a convenient and popular spot, always busy with hawkers and pilgrims, and a good place to hire a boat. It's one of the holiest ghats, the site of ancient sacrificial rite: the name literally means "ten-horse sacrifice." **Ganga Arti** is an *arti* (prayer ceremony) performed at Dashashvamedh Ghat every night at sunset. Priests clad in saffron and white robes blow conch shells and perform a synchronized ritual with *diyas* (lamps), flowers, and incense. The steps fill with people singing Vedic hymns, lighting lamps, and praying along with the priests; if you're out on a boat at this time, you can take in the whole scene without having to deal with the crush on the ghat itself. ⊠ *East of Godaulia Crossing, Chowk.*

Durga Temple. This 18th-century shrine, dedicated to the goddess Durga, Shiva's consort, stands beside a large, square pool of water due west about a kilometer from Assi Ghat. The multilevel spire (five lower ones, and one on top) symbolizes the belief that the five elements of the world (earth, air, water, fire, and ether) merge with the Supreme. The shrine is also called the Monkey Temple because there are monkeys everywhere, and they'll steal anything (keep all food and water out of sight). ⊠ *Durgakund Rd.* ⊙ *Daily sunrise–noon and 2–sunset.*

NEED A BREAK?   **Pizzeria Vaatika Café.** The café, an easygoing, inexpensive outdoor eatery with tables looking out on Assi Ghat, serves excellent thin-crust vegetarian pizza made in a wood-fire oven with real mozzarella, as well as homemade pasta dishes, bona fide espresso, and fresh homemade apple pie. ⊠ *B-1/178 Assi Ghat* ☎ *98380–94111, 94513–97331.*

Kashi Vishvanath Temple. Known as the Golden Temple because of the gold plate on its spire—a gift from the Sikh Maharaja Ranjit Singh of Punjab in 1835—this is the most sacred shrine in Varanasi. It's dedicated to Shiva, whose pillar of light is said to have appeared on this spot. Foreigners are only admitted through Gate 2, and are required to bring passports and register prior to entering. Various forms of the *arti* prayer ceremony are performed outside at 2:30 am, 11:30 am, 7:30 pm, and 11:30 pm. It's in the Old City above the Ganges, between Dashashvamedh and Manikarnika ghat: to get here, walk from Dashashvamedh Road down the relatively broad, shop-lined lane (Vishvanath Gali, the main sari bazaar) to Vishvanath Temple. The lane turns sharply right at a large idol of the elephant-head god Ganesh, then passes the brightly painted wooden entrance to the 1725 **Annapurna temple** (Annapurna was Vishvanath's consort), on the right. On the left, look for the silver doorway, which is usually manned by a police officer—this is the entrance to the Kashi Vishvanath Temple. The present temple was built by Rani Ahalyabai of Indore in 1776, near the site of the original shrine, which had been destroyed by the emperor Aurangzeb. Nearby is the **Gyanvapi Mosque,** built by Mughal emperor Aurangzeb after he destroyed the temple that stood here: the building's foundation and rear still show parts of the original temple. As a result of Hindu revivalist attempts to reconsecrate the site of the former temple, the area is usually staffed with police and fenced with barbed wire. It's normally very sedate, however, and is an important starting point for Hindu pilgrims. Nonpilgrims aren't allowed into the inner sanctum. ⊠ *Vishvanath Gali* ⊙ *Daily 4 am–11 pm.*

Ramnagar Fort and Palace. Across the Ganges from the river ghats is the 17th-century, red sandstone palace of the Maharaja of Varanasi, who still lives here (if the flag is up, he's in residence) and performs ceremonial and charitable functions. Inside, there are some interesting collections—stop at the Durbar Hall and the Royal Museum—but the place is sadly run-down and the objects are not well maintained. It's sort of fascinating, though, to see the state of decay: a case full of beautiful black musical instruments, for example, is so completely white with dust and the case so covered with grime that it's almost impossible to see anything, and the royal costumes are ratty. Still, there are palanquins and howdahs in ivory, goldplate, or silver (completely tarnished); old carriages and cars; furniture; portraits of maharajas; and arms from Africa, Burma, and Japan. The palace was built to resist the floods of the monsoon, which play havoc with the city side of the river. (It should cost about Rs. 1,200 to take a taxi here and have him wait for an hour or two; negotiate beforehand.) Note that the fort is closed to visitors during monsoon season if the weather is bad. ⊠ *End of Pontoon Bridge, off Ramnagar Rd.* ☎ *542/250–5033 tourism office* ▨ *Rs. 150* ⊙ *Daily 10–5.*

Sankat Mochan Temple. One of Varanasi's most beloved temples—as well as one of its oldest—Sankat Mochan (Deliverer from Troubles) was built in the late 16th century. Though the city has encroached all around it, the building still stands in a good-size, tree-shaded enclosure, like temples elsewhere in India. (Most temples in Varanasi are squeezed between other buildings.) Although most of the city's major shrines are dedicated to Shiva or various aspects of the mother goddess, Sankat Mochan belongs to Hanuman, the monkey god, revered for his dedicated service to Rama, an incarnation of Vishnu whose story is told in the *Ramayana.* The best time to see Sankat Mochan is early evening, when dozens of locals stop for a brief visit at the end of the workday, and on Tuesday and Saturday—days sacred to Hanuman—when worshippers come in large numbers to pay their respects. ⊠ *Durgakund Rd.* ⊙ *Daily 5 am–noon and 3–9.*

Shitala Temple. This unassuming but very popular white temple near Dashashvamedh Ghat is dedicated to Shitala, the goddess of smallpox, who both causes and cures the disease. Despite the eradication of smallpox, Shitala is still an important folk goddess in North India. ⊠ *Shitala Ghat* ⊙ *Daily sunrise–sunset.*

CLOSE UP

The Economics of Burning

Public cremation is the norm for Hindus throughout India, but the spiritual implications of being cremated in Varanasi make dying here an especially celebratory occasion. The idea is that because the Ganges is so holy, a spiritual cleansing in this water means easier achievement of moksha, *the* release from the cycle of rebirth. In Varanasi bodies are wrapped in silk or linen—traditionally white for men, red or orange for women—and carried through the streets on bamboo stretchers to the smoking pyres of the burning ghat. Then, after a brief immersion in the Ganges and a short wait, the body is placed on the pyre for the ritual that precedes the cremation. Funeral parties dressed in white, the color of mourning, surround the deceased. **Photographing funeral ghats is strictly forbidden**, but you are allowed to watch.

Dying in Varanasi will get you closer to achieving purification and moksha—but even here, there are still obstacles to achieving the ultimate release from the cycle of rebirth, and money is the most common problem. A proper wood cremation ceremony, even in one's hometown, involves basic **expenses that much of India's poor majority simply cannot afford**. The most expensive aspect is the wood itself, costing about Rs. 200 for 40 kilograms. With a minimum requirement of about 300 kilograms, the price of wood cremation starts at Rs. 1,500. Other supplies include ghee (clarified butter), sandalwood powder, and cloth to prepare the body—and there's a tax to be paid, too. The total price for the ritual usually comes to around Rs. 3,000. Add to that the cost of traveling to Varanasi, and the prospect of honoring the dead at the bank of the Ganges becomes financially daunting—many of the poorest people in India make less than Rs. 2,000 a month.

To help with cost, traditional funeral pyres share space at the burning ghat with Varanasi's one electric cremation center. Burning a body here costs just Rs. 500, a fraction of the cost of wood cremation, though still expensive by Indian standards. A lack of money, in fact, is probably the best explanation for a body drifting by during a boat ride on the Ganges. It's unlawful to offer dead bodies to the river now, except in the case of a pregnant woman, a child younger than 5, someone with smallpox, someone who has been bitten by a cobra, or a holy man—Hindus believe that **gods live inside these bodies**, so they can't be burned. But in the absence of money for a cremation, poor relatives often have no other choice but to break the law if they want to honor the dead in the holiest of waters.

WHERE TO EAT

$$$$ ✕ **1951.** Situated in the plush Clarks hotel, this upmarket restaurant **ECLECTIC** that's decorated in tones of white and dark wood is best for its Indian food, though there are plenty of fusion and multi-cuisine choices on the menu. The chef cooks up innovative items in the live kitchen, such as the cuts of chicken rolled in basil and green chilli pesto, then cooked in a tandoor. For a more local experience, try the Banarasi *thali*—a platter with rice, vegetable curries, *dal* (lentils) and yogurt; there's a version for meat-eaters as well. $ *Average main: Rs. 800* ⊠ *Clarks Varanasi Hotel, The Mall, Cantt* ☎ *542/250–1011.*

$

CAFÉ

✗ **Bread of Life Bakery.** Handily located behind the Shivala Ghat, this is an impressive haven for homesick Western palates and a great place for breakfast after a morning boat ride—the pancakes are real and so is the maple syrup, which is a rare thing in India. Stop in anytime to write postcards over coffee and chocolate-chip cookies, apple strudel, an éclair, or some Black Forest cake. Simple lunches and dinners include omelets, quiches, sandwiches, soups and stews, pastas, and some Chinese dishes. All profits of the café and the art gallery upstairs go to charities, or are used for the employees' education. $ *Average main: Rs. 200* ⊠ *B-3/322 Shivala* ☎ *542/227–5012* ▭ *No credit cards.*

$$

ECLECTIC

✗ **Canton Royale.** Behind the colonial facade of the Surya Hotel, the Canton Royal is a simple but elegant restaurant, with vaulted ceilings, statues, and framed pictures of Benarasi royalty. The menu is eclectic, spanning European, Mediterranean, Mexican, and Chinese, but the Indian is the best. The tandoori chicken and mutton curry are both delicious, and the *aloo dum Banarasi* (potatoes stuffed with paneer in a spicy tomato gravy), a dish native to Varanasi, is recommended. You can dine inside or in the lovely gardens. $ *Average main: Rs. 450* ⊠ *Surya Hotel, S-20/51A-5 The Mall* ☎ *542/250–8465, 542/250–8466* ⊕ *hotelsuryavns.com.*

$

MIDDLE EASTERN

✗ **Haifa.** Situated at the lobby level of Hotel Haifa, this restaurant's specialty is Middle Eastern food. It's basically a long room with nondescript tables and lots of tourists flowing in and out—and no wonder, because it's incredibly cheap and the only place in town to sample freshly made Middle Eastern treats. An entire Middle Eastern "thali" consisting of hummus, baba ghanoush (eggplant mashed with spices and olive oil), *labneh* (strained yogurt), falafel, and potato costs Rs. 200. In case you're sticking to Indian, there's plenty of that, too, along with Chinese and continental, also at affordable prices. $ *Average main: Rs. 200* ⊠ *B-1/107 Assi Ghat* ☎ *542/231–2960.*

$$

ASIAN FUSION

Fodor's Choice

★

✗ **I:ba Café.** At this unexpected oasis away from the chaos of the ghats, you can find good Japanese food and great cold coffee, perfect after a hot walk. Dark wood accents, warm yellow lights, and pleasing jazz music set a stylish scene—cane "tikki roofs," cozy floor couches, dangling bells, dry corn husks. A Japanese and Indian husband-wife team run the operation, serving varied cuisines, including Indian, Thai, and Korean, as well as pizzas and pastas, but the Japanese is the best: delicious vegetable tempura, tasty chicken *gyoza* (dumplings), teriyaki chicken, sticky rice bowls, and a variety of ramen (noodle) dishes. The nonvegetarian items on the menu are limited to chicken and mutton; no beef or fish is served here. $ *Average main: Rs. 350* ⊠ *B3/335B, Shivala* ☎ *0542/227–7523.*

$

SOUTH INDIAN

✗ **Kerala Cafe.** As the name implies, South Indian food is on the short menu at this no-frills, popular little diner that's lined with narrow, dingy booths and filled with mostly Indian pilgrims. The specialty is dosas—specifically masala dosas—and they're terrific, full of juicy chunks of potatoes, onion, and peas. In addition to choices like plain, tomato, or coconut *uttapams* (Indian-style pancakes), *idlis* (steamed bread made of rice flour), and *vadas* (deep-fried savory "doughnuts"), there's a great lemon rice with peanuts and a sprinkling of coriander leaves, and beautiful puffy *pooris* (fried bread) as big as your head. It's open for breakfast. $ *Average main: Rs. 200* ⊠ *Bhelupura Crossing* ⊟ *No credit cards.*

$ ✕ **Lotus Lounge.** There's a wonderful view from this simple outdoor ter-
INTERNATIONAL race restaurant, which is right along the Ganges. The setting itself is simple—a mix of tables and chairs on white Moroccan tiles, and tables with floor seating; the only real adornment is a large mural of the Buddha. The food is as pleasing as the view, with an eclectic menu of dishes including chicken schnitzel, vegetable moussaka, Thai coconut curry, and mushroom *makhani* (made with lots of butter). The mushroom and spinach Indian pakoda (fritters) with fig dip and the eggplant slices with spicy yogurt sauce are both delicious. $ *Average main: Rs. 280* ⊠ *D14/27 Mansrowar Ghat* ☎ *No phone* ⊟ *No credit cards.*

WHERE TO STAY

There are two options in Varanasi: you can stay near the water, where most of the lodgings are smaller and right in the midst of the action; or you can stay in the Cantonment area, about a 20-minute rickshaw ride away, where the more established, larger hotels are located. The latter area has less character, but it's definitely quieter and less chaotic.

WATERFRONT

$$ 🛏 **Hotel Ganges View.** Still the residence of a well-to-do family, this guest
B&B/INN house has small, beautiful rooms with quirky charm—one has a jungle painting and stone shrine (with goddess) that you sleep under—and a great veranda overlooking the river and Assi Ghat. **Pros:** the veranda is the best place in town to watch the endless stream of pilgrims and tourists. **Cons:** it's pretty noisy, particularly in rooms without a/c; narrow stairs to the front door make access difficult. $ *Rooms from: Rs. 4500* ⊠ *Assi Ghat* ☎ *542/231–3218, 542/329–0289* ⊕ *www.hotelgangesview.com* ⤶ *15 rooms* ⦿⧸ *Breakfast.*

$$$ 🛏 **Jukaso Ganges.** Accessed by boat from the nearby Dasaswamedh
HOTEL Ghat, this stunning sandstone heritage hotel on the Ganges is perfect for a romantic getaway or a personal retreat. **Pros:** excellent river views, including from the yoga meditation room; complimentary transfer to Dasaswamedh Ghat to watch the Ganga Arti prayer ceremony. **Cons:** boat access impossible during monsoon, and it's quite a trek overland; monsoon floods the lobby. $ *Rooms from: Rs. 9500* ⊠ *CK 1/14 Patni Tola Chowk, Between Mehta Hospital and Bhosle Ghat* ☎ *542/240–6667 to 6668* ⊕ *jukaso.co.in* ⤶ *15 rooms* ⦿⧸ *Breakfast.*

$$$ 🛏 **Palace on Ganges.** In this century-old building on Assi Ghat, rooms
HOTEL are styled after Indian states—Gujarat (brightly colored drapes studded with mirrorwork), Rajasthan (elaborately carved doors and furnishings), Assam (lots of bamboo)—while delivering modern comforts. **Pros:** magnificent view from the rooftop; library well-stocked with cultural and history books. **Cons:** you'll have to climb a flight of stairs just to get to the front door; expect to pay more for rooms with a view. $ *Rooms from: Rs. 8000* ⊠ *B-1/158 Assi Ghat* ☎ *542/231–4304 to 05* ⊕ *www.palaceonganges.com* ⤶ *24 rooms* ⦿⧸ *Breakfast.*

$ 🛏 **Pradeep.** A shining example of inexpensive lodging in an expensive
HOTEL tourist town, the Pradeep Hotel is in the heart of chaotic Varanasi, just

1.5 km (1 mile) from the ghats. **Pros:** economical; warm and sincere service. **Cons:** some rooms don't have windows; rooms near the road are noisy; usually quite crowded. $ *Rooms from: Rs. 2600* ✉ *Jagatganj* ☎ *542/220–4963, 542/220–4594, 542/220–7231* ⊕ *www.hotelpradeep. com* ➣ *45 rooms* ⦿ *No meals.*

$$$$ ⌂ **Suryauday Haveli.** Built in the style of a traditional Nepali courtyard
HOTEL by the royal family of Nepal, this boutique property sits directly on the banks of the Shivala Ghat. **Pros:** complimentary boat ride to Dashash-wamedh Ghat in the evening to watch the Ganga Arti prayers; luxuri-ous rooms; excellent service. **Cons:** windows in all the rooms are a bit small; a long, narrow flight of stairs to reach the main entrance; expen-sive. $ *Rooms from: Rs. 12000* ✉ *B-4/25 Shivala Ghat, Nepali Kothi* ☎ *542/654–0390, 542/227–6820, 80/4130–6352 reservations* ⊕ *www. suryaudayhaveli.com* ➣ *13 rooms, 1 suite* ⦿ *Breakfast.*

CANTONMENT

$$$ ⌂ **Clarks Varanasi.** With upscale amenities amid lots of greenery, Clarks
HOTEL makes a good choice for a quiet stay. **Pros:** a 24-hour coffee shop and well-stocked shopping arcade. **Cons:** a bit far from the unique hustle and bustle of Varanasi—which isn't all bad. $ *Rooms from: Rs. 7500* ✉ *The Mall, Cantt* ☎ *542/250–1011 to 1020* ⊕ *www.clarkshotels.com* ➣ *101 rooms, 2 suites* ⦿ *Breakfast.*

$ ⌂ **Hotel Cresent Villa.** With its contemporary Western interior design,
HOTEL this hotel doesn't have much local character, but it's clean, affordable, and within walking distance of the Ganges and the ghats. **Pros:** close to the river; free Internet. **Cons:** lacking in personality; some areas could use a bit of maintenance. $ *Rooms from: Rs. 3500* ✉ *126-A Lane No. 6, Ravindrapuri Colony, Bhelupura* ☎ *542/227–6191 to 94* ⊕ *www. cresentvilla.com* ➣ *11 rooms* ⦿ *Breakfast.*

$$$ ⌂ **Radisson Hotel Varanasi.** Plush and always lively, this hotel in the rela-
HOTEL tively noise-free Cantonment is a favorite for its luxurious settings,
Fodor'sChoice upscale amenities, and free Wi-Fi (rare in these parts). **Pros:** free Wi-Fi
★ throughout the property; good breakfast buffet at the cheerful East-West restaurant. **Cons:** pool is rather small; view from rooms is nothing special. $ *Rooms from: Rs. 8000* ✉ *The Mall, Cantt* ☎ *0542/250–1515* ⊕ *www.radisson.com* ➣ *114 rooms, 2 suites.*

$$$$ ⌂ **Taj Gateway Hotel Ganges.** Rooms at the Gateway are spacious and
HOTEL modern, done in soft colors with brass-accented furniture and eclec-tic Indian art. **Pros:** lots of space to take peaceful walks without fear of being run over in this crowded city; poolside barbecue in winter. **Cons:** a tour-group magnet. $ *Rooms from: Rs. 12000* ✉ *Nadesar Pal-ace Grounds* ☎ *542/666–0001 to 0019* ⊕ *www.tajhotels.com* ➣ *120 rooms, 10 suites* ⦿ *Breakfast.*

$$$$ ⌂ **Taj Nadesar Palace Hotel.** This restored heritage palace provides
RESORT the most luxurious accommodations in Varanasi, as it did in its hey-
Fodor'sChoice day, when guests of the Maharaja of Benaras included Queen Eliza-
★ beth, Lord Mountbatten, Jawaharlal Nehru, and the King of Persia. **Pros:** extraordinarily luxurious; you will feel like royalty here. **Cons:** extremely expensive. $ *Rooms from: Rs. 38000* ✉ *Off Raja Bazar Rd., Cantt* ☎ *542/666–0002, 542/250–3016* ⊕ *www.tajhotels.com* ➣ *10 suites* ⦿ *No meals.*

4

SHOPPING

The city's shops are open generally from 10 to 8; the larger shops close on Sunday, but the street sellers and smaller shops are open daily. One of India's chief weaving centers, Varanasi is famous for its silk-brocade saris, which start at around Rs. 2,000. Some saris are still woven with real gold and silver threads, though in most noncustom work the real thing has been replaced by artificial fibers.

Weaving is typically a family business, and most weavers are Muslims who belong to the Ansari community. Kamalan Tours organizes visits to the traditional silk houses where you can interact with weavers and watch them weave silk using foot-powered looms.

Cottage Industries Exposition. Come here for excellent Varanasi weaves in silk and cotton, a vast rug room, plus brass wares and Kashmiri embroidered shawls. Everything is expensive. ⊠ *Mint House, Nadesar, across from Taj* ☎ *542/250–7626.*

Dharam Kumar Jain & Sons. Operating out of a house near Thatheri Bazaar, this company has an extraordinary private collection of old brocade saris, pashmina shawls, and other textiles. ⊠ *K 37/12 Sona Kuan* ☎ *0542/233–3354.*

Mehta International. In the Cantonment area around the corner from the Radisson, this is a large showroom with a wide selection of fine saris, scarves, bed covers, fabric, and some elaborately worked tapestries. ⊠ *S 20/51 Varuna Bridge, behind Radisson Hotel* ☎ *542/250–5589.*

Thatheri Bazaar. Among the brass vendors, on a small lane 50 meters north of the Chowk, some shops sell silks and woolens to a local crowd. ⊠ *Varanasi, Uttar Pradesh.*

Vishvanath Gali. Most hotels sell silk-brocade saris in their shops, but the main bazaars for silks and saris are in Vishvanath Gali—the lane leading from Dashashvamedh Road to the Kashi Vishvanath Temple, where the customers are mainly pilgrims and tourists. Try to go early—it gets quite crowded in the afternoon. ⊠ *Varanasi, Uttar Pradesh.*

NIGHTLIFE AND PERFORMING ARTS

Nagari Natak Mandal. Music and dance performances during November's Ganga Mahotsav festival are held here. Concerts of some of Varanasi's—and India's—best musicians are also infrequently hosted here throughout the year. Ask your hotel to check the local Hindi newspaper, *Aj,* for events while you're in town, or check the English-language papers and websites yourself. ⊠ *Kabir Chowra.*

SARNATH

11 km (7 miles) north of Varanasi.

Sarnath is where the historical Buddha, Siddhārtha Gautama (ca. 563–ca. 483 BC) first taught the Buddhist dharma. In 528 BC, about five weeks after having attained enlightenment at Bodh Gaya, he came to Sarnath and preached his first sermon (now called Dharma Chakra Pravartan, or Set in Motion the Wheel of Law) in what is today Sarnath's Deer Park.

Legend has it that the Buddha was incarnated as King of the Deer in the deer park—the name "Sarnath" comes from Saranganath, which means "Lord of the Deer." In the Deer Park you can buy some carrots for a few rupees and feed the current denizens.

When the Buddha arrived at Sarnath, he revealed his Eightfold Path, which is meant to lead to the end of sorrow and the attainment of enlightenment. Three hundred years later, in the 3rd century BC, the great Mauryan emperor Ashoka arrived in the area; he was a convert to Buddhism and had made it the state religion. In Sarnath he had several stupas (large, mound-shape reliquary shrines) built, along with a pillar with a lion capital that was adopted by independent India as its national emblem—it's called the Ashoka pillar. The wheel motif under the lions' feet represents the *dharma chakra*, the wheel (*chakra*) of Buddhist teaching (*dharma*), which began in Sarnath. The chakra is replicated at the center of the Indian national flag.

Sarnath reached its zenith by the 4th century AD, under the Gupta dynasty, and was occupied into the 9th century, when Buddhist influence in India began to wane. By the 12th century Sarnath had more or less fallen to Muslim invaders and begun a long decay. In 1836 Sir Alexander Cunningham started extensive excavations here, uncovering first a stone slab with an inscription of the Buddhist creed, then numerous other relics. It was then that the Western world realized that the Buddha had been an actual person, not a mythical figure. Most of the sites are in a well-manicured park behind a gate (admission is Rs. 100).

GETTING HERE AND AROUND
Sarnath is an easy taxi or auto-rickshaw ride from Varanasi; be prepared to bargain. A taxi from the Cantonment area should take around 45 minutes and cost between Rs. 600–Rs. 800.

EXPLORING
Chaukhandi Stupa. The first monument you come to in Sarnath, on the left-hand side of Ashoka Marg on the way to the park, is this Buddhist shrine that is believed to have originally been a terraced temple during the Gupta period (the 4th to 6th century). Govardhan, the son of Raja Todarmal (who later became a governor under Akbar's rule), built an octagonal tower to commemorate the visit of Emperor Humayun, the father of Emperor Akbar. The event is recorded in Arabic in a stone tablet above the doorway on the north side.

Dhamekh Stupa. Dappled with geometric and floral ornamentation, the stone-and-brick Dhamekh Stupa is the largest surviving monument in Sarnath, at 143 feet in height and 92 feet in diameter at the base. Built around 500 AD, Dhamekh is thought to mark the place where the Buddha delivered his sermon, though excavations have unearthed the remains of an even earlier stupa of Mauryan bricks of the Gupta period (200 BC). An Ashoka pillar with an edict engraved on it stands near the stupa.

Mulagandha Kuti Vihar Temple. Built in 1931 by the Mahabodhi Society, the temple joins the old foundations of seven monasteries. The walls bear frescoes by a Japanese artist, Kosetsu Nosu, depicting scenes from the Buddha's life, and relics of Sakyamuni Buddha are enshrined here.

On the anniversary of the temple's foundation—the first full moon in November—monks and devotees from all parts of Asia assemble here. The temple is behind a separate gate just outside the park.

Sarnath Archaeological Museum. At the entrance to this excellent museum is Ashoka's Lion Capital, moved here from its original location in the park. The museum represents the oldest site in the history of India's Archaeological Survey. Other beautiful sculpture is here as well, including lots of Buddhas; still more of Sarnath's masterpieces are in the National Museum, Delhi, and the Indian Museum, Kolkata. ⊠ *Ashoka Marg at Dharmapal Marg* ☎ *542/259–5095* ⊕ *www.sarnathmuseumasi. org* 🖾 *Monument Rs. 100; museum Rs. 5* ☉ *Sat.–Thurs. 9–5.*

5

RAJASTHAN

WELCOME TO RAJASTHAN

TOP REASONS TO GO

★ **Appreciate Jaipur's Pink architecture:** Dusty-pink Jaipur is the gateway to Rajasthan's beautiful palaces, forts, culture, and food.

★ **Marvel at the diversity of Rajasthan's landscapes:** You can travel from the golden sand dunes in Jaisalmer to Udaipur's lovely Lake Pichola, which is set against the Aravali Mountains.

★ **Admire the Massive Mehrangarh Fort:** Standing dramatically on a hill, this massive fort is one of Jodhpur's most imposing treasures.

★ **Make a palace your home:** Spend a night in one of the many opulent palaces and forts that have been converted into heritage hotels around Rajasthan and experience Rajput grandeur.

★ **Go on a shopping spree:** Hopefully, there's room in your suitcase for the jewelry, clothes, fabric, carpets, leather-bound journals, silver, and everything else that has caught your eye—or buy an extra bag to hold your goodies.

1 Jaipur and Nearby.
The modern and ancient worlds collide in Rajasthan's bustling capital. Highlighted by the Hawa Mahal and the City Palace, this town is both an architectural delight and a shopping hot spot for carpets, textiles, handmade paper and jewelry. Excursions from Jaipur include the Shekhawati region, known as India's open-air art gallery because of the frescoes on the walls of the old *havelis*, or ancient homes of merchants.

2 Udaipur and Nearby.
With the Lake Palace floating in the middle of Lake Pichola, the White City is charming and serene. If you're feeling adventurous, you can hike up to Monsoon Palace for stunning bird's-eye views. From here there are spectacular day trips like the Jain temples at Ranakpur and Mount Abu, and the medieval citadel of Chittaurgarh.

HARYANA

DELHI
DELHI

Churu

Jhunjhunun

Fatehpur

Narnaul

UTTAR
PRADESH

Nawalgarh

SHEKHAWATI

Sikar

Alwar

Shahpura

Sariska
National
Park

Agra

1 Jaipur

Dausa

Hindaun

Dhaulpur

Ajmer

Karauli

Chambal River

Tonk

Beawar

Sawai
Madhopur

Ranthambhore
National Park

Bhilwara

Bundi

Banas

Kota

Chittaurgarh

Baran

Parbati

Nimbahera

0   50 mi

0   50 km

Banswara

MADHYA
PRADESH

A R A V A L I   H I L L S

GETTING
ORIENTED

The largest state in India, Rajasthan is in the northwestern part of the country, sharing a border with Pakistan. The Aravali mountain range runs north–south almost the entire length of the state. The hot, dry northwest region is dominated by the Thar Desert; the milder south is known for its lakes and greenery. Jaipur, the state capital, is an hour's flight from New Delhi—options for traveling around Rajasthan include air, train, and road.

5

3 Jodhpur. The blue houses in the Old City here contrast with the desert landscape and the regal Mehrangarh fort. The congested Old City is fun to explore, and the fort is a short auto-rickshaw ride away.

4 Jaisalmer and Nearby. The Golden City is synonymous with its majestic fort, and a visit here just isn't complete without a jeep or camel safari, or a visit to the Sam Sand Dunes.

EATING WELL IN RAJASTHAN

A major part of Rajasthan is also known as Marwar (literally "the land of dead" because not much grows there), and traditional cuisine revolves around the robust plants of the desert and the scarcity of water.

(top left) Creamy safed maas; (top right) A Rajasthani thali (plate); (bottom right) Ghevar, a popular sweet

The lack of fresh green vegetables led to the use of gram (chickpea) and millet flour and the development of dry, long-lasting foods, and because water was scarce, many dishes were cooked in ghee (clarified butter) or milk, making them quite rich. Food tends to be heavily spiced, too, perhaps for preservation. The area was predominantly Hindu and Jain—both vegetarian religions—but besides the restrictive but rich meat-free cuisine, the ruling Rajputs were avid hunters and contributed a variety of game dishes, many heavily influenced by the Mughals.

Tourist areas in Rajasthan—besides the better hotels—are a bit thin on authentic eating out options, especially for nonvegetarian fare, but *thali* meals (with a variety of different dishes) are usually available at casual eateries and offer a taste of Marwari home cooking. You'll also find a dazzling range of snacks and sweets.

COOKING SCHOOL

There are several places In Udaipur and Jaipur, where travelers can pick up the basics of Rajasthani cooking: **Spice Box** (⊕ www. spicebox.co.in); **Hotel Krishna Niwas** (⊕ www. cookingclassesinudaipur. com); **Shashi Cooking Classes** (⊕ www. shashicookingclasses. blogspot.com); **Jaipur Cooking Classes** (⊕ www.jaipurcooking-classes.com).

LAAL MAAS

A dish fit for Rajasthani royalty, **laal maas** (literally "red meat") is the state's best-known nonvegetarian entrée. This spicy dish is usually made with goat, marinated in ginger, garlic, and yogurt, then cooked in ghee with red chilli powder. It's sometimes confused with a similar dish called *jungli maas* (wild meat), which is more of a confit, and probably originated on hunting trips where only basic, nonperishable ingredients were available.

SAFED MAAS

The yin to *laal maas*'s yang, **safed maas** or "white" meat is another goat or lamb main dish—creamy white and wonderfully fragrant. The parboiled meat is massaged with yogurt before being sautéed in a fry-up of ghee, onion, ginger, garlic, cardamom, cloves, cinnamon, white peppercorn, and red pepper seeds. The meat is then finished with a paste of poppy seeds, cashew, almond, milk solids (*khoya*), and a hint of saffron or rosewater.

A true desert dish, **daal baati churma** is a staple of Rajasthani cuisine. The rustic *baati* is a ball of unleavened bread made of wheat, semolina, and ghee. Traditionally, these are cooked on coals to form a firm, slightly squashed sphere, which may be stuffed with peas and other fillings. *Baati* is eaten with a hot mixed-lentil dal. *Churma* is a sweet

accompaniment of ground-up wholewheat *baati* or other bread mixed with ghee and melted *jaggery* (unrefined sugar).

GATTE KI SABZI

One of Rajasthan's vegetable substitutes, *gatte* are sausage-shape gramflour dumplings that are spiced and then boiled. *Gatte* can be eaten in a variety of ways, but the most typical dish is **gatte ki sabzi**, in which the dumplings are fried before they're mixed into a curry of yogurt, with a little more gram flour for thickening, and some mild spices. If you like this, try curry dishes made from pappadams or *mangodi* (sundried ground-lentil dumplings).

GHEVAR

One of the most eye-catching of Indian sweets, **ghevar,** which look like halved bagels with the cratered surface of an English muffin—can be seen stacked up on confectionary shelves, especially around the Teej festival in late summer. Crispy, with a slightly soft interior, the *ghevar* is made from batter that gets its riddled texture from the bubbling heat of the ghee in which it is deep-fried. The crisp golden disc is then soaked in sugar syrup flavored with the freshtasting screwpine flower essence (*kewra*) and sometimes topped with silver leaf, spice, and nuts.

CAMELS: SHIPS OF THE DESERT

Taking a camel ride in the Thar desert is one of the most unforgettable experiences of a trip to India. If you can, start off before sunrise, so that you can watch the sun come up over the sand dunes.

(top left) A colorfully outfitted camel; (top right) Sunset in the Thar Desert; (bottom right) Camel safari

Camels are an indispensable part of the local landscape and economy in Rajasthan, and you'll see them wherever you go in the state—approximately half a million camels live here. Apart from pulling loads (and that includes tourists on safaris), camels are also highly valued for their milk, meat, hair, leather, and even their droppings (used for fertilizer and dried for cooking fuel).

Camel owners usually dress their animals with flair: red, green, and gold saddle covers and tasseled bridles are signs of the well-dressed camel. They're also rather gentle creatures—contrary to popular belief—and you'll no doubt form a bond with yours.

⇨ *For camel-safari tour contacts, see listings throughout the chapter, and in the Tours section of the Planning information.*

DESERT SUPERFOOD

Camel milk is rich in nutrients, and is a common food source for desert people worldwide. In India's desert regions the milk is consumed regularly, and a few enterprising people—Saras Dairy, for instance—even create camel-milk ice cream. Fans claim that it's easier to digest than cow's milk, but some travelers have reported tummy aches after consuming camel-milk products.

WHERE TO GO ON SAFARI?

It's easy to book a camel safari once you're in Rajasthan: Jaisalmer is the most popular place to take a safari, but other destinations like Pushkar and Jodhpur are good, too. You can choose to go for anything from several hours to several days, or even several weeks. On a day trip, your guide will probably take you through a local village, maybe stopping for something to eat.

SIMPLE OR LUXURY

Overnight safaris range from simple and inexpensive—a one-night trip to a local campsite—to luxury glamping ("glamorous" plus "camping") excursions. A lower-end, one-night safari will cost from around Rs.1,500, which includes a camel, a guide, a cot under the stars, and a basic dinner of dal and rice. Higher-end tours cost at least twice as much, and include more comfortable tented accommodations, multicourse meals, and even a jeep service to carry supplies and luggage between campsites. Water is not always included, so check to see if you need to pack your own.

WHAT TO BRING?

It's important to come prepared, be it a day trip or a longer safari. The desert sun is very strong, so wear sunglasses, a brimmed hat, and high-power sunscreen (ideally one that doubles as an insect/mosquito repellent) even if you don't generally get sunburned. Long-sleeved

shirts and full-length trousers are also a must—both for sun protection and to stop your legs from chafing. Wear solid shoes or boots with socks to avoid bites from small insects that live in the sand. Pack a scarf to protect your face in case of a sandstorm.

WHEN?

Overnight camel safaris typically run from late August to mid-April; in May, June, and July temperatures in the Thar Desert peak above 120 degrees, which is dangerously hot for anyone from outside the desert to make such a venture. Only male camels are used during the winter mating season, as adding females into the mix can cause the animals to bolt or even attempt mating, regardless of whether there's a rider on their back.

LEARNING TO RIDE

Although learning to ride a camel is easier than learning to ride a horse, it still takes a bit of getting used to. On short trips you might be tied to your guide's camel; on a longer trip, you will be taught to "drive" the camel yourself. Camel bridles are attached to pegs in the camel's nose, and camels are steered with reins. Camels have remarkably sensitive flanks, so you won't need to kick the way you would with a stubborn horse—a little practice and a few nudges with your legs is usually enough to get your steed to pick up the pace.

RAJASTHAN'S HOLY SITES

Although Rajasthan is best known for its forts, palaces, and desert expanses, this huge state is also home to some of India's most awe-inspiring sacred sites.

(top left) The Pushkar Brahma temple; (top right) The main gate of the Karni Mata Temple; (bottom right) Inside one of the Jain temples at Ranakpur

The Jain temples in the southern part of Rajasthan are popular destinations; visitors marvel at the white-marble architecture and intricately carved designs that embellish the temples walls and pillars. The best-known Jain holy sites in the state include the temples at Ranakpur near Udaipur and at Dilwara in Mount Abu. There are also a number of significant Hindu temples in Rajasthan. Pushkar has one of the world's few temples dedicated to Bramha, the god of creation in the Hindu trinity. The Eklingji temple complex near Udaipur was built by royalty and is dedicated to Shiva (the destroyer). Not everyone, however, feels the need to actually visit the Karni Mata temple at Deshnoke (popularly known as the Rat Temple among tourists) near Bikaner: it's known as an abode for thousands of rats, which are considered sacred. A popular Muslim pilgrimage site is just outside Pushkar, in Ajmer: Dargah Sharif is the shrine of Sufi saint Khwaja Moinuddin Chisti, and is among the most important pilgrimage sites for South Asian Muslims.

SWASTIKAS

Visitors to Rajasthan are often shocked to see images of the swastika—a symbol associated with Nazism in the West—on walls, doorways, and temples. The swastika is sacred to Hindus, Buddhists, and Jains, who place it prominently in all of their temples and holy books. Sadly, Hitler misappropriated the holy symbol, turning it on its side and making it into his party's logo.

DARGAH SHARIF

In Ajmer's Old Town the white-marble Dargah Sharif is one of the finest examples of Mughal architecture in the state. This is the shrine of Hazrat Khwaja Moinuddin Chisti, a Sufi saint of Persian descent who is best known for his service to the impoverished. Chisti's shrine is sacred to Muslims, but visited by people of all faiths. Every year, pilgrims from across the subcontinent flock to Dargah Sharif to commemorate the Chisti's Urs, the anniversary of the saint's death.

DILWARA TEMPLES

The five temples of Dilwara in Mount Abu attract Jain pilgrims from across the country and people of all faiths with an interest in art and architecture. Each temple is devoted to a different *tirthankar* (enlightened being who is repeatedly reborn to impart the knowledge he has gained) from the Jain faith. The pillars, arches, and domes represent some of the finest marble artisanship in the country.

RANAKPUR TEMPLE

Between Udaipur and Jodhpur, this magnificent Jain temple venerates the *tirthankar* Rishabha. The four sides symbolize the four directions, each with a similar facade, and the interior features an almost mazelike series of 1,444-plus intricately carved marble pillars. There's also a small, much older temple, dedicated to the sun.

EKLINGJI TEMPLE COMPLEX

A pleasant drive from Udaipur through the Aravali Mountains, Eklingji village is famous for its 108-strong temple complex, the highlight of which is the 15th-century Shiva Temple (some parts date back to the 8th century). There's a unique four-sided, four-faced black-marble image of Shiva here, miniature replicas of which will be eagerly offered to you in the village bazaar. Every Monday evening the Maharaja of Udaipur visits the temple privately.

PUSHKAR BRAMHA TEMPLE

It seems like there's a temple every few feet in Pushkar—many restrict access to foreigners and non-Hindus, but the most famous temple, the red-spired 14th-century Brahma Temple, allows people of all backgrounds. The town's lake is also a holy spot unto itself, and many of Pushkar's priestly residents earn a living performing *pujas* (ceremonies) at the shore.

KARNI MATA TEMPLE

Near Bikaner, the town of Deshnoke is home to the Karni Mata temple, dedicated to a 14th-century female sage who was believed to be an incarnation of the goddess Durga. The temple is best known, however, for its large population of rats, which some people estimate at being around 20,000. The rodents are considered sacred, and are fed by the temple's caretakers.

SHOPPING IN RAJASTHAN

When it comes to shopping, Rajasthan has something for everyone. From elegant silk saris to kitschy wooden camels, even the most frugal visitor is likely to leave the state with some goodies tucked in their luggage.

(top left) Indian bangles at a market in Jodhpur; (top right) Handmade leather shoes; (bottom right) Bandhani fabric

Rajasthan is well known for its craftspeople, and each region has its own distinct specialties. Jaipur is at the hub of the state's tourism industry and has handicrafts from across the state but is most famous for its jewelry; if you want something with a local flair here, pick up a piece of blue pottery or a pair of emerald earrings. Jodhpur is a good place to shop for appliquéd cloth, glass bangles, mirrored, sequined bedspreads and wood furniture. Udaipur is known for miniature paintings and marble work. In Jaisalmer it's camel leather—patchwork bed covers, shoes, purses, and even book covers are made from the desert animal's hide. Yellow sandstone statues are also popular here. The best deals can be found in local markets—large private emporia and shops in "craft villages" tend to mark their items up to recover the huge commissions they pay to travel agents, guides, and taxi drivers.

BUYER BEWARE

Every year, unsuspecting tourists fall prey to shady self-professed "gem dealers," who befriend foreign visitors and try to get them to transport gems back to their home countries. The victims are then asked to leave a deposit for the jewels, which are inevitably nothing more than tin and glass. Most tourists don't realize they've been scammed until they're thousands of miles away.

JEWELRY

Rajasthan has been known for its fine selection of jewelry for centuries, and you're sure to find something special, no matter what your budget. The state is a major exporter of precious and semiprecious gems, and good deals on precious jewelry abound—just make sure you buy from a reputable source. Popular purchases include glass bangles, silver anklets, rings, pendants, and *meenakari* (enamel) rings and bracelets. More traditional are the *kundan* pieces: elaborate gold and gem jewelry with designs dating from the Mughal era.

LEATHERWORK

Handcrafted leatherwork is popular in Rajasthan, and you can find purses, journals, and traditional slippers, or *jootis*, at bargain prices. Shopkeepers always claim that their products are made from camel hide, but sometimes cowhide is passed off as camel leather to avoid offending Hindus. Watch out for overly pungent leathergoods (sniff before you purchase), and if you do end up with something smelly, seal the item in a plastic bag along with some fabric-softener/dryer-sheets and baking soda.

PAINTINGS

Rajasthan is famous for paintings in the *phad, pichwai,* and miniature styles. The *phad* is a red, green, and yellow scroll depicting the life of a local hero; the dark and richly hued *pichwais*, hung

in temples, are cloth paintings depicting Lord Krishna in different moods. Miniature paintings are created using squirrel-hair brushes on paper, silk, marble, or bone, and usually depict wildlife and courtly scenes, or illustrations of religious stories and mythological themes.

POTTERY

Pottery is a huge industry in Rajasthan, and the blue pottery here is quite famous. Most people believe that blue pottery originated in Rajasthan, but it's actually of Turko-Persian origin and only emerged in India in the 18th century. The craft nearly went extinct, but was revived in the 1960s and 1970s. The name blue pottery is misleading—although blue is the traditional hue for this kind of work, it's available in an array of colors.

TEXTILES

Rajasthan has a rich textile tradition. *Bandhani* (tie-dye) has its origins in this part of the country, but don't expect to find the psychedelic designs popular in 1960s America—Rajasthan's tie-dyes are often only one or two colors embellished with tiny white circles. Handmade block-printing is also popular, and is made by using wooden stamps (mostly with patterns of paisley, elephants, or camels) to transfer natural dyes onto fabric. Detailed embroidery and appliqué, often featuring mirror work, are also popular.

5

Updated by
Vaihayasi
Pande Daniel

Steeped in tales of chivalry and romance, and famous for its striking desert landscape, massive forts, and fabulous palaces, Rajasthan represents, for many, the quintessential India. With the legendary cities of Jaipur, Jodhpur, Udaipur, and Jaisalmer, built by the mighty Rajput warriors, and the indigenous tribal and artisan communities, Rajasthan is a unique combination of royal and tribal India.

The variety of Rajasthan's landscape is unparalleled: the region is packed with awe-inspiring forts, sparkling palaces, tranquil lakes and gardens, and exquisite temples and shrines. The crafts and folk art produced here are world-renowned. Once called Rajputana ("Abode of Princes"), this vast land consisted of more than 22 princely states before most of them were consolidated into modern Rajasthan in 1949. Each of the 22 states was ruled by a Rajput, an upper-caste Hindu warrior-prince, and the Rajputs were divided into three main clans: the Suryavanshis, descended from the sun; the Chandravanshis, descended from the moon; and the Agnikuls, who had been purified by ritual fire. When they were not fighting among themselves for power, wealth, and women, the Rajputs built the hundreds of forts, palaces, gardens, and temples that make this region so enchanting.

The Rajputs' contribution to cultural life in Rajasthan lives on to this day, and with the amalgam of so many states, each with its rituals and ways of life, Rajasthan is extremely culturally diverse. Communities vary in everything from the colors of their sandstone buildings to the languages they speak—a local saying has it that you hear a new dialect every 4 km (2½ miles). Travelers will notice the brilliant colors of the local women's *lehangas* (long skirts with separate veils), designed to stand out against the starkness of the desert. Women also wear elaborate jewelry, and Rajasthani men are famous for their turbans—called *saafas*—which vary in style from region to region and caste to caste; the style of wearing high turbans with a tail is preferred by Rajputs, for instance, while *pagris* (compact turbans, often orange) are worn by businessmen. Even facial hair is unique in these parts: Rajputs, in particular, sport long, Salvador Dalí–like handlebar moustaches.

Although Rajasthan has many social problems, most notably widespread rural poverty, low literacy rates, and child marriages, its cities and people remain lively. Cultural festivals, crafts fairs, and religious gatherings take place throughout the year. With its bright colors and rich folk traditions, and the sheer variety of experiences it has to offer the traveler, Rajasthan easily earns its place as one of India's most popular tourist destinations.

PLANNING

WHEN TO GO
HIGH SEASON: OCTOBER TO FEBRUARY
The high season officially begins in October, though many tour groups begin arriving in August and September during the rains. Monsoon days can be quite hot between showers. The peak is November through mid-February when the weather is at its best, the days are perfect for sightseeing and evenings are pleasant—and can even be chilly in the desert areas. Temperatures rarely rise above the mid-80s, but the sun is still strong, so cover up if you're susceptible to sunburn. Many hotel rates are close to double those charged in low season, and monuments are crowded with group tours with the busiest periods being around Christmas and around Diwali when Indian tourists are holidaying. This is also when the Ranthambhore National Park is open and the winter migratory birds come to Bharatpur (Keoladeo Ghana) Bird Sanctuary.

LOW SEASON: MAY TO JULY
These summer months can be unbearably hot, with temperatures, particularly in desert cities like Jaisalmer and Jodhpur, at times soaring close to 120 degrees. It's almost impossible to endure a full day of sightseeing or be out in the sun for more than an hour or two. As a result most hotels are vacant and offer great deals—often less than half their usual rates—and the monuments are close to deserted.

SHOULDER SEASON: AUGUST TO SEPTEMBER AND MARCH TO APRIL
As long as you don't mind the monsoon, this is not a bad time to visit. The weather is neither at its best nor its worst, and crowds can easily be avoided. However, hotel deals are not as highly discounted as in the low season, and the wildlife parks are closed.

GETTING HERE AND AROUND
Rajasthan is India's largest state, and if you try to cram too much into one trip you may find yourself spending more time on the road than at your destinations. It can be helpful to use a travel agent for advice on getting around—they're seemingly everywhere you look in the touristy parts of Rajasthan's major cities, and they can help you reserve train and bus tickets for a nominal fee, and most are happy to offer destination advice, though not always unbiased as far as accommodations are concerned.

AIR TRAVEL
There are domestic airports in Jaipur, Jodhpur, and Udaipur (there's also a new airport in Jaisalmer, but civilian flights are still suspended as of this writing). Popular domestic airline carriers to these three cities

include Jet Airways, Air India, IndiGo, Go Air, and SpiceJet. Note that air connections *between* cities in Rajasthan are nonexistent and must be made via Delhi or Mumbai.

Jaipur's Sanganer Airport is about 13 km (8 miles) south of town; a taxi into town costs about Rs. 250 if you call for a radio taxi, or Rs. 360 for a private non-a/c taxi and Rs. 400 for a private a/c taxi. Jodhpur's airport is 5 km (3 miles) from the city center; a taxi into town costs about Rs. 600. Udaipur's Dabok Airport is 25 km (16 miles) from the city center; the ride costs about Rs. 750. You can also book and pay for a car to pick you up from the airport online (⊕ *www.makemytrip. com* or *www.savaari.com*).

BUS TRAVEL

If convenience and a cheap price are more important to you than a super-comfortable journey, travel by bus—but keep in mind that the quality of buses in India varies widely. The state-run Volvo buses are a good option for intercity travel. Some "tourist" buses end up picking up hitchhikers, so by the time you reach your destination people are sitting in the aisles and sometimes even on the roof. If you don't mind an adventure, or if you have no other choice, by all means take a bus. Otherwise, take a train (equally cheap) or rent a car and driver. The easiest way to get a bus ticket in advance is not from the bus stations, but from many of the private vendors in tourist areas. Your hotel reception or concierge might be able to help (for a fee).

CAR AND DRIVER TRAVEL

It's not cheap, but having a car and driver to yourself is highly efficient if you're short on time, as distances between points of interest are usually long, and direct trains can sometimes be hard to come by. It is also the best option if you plan to visit more than one city in Rajasthan. Plan to start early, when traffic on highways (and through toll plazas) are reduced and so you are not traveling after dark. You can hire a car and driver through your hotel or a recognized travel agent—hiring through your hotel is usually more expensive, depending on the class of the hotel, because the hotel will tack on a finder's fee. Car rates are extremely variable so do shop around. An a/c sedan car and driver should cost about Rs. 15 to Rs. 17 per km (½ mile), not including tolls for a minimum of 250 km per day. An extra Rs. 200 to Rs. 300 per day is usually tacked on for overnight trips and you should offer to pay for your driver's meal if you stop for one. A small tip at the end of the trip is customary if you are satisfied with the service provided. If you organize a car directly through the driver, it will be cheaper, but check the vehicle and driver out properly the day before you start. Expect to spend about Rs. 5,000 for a tour of the region from Delhi to Jaipur in a sedan air-conditioned car with room for three passengers or about Rs. 6,500 in an air-conditioned larger vehicle that can carry five passengers. Because the driver has to return to his point of origin, you pay the round-trip fare even if you're going one-way. To hire a car for a day of city driving expect to pay Rs. 2,000 for eight hours or 80 km, whichever comes first for an a/c sedan plus tips and money for the driver's lunch.

ROAD
CONDITIONS
Aside from major national highways crossing through Rajasthan, the state highways are not in very good shape, and the going is slow: The Delhi–Jaipur Highway (NH–8) is well paved, but once you're off the highway the roads are full of potholes, and it takes a long time to travel even short distances. When calculating driving time, plan to cover 40 kph–50 kph (25 mph–31 mph) at best. That said, driving is an excellent way to see the Indian countryside and glimpse village life.

Jaipur is a five- to six-hour drive from Delhi on National Highway (NH) 8. This is a congested industrial road with a high accident rate, so prepare for a trying experience.

Road surfaces are rough in and out of Jodhpur, and the going is slow. Don't expect to average more than 40 km (25 miles) per hour—Jodhpur-Jaipur is a seven-hour drive, Jodhpur-Jaisalmer is a five-hour drive, and Jodhpur-Udaipur is a six-hour drive. Udaipur is on National Highway 8, one of the better roads, which links Mumbai and Delhi, but in sections is rough. Again, expect your road speed to top out at 40 kph (25 mph). Journeys between Udaipur and Jaipur take seven hours or more. The Jodhpur-Jaisalmer road is in very good condition and it is possible to do 50 km–60 km per hour.

TAXIS AND AUTO-RICKSHAW TRAVEL

Taxis are unmetered in Jaipur, Jodhpur, and Udaipur, so ask your hotel for the going rate and negotiate with the driver before you set off (and in Jaipur use dial-a-cabs); hire one through your hotel or the RTDC's Tourist Information Center (⇨ *See Visitor Information, below, for contacts*). Depending on the distance to be covered, a taxi for half a day will cost about Rs. 900, and for a full day about Rs. 1,800. A full day usually equates to 8 hours and 80 km (50 miles) within the city limits; a set sightseeing city tour may cost less.

Auto-rickshaws in Jaipur are metered, but the meters are hardly ever used. Insist on setting the price in advance and negotiate—settle for no more than Rs. 10 per km (½ mile). Auto-rickshaws in Jodhpur and Udaipur are unmetered, so agree on a price before departing. You can also hire an auto-rickshaw by the hour, for about Rs. 150 per hour. Note that all of these rates go up by 25% to 50% after 11 pm.

TRAIN TRAVEL

In Rajasthan if you want to travel overnight, it's safer and more comfortable to take the train than a bus or car. Trains offer classes of service for all budgets (seats and sleepers, air-conditioning and non-air-conditioning, reserved and unreserved). Trains do get crowded, though, during peak season, and you may want to investigate special "tourist quotas" that set aside seats for foreign travelers. Check with a travel agent rather than deal with the crowds and administrative chaos at the train station, and book as far ahead as possible. Book online at ⊕ *www. indianrail.gov.in*.

Trains are the best method of getting to Jaisalmer. The Shatabdi Express, an air-conditioned chair-car train (the local term for a train carriage with only seats, no sleeping arrangements), travels every morning from New Delhi, departing at 6:05 am to arrive at Jaipur by 10:35 am. The Double Decker leaves Delhi S Rohilla station at 5:35 pm and reaches

Jaipur at 10:05 pm. The Garib Nawaz Express leaves Delhi Cantt station at 1:35 pm and arrives at 7:05 pm on Monday, Wednesday, and Saturday. Daily trains connect Udaipur with Jaipur, Ajmer, Chittaurgarh, Ajmer (Pushkar), and Delhi. Trains also run out from Delhi to Jaisalmer and Jodhpur as well as Jodhpur to Jaisalmer, but they're significantly slower than the road routes. The famed Palace on Wheels is a luxury train that runs across the state, connecting major sights. Note that if the train is running behind schedule, you might miss some sites.

Train Information Indian Railway Catering and Tourism Corporation Ltd ☎ 11/3934-0000 ⊕ www.irctc.co.in. **Palace on Wheels** ☎ 11/468-68686 in Delhi, 888/463-4299 U.S. and Canada, 800/845-6201 in Europe, 11/257-53628 in Delhi ⊕ www.palaceonwheelsindia.com.

EMERGENCIES

If you need a doctor or a 24-hour pharmacy, ask at your hotel: they'll know the closest place and can send someone to get medicine, or find a doctor. There are emergency help lines and ambulance numbers for all major cities—108 is the emergency number for ambulance service in Rajasthan.

MONEY MATTERS

Almost all ATMs take foreign credit cards, and are widely available. In major cities it's also possible to get a credit-card advance from a bank. Nearly all hotels exchange foreign currency for their guests. You'll get better rates at banks, but the hassle of waiting in line may outweigh the money-saving. There are also Thomas Cook and Western Union kiosks in all four major cities, open daily.

RESTAURANTS

Rajasthan's culinary traditions are heavily influenced by its desert setting and lack of a variety of fresh vegetables and in some parts of the state, sweets open the meal. Food tends to be highly spiced, perhaps for preservation. Instead of the rice and vegetables that are popular in regions with more rainfall, Rajasthani cuisine includes a lot of lentils, millets, and corn.

HOTELS

The most opulent hotels in India—and perhaps in the world—are in Rajasthan. You can live like a king, waited on hand and foot, in one of several converted palaces, surrounded by glittering mirrored walls, tiger skins, and stained-glass windows. Rajasthan is also famous for Heritage Hotels, a group of castles, forts, and havelis that have been converted to elegant accommodations. *Hotel reviews have been shortened. For full information, visit Fodors.com.*

WHAT IT COSTS IN RUPEES			
$	**$$**	**$$$**	**$$$$**
Restaurants	under Rs. 300	Rs. 300–Rs. 499	Rs. 500–Rs. 700	over Rs. 700
Hotels	under Rs. 4,000	Rs. 4,000–Rs. 5,999	Rs. 6,000–Rs. 10,000	over Rs. 10,000

Restaurant prices are the average cost of a main course at dinner or, if dinner is not served, at lunch. Hotel prices are the lowest cost of a standard double room in high season.

TOURS

It's usually easiest to book tours through your hotel or a travel agent, although a few operators allow direct booking. Shop around—sometimes agents will try to undercut the competition by offering small discounts on their offerings: there are usually several agents next to each other on the same street, so you can go from one to another. Rajasthan Tourism Development Corporation also organizes city tours and excursions.

Tour Contacts Karwan Tours. This Jaipur company can also help with general travel arrangements, including a hired car with driver to any location in Rajasthan. ✉ *Bissau Palace Hotel, outside Chandpol gate, near Saroj Cinema, Jaipur* ☎ *141/235–2785* ⊕ *www.karwantour.com.* **Le Passage to India.** This company functions both as an agent and as an operator, and offers custom tours as well as reliable cars and drivers in all major Rajasthan towns. ✉ *101 Ganpati Plaza, M.I. Rd., Jaipur* ☎ *141/511–5415, 982/905–1387* ⊕ *www.lepassagetoindia. com* ✉ *14/21 Lake Palace Rd., 1st fl., Udaipur* ☎ *0294/510–0422, 0294/510–0432* ⊕ *www.lepassagetoindia.com* ✉ *Shop 04, Geeta Ashram Rd., Hanuman Circle, Jaisalmer* ☎ *299/225–0355, 299/225–0354* ⊕ *www.lepassagetoindia. com* ✉ *Airport Rd., Ratananda circle, opposite R.S.E.B. substation, Jodhpur* ☎ *291/251–0859* ⊕ *www.lepassagetoindia.com.* **Parul Tours and Travels.** ✉ *32 Lal Ghat, opposite Kankarwa Haveli, Udaipur* ☎ *0294/242–1697* ⊕ *www. rajasthantravelbycab.com.* **Royal Desert Safaris.** In Jaisalmer, Royal Desert Safari organizes treks, camel safaris, and nights in the desert around Bikaner, Jodhpur, and Jaisalmer, as well as visits to traditional villages, craftspeople's homes, little-known fairs, and ashrams. ✉ *Nachna Haveli, Gandhi Chowk, Jaisalmer* ☎ *2992/252–538* ⊕ *www.campsandsafaries.com.* **Savaari Car Rentals.** Book cars online, including airport pickups, short-distance city driving, or long hauls. ☎ *904/545–0000* ⊕ *www.savaari.com.* **Virasat Exeriences.** Run by enterprising local youths, this company organizes meticulously designed walking tours that bring alive diverse elements of the city's living heritage that underpin the main monuments. The off-beat tours—a leisurely two- to three-hour walk, including a break for tea and food sampling—begin (morning and evening) at the heart of the old walled "Pink" city, and explore hidden, derelict, abandoned homes, temples, monuments, and buildings. The knowledgeable guides point out living crafts, culture, and traditional cuisines (including sweet making) with a historical perspective, and walks can be customized to specific interests. The fee includes all admission fees, temple donations, food sampling and tea; tip of Rs. 100 per person, to a maximum Rs. 500 for a group, is customary. Virisat Experiences also organize tours in Jodhpur and Udaipur. Book at least one day ahead. ✉ *Om Niwas Hotel, E-23 Kaushalya Marg, Bani Park, Jaipur* ☎ *141/510–9090, 941/406–6260 Vipul, 966/720–0797 Akshay* ⊕ *www. virasatexperiences.com* 💳 *Rs. 1500.*

VISITOR INFORMATION

Many hotels provide regional information and travel services. In Jaipur, Jodhpur, Udaipur, and Jaisalmer the Tourist Information Centers of the Rajasthan Tourism Development Corporation (RTDC) provide information, travel assistance, and guides and are open from 10 am to 6 pm. *Jaipur Vision* and the *Jaipur City Guide*, available in most hotels, are periodicals with visitor information and up-to-date phone numbers.

Festivals in Rajasthan

The dates of most of Rajasthan's festivals are determined using the Hindu calendar, so timing varies from year to year.

Jodhpur's RIFF (Rajasthan International Folk Festival) and Jodhpur's Marwar Festival is usually in late October or November.

The Jaipur Literature Festival in January attracts authors from around the world and is considered one of the most vibrant book festivals in the world, given its size, location and the number of people attending; speakers have ranged from the Dalai Lama to Amartya Sen, Oprah Winfrey, Michael Ondaatje, Orhan Pamuk, Pico Iyer, Gloria Steinem, V S Naipaul (expected 2015), Jhumpa Lahiri, Jonathan Franzen, Ved Mehta, William Dalrymple, and Tom Stoppard.

Tourist Offices Rajasthan Tourism Development Corporation ✉ *Paryatan Bhawan, Khasa Kothi Hotel Campus, M.I. Rd., Jaipur* ☎ *141/511–0598, 141/515–5100* ⊕ *www.rajasthantourism.gov.in.*

PLANNING YOUR TIME

The ideal way to see Rajasthan is first to fly to Jaipur, Jodhpur, or Udaipur and then tackle nearby towns by train, bus, or private car. Ideally you should start at Jaipur, make your way around by car, and end up in Udaipur, from where you can fly to Mumbai or Delhi. Overnight train journeys between major cities in air-conditioned sleeper coaches are a cheap way to travel without wasting too much time or money on hotel stays. For instance, you could also start in Jaipur and work your way to Udaipur, then to Jodhpur, Jaisalmer, and back to Delhi via Jodhpur.

EXPLORING RAJASTHAN

You could easily spend months in Rajasthan. The state's southwestern corner centers on Udaipur, a hilly town of palaces and artificial lakes, with the nearby hill station of Mount Abu, while central Rajasthan is anchored by Jodhpur, home to a glorious fort and the eye-catching blue houses, said to be of the Brahmin caste. Jaipur, the state capital, is in the east, toward Delhi. Western Rajasthan, largely given over to the Thar Desert, can best be explored via camel or jeep from the golden city of Jaisalmer. In the northeast, between Jaipur and Delhi, the Shekhawati region is home to lovely painted havelis, the mansions of prosperous merchants. The southern and eastern regions also have a number of good wildlife parks.

Dancers at Jaisalmer's Desert Festival

JAIPUR AND NEARBY

Jaipur, the state capital, is worth a few days' visit: it's a delightful mixture of modernity and folk tradition. Don't be surprised to see camels pulling carts on the main streets, mingling with vehicular traffic. With its towering forts and impressive city palace, Jaipur is a good indicator of what to expect as you progress to interior Rajasthan. It's also a good base from which to visit other towns and parks in the region. The craft villages of Sanganer and Bagru, just outside Jaipur, are populated almost entirely by artisans, and you're free to stop in and watch them make fine paper and block-print textiles by hand. The Hindu pilgrimage town of Pushkar is known for its annual camel festival, held in November or sometimes slightly earlier. For an unusual experience, take a short overnight trip out of Jaipur to Bundi, as famous for its intricate stepwells and charming little lanes as it is for being one of Rudyard Kipling's former residences and the place that inspired him to write *Kim*. To escape civilization altogether, go bird-watching at Bharatpur's Keoladeo National Park or on a tiger safari at Ranthambhore (which may or may not result in spotting a tiger).

JAIPUR

261 km (162 miles) southwest of Delhi; 343 km (213 miles) east of Jodhpur; 405 km (252 miles) northeast of Udaipur.

There is a Rajasthani proverb that asks, *"Je na dekhyo Jaipario, To kal men akar kya kario?"* ("What have I accomplished in my life, if I have not seen Jaipur?").

The Brave Rajputs

For centuries, many Hindu Rajputs valiantly resisted invasion, including attempts by the Muslim Mughals. Their codes of battle emphasized honor and pride, and they went to war prepared to die. When defeat and killing of their men folk on the battlefield was imminent, the Rajput women would perform the rite of *jauhar*, throwing themselves onto a flaming pyre en masse rather than live with the indignity of capture. With the exception of the princes of Mewar, major Rajput states like Jaipur, Bikaner, Bundi, and Kota eventually gave up, stopped fighting and built strong ties with the Mughals. The Mughal emperor Akbar was particularly skilled at forging alliances with the Rajputs. Those kingdoms who sided with Akbar quickly rose in importance and prosperity.

"THE VICTORY BELONGS TO AKBAR"

Raja Man Singh I of Jaipur was the first to marry his aunt to Akbar. As the emperor's brother-in-law and trusted commander-in-chief, Man Singh led Mughal armies to many victories, and both rulers benefited immensely. A traditional saying: *"Jeet Akbar ki, loot Man Singh ki"* translates as "The victory belongs to Akbar, the loot to Man Singh." In addition to securing wealth, these marriages opened the Rajput households to the Mughals' distinctive culture. The same people who initially sacrificed their lives to resist the Mughals quickly adapted themselves to Mughal domination and were influenced by Mughal aesthetics.

A GOLDEN AGE

Skilled craftsmen from the Mughal courts were enticed to Rajasthan to start craft schools, fomenting what would become a golden age of Indian art and architecture. The Mughals' influence in Rajasthan is still visible in everything from food to architecture, from intricate miniature paintings to musical styles, and from clothing to the tradition of *purdah* (covering the head and face with a veil).

DECLINE

The beginning of the 18th century marked the decline of the Mughal period, and with it came the decline of the Rajputs. The incoming British took advantage of the prevailing chaos. The princes made treaties with the British in 1818 and were allowed to govern with a deceptive sovereignty. As a result, Rajasthan escaped overt colonization. The British introduced significant administrative, legal, and educational changes in Rajasthan, and exposed the Rajputs to new levels of excess. The influence extended to Rajput children: sons were sent to English universities, and daughters to finishing schools in Switzerland.

DEFENDING THE RAJ

While the rest of India launched its struggle for independence, many Rajput princes ended up defending the Raj. Unwilling to give up their luxury and power, they did their best to suppress rebellion outside their own kingdoms by sending soldiers to help the British forces. When India became independent, the Rajput princes and kings merged their kingdoms into one state as part of the new nation, but they were allowed to keep the titles to their palaces, forts, lands, and other possessions.

Flanked on three sides by the rugged Aravali Hills, and celebrated for the striking, if somewhat run-down, pinkish buildings in the old part of the city, Jaipur is the capital of Rajasthan and these days a big city, modernizing very fast, and a good starting point for a trip through the region. It's a spirited place: a jumble of colorful Jaipuri natives attired in traditional clothes—*ghagha-ras* (skirts), complex turbans, and sturdy *jutis* (pointed shoes)—side-walk shops overflowing with pot-tery and dyed or sequined fabric, and streets packed with camel carts, cycle-rickshaws, and wandering cows. The salmon-color Old City

ROYALTY TURNS TO REALTY

After India's independence in 1947, the royal families of Rajas-than found it difficult to maintain their imposing forts and regal palaces without the special privi-leges they enjoyed under British rule. Now many of these beautiful palaces have been converted into five-star hotels—a creative way to maintain some of these historic sights while offering a taste of royal living to those who can afford it, be it only for a night.

is where you'll spend most of your time: most of the sights you'll want to see are here, and it's full of appealing bazaars with colorful textiles and trinkets—look for *lac* (resin) bangles, steel utensils, and copper ornaments—and *mehndi* (henna) artists as well umpteen places to have snacks or tall glasses of lassi. Mirza Ismail (or M.I. Road as it's popularly known) is the main drag. It's a bit touristy and rather hectic in the Old City, so be prepared to deal with noise, chaos, a lot of touts and bargain hard if you want to purchase something at one of the bazaars.

Jaipur was named after Maharaja Sawai Jai Singh II, an avid scientist, architect, and astronomer who founded the city in 1727 when he moved down from Amber, the ancient rockbound stronghold of his ancestors. It's known for being one of the first planned cities in the world. Part of the city is still enclosed in 20-foot-high fortified walls, which have eight gates.

GETTING HERE AND AROUND

Although you can fly to Jaipur, most people get here either by train or road. The train station and the city's main bus stand are less than half a mile apart, so if you don't have much luggage and need to transfer from a bus to train, or vice versa, you can easily walk from one to another.

To get around in the city, auto-rickshaws are your best bet although prebooked cabs, though slightly more expensive are hassle-free and air-conditioned; cycle-rickshaws are equally good for short distances especially in the old city—just be sure to negotiate a fare before you climb aboard. Note that parts of the walled Pink City get very con-gested during rush hours, so you may find it easier to walk through this part of town.

TIMING

Two full days is enough to take in many of Jaipur's major sights, with a little bit of time left over for shopping. You could easily, however, extend your stay here to three or four days, and take day or overnight trips to smaller towns in the surrounding regions.

Jal Mahal

Samrat Gate

Zorawar Sing Gate

Gangapol Gate

RAMACHANTRA COLONY

Moti Katra Bazaar

Hawa Mahal Bazaar

Chota Niias Road

Ramgani Bazaar

Haldion ka Rasta

Surajpol Bazaar

GHST DARWAZA

Suraj Pol Gate

Gangauri Bazaar

Gandha Gali Ka Rasta

Rasta Balaji Ki Kothi

Agra Road

JANTA COLONY

Ghat Gate

Nahargani Bazaar

NH 8 Bypass Road

ADARSH NAGAR

Adarsh Nagar Rd.

Govind Marg

Ghat Ki Guni

TO → GALWAR BAGH

NH 8 Bypass Rd.

Exploring ▼

Hotels & Restaurants ▼

5

KEY

1 *Exploring*

① *Hotels & Restaurants*

ESSENTIALS

Taxi Companies **Meru Cabs** ☎ *141/4422–4422.* **Metro Cabs** ☎ *141/424– 4411* ⊕ *www.metrocabs.in.* **Ola Cabs** ☎ *141/335–53355.*

Tourist Offices **Government of Rajasthan Tourist Office** ✉ *Paryatan Bhawan, Khasa Kothi Hotel Campus, M.I. Rd.* ☎ *141/511–0598* ⊕ *www. rajasthantourism.gov.in.*

EXPLORING

TOP ATTRACTIONS

FAMILY

Fodor's Choice

★

Amber (Amer) Fort and Palace. Surrounded by ramparts, this dramatically beautiful fortress is perched on a hill near the rippleless Maota Lake and grows more alluring as you approach it. Raja Man Singh began building it in 1592; Mirza Raja Jai Singh and Sawai Jai Singh continued the construction over a period of 125 years. For centuries the fortress was the capital of the Kachhawah Rajputs, but when the capital shifted to Jaipur in the early 18th century, the site was abandoned. Although the fort is in ruins, the interior palaces, gardens, and temples retain much of their pristine beauty. Both the art and the architecture combine Rajput and Mughal influences in felicitous ways; the old rainwater harvesting and lifting systems have been renovated and are particularly worth a look. You approach the palace complex by walking or, if you arrive very early, by riding an elephant (available from 7 am until 11 am only, Rs. 800 for two) up an incline to the **Singh Pole** gate and **Jaleb Chowk,** the preliminary courtyard—or you can drive up from the rear end into Jaleb Chowk. Try to leave your hotel for Amer by 8:15 and reaching the fort entrance by 8:45 to beat both the heat and crowds, and see the elephant parade. You will then need to set aside just an hour to tour the fort. ■ TIP→ To get the most from your visit, pick up an audio guide at the ticket window.

Two flights of stairs lead up from Jaleb Chowk; to start, skip the one leading to the Shiladevi Temple and take the one leading directly to the palace. In the next courtyard, the pillared **Diwan-i-Am** (Hall of Public Audience) contains alabaster panels with fine inlay work—the kind of craftsmanship for which Jaipur is famous. Typical of the Mughal period, the rooms are small and intimate, whereas the palace's successive courtyards and narrow passages are characteristically Rajput. In one corner is an interesting hamam (Turkish bath) area.

One of the elaborately carved and painted gates is known as **Ganesh Pol,** after the elephant god Ganesh. From a latticed corridor above it, the queen—always in purdah, or hiding—would await the king's return from battle and sprinkle scented water and flowers down upon him. Each room shows some vestige of its former glory, especially the **Sheesh Mahal** (Palace of Mirrors), with glittering mirror work on the ceiling. Narrow flights of stairs lead up to the lavish royal apartments, and beyond the corridors and galleries there'll find the small, elegant **Char Bagh** garden. Take in the views of the valley, the palace courtyards, the formal gardens abutting the octagonal pool next to the lake, and the vast **Jaigarh Fort,** the ancient fortress on the crest of the hill above you. Also on the upper floor is **Jas Mandir,** a hall with filigreed marble *jalis* (screens) and delicate mirror and stuccowork.

On your way out, peek into the 16th-century **Shiladevi Temple** to the goddess Kali, with its silver doors and marble carvings. Raja Man Singh installed the image of the goddess after bringing it here from lower Bengal (now Bangladesh). Exit the palace by the gate near the temple, and just a few minutes down the road is the 16th-century **Jagat Shiromani** temple. Dedicated to Krishna, this exquisitely carved marble-and-sandstone temple was built by Raja Man Singh I in memory of his son. Amer village has several other old temples and buildings. Within the fort is a cafe and a few legitimate government-run handicraft stores. ✉ *Delhi Rd., 11 km (7 miles) north of Jaipur, Amber* ☎ *141/253–0844, 141/253–1042, 141/253–0293* ⊕ *www.rajasthantourism.gov.in* ✉ *Rs. 200; camera and video free; sound-and-light show Rs. 200* ☉ *Daily 8–5:30; sound-and-light shows daily 7:30 pm (English) or 8:30 pm (Hindi).*

City Palace. This complex of pavilions, courtyards, and chambers was begun by Jai Singh II in 1727, and wings were added by later maharajas. If you're standing in the outer courtyard, the marble and sandstone building directly in front of you is the **Mubarak Mahal** (Guest Pavilion), built by Maharaja Madho Singh in the late 19th century. Now a museum, it's an ideal place to admire at close range some of the royals' finest brocades, silks, and hand-blocked garments and robes, many made in nearby Sanganer and some dating from as far back as the 17th century. The collection also includes musical instruments. The **armory** in the northwest corner of the courtyard has one of India's best collections of arms and weapons, including an 11-pound sword belonging to Akbar's Rajput general. Some of the paints used on the beautiful, 18th-century ceiling are believed to have been made from crushed semiprecious stones. The **Bhaggi Khana** (carriage museum) offers a peek into the royal family's horse-drawn vehicles and palanquins.

In the inner courtyard, through the gateway guarded by two stone elephants, is the art gallery, housed in the cavernous **Diwan-i-Am** (Hall of Public Audience). Built in the late 18th century, the building has a magnificent, vintage-1930s painted ceiling, rows of gray marble columns inside the courtyard, the second-largest chandelier in India, and two silver pots so large that they are mentioned in the *Guinness Book of World Records*. The art includes scores of miniatures from the Mughal and various Rajput schools, rare manuscripts, and 17th-century carpets from the Amber Palace. From the inner courtyard, enter the Zenana (ladies') courtyard on the left to see the seven-story **Chandra Mahal** (Moon Palace). Built by Jai Singh II, this attractive cream-color building was the official residence of the last maharaja, "Bubbles" (bestowed that nickname by his British nanny because of the amount of champagne that was consumed when he was born in 1931)—Lieutenant Colonel Sawai Bhawani Singh—who passed away in 2011; his family still lives on the upper floors. The ground floor, that is open to visitors, has sumptuous chandeliers, murals, and a painting of an old maharaja. ⚠ Watch out for touts claiming that you need a guide to tour the palace—you don't. There are official guides available for Rs. 200 and audio guides for Rs. 90 in eight languages at the ticket window. ✉ *Center of Old City, enter complex at Virendra Pole gate, Pink City* ✉ *Palace Rs.*

300; camera free; video camera Rs. 200 ☉ *Daily 9:30–5 (last tickets sold before 5).*

Hawa Mahal. Jaipur's photogenic Palace of Winds was built by Maharaja Sawai Pratap Singh in 1799 so that the women of the court (the zenana) could discreetly take some air and watch the activity on the street below. Every story has semi-octagonal overhanging windows, and each has a perforated screen. This curious five-story structure, named after the westerly winds that blow cool breezes through the 953 windows, or *jharokas,* is just one room wide, so the wind easily passes through the building and cools the interior (servants also threw water on the lattice, so any breeze would be cooled by the water, and would lower the temperature). The building facade has a delicate honeycomb design with close to 1,000 windows, and is fashioned from pink sandstone. If you are short of time you don't necessarily have to go into the *mahal,* though viewing it from the outside is most striking at sunset or sunrise. The entrance is at the side. ⊠ *Sireh Deorhi Bazaar, Pink City* ☎ *141/261–8862* 🎫 *Rs. 50 (free Mon.)* ☉ *Sat.–Thurs. 9–4.*

NEED A BREAK?

Laxmi Misthan Bhandar. LMB is a sweet shop famous all over Rajasthan for its fresh and sumptuous sweets, including *ghevar* (a flour-based disc-shaped cake), *mave ki kachori* (a milk and raisin and nut-filled pastry), *churma, pheeni,* and savory snacks like *raj kachori* and samosa, though the sugar-laden delicacies may be a bit too sweet for the average foreign visitor. LMB also has a famous but mildly shabby vegetarian restaurant adjoining the sweet shop. The *shahi* (royal) thali has an impressive 15 items. ⊠ *Johari Bazaar, Ajmer Rd., Behind Hawa Mahal, Pink City* ☎ *141/256–5844.*

Jantar Mantar. The scholarly Sawai Jai Singh II was well aware of European developments in the field of astronomy and wanted to create one of the world's finest observatories. He supervised the design and construction of five remarkable facilities in northern India, of which this is the largest and best preserved. Built in 1726 out of masonry, marble, and brass, it's neatly laid out and equipped with simple solar instruments called *yantras,* which look like large, abstract sculptures, and are remarkably precise in measuring complex celestial data like time, the location of stars, angles of planets, and predicting forthcoming eclipses. Such accuracy was desired for creating astrological predictions. If you don't have a guide with you, try to recruit one to explain how these devices work, as they're fascinating and, for nonscientists, somewhat complicated. Avoid the observatory at noon, as it can be very hot. ⊠ *Tripoliya Bazaar, near entrance to City Palace, Pink City* ☎ *141/261–0494* ⊕ *www.rajasthantourism.gov.in* 🎫 *Observatory Rs. 200; camera free* ☉ *Daily 9–4:30.*

Nahargarh Fort. The scenic hilltop location of Naharharh Fort provides breathtaking views of Jaipur and its natural defenses. One of the main reasons to arrive here after doing a round of Jaigarh and Amer, a few kilometers away, is to take in the views. Initially built by Sawai Jai Singh in 1734, it was enlarged to its sprawling, present-day glory in 1885

by Sawai Madho Singh, who commandeered it as a lookout point. Cannons placed behind the walls recall the days when artillery was positioned against potential attackers below. During the 1857 revolt, several Britishers took refuge here. The palace of nine queens—with nine separate apartments for the wives of Maharaja Ram Singh—within the fort is also worth a short visit. ⊠ *10 km (6 miles) north of Jaipur off Amber Rd.* ☎ *141/513–4038, 141/513–7686* ⊕ *www.rajasthantourism.gov.in* ☑ *Rs. 50; camera fee Rs. 30; video camera fee Rs. 70* ☉ *Fort daily sunrise–sunset; palace daily 10–5:30.*

WHAT'S WITH THE PINK?
The buildings of Jaipur were originally colored yellow, which you can still see on the backs of the buildings—the capital was painted pink (really more of a salmon color), however, when Prince Albert, consort of Queen Victoria, visited India in the middle of the 19th century. The idea stuck, and by law buildings in the Old City must still be painted pink. As a result Jaipur is commonly referred to as the Pink City.

5

WORTH NOTING

Albert Hall Museum. The oldest museum in Jaipur, inside the Ram Niwas Bagh, is worth a visit just for its breathtaking architecture—the sandstone-and-marble 19th-century Indo-Saracenic-style building was designed by Sir Samuel Swinton Jacob, the father of that movement that merged popular Indian and Victorian architecture of that era, and who was one of Rajasthan's great builders (he built the Rambagh Palace as well). Named in honor of Victoria's son Prince Albert (who became Edward VII) who came visiting shortly after it was built, the exteriors and gardens offer a glimpse of what the then New Jaipur (completed circa 1887) was like. The museum's enormous collection includes folk arts, miniature paintings, textiles pottery, traditional costumes, marble carvings, coins, musical instruments, ivory, and visual explanations of Indian culture and traditions. ⊠ *In Ram Niwas Gardens, Adarsh Nagar* ☎ *141/257–0099* ⊕ *alberthalljaipur.gov.in* ☑ *Rs. 150; audio tour Rs. 124; camera free* ☉ *Daily 9–5.*

Chokhi Dhani. About a 45-minute drive from Jaipur, this large replica cultural village (⇨ *See also Jaipur's Village Complexes*) includes a huge buffet meal in the admission price, consisting of pretty much every regional vegetarian dish you can imagine as well as a huge selection of sugary desserts. Come hungry and expect to sit on benches or on the floor in a lantern-lit hut to eat. If you are uncomfortable sitting on the floor there is inside seating at chairs and tables in a/c comfort. Performance tents and clearings around the compound host a vibrant Rajasthani pageant—traditional dances, including the dramatic fire dance, folk singing, *katputli* (puppet shows), and juggling. Tipping is discouraged. Camel and elephant rides are available for an extra fee, and there are plenty of vendors selling every type of Rajasthani tchotchke under the sun; salesmen can be irritatingly pushy. There's a less interesting hotel on-site, although not in authentic village style—it's much more luxurious—and its restaurant and bar, serving regular Indian fare, offer an alternative to the buffet. It gets very busy at weekends and holidays. ⊠ *Tonk Rd.,*

19 km (12 miles) south of Jaipur via town of Vatika ☎ 141/516–5000, 141/516–5015 ⊕ www.chokhidhani.com ✉ Rs. 500 alfresco and Rs. 700 a/c, including dinner and cultural show ☉ Daily 5:30 pm–11 pm.

Jaigarh Fort. Originally the royal treasury, this dramatic-looking fort has large water tanks for storing rainwater that's been channeled down the hill from imposing Nahargarh. There are fantastic views of Jaipur from the watchtower. Star attraction of the fort is the Jaivana Tope, the largest wheeled cannon in the world, measuring over 20 feet long and weighing in at around 50 tons. The mighty Jaivana was unsurpassed for power in its day; one of its cannon balls was found 35 km (22 miles) from here. This fort was responsible for the defence of Amer Fort (which is at a lower elevation) and its armory and museum showcases the weaponry it once had as well as photographs. Guides are available at the entrance—an English-speaking one will charge about Rs. 100. For a small fee you can enter the fort and reach the top (where the cannon is) by car and save yourself a long, uphill walk. ✉ *About 7 km (4 miles) from Jaipur, off Amber Rd.* ☎ *141/267–1848* ✉ *Fort Rs. 85; camera fee Rs. 50; video camera fee Rs. 200; vehicle Rs. 50* ☉ *Daily 9–4:30.*

Jawahar Kala Kendra. Jaipur's center for arts and crafts was founded by the state government with a specific vision: to create a space for understanding and experiencing culture and folk traditions amid the chaos of urban life. The center also hosts occasional theatrical and musical performances. You can drop by to meet some of the locals who exhibit and perform here, or just to collect information on cultural events. ✉ *Jawaharlal Nehru Marg, opposite Jhalana Institutional Area, Moti Dhungri* ⊕ *jawaharkalakendra.rajasthan.gov.in* ☉ *Daily 10–6; concerts some evenings; offices weekdays only.*

Kanak Vrindavan Gardens. This picturesque set of gardens and temples is just below the majestic Amber and Nahargarh forts and is nearly 300 years old. It was established by Jaipur maharaja Sawai Jai Singha. From here you can get a good look at the Jal Mahal Palace in Man Sagar Lake. The gardens also make a great picnic spot, especially if you like to people-watch. A few Bollywood films have been shot here, such as the famous romantic film *Lamhe*. ✉ *Amber Rd., Man Sagar* ✉ *Rs. 15.* ☉ *Daily 9–7.*

Sisodia Rani ka Bagh. On highway NH 11 that heads to Bharatpur and Agra stands one of many palaces built for the *ranis*, or queens, of Sawai Jai Singh II. Built in 1728, the palace, though in a state of disrepair, still looks lovely against the backdrop of hills. The palace is furnished with murals illustrating hunting scenes and the romantic legend of Krishna and Radha, while the terraced Mughal gardens are dotted with fountains and frequented by prancing peacocks and monkeys. Stop by on your way down the Bharatpur-Agra road. ✉ *8 km (5 miles) east of Jaipur on road to Bharatpur* ✉ *Rs. 50* ☉ *Daily 8–6.*

WHERE TO EAT

$$

INDIAN

✕ **Copper Chimney.** Taking its name from the faux copper chimney at its center, this mildly faded restaurant has a loyal clientele of business people and international tourists. It is best known for its standard heavy, North Indian dishes and kebab starters. The *mutter paneer* (peas

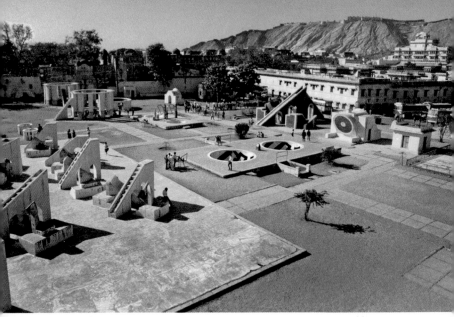

The Jantar Mantor Observatory in Jaipur

with cheese) with butter *naan* and *handi* meat (slow-cooked mutton), *rogan josh* (Kashmiri-style spiced, buttered mutton) is exceptional. This is also a good place to try the traditional *laal maas* (mutton in gravy), Rajasthani-style *kadai* chicken (cooked in a heavy wok, and spicy), or *tandoor* (clay oven) meat dishes. The nine-item vegetarian or non-vegetarian *thali* (Rs. 440) is good value for money. Alcohol is served. $ *Average main: Rs. 450* ✉ *Maya Mansion, M.I. Rd., near G.P.O., Panch Batti* ☎ *141/237–2275.*

$

SOUTH INDIAN

✕ **Dasaprakash.** This glass- and wood–dominated environment is the best place to tuck into South Indian specialties such as *dosas, idlis, upma,* and *vadas,* piping hot. *Thalis* (a set selection of dishes) offer great value for money. $ *Average main: Rs. 170* ✉ *5, Kamal Mansion, M.I. Rd., Panch Batti* ☎ *141/237–1313* ⊕ *www.dasaprakash.in* ◷ *Daily 11–11.*

$$$$

INTERNATIONAL

✕ **Frangipani.** The sumptuous Mughal-style gardens of Taj's Jai Mahal Palace are the site of an *alfresco* barbecue restaurant—the Frangipani—that only opens in the evenings. The many frangipani bushes nearby was the inspiration for its name. It is open from October to March when the weather is pleasant. For approximately $30 per head they offer unlimited, eclectic selection of barbecue and grill delights like rosemary lamb chops, fish *kasundi* (fish marinated in mustard), *achari gobhi* (pickled grilled cauliflower), *seekh kabab* (minced mutton kebab), button mushrooms in pesto, barbecue chicken legs, prawn *shaslik* (kebabs) and more, as well as soups, salad and dessert $ *Average main: Rs. 1800* ✉ *Jai Mahal Palace, Jacob Rd., Civil Lines, Jaipur* ☎ *141/660–1111* ⊕ *www.tajhotels.com* ⚑ *Reservations essential* ◷ *Closed Apr.–Sept..*

Jaipur's Village Complexes

Rajasthan is a largely rural state, and the local villages still maintain unique lifestyles, with traditional entertainments and ways of life. It's a fascinating other world from what Westerners are used to. Travelers with little time and limited personal contact with the locals, though, aren't generally going to get invited to an authentic village to see how people really live—and language barriers can be an issue if you do. A popular alternative is to visit what is known as "village complexes," essentially artificial replicas of the real thing that feature souvenir stands, cultural entertainment programs, and regional cuisine. Popular with Indian and overseas tourists alike, these villages feel a bit like theme parks, but the cuisine and traditional entertainment is authentic, so they're quite worthwhile. A good one to visit when you're in Jaipur is Chokhi Dhani. Chokhi Dhani is a large, over-the-top complex that has a feast of local delicacies and entertainment in the admission price, but there is an extra charge for camel and elephant rides—and, of course, there will be shopping opportunities.

$$$
INDIAN
×**Indiana.** Off one of Jaipur's main arteries, MI road, this garden restaurant offers continental, Indian and Chinese cuisine. The restaurant attracts tourists more for its open-air ambience and Rajasthani dances (nightly at 7 pm) than for the food, though their boneless butter chicken is justifiably well known. Dishes tend to be mild in deference to non-Indian visitors: if you like spice, request it. ⑤ *Average main: Rs. 600* ✉ *J2-34 Mahaveer Marg* ☎ *141/236–2061, 141/236–2062* ⊕ *www.indianajaipur.com.*

$
NORTH INDIAN
×**Natraj.** This all-vegetarian restaurant, popular with locals, is a terrific place for Indian tea and dessert, although it's a little rough around the edges, and one of the few places open for breakfast—if you're in the mood for stuffed *paranthas* (whole wheat flatbread) or *idlis* (South Indian steamed rice cakes). They serve up many types of *thalis* with a good assortment of vegetables and breads—one of the best on M.I. Road and good value. No alcohol is served. ⑤ *Average main: Rs. 300* ✉ *6, M.I. Rd., just past Panch Batti* ☎ *141/237–5804, 141/510–2804.*

$$$
INTERNATIONAL
×**Niros.** This Jaipur institution might be the most popular restaurant among the upper middle class and one of the city's oldest restaurants. Amid mirrors (on the ceiling, too), dimmed lights, and marble floors, it serves decent Indian and Chinese food, as well as continental dishes. Specialties include *reshmi* kebab (skewered boned chicken), *paneer tikka* (soft Indian cheese with skewered tomatoes, onions, and green peppers), and chicken and mutton *tikka masala* (simmered in a spicy tomato-and-butter sauce). They serve beer and wine, or try a cold coffee topped with ice cream. During peak tourist season reservations are advisable. There are seats outside if you have to wait for a table. ⑤ *Average main: Rs. 600* ✉ *M.I. Rd., next to Bank of Baroda, Panch Batti* ☎ *141/237–4493, 141/221–8520* ⊕ *www.nirosindia.com.*

Important residents hanging out in front of the wall to Jaipur's Old City

$$$$
NORTH INDIAN
Fodor's Choice
★

✕**Peshawri.** Considered one of the city's best (and most expensive) restaurants, Peshwari entices with melt-in-your-mouth, exquisitely spiced and marinated kebabs and other northwest frontier foods. The dining area has an outdoorsy, *dhaba* look—wood beams, shining copper platters, and pots hang on the walls and seating is at log tables matched with stools. Other menu highlights include *paneer tikka, chicken makhani,* and the *dal bukhara,* served with an assortment of *rotis* and *naans.* Part of ITC, a luxury hotel chain known for its excellent cuisine, Peshwari has branches in other cities in India. ⑤ *Average main: Rs. 2000 ⊠ Palace Rd.* ☎ *141/510–0100* ⊕ *www.itchotels.in* ⌂ *Reservations essential.*

$$
SOUTH INDIAN

✕**Rainbow.** An upgraded *dhaba* (roadside eatery), this unprepossessing spot located on the way to Amer Fort is an attractive and convenient stop after a heavy morning of fort-viewing. Air-conditioned and kept spotlessly clean by its house-proud and attentive owners, it serves north Indian specials like *palak paneer* (spinach with cottage cheese), garlic *naan, kadhi pakoda* (yogurt curry with chickpea dumplings), *achari aloo* (spiced potatoes), vegetable curry (stuffed potato dumplings in gravy) on its mostly vegetarian menu. ⑤ *Average main: Rs. 300 ⊠ 72, near post office, Ramgarhmod, Amer Rd.* ☎ *141/267–2237* ⊕ *www. rainbowmulticuisine.com.*

$$$
CAFÉ

✕**Steam.** The pizzas here are as memorable as the locale—the restaurant is located within the bogeys (rail compartments) of an out-of-service steam-engine-driven train surrounded by a mock platform. Hop aboard the train or dine on the Victorian-era platform on Mediterranean or Mexican bites (quesadillas, burritos) or pastas or pizza, surrounded by black-and-white historical train photographs. Try the mandarin *kulfi* (a frozen dairy dessert). It is on the grounds of the Rambagh Palace hotel. ⑤ *Average main: Rs. 750* ✉ *Rambagh Palace, Bhawani Singh Rd.* ☎ *141/385–5700* ⊕ *www.tajhotels.com* ⚷ *Reservations essential* ⊘ *Daily 7 pm–midnight.*

$$$$
INDIAN
Fodor'sChoice
★

✕ **Suvarna Mahal.** Once the maharaja's throne room, this grand hall has a soaring, frescoed ceiling, tapestry-covered walls, carvings, gold-plated silverware, and a staff eager to elaborate on the history and decor as well as the menu. It is easily one of India's most elegant restaurants and service is impeccable. The specialties are dishes from the royal kitchens of Hyderabad, Punjab, Awadh, and, of course, Rajasthan; try *murgh tikka zaffrani* (chicken marinated in yogurt and saffron and cooked in a tandoor) and *dahi ka mass* (lamb cooked in a yogurt-base curry) or *sikandari raan* (leg of lamb). The Hyderabadi biryani is divine. ⑤ *Average main: Rs. 2000* ✉ *Rambagh Palace, Bhawani Singh Rd., Rambagh* ☎ *141/221–1919* ⊕ *www.tajhotels.com* ⚷ *Reservations essential* ⛙ *Jacket and tie* ⊘ *No lunch.*

WHERE TO STAY

$$$
HOTEL
Fodor'sChoice
★

▥ **Alsisar Haveli.** This gorgeous and opulent haveli—one of the most popular family-run heritage hotels in Jaipur—in the heart of the Old City, tucked away in a narrow alley that keeps out urban noise, is a pretty sanctuary with a pool, numerous courtyards, and alcoves in which to chill out. **Pros:** good value; jeep and camel safaris can be arranged; spacious property close to historical sites. **Cons:** some rooms are dark and lighting is a bit depressing; staff can be slow to respond; Wi-Fi only in the lobby. ⑤ *Rooms from: Rs. 7460* ✉ *Sansar Chandra Rd., Chandpol* ☎ *141/236–4685, 141/510–7167, 141/510–7157* ⊕ *www.alsisarhaveli.com* ⇰ *45 rooms* ⑩ *No meals.*

$
HOTEL

▥ **Arya Niwas.** Trusted, reliable, comfortable, and probably the most efficient family-run hotel in Jaipur, the Arya Niwas has that ideal combination of convenience to the heart of the city and cushioning from its noise and chaos. **Pros:** centrally located; value for money; efficient. **Cons:** serves only vegetarian food and no alcohol; busy hotel; bathrooms could be cleaner. ⑤ *Rooms from: Rs. 1859* ✉ *Sansar Chandra Rd., behind Amber Tower, off M.I. Rd.* ☎ *141/407–3450, 141/407–3400* ⊕ *www.aryaniwas.com* ⇰ *91 rooms* ⑩ *No meals.*

$$
HOTEL

▥ **Diggi Palace.** In Jaipur's leafy C-Scheme neighborhood, this is the venue for the famous Jaipur Literature Festival every January; the rest of the year it's a peaceful, intimate and a charming alternative to staying in the rowdy Old City. **Pros:** great value; walking distance to the Old City; lovely atmosphere. **Cons:** Even the high-end rooms lack the opulence it could offer. ⑤ *Rooms from: Rs. 6000* ✉ *Shivaji Marg, Sawai Man Singh Rd., C-Scheme* ☎ *141/237–3091* ⊕ *www.hoteldiggipalace. com* ⇰ *70 rooms, 30 suites* ⑩ *Breakfast.*

$$$
HOTEL

▥ **ITC Rajputana.** The ITC chain's large, sumptuous Rajputana, centrally located, offers luxurious refuge from hectic downtown Jaipur. **Pros:** great dining options, especially the Peshawri; well-priced. **Cons:** slightly impersonal; not a traditional Rajasthani environment. ⑤ *Rooms from: Rs. 9000* ✉ *Palace Rd., Gopalbari* ☎ *0141/510–0100* ⊕ *www.itchotels. in/hotels/itcrajputana.aspx* ⇰ *218 rooms, 16 suites* ⑩ *No meals.*

$$$$
HOTEL

▥ **Jai Mahal Palace.** Built in 1745, and today managed by the Taj group, many rooms at this gracious historic palace hotel overlook 14 acres of lavish Mughal-style gardens. **Pros:** royal, historical environment; tented spas; open-air Frangipani barbecue restaurant; the occasional elephant polo match. **Cons:** expensive. ⑤ *Rooms from: Rs. 16900* ✉ *Jacob Rd., Civil Lines* ☎ *141/660–1111* ⊕ *www.tajhotels.com* ⇨ *100 rooms, 6 suites* ❙○❙ *No meals.*

$$
RESORT
Fodor's Choice
★
🏨 **Neemrana Fort Palace.** This 15th-century Rajput fort, now a heritage hotel, set in 6 acres across many level, is one of the finest retreats in India, perched on a plateau in the Aravali Hills in Alwar district with stunning views. **Pros:** lovely views and stunning sunsets; complimentary morning and afternoon tea with cookies; spa. **Cons:** fixed mealtimes; original building full of stairs and steep ramps; can get crowded on weekends; no room service. ⑤ *Rooms from: Rs. 4000* ✉ *Neemrana village, 150 km (94 miles) north of Jaipur, off NH–8* ☎ *1494/299–900, 11/2435–6145, 11/4666–1666* ⊕ *www.neemranahotels.com* ⇨ *31 rooms, 36 suites* ❙○❙ *Breakfast.*

$$$$
RESORT
Fodor's Choice
★
🏨 **Oberoi Rajvilas.** This fabulous 32-acre luxury retreat, 20 minutes outside Jaipur, is a destination unto itself, whether you want to splash out on a private villa with its own pool, enjoy a spacious standard room, or revel in a romantic luxury tent with rich wood fittings on grounds that are home to hundreds of peacocks. **Pros:** large spa and beautiful pool; impeccable, personal service; lavish breakfasts; **Cons:** expensive; far from the airport; traffic jams hamper getting in and out of Jaipur for sightseeing. ⑤ *Rooms from: Rs. 40539* ✉ *Goner Rd., Babaji-ka-Mod, 18 km (11 miles) from Jaipur* ☎ *141/268–0101* ⊕ *www.oberoihotels. com 71 rooms, 3 villas, 13 tents* ❙○❙ *Breakfast.*

$
B&B/INN
🏨 **Pratap Bhawan Home Stay.** Perfect for foodies, wildlife enthusiasts, and those who like to engage with locals, this cozy homestay, in an upscale residential area, is run by an energetic young couple, the Rathores—one a naturalist who runs wildlife tours, the other a food enthusiast who offers cooking and *rangoli* (a form of folk art) classes. **Pros:** warm, personal service from knowledgeable owners; home cooking; good value. **Cons:** simple, basic facilities; locomotive horns from nearby railroad can disturb light sleepers. ⑤ *Rooms from: Rs. 2500* ✉ *A-4 Pratap Bhawan, Jamnalal Bajaj Marg, C-Scheme* ☎ *98298–74354 cell phone, 98290–74354 cell phone* ⊕ *www.pratapbhawan.com* ⇨ *4 rooms* ❙○❙ *Breakfast.*

$$$$
HOTEL
Fodor's Choice
★
🏨 **Rambagh Palace, Jaipur.** Set on 47 acres of lawns punctuated by arcaded patios with fountains, courtyards, long colonnades, and prancing peacocks, this wistfully romantic palace was one of the first in Jaipur to be converted into a heritage hotel (run by the Taj group) and is one of the most elegant properties in India. **Pros:** lovely original indoor pool and newer outdoor pool; efficient, helpful service; excellent dining options. **Cons:** not walking distance to the tourist sites; Wi-Fi not free; rooms above restaurant can be noisy. ⑤ *Rooms from: Rs. 41000* ✉ *Bhawani Singh Rd., Rambagh* ☎ *141/238–5700* ⊕ *www.tajhotels. com* ⇨ *79 rooms, 33 suites* ❙○❙ *Some meals.*

$$$$
HOTEL
Fodor's Choice
★
🏨 **Samode Haveli.** Hidden amid the lanes of the Pink City, this stately and rambling heritage hotel preserves its Rajasthani character and harbors a few surprises, including elegant gardens and a beautiful open-air pool with pool-side bar. **Pros:** charmingly decorated main dining room; huge rooms; grounds have swings for kids. **Cons:** fancier rooms are very

The Anokhi museum in Jaipur, affiliated with the popular shop, is a great place to learn about Indian textiles.

expensive; vehicle access problematic during rush hours; no Wi-Fi in the rooms. $ *Rooms from: Rs. 13500* ⊠ *Near Gangapole, Pink City* ☎ *141/263–2407, 141/263–2370, 141/263–1942* ⊕ *www.samode.com* ⟳ *39 rooms* ❍❚ *Breakfast.*

$$$$
RESORT
Tree of Life. This haven from the chaos of Jaipur, nestled in the Aravali hills yet within an hour's drive of the city sights, offers secluded villa accommodations, spa treatments, and a chance to interact with the community. **Pros:** professional, personal service by owner and staff; stylish and modern; cooking lessons offered. **Cons:** 15 km from Jaipur; not best suited to one-night stays. $ *Rooms from: Rs. 14700* ⊠ *Delhi–Jaipur Hwy., Kukas, Kacherawala* ☎ *1426/21–7561, 1426/217–562* ⊕ *www.treeofliferesorts.com* ⟳ *13 rooms.*

NIGHTLIFE AND PERFORMING ARTS

If you want a night on the town, your best bet is one of the hotel bars, which are usually open from about 11 am to 3 pm and 7 pm to 11:30 pm. Many hotels stage cultural programs for their guests, such as the dance performances with dinner at the Panghat Lawnt Hall, at the Rambagh Palace.

The Fire Ball (TFB). Hotel nightclubs usually open around dinnertime and shut by midnight, but this place is open 11–11. A local crowd will come here to dance on Saturday (the only night there's a disco); otherwise it's just a pub. They have happy hours with drinks 50% off on certain days. ⊠ *Ramada Hotel, Govind Marg, Raja Park* ☎ *141/406–6666* ⊕ *www.ramadajaipur.com.*

Polo Bar. Sip a choice single malt or savor your cigar in an atmosphere rich in history. Rambagh Palace's Polo Bar is an extremely elegant place to have a drink—vistas of sweeping, peacock-dotted lawns and lots of old photographs that are testimony to Jaipur's long relationship with polo. There's a small fountain inside the bar. ⊠ *Rambagh Palace, Bhawani Singh Rd.* ☎ *141/238–5700* ⊕ *www.tajhotels.com.*

Rajmandir Movie Theater. This historic art deco movie theater is the place to experience Bollywood films. Widely visited by Indian and foreign tourists (the films are in Hindi without subtitles, but you get the gist of the action even if you don't understand the language), Rajmandir is still constantly flooded with locals, who sing, cheer, and whistle throughout each film. Shows are usually at 12:30, 3:30, 6:30, and 9:30, but times may vary by 15 to 30 minutes, according to the length of the film. Tickets for popular new releases sell out quickly on weekends, but you can buy in advance—your hotel reception or concierge should do this for you for a small fee. ⊠ *16 Bhagwandas Rd., next to McDonald's, near Panch Batti* ☎ *141/237–9372, 141/237–4694.*

Ravindra Rang Manch. In the heart of the city, surrounded by gardens, this theater and cultural organization, hosts occasional dinner-and-dance programs. It also plays host to famous classical musicians and theater groups performing Indian classics and epics at the open-air amphitheater, specially during and around Indian festivals like Holi and Diwali. Most are free or with nominal charge; some are by invitation. Programs are listed in local newspapers. ⊠ *Ram Niwas Gardens* ☎ *141/261–9061.*

SHOPPING
ARTS AND CRAFTS
Artchill. This is Jaipur's leading gallery of contemporary art. There's a larger branch with an exhibit area of more than 5,000 square feet, in Amber Fort, with a wide-ranging collection of oil paintings, watercolors, and graphics by eminent artists such as Jatin Das, Arpana Caur, and Paritosh Sen. Open daily. ⊠ *Lakshmi complex, M.I. Rd., Panch Batti* ☎ *141/403–4964, 982/901–1964 cell phone, 141/253–0025* ⊕ *www.artchill.com.*

The Friends. This little gift shop at Johari Bazaar next to Laxmi Mishthan Bhandar has a well-curated selection of small handicrafts that make good gifts and souvenirs. ⊠ *95, Johari Bazaar, Jaipur* ☎ *141/257–2655.*

Khadi Ghar. A good place to pick up practical gifts, this national cooperative sells natural herbal soaps and shampoos, oils, incense, Khadi (hand spun/woven) textiles and clothing, leather goods, and handicrafts. ⊠ *320 M.I. Rd.* ☎ *141/237–3745* ⊗ *Closed Sun.*

Khazana Walon ka Rasta. For specialty shops, wander through this lane in the old Pink City (accessible through Chandpol gate), and watch stone-cutters create artworks in marble. Bargaining is recommended. ⊠ *Chandpol.*

P.M. Allah Buksh and Son. Established in 1880 and still selling the finest hand-engraved, enameled, and embossed brassware—including oversize old trays and historic armor—this is a great place to look for antique metalwork. ⊠ *M.I. Rd., Panch Batti* ☎ *141/401–2786.*

Rajasthali. If you have limited time and lots of gifts to buy or don't relish bargaining, head to this enormous, government-run emporium in the center of Jaipur. It's always flooded with crafts and textiles, though you might have to sift through a bewildering variety before you find what you want. Open from 11 am to 8 pm. ⚠ Be aware that touts and rickshaw drivers may try to take you to fake Rajasthali showrooms, which are privately run by the same name and charge exhorbitant prices. ✉ *M.I. Rd., opposite Ajmeri Gate* ☎ *141/237–2974* ⊕ *www.rajasthali. gov.in* ☽ *Closed Sun..*

Tilak Gitai. A special treat for lovers of miniature paintings is a trip to the home of award-winning artist Tilak Gitai, who creates exquisite miniatures in classic Mughal, Rajput, Pahari, and other styles. Using antique paper, Gitai applies colors made from semiprecious stones, then real gold and silver leaf, in designs so fine he'll give you a magnifying glass to admire them. This is not a quick visit, but it's a great way to spend a few hours with a friendly Rajasthani family and learn about Indian art. Prices start at a few hundred rupees and soar to a few hundred thousand. ✉ *E-5 Gokhle Marg, C-Scheme* ☎ *141/237–2101.*

NEED A BREAK?

Lassiwallah. Across the street from Niros restaurant is the well-known Lassiwallah—on the periphery of a long chain of imposters, the real thing can only be found under the sign "Kishan Lal Govind Narayan Agarwal." It opens early in the morning and you may have to wait behind a line of locals waiting to get their daily glass of lassi. Served in disposable red-clay cups (which means they haven't been washed with unclean water), the delicious lassis come with a dash of hard cream on top. As with any street food, there's no absolute guarantee it is hygienic but the popularity of the place (they sometime sell out by 3) should reassure you. ✉ *M.I. Rd., across from Niros, Panch Batti* ☎ *141/237–8682, 982/902–0356.*

BEAUTY

Forest Essentials. India's answer to L'Occitane is cheaper and has a wide range of ayurvedic as well as naturally made and herbal products, including fragrances, oils, creams, soaps, and skin and beauty products. ✉ *341 M.I. Rd.* ☎ *141/402–9284* ⊕ *www.forestessentialsindia.com.*

JEWELRY

Amrapali Jewels. A favorite among trendy and wealthy Indians for its whimsical silver and ornamental trinkets, as well as semiprecious stone artifacts. ✉ *M.I. Rd., Panch Batti* ☎ *141/237–7940, 141/236–2768* ⊕ *www.amrapalijewels.com.*

Bhuramal-Rajmal Surana Showroom. For precious jewels, including gold ornaments, seek out this showroom, known worldwide for its *kundan* (a glasslike white stone) and *mina* (enamel) work. It has some reasonably priced silver jewelry featuring traditional patterns on contemporary styles. ✉ *368 J.L.N. Marg, Moti Dhungri* ☎ *141/257–0429, 141/257–0430* ⊕ *www.suranas.com.*

Chameli Valon ka Rasta. If you're willing to bargain, head for this lane within the walls of the old city to negotiate for silver and semiprecious jeweled ornaments, trinkets, and small toys. ✉ *Off M.I. Rd.*

CLOSE UP

Shekhawati, Rajasthan's Open-Air Art Gallery

Known as Rajasthan's open-air art gallery because of the frescoes painted on the walls of ornate havelis in the region, Shekhawati—about 160 km (100 miles) from Jaipur or 200 km (124 miles) from Delhi—makes an intriguing stop on the way to Delhi or a day-trip from Jaipur provided one hits the road early. Influenced by the Persian, Jaipur, and Mughal schools of painting, Shekhawati's frescoes, many of which date back to the early 19th century, illustrate subjects ranging from mythological stories and local legends to hunting safaris and scenes of everyday life. You'll even find illustrated experiences with the British and cars or planes. The introduction of photography in 1840 gave Shekhawati's painters still more to work with.

TIME-TESTED TECHNIQUES

The painters were called *chiteras* and belonged to the caste of *kumhars* (potters). Initially, they colored their masterpieces with vegetable pigments; after mixing these with lime water and treating the wall with three layers of a very fine clay, the chiteras painstakingly drew their designs on a last layer of filtered lime dust. Time was short, as the design had to be completed before the plaster dried, but the technique ensured that the images wouldn't fade.

ORNATE BACKDROPS

The havelis themselves are quite spectacular, with courtyards, exquisitely latticed windows, intricate mirror work, vaulted ceilings, immense balconies, and ornate gateways and facades. They date from the British Raj, during which traditional overland trading routes to Central Asia, Europe, and China were slowly superseded by rail and sea routes. Only a handful

of the havelis have survived—some have been restored by their owners, and a few have been converted into hotels. In **Sikar**, formerly the wealthiest trading center, look for the Biyani, Murarka, and Somani havelis. **Lachhmangarh** features the grand Char Chowk Haveli, particularly evocative of the prosperous Marwari lifestyle. In the village of **Churi Ajitgarh**, unusually erotic frescoes are painted behind doors and on bedroom ceilings in the Shiv Narain Nemani, Kothi Shiv Datt, and Rai Jagan Lal Tibrewal havelis. The frescoed temples of **Jhunjhunu** make for interesting comparisons: visit Laxmi Nath, Mertani Baori, Ajeet Sagar, and Qamrudin Shah Ki Dargah Fatehpur. Warrior-statesman Thakur Nawal Singh founded **Nawalgarh** in 1737, and the town has some of the best frescoes in Shekhawati, in the Aath, Anandilal Poddar, Jodhraj Patodia, and Chokhani havelis, as well as at the Roop Niwas Kothi hotel.

HOW TO VISIT

Hire a guide from Delhi or Jaipur, making sure they know the Shekhawati area; get an early start to make the most of your time, and be prepared to spend a lot of time driving from site to site, since the havelis are quite spread out. *The havelis listed above are the ones to prioritize.*

5

Gem Palace. Shop here for Jaipur's best gems and jewelry, and a small collection of museum-quality curios, and you'll join the ranks of a royal clientele that includes Prince Charles and many members of Rajasthan's royal families. Even the princess of Jaipur, Maharani Gayatri Devi, might have been found here bargaining for a good deal. Prices range from US$2 to US$2 million. ⊠ *M.I. Rd., Panch Batti* ☏ *141/237–4175.*

Jaipur Jewellery House. This Johari Bazaar jeweler has an extensive and attractive collection of well-priced silver jewelry especially very unusual earrings with semiprecious stones. They are very polite and patient and do not push you towards buying. Bargain their prices down some. ⊠ *81, Johari Bazaar* ☏ *141/257–5078.*

Motisons. Less a shopping experience and more a Jaipur experience, head here to see the kind of jewelry the city is known for. The showroom, in a phantasmagoric petal-shape modern mahal, has an enormous collection, including high-end pieces. It's considered one of the city's best addresses. The Kundan jewelry is of particular interest. ⊠ *Motisons Tower, Tonk Rd.* ☏ *141/425–2824.*

POTTERY

Jaipur Blue Pottery Art Center. A broad selection of Rajasthan's fetching blue pottery is available here, including a large selection of tiles, bathroom fittings, cups, plates, and decorative items. Clay pots are made on the premises. ⊠ *Amber Rd., near Jain Mandir* ☏ *141/263–0116.*

Neerja International. The blue pottery here is particularly funky—the designer, owner Lela Bordia, has been at the forefront of the movement to keep the craft alive for more than three decades, and has exhibited all over the world. Her wares are made in nearby villages, helping to create jobs in rural areas. ⊠ *Anand Bhawan, Jacob Rd., Civil Lines* ☏ *141/411–2609* ⊕ *www.neerjainternational.com.*

Sakshi. This store has an excellent collection of block-printed cloth items, and you can also watch the printing process happening. Next door is a selection of exquisite blue pottery items including tiles; well priced. ⊠ *Laxmi Colony* ☏ *141/273–1862, 141/263–0116.*

TEXTILES

Fodor'sChoice ★ **Anokhi.** This is a leading shop for elegant ethnic wear, mostly in cotton, some silk, with hand-block prints and paisley patterns. The selection includes both Indian and casual Western and it has the prettiest *lehengas* (skirts) in the state. They have a great range of *kurtis* (short kurtas). You can also get beautiful bedspreads, quilts, and cloth bags here. ⊠ *C-11, KK Sq., Prithviraj Rd., 2nd fl., C-Scheme* ☏ *141/400–7244, 141/400–7245* ⊕ *www.anokhi.com.*

QUICK BITES

Anokhi Cafe. The café attached to the Anokhi store, at C Scheme, is a perfect place for a break, to rest limbs weary from sightseeing or shopping. They serve a variety of cool drinks, chai, and vegetarian quick bites— sandwiches, pizza, and pastas. ⊠ *C-11, KK Sq., Prithviraj Rd., C-Scheme* ☏ *141/400–7244* ⊕ *www.anokhi.com.*

Cottons. Managed and staffed by women, Cottons carries simple, attractive clothes for men and women, as well as small bags, quilts, and

A painted *haveli* in Shekhawati

other decorative household items. Open daily 10–8 (Sunday 11–6:30) ✉ *Hari Bhawan, 4 Achrol House, Jacob Rd., Civil Lines* ☎ *141/222–5481* ⊕ *www.cottonsjaipur.com.*

Fab India. This shop sells great cottons for men, women, children, and the home. They specialize in tailored cottons in vegetable dye prints. You can find men's tropical shirts or kurtas for both sexes, and they do saris as well as silks. Prices for clothing begin at about Rs. 500. Open 10:30–10 daily. ✉ *B-4-E C-Scheme, opposite Gate 4, Prithviraj Rd* ☎ *141/511–5997.*

Krishna Textiles. A wide selection of Rajasthani-printed fabrics by the meter, bedcovers, shawls, pillow covers, and other items are the specialty of Krishna Textiles. Leather bags are also available. ✉ *H-99C RIICO Industrial Area, Mansarovar* ☎ *141/401–9708.*

Salim's Paper. Whatever handmade paper you've seen back home may well have come from Salim's, a factory where you can see each step of the process. Some of the thick, beautiful papers are made with crushed flower petals; it's fun to see them thrown into the mixture of cotton and resin. At their showroom you can buy an enormous range of pretty paper products–gift bags, wrapping paper, gift tags, Christmas stars, albums, and gift boxes. ✉ *Gramodyog Rd.* ☎ *141/273–0222, 141/273–0444, 141/273–333* ⊕ *www.handmadepaper.com.*

Soma. Catering to the ultra-elegant crowd, Soma is filled with vibrant colors. Here you'll find chutneys, clothing for women and children, and decorative fabrics, including fabulous, hand-painted white cloth lamp shades. ✉ *A5, Jamnalal Bajaj Marg, 2nd fl., C-Scheme* ☎ *141/235–2391* ⊕ *www.somashop.com.*

Zari. For exquisite but expensive formal wear embellished with *zari* (silver filigree embroidery), head here. Their *kurtis* (short tunics) are also special. ✉ *10/11, Narayan Singh Circle, opposite City Pulse Mall* ☎ *141/511–2276* ⊕ *www. zarijaipur.com.*

OFF THE BEATEN PATH

Sanganer (16 km [10 miles] south of Jaipur on Tonk Rd., near the airport) and Bagru (35 km [22 miles] southwest of Sanganer on Ajmer Road) are crafts towns that you can visit to see Rajasthani artisans in action. In Sanganer nearly every family is involved in the production of block- and screen-printed textiles, blue pottery, or handmade paper.

Bagru is famous for its hand-printed cloth industry, and the simple, popular designs made here feature earthen colors of green, brown, black, and blue.

> ■**TIP**→ Come out here to see artisans in action, but don't expect to get much better deals than in town just because you are buying from the source—the products here are marked up to cover the huge commissions they dole out to taxi drivers.

> **TIGER, TIGER**
>
> There are three national parks in the Delhi/Jaipur area. Ranthambhore (161 km [100 miles] south of Jaipur) is your best bet if tigers are your priority, but you'll still only have a 30% to 40% chance of seeing one. Keoladeo National Park in Bharatpur (150 km [93 miles] east of Jaipur, 55 km [34 miles] west of Agra) is mainly a destination for bird-watchers, though there are also some interesting flora and fauna. There is also Sariska, which is the closest park to Jaipur (110 km [68 miles]) but there are no tigers and it's not well-run or worth a visit.

RANTHAMBHORE NATIONAL PARK

161 km (100 miles) south of Jaipur.

Half of the world's endangered tiger population lives in India and one of the national parks where the odds of seeing a tiger are much higher is Ranthambhore in eastern Rajasthan. Once a game reserve of the royal families of Jaipur and Karauli it was (mis)managed by their *shikar khaana* (hunting department). The 20th century saw India's tiger population decrease from an estimated 40,000 to 1,800 and areas like Ranthambore were the scene of exotic tiger hunts where the entire court showed up on as many as 40 elephants to slay prodigious amounts of big game. Today, Ranthambore with its royal ruins and mixed vegetation—sand, scrub, grassland, hills—forms a dramatic background for tiger viewing and photography.

EXPLORING

Fodor's Choice ★ **Ranthambhore National Park.** If you want to see a tiger in the wild, Ranthambhore, in the Sawai Madhopur district and once the royal game reserve of the Maharaja of Jaipur, is the best park in Rajasthan to visit. The park (392 square km [151 square miles]) is part of the larger Ranthambhore Tiger Reserve which encompasses 1,334 square km (515 square miles) of rugged terrain bordered by the Chambal and Banas rivers and is home to a vast ecosystem of flora and fauna. To protect the fragile environment only a limited section of both the reserve and the park is open to visitors. Ranthambhore is noted for its tiger and leopard populations, although you still have only a 30% to 40% chance of seeing a large cat on any given expedition. The best time to see tigers is right before the monsoon, in summer, when the tigers emerge to drink at small water holes—when it's dry and the water table is low, the tigers are forced out of hiding to quench their thirst. What you will definitely see are numerous peacocks, *sambar* (large Asian deer), *chital* (spotted deer), *chinkara* (gazelles), *nilgai* (blue bull or Asian antelope), wild boar, jackals, crocodiles, and often sloth bears.

Sighting a wild tiger in Ranthambhore is an exciting experience even if you never come face to face with the king. First, of course, you will hear the jungle sounds that warn of a tiger's presence. Monkeys and peacocks scream loudly and the deer in the area become agitated and nervous. Ranthambhore became a national park in 1972 under the Project Tiger program, which was launched in an effort to save India's dwindling population of Bengal Tigers. Despite stricter conservation efforts that are slowly producing results, the tiger population in Ranthambhore is small: a 2014 census put the park's tiger population at around 61, although the number varies from source to source. Sighting a leopard is much more difficult, as these cats live on high, inaccessible slopes and are extremely shy.

The park is run by the Indian government, and the rules are happily inflexible: you can only enter the park in an official government jeep, and the jeeps keep strict hours, daily from 6:30 am to 9:30 am and 3 pm to 6 pm. (the timings may vary by 30 minutes during summer and winter months when the park opens later in the morning). Book a jeep in advance, or online (90 days before), or save yourself the hassle and book through your hotel (it's worth the service charge). Government regulations state that visitors must keep minimum distance of 20 meters from all wildlife (50 meters if you're in a vehicle) and that vehicles may only remain at a sighting point for up to 15 minutes.

You can also explore the surrounding region: the 10th-century **Ranthambhore Fort,** perched on a nearby hill, is one of Rajasthan's more spectacular military strongholds and how the reserve got its name. Dastkar, a craft-and-textile shop on the Ranthambhore Road, is run by a nongovernment legitimate cooperative organization.

The government-run heritage **Castle Jhoomar Baori** (12 rooms and two suites, Rs. 3,600–Rs. 7,500) offers the chance to spend a night near the animals, but little else. It can be booked through Rajasthan Tourism Development Corporation (RTDC) offices across the state. A better option is to stay at one of the hotels along Ranthambhore Road and take a morning safari. The neighboring town of Sawai Madhopur has numerous hotels, but most are basic. ☎ 7462/220–808 *Sawai Madhopur Tourist Information Center* ⊕ *sawaimadhopur.nic. in/ranthambhor_national_park.htm* ✉ *Rs. 1,200 per person entry and Rs. 999 jeep charges per head; up to 6 people per jeep; camera or video Rs. 400* ☉ *Oct.–June.*

WHERE TO STAY

$$$$
RESORT
Fodor's Choice
★
🕍 **Oberoi Vanyavilas.** On the edge of the Ranthambore Tiger Reserve, this is ideal for those who want to "camp" in sheer luxury—one of the best resorts not just in the area but in all of India. **Pros:** natural surroundings and camping-like experience that doesn't skimp on luxury; hospitable staff. **Cons:** expensive. ⑤ *Rooms from: Rs. 44500* ⊠ *Ranthambhore Rd., Sawai Madhopur* ☎ *7462/223–999* ⊕ *www.oberoihotels. com* ⤙ *25 tents* ☉ *Closed July–Sept.* 🍽 *No meals.*

$$$
RESORT
🕍 **Ranthambhore Regency.** This is the most comfortable mid-price place on the Ranthambhore Road, 10 km (6 miles) from the park, in an elegant heritage-style building. **Pros:** friendly staff; local advice; pool. **Cons:** meals are buffet-only. ⑤ *Rooms from: Rs. 7500* ⊠ *Ranthambhore Rd., Sawai Madhopur* ☎ *7462/223–456, 7462/221–176* ⊕ *www. ranthambhor.com* ⤙ *73 rooms, 10 cottages* ☉ *Closed July–Sept.* 🍽 *All meals.*

$$$$
RESORT
🕍 **Vivanta by Taj – Sawai Madhopur.** This small, intimate art deco lodge, the only heritage hotel in Ranthambhore, is convenient for the national park as well as being something of a destination in its own right. **Pros:** near the train station; just a 20-minute drive to the park. **Cons:** rooms are not particularly elegant or fancy. ⑤ *Rooms from: Rs. 14000* ⊠ *Ranthambhore Rd., Sawai Madhopur* ☎ *7462/220–541, 7462/223–500* ⊕ *www.vivantabytaj.com* ⤙ *36 rooms, 12 suites* 🍽 *Multiple meal plans.*

BHARATPUR

150 km (93 miles) east of Jaipur; 55 km (34 miles) west of Agra; 18 km (11 miles) west of Fatehpur Sikri.

Once the capital of a Jat kingdom, this town, which is very close to the border of Uttar Pradesh, is most famous for its proximity to the Bharatpur bird sanctuary, once a royal reserve, now renamed Keoladeo National Park. Bharatpur town has interesting bazaars, a fort, and several havelis in its vicinity.

EXPLORING

Keoladeo National Park. Founded by the Jat ruler Suraj Mal in 1733, the city of Bharatpur is famous for the Keoladeo National Park (also known as the Ghana Bird Sanctuary), once the duck-hunting forest of the local maharajas. This UNESCO World Heritage site is home to many mammals and reptiles—blue bulls (antelope), spotted deer, otters, and Indian rock pythons—but birds, especially waterbirds, are the main attraction. It's an ornithologist's dream—29 square km (10 square miles) of forests and wetlands with 400 species, more than 130 of which are resident year-round, such as the Saras crane, gray heron, snake bird (Indian darter), and spoonbill. In winter, birds arrive from the Himalayas, Siberia, and even Europe.

The best way to see the park is on foot or by boat (Rs. 200 per person, per hour, depending on boat type, though these are usually unavailable due to lack of rains even in the monsoon; check at entrance), but there are plenty of other options. The park's main artery is a blacktop road that runs from the entrance gate to the center. Surrounded by marshlands but screened by bushes, this road is the most convenient viewpoint for bird-watching and is also traveled by cycle-rickshaws (the best option Rs. 100 per hour, but drivers usually expect more, plus a tip of at least Rs. 50), bicycle (Rs. 60 per trip), and the park's electric bus (Rs. 200 per person). The rickshaw drivers, trained by the forest department, are pretty good at finding and pointing out birds. You can also rent a bicycle and head into more remote areas; just remember that most roads are unpaved. The excellent guides at the gate (Rs. 150 per hour; Rs. 250 for groups of five or more) are familiar with the birds' haunts and can help you spot and identify them.

Try to bring a bird guidebook: former royal-family member Salim Ali's *The Birds of India* is a good choice. The best time to see the birds is early morning or late evening, November through February; by the end of February, many birds start heading home. Stick around at sunset, when the water takes on a mirrorlike stillness and the air is filled with the calls of day birds settling down and night birds stirring.

⊠ *5 km (3 miles) south of city center* ☎ *5644/222–777* ⊕ *whc.unesco. org/en/list/340* 🎟 *Rs. 400, video camera fee Rs. 200* ⊘ *Daily 6 am–6:30 pm (entry before 5:30 pm).*

Lohagarh Fort. In Bharatpur's Old City, this solid-looking fort, surrounded by a deep and wide moat, is also known figuratively as the Iron Fort, though it's built of mud. It has a colossal metal door. The structure might seem fragile, but it was tested and found invincible by a British siege in 1805: armed with 65 pieces of field artillery, 1,800 European soldiers and 6,000 Indian sepoys did manage to win the battle, but they failed to break down the impregnable fort. There are palaces inside the fort and a museum that showcases wall paintings and pieces of sculpture and toys excavated nearby and dating from the 2nd century. ☎ *05644/228–185* 🎟 *Fort free; museum Rs. 50* ⊘ *Daily 10–5.*

WHERE TO STAY

$$$
HOTEL
🏨 **Laxmi Vilas Palace Hotel.** Rural and old-fashioned, this cozy, memorable heritage hotel is the best place to stay in the city and is still home to descendants of the former maharaja of Bharatpur. **Pros:** excellent value; impressive architecture. **Cons:** lacks the luxury of fancier hotels in its category; slow service. $ *Rooms from: Rs. 7000* ⊠ *Old Agra Rd., Kakaji Ki Kothi* ☎ *5644/231–199, 5644/223–523* ⊕ *www.laxmivilas. com* 🛏 *46 rooms, 23 suites* ⊘ *Breakfast.*

PUSHKAR

146 km (90 miles) southwest of Jaipur.

Fodor's Choice
★
With more than 500 temples, Pushkar is one of Hinduism's holiest sites and an interesting place to visit even when the famous camel fair (in October or November) isn't being held. The focus of the town is its placid lake and the ghats, havelis, crumbling buildings and temples, all whitewashed a splendid white, that edge the lake. Parts of the town have the vibe of a Rajasthani Varanasi and indeed this place is almost as sacred. But like many Indian towns Pushkar has several flavors. In its narrow car-free main bazaar, sadhus, tribals, hippies, the dreadlocked,

backpackers, pilgrims, monkeys, beggars, and five-legged cattle (such birth deformities are considered lucky) vie for space with shops selling everything from religious paraphernalia to water bongs and chillams. Although goods from all over Rajasthan find their way to the bazaar, because Pushkar is such a holy city, no alcohol or meat can be sold here—some restaurants get around the alcohol restriction by serving beer in coffee mugs to their regular customers, but by no means should you count on being able to get anything alcoholic. Alcohol and nonvegetarian food is served in hotels located beyond the city limits.

There are a few interesting types of handicrafts to shop for. Look for interesting tiny wooden chests of drawers, wooden re-created antique telephones, trays, and other such knickknacks. Rajguru Emporium, opposite the Brahma temple has a nice collection Pushkar crafts; bargain some.

GETTING HERE AND AROUND

Pushkar, best reached by road or by train via Ajmer (shuttle trains link Ajmer with Pushkar). The town is quite small, and everything worth seeing is in walking distance or you can take an auto (negotiate the fare beforehand).

ESSENTIALS

Tourist Offices Rajasthan Tourism Tourist Information Centre ⊠ *Hotel Sarovar, Pushkar Lake,* ☎ *0145/277–2040.*

EXPLORING

Bathing ghats (*flights of steps*). Many of the marble bathing ghats on the holy Pushkar Lake—a must-visit—were constructed for pilgrims by royal families who wanted to ensure power and prosperity in their kingdoms throughout Rajasthan by appeasing the gods. It is believed that the waters of the lake are healing powers and that the water near different ghats have different powers. There are 52 ghats in all with various degrees of significance. When you pass an entrance to a ghat, be prepared for a priest (or 10) to solicit you by simply offering you a flower—he'll want you to receive a blessing, known as the "Pushkar Passport." He'll lead you to the water's edge, say a prayer, and will ask you to recite a blessing in Sanskrit (you'll repeat after him). Then he'll paste a *tilak* (rice and colored powder dot) on your forehead and tie a religious red thread (denoting a blessing) to your wrist. After the ceremony, you're expected to give a donation or *dakshina*: don't give more than Rs. 100 (or you can negotiate the sum as soon as he approaches you). Once you have the passport no other priest will bother you.

The ghats get extra busy during auspicious pilgrimage times, especially during the Kartik Purnima, the full moon during the Hindu month of Kartik, around November (also the time of the Pushkar Camel Fair): there may be tens of thousands of people here bathing and getting blessings from local Brahmins. The peaceful parts of the ghats can be accessed from the eastern shore of the lake, close to Sunset Café.

Note: The ghats are considered very sacred places, so be sure to follow etiquette—taking off shoes and being respectful. ⊠ *Pushkar.*

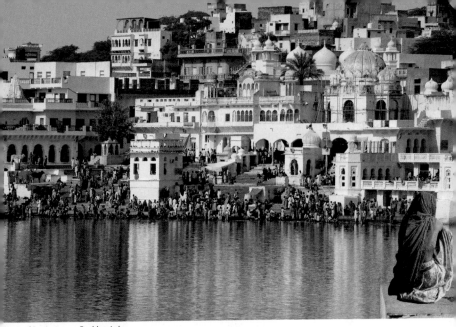

Looking out over Pushkar Lake

Brahma Temple. In the center of town, not on the lake, this is one of India's most important temples in spite of its unimpressive architecture and more modern feel postreconstruction. The building is newer but the shrine dates back to the 14th century. Pilgrims visiting the temple climb a long stairway into the walled area to take the blessings of the god—in the form of small sugar balls. Predawn and postsunset *aartis* (special rounds of worship) are held and are atmospheric. Shoes, bags, cameras, and video cameras are not allowed in the temple—it is best to leave in the car with your driver if reliable or back in your hotel and deposit your shoes at the temple shoe stalls (for Rs. 20–Rs. 40). Mind your wallets and phones. Don't think of visiting the inner sanctum of the temple during auspicious festival times but do view from afar. ⊠ *Pushkar* ☉ *Opens 6 am (slightly later in winter). Closed 1:30 pm–3 pm and after 9 pm.*

FAMILY

Fodor'sChoice

★

Camel Fair. If you really want an experience, go to Pushkar during its famous five-day annual Camel Fair, the largest in the world. Every October or November—depending on the lunar calendar—during the full moon (Kartik Purnima), people flock here by the many thousands to see the finest camels parade around the fairground, edging the sand dunes, in colorful costumes. People come to buy, sell, and trade camels, and to race one camel against another, and it is a treat to see Rajasthanis, who already dress in bright colors, kitted out in their best. A good male camel goes for at least US$400 although some of the popular Marwari horses go for much more. Other types of livestock are also sold. In addition to the camel activities, there are cultural programs, cricket matches, competitions during the day and all kinds of spontaneous music, dance and folk performances in the evenings. The town is packed during festival time, so make sure you reserve a room at least several weeks—if not much longer—ahead of time. Several tented camps with modern conveniences also mushroom during the fair. Contact the Rajasthan Tourism Development Corporation (RTDC) in Jaipur for more details. ✉ *Pushkar* ⊕ *www.pushkar-camel-fair.com.*

Dargah Sharif. The shrine of the 13th-century Sufi saint Khwaja Moinuddin Chisty is in the heart of Ajmer, a city about 11 km (7 miles) southeast of Pushkar. The shrine is very significant for South Asian Muslims—visiting it means the chance to set your soul free eternally—and is visited by Muslims and non-Muslims alike. The busiest time is during Urs, the anniversary of the saint's death, which takes place during six days in the Islamic month of Rajab starting with the day of the full moon. The custom when you visit this shrine is to offer flowers, sugar balls, beads, and a *chaadar* (ornate scarf)—the beads and sweets will be blessed and given back to you. Sufiism is a more mystical and less austere aspect of Islam that is embraced vigorously in these parts.

Be prepared to deal with crowds and aggressive beggars on the street leading to the dargah whenever you visit. Ajmer itself isn't much of a destination, so most people bypass it on their way to Pushkar, then backtrack for a half-day visit to the shrine; the drive to Ajmer to Pushkar is scenic and descends through some minor hills offering views of Ajmer and its lake. The shrine is located at the end of a narrow lane and is not very accessible. Have the driver (if you have a car) park on the wider main road and hire an auto (tuk tuk) for Rs. 150 or so (let the driver negotiate a price, if possible) to take you to the dargah and back. Shoes, purses, rucksacks, cameras, and video cameras are not allowed in the dargah—it is best to leave those items in the car with your driver (if reliable) and deposit your shoes at the shrine shoe stalls (for Rs. 50, and you get a basket of flowers to offer inside). Mind your wallets and phones. Women and men need to cover their heads inside the shrine and must be dressed appropriately (no skirts, shorts, sleeveless tops).

While you're here, the 19th-century **Nasiyan Temple** is worth a visit as well: the detailed display depicting the Jain story of the world's creation inside the temple is mesmerizing. It's near Agra Gate, or just ask people how to find the Jain temple. ✉ *Ajmer* ⊕ *dargahajmer.com.*

Savitri Temple. Make an early start to check out the Savitri Temple on a hill overlooking Pushkar Lake. The 1.5 km climb up the long flight of stairs leading up the hill takes between a half-hour and an hour, and the outstanding view at sunrise is worth it. A ropeway (cable car) to the top is planned. △ **Be careful of menacing monkeys, which tend to grab anything edible; don't venture out to the temple if it is getting dark—it may be badly lit and dangerous.** ✉ *Pushkar.*

WHERE TO EAT

$
ECLECTIC
✕ **Café Enigma.** This four-story, family-run restaurant is a good choice for continental cuisine (think veggie burgers and Israeli salads) as well as Indian classics, with spice levels suited to the Western palate. Their pizzas and pastas are also popular. It's also a good place for breakfast—they usually stock a few pastries from the nearby bakery, and

their *paranthas* (potato-stuffed flatbreads) are fresh and not too oily. They also serve "real" filter coffee. Sit up on the rooftop terrace for views of Pushkar and the surrounding desert. $ *Average main: Rs. 150* ✉ *Near Old Rangji Temple, Choti Basti, Pushkar* ☎ *99834–41449* ▭ *No credit cards.*

$$ ✕ **Out of the Blue.** This quirky vegetarian restaurant near the Brahma
INTERNATIONAL Temple has devis painted on its walls, chilled trance music in the background, and a lengthy menu. A favorite with backpackers, it serves pizzas, *thalis*, extensive breakfasts, grilled sandwiches, crepes (vegetable, sweet or salty), many flavors of *lassi* (chocolate, rose, mixed fruit), pasta, Mexican food, and Israeli food. They bake their own bread. You can eat downstairs in air-conditioned comfort or head to the rooftop and have a meal with a view. $ *Average main: Rs. 400* ✉ *Kapra Bazar, Pushkar* ☎ *978/408–9600* ▭ *No credit cards.*

$$$ ✕ **Prince's Restaurant.** This lakeside vegetarian restaurant inside the Hotel
INDIAN Pushkar Palace is popular with large tour groups and has buffet service for all three meals, plus a few snack and à la carte options. The main reason to come here is for the restaurant's terrace garden, which looks out over Pushkar's sacred lake; there are sometimes music and dance performances staged here at dinnertime, which add to the atmosphere. There's also indoor seating for hot days that have a view of the bathing ghats. $ *Average main: Rs. 600* ✉ *Hotel Pushkar, Choti Basti, off Pushkar Bazaar (main street), Pushkar* ☎ *145/277–3001, 145/277–2401* ⊕ *www.hotelpushkarpalace.com.*

$$ ✕ **Sunset Café.** If you like to people-watch, this small terrace restaurant
INTERNATIONAL with lovely lake views is the place to be. Come in the early evening, when scores of tourists and locals gather in front of the restaurant on Pushkar Lake's eastern shore to watch the sun set. There's a bohemian atmosphere: expect to see an eclectic mash-up of dreadlocked backpackers, ornately adorned desert dwellers singing and dancing, and plenty of local priests eager to perform *pujas* (Hindu ceremonies). The menu mixes Indian, Italian and Mexican dishes. The veg sizzlers, lasagna, and banana pancakes are particularly popular here. $ *Average main: Rs. 450* ✉ *Parikrama Marg, next to Pushkar Palace, Choti Basti, Pushkar* ☎ *145/277–2382, 145/277–2725* ▭ *No credit cards.*

WHERE TO STAY

$$$ ⌂ **Ananta Spa and Resorts.** Spread across 9 acres, this is Pushkar's loveli-
RESORT est, and most expensive, hotel. **Pros:** peaceful; not that far from the city but away from its bustle; meandering pool; spa. **Cons:** 4 km from the main town; expensive—during the Pushkar Fair rates more than triple. $ *Rooms from: Rs. 8000* ✉ *Leela Sevri, Ajmer Pushkar Rd., Pushkar* ☎ *145/305–4000* ⊕ *www.anantahotels.com* ⟿ *73 rooms* ⟐ *Breakfast.*

$$$ ⌂ **Jagat Palace.** The bearded guard, brandishing a spear and offering
HOTEL a salute as you arrive, is a good indication of the style of service at this mildly eccentric haveli-style hotel, with a promising view of the dunes outside Pushkar from some parts of the property. **Pros:** interesting ambience; good value except during Pushkar Fair; elevator. **Cons:** slightly out of the city; service a bit slow; charmless lighting in some rooms. $ *Rooms from: Rs. 6500* ✉ *Behind Ramdwara, Pushkar*

Evening falls at the Pushkar camel fair

📠 *145/277–2001, 145/277–2401* ⊕ *www.hotelpushkarpalace.com* 🛏 *84 rooms* ¶◎¶ *Breakfast.*

$
B&B/INN

🖼 **Master Paradise.** This oversized pink bungalow in a neat garden, in the leafy Pacnh Kund road enclave of Pushkar, surrounded by hills, is a charming surprise in a town short of attractive hotels. **Pros:** pool; elevator; close to the desert; well priced. **Cons:** 3 km (2 miles) from the main town. $ *Rooms from: Rs. 2525* ⊠ *Master Colony, Panch Kund Rd., Pushkar* 📠 *145/277–3931, 145/277–3933* ⊕ *www.masterparadise. com* 🛏 *63 rooms, 2 suites* ¶◎¶ *Breakfast.*

$$
HOTEL

🖼 **The Pratap Palace.** This eye-catching edifice in a delicate pink stone on a low hill is one of the first landmarks visible as you enter the out-skirts of Pushkar town coming from Jaipur, while inside, vast expanses of marble and white gives a sensation of immense space and grandeur. **Pros:** nice pool; lovely ambience; well priced. **Cons:** far from town; rooms could be slighty more luxurious; hotel needs more facilties to keep guests busy. $ *Rooms from: Rs. 5000* ⊠ *Village Hokra, Pushkar Byepass, 10.8 km (6.7 miles) from town, Pushkar* 📠 *1452/970–202* ⊕ *www.thepratappalace.com* 🛏 *80 rooms, 8 suites* ¶◎¶ *No meals.*

$$$
HOTEL

🖼 **Pushkar Palace.** In the best location in town, this charming, small palace sits above its own ghat (private stairs leading down to the lake) and has fabulous, panoramic views of Pushkar. **Pros:** lakeside loca-tion; good food; great views. **Cons:** no meat or alcohol served; as else-where, room rates skyrocket during the Pushkar festival and all meals must be included at this time; no pool; lacks the polish of a luxury hotel. $ *Rooms from: Rs. 7000* ⊠ *Choti Basti, off Pushkar Bazaar (main street), Pushkar* 📠 *145/277–3001, 145/277–2401* ⊕ *www. hotelpushkarpalace.com* 🛏 *50 rooms, 17 suites* ¶◎¶ *Breakfast.*

UDAIPUR AND NEARBY

Romantic Udaipur, the major city here, warrants several days or more since the Aravali Hills and the Mewar region are home to several fascinating day-trip or overnight destinations, including the impressive medieval citadel of Chittaurgarh and the remarkable fort at Kumbalgarh. There are several famous temples and religious sites in the area, too, including the spectacular Jain Temples in Ranakpur and Mount Abu and the Shiva temple complex at Eklingji. An overnight trip is recommended for a visit to Mount Abu. Udaipur is a famous white marble center; make time to visit Bhuwana on the outskirts to purchase some wonderful carved marble handicrafts.

UDAIPUR

405 km (251 miles) southwest of Jaipur; 335 km (207 miles) southeast of Jodhpur.

Fodor's Choice
★

Romantic old-world charm, soothing lakes, and fairy-tale palaces are what draw so many visitors to Udaipur, known as the City of Lakes. It was founded in 1567, when, having grown weary of repeated attacks on the old Mewar capital of Chittaur—Chittaur is the historic name of the area, and Chittaurgarh literally means "the fort of Chittaur"—Maharana Udai Singh asked a holy sage to suggest a safe place for his new capital. The man assured Udai Singh that the new base would never be conquered if it was established on the banks of Lake Pichola, and thus was born Singh's namesake, Udaipur.

Despite being one of Rajasthan's largest cities, with a population of less than half a million people, modern Udaipur still feels like a small town. Added perks are the weather, which is balmy year-round except for a spot of summertime heat between April and mid-June, and the fact that the locals are extremely friendly. To enjoy this city's hospitality, book a stay in a palace or a haveli (the bigger the better). Five main gates lead into Udaipur's Old City: they are Hathi Pol (Elephant Gate) to the north; Kishan Pol to the south; Delhi Pol to the northeast; Chand Pol (Moon Gate) to the west; and Suraj Pol (Sun Gate) to the east.

Anchoring Udaipur's Old City are the famed City Palace and Lake Palace—the latter in the middle of Lake Pichola, and now a hotel run by Taj Hotels Resorts and Palaces. The Old City itself is built on tiny hillocks and raised areas, its lanes full of twists and turns, with plenty of charming little niches to be discovered. The major landmarks in the new section are Chetak Circle, Sukhadia Circle, and Sahelion Ki Bari gardens.

GETTING HERE AND AROUND

You can reach Udaipur by air from Delhi or Mumbai (not Jaipur) or by train (the super-fast Shatabdi connects Udaipur and Jaipur) or by road. Most of Udaipur's top attractions are on the east shore of the lake, in the Old City, and if you stay near the Jagdish Temple or the City Palace, in the heart of the Old City, you'll be able to reach most of the sites on foot. If you follow the main road downhill from the Jagdish Temple, you'll wind up at the Ghanta Ghar (clock tower)—the road continues

north all the way to the city center in the newer, and far less enchanting, part of Udaipur. The easiest way to get from one side of the lake to the other is to cross the small bridge at Chand Pol, on the narrow northern edge. Auto-rickshaws are also widely available—don't pay more than Rs. 150 for a ride anywhere within the main city.

TIMING
While you can get through most of the sights if you stay here for only two days, three or four will give you time to explore the Old City's many winding lanes or take a day trip.

ESSENTIALS
Taxi Companies Travels to India ⊠ *Lok Kala Mandal, Chetak Circle* ☏ *294/241–5881* ⊕ *www.travelstoindia.com.*

Tourist Offices Government of Rajasthan Tourist Office. Staff in this office are helpful and patient and can advise you on what places to visit in Udaipur, and details about the sights. ⊠ *Fateh Memorial, Suraj Pol* ☏ *294/241–1535* ⊕ *www.rajasthantourism.gov.in* ⊙ *10:30–6, Mon.–Sat.*

EXPLORING
TOP ATTRACTIONS
City Palace. The sprawling maharana's palace—the largest in Rajasthan—stands on a ridge overlooking the lake and the view of the city and Lake Palace from the top is one great reason to come here. Begun by Udai Singh and extended by subsequent maharanas, the sand-color City Palace rises five stories tall, with a series of balconies. Cupolas crown its octagonal towers, which are connected by a maze of narrow passageways. The City Palace is part of a complex of palaces—two have been converted to hotels and one houses the current titular maharana, Arvind Singh of Mewar. Part of the palace houses a museum; its entrance is near the Jagdish Mandir; the entrance to the City Palace Hotel is at the bottom of the hill, to the south. The rooms inside the City Palace Museum contain decorative art: beautiful paintings, colorful enamel, inlay glasswork, and antique furniture. One of the more interesting features is the private bathroom of the maharaja on the third floor which has a tree growing nearby and a grand padded toilet seat. It's useful to have the explanatory site publication, available in the book shop, or get an audio guide at the admission point. The hour-long sound-and-light show held at the palace's Manek Chowk chronicles the history of the House of Mewar. The English-language version is shown from September to March at 8 pm (April to August it is in Hindi), but check ahead, as timings can change without notice. ⊠ *City Palace Complex* ☏ *0294/252–8016* ⊿ *Rs. 100, or Rs. 275 with audio guide; camera fee Rs. 225; video fee Rs 225* ⊙ *Daily 9:30–4:30.*

Jagdish Temple. This 17-century imposing Hindu temple, the oldest in the city, was commissioned by Maharana Jagat Singh and is a major landmark in Udaipur's Old City for its architecture and height—the *shikhar* (or dome/spire) alone is 79 feet. It's usually abuzz with devotees and tourists, especially during the morning and evening *aarti* (prayer ceremony), when vendors set up makeshift flower stalls along the temple walls and sell offerings of marigolds. The temple is dedicated to Jagdish (an incarnation of Vishnu), and referred to as Jagdishji. Songs sung in

5

his praise are often played through loudspeakers high on the temple's edifice. You're welcome to step inside, although the engravings on the temple's exterior walls are more interesting to look at. ⊠ *Jagdish Mandir, just north of City Palace* ☉ *Daily sunrise–sunset.*

Fodor's Choice **Lake Pichola.** You can't leave Udaipur without seeing the stunningly
★ romantic **Lake Palace** (Jag Niwas), which seems to float serenely on the waters of Lake Pichola. A vast, white-marble fantasy, the palace has been featured in many Indian and foreign films, including the James Bond film *Octopussy*. Unfortunately, the palace's apartments, courts, fountains, and gardens are off-limits unless you're a guest at the Taj Lake Palace Hotel *(⇨ Where to Stay, below)*. The equally isolated, three-story **Jag Mandir Island Palace** occupies Jag Mandir Island at the southern end of the lake, and is open to visitors from 10 to 6 (take a boat over). This palace has an elegant restaurant, the Darikhana (it serves Indian and continental cuisine, and is only open for dinner), as well as a more casual all-day café. Built and embellished over a 50-year period beginning in the 17th century, Jag Mandir is made of yellow sandstone, lined with marble, and crowned by a dome. The interior is decorated with arabesques of colored stones. Shah Jahan, son of the Mughal emperor Jahangir, took refuge in Jag Mandir after leading an unsuccessful revolt against his father. Legend has it that Shah Jahan's inspiration for the Taj Mahal came from this marble masterpiece. One-hour motorboat cruises (Rs. 430 morning rides, or Rs. 680 for afternoon ride), start at the City Palace including a stop at Jag Mandir, leave from the jetty on the hour (daily 10–6) check for the exact spot at ticket counter; book a day ahead during the busy season. ☎ *294/252–8016.*

NEED A BREAK?
Suryadarshan. Overlooking Lake Pichola from a gallery adjoining the magnificent Durbar Hall in Fateh Prakash Palace, Suryadarshan serves high tea between 2 pm and 5 pm. If you're visiting the expensive Crystal Gallery above the restaurant, your Rs. 550 ticket also includes a drink at the Surya Darshan Bar. The Crystal Gallery houses the palace's early-19th-century collection of Birmingham crystal, with everything from wine decanters to beds. Suryadarshan is open daily from 10:30 to 6:30. ⊠ *Fateh Prakash Palace, City Palace Complex* ☎ *294/252–8016 to 8019.*

Neemach Mata. This hilltop temple in the new part of town is dedicated to the goddess of the mountain, also considered an avatar of Ambaji, and the climb to its summit (no vehicles are allowed) is rewarded by a beautiful view of the whole city and the Fateh Sagar lake. The shrine dates from the 17th century although the building is newer. It's a steep, 20-minute climb on a paved, zigzag path, but you can pause often on the way up to take in the view (and catch your breath). Wear comfortable shoes. ⊠ *North of Fateh Sagar Lake.*

Sajjan Garh. High in the Aravali Hills just outside Udaipur, this fort–palace glows golden orange in the night sky, thanks to the lights that illuminate it. Once the maharana's Monsoon Palace, it's now rather dilapidated, and serves as a radio station for the Indian Army. The panoramic view is spectacular from the fort's lofty tower, and locals claim you can see distant Chittaurgarh on a clear day. The winding road to the

Udaipur's City Palace

top of Sajjan Garh, surrounded by green forests, is best covered by car (you can take an auto-rickshaw, but the ride will be long and bumpy). On foot, it's a 45 minute uphill walk. A fee is required for vehicles at the gate leading up the hill. ☎ *294/245–3686* 🎫 *Rs. 160; camera Rs. 100; vehicle fee Rs. 130* ⊘ *Daily 8–6.*

OFF THE BEATEN PATH

Shilpgram. This rural arts-and-crafts village near Fateh Sagar lake 5 km (3 miles) west of Udaipur contains a complex with 34 re-creations of furnished village huts (authentic right down to their toilets) from various states across India, including Rajasthan, Gujarat, Maharashtra, and Odisha, with tribal relics on display. The town comes alive in late December with the nine-day **Shilpgram Utsav,** when artists and crafts-people from around the country arrive to sell and display their works. Puppet shows, dances, folk music, and handicrafts sales take place year-round, however. You can tour parts of the compound on a slow camel ride. There is a basic *dhaba* (eatery) on site. Closed August 15 and January 26. ⊠ *Rani Rd., near Fateh Sagar Lake* ☎ *294/243–1304* ⊕ *www.shilpgram.org* 🎫 *Rs. 50; camera fee (still and video) Rs. 50* ⊘ *Daily 11–7.*

WORTH NOTING

FAMILY **Bagore ki Haveli.** It's fun to explore the many rooms and terraces of this elegant 18th-century haveli on Gangaur Ghat. It was built by a prime minister of Mewar. One-hour folk-dance performances are organized every evening at 7 (time may change, so check on arrival)—get there at least 30 minutes early for good seats. ⊠ *Gangaur Ghat* ☎ *294/242–2567* 🎫 *Rs. 50; dance performance Rs. 100; camera fee Rs. 100; video camera fee Rs. 100* ⊘ *Daily 9.30–5; dance performance at 7 pm.*

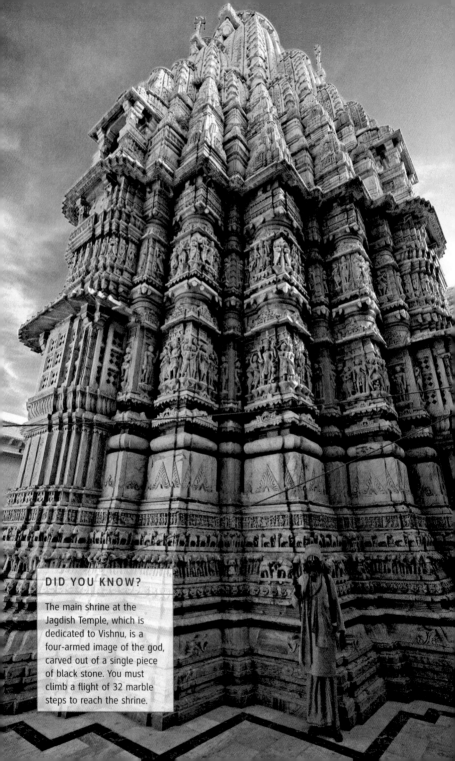

DID YOU KNOW?

The main shrine at the Jagdish Temple, which is dedicated to Vishnu, is a four-armed image of the god, carved out of a single piece of black stone. You must climb a flight of 32 marble steps to reach the shrine.

FAMILY **Bharatiya Lok Kala Mandal.** This folk-art museum displays a collection of puppets, dolls, masks, folk dresses, ornaments, musical instruments, and paintings. The museum is known for its interesting 7 pm puppet show—this is the reason to come here, because the museum itself is not well maintained. ⊠ *About 500 yds. north of Chetak Circle, Panch Batti, near Mohta Park* ☎ *0294/252–9296* ⊠ *Museum Rs. 45 with camera; evening program Rs. 50 (prices subject to change)* ☉ *Daily 9–7.*

Karni Mata Ropeway. Udaipur bursts with pride at having a cable car; one of the few places in India to have one. You can take the ropeway (as it is called locally), to the top of Machchala Hill near Karni Mata temple and feast your eyes on the view of the city lakes and palaces. ⊠ *Deen Dayal Park, Doodh Talai* ⊕ *www.udaipurropeway.com* ⊠ *Rs. 78 per head.*

Vintage and Classic Car Collection. The City Palace has an attached antique car musuem with a small selection of two dozen or or so old automobiles in working condition on display; they belong to the local royal Mewar family. Look out for the 1939 Cadillacs, 1936 Vauxhall, and the Rolls-Royces. After a spin around the museum you can have lunch at the garden barbecue restaurant nearby. ⊠ *City Palace* ☎ *294/241–9021* ⊕ *www.hrhhotels.com/regal-visits* ⊠ *Rs. 250* ☉ *Daily 9–9.*

WHERE TO EAT

$$$ ✕ **1559 AD.** Named after the year when Udaipur was founded, 1559
ECLECTIC occupies an elegant colonial bungalow, with the option of dining alfresco in the large garden. Specialties include Rajasthani game birds (farmed, not hunted), prepared in traditional Indian and European styles, as well as salmon, rack of lamb, and baby back ribs. Vegetarian specials are malai kofta and paneer dishes. They also do pastas and pizzas. There's a café with an authentic espresso machine and a bar with a decent selection of wines. Last order is 10:30. ⑤ *Average main: Rs. 700* ⊠ *P.P. Singhal Marg, near Fateh Sagar* ☎ *294/243–3559* ⊕ *www.1559ad.com.*

$$$ ✕ **Ambrai.** Right on the shore of Lake Pichola opposite Lal Ghat, this
INDIAN lively outdoor restaurant with a pleasant bar has a hidden approach via narrow lanes and stunning views of the City Palace complex and the Lake Palace. It serves Rajasthani standards such as *paneer do piaza* (soft white cheese in an onion gravy), *laal maas* (spiced mutton), and mutton *rajputana* (spicy, Mewari-style) along with decent continental and Chinese dishes. If you're here at dinner, ask that a mosquito repellant coil is placed under your table. ⑤ *Average main: Rs. 700* ⊠ *Amet Haveli, opposite Lal Ghat* ☎ *294/243–1085* ⊕ *amethaveliudaipur.com* ⚘ *Reservations essential.*

$ ✕ **Apani Dhani.** About half an hour's drive out of the center of town,
INDIAN and an upwards climb on a hillock, this is the place to have a traditional vegetarian Rajasthani *thali*, sitting cross-legged on the ground in a hut. The local delicacies—*daal baati* (unleavened wheat bread eaten with lentils), *bajra roti* (millet *rotis*), garlic chutney, *sangri* (a desert vegetable)—are tasty and especially authentic. Service is warm, but this is an experience for the brave—it is about sitting in a rural roadside setting where amenities are basic. There's a puppet show, Rajasthani

folk dancing, and a handicraft shop. ⑤ *Average main: Rs. 250* ⊠ *Pratap Nagar ByPass* ☎ *935/250–6351* ⊕ *apnidhani.com.*

$$$ ✕ **Cafe Brewmen.** Stop by this lounge, centrally located near a city garden
INTERNATIONAL   and close to Fateh Sagar Lake, for some interesting blends of coffee or a quick bite or to chill and get comfortable in their sofas. Sandwiches, burgers, and pizzas are on the menu and Wi-Fi is free. It's a lively café and a tad noisy at times. ⑤ *Average main: Rs. 500* ⊠ *Hitawala Complex, Saheliyo Ki Bari* ☎ *294/242–1571.*

$ ✕ **Café Namaste.** This little roadside bakery and café, with courtyard
CAFÉ   or rooftop seating, sells fresh pastries and cakes, as well as delicious, real espresso—a rarity outside of India's major cities. If you come for breakfast, try the baked beans on toast or the soft cinnamon rolls, apple crumble, or date-and-walnut pie. The café is on a busy thoroughfare, but you can take your coffee and pastry upstairs to their sister venue Natural City View, (same menu). They also serve international dishes at lunch and dinner. ⑤ *Average main: Rs. 290* ⊠ *339 Ashoka Haveli, Gangaur Ghat Marg, Udaipar* ☎ *294/242–2303.*

$$$ ✕ **Jagat Niwas Palace Terrace Restaurant.** In a converted haveli at the end
NORTH INDIAN   of one of Lal Ghat's labyrinthine lanes, this restaurant has retained the mansion's lovely design and has spectacular views of the Lake Palace, especially at night, when the vistas capture the incredibly romantic essence of the city. To see the brilliantly illuminated palace seemingly float on the water from a cushioned alcove is a signature Udaipur experience. There is a good range of continental, Chinese, and Indian food; wine, cocktails, and beer available—*Fish à la Jagat* is a highlight during fishing season; otherwise try the *laal maas* (red meat curry), *subz galouti kabab* (vegetarian kebabs), or cannelloni paprika. Service can be slow. There's nightly live music during peak season. ⑤ *Average main: Rs. 600* ⊠ *23–25 Lal Ghat* ☎ *294/242–2860, 294/242–0133* 🖶 *294/241–8512.*

$ ✕ **Maxim's.** On a rooftop—there are many steps to climb—with views
VEGETARIAN   of the Jagdish Temple (and not much more), this well-liked backpacker establishment borrows its name, audaciously, from the famous Parisian restaurant. This Maxim's is strictly vegetarian, with a huge selection of Indian dishes—from Chinese food to baked beans on toast. Adventurous eaters might try the Rajasthani Pizza, a greasy concoction of cheese, veggies, and tomato sauce, sandwiched between two chapattis and deep-fried. The lassis here are some of the best in town. Beer is available. ⑤ *Average main: Rs. 250* ⊠ *Near Jagdish Temple, Jagdish Chowk* ☎ *94/1423–9762* ▬ *No credit cards.*

$$ ✕ **Palki Khana.** Inside the City Palace complex, this casual café, is a
EUROPEAN   perfect postmuseum stop—sit outside under Rajasthani umbrellas if you like to people-watch. The menu emphasizes standard continental café fare, such as salads, sandwiches, pizza, and pasta; try the yummy "mochachillo" (espresso shake) for a caffeine kick. Beer and an extensive variety of international and Indian wines are also available. If you have tickets for the sound-and-light show, you can watch it over dinner (Rs. 400; reservations required) on the patio; if you want dinner but don't have show tickets, you'll have to wait until the café reopens at 9 pm. ⑤ *Average main: Rs. 700* ⊠ *Shiv Niwas Palace, City Palace Complex* ☎ *294/252–8016, 294/252–8017* ⊕ *www.hrhhotels.com.*

$$ ✕ **Rainbow Restaurant.** Popular with younger tourists and backpackers,
INDIAN   this family-run restaurant is a great place for Lavazza coffee and supe-
rior juices—the menu has an incredibly long list of fresh fruit juices
and "mocktails." Tandoori food is the favorite here—try the *chicken
palak* (chicken cooked curry style in spinach sauce), served with high-
quality basmati rice. Other stars of the menu are the butter chicken and
the *paneer masala*. It's also a good spot from which to gaze over Lake
Pichola and the Lake Palace as the sun goes down. $ *Average main: Rs.
400* ✉ *27–28 Lal Ghat, Lake Pichola* ☎ *946/063–1484.*

$$ ✕ **Savage Garden.** This Mediterranean-hued, three-story place is tucked
ITALIAN   away in the heart of Udaipur's Old City, with seating inside, out on
an airy veranda, and in the relaxed courtyard. The menu, just a page
long, is a refreshing change from the sheaves of standard Indian, Chinese, and continental options elsewhere. Owned by a German expat,
the restaurant specializes in homemade pastas, some with an Indian
(spicy) twist, and all dishes are freshly prepared using filtered water.
Try the grilled fish, or Chicken Wajid Ali (stuffed with cheese, butter,
dry fruits, and served with carrot rice). Beer and wine are available,
as is free Wi-Fi, and a selection of unusual locally made cutlery is for
sale. $ *Average main: Rs. 450* ✉ *22, inside Chandpol* ☎ *294/242–5440*
▬ *No credit cards.*

WHERE TO STAY

$$$$ ⬚ **Fateh Garh.** Environmentally friendly, community-minded, luxuri-
RESORT   ous, and with an interesting backstory, this is one of Udaipur's notable
boutique hotels, perched atop a hill adjacent to the Monsoon Palace.
Pros: friendly, polite service; great food; scenic location. **Cons:** a long
drive away from the Old City since it is out in the wilderness; policy
of employing locals can affect efficiency. $ *Rooms from: Rs. 14000*
✉ *Sisarma 6 km (4 miles) from Udaipur* ☎ *294/241–3845* ⊕ *www.
fatehgarh.in* ⤴ *48 rooms, 3 suites* ✦ *Some meals.*

$$$$ ⬚ **Fateh Prakash.** Part of the haughty City Palace complex, this 19th-cen-
HOTEL   tury retreat on the eastern bank of Lake Pichola looks across the water
at the Lake Palace, and oozes stateliness and history—royal portraits,
antiques, chandeliers, ornate ceilings and an abundance of crinkled-
edged arches set the tone. **Pros:** well located and close to city sights;
regal address. **Cons:** service, though warm, can be spotty. $ *Rooms
from: Rs. 20000* ✉ *City Palace Complex* ☎ *294/252–8016, 294/252–
8017, 294/252–8018* ⤴ *35 rooms, 18 suites* ⊗ *www.hrhhotels.com/
grand_heritage/fateh_prakash_palace/index.aspx* ✦ *Breakfast.*

$$ ⬚ **Jagat Niwas Palace Hotel.** Overlooking Lake Pichola, this airy white-
HOTEL   washed 17th-century haveli hotel is one of the best medium-budget
Fodor'sChoice   places to stay in Udaipur, you'd be hard pressed to find better value (or
★   better views). **Pros:** unsurpassed views of the lake and Aravali Hills; best
value in town; short walk from shopping and restaurants. **Cons:** narrow
approach only by auto-rickshaw; no pool or elevator. $ *Rooms from:
Rs. 4250* ✉ *23–25 Lal Ghat* ☎ *294/242–2860, 294/242–0133* ⊕ *www.
jagatniwaspalace.com* ⤴ *28 rooms, 3 suites* ✦ *No meals.*

$$ ⬚ **Lake Pichola Hotel.** For the price, this hotel has some great features,
HOTEL   including a rooftop pool and Upre restaurant where one can spend the
day, rooms with private terraces, suites with Jacuzzi or steam room,

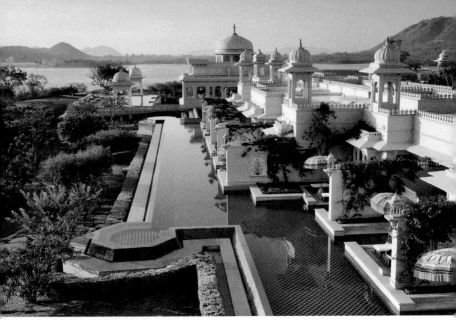

The private pools of the Oberoi Udaivilas hotel

and a wonderful lakeside location. **Pros:** city and lake views; good service; well priced, well located right in the old city so shops and cafés are nearby; elevator. **Cons:** difficult approach through narrow, crowded lanes; noisy at times. ⑤ *Rooms from: Rs. 4200* ✉ *Outside Chandpol, on western side of Lake Pichola* ☎ *294/243–1197* ⊕ *www.lakepicholahotel.com* ➵ *32 rooms, 3 suites* †○† *No meals.*

$$$$
HOTEL
Fodor's Choice
★

🏨 **The Oberoi Udaivilas.** On Lake Pichola, with sublime views of the Lake Palace, City Palace Complex, and ghats, this is one of India's most luxurious (and expensive) hotels—a contemporary palace in its own right, set in 30 acres, reflecting the beauty of Mewar artistry. **Pros:** luxurious spa; great service and surroundings; expansive garden and sanctuary. **Cons:** extremely expensive; rather remote from the old city (but a boat provides a shortcut). ⑤ *Rooms from: Rs. 40000* ✉ *Haridasji ki Magri* ☎ *94/243–3300, 800/562–3764 reservations from U.S. and Canada* ⊕ *www.oberoihotels.com* ➵ *87 rooms, 5 suites* †○† *No meals.*

$$$$
HOTEL

🏨 **Shiv Niwas Palace.** Once the royal guest house, where the maharaja of Udaipur had his guests stay, gracious Shiv Niwas on Lake Pichola is another part of the City Palace complex, and still features plenty of antiques and royal memorabilia in its decor. **Pros:** pretty pool and poolside restaurant with live music; spa; centrally located. **Cons:** some rooms lack views; a touch expensive for what you get. ⑤ *Rooms from: Rs. 15000* ✉ *City Palace Complex* ☎ *294/252–8016, 294/252–8017, 294/252–8018* ⊕ *www.hrhhotels.com/grand_heritage/shiv_niwas_palace/index.aspx* ➵ *36 rooms, 17 suites* ▭ *No credit cards* †○† *Breakfast.*

$$$$ ⌂ **Taj Lake Palace.** This exclusive 250-year-old white-marble palace—
HOTEL location for the James Bond film *Octopussy*—floats like a vision in
Fodor'sChoice the middle of Lake Pichola, and you arrive, of course, by boat. **Pros:**
★ exemplary service to match unique palatial setting; boat service to shore
available all hours; spa on a boat. **Cons:** astoundingly expensive, and
taxes can push up food and beverage costs by 25%. $ *Rooms from: Rs.
36000* ⌧ *Lake Pichola* ☎ *294/242–8800* ⊕ *www.tajhotels.com* ⌁ *66
rooms, 17 suites* |◎| *Some meals.*

$$$ ⌂ **Trident Hilton.** A relatively affordable option among Udaipur's luxury
HOTEL hotels, the Trident is removed from the downtown bustle, amid acres of
beautiful gardens on Lake Pichola. **Pros:** heated pool is pleasant day or
night; peaceful; attentive service always comes with a smile; well priced
for a luxury hotel. **Cons:** uninspiring rooms are on the small side; loca-
tion is not central; busy hotel. $ *Rooms from: Rs. 9500* ⌧ *Haridasji Ki
Magri, Mulla Tulai* ☎ *294/243–2200* ⊕ *www.tridenthotels.com* ⌁ *141
rooms, 4 suites* |◎| *No meals.*

$$ ⌂ **Udai Kothi.** Who can pass up regal accommodations at cut-rate prices,
HOTEL particularly when its rooftop is one of the liveliest places in town?
Pros: great value for the money; beautiful rooftop pool; elevator. **Cons:**
only the suites have lake views; a long walk from the main sites; not
a historical haveli. $ *Rooms from: Rs. 4000* ⌧ *Hannuman Ghat, out-
side Chandpol* ☎ *294/243–2810 to 2812* ⊕ *www.udaikothi.com* ⌁ *42
rooms, 7 suites* |◎| *No meals.*

SHOPPING

Udaipur's main shopping area is around the Jagdish Temple. You'll
discover interesting nooks and crannies here, but watch out for touts.
There are plenty of stores to explore and items to buy, including leather-
bound journals, marble crafts, wooden toys, silver, Udaipuri and Gujarati embroidery, large *pichhwais* (large cloth paintings with lord Krishna
themes done by painters in a group) from Nathdwara, and miniature
paintings in the Mughal and Rajput styles, though most of these paintings are machine-made prints, a fact reflected in the wide disparity in
prices between originals and others. If you want to buy original art,
ask the proprietor to show you his best pieces—and plan to bargain.

ART

B.G. Sharma Art Gallery. Udaipur has many galleries that exhibit original work by burgeoning artists, which attracts serious art buyers. This
gallery was started by B.G. Sharma, one of the preeminent miniature
painters of India. Unlike most artists of miniature paintings, Sharma
produced original ideas rather than copying traditional pictures, and
made a huge contribution to advancing the Mughal, Kishangarh, and
Kangra painting styles. Now his sons run the business but some of
Sharma's legacy remains. As well as creating miniatures themselves in-
house, they also sell the work of other painters. Check the authenticity
of anything you want to buy. ⌧ *3 Saheli Marg* ☎ *294/241–9201* ⊕ *www.
bgsharmaart.com* ⊙ *Closed Sun.*

Gallery Pristine. Specializing in both contemporary and folk art, this gallery has many small pieces by Shail Choyal, a guru of contemporary
Indian painting. Other highlights include the stylized work of Shahid

Parvez, a well-known local artist. ⊠ *60 Bhatiyani Chohatta, Palace Rd.* ☎ *294/242–3916.*

Ganesh Art Emporium. This is a trendy little shop focusing on a gifted young artist, Madhu Kant Mundra, whose oeuvre includes more than 125 funky representations of Lord Ganesh. Don't miss the artistic refrigerator magnets, sculptures, and antique photographs. ⊠ *152 Jagdish Rd.* ☎ *294/242–2864.*

Kamal Sharma Art Gallery. You can often see the artist at work here. Kamal Sharma paints mainly birds and animals on paper, marble, silk, and canvas, in contemporary and traditional styles. All the works are for sale. ⊠ *15-A New Colony, Kalaji-Goraji* ☎ *294/242–3451* ⊕ *www. kamalsharma.net.*

HANDICRAFTS

Bhuwana. A suburb of Udaipur on the road exiting the city toward Jaipur (15–20 minutes away from the city center), Bhuwana is the place to buy something carved in marble, be it an elephant almost as large as your car or a small knickknack like a soap tray or serving dish. There are rows and rows of shops here where with a little bargaining you will get a good deal. Marble workshops are attached to many of the stores and you may be able to see artisans at work. ⊠ *Bhuwana.*

Rajasthali. If your time is limited, head straight to the area around the Jagdish Temple, where you'll find an array of shops stocking an almost overwhelming variety of leather-bound journals, deity statues, and knickknacks; if bargaining isn't your thing, though, head to an emporium instead. The government-run Rajasthali emporium sells high-quality Rajasthani arts and handicrafts, and is a good place to pick up a wool-stuffed washable quilt with a Rajasthani motif. The showroom at Jagdish temple is a bit run down and looks dusty with limited items but the prices here are fixed. ⊠ *Jagdish Chowk, near Jagdish Temple* ☎ *294/241–5346, 294/242–9068* ⊙ *Closed Sun.*

Sadhna. One of the oldest NGOs in India, working for the advancement of the village poor, Sadhna works with rural women in the Udaipur district and trains them to produce traditional appliqué work on cushion covers, bedspreads, silk stoles, bags, kurtas, light quilts, and jackets. Sadhna has gained popularity over the years, and the women also tour around the country to exhibitions in major cities during festivals. There's another branch near the Jagdish Temple in the Old City. ⊠ *Seva Mandir Rd., Old Fathepura* ☎ *294/245–4655* ⊕ *www.sadhna. org* ⊙ *Closed Sun.*

University of Arts. While you're in the Jagdish Temple area, make sure you check out the collection of more than 500 handmade wooden puppets in varying shapes and sizes at this small shop. Ask the folk artist proprietor, Rajesh Gurjargour, an excellent puppeteer, for a private demonstration. Embroidered jackets, handcrafted soft toys, and knickknacks are also for sale. ⊠ *166 Jagdish Marg, off City Palace Rd.* ☎ *294/242–2591, 941/475–7429.*

JEWELRY

Ganta Ghar. From Jagdish Temple, stroll down to the Ganta Ghar (clock tower) and the area around it, a base for silver jewelry. Browse freely, but take care not to purchase items that are merely coated with silver-tone paint. Most of the silver shops here are run-of-the mill and offer little variation in style and price.

Gehrilal Goverdhan Singh Choudhary. More unusual jewelry is on offer here, with a good selection of antique jewelry as well as contemporary designs with stonework. Goverdhan Singh has been collecting jewelry from tribal sources for a decade. Choudhary has been in the business more than two decades, and has exhibited several times abroad. Open 10:30–6:30. ⊠ *72 Jagdish Marg* ☎ *294/241–0806* ☉ *Closed Sun.*

NEED A BREAK? | **Lala Misthan Bhandar.** Next door to Gehrilal Goverdhan Singh Choudhary, near the Clock Tower, is a sweet stall, Lala Misthan Bhandar, where you can satisfy your sweet tooth and refuel with the best *gulab jamun* (fried milk balls in syrup) and *imarti* (pretzel-shape pastries dipped in sugary syrup) in town, its open late till 10 pm. ⊠ *Jagdish Chowk, Near Ghantaghar.*

RANAKPUR

96 km (60 miles) northwest of Udaipur.

This small, out-of-the way village in the woodlands of the Aravali range is famous in all of Rajasthan for its astounding-looking Jain temples. It is said that site for the temples was gifted to the Jain merchant community by a Mewar king, Rana Kumbha in the 15th century, which how the place got its name. The temples are meticulously maintained by descendants of the original community and Ranakpur is an importance pilgrimage point for all Jains.

EXPLORING

Fodor's Choice ★ **Ranakpur Jain Temple.** A three-hour-plus uphill drive on winding roads from Udaipur, the 15th-century Jain Temple at Ranakpur is one of the most stunning examples of Jain temple architecture in the country. It is dedicated to Adinath, also called Rishabha, the first Jain *Tirthankar* (a holy person who has attained enlightenment and takes rebirth to pass on the knowledge to others), and is a less-crowded, more convenient, and perhaps more impressive alternative to Dilwara at Mount Abu. This white marble temple complex, rising out of the forest, is simply breathtaking. Not surprisingly the temple took 65 years to build. after (legend has it) it appeared in a dream to a minister of the Mewar kings. One of the five holiest places for India's Jains, the three-story temple is surrounded by a three-story wall and contains 27 halls supported by 1,444 elaborately carved pillars—no two carvings are alike. The relief work is some of the best in all of India. Below the temple are underground chambers where statues of Jain saints were hidden to protect them from the Mughals. As you enter, look to the left for the pillar where the minister and the architect provided themselves with front-row seats for worship. On one of the pillars is a carving of the creator of the temple. Another pillar is intentionally warped, to separate human works from divine ones—the builders believed only gods could be perfect, so they intentionally added imperfections to some of the columns to avoid causing insult. Outside are two smaller Jain temples and a shrine adorned with erotic sculptures and dedicated to the sun god. There are a few priests around who speak a little English and who act as guides; in return, you should make a small donation. Leather items— shoes, belts, wallets, and more—are not allowed inside the temple. They request menstruating women not to enter (though many modern Jain women ignore this), and there are strict instructions about dress code. You can use a camera but they do not allow photographs of the deity. ■TIP➜ Although there are a couple of hotels in the vicinity, Ranakpur is best visited as a day trip from Udaipur, maybe stopping at Kumbalgarh Fort, 32 km (20 miles) away en route since Ranakpur opens to tourists late in the day. ▣ *Temple free; camera free; video camera fee Rs. 150. Leather not allowed in temple and can be deposited at entry counter* ◷ *Non-Jains, daily noon–5.*

WHERE TO STAY

$$$ **Fateh Bagh.** A short drive from the Jain temple (the main reason to
HOTEL stay here is to avoid taking on the twisting round-trip between Ranakpur and Udaipur in one day), this dramatic-looking royal retreat offers traditionally decorated, enormous rooms; some of the suites have Jacuzzis. **Pros:** serene setting; lovely pool. **Cons:** in the middle of nowhere. ⑤ *Rooms from: Rs. 7200* ⊠ *Ranakpur Rd., Pali district* ☎ *293/428–6186* ⊕ *hrhindia.com* ⬎ *11 rooms, 7 suites* ⦿ *No meals.*

KUMBHALGARH

84 km (52 miles) north of Udaipur.

Perched high on a forested hilltop is the fort destination of Kumbhalgarh, 3,600 feet above sea level. The long Mewar dominance of this area of the country rested on the dynasty's skill of fortress building, and the fort is the main attraction here.

EXPLORING

Kumbhalgarh. When you set eyes on this formidable, isolated fort in a dramatic setting, you will understand its role in the history of these parts, and why it's venerated as a symbol of Rajput valor. This citadel, situated some 3,600 feet above sea level, was well equipped to withstand any kind of siege and was largely the reason the Rajasthani state of Mewar was able resist conquest by Mughal forces time and time again. Although there's less to see here than at Chittaurgarh, it's worth a visit; the countryside that separates it from Udaipur makes for a beautiful, and not too bumpy, drive through lovely scenery. It's also close enough to Ranakpur to visit both in one day.

Built by Maharana Kumbha, one of the mightiest rulers of Mewar, in the 15th century, the fort's massive ramparts run 36 km (22 miles) and can be seen from a distance. The outer wall encloses an area of 83 square km (32 square miles) and you enter through colossal gates (Ram Pol) that might have scared off any enemy. The views of the countryside from Badal Mahal (Cloud Palace)—the fort is one of the highest points in the state–are far-reaching. At one time its ramparts nearly encircled an entire township, with nearly 400 temples (you can still see many of them today), self-contained to withstand a prolonged attack. There's a small, bland café that serves light snacks and drinks. Take a hat and water. ☒ *Kumbhalgarh, Rajasthan* ☏ *Entry Rs. 100; camera fee: Rs. 100* ☉ *Daily 8–5.*

Kumbhalgarh Sanctuary. Surrounding the fort, the modern-day Kumbhalgarh Sanctuary is home to wolves, leopards, jackals, nilgai deer, sambar deer, and various species of birds, and makes for great treks. Inquire at the Government Tourist Office in Udaipur if you're interested in going on a two-hour morning jeep safari here. ☒ *Kumbhalgarh, Rajasthan.*

MOUNT ABU

185 km (115 miles) west of Udaipur.

Once the summer escape of Rajasthani royalty, who each had their over-sized haveli here (they can still be seen today), today Mount Abu is one of India's more popular, read crowded, hill stations. This is one of the few towns in Rajasthan where you can dine sumptuously on Gujarati food, given the proximity to the Gujarat border.

GETTING HERE AND AROUND

The road to Mount Abu is winding and rough in some areas, so make sure to leave early in the morning, without breakfast, if you're making a day trip from Udaipur or arriving here from Ahmedabad. Ideally, you should plan for an overnight stay.

EXPLORING

High in the Aravali Hills, Mount Abu situated on Nakki Lake is Rajasthan's only hill station, and it attracts hordes of tourists from the neighboring state of Gujarat, who come to enjoy the town's cool climate and pretty lakes. It's also a great place to stop if you like taking long walks or are simply looking to escape the heat during the unforgiving premonsoon months (April and May). The town's beautiful Dilwara Jain Temples brings plenty of pilgrims and admirers of art.

Mount Abu's ashram-cult hot spot, **Brahma Kumaris Spiritual University,** attracts thousands of followers from all over the world—members of the sect don white robes or saris and study spiritual knowledge or Raja yoga meditation—you'll see them around town.

Dilwara Temples. The magnificent, awe-inspiring Dilwara Temples, a group of five built of marble between the 11th and 13th centuries, have made Mount Abu a major pilgrimage center for Jains. Admire the stunning intricacy of the carving that covers every inch of the temples, from doorway to dome. Each temple is dedicated to a different Thirthankar (enlightened ascetic). The 13th-century Luna Vasahi and the 11th-century Vimal Vasahi temples are of special note. The highlight of the Luna Vasahi is its ceilings, covered with interconnected marble carvings; the Vinak Vasahi, with its beautiful white-marble columns and dome, is equally splendid. Non-Jains can visit between noon and 6 daily. Leather bags and shoes, and cameras are not allowed in the temple. Entry is free. ☒ *Dilwara Rd., Mt. Abu.*

Guru Shikhar. Past Peace Park, on Guru Shikhar Road, is Guru Shikhar, the highest point between South India's Nilgiri Hills and the Himalayas, in the north. From here you can enjoy excellent views of the country-side. It takes half an hour to reach here from Mount Abu town. ⚠ **Don't venture this way after dark—the winding forest roads make for hazardous driving.** ✉ *About 17 km (10 miles) out of Mt. Abu.*

Nakki Lake. The sacred Nakki Lake, resting between green hills, is said to have been carved out by the gods' fingernails. Several types of boats ply the lake; rides cost approximately Rs. 400 for half an hour. Around the shores of the lake are stalls selling local handicrafts. At Sunset Point, just southwest of the lake, you can take in a romantic Mount Abu sunset, but don't expect peace and quiet in the Indian tourist high season—this is a major beauty spot, and you'll likely be joined by plenty of others. ✉ *Nakki Lake, Mt Abu.*

WHERE TO STAY

$$$
HOTEL

Cama Rajputana Club Resort. Cradled in the Aravali hills, this late-19th-century club is where British officers and royalty from Gujarat and Rajputana came to escape the summer heat, and now it combines modern amenities with country style. **Pros:** rooms belonging to the old club property are old world; lovely lawns; pool. **Cons:** new blocks have modern rooms with nondescript furnishings. ⑤ *Rooms from: Rs. 9000* ✉ *Adhar Devi Rd.* ☎ *2974/238–205, 2974/238–206, 079/560–1234 reservations* ⊕ *www.camahotelsindia.com* ⤴ *42 rooms, 2 suites* ⑩ *Some meals.*

$$$
HOTEL

Palace Hotel (Bikaner House). Besides once being the summer residence of the Maharaja Ganga Singhji, the maharaja of Bikaner, this was for decades also the center of Mount Abu's aristocratic social life and it's still an elegant and hospitable getaway. **Pros:** service is excellent; free Internet; lovely grounds; billiards. **Cons:** no pool; conferences may have an impact on the experience. ⑤ *Rooms from: Rs. 9600* ✉ *Delwara Rd.* ☎ *2974/235–121, 2974/238–673* ⊕ *www.palacehotelbikanerhouse. com* ⤴ *31 rooms, 18 suites* ⑩ *Multiple meal plans.*

CHITTAURGARH

112 km (69 miles) northeast of Udaipur.

Chittaurgarh was for hundreds of years an important Rajput capital until it fell to Muslim conquerors from the north. Indian history books have made Chittaurgarh one of the most famous places in India, and the town attracts hordes of Indian tourists and students. Chittaurgarh town itself is an ugly, nondescript place.

EXPLORING

Chittaurgarh. If any one of Rajasthan's many forts perched grandly on a hill were to be singled out for its glorious history and chivalric lore, it would be Chittaurgarh. It's also gargantuan in size, and there's plenty to explore on a day-trip from Udaipur. This was the capital of the Mewar princely state from the 8th to the 16th centuries, before Maharana Udai Singh moved the capital to Udaipur, and the sprawling hilltop fort occupies roughly 700 acres on a hill about 300 feet high. It was besieged and

sacked three times: after the first two conquests, the Rajputs recovered it, but the third attack clinched it for the Mughals for several decades.

The massive fort encompasses the palaces of the 15th-century ruler **Rana Kumbha,** where Udaipur's founder Udai Singh was born, as well as tiny picturesque palace of **Rani Padmini** surrounded by a small lake and some pleasant gardens. Legend has it that Khilji fell in love with Padmini by gazing at her reflection in the pond in front of her palace. The magic of this fort is to visit her palace and actually visually re-create that very famous scene of history.

Also worth visiting in the fort are the victory towers—the ornate **Vijay Stambh** and **Kirti Stambh**—and a huge variety of temples, including **Kunbha Shyam, Kalika Mata,** and the **Meera temple** associated with the devotional poetess Mirabai. The **Fateh Prakash Mahal** displays some fine sculptures. Plan to spend at least half a day in Chittaurgarh. Note that the sites are spread out and it can get quite sunny, so you may want to drive between some points and it is best to hire an auto-rickshaw to do the circuit (about Rs. 300). You can find a guide for Rs. 200 by the Rampole entrance to the fort or near the Rana Kumbha. ⊠ *Rajasthan* ☎ *147/224–1089* ☉ *Daily 9–6.*

WHERE TO STAY

$ ⌖ **Bassi Fort Palace.** This eccentric 16th-century fort 20 km (12 miles) HOTEL   from Chittaurgarh was converted into a heritage hotel by descendants of the Chundawat royals who once defended Mewar. **Pros:** elegant common areas; period furniture; spacious, comfortable rooms; close to Bassi wildlife sanctuary. **Cons:** no pool or Internet; service lacks finesse; far from Chittaurgarh. ⑤ *Rooms from: Rs. 2400* ⊠ *On Udaipur Chittaurgarh-Bundi-Kota NH–76, Bassi* ☎ *1472/225–321, 1472/225–606* ⊕ *www.bassifortpalace.com* ⇥ *15 rooms, 2 suites.*

BUNDI

210 km (130 miles) south of Jaipur; 279 km (173 miles) from Udaipur.

Fodor's Choice   Pretty Bundi in southeastern Rajasthan is famous for its baoris or step-
★   wells and art as well as its fort and palace. The town once had more than 50 stepwells, providing its only source of water. Many of the town's old buildings and havelis are today painted a striking indigo blue.

GETTING HERE AND AROUND

Although Bundi can easily be reached by train from Jaipur (via Kota), it's even more convenient to rent a taxi with a driver and get there by road (it's about a five-hour drive). Bundi can be done as a day-trip, but it's more relaxing if you spend the night. The town is small enough to be navigated on foot, and most of the attractions are within a mile of each other. If you get tired of walking, auto-rickshaws are easy to find (negotiate a price suggested by your hotel before climbing in).

EXPLORING

The magical little town of Bundi, with its winding lanes and unusual step wells, appears to have been plucked straight from a fairy tale. It's a perfect getaway from the commotion of Jaipur.

One of the murals depicting the life of Lord Krishna, at Bundi Palace

The area now known as Bundi was populated by tribal people until the 13th century, when it was taken over by a clan of Rajputs, and after that was ruled by various dynasties like the Chauhans who were Hada Rajputs until the town was incorporated into the Republic of India after India's independence from the British. Rudyard Kipling is Bundi's most famous former resident, and it is popularly believed that it was during his stay in the little town that he decided to write *Kim*.

Most popular is the 14th-century **Taragarh** (Star Fort), tucked into a hillside above the town (but still within about 1½ km [1 mile] of the center). The run-down, poorly maintained fort, taken over by monkeys, was originally constructed to defend the principality of Bundi from invasion, although these days its biggest draw is its great views of the town and the surrounding countryside. Sunset is the best time to visit, but don't forget a flashlight for the way down. Don't carry food or you will attract monkeys, and carry an umbrella or a stick. **Bundi Palace** is another must-see, both for its impressive architecture and the amazingly well-preserved murals depicting the life of Lord Krishna that grace its interior walls. The palace also has its own *chitrashala* (art gallery), where beautiful old paintings are displayed. Bundi is also well-known for its dozens of *baoris* (step wells), many have fallen in disrepair, which were used by local women to gather water in large vessels in the days before indoor plumbing and hand pumps. The most interesting of these is the steep **Raniji ki Baori** (Queen's Well), which is covered with carvings and stone latticework. The interiors of the nearby identical twin step wells, **Nagar Sagar Kund**, feature banister-free flights of stairs that crisscross down into the well bellow—though you're not allowed to descend,

WHERE TO STAY

$$$ ◫ **Hotel Braj Bhushanjee.** Family-owned and operated, this hotel in a
HOTEL 200-year-old sprawling haveli preserves many of its original features, including carved stone-work, striking Bundi School of Painting murals, and other artwork making a stay here quite like living in an art gallery. **Pros:** excellent location; warm staff. **Cons:** only vegetarian food served; no alcohol. ⑤ *Rooms from: Rs. 6500 ⊠ Below palace, opp. Ayurvedic Hospital, Bundi, Rajasthan ☎ 0747/244–2322, 0747/244–2509 ⊕ www.kiplingsbundi.com ⇆ 18 rooms* ⦿⧵ *Breakfast.*

$ ◫ **Hotel Bundi Haveli.** This boutique heritage hotel, furnished with
HOTEL antiques, is in the heart of the town, with great views of the palace and fort. **Pros:** charming character; clean. **Cons:** staff is not always professional; restaurant is expensive. ⑤ *Rooms from: Rs. 2500 ⊠ 107 Balchand Parra, near Naval Sagar Lake, Bundi, Rajasthan ☎ 747/244–6716, 747/244–6046, 941/403–0426 ⊕ www.hotelbundihaveli.com ⇆ 12 rooms, 2 suites* ⦿⧵ *No meals.*

JODHPUR

343 km (215 miles) west of Jaipur; 266 km (165 miles) northwest of Udaipur.

Jodhpur, Rajasthan's second-largest city, is known as the Blue City because of the pale blue-painted narrow and tall houses of the jumbled and entrancing medieval Old City, which are especially impressive when viewed from the ramparts of Mehrangarh Fort.

There isn't that much to do in Jodhpur, aside from a few sites including the incredible Mehrangarh Fort, and some textile shopping, and many people use the city as a jumping-off point for Jaisalmer, or as a place to overnight on the way to Jaipur or Udaipur. It is also a great city to do a village tour, an opportunity you might not get in larger cities like Udaipur and Jaipur.

Check at the fort if any heritage tours are available. If you have time, Jodhpur is an especially good place from which to take a camel safari into the desert.

GETTING HERE AND AROUND

Getting around Jodhpur is relatively easy. The older part of the city that extends between the clock tower and the base of the Meherangarh Fort consists of narrow lanes, and it's faster and easier to hail an auto-rickshaw (they charge about Rs. 100 for a round-trip) to wander this part of town, since cars cannot enter. You can also walk the shorter distances in the quieter lanes or in the early morning but at other times traffic moves rapidly and

JODHPUR'S SWEETNESS

Jodhpur's famed tradition of hospitality, known as *mithi manuhar,* frequently takes the form of offers of food. Such items, especially *mithai* (sweets), are not to be missed. When you're offered a *mave ki kachori* (milk-based pastry), *besan ki barfi* (a fudgelike sweet made of chickpea flour), *mirchi bada* (fried, breaded green peppers), or *kofta* (deep-fried balls of potatoes or vegetables), don't resist: the offer will be repeated until you take some.

Jodhpur

Old City Walls

Padamsar
Talab
Ranisar
Talab

1

Fort Rd.

Bait ka
Talab

Fateh
Sagar

Nagouri
Gate

Bhagat Sing Marg

2

Mandore Rd.

3

Mahamandir
Station

4

Mansagar

65
61

PAOTA

Hanwant
Garden

Old City
Walls

Gulab
Sagar

Sadar & Girdikat
Bazaar

Clock Tower

Paota
Circle

112

Banar Road

OLD CITY

Nai Sarak

Mertia Gate

Umaid Garden
Museum & Zoo

65
61

112

Central Bus Stand

Sojati Gate

High Court Road

65

Jalari
Gate

112

Station Rd.

Mahatma Gandhi Hospital Rd.

Jodhpur
Station

JNV
University

Ratanada Road

Gausala Road

65
61

RATANADA

5

| 0 | | 1/4 mi |
| 0 | | 500 m |

dangerously, and you will feel more comfortable in an auto-rickshaw even if it is a bumpy, careening ride. For attractions farther afield, auto-rickshaws can easily be hailed on the street.

TIMING

You could squeeze in all the main attractions in one full day, though this won't leave you much time to shop or really get a feel for the city, so try to spend two days here.

ESSENTIALS

Tourist Office Government of Rajasthan Tourist Office ⊠ *RTDC Hotel Ghoomer Campus, High Court Rd.* ☎ *291/254–5083* ⊕ *www.rajasthantourism. gov.in.*

EXPLORING

Jaswant Thada. The royal marble crematorium was built in 1899 for Maharaja Jaswant Singh II. Capping the enormous white structure are marble canopies under which individual members of the royal family are buried. You may see people bowing before the image of the king, who is considered to have joined the ranks of the deities. A peaceful spot to stop, either on your way up to the fort or on your way down. ⊠ *500 yds. northeast of Mehrangarh Fort* ☎ *291/254–8790* ⊕ *mehrangarh.org/mmt/t_thada.htm* 🎫 *Rs. 30; cameras Rs. 25; video cameras Rs. 50* ⊙ *Daily 9–5.*

Mahamandir. Built in 1812 just outside Jodhpur, this old, walled monastery complex (*mahamandir* means "great temple"), which is not very well maintained, also called Natho ka Mandir, still contains a few hundred houses and a school. The monastery belongs to the Nath community, warrior-priests who worked closely with the royal family to arrange support in times of war. Mahamandir is best known for the 84 beautifully carved pillars that surround it. Prayers are offered morning and evening in the main temple. Located in the Mahamandir area of town near the railway tracks and a bit difficult to locate. Check locally for best times to visit. ⊠ *Mahamandir, on way to Mandore, 4 km (2½ miles) northeast of Jodhpur.*

Mandore Gardens. Within the old Marwar capital at Mandore, these gardens house the exquisitely sculpted red-sandstone, carefully looked-after *davals* (memorials or cenotaphs also called *chhatris*) to former rulers, the most impressive being the one dedicated to 18th-century maharaja Ajit Singh. The Hall of Heroes depicts 16 colorfully painted heroes and deities carved from a single piece of stone. The small **museum** on the grounds has sculptures from the 5th to the 9th centuries as well as ivory and lacquer work. It's definitely worth a visit here for the *davals*, but the gardens are not well maintained and full of trash, and are no longer the picnic-spot destination they used to be. There is also a temple devoted to the 330 million Hindu gods. A tranquil place to visit except on weekends and holidays when locals arrive here for outings. There are many monkeys, and people seeking alms. ⊠ *Mandore, 8 km (5 miles) north of Jodhpur* 🎫 *Gardens free; museum Rs. 50* ⊙ *Gardens: daily sunrise–sunset. Museum: Sat.–Thurs. 9–6.*

NEED A BREAK?

Shri Mishrilal Hotel. In the highly competitive world of lassi wallahs, only the strong survive and this one has survived since 1927, making it the oldest in Jodhpur. Look past the simple interior and neon lighting, and choose a flavor, make sure to specify whether you want salty (*khara*) or sweet (*makhani*) and how sweet, and note that the lassis here are consumed with a spoon. They also sell typical Jodhpuri sweets and snacks and are well-known for their soupy, milky *rabri* (thick pudding made from milk and cream). ⊠ *Ghanta Ghar (Clock Tower), Sadar Market* ☏ *291/254–0049.*

Fodor's Choice
★

Mehrangarh Fort. This enormous hilltop fort was built by Rao Jodha in 1459, when he shifted his capital from Mandore to Jodhpur. Looking straight down a perpendicular cliff, the famously impregnable fort, about 500 feet above the city, is an imposing landmark, especially at night, when it's bathed in yellow light. Approach the fort by climbing a steep walkway, passing under no fewer than eight huge gates—if you're not up for the hike, you can take an auto-rickshaw instead for about Rs. 150, or take the elevator (Rs. 35) up two levels from the ticket office. The first gate, the Victory Gate, was built by Maharaja Ajit Singh to commemorate his military success against the Mughals at the beginning of the 18th century; the other seven commemorate victories over other Rajput states. The last gate, as in many Rajput forts, displays the haunting handprints of women who immolated themselves after their husbands were defeated in battle. Inside the fort, delicate latticed windows and pierced sandstone screens are the surprising motifs. The palaces—**Moti Mahal** (Pearl Palace), **Phool Mahal** (Flower Palace), **Sheesh Mahal** (Glass Palace)—and the other apartments are exquisitely decorated; their ceilings, walls, and floors are covered with murals, mirror work, and gilt and you should not miss viewing these chambers. The palace museum has exquisite rooms filled with lavish royal elephant carriages (*howdahs*), palanquins, thrones, paintings, and even a giant tent. It also has an interesting weapons gallery. From the ramparts there are great views of the city; the blue houses at sunset look magical. Another option is to take a zip-line tour around the fort with **Flying Fox** (⇨ *See contacts in Sports and the Outdoors*); it's not for the fainthearted. The fort is possibly the best-maintained historic property in all Rajasthan, and offers an audio tour with headphones (included in the admission price for foreigners). There are two shops, open 9 to 5, run by the Mehrangarh Trust, that can be accessed without visiting the fort, that sell expensive but very attractive handicrafts. There's also a small craft bazaar that offers a variety of bargains. Apart from the fine-dining rooftop restaurant Mehran Terrace, there are also two cafés. For an extra Rs. 30 one can visit 200-year-old Chokelao Bagh, well-laid out palace gardens. ⊠ *Fort Rd.* ☏ *291/254–8790, 291/254–8992* ⊕ *www.mehrangarh.org* ✎ *Rs. 400 (including audio tour and lift); camera fee Rs. 100; video fee Rs. 200; guides for up to 4 people Rs. 225* ☉ *Daily 9–5.*

Umaid Bhawan Palace Museum. Built between 1929 and 1942 at the behest of Maharaja Umaid Singh during a long famine, this public-works

5

project employed 3,000 workers. Now part museum, part royal residence, and part heritage hotel, its art-deco design makes it unique in the state. Amazingly, no cement was used in construction; the palace is made of interlocking blocks of sandstone, something to admire when you stand under the imposing 183-foot-high central dome. The museum's collection includes a model of the palace, royal finery, collections of palace crockery and cut glass, menus, a sample of palace rooms (dining room and lounge), miniature paintings, stuffed big cats, and a large number of clocks. There's a photographic history of how the palace was designed as well as some grand old photographs of the palace, the royal family, and famous visitors. You may catch a glimpse of the titular Maharaja of Jodhpur, who still lives in one large wing, but you certainly won't miss the magnificent peacocks that strut around the palace's marble *chattris* (canopies) and lush lawns. ⊠ *Umaid Bhawan Palace, Airport Rd.* ☎ *291/251–0101* 🖾 *Rs. 50 (free to hotel guests); camera fee Rs. 30* ☉ *Daily 9–5.*

WHERE TO EAT

$$$ ✕ **Chokelao Mehran Terrace.** Sip a chilled beer or wine and enjoy spec-
NORTH INDIAN tacular views of Jodhpur city at this romantically lit restaurant high up within the royal Mehrangarh Fort. Notable more for its ambience than the food or the length of its menu, this touristy outdoor eatery is as good an option as any within the Old City, and it's specially fitting after an evening tour of the fort. Try the traditional Rajasthani food (tasty elegant veg and nonveg thalis), as well as standard tandoori favorites like mutton kebab and paneer tikka. On monsoon days they use indoor a/c dining areas. It opens at 7 pm. ⑤ *Average main: Rs. 250* ⊠ *Mehrangarh Fort* ☎ *291/255–5389, 291/254–8790* ▭ *No credit cards* ☉ *No lunch.*

$$$$ ✕ **Darikhana.** The mood in the evenings at this twinkling, partly open-air
INTERNATIONAL haveli restaurant, located in the shadow of the lit Mehrangarh Fort, is memorably romantic. They serve both Indian and international food, including pastas, Mediterranean, and Thai dishes. Popular Indian dishes are the traditional Rajasthani *laal maas* (spiced well-marinated mutton), chicken curry, *dahi kebab*, and their paneer dishes. The chicken teriyaki and wild mushroom risotto are also delicious. Service is good, and there's a wide variety of drinks. ⑤ *Average main: Rs. 1000* ⊠ *Raas, Tunwarji ka Jhalara, Makrana Mohalla* ⊕ *raasjodhpur.com* ⚲ *Reservations essential.*

$ ✕ **Janta Sweet Home.** Jodhpur's most famous sweet shop, bustling Janta
INDIAN Sweets is a hot favorite with locals and a good place to sample regional delicacies. Test your chilli tolerance level with the spicy *mirchi bada*, a huge pepper that's been breaded and deep-fried. For something sweeter, try the local specialty: *mawa kachori* (a pastry filled with nut-based milk solid), *ghevar* (disc-shape sweet), *rabri laddu* (milk balls). It buzzes till 11 pm so you might want to stop here for dessert. There's another branch of Janta near the railway station. ⑤ *Average main: Rs. 150* ⊠ *3 Nai Sarak* ☎ *291/263–6666, 291/262–5559* ⊕ *www.jantasweethome. com* ▭ *No credit cards.*

$$ ✕ **Jhankar Choti Haveli.** Although this little garden restaurant located in
VEGETARIAN a bungalow (as opposed to a hotel) is not as old as some of Jodhpur's

landmark eateries, it has quickly established itself as a popular spot for travelers to relax and meet new people over a cup of rich *masala chai*. Owned by a Jain, the restaurant is strictly vegetarian and alcohol-free, but even meat eaters will marvel at the Indian house specialties, which are well priced. Go for a thali or vegetable biryani. They also serve pizzas. Jhankar is at its best after dark, when tiny twinkling lights strung through the trees lend a whimsical air to the setting. They have a rooftop dining area as well. Wi-Fi is available. ⑤ *Average main: Rs. 300* ✉ *Jhankar Choti Haveli, Makarana Mohalla* ☎ *291/261–2590.*

$$$$
INTERNATIONAL
✕ **Latitude.** One of the better attempts at upscale cuisine in Jodhpur, the restaurant is a part of Taj group's Hari Mahal hotel. The neo-Mughal-style restaurant serves continental and Indian food, with a few Rajasthani specialties, and there is a buffet (evenings) as well as à la carte options. Pasta dishes are a nice break from the usual Indian fare: the penne *arrabiata* is particularly good as is the spinach lasagne. They offer both north Indian and Rajasthani *thalis* for Rs. 700. On most nights live Indian classical music is performed. ⑤ *Average main: Rs. 1200* ✉ *Vivanta by Taj – Hari Mahal Hotel, 5 Residency Rd.* ☎ *291/243–9700* ⊕ *www.vivantabytaj.com* ⚄ *Reservations essential.*

$$$
NORTH INDIAN
✕ **On the Rocks.** This jungle-theme restaurant is aptly named, not because it has a well-stocked bar, but because the ground inside the mostly outdoor restaurant is covered in gravel. The rich, hearty food is popular with locals as well as tour groups, and at weekends crowds swing to the music in the cavelike bar, Rocktails. On the same road as Ajit Bhawan hotel and close to numerous shopping boutiques, it's an ideal rest stop for a quick drink or lunch. ⑤ *Average main: Rs. 450* ✉ *Circuit House Rd., next to Ajit Bhawan Hotel* ☎ *291/510–2701.*

$
NORTH INDIAN
✕ **Pokar Sweets.** Arrive here, even as early as 6 am, for an old north Indian favorite—piping hot puris and *alu* (deep-fried wheat bread served with potato curry). They also have traditional Jodhpuri sweets, snacks, dosas, and more and are open beyond midnight. Don't expect ambience. ⑤ *Average main: Rs. 200* ✉ *Near Pokar Hotel, High Court Rd.* ☎ *982/902–3001* ▭ *No credit cards.*

$$$$
INTERNATIONAL
✕ **Risala.** If you're looking to feel (and splurge) like royalty, head to this elegant, formal dining room adorned with portraits from the royal collection—or opt for the balcony overlooking verdant gardens. If you like seafood, you're in luck, the prawn curry in a tomato cream sauce is perhaps the best dish here. The roast chicken, roast lamb and pastas are also very well done, while desserts are superb. Service is impeccable. The extensive drinks menu includes internationally sourced wines. Non-hotel guests may have trouble securing a reservation during the busy season; call ahead. ⑤ *Average main: Rs. 2600* ✉ *Umaid Bhawan Palace, Airport Rd.* ☎ *291/251–0101* ⚄ *Reservations essential.*

WHERE TO STAY

$$$
RESORT
⌂ **Ajit Bhawan.** This small, enchanting palace and village complex has several intriguing perks, like a garage full of royal vintage cars available for rent. **Pros:** warm and inviting; cozy bar; free Wi-Fi; paths and lanes connecting rooms create a spacious outdoor feel; large rooms. **Cons:** far from the Old City; tented rooms can be noisy; service can be

slow during peak times. ⑤ *Rooms from: Rs. 9300* ⊠ *Circuit House Rd.* ☎ *291/251–0674, 291/251–3333* ⊕ *www.ajitbhawan.com* ↝ *68 rooms, 24 suites, 10 tents* ⑩ *Breakfast.*

$ **Devi Bhawan.** One of the more moderately priced hotels in Jodhpur,
HOTEL Devi Bhawan is run by a friendly young couple, Prithviraj and Rambha Singh. **Pros:** on a quiet street away from the city; good service; excellent value; free Wi-Fi. **Cons:** not as many facilities as other places; Old City is far but reception can organize an autorickshaw. ⑤ *Rooms from: Rs. 2500* ⊠ *1 Ratanada Circle, Defence Lab. Rd.* ☎ *291/251–1067* ⊕ *www. devibhawan.com* ↝ *25 rooms* ⑩ *No meals.*

$$$ **Fort Chanwa.** This century-old, somber red fort in the dusty village of
HOTEL Luni is now a heritage hotel offering a real get-away-from-it-all experience. **Pros:** charming fort stay; good value. **Cons:** far from anything. ⑤ *Rooms from: Rs. 6500* ⊠ *58 km (36 miles) south of Jodhpur, District Jodhpur, Luni* ☎ *293/128–4216, 291/243–2460 reservations* ⊕ *www. fortchanwa.com* ↝ *75 rooms* ⑩ *Breakfast.*

$ **Hotel Haveli.** An affordable option for those interested in staying
B&B/INN in the heart of the Old City, this hotel also has a rooftop restaurant with excellent views of the city. **Pros:** entrance on quiet street in the otherwise bustling Old City; impressive facade; well-priced. **Cons:** no pool; multistory building with no elevator; can feel cramped; access by auto-rickshaw. ⑤ *Rooms from: Rs. 1090* ⊠ *Makrana Mohalla, behind clock tower, opposite Toorji Ka Jhalra (a step well)* ☎ *291/261–4615, 291/264–7003* ⊕ *www.hotelhaveli.net* ↝ *25 rooms* ⑩ *Breakfast.*

$ **Juna Mahal.** The nearly 400-year-old Juna Mahal, owned by a priestly
B&B/INN family once attached to Jodhpur's royal temples, is tucked away from the congestion in one of the upper streets of the Old City and resembles a carved dollhouse. **Pros:** initmate, cozy, homey lodging. **Cons:** deep in the Old City; lots of steep steps; rooms and bathrooms are small. ⑤ *Rooms from: Rs. 1550* ⊠ *Ada Bazaar, Daga St.* ☎ *291/244–5511* ⊕ *www.junamahal.com* ↝ *5 rooms* ⑩ *Breakfast.*

$ **Karni Bhavan.** Outstanding hospitality is the hallmark of this homey
HOTEL hotel, but you'll enjoy the interestingly themed rooms and the dinners with entertainment, too. **Pros:** large airy rooms; fabulous hospitality. **Cons:** away from action in the Old City; no gym or spa; ordinary pool; no kettle in the room. ⑤ *Rooms from: Rs. 3720* ⊠ *Palace Rd., Ratnada* ☎ *291/251–2101, 291/251–2102* ⊕ *www.karnihotels.com* ↝ *30 rooms, 4 suites* ⑩ *No meals.*

$$ **Pal Haveli.** This 300-year-old rambling haveli (family home) is in
HOTEL the heart of the chaotic labyrinth of central Jodhpur, with views of the Mehrangarh Fort above, and scores high on location and heritage. **Pros:** centrally located; fairly priced; kettle in the room. **Cons:** no pool; congested traffic can make getting in and out difficult and must be done by auto-rickshaw. ⑤ *Rooms from: Rs. 5600* ⊠ *Gulab Sagar, near clock tower* ☎ *291/329–3328, 291/263–8344 cell phone* ⊕ *www.palhaveli. com* ↝ *20 rooms* ⑩ *Breakfast.*

$$$$ **Raas Jodhpur.** Located on the periphery of the older northeastern
RESORT quarter, with marvelous views of Meherangarh, the hotel, a skillful blend of old and new, is away from the thick of the commotion of Jodhpur, but still offers a real flavor of the city. **Pros:** location; views;

Inside Jodhpur's Mehrangarh Fort

spa; romantic dining areas. **Cons:** you need to get here by auto-rickshaw but hotel can make special arrangements; some rooms don't have fort views; expensive. *⟨$⟩ Rooms from: Rs. 19800 ⊠ Tunwar ji ka Jhalara, Makrana Mohalla ☎ 291/263–6455 ⊕ raasjodhpur.com ⤶ 38 rooms, 7 suites ⟨†⟨○⟩⟩ Breakfast.*

$$$ ⛫ **Rohet Garh.** This 17th-century desert fortress 40 km (25 miles) south
HOTEL of Jodhpur is both a heritage hotel and the home of its Rajput family, whose members are your hosts. **Pros:** rooms are spacious and the suites are exceptionally large with tons of character; the bar area is like a semi-outdoors living room and has lovely views of the gardens. **Cons:** small pool; not much to do at the hotel unless you venture out on an organized village safari. *⟨$⟩ Rooms from: Rs. 9500 ⊠ Pali district, Rohet Garh Village ☎ 2936/268–231, 291/243–1161 reservations ☎ 291/264–9368 ⊕ www.rohetgarh.com ⤶ 32 rooms, 6 suites ⟨†⟨○⟩⟩ Breakfast.*

$$$$ ⛫ **Umaid Bhawan Palace.** You can live like (and with) royalty at this mag-
HOTEL nificent palace—one of Rajasthan's grandest hotels—which has featured
Fodor's Choice in many movies and hosted at least one international celebrity wedding.
★ **Pros:** a haven away from the city; impeccable, over-the-top service; the massive lawn is great for walks; excellent restaurants. **Cons:** very expensive; not close to the Old City; some rooms lack privacy. *⟨$⟩ Rooms from: Rs. 96284 ⊠ Off S.H.61, north of Jodhpur Airbase ☎ 291/251–0101 ⊕ www.tajhotels.com ⤶ 22 rooms, 42 suites ⟨†⟨○⟩⟩ Breakfast.*

$$$$ ⛫ **Vivanta Hari Mahal by Taj.** Outside the Old City, this bustling hotel
HOTEL offers a respite from the hustle and bustle, and what it lacks in excitement, it makes up in hospitality and subdued charm—and children will enjoy the nightly puppet show. **Pros:** friendly service; large closets. **Cons:** far from the Old City; busy hotel; lobby is noisy; not a real

palace. ⑤ *Rooms from: Rs. 16000* ✉ *5 Residency Rd.* ☎ *291/243–9700* ⊕ *www.tajhotels.com* ⟿ *93 rooms, 1 suite* ⦿| *Breakfast.*

NIGHTLIFE AND PERFORMING ARTS

If you're looking for nightlife, you'll find Jodhpur rather sedate; your best bet is one of the hotel bars, which are usually open from 11 am to 2:30 pm and 6 pm to 11 pm, though some bars, like the Trophy Bar at the Umaid Bhawan Palace, are only open to hotel guests.

Geoffrey's. This fully equipped bar is reminiscent of an English pub. It's popular among the upwardly mobile Jodhpuri crowd as well as with hotel guests. ✉ *Park Plaza Hotel, Airport Rd., Ratanada* ☎ *291/510–5000* ⊕ *www.sarovarhotels.com* ⊘ *11–11.*

Mehrangarh Fort. Festivals and exhibits are hosted here throughout the year such as sufi music festivals and flamenco; inquire at the Tourist Information Center *(⇨ See Planning section)* or your hotel to see if anything is going on while you're here. ✉ *Fort Rd.* ☎ *291/254–5083 Tourist Information Center.*

SPORTS AND THE OUTDOORS

Many hotels offer not-to-be missed excursions to outlying villages, and most can arrange camel and jeep safaris on request.

Blue House Guest House. If your hotel doesn't arrange excursions, try Manish Jain at the Blue House Guest House; he organizes reasonably priced trips. ✉ *Sumer Bhawan, Moti Chowk* ☎ *291/262–1396* ⊕ *www.guesthousejodhpur.com.*

FAMILY **Flying Fox.** This expat-owned outfitter runs zip-line tours of Mehrangarh Fort, an extraordinary way to get dramatic views of the city. If you book three days in advance you get a discount. Lower age limit is 10 years. ✉ *Mehrangarh Fort* ☎ *98109–99390 cell phone, 291/211–1989* ⊕ *www.flyingfox.asia.*

SHOPPING

Lalji Handicrafts Emporium. Woodwork, antiques, leatherwork, and brass furniture feature in the collection here, which also includes unique painted boxes and *jharokhas* (carved doorways or windows) made of dark wood with brass decoration. This place is a joy if you love antiques. ✉ *Opposite Umaid Bhawan Palace* ☎ *291/251–1378* ⊕ *www.laljihandicrafts.com.*

Maharani Textiles and Handicrafts. Come here for a beautiful array of shawls, bedcovers, cushion covers, and wooden handicrafts. Bargain hard and ignore tales about supplying to global designers. They have another showroom on Circuit House Road opposite Ummaid Bhawan Palace. ✉ *Tambaku Bazaat* ☎ *291/265–3152* ⊕ *Daily 11–8.*

M.V. Spices. A wide selection of spices are available here, clearly marked and packed in plastic for travelers with a passion for cooking Indian food. There's also an outlet on Nayi Sadak, which is easier to find than the main shop, and a stand at the entrance to Mehrangarh Fort. ⊠ *Shop 209B, Sadar Market, near clock tower* ⊕ *www.mvspices.com.*

National Handloom Corporation. For textiles, including cotton dress fabric, and other handicrafts—hidden among the rows of discounted toasters and kitschy house decorations—check out this four-story emporium. ⊠ *Nayi Sadak* ☎ *291/506–1103, 291/503–1198.*

Sadar Bazaar. Jodhpur's vibrant bazaars are among the city's key sights, particularly Sadar Bazaar and the Girdikot Bazaar, near the clock tower. Wandering among the tiny shops dotting these crowded, narrow lanes in the heart of town, you'll get a real feel for the life and color of Marwari jewelry, underwear, steel utensils, kitchenware, leather shoes, trinkets, wedding clothes—you can find just about everything here (including locksmiths and indigenous dentists sitting side by side on the street), many of the local spice merchants here deal in saffron and other spices from all over India. Beware of tourist markups and young men guiding you to their "uncle's store." There are also plenty of stores to shop in if you don't like haggling in bazaars—most notably the government-run emporium.

RANI BAGH

For boutique shopping, visit Rani Bagh, a cluster of high-end retail shops just outside the Ajit Bhawan hotel that sells antiques, silver jewelry, and clothing. Do bargain here, too. If you take a village tour you can do some of your best shopping—pottery, rugs, applique or patchwork fabrics and furnishings, vegetable dye–printed cloth, at good prices—buying from the craftsman directly in the countryside.

Anokhi. The local outlet of the popular brand Anokhi sells good-value Western clothes with an Indian flair, including cotton and hand block prints. ⊠ *Shop No. 5, Rani Bagh, Ajit Bhawan, Circuit House Rd.* ☎ *291/251–7178, 291/251–7179* ⊕ *www.anokhi.com* ☾ *Closed Wed. May–July.*

Bhandari Exports. Wood items are designed according to customer requirements, while maintaining the roots of the artisans' creative process. Antiques are also sold. ⊠ *Old Police Line, Raika Bagh* ☎ *291/251– 0621, 982/922–1777.*

Gems & Jewels Palace. This good local jewelry store specializes in traditional bridal jewelry styled according to Rajasthani royal tradition. ⊠ *Rani Bagh, Ajit Bhawan, Circuit House Rd.* ☎ *291/251–6666.*

Roopraj Durries. Buy your beautifully, painstakingly woven durry from the man who weaved it at Salawas village. At this peaceful, pretty and fairly remote hamlet of thatched homes you can see step by step how these colorful rugs are made by hand and choose from a huge selection. It is a memorable experience to witness this dying art—younger generations are not investing in the business. You can pay by credit card and they ship internationally. ⊠ *Roopraj Durries Udhyog, Salawas* ☎ *998/240–0416* ⊕ *www.rooprajdurry.com.*

Shriganesham Exports. This showroom, attached to the workshop where patchwork quilts and bedcovers are produced, has an exquisite range of textile and soft furnishings, tablecloths, bedcovers, applique work, and shawls. They also have a shop in town at Budhiya Kothi in Rai ka Bagh, but here, a short distance out of town, you can see how it happens. ⊠ *Plot 9, oppoiste Royal Honda, NH 65* ☎ *291/265–7981, 291/265–7980.*

Tulsi. Worth a stop for classic and contemporary textiles and home furnishings. ⊠ *Rani Bagh, Circuit House Rd., next to Ajit Bhawan Hotel* ☎ *291/510–2583* ⊕ *www.neerukumar.com.*

JAISALMER AND NEARBY

The stark, compelling beauty of the Thar Desert draws travelers to far-western Rajasthan—for good reason. Jaisalmer is a picture-perfect medieval city resplendent with golden homes and havelis and a towering citadel, which is an intriguing town in its own right, and is an excellent base for camel safaris into the desert and for day-trips to the photogenic Sam Sand Dunes and Desert National Park. It is easily one of India's most unforgettable destinations, and well worth the journey to this farthest corner of the state.

JAISALMER

663 km (412 miles) northwest of Udaipur; 285 km (177 miles) northwest of Jodhpur; 570 km (354 miles) west of Jaipur.

Fodor's Choice ★ Jaisalmer seems like a mirage: its array of sandstone buildings are surrounded by the stark desert and illuminated in a gold hue by the sun. The ancient city is defined by its carved spires and palaces and the massive sandcastle-like fort that towers over the imposing wall that encircles the town. Jaisalmer is a remote and unusual city; it's out of the way, but it's worth it if you want to see a different side of India, and take a camel safari.

Founded in 1156 by Rawal Jaisal, Jaisalmer is on the western edge of Rajasthan's Thar Desert, about 160 km (100 miles) east of the India–Pakistan border. The city started as a trade center: from the 12th through the 18th centuries, rulers here amassed their wealth from taxes levied on caravans passing through from Africa, Persia, Arabia, and Central Asia. Smugglers were also known to frequent Jaisalmer to work the profitable opium trade. The rise of Mumbai (known then as Bombay) as a major trading port in the 19th century, however, began to eclipse Jaisalmer. And when British India was partitioned into Pakistan and India at independence Jaisalmer's importance waned further when it lost its close access to the port town of Karachi (that went to Pakistan) and slowly became the sleepy place it is today.

Today Jaisalmer draws travelers attracted by the city's fairy-tale architecture and the mystery and harsh, remote charm of the desert. At night the golden fort is bathed in light, which illuminates its seemingly impregnable walls (most of the buildings inside are made out of yellow sandstone).

Jaisalmer is also known for its ornate 19th-century havelis—city mansions with facades so intricately carved that the stonework looks like lace. It's also worth wandering through the mazelike alleys and bazaars, in both the fort and off Gandhi Chowk, although the shopkeepers here can be at times annoyingly pushy, perhaps because they see fewer tourists than elsewhere in Rajasthan you will find a very eclectic selection of handicrafts to choose with more items of leather and patchwork.

Camel safaris are a good way to see the desert. These are great fun, but choose your outfitter carefully—don't skimp and choose a cheap one and choose a tour that offers a vehicle to take you to the desert. Take a light scarf to protect your face in case of a sandstorm, wear sunglasses, and use sun protection lotion.

Staying inside the fort area is the most atmospheric and memorable, but most of the hotels and guesthouses are outside its golden walls; if you do choose to stay in the fort know that this part of town is easily and painlessly accessed by auto-rickshaw only (Rs. 50 from the fort gates to the central square in the fort).

GETTING HERE AND AROUND

Jaisalmer is not easy to reach. There is an airport that has recently been completed but not opened and at this writing there are no commercial flights. From Jodhpur, Jaisalmer is about five hours by car and more than six hours by train; from Jaipur the train ride is about 12 hours; from Delhi it's a grueling 17–18 hours by train. There are no direct trains to Jaisalmer from Udaipur.

With clean lanes, little traffic, and few crowds, Jaisalmer's fort and the surrounding areas are easily covered on foot (heat permitting), although you can also take an auto-rickshaw from the base of the fort to other parts of town. Rickshaws are not metered, so be sure to bargain and fix a price before setting off.

TIMING

Spend at least two nights in Jaisalmer. If you plan to go on a camel safari, set aside at least one extra night for this.

ESSENTIALS

Taxi Companies Hanuman Travels ✉ *Hanuman Circle* ☎ *2992/250–340.* **Swagat Travels** ✉ *Hanuman Circle* ☎ *2992/252–557, 2992/252–057.*

Tourist Offices Tourist Reception Centre ✉ *Near Gadsisar Lake Circle* ☎ *2992/252–406* ⊕ *www.rajasthantourism.gov.in.*

EXPLORING

Bada Bagh. Outside of Jaisalmer proper, on the Ramgarh road, and on the shore of a small artificial lake, this site is home to a collection of picturesque yellowstone cenotaphs (*chhatris*) of Jaisalmer's Rajput rulers. There are royal cenotaphs in the overgrown gardens as well, with canopies under which members of the royal family are buried. Take your shoes off before climbing up to enter a cenotaph. Notice the beautifully carved ceilings and equestrian statues of the former rulers. This is a half-hour excursion and only worth a look if you have time to spare. Make sure you, or the driver of the vehicle you take, knows the way; incorrect signage on this road can lead to unnecessary detours. ✉ *6 km (4 miles) northwest of Jaisalmer* ☎ *2992/252–406* 🎫 *Rs. 50; camera fee Rs. 50; video camera fee Rs. 50* ⊙ *Daily 9–6.*

Desert Culture Centre. Near Gadsisar Lake, this small museum is run by local historian and teacher NK Sharma, who also runs the Folklore Museum, and admission to this interesting anthropological museum is included in the Folklore Museum entry fee (the two museums are slowly merging and will be in the same building in the future, so check before you visit). The culture center has a collection of artifacts about music, culture, and life in the desert including camel decorations and an interesting opium-mixing box. They host daily puppet shows at 6:30, with another at 7:30 pm during peak season. ⊠ *Gadsisar Circle* ☎ *2992/253–723* ✎ *Rs. 50 and includes entry to puppet show (free with admission to Folklore Museum); camera Rs. 50* ☉ *Daily 10–5.*

Fodor's Choice
★ **Golden Fort (Sonar Qila).** Jaisalmer's dazzling 12th-century fort, often likened to an oversized sandcastle, is unquestionably the most charming aspect of an already very charming city. Some 250 feet above the town, on Trikuta Hill, the fort has been inhabited for centuries and is a little town of its own; it's protected by a 30-foot-high wall and has 99 bastions, and several great *pols* (gateways) jut outward from the battlements. Built of sandstone and extremely brittle, the fort is rumored to be an architectural time bomb, destined to collapse in the face of a particularly aggressive sandstorm. So lovely is this structure that the poet Rabindranath Tagore (1861–1941) was inspired to write a poem *Sonar Kila* after seeing it; this, in turn, inspired another creative Bengali—Satyajit Ray made a famous film by the same name.

Inside the web of tiny lanes are Jain and Hindu temples, palaces, restaurants, shops and charming havelis. The fort is very clean and has a sleepy, time-has-stood-still vibe to it. The seven-story **Juna Mahal** (Old Palace), built around 1500, towers over the other buildings and is now home to the **Jaisalmer Fort Palace Museum and Heritage Centre.** A visit to the museum is worth the time: enter via the **Satiyon ka Pagthiya** (Steps of the Satis), where the royal ladies committed *sati,* self-immolation, when their husbands were slain.

Cars and larger vehicles are not allowed in the fort so you most hire an autorickshaw (Rs. 50) to take you. The walk up is also pleasant in cool weather. ✎ *Free. Museum Rs. 300, includes audio tour; camera free; video camera fee Rs. 200. Jain temples Rs. 30, camera fee Rs. 70; video camera fee Rs. 130* ☉ *Fort always accessible. Museum daily 9–5. Jain temples daily 8 am–noon.*

Jain temples. Make sure to visit the seven intricately decorated Jain temples within the fort. They were built from the 12th to 16th centuries, and house thousands of carved deities and dancing figures in mythological settings. The carvings of both the exteriors and the interiors are notable. There are a few rules to observe: photographing some sculptures is not allowed; you'll have to leave any leather items at the gate; food, shoes, and cell phones are not allowed; and menstruating women are asked not to enter the temple. ⊠ *Inside Fort* ✎ *Rs. 200, including camera fee* ☉ *Daily 8–noon.*

Gyan Bhandar. Within the fort, the Jain temple complex library contains more than 1,000 old manuscripts—some from the 12th century, written on palm leaf, with painted wooden covers—and a collection of Jain, pre-Mughal, and Rajput paintings.

Patwon-ki Haveli. Outside the fort, about 1½ km (1 mile) from the Gopa Chowk entrance, are the Patwon-ki Havelis—literally "five mansions"—a string of connected grand, beautifully carved homes built by the Patwa brothers in the 1800s. The Patwas were highly influential Jain merchants who dealt in brocade (although it was rumored that they actually made their money on opium) back when Jaisalmer was an independent principality. The Patwa brothers forbade the repetition of any motifs or designs between their mansions, so each is distinctive. The first of these is arguably the most elaborate and magnificent of all—in addition to exquisitely carved pillars and expansive corridors, one of the apartments in this five-story mansion is painted with beautiful murals. ⊠ *Near Mahavir Bhawan* 🔖 *Rs. 120; camera fee Rs. 100; video camera fee Rs. 100* ⊙ *Daily 9–6:30 (part of complex closed Sun.).*

Sam Sand Dunes. No trip to Jaisalmer is complete without a visit to this photographer's feast. Although the dunes have become somewhat touristy in recent years, with hawkers of all sorts dotting the sand, their wind-carved ripples still create fantastic mirages, and it's still a magical place to be. Many famous Hindi films were shot here. Take a camel safari to the dunes, if you can cope with the heat and the time it takes to get here (all day); riding a camel is a bumpy business. Alternatively, look for "parked" camels a few kilometers before you reach Sam, and take a short ride to the dunes. For those who do not want to ride a camel you can opt for a cart. These short camel or camel cart rides can cost up to Rs 800 if you don't book your excursion through a camel safari agent. Expect some amount of heckling from persistent camel owners and girls offering to dance or sing for you, but don't let it put you off staying for the sunset, which is often spectacular. A peculiar sort of peace descends on the dunes in the late evening, when the icy cold desert wind begins to blow, and this is the most enjoyable part of the dunes experience. Note there are no hotels here, but there are a few permanent camps, for which you may need to book in advance (⇨ *See Royal Desert Safaris, under Tour Contacts*); otherwise you must return to Jaisalmer at night. In summer or monsooon the going can be tough—heat, rain, sandstorms—but still try and take in a ride. ⊠ *42 km (26 miles) west of Jaisalmer.*

WHERE TO EAT

$ × **8 July Restaurant.** Run by an eccentric Indo-Australian and his wife
CAFÉ Rama Bhatia, this second-floor vegetarian restaurant serves simple snacks, pizzas, vegetable dishes, waffles, and wonderful coffee milk shakes throughout the day—the ice cream and freshly baked bread is made on the premises. Indian dishes on the menu include egg curry and *pav bhaji* (vegetable curry with bread), a popular street-food snack served throughout Maharashtra and Mumbai. Homesick Brits and Australians should note that Marmite and Vegemite can be purchased here. The restaurant is just inside the fort, up a staircase, and has beautiful views of Jaisalmer's Old Palace opposite. ⑤ *Average main: Rs. 100* ⊠ *Fort* ☎ *2992/252–814* ▭ *No credit cards.*

$ × **Jaisal Italy.** At the base of the fort, this little Italian restaurant has a
ITALIAN lovely vibe. The interior is simple yet far from rustic, and the open rooftop area is perfect for people-watching. It also has a huge advantage: it

Jaisalmer

Train Station

Old City Walls

Malka Pol

Kishangal Pol

Mahangarh Road

Gandsisar Road

Barmer Road

Gadsisar Lake

Bus Stand

Gadisar Pol

Tilon Ki Pol

Bakta Market

Fort Rd

Jaisalmer Fort Gate

Jaisalmer Fort Palace Museum

Old City Walls

Gandhi Chowk

Fort Road

Fort Walls

Gadisar Road

Amar Sagar Pol

Hanuman Circle

Hanuman Circle Road

Shahid Poonam Singh Stadium

Sam Road

Ram Gargh Rd

Jawahar Niwas Palace

Government Archaeological Museum

1/4 mi

300m

0

0

Bada Bagh **2**
Badal Vilas **3**
Desert Culture Centre **7**
Golden Fort **5**
Jain temples **4**
Patwon-ki Haveli **6**
Sam Sand Dunes **1**

is one of the only restaurants with an indoor area with air-conditioned comfort. The menu focuses on well-cooked vegetarian Italian pasta dishes and pizza, as well as good espresso and tiramisu. They also serve Spanish-style tortillas, quite a rarity in India. Beer is available. ⑤ *Average main: Rs. 250* ⊠ *By First Gate of fort* ☎ *2992/253–504* 🖃 *No credit cards.*

$ ✕ **K.B. Cafe.** Rajasthani vegetarian food is the specialty at this small
NORTH INDIAN family-owned rooftop restaurant, but don't expect the palate-burning dishes that Rajasthan is known for—the spice levels here are significantly toned down to suit westerners. If you haven't yet tried quintessentially Rajasthani dishes *dal bati churma* (lentils, rolls, and sweetened wheat and butter paste, sort of the Rajasthani equivalent of bread and butter) or *ker saangri* (desert vegetable), this is the place to do so. For a taste of something local, try the Marwari Thali, an assortment of regional vegetarian dishes served with rice and chapatis. The café has Wi-Fi. ⑤ *Average main: Rs. 150* ⊠ *K.B. Lodge Hotel, opposite Patwon ki Haveli* ☎ *2992/253–833* 🖃 *No credit cards.*

$ ✕ **Little Tibet.** Most of the restaurants within the fort are vegetarian for
CAFÉ historical reasons—mainly vegetarian Brahmin families lived in the fort. But a small section, where Rajput families live, have a few nonvegetarian restaurants—Little Tibet is one of them. It serves a mix of Tibetan (momos, vegetable and meat, great thukpa soups), Chinese, and Indian, with a few global items thrown in. The Indian nonvegetarian food is competently cooked if not hugely exciting; Tibetan fare is better. You can either eat at the main level or climb up to the rooftop, lit with fairy lights, and eat under the stars. It stays open later than most places inside the fort. ⑤ *Average main: Rs. 250* ⊠ *Fort Kotri Para* ☎ *779/195–7921* 🖃 *No credit cards.*

$$ ✕ **Saffron Restaurant.** The emphasis here is on traditional Rajasthani
ECLECTIC dishes, Indian, and tandoor (Indian clay oven roasts), especially chicken delicacies. They offer a special Nachana *thali* (vegetarian and nonvegetarian). Continental specialties include roast chicken with potatoes, as well as a selection of gratins and sizzling platters. There's also a large selection of all-day breakfast dishes. The restaurant sells beer, wine, and other alcohol at very affordable prices. ⑤ *Average main: Rs. 400* ⊠ *Nachna Haveli Hotel, Goverdhan Chowk* ☎ *2992/252–110, 2992/255–565* ⊕ *www.nachanahaveli.com.*

$ ✕ **Vyas Meal Service.** Mrs. Vyas, well into her 70s, cooks some of the
NORTH INDIAN best food in Jaisalmer. You need to go to her little home inside the fort early in the morning and request her to cook your lunch or dinner, and come back to her home to have it in a family environment. Homemade Indian food is the best Indian food you can eat—so jump at the chance to sample it. ⑤ *Average main: Rs. 300* ⊠ *Vyas Para, near Ristorante Italiano, Fort.*

WHERE TO STAY

$$ 🏠 **Garh Jaisal.** This cozy haveli hotel, inside the 11th-century fort, is
B&B/INN run like a homestay by the family who owns it, and makes for a special stay. **Pros:** location; quiet, clean surroundings. **Cons:** no meals apart from breakfast; rooms have no TVs or phones. ⑤ *Rooms from: Rs.*

5450 ⊠ Fort Kotari Para ☎ 2992/253–836 ⊕ hotelgarhjaisal.com ↩ 7 rooms ⯑⊙⯑ Breakfast.

$$$
HOTEL
🏨 **Gorbandh Palace.** This expansive retreat run by the royal family of Udaipur's efficient hotel company Historic Retreat Hotels is a good option if you're looking for a break from the city center. **Pros:** spacious property; nice pool; well priced; music evenings in season. **Cons:** slightly institutional and bland rooms; corridors could do with better lighting; hotel lacks intimacy. ⑤ *Rooms from: Rs. 7200 ⊠ 1 Tourist Complex, Sam Rd. ☎ 2992/253–801 to 807 ⊕ www.hrhindia.com ↩ 83 rooms, 3 suites ⯑⊙⯑ Breakfast.*

$$$
HOTEL
🏨 **Killa Bhawan.** The location of this ancient hotel, built into the walls of the fort, could not be better: the views are great, and with their rainwater harvesting system they are admirably eco-friendly. **Pros:** fabulous views from the terrace; room rate includes breakfast; excellent service. **Cons:** steep stairs; no TVs and phones in the room; some rooms have common bathrooms. ⑤ *Rooms from: Rs. 8510 ⊠ Fort, 445 Kotri Para ☎ 02992/251–204 ⊕ www.killabhawan.com ↩ 8 rooms, 3 suites ⯑⊙⯑ Breakfast.*

$
B&B/INN
🏨 **KB Lodge.** Famous for its traditional Rajasthani *thali*, available in its rooftop eatery, accommodations are equally authentic and striking at comfy KB, located smack in the center of town near the historic Patwon-ki-Haveli. **Pros:** well located; good pricing; close to restaurants and sights. **Cons:** not particularly atmospheric. ⑤ *Rooms from: Rs. 2128 ⊠ Patwon ki Haveli ☎ 2992/253–833 ⊕ www.killabhawan.com ↩ 6 rooms ⯑⊙⯑ Breakfast.*

$$$
HOTEL
🏨 **Mandir Palace.** Like something out of a fairy tale, this rambling 200-year-old palace-hotel at Gandhi Chowk has a breathtakingly beautiful carved exterior that incorporates turrets, arched doorways, windows, and balconies. **Pros:** in the center of town near the better restaurants; authentic ambience; nice pool. **Cons:** rooms do not reflect the character and heritage of the place. ⑤ *Rooms from: Rs. 8000 ⊠ Gandhi Chowk ☎ 11/46035500, 2992/252–788, 2992/252–951 ⊕ www.welcomheritagehotels.in ↩ 28 rooms, 6 suites ⯑⊙⯑ Breakfast.*

$
HOTEL
🏨 **Nachana Haveli.** A 10-minute walk from the Golden Fort, this 18th-century haveli exudes old-world charm and is owned and run by descendants of the Maharaja Kesri Singh, who ruled over Jaisalmer during the 1700s. **Pros:** central; reasonably priced; free Wi-Fi. Saffron, one of the better restaurants of the city is on the rooftop. **Cons:** no pool; basic amenities; some windowless rooms; steep steps to the restaurant. ⑤ *Rooms from: Rs. 3500 ⊠ Gandhi Chowk ☎ 2992/252–110, 2992/255–565 ⊕ www.nachanahaveli.com ↩ 12 rooms, 2 suites ⯑⊙⯑ No meals.*

$$$
RESORT
🏨 **Suryagarh.** Like a mirage in the desert, this contemporary, elegant fort rises out of the sand, luring you to its ramparts—once inside, the interior is equally impressive. **Pros:** scenic location; atmospheric; elevator. **Cons:** 13 km (8 miles) out of Jaisalmer in the middle of nowhere. ⑤ *Rooms from: Rs. 8998 ⊠ Kahala Phata, Sam Rd. ☎ 2992/269–269 ⊕ www.suryagarh.com ↩ 62 rooms, 28 suites ⯑⊙⯑ Breakfast.*

$$
B&B/INN
🏨 **Victoria.** There are very few comfortable lodgings inside Jaisalmer fort, but this is one of them. **Pros:** well-located and well-priced. **Cons:** only breakfast is served; service is patchy. ⑤ *Rooms from: Rs. 4551 ⊠ Kund*

Para ☎ *2992/252–150, 2992/253–844* ⊕ *www.hotelvictoriajaisalmer. com* ⤴ *11 rooms* |◎| *Breakfast.*

CAMEL SAFARIS

Safari prices and types of excursions vary dramatically depending on the itinerary and the level of tourist crush. Camel safaris are slow; if you're pressed for time, try combining them with jeep travel and accomplish it in one evening. One option is to contact the Rajasthan Tourism Development Corporation's Tourist Reception Center (☎ *2992/252–406*) for reservations.

Royal Desert Safaris. The oldest and most-established agent in town offers trips to nearby villages and overnight sojourns in the desert. ✉ *Nachna Haveli, Gandhi Chowk* ☎ *2992/252–538, 2992/251–402* ⊕ *www. campsandsafaris.com.*

⇨ *For more about camel safaris, see the "Camels: Ships of the Desert" boxed feature.*

SHOPPING

Jaisalmer is famous for its mirror work, embroidery, and woolen shawls. Local artisans also make attractive, good-quality wooden boxes, silver jewelry, leather items, patchwork bedcovers, mats and cushion covers, trendy cotton clothing, and curios. The main shopping areas are **Sadar Bazaar, Sonaron Ka Bas, Manak Chowk,** and **Pansari Bazaar,** all within the walled city, near the fort and temple areas. Sonaron Ka Bas, in particular, has exquisite silver jewelry. Avoid solicitors dispensing advice, take time to browse carefully, and bargain hard.

Khadi Gramudyog. This shop has *khadi* (hand-spun cotton) shawls, Nehru jackets, scarves, and rugs. There is also a branch outlet at Hanuman Chowk. ✉ *Dhibba Para, near fort, in walled city.*

Suresh Photo Studio. This little photographic shop has been around for umpteen years and sells lovely old and framable prints of Jaisalmer. It's not to be missed. ✉ *Katchery Rd., near Patwon ki Haveli* ☎ *2992/252–814.*

MUMBAI

WELCOME TO MUMBAI

TOP REASONS TO GO

★ **All of India in one city:** Mumbai is both modern and old-fashioned, rich and poor, beautiful and ugly—all of India concentrated in one metropolis.

★ **One big feast:** From down-home seafood joints to upscale temples of gastronomy, many of Mumbai's restaurants are the best in India.

★ **Experience India's bazaars:** The buzz of a typical Indian bazaar is fascinating, and Mumbai is packed with them; time to get shopping.

★ **Check out Chowpatty:** No visit to Mumbai would be complete without a nighttime stroll along this carnivalesque stretch of beach.

★ **The Ancient Caves of Ajanta and Ellora:** Take a side trip to see the awe-inspiring carvings and paintings here, using Aurangabad as a base.

1 Colaba. The tip of Mumbai's peninsula is one of the oldest parts of the city, home to the majestic Taj Mahal Palace Hotel, the Gateway of India, and the Colaba Causeway, the city's main commercial drag.

2 Fort and Marine Drive. From the winding lanes of quaint Kala Ghoda (a tiny enclave within the Fort District) to the long promenade of Marine Drive, this neighborhood provides a good wander, and the best seafood in town.

3 Malabar Hill and Nearby. Mumbai's richest neighborhood also houses some of the city's most important holy sites.

4 Central Mumbai. A bit of a no-man's-land when it comes to sightseeing, the densely populated center of the city does have a number of choice dining and lodging options.

5 CST and Nearby. In the shadow of Mumbai's massive Victorian train station, this is where you'll find the city's best street food and the biggest, busiest bazaars.

6 Elephanta Island. Just a short ferry ride from South Mumbai lie the ancient caves of Elephanta: a historic getaway from the ultramodern city.

6

GETTING ORIENTED

Mumbai is not only India's largest city, it's also one of the largest cities in the world, both in size and population. Nearly 20 million are crammed into an area of a little more than 4,000 square km (1,600 square miles)—that's about 5,000 people per square km (11,000 people per square mile). On a peninsula jutting out of the western coast of India and facing the Arabian Sea, in the state of Maharashtra, Mumbai is roughly equidistant from the three other main Indian cities of New Delhi, Kolkata, and Chennai.

7 Juhu, Bandra, and the Western Suburbs. The neighborhoods along the northwestern side of the peninsula and on the suburban train line are growing fast. Juhu, probably the northernmost suburb tourists are likely to visit, offers a number of nice hotels, and Juhu Beach—great for a sunset walk. Bandra is home to Bollywood's studios, and where most of India's biggest celebrities live. Other suburbs have restaurants that make a visit worthwhile.

8 Aurangabad and the Caves. Aurangabad, about 400 km (250 miles) east of Mumbai, is a base for exploring the astounding cave temples of Ellora and Ajanta.

EATING WELL IN MUMBAI

Mumbai has a robust tradition of eating out for cheap—you can dine out on a dime at working-class diners or stretch your dollar at bars and cafés—but it's also a modern metropolis with an exciting, extensive, and relatively affordable cosmopolitan dining scene.

(top left) A plate of *bhel puri*; (top right) Potato snacks on display in the Zaveri bazaar; (bottom right) A bowl of lamb *dhansak*

With its origins as a fishing village, Mumbai is blessed with a strong coastal culinary tradition. And because it's also a historic port of commerce, Mumbai also has absorbed influences from foreign traders and settlers (among them, Portuguese, Iranians, and Brits) and Indian communities that came here for trade. Maharashtrian food, marked by the use of peanuts, coconut, and chillies, dominates home cooking and the city's street-food options. Also significant are the culinary traditions of the Gujarati Hindus, Jains, and Parsis—the first two for their elaborate vegetarian contributions and the latter for its Persian- and British-influenced dishes. Regionally themed *thalis* (platters with lots of small dishes) are a popular way to sample an assortment of dishes from distinct cuisines.

DABBAWALAS

Dabbawalas, or tiffin carriers, are a symbol of Mumbai's industriousness. An institution since the late 1800s, they ensure that hundreds of thousands of professionals get fresh, home-cooked meals delivered daily to their offices. Wives and mothers fill containers, which are picked up and delivered by foot, bicycle, and train via a supply chain organized by an efficient system of coded marks.

BHEL PURI

Probably the most common street food you'll see in Mumbai is **bhel puri;** the crunchy, piquant, puffed-rice snack is sold on almost every street corner. Best savored during a stroll on Chowpatty Beach, *bhelwallas* blend the puffed rice with onion, tomato, coriander, and a sprinkling of powdered spices like cumin, rock salt, and chilli powder; a chutney made of tamarind, dates, and jaggery (unrefined brown sugar); and a chutney made of coriander, mint, green chillies, and peanuts. The addictive combination is tossed with fine shreds of fried gram (chickpea) flour and, sometimes, raw mango, then served on stitched-leaf plates.

PAV BHAJI

Pav, the local word for leavened bread, comes from the Portuguese *pão*; "bhaji" is a curried vegetable dish. The combination, **pav bhaji,** is served late into the night on Mumbai's streets, but also in fast-food places and some hotel restaurants. A spicy mash of potato that's been fried and simmered into an orange paste is sopped up with soft white-bread rolls that have been lightly toasted with butter on a griddle. Slivers of raw onion, a squeeze of lemon, and a coriander garnish add a sharp kick.

DHANSAK

The flagship dish of the Parsi community, **dhansak** is a labor-intensive production

that constitutes the big weekend meal. This stew always includes lentils and is usually made with lamb and vegetables like radishes and gourds. Dhansak lends itself to adaptation, though, and can be made with fish, chicken, or paneer. It's a filling dish that can be eaten with bread or rice.

BATATA VADA

Mumbai's answer to french fries, **batata vada** are mashed-potato patties coated with batter and deep-fried into a crisp-and-soft salty snack that's irresistible when fresh. Both the potatoes (*batata*) and the gram-flour batter are spiced, and the fritters are served with green chilli chutney. Every Mumbai barfly has his favorite go-to spot for a postdrinking *vada pav*: a *batata vada* sandwiched in a greasy, fried-bread bun. Yum.

MODAK

An unusual dish found in Mumbai and parts of south India is **modak,** a type of sweet dumpling. In Maharashtra, modak are usually prepared for the late-summer Ganesh Chaturthi holiday, as they're thought to be the favorite treat of the elephant-headed god celebrated on this day. Filled with coconut and unrefined sugar, these rice-flour dumplings can be steamed and eaten with ghee. Another version less particular to this region uses different flour and deep-fries the dumplings.

THE BAZAARS AND MARKETS OF MUMBAI

Mumbai is not a city for sightseeing in the traditional sense—it's more a destination that you need to experience through your five senses, and there's no better way to do this than by going shopping in one of the city's teeming bazaars.

(top left) Produce at Crawford market; (top right) A relics shop in Chor Bazaar; (bottom right) Flower garlands for sale

No one comes to Mumbai to shop at luxury boutiques—indeed, the locals don't, either, because high import taxes make it cheaper to buy name brands like Gucci abroad—they come to experience the racing pulse and frenzied pace of the markets. From handcarts tottering down crowded lanes, overloaded with antiques in Chor Bazaar, to succulent street food on the by-lanes of Bhendi Bazaar, to the overwhelming madness of the wholesale trade at Crawford Market, to the glittering gold of Zaveri Bazaar, Mumbai knows how to shop. If you consider yourself a bargainer, this is the place to test your skills—Mumbai merchants are some of the trickiest in the world, so be prepared to cut whatever price you're quoted in half, and then in half again.

THE ART OF THE BARGAIN

Unlike other parts of the world, where bargaining can sometimes take on a mean-spirited tone, in India the back-and-forth is part of the joy of shopping. Here bargaining is a game both you and the merchant are in on, so have fun with it: he's going to go extremely high, so you should go extremely low, then walk away when he won't come down. He'll likely call you back, with a smile on his face.

ANTIQUES, CHOR BAZAAR

Tourists—and locals—spend hours in crowded Chor Bazaar for the chance to dig out a hidden gem, lost for ages beneath mountains of ancient antiques. Although the market's best finds are probably long gone, there is still the chance you might get lucky with vintage furniture or prints from decades gone by, but only if you bargain, and bargain hard. *Chor* is the Hindi word for thief, and if you're not firm—or don't have a local to help you with your purchasing—you're likely to get taken for a ride. ■TIP→ Do a round of the bazaar, taking notes on the items you like and which stall they're in; then, if you have a local friend, send him or her around the next day to buy the items for you, at a fraction of the quoted price.

ANYTHING AND EVERYTHING (IN BULK), CRAWFORD MARKET

For an all-encompassing Mumbai market experience, look no farther than Crawford Market, where you can find everything from household goods to wholesale vegetables to live poultry to knickknacks—it's definitely worth checking out, even if you're not planning to buy any of the above. To see Crawford in all its glory, go on a weekday, when the market, housed in a 140-year-old British Raj–era building, is packed with housewives (or, more likely, their maids) bargaining over the price of Alfonso mangoes, tableware sets, and

plastic bags. ■TIP→ Steer clear of the area that sells pets if you're sensitive; the dogs, cats, and birds in this section of the market are not treated very well, and the scene can be depressing.

CLOTH, MANGALDAS MARKET

More than 1,000 shops cram the far side of Crawford Market, in an area called Mangaldas, where the best fabrics in town are available at rock-bottom prices (sold by the bolt). If you're looking to get Indian clothing made, this is the place to pick up the fabric you need. If you sew a little yourself, Mangaldas is a must-visit.

STREET FOOD AND JEWELRY, ZAVERI AND BHENDI BAZAARS

This pair of bazaars blend into one another, north of Crawford Market, and if you're looking for gold or, better yet, the best street food in Mumbai, this is the place to go. Shady is the name of the game here—from the money-laundering operations that most of the jeweler's in Zaveri engage in to the questionable hygiene of most of the street-food stalls on Khao Galli and Muhammad Ali Road; but if you want a great deal on jewelry, or have the stomach and the desire to taste the best of what Mumbai's carnivorous side has to offer, this is it.

6

MUMBAI'S HOLY SITES

Although it's not generally known for its religious heritage, Mumbai has a holy legacy going back hundreds of years, with sites dedicated to most of the world's major religions scattered throughout the city.

(top left) The Knesseth Eliyahoo synagogue; (top right) At the Haji Ali shrine; (bottom right) Mount Mary church, in Bandra

Not surprisingly, Hindu sites dominate any religious-oriented tour of Mumbai—from Siddhivinayak, central Mumbai's grand temple to Lord Ganesha, to Malabar Hill's peaceful, isolated Banganga water tank—but the city is also home to one of the world's most unique mosques (Haji Ali Shrine, whose location in the Arabian Sea means it's only accessible during low tide) and colorful synagogues (the sky-blue Knesseth Eliyahoo synagogue in Kala Ghoda). So if you need a break between booming bazaars and bumping bars—though, to be fair, some of these sites are likely to be just as busy as the hottest clubs in town—wander over to one of Mumbai's many temples, churches, mosques, or synagogues.

PAYING RESPECTS

How to be suitably respectful in a place of worship can be a little confusing—whether to take off your footwear, cover your head, or remove your hat. Keep the following in mind: If you see a pile of shoes outside a temple, remove yours as well; if you see a collection box in front of an idol, drop in a coin or two; and if you're still not sure what to do, ask a local.

HAJI ALI SHRINE

One of the most unusual mosques in the world lies in the middle of the Arabian Sea, just off one of Mumbai's busiest intersections. At high tide it looks like an isolated island in the middle of a bay. But during low tide the narrow 1 km (½-mile) pathway to the 500-year-old tomb is revealed. It's especially busy on Thursday and Friday, when upward of 40,000 pilgrims visit the site.

BANGANGA WATER TANK

According to the Hindu epic the *Ramayana*, the god Rama stopped at this spot while searching for his wife Sita, and asked his brother Lakshmana for some water. Lakshmana shot an arrow into the ground and water gushed out, creating what would become Banganga. The first tank, used for storing rainwater, is said to have been built here in the 11th century, and a more formal version was constructed in the 1700s. The current tank, built in the early 20th century, is a serene spot.

SIDDHIVINAYAK TEMPLE

Siddhivinayak Temple. Pilgrims travel from far and wide—often on foot—to visit the Siddhivinayak Temple, dedicated to Ganesh, the elephant-headed god. The shrine is renowned throughout the Hindu world for its purported wish-granting properties, and attracts worshippers of every stripe—from Bollywood beauties to industrial titans

to slum dwellers. Tuesday is Ganesh's day, and the road to the temple is especially busy then. ✉ *Prabhadevi, Central Mumbai* ☎ *22/2437–3626* ⊕ *www. siddhivinayak.org.*

KNESSETH ELIYAHOO SYNAGOGUE

This pale, light blue synagogue stands out among the gray and brown British Raj buildings of winding Kala Ghoda. It's worth a visit more for its exteriors than its interiors—the sparsely attended services are a sign of Mumbai's dwindling Jewish population.

JAIN TEMPLE

Officially known as Babu Amichand Panalal Adishwarji Jain Temple, but usually just referred to as the Jain temple, this small but very opulent (thanks to its diamond merchant benefactors) temple sits atop Malabar Hill, full of ornate sculptures and elegant frescoes, and topped with an arched dome extravagantly emblazoned with the 12 signs of the zodiac. The Jain temple is a testament to the wealth and status of a people who make up but a fraction of 1% of the Indian population.

CATHOLIC BANDRA

Tucked between Bandra proper and Bandra Reclamation is the Catholic village of Bandra—a small slice of Goa here in the big city. With tiny, winding lanes, small bungalows, a few churches, and a simple, village atmosphere, it makes for a charming place to wander.

Updated by Michael Edison Hayden

Mumbai, sometimes called the Maximum City, after Suketa Mehta's 2004 nonfiction book of the same name, encapsulates the dynamism and chaos of modern India better than any other city. In this sprawling, muscular place by the sea that you'll find everything from succulent street food to haute cuisine, bargain-basement bazaars to haute couture, humbling poverty to staggering wealth, sacred temples to hedonistic nightclubs. Mumbai *is* in many ways the New York City of India, and the many of the locals carry the same kind of chip on their shoulders—despite the madness, they wouldn't trade it for any other place on Earth.

Mumbai is a city of extremes, where slum-dwelling strivers making dollars a day serve Bollywood stars and industrial billionaires. It's a 24-hour city stocked with some of the best late-night street food in the world, as well as fine-dining restaurants of renowned chefs. It's a cosmopolitan city of people from all over India that's nonetheless home to strident parochialism. It's a city of dreams for millions of Indians that, at the same time, affords so few any measure of comfort. And it's a beautiful city of silver towers when viewed by twilight from the Bandra-Worli Sea Link bridge over the Arabian Sea, but that sight quickly turns into a maze of winding, dirty streets and alleys when viewed up close.

Sensory overload is the name of the game on the island formerly known as Bombay (and yes, most locals still call it by its previous moniker). The first thing that hits you when you arrive at the airport is the smell—spicy, fishy, and, to be honest, often not altogether pleasant. Next comes a crazed cab ride through the seemingly lawless streets (should your driver run a red light or, just as likely, drive on the wrong side of the road, try to remain calm). Then a traffic jam in the midst of a veritable symphony of honking, in which barefoot children, often holding infants, and tragically disfigured men and women knock at your window, begging for change. Persevere through, though; embrace and try to understand the natural hazards of the developing world, and you'll find yourself in the middle of a beautiful, often inspiring city.

PLANNING

WHEN TO GO

HIGH SEASON: DECEMBER TO MARCH
Every year, Mumbaikars wait for the one-month period between mid-January and mid-February when the weather turns breezy and clear—a welcome respite from the sweltering heat (or pouring rain) that otherwise swamps the city. If you hit that sweet spot, you're golden—and you'll have also just missed NRI season, when the Non-Resident Indian relatives of locals visit from abroad during Christmas vacation (and prices explode). Because most tourists arrive in Mumbai in winter, it's important to make hotel and transportation arrangements ahead of time.

LOW SEASON: APRIL TO MID-SEPTEMBER
Mumbai's first summer starts at the tail end of March, increasing in heat and humidity until the monsoon breaks the cycle to cool things off, usually in mid-May; the rainy season lasts until mid-September, when another hot season comes around. None of these times are particularly pleasant—it's ungodly hot, then raining buckets, and then ungodly hot again. But those willing to test their mettle will find two joyous surprises: low hotel prices, and a monsoon that is not nearly as bad as you'd imagined (though hardly a walk in the park).

SHOULDER SEASON: MID-SEPTEMBER TO NOVEMBER
The Hindu festival season, when there seems to be (and often is) a religious holiday every other day, begins in August, but really starts rolling in September, attracting both domestic and international tourists. It will be hot and loud, but the Ganpati festival—during which Hindus transport massive, colorful idols of the elephant-headed god, Ganesh, to the sea—and other such festivities may just make it worth the sweat.

GETTING HERE AND AROUND

AIR TRAVEL
Mumbai's international airport, Chhatrapati Shivaji International Airport is 30 km (19 miles) north of the city center. The domestic airport is at Santa Cruz, 4 km (2½ miles) away from the international airport. (Some domestic Air India flights leave, somewhat inexplicably, from the international airport. Many a domestic traveler has missed a flight by neglecting this crucial information, so always double-check your ticket before making your arrangements.) Arrive at the airport at least 75 minutes before takeoff for domestic flights, two to three hours before international flights (some airlines require three hours), and give yourself a cushion of time when leaving to avoid being stuck in the city's notoriously unpredictable highway traffic—it's better to wind up with some extra reading time at the gate than to endure the horror of having to watch your plane take off from the backseat cushion of a sweltering, motionless taxi. ■TIP➔ **Mumbai airports are usually packed to their gills, and there are long lines for scanning luggage and checking in.**

However, in recent years a huge effort has been put into renovating both airports (international and domestic), and things are finally looking up. The recently renovated domestic airport is now one of India's finest, and is of international standard. Both airports have 24-hour business centers available to holders of major credit cards.

Most international flights arrive in the middle of the night. Be prepared: Airports in Mumbai, like those in Delhi, Kolkata, or Chennai, are still poorly run, compared to those in other countries. Because airports typically run at or beyond capacity, many flights arrive at the same time, and luggage belts and trolleys are few. Your luggage may arrive after an interminable wait. ■TIP➔ Make sure you secure a free baggage trolley first and send the touts (and assorted individuals posing as porters, luggage loaders, personal trolley pushers, hotel/taxi providers, or customs clearance aids) packing. Station yourself close enough to the right belt; check any stacks of luggage lined up against the wall in case your suitcases have come earlier.

If you have a lot of luggage, you can get a porter as soon as you disembark—right at the door of the airplane—they work for the airport and are identifiable by their uniforms. If you hire one, get his name, and he will meet you after you go through immigration, at the baggage belt. Do not negotiate rates beforehand—if he tries to do so, hire someone else. Pay him between Rs. 100 and Rs. 300 depending on how helpful he's been.

Immediately after you exit the customs hall there is a row of tourist counters for hotels, taxi hire, car hire, tourist information, cell-phone-cards, and currency exchange booths. If someone is meeting you at the airport, understand that he or she will have no idea when you will emerge from the airport, given the wait at immigration or at the baggage concourse, so don't panic.

AIRPORTS AND TRANSFERS The trip from Chhatrapati Shivaji International Airport downtown to south Mumbai can take anywhere from 40 minutes if you arrive before 7:30 am or after 11 pm (many international flights arrive around midnight) to two hours, when traffic is at its worst. Some hotels provide airport transfers starting at Rs. 1,000 and going up to Rs. 3,000; some offer complimentary transfers if you're staying in a suite or on an exclusive floor or if the hotel is close to the airport.

To avoid hassles with taxis over prices, we strongly recommend heading to the prepaid-taxi counter outside the baggage-and-customs area to hire a regular cab, either air-conditioned or non-air-conditioned. Your rate is determined by your destination and amount of luggage, and is payable up front; Rs. 450 by day and Rs. 500 at night should get you to the center of town from the international airport, and from the domestic airport Rs. 50 less (tips aren't necessary and if your driver tries to charge you extra, show him the slip and firmly say "prepaid"). If you want an air-conditioned taxi and do not spot one, call Group Mobile Cool Cab Service or Gold Cabs, but remember, you'll have to wait even longer. Air-conditioned taxi fares are 25% higher than non-air-conditioned cabs. A trip to Colaba, for example, from the international airport will set you back Rs. 450 by day and Rs. 500 at night, and from the domestic airport Rs. 50 less. A word to the squeamish: Most of the standard black-and-yellow cabs operating in Mumbai were built well over 20 years ago and seem to be held together by little more than duct tape and the driver's ingenuity. If you end up with an old Prestige (modeled on a Fiat), expect to see dirty, smelly upholstery (the drivers also sleep in the cars), a jerry-rigged trunk, and, quite possibly, a hole or two in the rusted metal floor. If you're on a budget, it's the way to go; but if you can afford it, spring for an overpriced Avis car, which includes a driver.

■ **TIP➜** Even though metered taxis are available outside the domestic airport, and a police officer notes the taxi's license plates before dispatching you on your way, we advise against taking one. The cabbies waiting at the domestic airport are often cheats with meters that run double-time.

A metered (not prepaid) taxi from the domestic airport to the downtown/south Mumbai area should cost Rs. 400, and from the international airport about Rs. 500 (more expensive at night). In any case, do not take a taxi that's outside the queue, or accept the offer of a taxi that's parked somewhere that requires you to walk out of the main airport area.

Finally, keep in mind that the route over Mumbai's Bandra-Worli Sea Link will cost you an extra Rs. 55, exclusive of what you've prepaid. The bridge, which cuts travel from the leafy Bandra to not-quite-midway-point Worli from 40 minutes to 7, offers stunning views of the ever-growing Mumbai skyline, and is definitely worth the extra money to save time.

Airport Information Chhatrapati Shivaji International Airport ✉ *Airport* ⊕ *www.csia.in.* **Gold Cabs** ☏ *22/3244–3333, 22/3244–9999* ⊕ *www.mumbaigoldcabs.com.* **Group Mobile Cool Cab Service** ☏ *22/2490–5151, 22/2490–5152.*

BUS TRAVEL

Mumbai has a good bus system for traveling within the city, but navigating long routes and big crowds make it highly inadvisable for most short-term visitors.

CAR TRAVEL

Fairly good roads connect Mumbai to most major cities and tourist areas. Hiring a car and driver gives you a chance to watch the often-beautiful surroundings whiz by. Note that the driving can also be loud, hair-raising, and is definitely less than time-efficient for long distances.

Some distances from Mumbai: Aurangabad 388 km (241 miles); Panaji (Goa) 597 km (371 miles); Delhi 1,408 km (875 miles); Kochi (Kerala) 1,384 km (860 miles).

CARS AND DRIVERS In certain areas, such as bazaars, you really have to walk for the full experience. Aside from these, having a car at your disposal is the most convenient way to travel around Mumbai, as you can zip (or crawl, depending on the time of day) around town without the repeated hassle of hailing taxis and haggling over fares. To arrange a hired car, inquire at your hotel's travel desk or contact a travel agency (you'll probably pay much more if you book through your hotel). You'll get lower rates

SOME MUMBAI HISTORY

Mumbai initially consisted of seven marshy islands—Colaba, Old Woman's Island, Bombay, Mazgaon, Worli, Mahim, and Parel—that belonged to the Muslim kings of the Gujarat sultanate. The Muslims passed the parcel to the Portuguese (who occupied much of western India in the 16th and 17th centuries), who in turn gave it in 1661 to England's King Charles II as part of a dowry in his marriage to the Portuguese Princess Catherine de Braganza. The British established a fort and trading post that grew quickly in size and strength.

Soon enough, land reclamation joined the seven small islands into one, grafting a prototype for today's multifarious metropolis—today the islands, except for Old Woman's Island, are neighborhoods within Mumbai.

The pride of the British in Bombay, and in their power over western India, is memorialized in the city's most celebrated landmark—the Gateway of India, built to welcome King George V to India in 1911. It's now near a statue of the young 17th-century Marathi leader, Shivaji.

from private agents like Adarsh, Euro Cars, or Travel House: Rs. 1,800 to Rs. 2,000 for a full day (8 hours, or 80 km [50 miles]) in a car (Uno or Indica; small cars) with air-conditioning, and Rs. 1,700 or more for an air-conditioned sedan car like a Maruti Esteem. Rates go up for Toyotas, Mercedes, and other luxury cars.

Contacts Adarsh Rent a Car ✉ *Kedia Apartment, 29/F, Dongarshi Rd., near Teen Batti, Malabar Hill* ☎ *22/6664–4488, 22/2368–3666* ⊕ *www. adarshrentacar.com.* **Euro Cars** ✉ *105 Madhava, Bandra Kurla Complex, Bandra East* ☎ *22/2659–2929, 22/4074–4074* ⊕ *www.eurocars-india.com.* **Travel House** ✉ *Crescent Business Park, 301/302, Andheri Kurla Rd., 3rd fl. Near Saki Naka Telephone Exchange, Andheri East* ☎ *22/4077–4071, 22/4077–4072* ⊕ *www.travelhouseindia.com.*

TAXI AND AUTO-RICKSHAW TRAVEL

Mumbai's sights are spread out, so getting around by taxi is a sensible—and cheap—option. You can flag down yellow-top black taxis anywhere in the city. Insist that the driver turn on the meter before setting off—in fact, if you turn the meter on yourself, the driver is less likely to scam you. Most cabs are equipped with digital meters nowadays, so you are less likely to deal with negotiating using the dreaded tariff cards. But if you do enter the rare cab without a working digital meter, ensure that they have a tariff card to consult before you drive off. Drivers must show riders the cards, which show how much you'll pay based on distance, but they sometimes "misplace" them, or whip out a chart for air-conditioned cabs, or show you fares chargeable after midnight. At this writing, the legal fare was Rs. 19 per kilometer, but negotiations were in the works to raise the rate. Consult with your hotel's front desk to confirm the up-to-date rate before leaving to sightsee via local taxi.

In the last few years on-call air-conditioned taxi services have been springing up—and the drivers are usually reliable. Meru and MegaCab are the best services, but even they can miss your scheduled pickup time, so book the car for at least a half-hour earlier than you actually have to leave if you're headed to the airport. Still, they're generally worth it for the sheer comfort.

You can hire an air-conditioned taxi for a full day (eight hours or 80 km [50 miles], whichever comes first) for Rs. 1,000, and a half day (four hours) for Rs. 550. Ask your hotel what the going rates are in case they've gone up. ■TIP➔ Hiring a car and driver often presents a more comfortable ride at a better value than hiring a taxi for extended periods of time. Also, because there is no contract, you're not locked in, and if you don't like a particular driver, you can hire a different one the next day. Both Mega Cabs and Meru Cabs have an automated phone system, but if you stay on the line you'll eventually speak to an agent, and they'll send a confirmation by text message.

Auto-rickshaws are permitted only in Mumbai's suburbs, where you can flag them down on the street. Oftentimes, there will only be rickshaws available to you on the streets beyond Bandra, so it helps to get accustomed to using them. (Highway riding can sometimes feel a bit nerve-wracking when you're being driven without a door against a sea of trucks.) Rickshaws almost universally have digital meters now, and the fare, as of this writing, is Rs. 15 per km.

Contacts Mega Cabs ☎ *22/4242–4242* ⊕ *www.megacabs.com.* **Meru Cabs** ☎ *22/4422–4422* ⊕ *www.merucabs.com.*

TRAIN TRAVEL

Mumbai has two main train stations for travel outside of Mumbai (they also both act as stations for the local railroad). Chhatrapati Shivaji Terminus (CST), more commonly called Victoria Terminus, is the hub of India's Central Railway line. Mumbai Central Station is the hub of India's Western Railway line. Make sure to go to the right train station.

To avoid the pandemonium at the stations, have a travel agent book your ticket; this costs a bit more but saves time and stress. Or book online: Indian Railways has a lumbering, heavily trafficked website (⊕ *www.indianrail.gov.in*), so instead go to ⊕ *www.yatra.com* or ⊕ *www.makemytrip.com*—India's versions of Expedia and Priceline— where you can now book Indian Railway tickets in a much more user-friendly format. For information on confirming a ticket or on arrivals and departures ask a local to make the phone call.

If you decide to book in person, head for the tourist counter established specially for foreign travelers. Eliciting information about trains on the telephone is usually impossible—local stations have no phone number, the national lines are usually busy, and the interactive voice-response numbers are in Hindi.

Train Information Chhatrapati Shivaji Terminus (*CST, Victoria Terminus, or VT*). ✉ *D. Naoroji Rd.* **Mumbai Central Station** ✉ *Adjacent to Tardeo, Central Mumbai.*

EMERGENCIES

Pharmacies (chemists) in Mumbai are usually open daily until about 9 pm, and a wide variety of medications, including those that may require a prescription in the West, are available here over the counter. Hotels

have house physicians and dentists on call. Your consulate can also give you the name of a reputable doctor or dentist and can assist you in locating the closest chemist. Otherwise, try the emergency room at Breach Candy Hospital or nearby Jaslok Hospital—both are privately run and have highly regarded doctors. Mumbai emergency services can't respond to an emergency as quickly as these services do in parts of the world with better roads and more manageable traffic.

Medical Care Breach Candy Hospital and Research Center ⊠ *60 Bhulabhai Desai Rd., Breach Candy* ☎ *22/2367–1888, 22/2367–2888.* **Jaslok Hospital** ⊠ *Dr. G. Deshmukh Marg, near Haji Ali, Peddar Rd.* ☎ *22/6657–3333.* **Lilavati Hospital** ⊠ *A-791, Bandra Reclamation, Bandra* ☎ *22/2642–1000* ⊕ *www. lilavatihospital.com.*

RESTAURANTS

Mumbai is India's melting pot, as well as its most cosmopolitan city, so it's no surprise that you can find nearly every regional Indian cuisine here, and some quality international food, too. You'll also find options ranging from casual to super chic.

Seafood from the Konkan coast—from Maharashtra south through Goa and all the way to Mangalore, in Karnataka—is a Mumbai specialty. The many seafood restaurants in Fort, from upscale Trishna to old-school Apoorva, have some of the best food in Mumbai. "Lunch home" is a typical Mumbai name for the slightly dingy seafood joints that bring in the crowds at lunchtime. North India is represented as well, with kebabs and tandoori. If you're looking for kebabs, head to restaurants specializing in Punjabi or Mughlai cuisine, or, if you have a fairly strong stomach, go to Khao Galli near Bhendi Bazaar; the late-night kebab snack option is Bade Miya behind the Taj Mahal Palace Hotel. Meat-heavy dishes from the North West Frontier (the area of undivided India that's partly in modern-day Pakistan) are also popular, and closely related to Mughlai food: check out Neel, at the Mahalaxmi race track in Central Mumbai, for upscale versions. On the other end of the spectrum are Gujarati vegetarian thalis—combination platters of various veggies and lentils, though the ones in Mumbai tend to be a bit oilier than those from elsewhere in India. Soam, at the top of Marine Drive, is a great upscale place for thalis, and they're less oily here. You may also encounter some Jain food, which is also vegetarian but cooked without any root vegetables—and that includes onions and garlic. You'll find authentic South Indian vegetarian food—*dosas* (fried, crepelike pancakes), *idlis* (steamed rice cakes), *wadas* (also spelled *vadas*; savory fried, and often flavored, lentil-flour doughnuts), and simple, light *thalis* (combination platters)—all over the city.

There are many multicuisine restaurants around the city—usually fairly cheap, tacky joints that make good kebabs, decent Indo-Chinese food, and terrible continental food. (One rule of thumb for smaller or unknown places is that the further you depart from the Indian palate, the more likely you are to be burned with an unsavory dish.)

People eat late in India. Lunch is generally around 1-ish, and dinner is anytime between 8:30 pm and midnight—if you're meeting local friends, expect to eat around 9:30 or 10 pm. If you plan on eating at

Playing cricket in one of Mumbai's public parks

7, reservations probably aren't necessary, and if you want to eat at 6, call ahead: your restaurant may not even be open for dinner yet. Locals generally dress for dinner. They aren't formal, but they are usually well turned out. Shorts and anything sloppy or grungy are only acceptable at cafés and dives.

It's worth noting, too, that if you're staying in South Bombay, there's no need to head out to the suburbs to eat. Nearby Lower Parel (roughly 25 minutes from Colaba Causeway by taxi), may lack tourist attractions, but it still manages pack in some of the more popular new eating and drinking hubs in the city.

The restaurant scene in Mumbai is always evolving. To keep an eye on the latest openings, as well as nightclub events, parties and food or drink festivals, check local papers, as well as the well-run local website Mumbai Boss (⊕ *www.mumbaiboss.com*).

HOTELS

In Mumbai, unlike elsewhere in India, even mid-range hotels can be shockingly overpriced, and a hotel shortage means that good deals are few. Many hotels in that middle range aren't quite up to Western standards of cleanliness, despite their high prices, but location means everything in Mumbai, and tourists may have to sacrifice a bit on substance to get proximity to the city's best attractions. Even hotels with the highest of prices can be full because of year-round demand, so you're well advised to make reservations a few months in advance.

Chains like the Taj, Oberoi, Hyatt, Marriott, InterContinental, Hilton, and Sheraton have huge hotels, most of them deluxe; these cater to leisure and business travelers, and movie stars with money to burn.

Whether you reserve with a hotel directly or through a travel agent, always ask for a discount. Note that tariffs quoted in this book and at hotels do not include 12% tax. Room rates at the luxury hotels fluctuate depending on occupancy, and they offer the rate of the day; the earlier you book, the better the rate you'll get. If you're paying cash, convert your currency beforehand—most hotels give poor exchange rates.

Most of Mumbai's hotels are collected around three locations: in South Mumbai, primarily in Colaba; near Juhu Beach in the suburbs (note that the beach has been cleaned up, but it's not clean enough for swimming—even though you might see some local boys going in); and in North Mumbai, near the airport. If you're going to be sightseeing, and you have the money, stay in South Mumbai rather than the suburbs. If you're here on business, the airport may be your ideal location, and there are several luxury hotels in the vicinity.

Mumbai's cheaper hotels, usually in South Mumbai, can be decent but are still probably overpriced for what you get. During the monsoon season (mid-May through late September), these hotels are overrun by large groups of vacationers from various Arab nations who come to Mumbai to enjoy the cooler weather and rain, during which time noise levels can be very high—solo women travelers should probably stay elsewhere during this time unless they really aren't going to be bothered by the stares.

Unless otherwise noted, all lodgings listed have a private bathroom, a room phone, and a television. We always list the facilities that are available—but we don't specify whether they cost extra: when pricing accommodations, always ask what's included and what costs extra.

Hotel reviews have been shortened. For full information, visit Fodors. com.

WHAT IT COSTS IN RUPEES				
	$	**$$**	**$$$**	**$$$$**
Restaurants	under Rs. 500	Rs. 500–Rs. 1,000	Rs. 1,001–Rs. 1,400	over Rs. 1,400
Hotels	under Rs. 6,000	Rs. 6,000–Rs. 9,000	Rs. 9,001–Rs. 13,000	over Rs. 13,000

Restaurant prices are the average cost of a main course at dinner or, if dinner is not served, at lunch. Hotel prices are the lowest cost of a standard double room in high season.

VISITOR INFORMATION

Don't count on hotels to stock general tourist information. The Government of India Tourist Office, near the Churchgate train station, has useful material; it's open weekdays 8:30–6, Saturday and holidays 8:30–2. There's information on trains, and the office oversees knowledgeable, multilingual tour guides, available directly from the office or through the MTDC (Maharashtra Tourism Development Corporation), or just about any travel agency. Rates are approximately Rs. 500 per half-day for groups of one to four, Rs. 700 for a full eight-hour day (your guide will have lunch when you do, and you should pay for his lunch).

Additional fees of Rs. 350 apply for trips beyond 100 km (62 miles), and for those involving overnight stays the rates could be still higher. Multilingual guides charge Rs. 300 extra, in addition to the regular fee. The MTDC is open daily 9–6. Both MTDC and the Government of India Tourist Office have 24-hour counters at the airports. The MTDC also has counters at Chhatrapati Shivaji Terminus (Victoria Terminus) and the Gateway of India (it's a booth where the boats to Elephanta Island dock). MTDC phone numbers are not that useful, as they are always busy—visit in person or check the website.

Tourist Offices Government of India Tourist Office ✉ *123 Maharishi Karve Rd., Churchgate* ☎ *22/2207–4333, 22/2207–4334, 22/2203–3144, 22/2203–3145 recorded tourist background on Goa, Mumbai, Ahmedabad, and Aurangabad* ⊕ *www.incredibleindia.org.* **Maharashtra Tourism Development Corporation** (*MTDC*). ✉ *Madame Cama Rd., opposite L.I.C. Bldg., Nariman Point* ☎ *22/2284–5678* ⊕ *www.maharashtratourism.gov.in.*

GANESH CHATURTHI

For two weeks every year, usually between August and September, Mumbai explodes with impromptu parades to celebrate Lord Ganesha, the elephant-headed god. During the Ganesh Chaturthi festival, idols of the god are worshipped throughout the city and then taken to the sea to be immersed—and no beach is quite as popular as Chowpatty. If you happen to be in Mumbai during this time, you'll witness thousands of people walking, dancing, and singing down the street toward Chowpatty, where elaborately adorned idols as small as 6 inches and as large as three stories are dunked into the water.

TOURS

Slum tours. In recent years tours of one of Asia's largest slums, Dharavi, have become something of a cottage industry in Mumbai, especially after the popularity of the 2008 movie *Slumdog Millionaire*, which was set here. While the idea may seem like voyeurism, many of the companies who conduct the tours do so on a not-for-profit basis, and have explicit no-camera-allowed policies. On such a tour you'll normally meet up with a guide at Churchgate or Mahim Station, and take the train with a group of no more than six other tourists to Dharavi, which is near the Mahim neighborhood. Here you'll see the variety of cottage industries—from jewelry making to recycling to leather working to blacksmithing—that make up an estimated $600 million annual economy. You'll see poverty, but Dharavi is not the kind of place you saw in those early scenes in *Slumdog*: it has a vibrant, functioning community, with its own post office, schools, temples, mosques, churches, and police force. It is, on balance, an incredibly safe place (and you'll be with a local guide) full of people striving for a better life in Mumbai, willing to live in cramped confines and not knowing where their next meal will come from—or even if there will be a next meal. The best of the tour operators, Reality Tours and Travel, explicitly takes no tips, and makes no profit: they use the fees (Rs. 400 per person) to fund a community center and a kindergarten in the area. ☎98/2082–2253 ⊕ *www.realitytoursandtravel.com.*

PLANNING YOUR TIME

Spending two days in Mumbai is like sprinting a marathon. Even though the city may lack much in the way of monuments and historic sites, this is a place you have to experience to understand (and enjoy). Try cramming all of Mumbai into two days and you're likely to end up hating it, but give it a little longer and the abstract cacophony will start to make more sense and, ultimately, grow on you. Otherwise, the only impression you're likely to get is: hot, crowded, smelly, filthy. Give it a bit of time, and you'll begin to appreciate the madness, as opposed to being overwhelmed by it. So, we suggest spending a week in Maharashtra, with 4–5 days in Mumbai and a weekend trip to the Ellora and Ajanta caves, 370 km (229 miles) northeast of the city—you can take a round-trip overnight train to Aurangabad, the best place to base yourself for trips to the caves; but for the time-crunched, one-hour flights are readily available. If you have an extra day or two, head up to the gorgeously green Matheran (110 km [66 miles] away) or one of the other quaint hill stations nearby, where Maharashtra's landscape fuses stark, semiarid mountains, and rock formations with lush, green countryside.

In Mumbai it's important to catch the flavor of the colonial city: This means walking around the Gateway of India, the Prince of Wales Museum, and Victoria Terminus. To take in a bazaar, head to Crawford Market or stroll down Colaba Causeway to do some bargain hunting. Lunching at a seafood restaurant in Fort and snacking at Chowpatty Beach off Marine Drive are both great experiences, as is people-watching with a beer at the Leopold Café in Colaba. A trip to the western suburbs—Bandra and Juhu, among others—will give you a good perspective on how Mumbai has grown, and where it's going next. A day trip to the ancient Elephanta Caves will show you where it came from.

In South Bombay—"Town" to the locals—colonial mansions, remnants of the British Raj, share space with towering high-rises, and long, rectangular parks, known as *maidans*. To the east, in the labyrinthine streets of Kala Ghoda, the sky-blue Knesseth Eliyahoo synagogue looms. South, the majestic Taj Mahal Palace Hotel holds court with the massive Gateway of India. On the western coast, the Queen's Necklace—as the lights along Marine Drive are affectionately known—stretches out past the carnival food and games of Chowpatty Beach to tony Malabar Hill, where the Hanging Gardens provide some of the city's best non-skyscraper views. Farther north, the Haji Ali shrine, a popular pilgrimage spot for Muslims the world over, sits in the middle of the Arabian Sea like an ancient island tomb. Beyond that, the Bandra-Worli Sea Link, finally finished in 2009, connects the south to leafy Bandra, the king of the western suburbs, where Bollywood stays and plays. In between, and beyond, lie the very things that make Mumbai so confounding, and alluring, and so quintessentially Indian.

6

THE GREAT BOMBAY NAME CHANGE

In the mid-1990s, Shiv Sena, the Hindu nationalist party in power in Bombay, decided to change the city's name to Mumbai, a name often used in local languages that derives from Mumba Devi, the patron Hindu goddess of the island's original residents, the Koli fishermen. Many residents still call their city Bombay, however. The renaming of the city was simply the grandest example of an epidemic that has swept the former Bombay in the last 20 or so years—Crawford Market became Mahatma Jyotiba Phule Market, Victoria Terminus became Chhatra-pati Shivaji Terminus, Marine Drive became Netaji Subhash Chandra Bose Marg. And those are just the big ones; indeed, nearly every road and lane in Mumbai has more than one name. Not only that, but each intersection often has its own name, too, and each individual corner might also have its own moniker (they're often named by local government officials or rich locals for members of their families).

The fact is, though, that as a tourist—and even as a local—you don't need to know any of the new names: No one calls Marine Drive anything but Marine Drive, and no one calls the Causeway anything but the Causeway. Although you will get the odd "CST" for Victoria Terminus, no one uses the new full name, so don't worry about pronouncing it: VT will do just fine.

EXPLORING MUMBAI

There's plenty to see in Mumbai, but it doesn't have much in the way of the stationary monuments that London, Paris, Delhi, and other major cities possess. The art of experiencing Mumbai lies in eating, shopping, and wandering through the strikingly different neighborhoods and the various markets. Think of Mumbai as a 50-km (30-mile) -long open-air bazaar.

Colaba, headed by Gateway of India, is the tourist district and main drag for visitors, and from the Gateway of India to Colaba Market, along the main road, is a walkable stretch of hotels, pubs, restaurants, and interesting shops. Churchgate and Nariman Point are the business and hotel centers, and major bank and airline headquarters are clustered in skyscrapers on Nariman Point.

The district referred to as Fort—which includes Mumbai's hub, Flora Fountain—is filled with narrow, bustling streets lined with small shops and office buildings, as well as colleges and other educational facilities. Another upscale residential neighborhood, Malabar Hill, north of Churchgate on Marine Drive, is leafy and breezy, with fine, old stone mansions housing wealthy industrialists and government ministers.

Shopping and people-watching are most colorfully combined in Mumbai's chaotic bazaar areas, such as Chor Bazaar, Zaveri (jewelry) Bazaar, and Crawford Market (aka Mahatma Jyotiba Phule Market). Many of the city's newest and trendiest shops and restaurants are now out in the suburbs—where more and more people have been moving due to

The Gateway of India, with the Taj Mahal Palace hotel in the background

soaring real-estate prices and a lack of space—but South Mumbai still retains some of the very best.

Some travelers opt to stay in the suburbs, either in Bandra, at the end of the Bandra-Worli Sea Link; or in Juhu, a popular coastal suburb between Mumbai and the airports (about 20 km [12 miles] north of the city center). Juhu's beaches aren't clean enough for swimming, and the place can be scruffy, but staying out here is a good way to observe everyday Indian life beyond the shadow of Mumbai's skyline. Sunday nights bring families down to the beach for an old-fashioned carnival, complete with small, hand-powered Ferris wheels, and lantern-lit snack stalls hawking sugarcane.

COLABA

Mumbai's main hot spot is full of bars, restaurants, and a long stretch of street stalls with everything from clothing to black-market DVDs to brassware and handicrafts set in front of name-brand stores from Nike, Puma, Lacoste, and many others. It's a bit of a one-stop shop for all of Mumbai. Beginning at Regal Circle, which is named for the 1930s art deco Regal Cinema, Colaba stretches southward, through winding lanes and bustling streets. You can stop by the Taj Mahal Palace Hotel for high tea and gaze out at the Gateway of India, standing sentinel over the sea, then wander up through cramped lanes filled with shops to the Colaba Causeway, South Mumbai's main drag. On the Causeway, you can haggle for knockoffs and bootlegs—start at one-third the asking price, at a maximum—or shop in the "official" stores if you're not in the bargaining mood, then stop in at Leopold Café or Café Mondegar

Colaba, Fort, and Marine Drive

MANDVI

BHULESHWAR

KALBADEVI

GIRGAUM

PYDHUNI

DHOBI TALAO

FORT

MALABAR HILL

Masjid

N. Natha St.

Jail Rd.

Yusuf Meherali Rd.

Mohamed

A. Rehman St.

Bhuleshwar Rd.

Kalbadevi Rd.

Vithalbhai Patel Rd.

Cavasji Patel Tank Rd.

Dr. Bahasaheb Jaikar

Jagannath Shankarsher St.

Sharma Rd.

Poddar Marg

Maharshi Karve Rd.

Charni Rd.

Marine Lines

Netaji Subhash Rd.

Marine Drive

Veer Nariman Rd.

Churchgate Station

Maharshi Karve Rd.

V. Thackersey Marg

Mahatma Gandhi Rd.

Mahapalika Marg

Lokmanya Tilak Rd.

S. Marg

fM Ln.

D. D. Sathe Marg

St. George Rd.

Dr. D. Naoroji Rd.

Patton Rd.

Police

P. D'Mello Rd.

Chhatrapati Shivaji Terminus (Victoria Terminus)

General Post Office

Municipal Corporation Building

Walchand Hirachand Marg

Sahid Bhagat Singh Marg

Flora Fountain

High Court

Rajabhai Clocktower

Oval Maidan

Back Bay

Custom Basin

7

6

KEY

⚓	Ferry
🚂	Rail Lines
🛈	Tourist Office

TO ELEPHANTA CAVES

see detail map

Taj Mahal Palace and Tower Hotel

Cooperage Maidan

COLABA

Sassoon Dock

Dhobi Ghat ◆

NARIMAN POINT

Cuffe Parade

1/2 mile
1/2 km

6

Colaba

Maharashtra Police Headquarters

Taj Mahal Hotel

COLABA

Colaba Bus Depot

for a beer, a snack, and some people-watching before heading deeper down into Colaba, where more stores, bargains, bars, and food await. Colaba is an easy place to end up spending an entire day just wandering, eating, drinking, and shopping with nothing particular in mind.

EXPLORING

Elephanta Caves. A quick 30-minute ferry ride from bustling South Mumbai, the Elephanta Caves make an ideal half-day trip for anyone who wants a quick glimpse of India's ancient history. Once you arrive at the island, you climb a steep hill, on rough-hewn steps, past trinket sellers and beggars, to get to Shiva Cave; greenery abounds. The temple, carved out of the basalt hillside, is 130 square feet. Inside, each wall has elaborate, 16-foot-tall rock carvings of Lord Shiva, the destroyer, in his many forms, depicting famous events from the Hindu epics. The main sculptures are on the south wall, at the back.

The central recess has the most outstanding sculpture, the unusual Mahesamurti, the Great Lord Shiva—an 18-foot triple image. Its three faces represent three aspects of Shiva: the creator (on the right), the preserver (in the center), and the destroyer (on the left). Other sculptures near the doorways and on side panels show Shiva's usefulness. Shiva brought the Ganges River down to Earth, the story says, letting it trickle through his matted hair. He is also depicted as Yogisvara, lord of Yogis, seated on a lotus, and as Nataraja, the many-armed cosmic dancer. The beauty of this stonework lies in the grace, balance, and sense of peace conveyed in spite of the subject's multiple actions. It's all very peaceful and serene. Then you step back outside and see the monkeys.

They are everywhere: climbing trees, hooting and hollering, looking for opportunities to get any human food you might be carrying—so we suggest you don't bring any with you (have lunch before you leave Mumbai, or wait until you get back). There are so many monkeys, and they are so comfortable around humans, that they almost distract you from the 1,500-year-old rock carvings. Almost.

It's unclear who did the carvings on Elephanta but it is known that the island was originally called Gharapuri; the Portuguese renamed it after a large stone elephant was found near where their boat landed (the figure collapsed in 1814 and is now in mainland Bombay's Victoria Gardens, also known as Jijamata Udyaan). Shortly before the temples were created, Mumbai experienced the golden age of the late Guptas, under whom artists had relatively free range. The Sanskrit language had been finely polished, and under the court's liberal patronage writers had helped incite a revival of Hindu beliefs. It was Shivaism—the worship of Shiva—that inspired the building of these temples.

The MTDC leads a tour, every day at 2 pm (book when you arrive), that is good but not essential, and runs a tiny restaurant on the island for refreshments and beer. In February they organize a dance festival here.

Getting here: Ferries for the one-hour trip (each way) depart daily every half hour from 9 to 2:30 from the Gateway of India and from noon to 5 from Elephanta Island, unless the sea is very choppy. ⚠ **It's not advisable to visit Elephanta during monsoon season.** ✉ *Gharapuri, Elephanta Island* 🚢 *Round-trip Rs. 100–Rs. 200 depending on type of seat* *or boat you choose; Rs. 250 tickets for entering caves can be purchased at Mahesh Travels at Gateway of India (22/2282–0139)* ☉ *Closed Mon.*

Gateway of India. Mumbai's signature landmark, this elegant 26-meter (85-foot) stone archway was hastily erected as a symbol of welcome to Queen Mary and King George V of England when they paid a visit to India in 1911. In the years following, artisans added decorative carvings and lovely *jharoka*-work (window carvings), finishing in 1923. Less than 25 years later, the last British troops departed from India through the same ceremonial arch. The monument serves as a launching point for boats going to Elephanta Island, and this is also where luxury liners like the *Queen Elizabeth 2* dock on their cruises. The majestic Taj Mahal Palace Hotel, built before the Gateway of India, in 1903, now stands just behind it. ⊠ *End of C. Shivaji Maharaj Marg.*

NEED A BREAK?

Kalash Parbat Hindu Hotel. For decades Bombayites have come to Kalash Parbat Hindu Hotel, which isn't actually a hotel, to indulge their craving for Indian-style vegetarian junk food, such as *chana bhatura* (giant *puris*, or puffed bread, served with spicy chickpea curry), *samosas* (stuffed vegetable turnovers), *sev puri* (deep-fried crackers layered with potato and chutney), *ragda pattice* (spicy potato cakes), *pani puri* (fried lentil-and-potato-stuffed puffs), and other intricate snack food. The place is a bit down-at-the-heels in looks, but the spectacular vegetarian dishes are all that matters. For those wary of trying Bombay street food, you'll find many of those same items on the menu here—just prepared more hygienically. ⊠ *Sheela Mahal, 1st Pasta La., off Colaba Causeway* ☎ *22/2287–4823, 22/2284–1972* ☉ *Daily 11–11.*

6

FORT AND MARINE DRIVE

Long, rectangular parks—known as *maidans*—split Marine Drive starting at the Fort neighborhood, each one filled from end to end with countless overlapping cricket games. At one end there might be a gentle match between players in full white regalia, while the next comparable stretch of land is filled with 10 side-by-side matches, barefoot players whipping the ball and hurling their bodies through the air, laughing and talking trash. To the west, past Flora Fountain and the surrounding street-side secondhand booksellers, you'll find Churchgate Station and the Queen's Necklace (as Marine Drive's curved line of street lights is called), where some of the city's best hotels sit. To the east, past the 130-year-old Gothic High Court building and Mumbai University's 260-foot Rajabhai Clocktower, in the labyrinthine streets of Kala Ghoda (a small area within the Fort neighborhood), the city's best seafood restaurants await, along with a completely incongruous, beautiful baby-blue synagogue. In Fort, the side streets are filled with vendors selling used books and bootleg software and DVDs, all at rock-bottom prices. Fort is a great place to see the kind of grandeur the British had in mind when they dreamed up "Bombay," and Marine Drive offers a wonderful walk along the Arabian Sea.

Crowds of people at Chowpatty Beach

EXPLORING

Fodor's Choice
★ **Chowpatty Beach.** Chowpatty Beach and the rest of long, elegantly curved Marine Drive are the essence of the mammoth, cheeky, beautiful seaside beast that is Mumbai. Chowpatty gives a taste of the bazaar and *mela* (festival) rolled into one. By day—weekday, that is—it's a quiet, uncluttered stretch of sand, but by night it transforms into a carnival of food and hawkers and touts and amusements of every kind, all lit up like Christmas Eve. In a rapidly changing city, it retains some of the simple pleasures in which Mumbaikars indulged before the economy skyrocketed—and it remains an equalizer of sorts, with parents of every class and caste bringing their families here for an evening of fun. For the casual traveler, it offers a window into the many colors—and smells and tastes and sounds—of Mumbai.

A hundred species of salespeople throng the beach in the evening, and especially on Sunday, selling everything from glow-in-the-dark yo-yos and animal-shape balloons to rat poison. Men stand by with bathroom scales, offering complacent strollers a chance to check their heft. Hand-operated Ferris wheels and carousels are packed with children. A few stalls nearby distribute Mumbai's famously satisfying fast food— crunchy *bhel puri* (puffed-rice snacks), *ragda pattices* (spicy potato cakes), and *pav bhaji* (fried vegetable mash eaten with bread). From the beach, walk southeast down Marine Drive toward Nariman Point and you'll bump into flotillas of evening strollers, cooing couples wandering past the waves in a daze, and dogs and kids being walked by their respective minders. Just about the only thing the area lacks is water that's safe for swimming. ⊠ *Chowpatty.*

NEED A
BREAK?
Cream Centre. This old and very popular vegetarian restaurant, one of a chain, is the best address in the city for delicious *chana bhatura*: the piping-hot, football-size puris made from white flour and yeast are served with a spicy chickpea concoction and raw onions and lemons. Just as good are the stuffed parathas, *lassis* (yogurt-based drinks), and refreshing fresh lime sodas. ✉ *Fulchand Niwas, 25B Chowpatty Seaface, opposite Chowpatty Beach, Marine Drive* ☎ *22/2367–9222, 22/2367–9333* ⊙ *Daily noon–midnight.*

Jehangir Art Gallery. Not a far stroll from Trishna and other famous restaurants, Mumbai's chief contemporary-art gallery hosts changing exhibits of well-known Indian artists. Some of the work is lovely, and all of it is interesting for its cultural perspective. There's usually plenty of art outside as well—when it's not monsoon season the plaza in front of the building is full of artists selling their work. ✉ *M.G. Rd., Kala Ghoda, Fort* ☎ *22/2284–3989* ⊕ *www.jehangirartgallery.com* 🎟 *Free* ⊙ *Daily 11–7.*

Knesseth Eliyahoo Synagogue. The attractive and ornate Knesseth Eliyahoo Synagogue is across from Jehangir Art Gallery and behind Rhythm House, at the southern edge of Fort. Built in 1884 for Bombay's community of Baghdadi Jews, it's sky blue, with lovely stained-glass windows and intricately constructed second-floor balconies. You can visit daily between 10 and 6:30, and are welcome for Sabbath prayers on Friday evenings. ✉ *V. B. Gandhi Rd., Kala Ghoda, Fort* ☎ *22/2283–1502* 🎟 *Donation of around Rs. 100 requested.*

NEED A
BREAK?
Café Samovar. Next to a bit of courtyard greenery in the Jehangir Art Gallery, Café Samovar is a popular, laid-back place for a fresh lime soda or a mutton samosa. Their meat-stuffed *parathas* (griddle-fried whole wheat pancakes) and chicken rolls are also tasty. ✉ *M. G. Rd., Kala Ghoda, Fort* ☎ *22/2284–8000* ⊙ *Mon.–Sat. 10–7.*

Marine Drive. Stretching for 3 km (2 miles) along the Arabian Sea, Marine Drive's promenade offers one of the best walks in Mumbai. After you've had your fill of the busy city, head out for a wander—if you're in the mood, you can stroll all the way from Nariman Point up to Malabar Hill. On the way, stop by **Dome**, on top of the InterContinental Hotel in Churchgate, for a sunset drink, or grab a snack at Chowpatty Beach, which is famous for Mumbai street food. If you're here at night, scope out the famed Queen's Necklace, as the streetlights along C-shape Marine Drive are affectionately known.

National Gallery of Modern Art. A great place to see the works of legendary Indian artists M. F. Hussein and F. N. Souza, this imposing, classical-looking circular building has interiors that bring to mind a shrunk-down version of New York's Guggenheim Museum. Built in 1911 by Gateway of India architect George Wittet, it was once the Sir Cowasji Jehangir Public Hall, and the venue for the concerts of violinist Yehudi Menuhin and the rallies of Mahatma Gandhi—the hall still has the acoustics to match. Modern Indian art is displayed in an uncrowded,

Mumbai's Jewish Heritage

Jews were once a prominent stream in Mumbai's population. It's believed there were three strains of Indian Jews—Maharashtrian (Bene Israel) Jews, Cochini Jews, and Baghdadi Jews. The Bene Israel Jews, considered by some to be the Lost Tribe of Israel, supposedly arrived (shipwrecked) in India in the early centuries of the Common Era (some say as far back as 500 BC) and settled along the Konkan coast south of Mumbai. The Cochini Jews, who were spice traders, arrived in approximately AD 1000 and settled in Kerala, in the town of Cochin (Kochi) on the Malabar Coast. Jewish immigration began in earnest in India, however, in the 1800s, and by the 1900s there may have been up to 50,000 Jews in India. These days there are about 5,000 left—most migrated to Israel in the 1950s. Baghdadi Jews, from Iraq and Syria, settled mainly in Mumbai and Kolkata; there's still a small but active population of Iraqi Jews in Mumbai.

Left behind by historic Jewish communities in Mumbai is an assortment of synagogues *(see Exploring listings).*

---

easy manner on four floors. It's not as spectacular as the Prince of Wales Museum across the street, but it's quiet, and worth a visit, especially if you're an art lover. On the top floor is Atul Dodiya's interesting interpretation of Bill and Chelsea Clinton's visit to India, hung alongside a portrait of Vladmir Putin on his visit. ✉ *M. G. Rd., near Regal Cinema, Fort* ☎ *22/2288–1969, 22/2288–1790* ⊕ *www.ngmaindia.gov.in* 🖼 *Rs. 150* ⊙ *Tues.–Sun. 11–6.*

NEED A BREAK?

Status. This is a convenient vegetarian spot along the seaside stroll to sample long, crispy dosas bathed in butter, in all their crackling perfection. Weight-watchers can opt for an oil-free version. Equally good are the *idlis* and *rava* (semolina) dosas. Alternatively, you can try the various *pulaus* (rice dishes), and thalis available on the lunch menu. ✉ *Regent's Chamber, Jamnalal Bajaj Rd., Nariman Point* ☎ *22/4031–8737.*

Prince of Wales Museum. Topped with Moorish domes, Mumbai's finest Victorian building and principal museum houses 30,000 artifacts, divided between art, archaeology, and natural history. While the building is stunning, the artifacts, most of which are extremely interesting, are unfortunately shown in a slightly dusty environment, with less-than-ideal lighting. The picture gallery contains scores of Mughal and Rajput miniature paintings, works by European and contemporary Indian artists, and copies of magnificent cave-temple paintings from Ajanta. ■TIP→ The museum was renamed the Chhatrapati Shivaji Maharaj Vastu Sangrahalaya, but don't ask for directions to this—no one uses that name. ✉ *M. G. Rd., near Regal Cinema, Fort* ☎ *22/2284–4519, 22/2284–4484* ⊕ *csmvs.in* 🖼 *Rs. 300* ⊙ *Tues.–Sun. 10:15–5:45.*

Malabar Hill and Environs

KEY

+—+— Rail Lines

Arabian Sea

Babulnath Temple **3**
Banganga Water Tank **6**
Haji Ali Shrine **1**
Jain Temple **5**
Kamala Nehru Park **2**
Mani Bhavan **4**

TOURING THE MALABAR HILL AREA

■TIP➤ Do this tour by taxi; it's totally acceptable to have your taxi driver wait for you—he may ask for extra money for "waiting time," and Rs. 50 or so should do the trick.

After checking the tides to time your visit just right, take a taxi to the **Haji Ali Shrine** and have your taxi wait for you while you walk out on the jetty. Then drive to **Kamala Nehru Park,** take some air, enjoy the views, and walk to the **Jain Temple.** From here you can either walk or take a taxi along Walkeshwar Road to the **Banganga water tank** area. Finally, have your taxi take you to **Babulnath Temple** and Gandhi's former home, **Mani Bhavan.**

This tour takes about three to four hours, depending on traffic.

MALABAR HILL AND NEARBY

This tony area is at the far end of Marine Drive, where some of the richest and most powerful people in Mumbai live. It's also probably the best place to see the sheer amount of money this city is made of—take, for instance, Antilia, the "quaint" house industrialist Mukesh Ambani recently completed on Altamount Road. Its $2-billion price tag, 560-foot height (27 floors), and 400,000 square feet of living space make it the most expensive, and largest, residential home on the planet. (That the 600-person-staffed behemoth is a mere 10 km [6 miles] from Dharavi, one of the largest slums in Asia, where 1 million people share less than 2½ square km [1 square mile] of land, highlights the extent of India's massive income gap.) Along the switchback roads of Malabar Hill you'll also find the ancient Babulnath Temple (a Shiva temple), the austere Jain Temple, the spring-fed Banganga water tank, and the verdant Hanging Gardens.

TOP ATTRACTIONS

Babulnath Temple. To get the flavor of a large, traditional Indian temple that's nevertheless jammed in the heart of a busy city, a visit to the Babulnath Temple is a must. And climbing the few hundred steps to reach the temple, perched on a hillside, will also reward you with a panorama of South Mumbai. The first Babulnath Temple was apparently built by Raja Bhimdev in the 13th century and named after the *babul* trees (a type of acacia native to India) that forested this area. The architecture of this imposing shrine, one of Mumbai's most important, isn't especially remarkable, but it's interesting to watch the melée of worshippers coming, going, and milling about. Outside are rows of flower sellers hawking a temple-visit kit—coconut plus flowers plus rock sugar—and a cluster of vendors concocting sweets in *karhais* (large woks) in the open air. Temple authorities are sometimes prickly about allowing foreigners into the innermost areas, but it's worth a try; more often than not they don't object. For Rs. 2 you can avoid the climb and take the elevator. ⊠ *Babulnath Rd.*

Banganga Water Tank. This serene, criminally under-visited temple complex is considered one of the city's holiest sites. It's also the oldest surviving structure in Mumbai. The small, somewhat dilapidated temples are built around a holy pool of water and surrounded by the ever-encroaching houses of Mumbai's newer residents. Cows and people mingle freely here, as do bathers who come to obtain the purportedly healing powers of the water. Life around here harks back to earlier, more traditional times. ✉ *Walkeshwar Rd., take lane just beyond Ghanshyamdas Sitaram Poddar Chowk* ✆ *Free.*

Mani Bhavan. This charming, old-fashioned three-story Gujarati house, painted brown and cream

> ### THE DHOBI GHATS
>
> *Dhobi ghats* are where washermen (dhobis) pound clothes clean day and night in enormous open-air laundries. Mumbai actually has several, but the Cuffe Parade ghat is the most conveniently located for tourists. If you're feeling more adventurous, a visit to Mumbai's main dhobi ghat, near Mahalakshmi Station, a kilometer (half mile) beyond the racecourse, may make for better photo ops; here about 200 dhobis are at work in an area covering 7 acres—it's best viewed from the railroad bridge leading into Mahalakshmi Railway Station.

and in a quiet, tree-shaded Parsi neighborhood on Malabar Hill, was the home of Mahatma Gandhi from 1917 to 1934. Now overseen and lovingly maintained by the Gandhi Institute, it houses a library and an interesting and attractively presented small museum on Gandhi's life and work. Gandhi's simple belongings are displayed in his room, including his original copies of the Bible, the Koran, and the Bhagavad Gita (a famous discourse within the ancient Indian epic, the *Mahabharata*); other displays include spectacular colorful miniature dioramas of his life, photographs, and some important and moving letters from the fight for Indian independence. Don't miss the humble and polite letter to Adolf Hitler asking him to not go to war. ✉ *19 Laburnam Rd., near Nana Chowk, Gamdevi* ✆ *22/2380–5864* ⊕ *www.gandhi-manibhavan. org* ✆ *Rs. 10* ⊙ *Daily 9:30–6.*

WORTH NOTING

Haji Ali Shrine. Set far out on a thin, rocky jetty in the Arabian Sea, this striking, dilapidated white shrine was built in honor of the Muslim saint Haji Ali, who drowned here some 500 years ago on a pilgrimage to Mecca. When a coffin containing his mortal remains floated to rest on a rocky bed in the sea, devotees constructed the tomb and mosque to mark the spot. The shrine is reached by a long walkway just above the water. ■ TIP➡ **At high tide the walkway is submerged, making the shrine unreachable. But walking there when the sea has completely receded is not too romantic, because the exposed rocks smell of garbage; choose a time in between.** The walkway is lined with destitute families and beggars ravaged by leprosy, some writhing, chanting, and (calling on the Muslim tradition of giving alms) beseeching you as you make your way down—this can be a deeply upsetting experience, but it's one that is unfortunately quintessentially Mumbai. Inside, the shrine is full of colored-mirror mosaics and crowded with worshippers praying over the casket, which is covered with wilted flower garlands. Men and women must enter through separate doorways. On many evenings a busker plays *quawalis* (a style of Muslim music) after the sunset prayers. There's no admission charge, but you may consider giving between Rs. 20 and Rs. 50 to the mosque charity box. The shrine closes at 10 pm. ⊠ *Off Lala Lajpatrai Marg, near Mahalaxmi Race Course, Central Mumbai.*

Jain Temple. What may be the most impressive temple in Mumbai belongs to the prosperous, strictly vegetarian Jains, the largely Gujarati followers of Lord Mahavira. The colorful interior of their main Mumbai temple is filled with marble, but at the same time it's understated and peaceful—check out the intricate work on the walls and ceilings. Jain worship here is rather different from the general chaos at Hindu temples; it's more introspective and humble in aspect, which reflects the Jain faith. At around 8 am daily, freshly bathed Jain devotees in swaths of unstitched off-white cloth walk here barefoot from their nearby— often quite ritzy—homes to pay homage to the splendid idol of Adinath, an important Jain prophet. (Jains show respect by arriving clean and without shoes—originally Jains used to wear only a silk cloth, the highest quality and hence most respectful material, but plenty now also wear cotton, and many others simply make do with ordinary clothes.) ⊠ *B. G. Kher Marg, Teen Batti, near Walkeshwar.*

Kamala Nehru Park. Children love playing on the "Old Woman Who Lived in a Shoe" structure here, at this small park on the eastern side of the top of Malabar Hill. It's primarily a children's playground—and an old-school one at that, so if your kids are used to the finer things, this park may seem impossibly quaint—but also has gorgeous views of the city below that are worth checking out if you happen to be in the area. From the special viewpoint clearing you can see all of Marine Drive and the Mumbai skyline, from Chowpatty Beach to Colaba Point—try to come up after dark to see why Marine Drive, sparkling with lights, is known as the Queen's Necklace. Just across the road another park, the **Hanging Gardens** (also known as the Pherozeshah Mehta Gardens), also has pleasant views and a topiary garden. A few minutes north of here, heading down the hill, are the **Towers of Silence**, where Mumbai's Parsis—followers of the Zoroastrian faith—dispose of their dead. Pallbearers carry the corpse to the top of one of the towering cylindrical bastions, where it is left to be devoured by vultures and crows (a roughly two-hour process) and decomposed by the elements. None of this is visible to would-be onlookers, even relatives, and high walls prevent any furtive peeping. ⊠ *B. G. Kher Marg* ☉ *Daily 6 am–9 pm.*

CENTRAL MUMBAI

Unlike most other cities, the center of Mumbai has few historical sites, though it does include Mahalaxmi, home of the city's racetrack. Densely populated, it also encompasses areas like Tardeo, Lower Parel, and Worli, but its cluster of gray tower blocks help keep it from being the sort of place many tourists are going to want to visit. However, it is home to some of the best restaurants, bars, and nightlife in the city, and that alone may warrant a trip.

EXPLORING

Magen Hassidim Synagogue. This is probably Mumbai's most active synagogue, but being in Byculla, it's not really much of a tourist destination and, as a Hasidic synagogue, may not be as open to visitors as some of the reform places of worship. This Bene Israel shrine is in the Muslim area of Madanpura. Although the communities of Baghdadi and Cochini Jews have dwindled to just a few thousand, the Bene Israel community continues to modestly prosper. The congregation and caretakers at this well-attended shrine (with about 750 members) can lend insight into the future of this community: Magen Hassidim is the face of India's modern Jews, the ones who generally don't plan to migrate to Israel and who are now part of the nation's mainstream. ⊠ *Maulana Azad Rd., near Fancy Market and Jula Maidan, Madanpura* ☎ *22/2301–2685.*

CST AND NEARBY

Colaba may have the Causeway, but the commercial hub of Mumbai is centered on the bustling bazaars near Chhatrapati Shivaji Terminus. CST—also often referred to by its colonial acronym, VT, which stands for Victoria Terminus—is a sight in and of itself; nearby you'll find three of Mumbai's most important bazaars and the city's best Muslim food. It's the perfect place to see a true slice of Bombay as it was before the high-rises, fancy hotels, and high-end restaurants moved in.

EXPLORING

Chor Bazaar (*Thieves' Bazaar*). This narrow thoroughfare, in the center of classic Muslim Mumbai, is lined with dozens of stores crammed with antiques and general bric-a-brac: clocks, old phonographs, brassware, glassware, and statues; some of it quite cheap. Over the years the value and breadth of much of this stock has dwindled, but there's still a chance that you'll find an unusual, memorable piece. Haggle. In the same lane a number of shops are engaged in the profitable business of constructing new furniture that looks old; many will openly tell you as much. Some shops do stock genuine antique furniture from old Parsi homes. Around the corner, stolen cell phones and car stereos are being hawked. The Thieves' Bazaar got its name because it's always been the kind of place that sold goods that fell off the back of the truck—or back of the camel—and even today you can't be too sure of the provenance of your purchases. Getting to the Chor Bazaar will take you on a tour of an interesting and very staunchly Muslim neighborhood, where life has a completely different flavor from elsewhere in the city. One street away is an interesting mosque belonging to the Bohri Muslims—the architecture and the people are a mix of Yemeni, Egyptian, Indian, and African—just ask people to point you in the direction of Bohri Masjid (or Mosque). ⊠ *Mutton St., off Sardar Vallabhbhai Patel Rd., off Mohammed Ali Rd., Mandvi, CST and Environs* ☉ *Sat.–Thurs. 11–7.*

CST (Chhatrapati Shivaji Terminus), aka Victoria Terminus. Built by the British in 1888, this is one of India's—and probably the world's—busiest train stations, overflowing at rush hour with enormous, surging,

CST and Environs

KAMATIPURA

Grant Rd.

Maulana Shaukatali Rd.

Ramchandra
Bhatt Marg

KHETWADI

KHARA
TALAO

5

Sandhurst
Rd.

Maulana Azad Rd.

Ibrahim Rahimtulla Rd.

Jail Rd. (East)

UMERKHADI

Vithalbhai Patel Rd.

Cawasji Patel
Tank Rd.

MANDVI

Keshavji Naik Rd.

Manson Rd.

Chowpatty
Beach

BHULESHWAR

GIRGAUM

Mohamed Ali Rd.

Yusuf Meherali Rd.

4

A. Rehman St.

3

Masjid

N. Nathai St.

Dr. Babasaheb Jaykar

KALBADEVI

Charni Rd.

Jagannath Shankarset Rd.

Bhuleshwar Rd.

Kalbadevi Rd.

G. Gandhi Marg

PYDHUNI

2

Maharshi Karve Rd.

K. Sharma

Lokmanya
Tilak Rd.

Dr. D. Naoroji Rd.

Pattoli Rd.

P.D Mello Rd.

Marine Lines

Police

Back Bay

A. Poddar Marg

DHOBI
TALAO

Maharshi Karve Rd.

Municipal
Corporation
Building

1

General
Post Office

Waitchand Hirechand Marg

Netaji Subhash Rd.

Marine Drive

Churchgate
Station

Dr. D. Naoroji Rd.

FORT

Shoorji
Vallabhdas Marg

Custom
Basin

Veer Nariman Rd.

Patil Marg

High Court

M. Gandhi Rd.

Sir Durab Tata Rd.

Jamshetji Tata Rd.

Madam Cama Rd.

Rajabhai
Clocktower

Oval
Maidan

Bhaurao Patil

Kala
Ghoda

Shaid Bhagat Singh

KEY

⛴ Ferry

├─┼─┤ Rail Lines

ℹ Tourist Office

Maharshi Karve Rd.

Cooperage
Maidan

Taj Mahal
Hotel

TO
ELEPHANTA
CAVES

Jamnalal Bajaj Marg

Free Press Journal Rd.

0 — 1/2 mile
0 — 1/2 km

CLOSE UP

A Good Walk of Mumbai's Markets

This walk is not for the timid: It will be harried, the traffic is usually crazy, and the streets are dirty, but this is Mumbai, and the experience can't be beat.

Start off at grand, Victorian **CST**, then head north, just past the station, to **Crawford Market** (renamed Mahatma Jyotiba Phule, which no one ever uses). This is one of Mumbai's biggest wholesale fruit, poultry, and vegetable markets—though you can also buy retail—and it teems with traders and local buyers. To get around, it's best to just ask a local to point you in the direction of what you're looking for (or a good landmark), because street names mean almost nothing in Mumbai, and the roads here are winding and confusing. ■TIP➜ You're about to enter the belly of the bazaar beast, so keep an eye on your wallet, and it's a good idea not to carry anything of great value with you. Head north and you'll end up on **Muhammad Ali Road,** the city's great Muslim ghetto, though its ragged appearance and generally filthy streets make it not for the faint of heart. Muhammad Ali Road begins to blend with **Bhendi Bazaar,** which, in turn, blends into **Zaveri Bazaar,** and these two bazaars contain all of Mumbai's best goldsmiths, as well as the city's not-so-secret money-laundering industry. Grab lunch in the air-conditioned confines of **Shalimar Restaurant** (✉ *Bhindi Bazar Corner, Masjid Bunder Sind Harsh Rd.* ☎ *022/2345–6630*) in Bhendi (order the *rand biryani,* a spicy rice dish made with goat leg), then hang a left to **Chor Bazaar,** where you'll dodge wooden carts piled high with goods and wind through the labyrinth of alleys, picking through thousands of shops and stalls for dirt-cheap antiques, vintage Bollywood posters, and furniture. ■TIP➜ If you can, bring a local with you and, after making a round together, have them go back and do the bargaining and purchasing for you, with you out of sight—they'll get much better deals without a foreigner around. Next, head back toward Muhammad Ali Road and Bhendi Bazaar for some of the best Muslim street food Mumbai has to offer. If you're strong of stomach, go to Haji Tikha Wali (ask a local, he's well known) for *kheeri tikka,* marinated cow udders grilled right in front of you. Or, if it's late at night, to Walliji Paayawala, for cooked, spicy goat hooves with coarse Irani bread. During the day, you can get *chana bateta,* chickpeas cooked with spleen (yes, we know how terrible all of this sounds, but this is seriously tasty food); there's a whole row of stalls—just go for the one with the longest line. If you're adventurous, and relish food from regions far and wide, you won't be disappointed. And, on the honestly off chance you end up spending the night on the toilet or are otherwise chastened, at least you'll do so knowing you tried the best there is.

Timing: This walk will take a full day, and, again, it's not for the faint of heart—or those unwilling to experience India on its own chaotic, messy terms. Note that Crawford Market is closed Sunday, and Muhammad Ali Road, Bhendi Bazaar, and Chor Bazaar are essentially closed—that is, completely empty of the Muslims who make up their majority—on Friday, their holy day.

6

scurrying crowds who use the suburban lines that also originate here (Mumbai's suburban trains carry 8 million people a day). Although it's been renamed Chhatrapati Shivaji Terminus, it's still commonly called Victoria Terminus or just V.T., and it bears a hefty statue of Queen Victoria on its imposing dome, the haughty structure combining Indian and Victorian–Gothic architecture for an Eastern version of London's St. Pancras station. Why visit? To spend a few minutes admiring the enormous, incredible building, which is even more arresting lit up at night. If you're brave, walk around the corner to the modern suburban extension of the station around rush hour—9 am or 5:30 pm—and experience Mumbai's maddening crowds. Even better, take a ride on a local train; many say you have not experienced Mumbai unless you have ridden one. ⊠ *D. Naoroji Rd.*.

Crawford Market. Renamed Mahatma Jyotiba Phule market decades ago, but still known by its original name, this building was designed in the 1860s by John Lockwood Kipling (father of Rudyard, who was born in this very neighborhood). The market's stone flooring supposedly came from Caithness, Scotland. Check out the stone relief depicting workers on the outside of the building. Come here early in the morning for a colorful walk through Mumbai's fresh-produce emporium, and if it's late spring or early summer, treat yourself to a delicious Alphonso mango— the experience has had many people rhapsodize that they've never truly had a mango until they ate one of these. Everything from cookies and party streamers to white mice and cane baskets is sold in other sections of the market—the meat section can be a bit hair-raising. In the middle lane (Sheikh Memon Street) of Crawford Market, is the chaotic **Mangaldas Market**, a covered, wholesale cloth market with a tremendous variety of fabrics at hundreds of indoor stalls. Across the street from the market's main entrance on the west, spread across a trio of lanes, is a smaller but popular bazaar area called **Lohar Chawl**, where the selection ranges from plastic flowers to refrigerators. ■TIP→ **If you're headed to the market during the monsoon, wear rain boots or shoes you don't mind getting dirty. The floors can become quite mucky.** ⊠ *D. Naoroji Rd., at L. Tilak Rd.* ⊗ *Mon.–Sat. 11:30–8.*

NEED A BREAK?

Rajdhani. Rajdhani serves up hot Gujarati and Rajasthani vegetarian thalis (combination platters; Rs. 299) in spartan, clean surroundings. It's just a tiny bit north of Crawford Market. Eat sparingly, because the restaurant uses a lot of ghee (clarified butter) in its dishes, which are also slightly (and authentically) sweet. ⊠ *Sheikh Memon St., Lohar Chawl, near Crawford Market, Mandvi* ☎ *22/2342-6919* ⊗ *Mon.–Sat., noon–4 and 7–10:30, Sun. noon–3:15.*

Shaare Rahamim (*Gate of Mercy*). North of Crawford Market via P. D'Mello Road, past Carnac Bunder and right next to the Masjid train station, is the hard-to-find Shaare Rahamim, built in 1796. The mildly dilapidated synagogue is still in use, and you're welcome to peek inside. ⊠ *254 Samuel St., Mandvi,* .

Zaveri and Bhendi Bazaars. Bombay's crowded, century-old jewelry markets have shops filled with fabulous gold and silver in every conceivable

Outside Victoria Terminus, Mumbai's main train station, officially known as Chhatrapati Shivaji Terminus (CST)

design. The two bazaars are so intermingled at this point that it's impossible to tell where one ends and the other starts. If you notice people walking past with plastic bags full of cash, try not to stare—this is also a major hub for (certainly illegal, widely known, wholly tolerated) money laundering, completely out in the open, with no security measures in place. You'll find the bazaars a little beyond Fort in the neighborhood of Kalbadevi—a 10-minute walk northwest of Crawford Market. ■TIP➔ One of the lanes leading off Zaveri Bazaar is called Khao Galli (literally "Eat Lane") and its endless food stalls feed most of the bazaar workers daily; it's here that you'll find some of Mumbai's best—and most unusual—nonveg street food. ⊠ *Sheikh Memon St., Kalbadevi, Elephanta Caves* ⊘ *Mon.–Sat. 11–7.*

Mumbadevi Temple. At the Bhuleshwar (the name of a neighborhood) end of Zaveri Bazaar is the six-century-old Mumbadevi Temple, a noisy, busy structure that houses the mouthless but powerful patron goddess who is the city's namesake. *Aarti*, evening prayers, take place at 6:30 pm. ⊠ *CST and Environs* ☎ *22/2242–4974.*

JUHU, BANDRA, AND THE WESTERN SUBURBS

The suburbs that make up the majority of Mumbai lie north of the island city, and spread out for miles on end, but visitors are likely only to visit the two main ones: Juhu and Bandra. Both house Mumbai's rich and famous, including most of its Bollywood stars (and studios). Being right in the middle of Mumbai, the main feature of **Juhu** is Juhu Beach, but it's not the kind of sandy oasis for swimming, or even sunbathing, even though it was recently cleaned up—you'll notice the locals, fully

QUICK BITE

For a quick and essential bite, Mumbai has hundreds of fast-food, piping-hot-idli-crispy-dosa restaurants run by the Mangalorean Shetty community, known for proficiency in this delicious cuisine, which is an absolute must-try. The cooked food in these places is generally clean (raw foods and the restaurant floor may be less so). Many a traveler has become so addicted to eating dosas for snacks and for breakfast that they had to resist the temptation to consuming nothing else. If you're new to India and worried about getting sick from the food, dip your dosa, idli or vada only in the hot sambar, and avoid the accompanying chutneys. Although the chutneys are quite delicious, cold and room-temperature dipping is better left for five-star hotels and fancier restaurants that cater to foreigners, where cleanliness is held to a slightly higher standard.

clothed, jumping around in the water, but theirs is a stronger constitution, so limit yourself to a sunset stroll. Instead, tourists are most likely to come here either for a hotel room or to sample one or two of its many bars and clubs. **Bandra,** the hub of hip Mumbai, is full of boutiques, trendy restaurants, and expats, and though it's low on sightseeing it's high on eating and drinking spots. If Bollywood's your thing, ask your cabbie or rickshaw driver to take you past the towering homes of superstars Shah Rukh Khan or Salman Khan, or past historic Mehboob Studios. If it isn't, stop in for a drink at one of the many watering holes on Waterfield Road. Beyond Juhu and Bandra, other suburbs, such as Khar and Santa Cruz, are only worth a trip for the culinary offerings of certain restaurants.

WHERE TO EAT

CENTRAL MUMBAI

$$$$
MILANESE
✕ **212.** Milanese head chef Alex Bignotti performed a neat little trick—he built a restaurant where expats and locals alike can sample an honest-to-goodness authentic Italian meal that satisfies experienced palates. Free of the missteps and processed-cheese chaos that often comes with European fare in India, this large restaurant on a commercial street in the Worli neighborhood looks sleek and hip, and its elegantly prepared food delivers simple pleasures done right. For starters, try the "cappuccino" of wild mushrooms, black summer truffles, and garlic bread. For the main course, the four-cheese brick-oven pizza is among the best in the city. $ *Average main: Rs. 2500* ⊠ *12 A, ground fl., Hornby Vellard Estate, Worli* ☎ *22/2490–1994* ✢ *F4.*

$$
BURMESE
Fodor's Choice
★
✕ **Burma Burma.** A trip to India can represent an opportunity for travelers to test the ropes at living vegetarian for awhile (veg options constitute literally half of every menu here), but few major restaurants in the city have mastered all the possibilities of vegetarian like the charming Burma Burma. Ankit Gupta, the owner, is half Burmese, and demands authenticity, so short of a separate flight to Myanmar itself, you're not

BEST BETS FOR MUMBAI DINING

With so many restaurants to choose from, how to decide? Fodor's writers and editors have chosen their favorites, by price, cuisine, and experience, in the lists below.

Fodor's Choice ★

Apoorva, p. 351
Britannia & Co., p. 351
Burma Burma, p. 340
Café Zoe, p. 344
Kebab Korner, p. 352
Neel, p. 345
Oh! Calcutta, p. 345
The Pantry, p. 353
Soam, p. 353
The Table, p. 350

By Price

$

Apoorva, p. 351
Britannia & Co., p. 351
The Pantry, p. 353
Soam, p. 353

$$

Burma Burma, p. 340
Oh! Calcutta, p. 345
Woodside, p. 350
Zaffran, p. 354

$$$

Café Zoe, p. 344
India Jones, p. 352
Kebab Korner, p. 352
The Table, p. 350
Trishna, p. 354

$$$$

Neel, p. 345

By Cuisine

AMERICAN

The Pantry, p. 353
The Table, p. 350

ASIAN

Burma Burma, p. 340
Busaba, p. 348
India Jones, p. 352

EUROPEAN

Café Zoe, p. 344
Suzette, p. 353

INDIAN

Apoorva, p. 351
Britannia & Co., p. 351
Kebab Korner, p. 352
Neel, p. 345
Soam, p. 353
Status, p. 330
Zaffran, p. 354

SEAFOOD

Apoorva, p. 351
Gajalee, p. 355
Mahesh, p. 352
Oh! Calcutta, p. 345
Trishna, p. 354

By Experience

BEST BRUNCH

Café Zoe, p. 344
The Pantry, p. 353

BEST HOTEL DINING

India Jones, p. 352

BEST VEGETARIAN

Burma Burma, p. 340
Soam, p. 353
Status, p. 330

BEST WITH KIDS

Café Zoe, p. 344

HOT SPOT

Busaba, p. 348
Café Zoe, p. 344
The Pantry, p. 353
Woodside, p. 350

MOST ROMANTIC

Aurus, p. 355

6

CLOSE UP

Mumbai's Greatest Seafood Hits

Clams, squid, prawns, lobsters, crabs, and fish, rubbed with a spicy red masala or spiked with a green masala or simmered in a thick fragrant coconut gravy: this is what you'll find emanating from kitchens along the Konkan coast of India, stretching from Mumbai to Mangalore to Goa. If you love seafood, help make your Mumbai trip memorable by sampling the best of the local seafood cuisine.

Here's a list of what to look for on menus:

■ Prawn *gassi*: small prawns simmered in a thick, tangy, spicy red coconut gravy

■ Prawn curry: thinner than a *gassi*, also red, with *kokum* (a sour berry)

■ Masala prawns: prawns marinated in garlic and spices and then panfried

■ *Teesri* masala: tiny clams cooked in a dry coconut masala

■ Bombay duck *bombil*: this Mumbai specialty has nothing to do with duck: Bombay duck is actually a type of fish that's dried out in the open—it's also extremely pungent and not for everybody. In this dish it's batter-fried with semolina, and is light and flaky

■ *Surmai*, pomfret, and *rawas*: these three famous, fleshy fish of the region are either marinated and fried, baked in a tandoor, or cooked into a curry

■ Masala crab: crab cooked in thick, almost dry, green or red masala

■ *Neer* dosa: a light crumpled soft-rice dosa meant especially for eating with seafood

■ *Kori* roti: a dry, crumbly rice roti

■ *Appam*: a Kerala-style steamed rice cake available in some Konkan joints

---

likely to find dishes as skillful as these in many other places. The restaurant serves excellent teas, *nanji kaukswe* (delicious noodles served in dry coconut powder), and *nanpeebya* (Burmese bread served with creamy white peas). For dessert, the *shway aye*, chilled coconut milk served in a glass with sweet bread, is a must try. Like all "pure veg" restaurants, however, no alcohol is served on the premises, so it's a much better place to visit before or after that cold beer you've been craving while walking around in the Bombay heat. ⑤ *Average main: Rs. 800* ⊠ *Kothari House, off M. G. Rd., Fort* ☎ *22/4003–6600* ⊕ *C3.*

$$$ ✕ **Café Zoe.** Rapidly becoming one of the city's most popular spots for
MODERN almost anything and everything, the roomy, open, yet strangely utili-
EUROPEAN tarian Café Zoe serves European and continental breakfasts, brunches, lunches, dinners, and drinks. Depending on what time you arrive at this converted industrial compound, the crowd may include young parents feeding their one-year-old daughter sweet bites of Belgian waffles, local journalists shoveling down hot minestrone soup while using the free Wi-Fi, second-date couples sharing a romantic dinner of seafood and pasta, or young partygoers drinking cocktails in a dim but sensuous atmosphere after midnight. What's even more impressive is that Zoe manages this incredible balancing act without seeming watered-down or tired. For dessert, the bread pudding, with a crispy, crème brûlée–style caramel coating, is superb—at any hour. ⑤ *Average main: Rs. 1200*

✉ *Todi Mills, Mathuradas Mills, Compound, Lower Parel* ☎ *22/2490–2065, 22/2490–2066* ⊕ *www.cafezoe.in* ✢ *F4.*

$$$$
NORTH INDIAN
Fodor's Choice
★

✕ **Neel.** Hand's down the best upscale Indian food in town for meat-eaters, this restaurant in a beautifully designed building at the track makes the journey to the city center utterly worthwhile. Portions are big—as are the prices—and the food is heavy but sophisticated. Start with a *seekh kebab* (minced chicken or mutton with spices) or the mutton *shorba* (bone-marrow soup), followed by *raan*, a North Indian–style leg of lamb with roasted apples, or *bindhi kali mirch* (spicy okra), and *dal makhani* (a buttery black lentil dish) with rice, or any of the dozen great breads—flaky *lachha paratha* is recommended. ⑤ *Average main: Rs. 1700* ✉ *Tote on Turf, Mahalaxmi Racecourse, Gate 5 or 7, Mahalaxmi, Central Mumbai* ☎ *22/3348–7642* ✢ *C1.*

$$$$
THAI

✕ **O:h Cha.** Thai can be hard to find in Mumbai, and that makes this restaurant, inside the suddenly bustling Mathuradas Mills Compound in Lower Parel, between Café Zoe and the Barking Deer Brew Pub, such a rare treat. The interior may be a tad on the drab side, since it's buried on the ground of an old factory and office and feels something like a postmodern war bunker, but Thai chef Pipat Niyomsin's food, which pulses with spice, is anything but. The *kang kaew waan*, a loud Thai green curry, is superb, as is the *pad pak si sa hi* (a wholesome combination of asparagus, broccoli, and shiitake and chewy snow-ear mushrooms, tossed in soy sauce), and the *pla kow nong ma nao* (steamed grouper in a blisteringly hot chilli–garlic sauce). Reservations are helpful for weekends and Friday meals, and there's a light but tasty prix-fixe lunch menu on tap for the office crowd, with Kingfisher beer included. ⑤ *Average main: Rs. 1700* ✉ *Senapati Bapat Marg, Mathuradas Mills Compound, Near Café Zoe, Lower Parel* ☎ *22/6633–4455* ✢ *F4.*

$$
INDIAN
Fodor's Choice
★

✕ **Oh! Calcutta.** Rarely packed, even on Saturday night, because it's in the infrequently visited center of town, Oh! Calcutta serves the city's best Bengali food in an upscale surroundings of dark-wood set off by simple black-and-white archival photos from the British Raj. The seafood is exquisite, and if it's all too unfamiliar, defer to the waiters—some of the best in the city—to choose something, based on your specifications. Start with *roshun bhapa maach*, a steamed *bekti* (a freshwater fish) marinated with *kashundi* (Bengali-style mustard), green chilli paste, and garlic. For a main course, you can't go wrong with the *aam kashundi kakra* (breaded and stir-fried crabmeat in an orange-mango mustard sauce). ⑤ *Average main: Rs. 800* ✉ *Rosewood Hotel, Tulsi Wadi La., near Tardeo A/C Market* ☎ *22/2353–9114* ✢ *F4.*

$$$
EUROPEAN

✕ **The Tasting Room.** Popular with rich Mumbai housewives—who pack the place for lunch during the week—this Mediterranean restaurant serves gourmet food in a relaxed setting. On the top-floor veranda of Good Earth (a designer furniture store), the Tasting Room shares its hosts' penchant for subtle Indian minimalism in warm earth tones. Although the ladies who lunch tend to get a little loud midday, dinner is quite the calm affair. The watermelon and feta salad is extremely popular, and makes a good starter, as do the port-poached beets. For mains, you can't go wrong with the ravioli stuffed with roasted pepper and asparagus. ⑤ *Average main: Rs. 1200* ✉ *Raghuvanshi Mansions,*

6

Street-Food Favorites

Unlike most other Indian cities that start snoozing as early as 8 pm, Mumbai buzzes around the clock. Food carts appear every few yards serving *chaats* (Indian street snacks), and even the simplest food is transformed into something impressive. The choices are enormous—there are hot, spicy vegetable sandwiches, slices of green mango peppered with masala, sizzling kebabs, Chinese noodles with vegetables, fresh strawberry milk shakes, carrot juice, *kulfi* (cream-based Indian ice cream), fresh-sliced mango with creamed, spicy boiled chickpeas, fried fish, potato turnovers, masala peanuts, coconut water, green-chilli omelets in buns, and an almost endless array of exotic snacks associated with Mumbai, *such as those listed here.*

Much of this snack food is created right at the side of the road on open grills and stoves and then assembled in front of you. As you would imagine, the hygiene is often a little suspect, but don't dare avoid it, or you may miss out on some of the best available street food on our planet. If you sample any of these street-side treats, follow some rules. Try food served hot on the spot. Avoid cold and room temperature sauces ("dry chutney" is often a helpful code for "no sauce" when ordering sandwiches like vada pav), and try to avoiding heavy dustings of herbs, such as coriander. If the plates don't look clean, or are dripping wet with unfiltered water, ask that food be either served or packed in a disposable container (a fresh plastic bag, a cup created from leaves, a paper plate, or newspaper) or bring your own container. Carry your own spoon and paper or plastic cup, if you want. And don't worry—the vendors usually understand enough English to see the process through. Finally, those vendors who attract the biggest crowds and fame are likely to be safer than those who are ignored.

MUMBAI'S STREET-FOOD CLAS-SICS

■ *Bhel puri*: Puffed rice tossed with cubes of boiled potatoes, slices of tomatoes, peanuts, tamarind sauce, chopped onion, and *sev* (a savory, deep-fried treat made of chickpea flour).

■ *Dahi puri*: Tiny, flat, white-flour *puris* (deep-fried bread) layered with boiled potatoes, three types of chutney made from tamarind, dates, and coriander leaves (cilantro), plus mung-bean sprouts and topped with curd and chopped cilantro leaves.

■ *Sev puri*: The same white-flour puris *as above*, or crackers, layered with boiled potatoes, three types of chutney made from tamarind, dates, and cilantro.

■ *Pani puri*: Deep-fried, globular puris, also known as *golgappas,* that have been cracked open and filled with date water, tamarind sauce, mung-bean sprouts, and potatoes.

■ *Ragda pattice*: Spiced and mashed potatoes shaped into cutlets and fried on a griddle. These are served with hot white-pea curry and a few sauces.

■ *Dahi bada*: Large flat dumplings of white lentils, which are deep-fried to make *badas,* and are then dipped in water to soak out the oil. The badas are broken into pieces and served spiced with a variety of masala powders, tamarind sauce, cilantro chutney, and yogurt.

■ *Pav bhaji*: Mashed potatoes that are fried on a hot griddle for an hour with peas, tomatoes, and butter—until it's become a juicy, spicy, potato mash. It's then served with sliced onions, lemons, and butter-fried buns called *pavs*.

■ *Vada (or wada) pav*: A cutlet made of mashed potatoes, spice, cilantro, and ginger that's coated in chickpea flour and deep fried—which is then stuffed into a pav lined with hot garlic and red-chilli chutney.

■ *Aanda pav*: A spicy omelet made with chillies, onions, masala, and a bunch of spices, which is then fried and slapped into a pav.

■ *Baida roti*: Minced meat mixed with beaten egg is wrapped in white-flour dough that's been tossed by hand into thin sheets; the square, layered pancake is then fried on a hot griddle with oil.

■ *Bheja fry*: Spicy red masala and tomatoes fried with goat brains—it's really tasty!

■ *Boti roll*: Spicy pieces of grilled lamb kebab, chutney, and sliced onions rolled into a *roomali* roti (a thin, hand-tossed, and roasted white-flour pita).

■ *Sheekh kababs*: Minced, spiced lamb cooked on a skewer barbecue-style and served with chutney.

■ *Chicken tikka*: Marinated chicken pieces that have been roasted on an open-air barbecue and are served with chutney.

■ *Mutton or chicken biryani*: Long-grained basmati rice simmered with spice and mutton or chicken for many hours.

■ *Masala dosa*: A lentil- and rice-flour pancake fried on a griddle with plenty of ghee (clarified butter) and stuffed with a spicy potato mixture.

WHERE IS IT SERVED?

Bade Miya *(see full listing in Where to Eat)*, next to Gokul Bar on Tullock Road, off Shahid Bhagat Singh Road (enter the lane next to Café Mondegar and take the next right) is an open-air stall that has been supplying hungry Mumbaikars with kebabs and *baida* (white-flour) rotis for more than 50 years; they're open through the night until the early morning. Also check out the Elco food stalls and the Elco Restaurant *(see full listing in Where to Eat)* in Bandra.

Head to Kailash Parbat or Swati Snacks *(see the Need a Break boxes for full contact info)* to sample bhel puris and sev puris. Also visit Shiv Shankar Tiwari's Dahi Puri stall on B. Road (aka Karmveer Pandit Shobhnath Mishra Marg) off Marine Drive, next to the InterContinental hotel.

And if you're near Churchgate Station at night, ask around for the omelet *pav* man, as his stand doesn't have a name. He makes the best *aanda pav* in town; he starts in the evening and is open into the wee hours of the morning.

6

Raghuvanshi Mills, Senapati Bapat Marg, Lower Parel ☎ 22/6528–5284 ✛ F4.

COLABA

$ ✕**Bade Miya.** Mumbai's most famous kebab joint has hit the big time.
INDIAN   Sitting behind the Taj Mahal Hotel for generations, always packed, always greasy, and always tasty, the owners of this late-night snack shrine have now expanded, adding a full new restaurant—with doors, windows, the works—in the Fort neighborhood of Horniman Circle. Still, you'll probably want to check out the original to understand what the fuss is all about. Try the chicken *bhuna* (shredded chicken in a spicy red-brown gravy), the chicken *baida* roti (a sort of Indian quesadilla, with chicken and egg), or, for the more adventurous, the *bheja* fry (fried goat brains in a spicy gravy). There's also a strictly vegetarian tandoor. ⑤ *Average main: Rs. 200* ✉ *Tullock Rd., behind Taj Mahal Hotel* ☎ 22/2202–1447 ▭ No credit cards ✛ C4.

$$$ ✕**Busaba.** "Pan-Asian" is a dirty term in the hands of most restaurants,
ASIAN   but this small, hip joint proves that it *is* possible to do it all, and do it well. The most popular dish, with good reason, is the Khao Suey, a Burmese coconut-based soup that you assemble yourself—you get a bowl of noodles, a bowl of broth, and small bowls of ingredients like chives, veggies, chicken, crushed peanuts, etc. The Korean *bibimbap* (a combination of vegetables, meat, and rice) and beef *bulgogi* are also great. Start with the beef tenderloin skewers, pepper prawns, or any of the *momos* (dumplings). ⑤ *Average main: Rs. 1200* ✉ *2 Mandlik Rd., near Cotton World, behind Taj Mahal Hotel and Palace* ☎ 22/3348–7621 ✛ C5.

$ ✕**Café Churchill.** Churchill's specializes in British-style comfort food,
BRITISH   perhaps a welcome break from all the Indian food you'll be eating. Dingy—but not dirty, the red-and-white vinyl interior fits the food, and although the cheap chow may be starchy and simple, sometimes roast beef and gravy with steamed veggies and mashed potatoes really hits the spot. The desserts, though, are some of the best Mumbai has to offer: at any given time you'll find five kinds of chocolate cake (brownie, truffle, you name it), and five kinds of cheesecake in the dessert case. You might be tempted to have dessert for dinner. ⑤ *Average main: Rs. 350* ✉ *103-B Colaba Causeway, opposite Cusrow Baug* ☎ 22/2204–2604 ▭ No credit cards ✛ C5.

$ ✕**Café Mondegar.** Just down the block from Regal Cinema, Monde's
CAFÉ   is similar in atmosphere and cuisine to its older brother, Leopold's, up the road. Always packed, it's a great place to grab an ice-cold Kingfisher draft and watch the crowds roll in—though unlike Leo's, they don't have a full liquor license. Avoid the characterless air-conditioned room and instead post up at one of the cramped tables in the main space, where the jukebox plays at full blast and the walls are covered with cartoon murals of Mumbai life. Continental and Chinese cuisine are available, or you could stick to the greasy french fries and onion rings. ⑤ *Average main: Rs. 200* ✉ *Colaba Causeway* ☎ 22/2202–0591, 22/2283–0586 ✛ C4.

$$ ✕**Delhi Darbar.** Classic no-frills Mughlai food draws vacationing Arabs
INDIAN   to this eatery; it has outlets throughout the United Arab Emirates,

though this one's the flagship. It's loud and bustling—not the place for a romantic dinner—but the real reason to come is the top-quality non-vegetarian food, not the atmosphere. Meat, kebabs, and rice dishes are guaranteed not to disappoint, but bonus points go to the *palak gosht* (mutton in creamy spinach), *murgh badami korma* (minced chicken kebabs), and mutton Kashmiri. Delhi Darbar also serves Chinese food, but it pales in comparison to the Mughlai dishes. ⑤ *Average main: Rs. 500* ⊠ *Colaba Causeway, near Regal Cinema* ☎ *22/2202–5656* ⊕ *www. delhi-darbar.com* ▭ *No credit cards* ✛ *C4.*

$ ✕ **Kala Ghoda Café.** Among the most beloved lunch spots for South
CAFÉ Bombay's workaday crowd, this quaint little café is the ideal spot to grab a soy latte and a quick bite while resting your feet. The fresh juices and salads are cheap but clean and safe for foreigners, the Wi-Fi is free, and the interior, while a bit cramped, is bright and pleasant. Best of all, the sandwiches, like the KGC Special (arugula, vegetarian mayo, and Padano cheese on grilled flat bread), are light but extremely tasty when snuggled up to a hot (or more preferably iced) cup of joe. The restaurant is opposite Trishna, and a stone's throw from the Jehangir Art Gallery in the heart of the Kala Ghoda neighborhood. ⑤ *Average main: Rs. 250* ⊠ *10 Ropewalk La., Kala Ghoda, Fort* ☎ *22/2263–3866* ⊕ *www.kgcafe.in* ✛ *C3.*

$$ ✕ **Konkan Café.** Styled as an haute version of a typical Mangalorean
SEAFOOD home—all red clay and bright green—Konkan is in the Vivanta by Taj hotel (still "Taj President" to taxi drivers). It does all the chow your average home might serve, but it's more refined, with cleaner flavors and elegant presentation: food is served on copper thali plates lined with banana leaves. The prawn *gassi* (Mangalorean curry) is spicy and delicious, and the crab dishes will not disappoint, but breads tend to be rather dry. Still, it's probably the only coastal restaurant to offer a great, if expensive, bottle of wine. ⑤ *Average main: Rs. 1000* ⊠ *Vivanta by Taj hotel, 90 Cuffe Parade* ☎ *22/6665–0808* ⊕ *www.vivantabytaj. com/president-mumbai/dining/konkan-cafe-restaurant.html* ⌂ *Reservations essential* ✛ *A6.*

$$ ✕ **Le Pain Quotidien.** This Belgian bakery, a stone's throw from the
BELGIAN Gateway of India, offers great breads, fresh ingredients, and a giant communal table. It has the best croissants and baguettes in the city, fresh, large salads (try the Caesar or Caprese), and its specialty: *tartines* (open-face sandwiches)—the roasted chicken and smoked mozzarella is recommended. There's a wine selection, too, and evening specials might include grilled salmon or seared lamb chops. It's a good option when you're sweating it out in South Bombay, or for those who need a break from Indian food and want to check email on the free Wi-Fi. ⑤ *Average main: Rs. 700* ⊠ *Dhanraj Mahal, C.S.M. Rd., Apollo Bunder* ☎ *22/6615–0202* ⊕ *www.lepainquotidien.in* ✛ *D4.*

$ ✕ **Leopold Café.** When it defiantly reopened just four days after the first
CAFÉ shots of November 2008 terrorist attacks were fired and 10 people were killed, the crowds were so big the police had to shut the place down all over again. (So defiant, in fact, that ownership has preserved bullet holes from the attack on its upstairs windows for people to see and snap pictures.) Order a bottle of ice-cold Kingfisher beer to wash

down the hearty, typical bar food—chicken tikka, french fries, that kind of thing. Surprisingly, the Chinese food is actually the better bet: the beef with chilli peppers can't be beat, and the chicken-fried rice and the chilli chicken are highly recommended. $ *Average main: Rs. 400* ⊠ *Colaba Causeway* ☎ *22/2282–8185, 22/2202–0131* ⊕ *www. leopoldcafe.com* ✛ *C5.*

$$ ✕ **Moshe's.** The jewel of the Moshe's empire, this elegant, European-style
CONTEMPORARY   restaurant is where chef Moshe Shek, a Mumbai Jew, puts his culinary skills on display. It offers some of the city's best international food— pastas in creamy sauces, eggplant *roulade,* crusty cheese garlic bread (baked on the premises), Israeli stuffed chicken, hearty soups, vegetarian sandwiches for lunch, and the highly recommended char-grilled *rawas* (Indian salmon). Some of the city's best pastries are also available: try the cheesecake. ■TIP➔ **Get an inside table—though the outdoor patio is lovely, it's sometimes engulfed in the stench of the fisherman's village across the road.** $ *Average main: Rs. 800* ⊠ *7 Minoo Manor, Cuffe Parade, off Wodehouse Rd.* ☎ *22/2216–1226* ⊕ *www.moshes.in* ⌂ *Reservations essential* ✛ *A6, D4.*

$$ ✕ **Ragaa.** On the ground floor of the Sea Palace Hotel, Ragaa serves
NORTH INDIAN   surprisingly good Indian food and also has outdoor seating for dining to the sound of the ocean. The service is not great, and it can take a while to get your drinks and food, but when they arrive they are cheap and of good quality. Try the spinach *chaat* (fried breaded spinach with spicy tomato on top), the buttery *dal makhani* (a rich, dark lentil dish), and the kebab platter. After your meal, head up to the rooftop bar for an after-dinner cocktail. $ *Average main: Rs. 600* ⊠ *Sea Palace Hotel, Sea Front* ☎ *22/6112–8080* ✛ *C5.*

$$$ ✕ **The Table.** One of Mumbai's best restaurants, the Table was launched
MODERN   by a pair of Indian restaurateurs and a young American chef from San
AMERICAN   Francisco. The lofted upper floor is perfect for romantic dinners, while
Fodor's Choice   below a large, eponymous, communal table extends from the bar for
★   a more lively and sociable setting. The small plates tend to be the best, with particularly high marks for the zucchini "spaghetti" in a light buttery sauce with almonds, the tuna tataki, the spicy lamb burgers, and the meatballs, smothered in sauce and topped with cheese and fried onions. The large plates don't disappoint either. $ *Average main: Rs. 1400* ⊠ *Kalash Peshi Bldg., Chhatrapati Shivaji Maharaj Marg, Apollo Bundar* ☎ *22/2282–5000* ⊕ *thetable.in* ✛ *C4.*

$$ ✕ **Woodside.** The only real bar in town (in the American sense, at least) is
BRITISH   modeled on an English pub, plays decent music (though sometimes too loud), has great snack food, and free Wi-Fi. It also has some of the best-priced alcohol in town and is the only such place that's neither a trendy lounge playing club music or a dingy permit room. It's also a great place to stop in after a day's walking. Try the pizzas—the four cheese is excellent, and the margherita's no slouch—the soy burgers, or Franco's meat balls (a lamb and pork mix in a tangy tomato sauce). Listed here is the original, but the establishment has become popular enough to expand into the suburbs as well, with a branch in Andheri as well. $ *Average main: Rs. 600* ⊠ *Indian Mercantile Mansion, Wodehouse Rd., Regal Circle* ☎ *22/2287–5752* ⊕ *www.woodsideinn.in* ✛ *C4.*

The Great Irani Cafés

Mumbai has a special breed of teahouse that's fast disappearing. Called "Irani joints" in local parlance, these corner shops were begun by the first waves of Zoroastrians, called the Iranis, who migrated to India in the 10th century from Persia to escape religious persecution. (Those who were part of later waves are referred to as Parsis.) In following centuries thousands and thousands more Zoroastrians arrived in India. A community of about 50,000 remains in the country today, the majority in Mumbai.

Irani cafés probably arose out of the Iranis' need for a place to gather and exchange news. Simply furnished with solid wood chairs and cloaked in the appearance of yesteryear, they remain places where customers can tarry over endless cups of sweet tea for just a couple of rupees. Visiting these seedy, century-old cafés is a chance to glimpse a culture that has all but vanished. The clientele is usually very ordinary Mumbai *wallahs* (dwellers), more often than not old-timers who have been having chai and buns for the last 40 years in the same spot. Equally eccentric is the menu, an odd selection of chai, "cutting chai" (a half-cup of tea), *bun-maska* (a bun with butter), and typical Parsi cutlets, patties, rolls, fruitcakes, and confectionery. Amid the ancient mirrors, upright chairs, marble tables, elaborate balconies, and portraits of the Prophet Zarathustra is sometimes a sign acquainting you with the dos and don'ts of the particular establishment. Beer is sometimes served. But credit cards? Goodness, no. Early or mid-morning is a good time to visit.

Traditional Irani cafés are dying out, almost overnight being converted to fast-food joints or else turning upscale and adding Chinese food or spaghetti to their menus. The few that are still left can be found in the Fort area.

FORT AND MARINE DRIVE

$
INDIAN
Fodor's Choice
★
✕ **Apoorva.** If you're searching for an authentic seafood "lunch home"— which implies unpretentious, tasty, and cheap—this old-school Kala Ghoda mainstay is spot on: slightly dingy, full of locals, with a too-cold a/c section that smells faintly of mothballs. The king prawn *gussi*, a spicy red masala dish, is the best thing on the menu, though the tandoori pomfret (an Indian Ocean fish) is a close second. Whatever main dish you choose—especially any fish with a dry green Hyderabadi treatment—order a couple of *neer dosa* as accompaniment: they are a little like rotis, but much lighter and fluffier, and made of rice; most Konkan restaurants have them, but none do them better than Apoorva. ⑤ *Average main: Rs. 400* ✉ *Vasta House (Noble Chambers), S. A. Brelvi Marg, near Horniman Circle, Fort* ☎ *22/33488071* ✛ *D3.*

$
INDIAN
Fodor's Choice
★
✕ **Britannia & Co.** Office workers come here for the world-famous chicken berry *pulao*—and Boman Kohnior, whose father founded the restaurant in 1923, still takes their orders. When he chants—and he will—"fresh lime soda sweet to beat the Mumbai heat!" you will order just that, but it's that pulao, with rice, chicken, gravy, and dried fruit, that will keep you coming back. Parsi food is only available in Mumbai, and this is one of the oldest Parsi restaurants that, thankfully, hasn't

6

tried to go upscale. It's simple, fast, heavy, blissfully unhealthy food served in a dingy-looking shop with simple tables. Be prepared to wait, as it often gets crowded here. ⑤ *Average main: Rs. 400* ⊠ *Wakefield House, Strott Rd., opposite New Custom House, Ballard Estate, Fort* 🕾 *22/2261–5264* ▭ *No credit cards* ⊘ *No dinner* ✛ *D3.*

$$
BURGER

✕ **Café Sundance.** Owned by the same crew that brought Italy to India with 212, this bright, bustling burger joint has quickly become one of the crown jewels of the South Bombay eating scene. Burgers and beer are the name of the game here, but the experience in delivering quality European fare shows in items like the four-tier vegetable lasagna, the crisp and salty french fries and the many varieties of salads. The portobello mushroom burger, built around a crunchy patty and packed with Camembert, comes recommended, as are the blackened fish-and-chips. The restaurant also has a handy location, just a stone's throw from Churchgate station and Eros, one of the city's classic art deco movie theaters. ⑤ *Average main: Rs. 800* ⊠ *42 Eros Cinema Bldg., Maharishi Karve Rd., Churchgate* 🕾 *22/3348–8040* ✛ *C3.*

$$$
MODERN ASIAN

✕ **India Jones.** Though the name implies something quite different, this restaurant actually serves pan-Asian food, and attracts a mix of couples and families out for a special occasion. A bubbling pond with wooden statues greets customers to an interior decked out with traditional Asian accoutrements—mini yellow catamaran sails over the lights, giant Japanese orchids, and various Asian scripts on the walls. For starters, try the Malaysian beef tenderloin satay, and follow with *da long xai* (ginger-flavored, wok-fried lobster with water chestnuts and asparagus) or just show up for lunch and its delicious all-you-can-eat dim sum menu. ⑤ *Average main: Rs. 1400* ⊠ *Trident Hotel, Nariman Point* 🕾 *22/6632–6330* ⊕ *www.tridenthotels.com* ✛ *A4.*

$$$
INDIAN
Fodor'sChoice
★

✕ **Kebab Korner.** Though they don't come cheap, the succulent kebabs at this hotel restaurant are perfect for those who don't want to risk Delhi belly (yes, even in Mumbai it's called that) at a hygienically challenged late-night spot. Elegant and subdued, with excellent waitstaff, the restaurant's only drawback is the minimum 25-minute wait for your food—but good things take time, and the chicken *seekh* kebabs (ground chicken and spices), Chilean sea bass served in a green *hariyali (spinach and mint)* masala, and the chicken *pahadi* kebab (chunks of saffron-tinged chicken topped with egg whites) are worth the wait. ⑤ *Average main: Rs. 1400* ⊠ *InterContinental Hotel, 135 Marine Dr., Churchgate* 🕾 *22/3987–9999* ⊕ *www.ichotelsgroup.com* ⊘ *No lunch* ✛ *B2.*

$$
SEAFOOD

✕ **Mahesh Lunch Home.** Somewhere between Apoorva and Trishna—geographically as well as atmospherically—Mahesh is another legendary Fort seafood restaurant that attracts the office-lunch crowd as well as packing them in during the evenings. Some of the character was stripped out of the place after they decided to go upscale, and the floor-to-ceiling marble might be a bit much, but the food remains reliably authentic. The traditional Konkan fare is excellent, including the prawn *gussi* (a spicy red curry), *rawas* (a local fish), and fried *kane* (a bony Mangalorean fish). It's also the best place in Mumbai to order snacky, deep-fried and delectable *koliwada* prawns. Decades into its existence, it's still *the* place for the freshest fish in town. There's another branch in

Juhu, on Juhu Tara Road. $ *Average main: Rs. 700* ✉ *8-B Cawasji Patel St., Fort* ☎ *22/6695–5559, 22/6695–5554* ⊕ *www.maheshlunchhome. com* ✛ *D3.*

$ ✕ **Natural.** Serving the best ice cream in town, Natural—which has the
CAFÉ taste of Indian *malai* (sweets so creamy they're almost like cheese)—seems to be everywhere. Established in 1984 in Juhu, Natural now has outlets throughout the country. Open until around midnight—depending on the shop—Natural shops attract students and families alike on most weekend nights. All of the ice cream is made with fresh fruit or nuts, and contains no preservatives; highly recommended are the tender coconut, roasted almond, or seasonal Indian fruit flavors like cinnamon-tinged *chikoo* (a caramel-flavored fruit also known as sapodilla), custard apple, or mango. $ *Average main: Rs. 200* ✉ *Jyoti Sadan, 137 Marine Dr., next to InterContinental Hotel, Churchgate* ☎ *22/2202–7426, 22/6610–8000* ⊕ *www.naturalicecreams.in* ▭ *No credit cards* ✛ *B2.*

$ ✕ **The Pantry.** Under the same ownership as Woodside, this restaurant
MODERN dispenses with the pubby atmosphere to focus on simple, rustic cuisine
AMERICAN using local ingredients. The food is excellent and reasonably priced considering how refined it is, and although it'd be nice if it had a wine license—the white interiors, open kitchen, and general atmosphere all scream "wine bar"—the excellent baked goods and mains more than make up for the lack of booze. Try the creamy potato pie, or the grilled chicken or pulled pork sandwich, along with the grilled *rawas* and literally any of the breads or pastries, and get ready for the best salads in town. $ *Average main: Rs. 450* ✉ *Yeshwant Chambers, Military Square La., Kala Ghoda, Fort* ☎ *22/2270–0082* ☾ *No dinner* ✛ *C3.*

$ ✕ **Soam.** Families, vegetarians, and foreigners who can't handle street
INDIAN food flock here for healthy Gujarati food. Granted, the use of ghee
Fodor's Choice (clarified butter) is quite liberal, but not all dishes use it—that includes
★ the various kinds of *chaat* (veggie and bread snacks). The spicy potato patties stuffed with peas and smothered in savory yellow *dal* are highly recommended, as is *palak moong dal* (yellow lentils sautéed with spinach), vitamin *bhel* (a light veggie salad), and spinach and cheese samosas. The modern take on classics doesn't deter the locals, and it's likely to be packed, but you'll soon get a seat amid the pale yellow walls, wooden benches, and loud aunties. $ *Average main: Rs. 400* ✉ *Sadguru Sadan, ground fl., across from Babulnath Mandir, Chowpatty, Marine Drive* ☎ *22/2369–8080* ✛ *E5.*

$ ✕ **Suzette.** India's French influence might be strongest in sunny Pondi-
FRENCH cherry, on the east coast, but with two Frenchmen at the helm, this tiny crepe joint can provide a taste of it right here in Mumbai. The space gets packed with office jockeys for weekday lunch, but they don't linger, so the longest wait time is 10 minutes. Try the Méditerranée, with grilled chicken, olive tapenade, mozzarella, and tomatoes, or the Italie, with arugula, a tomato coulis, mozzarella, and oregano, or build your own crepe from an extensive list of ingredients. Salads are washed in bottled water and safe. Sweet crepes come with various combinations of Nutella, jam, fruit, and cream. There's another branch in Bandra.

6

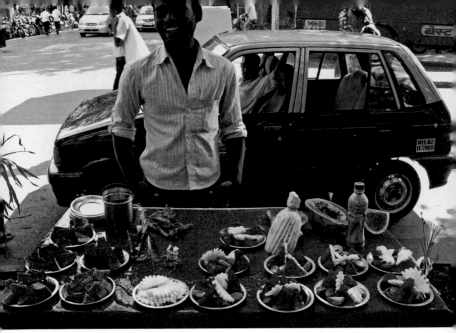

Sliced fruit for sale

$ *Average main: Rs. 400* ✉ *Atlanta Bldg., Nariman Point* ☎ *22/2641–1431* ⊕ *www.suzette.in* ✚ *A4.*

$$$
SEAFOOD
✕ **Trishna.** Four words: Butter; Pepper; Garlic; Crab. Even if that was all this legendary Kala Ghoda restaurant served, they'd be full year-round. The succulent crab is available in myriad treatments—with Indian and Western spices, green *hariyali* masala, black (spicier) Hyderabadi masala—and they maintain the quality that's made it a favorite with locals and tourists alike for more than 30 years. But there's so much more to the menu than crab, especially for fish lovers—prawns, squid, pomfret (a classic Indian Ocean fish) are there, too, and deliciously prepared. Ask the waitstaff for a recommendation; they're extremely helpful and know what's fresh to order. With good reason, this bustling place with a ho-hum interior has the best reputation of any seafood restaurant on the subcontinent. $ *Average main: Rs. 1200* ✉ *7 Rope Walk La., next to Commerce House, Kala Ghoda, Fort* ☎ *22/2261–4991* ⊕ *www.trishna.co.in* ☜ *Reservations essential* ✚ *C3* $ *Average main: Rs. 1200* ✉ *3/A Crystal Plaza, opposite Infiniti Mall and Cinemax, New Link Rd., Andheri* ☎ *22/3266–1146, 22/3266–1147* ☜ *Reservations essential* ✚ *C3.*

$$
INDIAN
✕ **Zaffran.** Oily, spicy biryani and tikkas draw crowds to this oddly nightclub/spaceship-looking joint near CST. This is a spot for the late-night foodie whose taste buds may be a bit more discerning than those of the people eating on the street in front of Bade Miya. The chow is unbelievably tasty, if completely traditional, and it comes fast and cheap. Try the chicken biryani, the chicken tikka, or the famous, creamy butter chicken. $ *Average main: Rs. 500* ✉ *B Block, Sitaram*

Bldg., Dr. D.N. Rd., Fort ☎ *22/2344–2690, 22/2340–1976* ⊕ *www. zaffranrestaurant.com* ⊗ *No lunch* ✛ *D2.*

$$$$ ╳ **Ziya.** Opened in 2010, Ziya quickly shot to the very forefront of
INDIAN   Indian cuisine, and although other modern, more traditionally minded restaurants (like Neel) have taken its place at the top of the heap, it remains one of the most exciting restaurants to hit India in ages. Here, traditional Indian flavors receive nouvelle cuisine treatment from Chef Vineet Bhatia, the first Indian chef to win Michelin stars. Try his "gourmand" tasting menu—7 to 10 courses that may include dishes such as mushroom *kichidi* (rice, yoghurt, and spices—like risotto, but mushier) with *makhani* (creamy red tomato curry) ice cream, or a smoked tandoori lamb chop with lemon-grass foam. ⑤ *Average main: Rs. 2500* ✉ *Oberoi, Nariman Point* ☎ *22/3348–7783* ⊕ *www.oberoihotels.com* ✛ *A4.*

JUHU, BANDRA, AND THE WESTERN SUBURBS

$$$$ ╳ **Aurus.** Juhu's most trendy nightspot for a long time running is also
EUROPEAN   one of its better fine-dining restaurants. Definitively loungey, it feels less forced and more elegant than most lounge bars in Mumbai, and the outdoor area, overhanging a nice stretch of Juhu Beach, has low white couches and sparkling candlelight. Inside, it's a bit too dim, but later on the dance floor fills up with some of Bollywood's most beautiful people, so stick around after your meal. The continental food has local influences, and runs the gamut from traditional pastas to molecular gastronomy. The signature dish—duck prepared by the *sous vide* method—is succulent, but the grilled New Zealand lamb shank is better. ⑤ *Average main: Rs. 1500* ✉ *Nichani Kutir, Juhu Tara Rd., near Reid and Taylor, Juhu* ☎ *22/6710–6666* ✛ *F2.*

$$$$ ╳ **Azok.** Shortly before Ziya stormed Mumbai's culinary world,
INDIAN   renowned chef Vineet Bhatia, hailed for his experimental fine-dining Indian food, quietly opened this lower-key version of his revolutionary Indian restaurant. Perched on the rooftop of an apartment building, Azok may look like a lot of the other outdoor lounges in the city, but rooftop dining is a rare treat in Mumbai, and the food heralds the future of Indian cuisine. Try the mustard tempered stir-fried prawns with wasabi, the lamb biryani, and the chicken tikka with creamy red *makhani* curry over penne pasta. ⑤ *Average main: Rs. 1600* ✉ *Oakwood Premier, 29/1 JR Mhatre Rd., opposite Iris Park, Juhu* ☎ *22/6623–8894* ⊕ *www.azokrestaurant.com* ⊗ *No lunch* ✛ *F1.*

$ ╳ **Elco Restaurant.** For decades the food stalls in front of Elco Market
INDIAN   have been serving some of the best—and cleanest—vegetarian street food Mumbai has to offer, and they were doing so well that the owners were able to open this two-floor restaurant inside the market, offering essentially the same food. Try the cheese *pav bhaji* for a heartier take on a Mumbai classic, the *ragda pattice,* and pretty much any of the other classics listed in the "Street Food Favorites." Finish off with a serving of sweet, doughy *gulab jamuns,* basically doughnut holes in a sweet syrup. ⑤ *Average main: Rs. 200* ✉ *C-84 Elco Market, 46 Hill Rd., Bandra* ☎ *22/2645–7677* ⊟ *No credit cards* ✛ *F2.*

$ ╳ **Gajalee.** Suburbanites love this quaint seafood joint near Juhu Beach,
SEAFOOD   which compares favorably with the best coastal restaurants Fort has

to offer. There are other branches across India, including one at the High Street Phoenix Mall, so those staying down south don't have to travel too far to enjoy the fried *surmai* fish (a type of mackerel), the savory crab stir-fry, the big, fresh grilled tiger prawns, or the "baby shark" masala (actually mori fish). The Phoenix Mall branch is sleek and modern, while the original Vile Parle location is a bit tacky and dated but better regarded (as most originals are). $ *Average main: Rs. 400* ✉ *Amrapali Shopping Centre, VL Mehta Marg, Vile Parle, Juhu* ☎ *22/2610–7040, 22/6696–0902* ⊕ *www.gajalee.com* ✛ *F2* $ *Average main: Rs. 400* ✉ *Phoenix Mills, Block 3 ABC, Senapati Bapat Marg, Lower Parel, near Big Bazaar (department store), Central Mumbai* ☎ *22/2495–0667, 22/2495–0668* ☾ *No dinner* ✛ *F2.*

$ | ✕ **Kareem's.** Popular with college kids, and tucked neatly off Carter
INDIAN | Road, Kareem's serves some of the best kebabs in the burbs—and it's a good option for those wary of eating street-side kebabs (which, honestly, take kebabs to a whole other level), or not up for a visit to Muhammad Ali Road, in the Muslim ghetto. Open-air, but decorated in unpretentious but modern, dark wood, Kareem's has a casual atmosphere, enhanced by the bench-style seating. Try the chicken tikka, the mutton *seekh* kebabs (minced meat wrapped around a skewer and cooked in the tandoor oven), and, for vegetarians, the *paneer tikka* (grilled cheese with peppers and onions). There's another on Colaba Causeway. $ *Average main: Rs. 300* ✉ *7A Gagangiri, off Carter Rd., Bandra* ☎ *22/2646–3501* ✛ *F3* $ *Average main: Rs. 300* ✉ *Shop 3 and 4, Radha Estate, 148 A, Shahid Bhagat Singh Rd., Colaba Causeway, near Sassoon Dock, Bandra* ☎ *22/2215–2206* ✛ *F3.*

$$$$ | ✕ **Pali Village Café.** Quality European bistro food—and the possibility of
EUROPEAN | seeing a Bollywood star or two—draws suburbanites as well as townies on date night to this converted two-story furniture store in Bandra, but it's the romantic, old-school charm of its interior that keeps them coming back for more. While the rest of Mumbai runs headlong into the future, this place harks back to Bombay's bungalow roots with simple wooden tables, wrought iron railings, and exposed brick. The pastas and sandwiches are well executed, as is the flat bread pizza and flavorful pitchers of sangria. But the real draw, however, is the panna cotta—one of the most delightful desserts the city has to offer. $ *Average main: Rs. 1500* ✉ *Pali Naka, next to Janata Lunch Home, Bandra* ☎ *22/2605–0401* ✛ *F3.*

$$ | ✕ **Salt Water Café.** This unpretentious restaurant in Bandra Reclama-
EUROPEAN | tion—a scenic, walkable section of Bandra—has a classic nouvelle cuisine menu and a simple rooftop terrace. The breakfast menu is long and trustworthy, and at night, the crab legs are excellent, and the drinks are relatively cheap. It gets crowded on weekends, so be sure to make a reservation, preferably for the terrace, where the cover of giant palm trees somehow blocks out the cacophony from noisy Chapel Road below. $ *Average main: Rs. 700* ✉ *Rose Minar Annexe, 87 Chapel Rd., near Mount Carmel Church, Bandra* ☎ *22/2643–4441* ✛ *F3.*

WHERE TO STAY

CENTRAL MUMBAI

$$$
HOTEL
Four Seasons. Extremely popular with businesspeople because of its central location between South Bombay and the western suburbs, India's tallest hotel—33 stories—has a luxury rooftop bar that is one of the city's hottest (and most expensive) night spots. **Pros:** central location between South Bombay and the suburbs; business-friendly; the city's best spa. **Cons:** unless you are on business nearby, it will take you an additional 20 minutes to reach town. $ *Rooms from: Rs. 11750* ⊠ *114 Dr. E. Moses Rd., Parel* ☎ *22/2481–8000* ⊕ *www.fourseasons.com/mumbai* ⇥ *176 rooms, 26 suites* �‖ *No meals* ✢ *F4.*

COLABA

$
HOTEL
Fodor'sChoice
★
Bentley's. The best deal in Colaba—a clean, quaint, simple tourist joint in a prime South Bombay location—is the kind of place young expats send visiting friends to stay if they don't have room. **Pros:** cheap and clean; friendly, helpful owner. **Cons:** basic, and can be a little musty. $ *Rooms from: Rs. 2000* ⊠ *17 Oliver St.* ☎ *22/2284–1474* ⊕ *www.bentleyshotel.com* ⇥ *55 rooms* �‖ *No meals* ✢ *C5.*

$$$
HOTEL
Fariyas. Just a few minutes on foot from the Gateway of India, the Fariyas is a solid mid-range hotel, well located in Colaba. **Pros:** well located; good views. **Cons:** smallish rooms; surprisingly expensive (though cheaper rates are often available online). $ *Rooms from: Rs. 10000* ⊠ *25 Devshankar V, Vyas Marg, off Arthur Bunder Rd.* ☎ *22/6141–6141* ⊕ *www.fariyas.com* ⇥ *87 rooms, 6 suites* �‖ *Breakfast* ✢ *C5.*

$
HOTEL
Sea Palace Hotel. The location of this mid-range hotel (with bargain prices given that it's Mumbai) is enough to make it a good choice—it's right on the waterfront near the Gateway of India. **Pros:** the staff is attentive; cheap; great location; airy, pleasant rooftop bar. **Cons:** could be classier. $ *Rooms from: Rs. 5200* ⊠ *26 P. J. Ramachandani Marg* ☎ *22/6112–8000* ⇥ *50 rooms, 3 suites* �‖ *Breakfast* ✢ *C5.*

$$$$
HOTEL
Fodor'sChoice
★
Taj Mahal Palace. Foreigners and wealthy Indians choose the Taj over other fancy hotels in town because it's a beautiful and regal landmark—worth visiting even if you don't stay here—with views past the Gateway of India to the Arabian Sea. **Pros:** it's an icon; location, location, location; city's best views. **Cons:** expensive; service can be disorganized. $ *Rooms from: Rs. 16000* ⊠ *Colaba* ☎ *22/6665–3366* ⊕ *www.tajhotels.com* ⇥ *565 rooms, 45 suites* �‖ *Breakfast* ✢ *C4.*

$$
HOTEL
Vivanta by Taj–President. Favored by business travelers, this hotel in the heart of charming Cuffe Parade also offers some great views, a choice of restaurants, and a hip bar. **Pros:** great in-house restaurants and pleasant neighborhood; well located. **Cons:** small rooms. $ *Rooms from: Rs. 8000* ⊠ *90 Cuffe Parade* ☎ *22/6665–0808* ⊕ *www.tajhotels.com* ⇥ *292 rooms, 20 suites* �‖ *Breakfast* ✢ *A6.*

FORT AND MARINE DRIVE

$$$$
HOTEL
InterContinental. Aside from the ideal Marine Drive location and some of the city's biggest standard rooms, service is a big plus point here, with personal concierges and a complimentary in-room massage for every

BEST BETS FOR MUMBAI LODGING

Fodor's Choice ★

Bentley's, p. 357
The Oberoi, p. 358
Taj Mahal Palace, p. 357

By Price

$

Bentley's, p. 357
Sea Green, p. 358
Sea Palace, p. 357

$$$

Four Seasons, p. 357
JW Marriott, p. 359
The Trident, p. 359

$$$$

InterContinental, p. 357

The Oberoi, p. 358
Taj Mahal Palace, p. 357

By Experience

BEST FOR BUSINESS

Four Seasons, p. 357
InterContinental, p. 357

BEST FOR KIDS

JW Marriott, p. 359

BEST HOTEL BAR

Four Seasons, p. 357
InterContinental, p. 357

BEST INTERIOR DESIGN

Novotel, p. 359

BEST LOCATION

Bentley's, p. 357
Fariyas, p. 357
The Oberoi, p. 358
Taj Mahal Palace, p. 357

BEST POOL

JW Marriott, p. 359
Taj Mahal Palace, p. 357

BEST SPA

JW Marriott, p. 359

BEST VIEWS

InterContinental, p. 357
The Oberoi, p. 358
Taj Mahal Palace, p. 357

guest. **Pros:** 500-square-foot rooms are standard; Dome and Kebab Korner restaurants are among the city's best; there are often good online deals. **Cons:** the Oberoi, its chief competitor, seems a touch more grand; usual rates are quite high. $ *Rooms from: Rs. 16000* ⊠ *135 Marine Dr., Churchgate* ☎ *22/3987–9999* ⊕ *www.ihg.com/intercontinental/hotels/ gb/en/mumbai/bomhb/hoteldetail* ⤳ *58 rooms, 11 suites* ⧖ *Breakfast* ✛ *B2.*

$$$$
HOTEL
Fodor's Choice
★
⚏ **The Oberoi.** Luxury and stellar service are the hallmarks here—every floor has a butler who will make reservations, collect your laundry, shine your shoes, supervise the room cleaning, and bring you chocolates. **Pros:** the world-famous restaurant Ziya; elegant rooms with views of the Arabian Sea. **Cons:** expensive. $ *Rooms from: Rs. 14000* ⊠ *Nariman Point* ☎ *22/6632–5757* ⊕ *www.oberoihotels.com* ⤳ *214 rooms, 73 suites* ⧖ *Breakfast* ✛ *A4.*

$
HOTEL
⚏ **Sea Green.** For those looking to save money but still get a glimpse of the shimmering waters off Marine Drive, consider this classic hotel, whose main virtue is that it's a remarkable bargain relative to its location, halfway between heavyweights like the Oberoi and the InterContinental. **Pros:** good location; nice views; large, clean rooms. **Cons:** antiquated and rather worn. $ *Rooms from: Rs. 3300* ⊠ *145 Marine Dr., Churchgate* ☎ *22/6633–6525, 22/2282–2294* ⊕ *www. seagreenhotel.com* ⤳ *34 rooms, 4 suites* ⧖ *No meals* ✛ *B3.*

$$$ 🖼 **The Trident.** The Oberoi's posh and slightly less luxurious cousin con-
HOTEL   tinues the same tradition of excellent service, and because room rates vary according to occupancy, it can be a great value in the off-season. **Pros:** cheaper than the Oberoi, though not significantly lower in qual-ity; a true high-rise with proper views. **Cons:** you're not staying at the Oberoi. $ *Rooms from: Rs. 11000* ⊠ *Nariman Point* ☎ *22/6632–4343* ⊕ *www.tridenthotels.com/mumbai-nariman-point/hotel.asp* ↝ *550 rooms, 40 suites* ❑ *No meals* ✛ *B4.*

JUHU, BANDRA, AND THE WESTERN SUBURBS

$ 🖼 **Citizen.** One of the cheapest decent hotels on the Juhu strip, and right
HOTEL   on the beach, the Citizen is a deal in a city where you seemingly pay for every square inch. **Pros:** good value for money; on the beach. **Cons:** far from South Bombay. $ *Rooms from: Rs. 5000* ⊠ *960 Juhu Tara Rd., Juhu* ☎ *22/6693–2525* ⊕ *www.citizenhotelMumbai.com* ↝ *45 rooms, 3 suites* ❑ *Breakfast* ✛ *F1.*

$$$ 🖼 **JW Marriott.** A grand, luxurious hotel where you can retreat from the
HOTEL   chaos of Mumbai but still be able to step out and experience it, though
FAMILY   the main sights are distant. **Pros:** airport transfers included in rates; well-appointed rooms; excellent meals. **Cons:** a bit far from city sights. $ *Rooms from: Rs. 11500* ⊠ *Juhu Tara Rd., Juhu* ☎ *22/6693–3000* ⊕ *www.marriott.com* ↝ *326 rooms, 29 suites* ❑ *Breakfast* ✛ *F1.*

$$$ 🖼 **Novotel.** Built in the 1970s, this Western-style high rise was com-
HOTEL   pletely renovated when Novotel took over in 2009, and the spacious lobby and large rooms now have a modern, sleek feel. **Pros:** beachside location; airport pick-up included in price; close to suburban malls. **Cons:** far from downtown. $ *Rooms from: Rs. 11000* ⊠ *Balraj Sahani Marg, Juhu* ☎ *22/6693–4444* ⊕ *www.novotel.com* ↝ *203 rooms, 12 suites* ❑ *No meals* ✛ *F1.*

NIGHTLIFE AND PERFORMING ARTS

NIGHTLIFE

No other city in India knows how to have a good time quite like Mum-bai. Here you'll find everything from dingy "permit rooms" (basically cafeteria-style rooms with a liquor license) so dirty they make an Ameri-can dive bar look like the Rainbow Room, and clubs so fancy they make the Rainbow Room look like a permit room. Whatever destination you choose, they all hold their own special charms. If you're in the mood for a cheap tipple, and you appreciate the character of a down and dirty dive bar, head to Gokul, behind the Taj Mahal Palace, it's the most tourist-friendly of Mumbai's permit rooms.

If you're more inclined to clubbing, Mumbai has lots to choose from—though club owners seem to have decided that the only option that works in this city are lounges with blaring music and tiny dance floors: be forewarned, though, that prices are steep, and you'll often pay New York prices, or more, for your drinks. Note, too, that many clubs and bars have "couples" policies, wherein a "stag" (lone man) is not per-mitted to enter without a woman. This might be a circuitous attempt to prevent brawls, pickup scenes, and prostitution—or just a club owner figuring that in a country where many more guys are allowed to stay out late than girls, a club full of dudes isn't going to attract much business. To avoid an unpleasant encounter at the door, check with your hotel staff to find out whether your destination club or bar will allow you to enter if you're a man traveling alone or in a group of men. Dress nicely and you'll probably get in; an advance call from your hotel concierge might also make your entry smoother.

One area where the suburbs have it over the city is nightlife, and the after-dark scene in the wealthy enclaves of Juhu and Bandra thrive on suburbia's young nouveau riche as well as city folk willing to travel for a good night out.

Revelry peaks from Thursday to Sunday nights, with an early-20s-to-mid-30s crowd. Pubs open daily at around 6 or 7 (except a few, which open in the afternoon) and close by 1:15 am or a little later, depending, honestly, on how much they've paid the local cops. Some places collect a cover charge at the door. As in any metropolis, the reign of a night-spot can be ephemeral. ■TIP➔ Ask a young hotel employee to tell you where the best clubs or bars are, as trends change quickly in Mumbai.

CENTRAL MUMBAI
BARS AND LOUNGES

Aer. The rooftop club at the Four Seasons is one of the most popular—and most expensive—bars in town, but it offers stunning views of the city in all directions, and is probably worth a drink. ⊠ *Four Seasons Hotel, 114 E. Moses Rd., Worli* ☎ *22/2481–8000.*

The Barking Deer. Stay long enough in Mumbai, and the words "cold beer on tap" start to sound like some distant faraway dream. This bar's founder Greg Kroitzsh, a transplant from Vermont, decided to quit whining about India's headache-inducing bottles of Kingfisher Strong, and make the dream real. The Barking Deer brews its own pale ale, as well as Bombay Blonde, a tasty lager, and the Belgian Wit, a crisp wheat beer. Kroitzsh keeps on hand a nice sampling of imported bottled beers, and the pub fare, like the eggplant Parm sandwich, is well regarded. Weekend nights tend to become overcrowded with partiers, but afternoons present a quiet opportunity to relax and reflect on your trip. The best part? Happy hour (from 4 to 8) is two beers for the price of one. There's free Wi-Fi, too. ⊠ *Mathuradas Mill Compound, Senapati Bapat Marg, Lower Parel* ☎ *22/614–17400* ⊕ *www.barkingdeer.in.*

Busaba. In addition to its Asian restaurant, which serves a mix of Burmese, Chinese, Vietnamese, and Thai, Busaba has a relaxed but small and attractive bar-lounge. There's another branch near Blue Frog and Café Zoe in Central Mumbai, if you're in the neighborhood. ⊠ *4 Mandlik Rd., near Cotton World, Colaba* ☎ *22/2204–3779* ⊠ *Mathuradas Mill Compound, N.M. Joshi Marg, near Blue Frog, Lower Parel* ☎ *22/6747–8974.*

The White Owl. The White Owl brewpub currently stands as a reminder of how tricky it is to get government permission to brew beer here. Huge brass tankers have sat unattended behind the clean, inviting black-and-white checkered bar since its opening. Bottles of imported ales, stouts, and lagers are served instead, however, and the atmosphere, pub food, and bar snacks, like hot, tangy sweet-potato-and-chives popcorn, make it well worth the visit. The brewing license is coming, we are told, but in the meantime, there are many reasons to keep coming back. ✉ *One Indiabulls Center, Tower 2 Lobby, Senapati Bapat Marg, Lower Parel* ☎ *22/2421–0231* ⊕ *whiteowl.in.*

CLUBS AND DISCOS

Blue Frog. International bands and local acts play Tuesday through Sunday nights at this spacious, trendy nightclub with top-notch acoustics. Munchies like onion rings, burgers, and cheese platters, as well as full meals like pasta are all available. The entry per head varies from free to Rs. 2,000, depending on whether there is an international or domestic act playing. ✉ *Mathuradas Mills Compound, Tulsi Pipe Rd. entrance, opposite Kamala Mills entrance, Lower Parel* ☎ *022/6158–6158* ⊕ *www.bluefrog.co.in.*

COLABA

BARS AND LOUNGES

Gokul. The safest destination to test out one of Mumbai's infamous permit rooms offers a no-frills, dingy atmosphere—this is the kind of place you want to hit up for super-cheap drinks (we're talking nearly retail prices per bottle, which you can order to your table) before you head to the club, or for a late-night drink postclubbing, if the owners have paid the cops enough to stay open past bar time that night. ✉ *10 Tulloch Rd., behind Taj Mahal Palace hotel and next to Bade Miya* ☎ *77381–12828, 22/2284–8206.*

Wink. One of the more popular bars in south Mumbai, Wink is on the spendy side, as is common with bars in high-end hotels. The main draw is its chill house music. ✉ *Vivanta by Taj–President Mumbai, 90 Cuffe Parade* ☎ *22/6665–0975.*

FORT AND MARINE DRIVE

BARS AND LOUNGES

Dome. With some of the best views of the city, the open-air Dome attracts a young, good-looking crowd who sit, amid candlelight, on plush white sofas and chairs. It's one of the best sunset-drink spots in the city, and the fact that the menu includes a selection from the excellent Kebab Korner only sweetens the deal. Drinks are fairly expensive, but if you're on a budget, grab a Kingfisher for Rs. 300. That's hardly a steal, but you're paying for the view. ✉ *InterContinental Hotel, 135 Marine Dr., Churchgate* ☎ *22/3987–9999.*

Eau Bar. Facing the Arabian Sea, this bar is elegant and more reserved than many of its peers, and attracts a rather high-class clientele for the live jazz band that plays each night. ✉ *The Oberoi Hotel, Nariman Point* ☎ *22/6632–5757.*

Geoffrey's. A relatively staid yuppie crowd likes to hang out in the clubby (in the British sense) setting here, but it's also one of the few bars with enough TVs to accommodate a big sporting event like Wimbledon or the World Cup. ✉ *Marine Plaza Hotel, 29 Marine Dr., Churchgate* ☎ *22/2285–1212.*

6

Song and Dance, Bollywood Style

Bollywood, the famously spirited and wildly popular Indian film industry headquartered in Mumbai, is the largest movie production center in the world. Its devoted Hindi-speaking patrons number in the tens of millions.

For almost 40 years, the blueprint of Bollywood movies hasn't changed much: boy meets girl, boy and girl dance provocatively, but never kiss; something keeps them apart, usually some sort of injustice, or something having to do with religion or family; a poorly staged fight ensues in which one man takes on an entire village, and, finally, love conquers all and the pair live happily ever after. Often a dream sequence is used as an excuse for what basically amounts to a music video, often shot in the Swiss Alps, wherein famous actors otherwise unaffiliated with the movie's plot will appear, and lip synch. You may also notice pieces of your favorite American films popping up, uncredited (one popular Bollywood movie includes pieces of all the following films: *The Godfather*, *Pulp Fiction*, *Reservoir Dogs*, and *Goodfellas*; another took the plot of *I Am Sam* and turned it into a post-9/11 film, and managed to fit in a subplot featuring a Katrina-like situation in the American South).

Hindi films play a special role in the lives of the Indian people. Sure, it's a lot of musical gobbledygook, but for the poor and the illiterate, paying a few rupees for three solid hours of fantasy is a terrific bargain—and middle- and upper-class Indians are no less attached to their movies and the gods of Bollywood. An on-location film shoot, or the arrival of a Hindi star at a restaurant, will attract mobs; these actors and actresses are the demigods of India. (You'll also find them on TV and billboards, hawking everything from cell phones to cement.) The lion of the industry, Amitabh Bachchan, one of India's favorite superstars—think of him as a cross between Burt Reynolds and Ben Kingsley—has a temple dedicated to him in West Bengal.

Moviegoing tips: Remember to stand up for the national anthem before the movie. You could try to brush up on your Hindi before you go, or have a local accompany you to provide a translation (you'll find that patrons talking in the movies is not uncommon, indeed, it's also not unusual for theatergoers to hold full-volume cell-phone conversations in the middle of the movie), but even though the movies are in a foreign language, the thin plotlines make it easy to follow along.

JUHU, BANDRA, AND THE WESTERN SUBURBS

BARS AND LOUNGES

The Hawaiian Shack. Small but popular, the Hawaiian Shack resembles a Goa beach spot and plays retro music. ✉ *339 16th Rd., opposite Pal's Fish Corner, off Linking Rd., Bandra* ☎ *22/3348–7834, 99672–11694* ✉ *Pipewalla Bldg., 4th Pasta La., Colaba* ☎ *22/2202–0455.*

Olive Bar and Restaurant. This candlelit nightspot draws Mumbai's who's who for bites of top-notch antipasts, risotto, seafood salad, and sips of caipiroskas (caipirinhas made with vodka instead of the rumlike cachaça). ✉ *14 Union Park, off Carter Rd., Bandra* ☎ *022/4340–8229* ⊕ *www.olivebarandkitchen.com.*

Vie. Great food as well as great beats—opt for the lounge on the beach. ✉ *102 Juhu Tara Rd., opposite Little Italy, Juhu* ☎ *22/2660–3003, 22/2660–4884* ⊕ *www.vie.co.in.*

MALABAR HILL AND NEARBY
BARS AND LOUNGES
The Ghetto. Among the most legendary dives in the entire city, complete with a pair of beat-up pool tables, black light, and a psychedelic mural of Jim Morrison. ✉ *30 Bhulabhai Desai Rd., Breach Candy, Malabar Hill* ☎ *22/2353–8418.*

PERFORMING ARTS

Nowadays, Mumbai's arts scene has gone as online as any other major city's, so your first stop should probably be the Internet. *You'll find the websites for all of the major playhouses below; check schedules accordingly.* For movies, go to ⊕ *www.bookmyshow.com* to book tickets at most Mumbai theaters. For some of the best cultural goings-on-about-town, check out the websites ⊕ *www.mumbaiboss.com* and ⊕ *www.bpbweekend.com.* If you're old-school, you can check out the fortnightly culture calendar "Programme of Dance, Music and Drama," available free at the Government of India Tourist Office. The daily *Times of India* usually lists each day's films, concerts, and other events; on Friday the paper publishes a guide to city events called *What's Hot* that can be purchased at any newsstand. The afternoon paper *Midday* publishes highlights of the coming week's events in its pullout *What To Do? Where To Go?*, also available online (⊕ *www.mid-day.com*). Program information and details usually appear on the Maharashtra Tourism Development Corporation's (MTDC) city-guide programs, shown regularly on hotel in-house TV stations.

Performance tickets in Mumbai are usually quite inexpensive (from free to Rs. 500) and can be purchased from box offices or from the ticket counter at Rhythm House (across the street from the Jehangir Art Gallery), an iconic Mumbai music store so legendary that locals write wistful essays about it. They still sell CDs and DVDs in the download era, and for now, people still buy them. The helpful staff is also a valuable source of info on what's happening around town.

National Centre for the Performing Arts (*NCPA*). The **Godrej Dance Academy Theater,** a main venue for classical Indian dance performances as well as workshops and master classes, is in this huge complex, along with the **Drama Opera Arts Complex,** a 1,000-seat auditorium that is Mumbai's ballet and opera theater. There are also several theaters, including the **Tata Theatre,** a grand 1,000-seat auditorium that regularly hosts plays, often in English, and classical concerts by major Indian and international musicians. It also boasts a spacious and well-regarded Mediterranean restaurant, Amadeus, that occasionally holds wedding functions. Note that some NCPA performances are open to members

6

only; a year's membership is Rs. 2,500. ✉ *Sir Dorab Tata Rd., Nariman Point* ☎ *22/2282–4567* ⊕ *www.ncpamumbai.com.*

FILM

Mumbai, aka "Bollywood," is the center of the Indian film industry—the largest film producer in the world. A typical epic Indian musical in the movie theater is three or so hours of song, tears, gun battles, and around-the-trees love dances; in other words, quite a spectacle. Most of these movies are in Hindi, but the plots are pretty basic, so you'll probably get the gist. Seeing a Bollywood movie in an Indian theater is an experience unlike what most Americans are used to: it's a very social scene, often with whole families or groups of friends talking and laughing and eating; indeed, the movie itself is often not the primary entertainment. It's definitely a unique experience, but not for everyone. And even if you go, don't feel obliged to stay to the end; the intermissions can be a convenient exit cue. The Inox is a convenient place to go, but there are other Bollywood theaters farther afield; check local entertainment listings.

Eros Cinema. First opened in 1938, and built with handsome red sandstone, Eros is among the last few of Mumbai's beautiful art deco cinemas, creating an opportunity to catch a Bollywood flick, visit a famous site, and travel back in time to a different era of India's history—in the same stop. ✉ *Cambata Bldg., (North Wing), 42 Maharishi Karve Rd., opposite Churchgate Station, Churchgate* ☎ *22/2282–6828* ⊕ *www. eroscinema.co.in.*

For English-language movies, there are several options around Mumbai:

Regal Cinema. One of the last in a dying breed of South Bombay's gorgeous art deco theaters, Regal is a tourist treasure in its own right, and well worth the price of admission, regardless of the quality of the film itself. Here, flowing curtains still draw open at the start of a film and intermissions bubble over with gossip about the Hollywood and Bollywood stars on screen, harking back to a charming, almost forgotten time in India's pop culture landscape. ✉ *Shaheed Bhagat Singh Rd., opposite Prince of Wales Museum, Colaba* ☎ *22/2202–1017.*

MUSIC AND THEATER

The Comedy Store. The popularity of stand-up comedy has been on the rise in Bombay ever since India received its own version of Comedy Central on cable back in 2011. Located in a luxury mall, this theater is a great place to catch local comics tuning up their act, and also plays host to a number of excellent plays throughout the year. ✉ *Palladium Mall, 462 Senapati Bapat Marg, 4th fl., Lower Parel* ☎ *22/3989–5050* ⊕ *www.thecomedystore.in.*

Nehru Centre Auditorium. Mumbai's second major venue regularly hosts theater, music, and dance performances. Interesting art films, some in English, are also screened here. ✉ *Dr. Annie Besant Rd., Worli, Central Mumbai* ☎ *22/2496–4676* ⊕ *www.nehru-centre.org.*

FAMILY **Prithvi Theatre.** Run by the famous Kapoor acting family (current Bollywood stars Kareena and Ranbir Kapoor are two of them), the theater stages plays each week, many in English, with reasonably priced tickets. They often host special programs for children, too. It's a 45-minute

Getaway to Matheran Hill Station

The most pleasant hill station to visit near Mumbai, Matheran, founded by British collector Hugh Malet, is cooler than Mumbai all year long due to the elevation, and it's particularly nice in the months leading up to and during the monsoon, when the hillsides burst into verdant bloom. One big attraction is the fact that Matheran is car-free, and the main forms of transportation are horses, hand-pulled rickshaws, and carts. The late Jimmy Lord, a crusty Parsi gentleman who established a Raj-style hotel (Lords Central) here, was responsible for the push to hang on to Matheran's heritage: he was at the forefront of campaigns to keep the hill station free of vehicles. Over the years this hill station has grown from a tiny hamlet to a budget tourist resort. Horseback riding on the country paths beyond town is a pleasant and popular pastime. Matheran is famed for its handmade shoes, and stalls and stalls of footwear dot the town. Equally famous is the historic "toy" train by which you get here—it's not a toy but, rather, runs on a narrower-gauge track.

drive north from downtown Mumbai, or 20 minutes from the airport in nontraffic hours. An evening at Prithvi, which has an arty café and a carefully curated bookstore, can make for one of the more memorable cultural experiences in the city. ⊠ *Janaki Kutir, Church Rd., Juhu* ☏ *22/2614–9546* ⊕ *www.prithvitheatre.org.*

SHOPPING

Mumbai is a shopper's town: in the same day, you can sift through alleys full of antiques in Chor Bazaar, haggle for trinkets on the Colaba Causeway, and stop in at the Brioni showroom at the Taj Mahal Palace Hotel for marked-up luxury goods (though we'd recommend you get your Chanel and Armani back home to avoid the huge import taxes).

The Causeway, Kemps Corner, and Breach Candy are all trendy shopping areas in South Mumbai; the latter two are chic and pricey. A walk down Colaba Causeway will probably take you past most of the things you want to buy in India—shoes, clothes, cheap knickknacks, cheap cotton clothing, jewelry, and wraps—displayed at stalls lining the road; more expensive items are found in the air-conditioned shops and boutiques behind the stalls on this same road.

The arcades in top hotels offer a little bit of everything for a lot more money than anywhere else, but the merchandise is beautiful and the pace unhurried (and it's climate-controlled). If you're looking for the kind of stuff you can't get anywhere else in the world, and a more vibrant experience, throw yourself into the middle of one of Mumbai's famous bazaars. After all, odds are you didn't come to India to visit the Louis Vuitton boutique.

The city's department stores are good for one-stop shopping, and Fabindia and the Bombay Store both have a large number of branches in the city.

Throughout Mumbai many smaller shops are closed on Sunday (some of the suburbs are closed a different day: in Worli, up to Bandra, they're closed Monday; and in Bandra, up to the suburbs, they're closed Thursday, although many areas are also in the process of switching to Sunday). Malls, however, are open every day. They are especially crowded on the weekend (mall-gazing—that is, large-scale window shopping—has become a new Mumbai leisure activity).

Once you've exhausted Mumbai proper, you can venture out to the suburbs, where prices tend to be lower and the malls more numerous. Linking Road in Bandra is a trendy place to shop, and Juhu's main strip, Juhu Tara Road, is lined with cutting-edge new boutiques, shops, art galleries, and restaurants.

Some good and cheap Mumbai buys: silver jewelry, handicrafts, handloom cotton and silk clothing and household items, eyeglasses, DVDs, CDs, and books.

CENTRAL MUMBAI

CLOTHING

Ensemble. This pricey store has exclusive men's and women's Indian and Western fashions, and lovely costume jewelry, all by high-profile Indian designers. Ask to see the rare Banarasi silk saris, in rich colors woven with real gold and silver thread. ⊠ *Paragon Centre, ground fl., opposite Century Mills, B-1, Worli* ☎ *22/2284–3227, 22/2287–2882* ⊕ *www.ensembleindia.com.*

DEPARTMENT STORES AND MALLS

Phoenix Mills. This ever-expanding shopping, entertainment, and dining area in an old mill is an island of prosperity and chic modernity amid slums and industry. The complex is divided into different segments. Phoenix Mills itself has department stores like **Big Bazaar**, outlet clothing shop **Pantaloons,** and Hamley's. Palladium is the luxury mall with stores like Burberry, Zara, Gucci, Diesel, and Royce, a company that sells high-end Japanese chocolates. Here too are a number of clubs (frequented by the teenage and college student set) and the Comedy Store, showcasing various comics of varying quality on a nightly basis. High Street Phoenix feature major international chains. If you get hungry, outlets of Indigo Deli, Moshe's and McDonald's, among many others, await. ⊠ *Phoenix Mills Compound, Senapati Bapat Marg, Lower Parel.*

COLABA

CLOTHING AND CUSTOM TAILORING

Amrapali Creations. Very prompt and efficient, Amrapali Creations usually makes Indian clothes, such as *salwar kameez* and sari blouses, but if you give them a sample to copy they can make you a Western-style outfit. ⊠ *Shop 38, Ruki Mahal, near H.P. Petrol Pump* ☎ *22/2288–5060.*

Indian Textiles Company. In the Taj Mahal hotel, this store sells quality silks, as does the Burlington store here. ⊠ *Taj Mahal Palace & Tower, Apollo Bunder* ☎ *22/2202–8783.*

Khubsons Narisons. Fine cotton and silk can be made into excellent shirts, trousers, or women's outfits in one day if need be. They also sell readymade women's clothing. There are two shops named Khubsons, back to back; make sure you have the right one (the one closer to Regal Cinema). ✉ *49 Colaba Causeway, opposite Colaba police station* ☎ *22/2202–0614.*

HANDICRAFTS AND HOUSEHOLD FURNISHINGS

Atmosphere. Exotic home furnishings and fabrics for the home are sold by the meter here. There's lots of expensive silk, and they'll organize tailoring for you. ✉ *Vaswani House, 7 Best Marg* ☎ *22/2283–1877, 22/2283–1936* ⊕ *www.atmospheredirect.com.*

Central Cottage Industries Emporium. The Mumbai branch of this government-owned chain is a decent place to buy souvenirs—though you won't be doing any bargaining, as all prices are fixed (and likely more than you'll pay elsewhere). It's therefore a good way to establish an upper bound for prices before you do any haggling in other places. It's packed with textiles, carvings, and myriad other traditional Indian handicrafts from all over the country, and there's a small but imaginative assortment of Indian costumes for kids, and traditional Indian toys. Mirror-work elephants, Indian dolls, wood and cane doll furniture, tiny brass tea sets, stuffed leather animals, and puppets can all be found on the second floor, as can kurtas and long skirt ensembles in cotton and silk. ✉ *Narang House, 34 Shivaji Marg, 1 block north of Taj Mahal hotel* ☎ *22/2202–6564, 22/2202–7537* ⊕ *www.thecottage.in.*

Good Earth. All sorts of housewares, including linens, pottery, and brass, are on offer here. There's one in Juhu, opposite the Marriott Hotel, and one in Lower Parel. ✉ *2 Reay House, adjacent to Taj Mahal Hotel* ☎ *22/2495–1954* ⊕ *www.goodearth.in.*

INCENSE AND PERFUME

Ajmal. You'll find a wonderful selection of rare Indian and French perfumes stored in huge decanters here. They also stock *agar* wood, a rare incense base, a kilo of which costs as much as a night at the Taj Mahal hotel. Sandalwood oil is also another fragrance stocked here. ✉ *4/13 Kamal Mansion, Arthur Bunder Rd.* ☎ *22/2285–6976* ⊕ *www.ajmalindia.com.*

JEWELRY

Mangal Palace Silver Shop. You'll find wonderful silver jewelry from all over India here, and there are some good bargains. ✉ *Colaba Market* ☎ *22/2283–4333, 22/2204–8928.*

CST AND NEARBY

BAZAARS AND MARKETS

Chor Bazaar. In this bustling but tiny flea market you can find exactly what you don't need but have to have—old phonographs, broken nautical instruments, strange toys, dusty chandeliers, furniture, and brass objects ranging from junky knickknacks to valuable antiques and curios. Keep an eye on your purse or wallet and come relaxed—it can be chaotic. ✉ *Mutton St., near Kutbi Masjid, off Mohammed Ali Rd., Mandvi.*

Zaveri Bazaar. A few blocks northwest of Crawford Market, this is the place to go for diamond, gold, and silver jewelry. The tumultuous streets are lined with tiny, decades-old family jewelry businesses. Duck into one and sip a customary cup of tea or coffee while a salesperson shows you the merchandise. Most shops are authentic, but beware of false silver and gold; it's difficult to spot the fakes, so it might be best to buy primarily for appearance and make intrinsic value a secondary consideration. ⊠ *Sheikh Memon St., Kalbadevi* ☉ *Mon.–Sat. 11–7.*

JEWELRY

Sheikh Memon Street. The most cost-effective place to buy jewelry is from a smaller outfit, such as **Narandas and Sons, Zaveri Naran Das,** or **Ram Kewalram Popley**—all on Sheikh Memon Street, which begins at Crawford Market and runs northwest through Zaveri Bazaar. Insist on knowing how many karats you're buying and whether or not the store will stand by the piece's purity. ⊠ *Kalbadevi.*

Tribhovandas Bhimji Zaveri. In business since 1865, this is said to be the largest jewelry showroom in India, with five floors of gorgeous 18-, 22-, and 24-karat gold, diamonds, and silver jewelry. ⊠ *241–43 Zaveri Bazaar, Kalbadevi* ☎ *22/2343–5656* ⊕ *www.tbztheoriginal.com.*

LEATHER AND SHOES

Daboo Street. Brave bargain-hunters should take a trip to chaotic Daboo Street for all sorts of leather goods. ⊠ *Off Mohammed Ali Rd., a 5-minute walk south from Chor Bazaar.*

FORT AND MARINE DRIVE

ART AND ANTIQUES

Gallery Chemould. An elegant gallery in the Fort district for those looking for a break, full of works by modern masters like Atul Dodiya and rolling exhibitions. ⊠ *Queens Mansion, G. Talwatkar Rd., 3rd fl., Fort* ☎ *22/2200–0211* ⊕ *www.gallerychemould.com.*

Natesan's Antiqarts Ltd. With branches in many Indian cities, this emporium sells magnificent but expensive curios, subcontinental antiquities, wood carvings, sculptures, and paintings, as well as a few smaller items at better prices. ⊠ *Shop #5, Taj Shopping Arcade, Taj Mahal Palace and Tower, Colaba* ☎ *22/2202–4165* ⊕ *www.natesansantiqarts.com.*

Phillips Antiques. Established in 1860, Phillips has the best choice of old prints, engravings, and maps in Mumbai. It also sells many possessions left behind by the British—Staffordshire and East India Company china, old jewelry, crystal, lacquerware, and sterling silver. The store is closed for an hour at lunchtime. ⊠ *Waterloo Mans, Main Rd., Gpo, Fort* ☎ *22/2020–5564* ⊕ *www.phillipsantiques.com.*

BAZAARS AND MARKETS

Fashion Street. This is a trove of cotton bargains in a long row of open-air stalls, with mounds of colorful, cheap, mainly Western clothing for all ages. The name is completely incongruous—there is nothing fashionable about this street, but the knock-offs are cheap. Come around 11 am, when the crowds are thinner and the sun has not yet peaked—and bargain. ⊠ *M.G. Rd., opposite Bombay Gymkhana, Fort.*

CLOTHING AND CUSTOM TAILORING

Anokhi. Colorful clothes with block-print designs from Rajasthan. ⊠ *Rasik Niwas, Metro Motors La., Dr. A.R. Rangnekar Marg, off Hughes Rd., Marine Drive* ☎ *22/2368–5761, 22/2368–5308* ⊕ *www.anokhi.*

6

CLOSE UP

Custom Tailors and Fine Fabrics

Mumbai's bazaars boom with some of the richest and widest varieties of cloth, and the Mangaldas Cloth Market has enough bales of material to carpet all of South Mumbai.

Buying clothes tailored to fit in Mumbai is not a difficult proposition: There are a number of tailors who can turn splendid fabric into custom-made clothing—Indian or Western—in a matter of hours, for ladies or men. The tailors are often armed with the latest catalogs and will faithfully copy a design from a picture. They're fast and competent, but be specific about what you want; their improvisations are not

likely to go over well. If you have a shirt or trousers to give as a sample, they can generally make an exact copy. Make sure you preshrink cotton material and any lining before you give it in for stitching (rinse for a few minutes and drip dry; colored cottons need to be rinsed by themselves for just a few seconds to prevent too much bleeding). Fix a rate beforehand, and give an earlier deadline than necessary to allow for refittings if needed. If the material needs a lining, buy it yourself. *See Clothing and Custom Tailoring listings under Colaba, Fort and Marine Drive, and Malabar Hill and Nearby.*

com ✉ *Govind Dham, 210 Waterfield Rd., Hughes Road* ☎ *22/2640–8261, 22/2640–8263.*

Christina. This is a tiny, classy boutique with exquisite silk blouses and shirts, scarves, ties, *dupattas* (long, thin scarves for draping), and silk-edge purses and wallets. ✉ *The Oberoi hotel section of Oberoi Shopping Centre, Nariman Point* ☎ *22/2282–5069.*

Roop Milan. Primarily a sari shop, Roop Milan also sells a huge variety of fine silks upstairs. ✉ *385 Laxmi Bldg., NC Kelkar Rd., Dadar West* ☎ *9820033363* ⊕ *www.roopmilan.net.*

Sheetal. This is probably the best suit shop in Mumbai, with an extensive collection of fabrics and impeccable tailoring. You can get a full suit made here in about five days if you ask them to expedite it, with a trial fitting, for about Rs. 12,000. ✉ *Lal Bahadur Shastri Rd., Bail Bajar, Sakinaka* ☎ *22/2385–6565, 22/2387–6114* ⊕ *www.sheetalindia.com.*

DEPARTMENT STORES AND MALLS

Bombay Store. A must for souvenir shoppers, the friendly Bombay Store sells clothing and accessories for men, women, and children, silk by the meter, housewares, organic wellness products, and gifts. There are a number of branches in the city, but the Fort one is the most expansive. ✉ *Sir Pherozeshah Mehta Rd., Fort* ☎ *22/2288–5048, 22/2288–5049* ⊕ *www.thebombaystore.com.*

Fabindia. This store showcases the best of Indian fabrics—*khadis* (homespun cotton), muslin, vegetable-dyed silks, and embroidered materials. You can find women's clothing (saris, *kurtas*, skirts, trousers, blouses, and *kurtis*) as well as men's shirts and *kurtas,* children's clothes, tablecloths, curtains, cushion covers—and napkins fashioned from these beautiful materials, some of which is also available by the meter. The

Fort location is the address to head to—it's in a high-ceilinged, period building, with a wide selection—but there are a number of branches all over the city. ⊠ *Jeroo Bldg., 137 M.G. Rd., Kala Ghoda, Fort* ☎ *22/2262–6539* ⊕ *www.fabindia.com* ⊙ *Daily 10–7:45.*

HANDICRAFTS AND HOUSEHOLD FURNISHINGS

Contemporary Arts and Crafts. There's a small but representative selection of Indian handicrafts at reasonable prices here. ⊠ *210 D.N. Rd., opposite Fort House, Fort* ☎ *22/2201 3379.*

JEWELRY

Tanishq. Owned by the Tata Group, a venerable and enormous Indian conglomerate whose founder built the Taj Mahal hotel, Tanishq is a reliable place to buy gold jewelry. The prices, however, are a little higher than elsewhere. ⊠ *Veer Nariman Rd., near Cricket Club of India (CCI), Churchgate* ☎ *22/2282–1621, 22/2282–6043, 22/2283–8801* ⊕ *www. tanishq.co.in.*

MUSIC

Rhythm House. If you want to take home some Indian recordings, especially classical music, head for local favorite Rhythm House; along with pop, jazz, and everything else, the beloved store has an excellent selection of *pacca gana* (classical vocal music), Indo-Western fusion music, Hindi film music, and Indian instrumental music, as well as English and Hindi DVDs and VCDs. ⊠ *40 K. Dubash Marg, Rampart Row, Kala Ghoda, Fort* ☎ *22/2285–3963* ⊕ *www.rhythmhouse.in.*

JUHU, BANDRA, AND THE WESTERN SUBURBS

CLOTHING

Linking Road. Starting from S.V. Road in Bandra all the way through a seemingly endless strip of stores, stalls, and tables of goods, you can bargain on belt buckles here in one minute, and then pick up a designer dress on sale the next. It's also one of the more decent strips in the city to buy women's shoes. ⊠ *Linking Rd., Bandra.*

OMO. OMO, short for On My Own, is a Bandra hotspot for women's clothing and silver jewelry. ⊠ *204 Sagar Fortune, Waterfield Rd., Bandra* ☎ *22/6698–1804.*

HANDICRAFTS AND HOUSEHOLD FURNISHINGS

Dhoop. Here you'll find a superb, unusual collection of handicrafts that includes upside-down incense holders and palm-leaf lampshades. If you're staying in Bandra, you're only 15 or so minutes away. ⊠ *101 Khar Sheetal Apartments, Dr. Ambedkar Rd. and Union Park, Khar* ☎ *22/2649–8646, 22/2649–8647* ⊕ *www.dhoop.co.in.*

MALABAR HILL AND NEARBY

CLOTHING AND CUSTOM TAILORING

Nalli. The Mumbai branch of the famous Chennai store has a fair selection of classic silk saris. Have a look at the authentic gold-embroidered saris from Kanchipuram, in Tamil Nadu, as well as the Bangalore saris and the uncut silk sold by the meter. ⊠ *Trimurti Apartments, Bhulabhai Desai Rd., Breach Candy* ☎ *22/2353–5577* ⊕ *www.nallisilks.com/ web/mumbai.*

CLOSE UP

The Deccan Odyssey

Following the success of Rajasthan's luxury Palace on Wheels train, India introduced a Maharashtra counterpart, the *Deccan Odyssey*. Traveling first-class on Indian trains in the heyday of the British Raj could be a comfortable, lavish experience, with chefs and attendants taking care of the passengers' every need, in royal surroundings, as the train chugged through breathtaking countryside. The feeling is replicated aboard this train. The longest version of the trip takes you over seven nights and eight days down the Maharashtra coast to Goa before you swing upward to Pune, and to Ajanta, Ellora, and the vineyards of Nashik before returning to Mumbai. The train has several restaurants, lounges, and even a gym, but reservations are quite pricey, ranging from US$1,500 to US$11,500 depending on your choice of accommodations and the length of your journey. For more information, visit ⊕ *www.deccan-odyssey-india.com.*

Raymond. This is an outlet for Raymond Mills, which makes some of India's finest men's suits. They can tailor a first-rate suit for about Rs. 8,000 in about a week. During the wedding season (winter) they can get very busy. ⊠ *Shop No. 15/16, ground fl., Baria Mansion, 136 L.T. Marg, Carnac Rd., Crawford Market* ☎ *22/2368–2644* ⊕ *www. raymondindia.com.*

AURANGABAD AND THE AJANTA AND ELLORA CAVES

Although they may never receive top billing on a brochure, an argument can certainly be made that the cave temples at Ajanta and Ellora, which rank among the wonders of the ancient world, make for as spectacular of a visit as one to Taj Mahal. The good thing about the reduced hype, of course, is that it translates to a less crowded and more intimate touring experience. And the best part for visitors of Mumbai? The sites are only a tidy weekend trip away.

A less-than-an-hour flight and a reasonably short drive can put you inside of a Buddhist cave filled with stunning paintings, or place you in front of a mighty temple carved from the hills, retelling the story of the Ramayana in intimate detail.

Dating back more than 2,000 years, the cave temples of Ajanta and Ellora represent the most elaborate and spectacular cave architecture in the entire country. Both have been listed as UNESCO World Heritage Sites. Here, between the 2nd century BC and the 9th century AD, thousands of monks and artisan laborers carved cathedrals, monasteries, and entire cities of frescoed, sculptured halls into the solid rock. Working with simple chisels and hammers, and an ingenious system of reflecting mirrors to provide light into the dark interiors, they cut away hundreds of thousands of tons of rock to create the cave temples and other carvings. The work of these craftsmen inspires awe for the precision of their

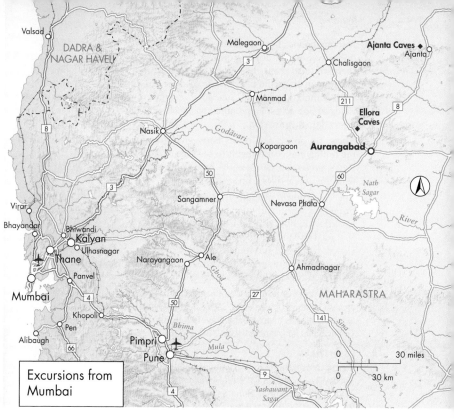

Excursions from Mumbai

planning and knowledge of rock formations, their dedication to creating all this so far from the rest of India, and the delicacy and sheer quantity of the artwork. The cave temples span three great religions—Buddhism, Hinduism, and Jainism.

To best appreciate the caves, allow one full day for each site, and remember Ajanta is closed Monday, and Ellora is closed Tuesday.

Suggested itinerary: A weekend trip to Ajanta and Ellora, while making your base in Aurangabad, makes for a perfect trip from Mumbai. If you leave Mumbai on Friday morning, you can have dinner in Aurangabad—it's best to estimate more time, rather than less, when it comes to travel in India—and then head out early the next morning for the Ajanta caves, about a two- to three-hour drive away, for the day. Sunday morning you can head to the much closer (about 30 minutes), and more crowded, Ellora Caves, then head back to Mumbai that evening.

⇨ *See the "Ajanta and Ellora Caves" feature in this chapter for more information.*

GETTING HERE AND AROUND
To get to Ajanta and Ellora, you can take a train, bus, or plane to Aurangabad.

BY AIR Aurangabad is about 45 minutes from Mumbai by air (about US$100, one-way), or 3½ hours from New Delhi (about US$125, one-way); there are also sometimes links between Aurangabad and Jaipur and Udaipur in the winter. Air India and Jet Airways fly to Aurangabad from Mumbai and Delhi. Schedules change every six months for these kinds of hop-and-a-skip flights, so check with the airlines for the most up-to-date information.

BY TRAIN There are only a few trains between Aurangabad and Mumbai, and the timing makes it difficult to see the caves in a timely manner. Indian Rail's *Tapovan Express* is the best option; it departs from Mumbai at 6:10 am and arrives a little after 1 pm.

VISITOR INFORMATION The Government of India Tourist Office, across from the train station, provides a warm and informative welcome to Aurangabad and is open weekdays 8:30–6 and Saturday and holidays 8:30–2. Ask for Mrs. I. R. V. Rao. The MTDC office in town (open Monday to Saturday 10–5:30; closed the second and fourth Saturday of the month) offers a variety of information about other destinations in Maharashtra, and they have a counter at the airport that's open when flights arrive.

Travel Agency and Tour Guide Contacts Blossom Travel Services ✉ *205 Mehar Chambers, Town Centre, Sector C-1, Aurangabad* ☎ *240/248–1955* ⊕ *blossomtravels.com.* **Saibaba Travels Aurangabad** ✉ *Shop No 88, Sindhi Colony, Jalna Rd., Aurangabad* ☎ *240/235–1612* ⊕ *www.saibabatravels.com.*

ESSENTIALS

Visitor Information Contacts Government of India Tourist Office ✉ *MTDC Holiday Resort, Station Rd, 1st fl., Aurangabad* ☎ *22/2204–4040* ⊕ *www. maharashtratourism.net.* **Maharashtra Tourism Development Corporation (MTDC)** ✉ *MTDC Holiday Resort, Station Rd., Aurangabad* ☎ *240/233–1513* ⊕ *www.maharashtratourism.gov.in.*

AURANGABAD

388 km (241 miles) east of Mumbai; 30 km (18 miles) southeast of Ellora; 100 km (62 miles) southwest of Ajanta.

With several excellent hotels, Aurangabad is a good base from which to explore the cave temples at Ajanta and Ellora, but not a fantastic city for restaurants, and not likely a place where you would likely go without its accessibility to those jaw-dropping attractions.

India is still India, however, and Aurangabad does have a few intriguing sites if you have extra time before or after visiting the caves.

The city is known for its *himru* (cotton and silk brocade) shawls and saris, and its gorgeously and painstakingly decorated Paithani *zari*, which are fine gold-embroidered saris—*zari* is the name for the gold metallic thread; and Paithani is a village very close to Aurangabad. If you're interested, pop into the Aurangabad Standard Silk Showroom or Aurangabad Silk, both near the train station; Ajanta Handicrafts in Harsul, on the highway to Ajanta; or Himroo Saris, on the highway to Ellora. An even better option to view Himru saris being woven is to venture over to the Himru Cooperative Society at Jaffer (also spelled

Zaffar) Gate, an area in the western part of Aurangabad: There you can see the entire process in action in a traditional environment. The saris (which can be cut up and tailored into other items) are more reasonably priced here.

EXPLORING

Bibi-ka-Maqbara. This 17th-century tomb is also known as the mini Taj Mahal; you can usually see it from the plane when you're flying into Aurangabad. A pale imitation of the original Taj Mahal, it is dedicated to the wife of the last of the six great Mughal emperors, Aurangzeb (founder of Aurangabad and son of the Taj Mahal's creator, Shah Jahan). It was supposed to be a shining, white-marble edifice, but money ran out, so only the bottom 2 feet of the monument were built with marble; the rest is stone with a facade of plaster. Somewhat awkwardly proportioned, the structure can be said to illustrate the decline of Mughal architecture. ⊠ *550 yards north of Old Town, beyond Mecca Gate* 🎫 *Foreigners US$3* ⊙ *Daily sunrise–10 pm.*

Daulatabad Fort. The imposing fort, built in 1187 by a Hindu king, is surrounded by seven giant walls more than 5 km (3 miles) long. Daulatabad was once called Deogiri, or "hill of the gods," but was changed to "city of fortune" when the sultan of Delhi overtook it in 1308. Devote at least half a day to this fascinating fort, considered one of India's most impressive. There's a wonderful view of the plains from the acropolis (fortified city) on the top. As you enter the fort you go through a labyrinth—note the moats, spikes, cannons, and dark maze of tunnels designed to make the fort as impregnable as possible. Equally interesting is the Jami Masjid (large mosque) inside; it was made from horizontal lintels and pillars taken from Jain and Hindu temples. Local Hindus put a lot of store in a *puja* (worship) done at the top of the fort and then down below, at the exit. ⊠ *13 km (8 miles) west of Old Town, on hwy. to Ellora Caves* 🎫 *Foreigners around US$3* ⊙ *Daily sunrise–6.*

WHERE TO EAT

Most of the better choices for restaurants in serve dishes representing multiple cuisine options—Indian (Mughlai and tandoori, or South Indian), Chinese, and the local variant of what passes for continental food. Stick with Indian cuisine outside the luxury hotels—Maharashtran and Hyderabadi fare is generally better prepared and tastier. Most restaurants here don't serve food outside typical meal hours.

$ NORTH INDIAN ✕ **Angeethi.** Named after a traditional Indian cooking vessel, this dark, cozy, slightly tacky restaurant serves Punjabi, continental, and Chinese food, and has a knack for tandoori items. Other specialties include chicken biryani, Afghani kebab *masala* (boneless chicken in a cashew sauce), and two-person *sikandari raan* (marinated leg of mutton). There are plenty of tasty vegetarian choices, too. Service is friendly but not terribly efficient. This is one of Aurangabad's most popular restaurants, and it gets busy on weekends. ⑤ *Average main: Rs. 400* ⊠ *6 Mehar Chambers, Jalna Rd., Vidya Nagar* ☎ *240/244–1988.*

$$ INTERNATIONAL ✕ **Madhuban.** Dark furniture, large paintings of Indian scenes, an abundance of green granite, crisp white tablecloths, and a chandelier composed of multiple *diyas* (traditional Indian lamps) set a regal tone at

Continued on page 386

AJANTA AND ELLORA CAVES

The centuries-old carved cave temples and cave paintings at Ajanta and Ellora are the product of awe-inspiring workmanship and span three great religions—Buddhism, Hinduism, and Jainism.

The caves at Ajanta and Ellora rank among the wonders of the ancient world. Here, between the 2nd century BC and the 5th century AD, great numbers (probably thousands) of monks and artisan laborers carved cathedrals, monasteries, and entire cities into the rock. Working with simple chisels and hammers, and an ingenious system of mirrors to send light into the interiors, the laborers cut away hundreds of thousands of tons of rock to create the cave temples and other carvings. The precision of the planning, the dedication of the laborers in such a remote location, and the delicacy and sheer quantity of the artwork make it obvious why both locations have been designated UNESCO world heritage sites.

CAVE PAINTINGS

Both Ajanta and Ellora have monumental facades and statues but Ajanta also has remarkable cave paintings that have survived the centuries. The paintings cover most of the cave surfaces, except the floor. They were created by spreading a plaster of clay, cow dung, chopped rice husks, and lime onto the rock walls, then painting pictures with local pigments: red ocher, copper oxide, lampblack, and dust from crushed green rocks. The paint brushes were made of twigs and camel hair. The caves are now like chapters of a splendid epic in visual form, recalling the life of the Buddha, and illustrating the life and civilization of the artisans.

(top) The magnificent Kailasa Temple, carved out of solid rock (left) The Ajanta cave painting of Padmapani, also known as "the one with the lotus in his hand"

THE AJANTA CAVES

Set in a wide, steep, horseshoe-shaped gorge above a wild mountain stream, the Ajanta caves reward travelers with a stunning glimpse into ancient India. Tucked in a setting that is lush and green after the monsoon, India's greatest collection of cave paintings dates back two millennia and is housed within massive carved stone caverns.

HISTORY

It's believed that a band of wandering Buddhist monks first came here in the 2nd century BC, searching for a place to meditate during the monsoons. Ajanta was ideal—peaceful and remote, with a spectacular setting. The monks began carving caves into the gray rock face of the gorge, and a new temple form was born.

Over the course of seven centuries, the cave temples of Ajanta evolved into works of incredible art. Structural engineers continue to be amazed by the sheer brilliance of the ancient builders,

(top) An aerial view of the Ajanta caves (right) A carving of a reclining buddha in an Ajanta cave

who, undaunted by the limitations of their implements, materials, and skills, created a marvel of artistic and architectural splendor. In all, 29 caves were carved, 15 of which were left unfinished; some of the caves were *viharas* (monasteries)—complete with stone pillows carved onto the monks' stone beds; others were *chaityas* (Buddhist cathedrals). All of the caves were profusely decorated with intricate sculptures and murals depicting the many incarnations of Buddha.

As the influence of Buddhism declined, the number of monk-artists became fewer, and the temples were swallowed up by the voracious jungle. It was not until about a thousand years later, in 1819, that an Englishman named John Smith, who was out tiger hunting on the bluff overlooking the Waghora River in the dry season, noticed the soaring arch of what is now known as Cave 10 peeking out from the thinned greenery in the ravine below. It was he who subsequently unveiled the caves to the modern world.

The paintings are dimly lit to protect the artwork, and a number are badly damaged, so deciphering the work takes some effort. The Archaeological Survey of India has, however, put a lot of effort into making the caves more viewable, including installing special ultraviolet lights to brighten certain panels. Shades and nets installed at the mouth of each cave keep out excess sun and bats.

PLANNING YOUR VISIT
A trip to the Ajanta caves needs to be well planned. You can see the caves at a fairly leisurely pace in two hours, but the drive to and from the site takes about two to three hours each way.

There's no longer direct access to the caves. All visitors are required to park their cars or disembark from their buses at a visitor center 3 km (2 mi) from the caves. From here, a Rs. 6 ticket buys you a place on frequently departing green Maharashtra Tourism Development Corporation (MTDC) buses to the caves (it's Rs. 10 for an air-conditioned bus, but they travel less frequently). The visitor complex has stalls with people hawking souvenirs, film, sodas, water, and packaged and fresh hot snacks—plus unknown guides that need to be firmly dismissed.

WHAT TO BRING AND WEAR
Come prepared with water, lunch or snacks, comfortable walking shoes (that can be slipped on and off easily, because shoes are not allowed inside the caves), socks to pad about the cave in so you don't get your feet dirty, a small flashlight, a hat or umbrella for the heat, and patience. Aurangabad can be hot year-round, and touring 29 caves can be tiring.

PRACTICAL INFOMATION

✉ 100 km (62 miles) northeast of Aurangabad; about a 2–3 hour drive.

🎟 Admission Rs. 250 foreigners $5, light fee Rs. 5 (includes all caves), video camera fee Rs. 25, parking Rs. 50. Flash photography and video cameras are prohibited inside the caves (shooting outside is fine). There is a cloak room at the visitor center where you can check bags for Rs. 5.

🕙 Tues.–Sun. 9 am–5 pm (Closed Monday); arrive by 3:30

VISITING THE AJANTA CAVES

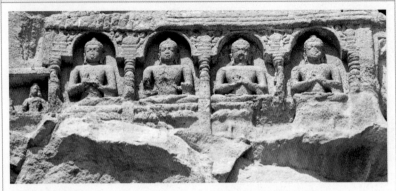

WHERE TO START

The caves are connected by a fair number of steps. It's best to start at the far end, at Cave 26, and work your way to Cave 1 to avoid a long trek back at the end. The initial ascent, before you reach the cave level, is also quite a climb, at 92 steps. Palanquins carried by helpers are available for the less hardy, for Rs. 400.

MOST IMPORTANT TO SEE

Opinions vary on which of the Ajanta caves is most exquisite: Caves 1, 2, 16, 17, and 19 are generally considered to have the best paintings; caves 1, 6, 10, 17, 19, and 26 the best sculptures. (The caves are numbered from west to east, not in chronological order.) Try to see all eight of these caves, at least.

Cave 1. Ajanta's most popular cave paintings are here; they depict the Bodhisattva Avalokitesvara and Bodhisattva Padmapani. Padmapani, or the "one with the lotus in his hand," is considered to be the alter ego of the Lord Buddha; Padmapani assumed the duties of the Buddha when he disappeared. Padmapani is often depicted with his voluptuous wife. When seen from different angles, the mag-

nificent Buddha statue in this cave seems to wear different facial expressions.

Cave 2. This cave is remarkable for the ceiling decorations and murals relating the birth of the Buddha. For its sheer exuberance, the painting of women on a swing is considered the finest. It's on the right wall as you enter, and when you face the wall it's on the left side.

Cave 6. This two-story cave has lovely detail. Climb the steep steps to the second floor, where there are pillars that emit musical sounds when rapped.

Cave 10. The oldest cave, this shrine dates from 200 BC, and is dominated by a large, squat *stupa* (a dome, or monument,

to Buddha). The exquisite brush-and-line work dates from AD 100: in breathtaking detail, the Shadanta Jataka, a legend about the Buddha, is depicted on the wall in a continuous panel. There are no idols of Buddha in this cave, indicating that idol worship was not in vogue at the time. (Cave 19, which dates from about the 5th century, does contain idols of Buddha, showing the progression of thought and the development of new methods of worship as the centuries wore on.) Guides and caretakers will enthusiastically point out the name of the Englishman, John Smith, who rediscovered the caves. His name, along with 1819 underneath, is carved on the 12th pillar on the right-hand side of this cave—though it's Cave 9, with its domed arch, that Smith first spotted.

Elevation

Cave 16. The monk-artists seem to have reached their creative zenith here; the continuous narrative spreads both horizontally and vertically, evolving into a panoramic whole—at once logical and stunning. One painting is especially riveting: known as *The Dying Princess*, it's believed to represent Sundari, the wife of the Buddha's half-brother Nanda, who left her to become a monk. This cave has an excellent view of the river and may have been the entrance to the entire series of caves.

Cave 17. This cave has the greatest number of pictures undamaged by time. Heavenly damsels fly effortlessly overhead, a prince makes love to a princess, and the Buddha tames a raging elephant (resisting temptation is a theme).

Other favorite paintings here include the scene of a woman applying lipstick and one of a princess performing *sringar* (her toilette)—this last is on the right-hand wall as you enter, and as you face the wall on the farthest right pillar.

Cave 19. Dating from about the mid 5th century, when Buddhism was in full swing, the stone sculpture on the exterior of this magnificent chaitya, or cathedral, is incredibly detailed. Inside, too, the faded paintings are overshadowed by the the sculptures. The standing Buddha is especially notable; compared with the stupas from earlier caves, this one is much more detailed and elongated.

Cave 26. This is the most interesting of the caves at the far end. An impressive sculpted panel of a reclining Buddha is on your left as you enter. It's believed to be a portrayal of a dying Buddha on the verge of

attaining nirvana. His weeping followers are at his side, while celestial beings are waiting to transport him to the land of no tomorrows (no rebirths).

Unfinished caves. Several unfinished caves were abandoned nearby but are worth a visit if you're up for the steep, 100-step climb (alternatively, you can walk up the bridle path, a gentler ascent alongside the caves). From here you have a magnificent view of the ravine descending into the Waghura River. An even easier way to reach this point is to stop your car as you return to Aurangabad, 20 km (12 mi) from the caves: take a right at Balapur and head 8 km (5 mi) toward Viewpoint, as it's called by the locals.

(top left) Religious figures carved out of the rock on the facade of an ancient Buddhist rock temple cave 26 (bottom left) Detail from Cave 2 (middle left) Buddha carving in Cave 6 (left) Inside Cave 26

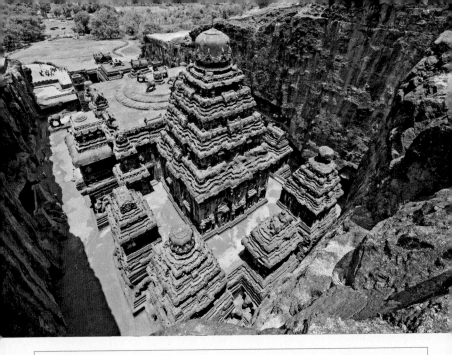

THE ELLORA CAVES

Unlike the cave temples at Ajanta, those of Ellora are not solely Buddhist. Rather, they follow the development of religious thought in India through the decline of Buddhism in the latter half of the 8th century, to the Hindu renaissance that followed the return of the Gupta dynasty, and to the Jain resurgence between the 9th and 11th centuries. Of the 34 caves here, the 12 to the south are Buddhist, the 17 in the center are Hindu, and the 5 to the north are Jain.

HISTORY

In the 7th century, religious activity shifted from Ajanta to a site 123 km (76 mi) to the southwest—known today as Ellora—although the reason for this move is not known. The focus at Ellora is sculpture, which covers the walls in ornate masses. The carvings in the Buddhist caves are serene, but in the Hindu caves they take on a certain exuberance and vitality—gods and demons do fearful battle, Lord Shiva angrily flails his eight arms, elephants rampage, eagles swoop, and lovers intertwine.

Unlike at Ajanta, where the temples were chopped out of a steep cliff, the caves at Ellora were dug into the slope of a hill along a north–south line, presumably so that they faced west and could receive the light of the setting sun.

WHEN TO GO?

Because Ellora is such a busy tourist destination, try to avoid coming here during school holidays from April to first week of June.

(top) Kailasa Temple (top right) Detail of a religious story carved into Kailasa (bottom right) One of the smaller rock-carved temples

The annual **Ellora Dance Festival,** held on one full moon night in December, draws top classical Indian dancers and musicians from around the country to perform outdoors against the magical backdrop of the Ellora Caves. For more information, ask at the tourist office or the Maharashtra Tourism Development Corporation.

PLANNING YOUR VISIT

Visiting the Ellora caves is in many ways easier than visiting Ajanta, though the rewards are different. Not only is Ellora closer to Aurangabad, when you get there, the line of caves is more accessible, all parallel to the road, and there are not many steps involved. Proximity to Aurangabad and the easy access makes seeing these caves a half-day's

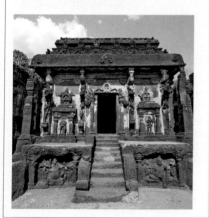

adventure; choose either early morning or late afternoon. The winding drive to Ellora is very pleasant, through low-slung hills past old ruins as well as Daulatabad Fort (try to squeeze at least a half-hour stop there, too).

WHERE TO EAT?

You're best off packing a lunch from Aurangabad, but there are two decent options around caves: The **Ellora Restaurant** (☎ 24/372–4441), by the entrance, is a convenient place to stop for a cold drink and a hot samosa. The outdoor patio has fruit trees (home to many monkeys) and pink bougainvillea flowers. The restaurant closes before the caves do. Outside Kailasa Cave (number 16), past the many souvenir stall, is the Hotel Kailas with its attached restaurant, **Kailas:** it's a simple cafeteria-style restaurant serving basic vegetarian Indian food until 9:30 pm. The food isn't great, but it's a bit nicer than the Ellora Restaurant.

6

IN FOCUS AJANTA AND ELLORA CAVES

PRACTICAL INFORMATION

✉ 30 km (18 miles) northwest of Aurangabad; about a 1/2 hour drive

🎫 Rs. 250, video camera fee Rs. 25

🕐 Wed.–Mon. (closed Tuesday), 6 am–6 pm

VISTING THE ELLORA CAVES

WHERE TO START

Although the caves are spread out over a large area, they're parallel to the road. Arrange with your driver to pick you up at several points: start at Cave 1 and work your way to 16, where you should have your driver meet you and take you to Cave 21. Then head to Cave 29. Another short drive will take you to the Jain caves.

MOST IMPORTANT TO SEE

Cave 16, the Kailasa temple, is the star attraction here but make sure to see caves from each of the three representative religions so that you can compare and contrast.

The southernmost caves are Buddhist.

Cave 2. The facade of this impressive monastery is deceptively simple, but the interior is lavish: gouged into the block of rock is a central hall with ornate pillars and a gallery of Buddhas and Boddhisattvas seated under trees and parasols.

Cave 5. The largest of the Buddhist caves, this was probably used as a classroom for young monks. The roof appears to be supported by 24 pillars; working their way down, sculptors first "built" the roof before they "erected" the pillars.

Cave 6. A statue of Mahamayuri, the Buddhist goddess of learning—also identified as

Saraswati, the Hindu goddess of learning—is the focus here, surrounded by Buddhist figures. The boundaries between Hinduism and Buddhism are fuzzy and Hindus worship and recognize some Buddhist gods and goddesses as their own, and vice versa: Hindus, for instance, consider Buddha the avatar of Vishnu.

Cave 7. This austere hall with pillars is one of Ellora's two-story caves.

Cave 10. The carvings here are impressive: the stonecutters reproduced the timbered roofs of the period over a richly decorated facade that resembles masonry work. Inside this shrine—the only actual Buddhist chapel at Ellora—the main work of art is

a huge sculpture of Buddha. Check out the high ceiling with stone "rafters" and note the sharp echo. The cave has been dubbed the Sutar Jhopdi or Carpenter's Cave and called a tribute to Visvakarma, the Hindu god of tools and carpentry.

Caves 11 and 12. These two caves rise grandly three floors up and are richly decorated with sculptural panels.

Starting with Cave 13, the Hindu caves are the successors to the Buddhist ones, and a step inside will stop you in your tracks. It's another world—another universe—in which the calm contemplation of the seated Buddhas gives way to the dynamic cosmology of Hinduism. These caves were created around the 7th and 8th centuries.

Cave 16. Ellora is dominated by the mammoth Kailasa Temple (also known as Kailasanatha, or Kailash) complex, or Cave 16. Dedicated to Shiva, the complex is a replica of his legendary abode at Mount Kailasa in the Tibetan Himalayas. The largest monolithic structure in the world, Kailasa reveals the genius, daring, and raw skill of its artisans.

To create the Kailasa complex, an army of stonecutters started at the top of the cliff, where they removed 3 million cubic feet of rock to create a vast pit with a freestanding rock left in the center. Out of this single slab, 276 feet long and 154 feet wide, the workers created Shiva's abode, which includes the main temple, a series of smaller shrines, and galleries built into a wall that encloses the

entire complex. Nearly every surface is exquisitely sculpted with epic themes.

Around the courtyard, numerous friezes illustrate the legends of Shiva and stories from the great Hindu epics, the Mahabharata and the Ramayana. One interesting panel on the eastern wall relates the origin of Shiva's main symbol, the lingam, or phallus. Another frieze, on the outer wall of the main sanctuary on the southern side of the courtyard, shows the demon Ravana shaking Mount Kailasa.

Cave 21. Of the Hindu caves north of Kailash, this cave, also called the Ramesvara, has some interesting sculptures, including the figurines of the river goddesses at the entrance. It's thought to be the oldest Hindu cave.

Cave 29. Past the seasonal waterfall, this cave, also called Dhumar Lena, is similar in layout to the caves at Elephanta, near Mumbai. Pairs of lion sculptures guard the staircases and inside are some interesting friezes.

The Jain caves are at the far end of Ellora, and definitely worth a visit, if just for the contrast. The Jain caves are more modest and subdued

than the Hindu caves, but have some lovely artwork carvings. Climb through the many well-carved chambers and study the towering figures of Gomateshvara (a Jain mythological figure) and Mahavira (an important Jain sage).

Cave 32. The most notable of the Jain caves is a miniature Kailash Temple, on two levels. The bottom floor is rather plain, but elaborate carvings surround the upper story.

(top left) Seven carved buddhas, Cave 12 (middle left) seated buddha, Cave 10 (top right) Detail on Kailasa Temple (bottom right) Cave 29 detail

Girija River

27
26
25
23
22
21
20
17
Cave 16
16
14
Cave 12
Cave 10
Cave 11
Cave 7
Cave 6
Cave 5
Cave 2
Elevation H
L

PLANNING YOUR VISIT TO THE CAVES

GETTING TO THE CAVES

To see the caves from Mumbai takes several days: you'll base yourself in Aurangabad, which is about 400 miles east of Mumbai (an hour-long flight), and make separate day trips to Ajanta and Ellora. Allow one full day for each site, and remember Ajanta is closed Monday, and Ellora is closed Tuesday.

If you can make it only to either Ellora or Ajanta, choose Ajanta: it's farther, but the comparative lack of crowds and the pristine serenity of the forest are worth it.

Suggested itinerary from Mumbai: A trip to Ajanta and Ellora, while making your base in Aurangabad, makes a perfect long weekend trip from Mumbai. If you leave Mumbai on Friday you can be in Aurangabad in the late afternoon, have dinner, and then head out early the next morning for the Ajanta caves, about a 2- to 3-hour drive away, for the day. Sunday morning, you can head to the much closer (about 30 minutes), and more crowded, Ellora Caves, then head back to Mumbai that evening.

Getting to Ajanta and Ellora from Aurangabad: From Aurangabad there are tour buses (check with the Government of India Tourist Office or the MTDC office) but this ends up being rather rushed. You're best off hiring a car and driver. An air-conditioned car for a full day will cost around Rs. 2,400 to Ajanta and Rs. 1,100 to Ellora. You can arrange a car for hire through your hotel a travel agent, or the Government of India Tourist Office; fix a price in advance.

HIRING A GUIDE

It's a good idea to hire a guide, who can explain the iconography and details about how the caves were built. The Government of India Tourist Office (✉ *Krishna Vilas, Station Rd., Aurangabad* ☎ *240/236–4999 or 240/233–1217* ⊕ *www. incredibleindia.org*) oversees about 45 expert, polite, multilingual tour guides. You can hire one through the tourist office; through the MTDC office (✉ *MTDC Holiday Resort, Station Rd., Aurangabad* ☎ *240/233–1513* ⊕ *www.maharashtratourism. gov.in*); or through a travel agent in Aurangabad.

For parties of one to four, the fees are about Rs. 1,000 for a full day to Ajanta, and about Rs. 750 for a full day to Ellora. Hiring a half-day guide (four hours) is about Rs. 450. An extra Rs. 400 or so is charged for trips of more than 100 km (60 miles). It's best to book ahead. There are also some guides availabe to hire at the ticket counters to the caves.

QUICK GUIDE TO THE CAVES

Ajanta	Ellora
Farther from Aurangabad (3-hour drive)	Closer to Aurangabad (½-hour drive)
Closed Monday	Closed Tuesday
29 caves were carved (15 are unfinished)	34 caves; Kailasa is the highlight
All Buddhist	Buddhist, Hindu, and Jain
Focus is on cave paintings	Focus is on sculpture
Caves chopped out of steep cliff	Caves dug into slope of a hill

Madhuban, one of Aurangabad's top restaurants. A wall of windows opens onto a garden of lovely tropical trees and flowers. The menu might include butter chicken and dal *makhani,* a rich black lentil dish; the Indo-Chinese food is tasty, too—the chilli chicken, a spicy concoction, is recommended—though the addition of Mexican and Italian food is hardly necessary. The buffet lunch is popular. $ *Average main: Rs. 900* ✉ *Welcomgroup Rama International Hotel, R-3 Chikalthana* ☎ *240/265–3095.*

$
INDIAN
✕ **Surya's Garden Court Restaurant.** About a 15-minute journey from the center of town, the Garden Court Restaurant is on a sprawling estate often used for weddings and private parties. The restaurant is open year-round, and serves great Indian food. Try the chicken *seekh* kebabs (minced chicken grilled in a tandoor), the chicken tikka masala and the *laccha parathas* (a flaky bread). Somewhat surprisingly, there's also some decent Mexican food here—the enchiladas have an Indian twinge to them, which turns out to be not a bad thing. $ *Average main: Rs. 400* ✉ *Beed Bypass Rd., near Dutta Mandir, Deolai* ☎ *240/224–2043, 240/696–0500* ⊕ *www.suryalawns.com.*

$$
INDIAN
✕ **Tandoor.** The hospitality of manager Syed Liakhat Hussain is one good reason to visit this brightly lit, busy, and cheerful restaurant that stays open late. The kebabs are another reason, especially the *kasturi* (chicken) kebab. People come to this local landmark for authentic and well-made tandoori food. Try the *murg tikka* (chicken kebabs), *paneer tikka* (cubes of white cheese baked in a tandoor), biryani, black *dal* (lentils), and the fresh, fried local fish. Shoot for lunch instead of dinner if you're coming by auto-rickshaw—later in the evening it's difficult to find transportation (it's far from the main hotels). $ *Average main: Rs. 500* ✉ *Shyam Chambers, Station Rd.* ☎ *9890–958466.*

$$$$
CHINESE
✕ **The Tea House.** This restaurant inside the local Taj is as good a place to sample the distinct flavor of Indo-Chinese—which blends powerful Indian spices and delicate Chinese preparation—as you're likely to find outside of Mumbai proper. The menu features an excellent array of teas (try the Darjeeling) and cocktails (their sweet but subtle Mojito is especially nice) and unlike most of the rest of the pack in Aurangabad, the atmosphere here is quiet and refined. While the small selection of main courses here tend to be either too salty or a bit underwhelming, the dim sum is superb, so we recommend sticking with that. Try the salt-and-pepper tofu, or the golden honey shrimp, paired with several of the excellent variety of dumplings on the restaurants expansive and delectable front-of-book menu. $ *Average main: Rs. 1600* ✉ *Vivanta by Taj–Aurangabad, 8-N 12 CIDCO, Rauza Bagh* ☎ *240/661–3737* ⊕ *www.tajhotels.com* ⚘ *Reservations essential* ☾ *No lunch.*

WHERE TO STAY

Most hotels in Aurangabad discount their rates if you ask. If you book directly, push for 15% off, or more—and make sure to ask whether the agreed-on rate includes breakfast and airport or train station pickup. Unless otherwise noted, all hotels listed are fully air-conditioned.

$
HOTEL
⌂ **Lemon Tree Hotel.** Every room at this attractive contemporary hotel, designed around a central garden, has a pool view, and either a patio or a balcony. **Pros:** well-lit, cheerful hotel; comfortable rooms; good

value; excellent food. **Cons:** small bathrooms. ⑤ *Rooms from: Rs. 4000* ⊠ *R 7/2 Chikalthana, Airport Rd.* ☎ *240/660–3030* ⊕ *www. lemontreehotels.com* ⇲ *102 rooms, 4 suites* ¶⊙¶ *Breakfast.*

$ ⊡ **The Meadows.** Accommodations at this resort-style hotel, which has
HOTEL   won architectural awards, are in simple cottages, each with a private patio, and though rooms are a bit spartan, it's wonderfully tranquil— and eco-conscious, too: biotechnology using plant roots purifies the air and wastewater. **Pros:** service above average; good value; airport pick-up; close to Ellora caves. **Cons:** far from the city. ⑤ *Rooms from: Rs. 4000* ⊠ *Aurangabad–Mumbai Hwy., Village Mitmita, Padeg-aon, 5 km (3 miles from city center)* ☎ *240/267–7412 to 16* ⊕ *www. themeadowsresort.com* ⇲ *48 cottages, 4 suites* ¶⊙¶ *Breakfast.*

$$ ⊡ **Vivanta by Taj–Aurangabad.** Convenient for the caves, this gleaming
HOTEL   Mughal palace, still called the Taj Residency by many, is all bright white marble and stone, inside and out—its windows and doors arch to regal Mughal points, and the grand dome over the lobby is hand-painted in traditional Jaipuri patterns. **Pros:** city's most elegant hotel; lovely ambi-ence. **Cons:** rather expensive; service can be disorganized. ⑤ *Rooms from: Rs. 6000* ⊠ *8-N 12 CIDCO* ☎ *240/661–3737* ⊕ *www.tajhotels. com* ⇲ *66 rooms, 2 suites* ¶⊙¶ *Breakfast.*

$ ⊡ **Welcom Hotel Rama International.** A long driveway through spacious
HOTEL   grounds leads to a place where efficient and friendly staffers create the kind of warm, intimate setting you'd normally associate with a smaller hotel. **Pros:** excellent value; attentive personal service; nice views; com-fortable rooms. **Cons:** small pool. ⑤ *Rooms from: Rs. 5000* ⊠ *R-3 Chikalthana* ☎ *240/663–4141* ⊕ *www.welcomhotelrama.com* ⇲ *132 rooms, 5 suites* ¶⊙¶ *Breakfast.*

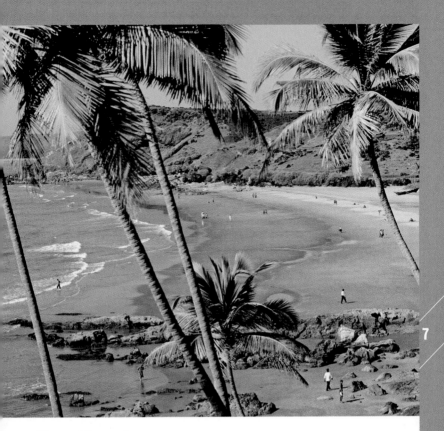

GOA

WELCOME TO GOA

TOP REASONS TO GO

★ **Sand and waves:** Goa's long, sandy, palm-fringed beaches are suited to more than just sun worship: scores of shacks serving cheap, cold beer and fresh seafood make it one long beach party.

★ **Goan cuisine:** If you like your spicing heavy and your seafood caught fresh, you'll love the food in Goa.

★ **Backwaters:** Rivers flow across Goa to the Arabian Sea. Escape the crowds at a heritage home or country inn in a town like Loutolim, for a couple of days of quiet nature walks, home-style cooking, and warm hospitality.

★ **Parties:** Goa's party scene is no longer as hedonistic as in years past, but during peak season there's usually an after-party (or three) to be found if you ask around a little.

★ **Portuguese architecture:** Goa was under Portuguese control until 1961, and its colonial past is stamped across its historic buildings, forts, churches, and charming Portuguese homes and mansions.

Fort Tiracol
Arambol
Pernem
Arambol Beach
PERNEM
Mandrem Beach
17
Chapora
Ashvem Beach
Morjim Beach
1
Vagator Beach
Arabian Sea
Anjuna Beach
Mapusa
Dicholi
Baga Beach
BARDEZ
Calangute Beach
Dr. Salim Ali
Candolim Beach
Bird Sanctuary
Sinquerim Beach
Bitona
Divar Is.
Fort Aguada
Panaji
Old Goa
TESWAD
17
Gama
Vasco Da
17A
Dabolim Airport
MORMUGAO
Bogmalo Beach
Grande Island
Cansaulim Beach
Majorda & Utorda
Colva
Benaulim
Varca
Cavelossim Beach

1 North Goa. For many visitors the heart and soul of Goa is in the bustling beaches and villages north of Panaji. You can find classic Goan beach life in many towns and villages dotting the coast, such as Candolim, Calangute, Baga, and Anjuna. And hotel rooms, restaurants, shops, and water sports are plentiful during the tourist season. Quieter beaches are north of the Chapora River in and around Mandrem; inland villages such as Siolim are lovely alternatives for experiencing Goa's less touristy, rural side.

2 Panaji and Central Goa. Whitewashed Catholic churches, palm-lined plazas, and the narrow streets of Panaji's historic Fontainhas—the Latin Quarter—feel decidedly more European than Indian. The grandiose churches of Old Goa and the temples in Ponda are best accessed from here.

3 South Goa. There are a few historic sights in and around Margao, but most people come to the south for the swanky upscale resorts that offer much quieter beaches. Colva and Palolem are catching up to the party trail of the northern beaches, and the area now has a slew of beachfront bars and restaurants. Loutulim, one of Goa's prettiest villages, is a charming alternative to go off the beaten path.

MAHARASHTRA

KARNATAKA

BICHOLIM

SATARI

Valpoi

4A

Ponda

Mandovi

4A

PONDA

Loutolim

GOA

SANGUEM

Margao
(Madgaon)

Dudhsagar
Falls

17

3

Chandor

SALCETE

Quepem

Sanguem

QUEPEM

Cabo de
Ramao
(Cape Rama)

17

CANACONA

Chauri

Palolem
Beach

17

Patnem

0   10 mi

0   10 km

GETTING ORIENTED

Goa is best described as short (just 105 km [65 miles] long) and sweet (full of friendly locals). The capital city, Panaji, divides the northern beaches from those in the south, and is the regional transportation and cultural center. Although Goa is India's smallest state (in area), its terrain manages to include sandy beaches, lazy backwaters, acres of emerald-green rice paddies, and thick palm forests, as well as steep, jungle-covered mountains. Its immense popularity means that it has much better tourist infrastructure than elsewhere in India, with plenty of hotel rooms, an increasing number of excellent, and very affordable, restaurants, decent roads, and fairly reliable cell-phone connectivity and electricity. Most of the country's development is along its coastline, where visitors will find all the resorts that have made Goa famous, as well as in its two major towns—Panaji in the center and Margao in the south.

7

EATING WELL IN GOA

Abundant seafood from the Arabian Sea, coupled with Goa's location on the spice route, ensures a wonderfully diverse cuisine.

(top left) Chicken vindaloo; (top right) The popular Goan sweet called *bebinca*; (bottom right) A dish of roasted cashews

Goan food is distinguished by the continued presence of Portuguese cooking techniques and ingredients. Chillies from the New World were incorporated into the local arsenal of spices relatively early, possibly with the arrival of Vasco da Gama in the late 15th century. The Portuguese also popularized eating pork, the use of vinegar, and certain desserts, and Goan Catholic eating habits continue to be influenced by these Portuguese methods, as well as those of the native Konkani-speaking inhabitants of the area.

The fact that Goa is a major tourist destination has also had an effect on the food you'll find here, and there are now plenty of international restaurants to be found, particularly in the north, where everything from Italian and Japanese to Greek and Mexican food can be found. There is also, of course, the gamut of Indian cuisines, from home-style Goan cafés to Punjabi restaurants that comparable to anything in North India.

CASH(EW) CROP

An important cash crop in Goa, cashew trees grow all over the state. The tree, which is native to Brazil, came to Goa with the Portuguese. A local liquor is distilled from the cashew tree's fruit: the cashew apple. The first distillation, called *arrack*, has lower alcohol content than the pungent *feni*, which is the third distillation and can be up to 80 proof. Goan distilleries also make a coconut feni.

BEBINCA

A layered glutinous dessert, **bebinca** is traditionally eaten on special occasions, but due to its popularity with tourists, it is available in Goa all year round. The dish most likely evolved in Goa, likely with some Portuguese influence, but it has since migrated to Portugal as well. Making bebinca is a slow process: a batter of refined flour, coconut milk, egg yolks, and sugar is poured and baked, in layers, in a low-heat oven. The slight caramelizing between layers makes for an attractive tiger-stripe treat. You can buy bebinca in vacuum-sealed packages to take home.

VINDALOO

A much-replicated Indian dish, vindaloo is the culinary pinnacle of the merging of Konkan and Portuguese cultures. A Portuguese meat dish cooked with red wine and garlic (*vinho* and *alhos*) was baptized in the fire of Goan spices and became vindaloo; the Goan version uses vinegar rather than wine for a slightly acidic-sweet taste. Vindaloo is originally a pork dish, but has since been adapted to chicken and lamb. It may include potatoes, too, and it generally incorporates red chilli for color and green chilli for spice.

SORPOTEL

A dish of Portuguese heritage that was adopted by Goan Christians, **sorpotel** (or *sarapatel*) is often somewhat toned down for tourists: it's an offal stew that is made using the liver, heart, and tongue of pork or other meats. By some accounts, the stew traditionally also includes the animal's blood, which some cooks still use as a thickener—but probably not in the version tourists encounter. This flavor is enhanced by the use of vinegar.

CHOURIÇO

If you happen to be in town on a market day, you might see strings of bulging Goan sausages gleaming dark red in the sun. Called **chouriço,** these are the local descendents of Portuguese chorizo, and are made with ground pork, vinegar, chilli, and other spices, and stuffed into casings. *Chouriço* can be very spicy or mild and varies in texture from dry to juicy. This type of sausage must be cooked, and is usually eaten with rice or pao, local Goan bread.

XACUTI

Chicken **xacuti** is one of Goa's most successful dishes outside of the state—and it can also be made with fish or lamb. It's a milder curry than some of the fiery red Goan curries. Coconut, white poppy, other seeds (peppercorn, cumin, and fennel), and warm spices like cinnamon, star anise, and cloves are roasted and then fried and simmered with the meat for an aromatic addition to rice or a piece of *pao*.

7

GOA BEACHES

With its crescent-shape beaches of white sand and dramatic swathes of cliffs that hug the coastline, Goa continues to be a draw for both domestic and foreign travelers.

(top left) A fishing boat on Palolem beach; (top right) Arambol beach in northern Goa; (bottom right) Sunset at the beach

The northern beaches at Baga, Calangute, and beyond draw the biggest crowds and have plenty of beachside shacks, trendy bars and restaurants, booming nightlife, easy access to water sports, and an abundance of discount clothing and swimwear. There's a Wednesday flea market at the former hippie enclave around Anjuna, while arresting sunset views await visitors to the cliffs at Vagator. The northern-most beaches of Ashvem, Mandrem, and Morjim are quieter and more scenic, though there's been a recent upswing in the number of cool little boutique hotels and the trendy bars around these beaches. Plush all-inclusive resorts dominate the southern coastline of Benaulim, Varca, and Cavelossim, where the beaches are quieter, cleaner and with much fewer shacks in evidence. Palolem beach, with its swaying palms and clean coastline, is becoming more popular but quality accommodations and dining options still lag behind its northern counterparts.

MONSOON SEASON?

Most visitors go to Goa for the beach and the sun, though monsoon season (June to September), with its frequent downpours, is atmospheric and remarkably lush. It's also when the crowds are thinner and the prices lower—though most of the beach shacks and some of the larger properties are closed. And if your dream is to lie out on the beach or by the pool, this definitely isn't the time for you to visit.

WHAT SHOULD I WEAR?

The steady influx of foreign visitors over the years means that bikinis on the beach are commonplace. However, anything more risqué, like going topless or nude, is not acceptable. When you leave the beach, drape a sarong or throw on a cover-up to avoid untoward attention. Wandering around town or sitting in a restaurant in only a bathing suit is not advisable. And wear your flip-flops if you're leaving the beach as streets and beach walkways can be dirty.

EATING AND DRINKING

Beach-shack dining is a signature experience in Goa—fresh seafood, a cold beverage, and a golden sunset. What more could you ask for? Stick to simple Goan dishes here, though, and save the bold ordering choices for the better restaurants in town.

RESTROOMS

Public restrooms can be dirty, so tuck some toilet paper in your beach bag, and bring some hand sanitizer unless your hotel is within walking distance. Facilities are cleaner at the nicer restaurants but you'll probably be turned away if you're not a paying customer.

WATER SPORTS

The beaches at Calangute, Baga, and Colva in particular offer plenty of options for water sports, including parasailing, windsurfing, jet-skiing, and banana boating.

BEACH CHAIRS

Beach chairs with umbrellas line the beaches in front of restaurants. If you're a customer these are free to use, otherwise you can ask to rent one for a small, and negotiable, fee.

HAWKERS

You'll find plenty of vendors and stalls selling knickknacks, souvenirs, food, and drinks. Stick to the bottled beverages and be cautious of inflated prices. Vendors can be a nuisance but a firm "No thank you," is all that's needed.

THE SUN

This is the tropics and the sun is strong. Wear good sunscreen and reapply often. Local brands with high SPF are available, but if you're particular about a specific brand, bring your own as prices here will be higher.

LIFEGUARDS

Major beaches have lifeguards during the day; smaller beaches do not. Undertows can be a danger in some areas, particularly in the monsoon season, so ask the lifeguards or the locals.

NEFARIOUS ELEMENTS

Goa's reputation for wild parties and easy drugs is not undeserved but you can avoid any associated annoyances by sticking to recommended hotels, restaurants, and bars. Again, if approached by anyone undesirable, a firm "No thank you" should send them on their way.

Updated by
Vandana
Verma

Beguiling white sands, fresh and spicy seafood, and a cold drink under a glowing sun is Goa at its charming best. But there's plenty more: striking Renaissance cathedrals in Old Goa, ancestral homes surrounding the ragtag city of Margao, the ornate Hindu temples of Ponda, and Panaji's Portuguese historic district.

Those who know India well will tell you that Goa, the smallest state in the Indian federation, is an anomaly—a territory that is decidedly its own entity, shaped by a unique set of circumstances and influences.

Goa wasn't much of a tourist spot until the early 1960s, with the arrival of the first hippies from Europe, who were lured by the laid-back culture and picturesque beaches of Anjuna, Calangute, and Vagator. The lax law enforcement made it easy for the beaches to quickly become the site of wild parties, cheap alcohol, and plenty of drugs. The Anjuna flea market was established soon after, in the 1970s, as many of the foreign tourists started selling secondhand goods to fund an extended stay. It was around this time that the beach shacks appeared as well: temporary structures that multitasked as restaurants, bars, hotels, bookstalls, shops, or just places to hang out all day.

The era of electronic music in the 1980s changed Goa into a hot spot for raves, and heady full-moon parties were all the rage for the subsequent decade. This golden age of raves has subsided in recent years due to increased government action. However, parties continue to rage on in a less publicized fashion—parties tend to move from the bars and clubs into a new slew of "after hours clubs" that go until dawn and beyond, you just have to discreetly ask around.

As Goa continued to attract more and more visitors, it caught the attention of well-heeled Indian tourists. Five-star hotels and resorts started popping up in the south, while package tours and charter flights from the United Kingdom and elsewhere in Europe became a common feature in the north. It soon became a hip destination for Indians, particularly in the 10 days over Christmas and the New Year, as the affluent flocked to Goa for private parties.

Today, with more and more Indians traveling abroad, this party scene has subsided to a certain degree, but it still remains enough of a party destination to justify sky-high hotel rates during that fortnight around Christmas and New Year's Eve. The next generation of long-term budget foreigners, meanwhile, has retreated to the northern beaches around Morjim. Here you might enter an Internet parlor and find a keyboard in Hebrew or signs in Russian.

All this tourism has had an undeniable influence on Goa's way of life, economy, and identity, and in some areas today you can find a Greek restaurant, a French-food shack, a German bakery, a pizza joint, and an Indian *dhaba* (fast-food joint) all within a 5-mile radius. Much of Goa has evolved to cater to every breed of tourist—top-notch restaurants, boutique hotels, lovely heritage homes, luxury resorts, funky beach shacks, cheap and noisy hotels, and business hotels for the corporate retreats and conferences. You can still get away from it all, or you can just dive in and savor its still-wild reputation. But now, more than ever before, Goa offers so many more options that the hippies might be the only ones complaining.

PLANNING

WHEN TO GO

HIGH SEASON: NOVEMBER TO LATE FEBRUARY

Goa's tourist season begins in November and peaks from the middle of December until after the New Year in January, when the skies are clear and parties are in overdrive. Anyone planning to visit over this time should prepare for sky-high lodging prices, and for beaches, hotels, and restaurants that are packed around the clock.

LOW SEASON: MAY TO OCTOBER

It's wise to avoid Goa in the months of May and October, when it is oppressively hot and humid, and very unpleasant even for the locals. During the monsoon months, from June through September, most of Goa's hotels, beach-shack restaurants, and bars shut down due to the torrential rains and strong winds; violent surf makes water sports impossible, and visitors will struggle to find places to dine that are open. Farther inland the forests are lush, as are the rice plantations, which lie near Goa's many rivers, and most of the larger hotels stay open—it's always worth asking for "monsoon specials" if you are headed to Goa at this time of year.

SHOULDER SEASON: LATE FEBRUARY TO APRIL

Those who visit in the early spring can still enjoy gorgeous weather and Goa's beauty without feeling as if they're just part of a crowd—and there's the added excitement of Carnival.

GETTING HERE AND AROUND

AIR TRAVEL

Most travelers get to Goa by booking an international flight to Mumbai or Delhi, then hopping a domestic flight to Goa's Dabolim Airport, about 29 km (18 miles) south of Panaji, the state capital. Direct flights are available from many of India's major cities, and most can be booked online.

Buses are infrequent, so it's usually best to take a taxi from here to your destination. You can arrange for a prepaid taxi service at a counter inside the airport, or go straight outside and hire a private cab. Many resorts include airport transfers, or you can prearrange it for a fee. Alternatively, a government taxi desk outside the arrivals hall can organize a prepaid taxi. This is a better option than trying to negotiate fares with persistent drivers yourself. Either way, the fare to Panaji should not exceed Rs. 700.

Airport Information Dabolim Airport
☎ *832/245-0723.*

FESTIVALS: CARNIVAL

Carnival time—in February, just before Lent—remains the local's official season for nonstop revelry, directed by King Momo ("King of Misrule"), a Goan appointed by his peers as the life of the party. Festivities include fanciful pageants (with some 50 floats depicting elements of Goa's folk culture, or more contemporary messages like preservation of the environment), hordes of musicians strumming the guitar or playing the banjo, and dancers breaking into the *mando* (a folk fusion of the Portuguese fado and the waltz)—all in streets spangled with confetti.

BIKE OR MOTORBIKE TRAVEL

If you're in reasonable shape and confident riding on potholed, heavily traveled roads, consider renting a bicycle for a jaunt to save on taxi fares, especially if you simply want to get from your hotel to the beach and back. Don't expect more than one gear or anything resembling what you're used to; check the tires and brakes. You can rent motorbikes at bus stops, train stations, markets, and beach resorts and cars at the airport—your hotel will be able to arrange one as well. You'll need an international driver's license to drive anything larger than a 55-cc engine. However, Indian drivers and roads being what they are, think long and hard before renting any motorized vehicle you intend to drive yourself.

BUS TRAVEL

Several private bus companies connect Goa with Mumbai, Pune, Bengaluru, and Mangalore. They are more expensive than public transit but definitely faster and more comfortable. Try Paulo Travels (☎ *832/663–7777* ⊕ *www.paulotravels.com*) for reliable service. Getting around Goa by bus is not advised unless you are traveling very light. Passengers are often packed in tight.

CAR TRAVEL

Goa can be easily explored from one end to the other by car. Everyplace is within a short drive of everyplace else.

TAXI AND AUTO-RICKSHAW TRAVEL

Goa has a unionized taxi system with fixed rates from point A to point B. They are expensive, but this is the best way to get around in Goa if money isn't a constraint. You don't really need to contact a tour operator, as there will usually be a taxi stand outside your hotel. If not, the hotel will call one for you from the nearest stand. Fares are not negotiable (in theory), and drivers charge a fixed rate displayed on a board at every taxi stand. If you are visiting a number of places and covering a lot of ground, it makes more sense to hire a taxi for a four- or eight-hour stretch (Rs. 1,500 for four hours), and pay an additional rate (Rs. 12) for every kilometer above 80 km (50 miles). Round-trip distances are calculated even for one-way journeys. Taxis levy a surcharge when they operate at night.

Most hotels can arrange taxis to take you around, either to the beach, restaurants, or shopping, and nothing is too far given the state's small size.

Auto-rickshaws, otherwise known as autos in India and "tuk-tuks" elsewhere in Southeast Asia, are easy to find. They cost less than taxis, but there are no fixed rates, so before climbing in ask a local or a knowledgeable visitor what the fare should be to your destination. Autos are best for short distances in town rather than for jaunts across the state.

TRAIN TRAVEL

You can take a train or bus to Goa from Mumbai, but be warned: such trips can be long—at least 12 hours by train, 17 hours by bus—crowded, and uncomfortable. (Be sure to take a bus or train with reserved seating.) The Konkan Railway (⊕ *www.konkanrailway.com*) runs lines to Mumbai in the north and Mangalore in the South. The Madgaon station in Margao is the main station, and there are smaller ones in Pernem, Thivim, Karmali, and Canacona. Book early online for train reservations: seats fill up quickly during the tourist season. Air-conditioned sleepers are best for overnight journeys.

For complete train schedules and fares, and to book tickets online, go to the Indian Railways website (⊕ *www.indianrail.gov.in),* where you can purchase and upgrade tickets, determine the kind of train you want, and review the rather extensive list of rules.

Train Information Karmali station ☏ *832/228–5798.* **Margao station** ✉ *2 km (1 mile) from main shopping area, Margao* ☏ *832/271–2790.*

English-Language Media Golden Heart Bookshop ✉ *Off Abade Faria Rd., Margao* ☏ *832/273–6339.* **Singbal's Book House** ✉ *Opposite Mary Immaculate Conception Church, Panaji* ☏ *832/242–5747.*

TOURS AND VISITOR INFORMATION

There are dozens of private tour operators in Goa. The most reliable are run by the Goa Tourism Development Corporation, which runs bus tours of both North and South Goa—departing from Panaji, Madgaon, and Colva Beach—as well as river cruises from the Santa Monica Pier in Panaji, and the Goa Department of Tourism. In Panaji, the Directorate of Tourism fields general inquiries. For assistance with reservations, including bus tours, contact the Goa Tourism Development Corporation (GTDC). There's also a 24-hour "Hello Information" number for Goa (☏ *832/241–2121),* which is extremely useful for finding phone numbers.

Contacts Department of Tourism ✉ *Tourist Home, Patto Bridge, Panaji* ☏ *832/243–8750* ⊕ *www.goatourism.gov.in.* **Goa Tourism Development Corporation** ✉ *Trionara Apartments, Dr. Alvares Costa Rd., Panaji* ☏ *832/242–4001 to 03* ⊕ *www.goa-tourism.com.*

RESTAURANTS

If you like seafood and spicy food in general, you're in luck. You can spend all your time happily eating nothing but searingly hot (spicy) fish day in and day out, in the state's best restaurants as well as at the beachfront open-air shacks. But since Goa has such a huge tourist culture, food can be prepared to your liking—simply grilled or fried or with less spice, if you prefer. Goan food is typically big on flavor, whether it's chilli, tamarind, or coconut that dominates the dish. Make sure you order your meat (pork or beef) cooked through, and only order meat in the better-known larger restaurants, not at the beach shacks. Seafood is usually safe everywhere as long as it's fresh. If you're vegetarian, you'll get by fine, but vegetables are not as plentiful in the Goan diet as are fish, seafood, and meat.

FIND IT ALL GOA

The best resource for up-to-date Goa information is Find All Goa (⊕ www.findall-goa.com), which provides detailed calendars for live music, tours, cruises, and cultural and sporting events, as well as useful information regarding plane and train departures. Exceptionally detailed maps of Goa's districts and towns (including walking paths) can be downloaded.

HOTELS

Goa has every kind of lodging, from super-exclusive posh resorts to beachside shacks appropriate only for beach bums and seen-it-all globe-trotters. Expect to get what you pay for, however, especially during peak season, from December to February, when the tourist hordes fill the hotels. Make sure you reserve a room far in advance of this time. During the monsoon season (June–October), prices drop by up to half and the resorts fill up with Indian visitors from the North. Unless noted otherwise, hotels have air-conditioning, TVs, and bathrooms with showers. *Hotel reviews have been shortened. For full information, visit Fodors.com.*

WHAT IT COSTS IN RUPEES			
	$	$$	$$$	$$$$
Restaurants	under Rs. 300	Rs. 300–Rs. 499	Rs. 500–Rs. 700	over Rs. 700
Hotels	under Rs. 4,000	Rs. 4,000–Rs. 5,999	Rs. 6,000–Rs. 10,000	over Rs. 10,000

Restaurant prices are the average cost of a main course at dinner or, if dinner is not served, at lunch. Hotel prices are the lowest cost of a standard double room in high season.

PLANNING YOUR TIME

It takes about a week to catch all of Goa's highlights—the beaches, Panaji, Old Goa, and the backwaters. If you're coming mainly for the beaches, a three- or four-day trip will suffice for swimming in the warm waters of the Arabian Sea, shopping at the colorful markets, and enjoying the flavors of Goan food. It's worth putting a day aside to see Panaji and to sample Goa's Portuguese ties firsthand, most apparent in the historic Fontainhas and Sao Tomé districts, as well as in the grand churches of Old Goa, built by the Portuguese in the 16th century.

A wonderful way to properly experience Goan life is to check in for two or three days at one of the state's heritage homes or properties. With antique-filled guest rooms, attentive service, and delicious home cooking, the best of these places amount to a pleasurable window into Goa's past. Ultimately, much of Goa's charm lies in its ability to be so flexible: here you can choose between a tranquil retreat from modern life or party central, a resort spot for a perfect tan, or a destination from which to explore India's heritage.

> ### MONSOON MASALA
>
> Chances are you've never experienced anything like the monsoon in Goa. The downpours are heavy and sudden, and the raindrops so huge and close together it's as if someone is throwing buckets of water on you from a second-floor window. The rain may last for days or a mere 30 minutes, disappearing as quickly as it came. Even so, if you're in Goa during a rainy spell, don't let it slow you down. Wear your flip-flops, bring an umbrella, and carry on, as the locals do.

EXPLORING GOA

Although it is the coastal areas that are the biggest draw for visitors to Goa, if you travel inland you'll find jungles, mountains, and agricultural areas. The north is known for its restaurants, bars and party-hearty beaches. In central Goa you'll find the mammoth ghost town that is Old Goa, as well as Panaji, the state capital. The less-traveled south is home to several high-end hotels and resorts, as well as small villages that allow a glimpse into Goa beyond the beach shacks and all-night parties.

Note that in addresses the terms *wadi, waddo,* and *vado* all mean "street."

NORTH GOA

Calangute, Baga, and Anjuna were important stops on the hippie trails of the 1960s and 1970s, and continue to be at the beating heart of Goa's party scene. This coastal stretch is increasingly built up, but there are still some quiet areas around Mandrem beach (north of the Chapora River). Nearby, atop the hills, are a few beautiful old forts built of laterite, the local pitted red stone; they offer beautiful vistas of the curvaceous coastline. The villages that sit a few miles inland have charming bed-and-breakfasts and inns with rustic flavor.

You may also want to take an excursion to one of the popular markets. On Wednesday the bustling market in Anjuna, not far from the beach, is filled with inexpensive jewelry, cotton sarongs, colorful shoulder bags, handicrafts marketed by vendors from Goa, Karnataka, and other Indian states, and food stalls selling everything from bean burritos and brownies to Middle Eastern platters with hummus and falafel.

7

There's also the Saturday night bazaar in nearby Arpora that is similar, and with even more food on offer, including whole roast chickens and Italian gelato. Goa's famed all-night beach parties are now history, but once the shacks close, follow the music (or the crowd) to the after-party, usually not publicized.

Goa's restaurant scene continues to refine and reinvent itself, with excellent restaurants serving both Goan and international cuisines. Stop by A Reverie in Calangute for its global fusion menu, Thalassa in Vagator for delicious Greek food, Ciao Bella in Assagao for a wonderful Italian meal, or Lila Café in Baga for a hearty morning-after recovery meal.

ARAMBOL, ASHVEM, MANDREM, AND MORJIM

48 km (30 miles) northwest of Panaji.

Fodor'sChoice ★ The sands of Arambol are far less congested than those at Baga and Calangute, and as a result the area has become home to a new generation of hippies and free-spirited travelers. You'll catch this bohemian vibe in the European cafés and cheap hotels and shacks that cater to long-haul visitors.

The beach, also known as Harmal, is rugged and lovely. The best stretch is tiny Paliem Beach, at the foot of Waghcolomb Hill. The scenery is spectacular: a freshwater pond stands at the base of the hillside barely 200 yards from the sea. The sea is rougher here than at other beaches—it's still good for swimming, but a bit more fun for those who like a little surf. To avoid the crowds when it's high season, walk past the pond, and you'll find quieter tidal inlets and rock ledges.

A little farther south are the lovely, quiet beaches of Ashvem, Mandrem, and Morjim. Divided by little creeks, the beaches have spectacular windswept stretches of sand, a far cry from the overcrowded beaches south of the Chapora River. Mandrem offers the most accommodation and entertainment options, including a couple of well-tended luxury shacks. Morjim is popular because of the Olive Ridley turtles, which use its dark sands as a nesting ground during the winter. Hatchlings emerge at night after an eight-week incubation period. Conservation efforts have proved difficult, and it's unclear whether turtles will continue to return to nest here. Ashvem is quiet and relaxing in the daytime, but once the sun goes down this is where you'll find the open-air beach parties in high season.

GETTING HERE AND AROUND
The best and fastest way of getting here is by taxi. A prepaid non-air-conditioned ride from the airport should set you back about Rs. 1,200 to Arambol. From Panaji, it should take you about 40 minutes for a Rs. 600 taxi ride. Most hotels will arrange taxis, rent motorbikes, or loan bicycles.

BEACHES
Arambol Beach. Perfect for those keen on sampling a taste of the 1970s hippie trail, and still favorite with Goa's free spirits, this North Goan beach has long, wide swathes of clean sand and shallow water that's great for paddling. Even in season you can find quiet stretches where

Goa's Past

CLOSE UP

Goa's coastal location has made it an influential trading post for many centuries. Hindu merchants flourished for centuries, trading spices, silk, pearls, horses, and ideas with Arab, East African, and Mediterranean cultures. Control of the region shifted between the Bahmani Sultanate of the Deccan Plateau and the Vijayanagar Empire in Hampi, to the east. Goa's fortunes were profoundly altered by the arrival in 1510 of Affonso de Albuquerque, a Portuguese explorer and naval officer who wrestled the tiny realm from the hands of the Sultan of Bijapur. For the next 450 years the Portuguese exerted major pressures as well as a strong influence on Goan culture, language, and religion—they converted many native Hindus and Buddhists to Catholicism by force. The Portuguese ruled with an iron first before, during, and after the rest of the Indian subcontinent was under the thumb of the British.

It was during this period, from the 16th to the 18th centuries, that the grandiose churches of Old Goa were built. The most illustrious structures here include Old Goa's Sé (cathedral) and the Basilica of Bom Jesus, where the remains of St. Francis Xavier lie in a silver casket entombed in a Florentine-style marble mausoleum. A string of cholera epidemics in this city built on swamps eventually saw its decline, and the Portuguese adopted Panaji as its new capital.

Although British-ruled India became a free country in 1947, the Portuguese retained their hold on Goa for 15 more years. They were finally driven out in 1961 through a land assault ordered by India's first Prime Minister, Jawaharlal Nehru. In comparison to some 30,000 Indian troops, the Portuguese force of 3,000 men was nominal.

In the decades since, Goa has retained its own identity, although tourism has changed it a great deal. In day-to-day life, Catholic traditions are evident in its whitewashed village churches, and European influence lives on in the Goans' love for pork, and even in local fashions. Goans, perhaps more than any other Indian state, are quite Western in their outlook, and it is that harmonious blend of East and West that sets it apart from most other parts of the country.

you can chill out, and with a few fun shacks spread out over the length of the beach, there's always fresh juice and light food to be had. **Amenities:** food and drink. **Best for:** solitude; sunrise; sunset; swimming. ✉ *Arambol Pernem.*

Ashvem Beach. The white sands here are perfect for uninterrupted lazing. Sandwiched between Morjim and Mandrem beaches, Ashvem has a fair few hippie beach shacks, but it still manages to hold onto its air of deserted idyll. Between September and February, this is a nesting spot for the Olive Ridley turtle, and if you're lucky you'll spot a few. No longer off the beaten track, the areas around the beach are now full of thatched beachside accommodations, like Yab Yum Resorts ⇨ *See Where to Stay listings.* And in season it's also home to some of Goa's best seasonal eating, notably at upscale La Plage ⇨ *See Where to Eat listings.* It's not as much of a destination for partyers as some of its neighboring beaches, and just a hop and a skip away from the beach are lush paddies and coconut groves. **Amenities:** food and drink. **Best for:** solitude; sunrise; sunset; swimming; walking. ⊠ *Mandrem.*

Mandrem Beach. This quiet hideaway in North Goa has the advantage of not being a popular destination on the tourist trail, which is why it's a top pick for honeymooners and for couples looking for a quiet getaway. There are a few beach shacks and the odd guesthouse in season, but you really have to make your own entertainment on this deserted stretch. **Amenities:** none. **Best for:** solitude; sunset.

Morjim Beach. Best known as a home to Olive Ridley sea turtles, serene Morjim Beach is popular with those keen to see a nesting site of the species. Known to be quiet and peaceful, it is easy to see the attraction for these endangered marine creatures. In recent years, however, the village of Morjim has also become home to most of Goa's Russian expatriates, earning itself the title of "Little Russia," and this influx has brought with it a less peaceful atmosphere. Although the beach is still quiet during the day, it now has a thriving nightlife. **Amenities:** food and drink. **Best for:** swimming; walking; partiers. ⊠ *Morjim.*

WHERE TO EAT AND STAY

$$ \
PIZZA

✕ **Fellini.** Firmly established as the definitive destination for pizza in North Goa, Fellini is tucked away in the busy lanes of Arambol—it takes some finding, but the pepperoni pizzas make it worth the hunt. They don't skimp on the mozzarella, and Fellini's salami pie commands a devoted following that traipses in from all over the North. Vegetarians should try the classic margherita or the spinach and mushroom options. The interior is no-nonsense, with shack-style tables and seating. It's best to skip right over the pasta section of the menu, because it's the giant calzones and pies that are the stars here. ⑤ *Average main: Rs. 500* ⊠ *Socoillo Vaddo, Main Arambol Beach Rd., Arambol Pernem* ☎ *0091/9881461224.*

$$$$ \
INDIAN

✕ **La Plage.** Don't let the casual air of the palm trees and simple white tables of this down-to-earth shack fool you. It serves excellent French food as well as comforting burgers and grills. Conceived in 2003 by three old friends, the restaurant has transformed from its humble six-table beginnings into a must-visit destination for any food-lover passing through Goa. Try the fresh fruit cocktails, the warm tiger prawn carpaccio or crispy sardine fillets with parsley, pine nuts, and lime zest; or the sesame-crusted tuna fillet with wasabi mashed potatoes and soy sauce, and finish with the chocolate thali, a sampler of their sweetest offerings. Dinner reservations are essential in the months of December and January. ⑤ *Average main: Rs. 1500* ⊠ *Ashwem Beach, Morjim* ☎ *98/2212–1712* ⊟ *No credit cards* ⊘ *Closed May–Nov.*

$$$$ \
HOTEL

▦ **Elsewhere.** On a 500-yard-long spit of outstretched private land, surrounded on three sides by the waters of the Arabian Sea and Otter Creek, is Denzil Sequeira's lovely ancestral property, a reminder of a forgotten Goa. **Pros:** semi-private beach; lovely property. **Cons:** a 60-yard bamboo footbridge is the only access route; reservations have to be made via email ⑤ *Rooms from: Rs. 45529* ⊠ *North Goa* ⊕ *www.aseascape.com* ⤺ *4 beach houses, 3 tents* ⊘ *Closed June–Sept.* ▨◎▮ *Breakfast.*

$$$ 🏨 **Siolim House.** For the old-world charm of an aristocratic family home,
HOTEL stay at this elegant Portuguese villa on the south bank of the Chapora River, now converted into an all-suites boutique hotel. **Pros:** tranquil rural setting; free Wi-Fi; palatial rooms. **Cons:** no TV; no a/c in some rooms; the mattresses on some beds are old. ⑤ *Rooms from: Rs. 7500* ✉ *Opposite Vaddy Chapel, Siolim, Bardez* ☎ *832/227–2138, 833/227–2941* ⊕ *www.siolimhouse.com* ↬ *7 suites* ⑩ *Breakfast.*

$$$ 🏨 **Yab Yum Resorts.** The property's signature thatched and dome-shape
RESORT roofs are tucked away in a shaded grove of palm trees—a fun and funky location that's minutes from lovely Ashwem Beach. **Pros:** quiet beach. **Cons:** no restaurant on premises. ⑤ *Rooms from: Rs. 5800* ✉ *Ashvem Beach, Mandrem* ☎ *832/224–7712, 832/651–0392* ⊕ *www.yabyumresorts.com* ↬ *5 cottages, 12 domes* ☉ *Closed late Apr.–Oct.* ⑩ *Breakfast.*

VAGATOR BEACH

25 km (16 miles) northwest of Panaji.

Jagged cliffs along sandy shores give a rugged wild atmosphere to the beaches at Vagator, which is split by a seaside headland that offers beautiful views on either side. On one side are the dark red walls of the old hill fort of Chapora, built in 1717, which was later taken twice from the Portuguese by the Marathas. (The Marathas ruled a principality that covers much of the modern-day state of Maharashtra, north of Goa.) The view from the ramparts is phenomenal, and farther up the shore are stretches of secluded sand. On the other side is beautiful Ozrant Beach, also called Mini-Vagator, near which you will find an impressive stone face of Shiva that was carved into a boulder by an unknown sculptor.

Little Vagator and Vagator come to life after dark. Beach shacks like Boom Shankar will have information on the ongoing beach parties. Nine Bar, above the beach, is for trance and techno lovers. This part of Goa has plenty of beach shack restaurants, but many disappear from one season to the next, or take on a different name. The best way to figure out where to eat is to ask fellow travelers for the name of the current favorite.

BEACHES

Vagator Beach. The dark sands of Vagator Beach lead on from the red cliffs that line it. Vagator is popular with both local and foreign tourists, and as a result visitors will find lots of vendors and stands selling snacks, sliced local fruit, trinkets, and souvenirs. Plenty of bars and shacks are on hand to cater to this mixed crowd, and in the high season most bars reverberate to the sounds of dance and trance music. Vagator's waters are choppier than some of North Goa's other beaches, which is why this beach isn't a top pick for swimmers. **Amenities:** food and drink; parking; toilets. **Best for:** sunset; partiers; walking. ✉ *Vagator.*

WHERE TO EAT AND STAY

$$$ ✕ **Ciao Bella.** This delightful Italian restaurant is one of Goa's best. The
ITALIAN Italian couple, Mario and Simona, who are at the helm here are hands-on hosts who tend to customers as well as cook, and their personal

A woman playing an alphorn at Arambol beach

touch is evident in every plate the kitchen sends out. With delicious homemade pasta and bread, a perfect plate of spinach-and-ricotta ravioli, giant portions of black tagliatelle with salmon, and a dessert list that includes a potent coffee granita, everything on the menu is fresh and fantastic. Go early to bag a table at the weekend, but service is so quick that you might not have too long a wait even if you forget. Ciao Bella is open all year round, but reservations are recommended in the high season. ⑤ *Average main: Rs. 800* ✉ *569 Assagao Baden Rd., Assagao, Bardez* ☎ *97/6755–7673* ⊗ *No lunch. Closed Mon.*

$$ ✕ **Thalassa.** Rugged Vagator Beach is the seductive backdrop for Mark-
GREEK etty Grana's popular whitewashed Greek restaurant, which is on top of a low cliff overlooking the rocky shores of Little Vagator. Thalassa's vibrant chef re-creates authentic food from her native Corfu, including much-loved dishes like *sofrito* (veal, slow-cooked in white wine and herbs) and *pastisada* (meat with tomato sauce and spices served with macaroni). The lamb dishes, such as the moussaka, are excellent. There are options for vegetarians, too: try the hot feta cheese, the risotto, or the mushroom saganaki, made with melted cheese. They also have fairly reasonably priced rooms on offer, although they need to booked well in advance. ⑤ *Average main: Rs. 800* ✉ *Little Vagator, Ozran Beach, Vagator* ☎ *98/5003–3537* ⊕ *www.thalassagoa.com* ▭ *No credit cards* ⊗ *No lunch. Closed late May–Sept.*

$$$ ▥ **Casa Vagator.** Perched on a hillside high above the Arabian Sea, this
HOTEL smart and stylish contemporary hotel overlooks the wild beauty of Vagator Beach, which guests can reach by following a winding path that descends rather sharply. **Pros:** far from the hustle and bustle of Goa's beach scene; striking sea views. **Cons:** lots of stairs; small pool;

CLOSE UP

Water Sports in Goa

Goa offers a variety of water sports, from adrenaline-generating Jet Ski rides and parasailing to more light-hearted banana boat and catamaran rides.

Parasailing. This is the most exciting water-sport experience in Goa: you take off and feel the wind hitting you across the lovely palm-fringed coastline. There are two ways to do it: either you take off and land on a winchboat in the water, or you descend onto the beach. You will find plenty of operators during the tourist season, but some of them have questionable safety standards. Use licensed operators at the luxury resorts if you happen to be staying at one, or use one of those with a history of operating in Goa. Parasailing around Sinquerim-Candolim-Calangute offers a spectacular view of Fort Aguada. Other recommended areas are near the Arrosim-Cansaulim and Utorda stretches, and Mobor Beach, in the south. From Miramar you can catch views of the Mandovi River

meeting the sea. Rides last for three to five minutes and cost between Rs. 400 and Rs. 1,000; boat-ride charges are extra. You need to be comfortable with both heights and water.

Jet-skiing and waterskiing. Water sports operators in Colva, Candolim, Calangute, Miramar, Arossim, Utorda, Benaulim, Mobor, and Rajbaga are also set up for jet-skiing. It's an exhilarating, energetic ride, which lasts from 2 to 15 minutes. Usually instructors accompany you on the rides, which cost around Rs. 1,500. If you want to go waterskiing, the cost is between Rs. 400 and Rs. 1,200 depending on the length of the ride and the time of year; operators are at Candolim, Calangute, Arossim, Utorda, Majorda, and Rajbaga.

Scuba diving and snorkeling. Goa is not a great location for these sports, but there are a couple of reputable places to try both. They can both also help you get PADI certified although the water in these areas isn't very clear.

7

---

the neighboring Nine Bar sometimes has thumping music at night. $ *Rooms from: Rs. 7000* ✉ *H. No. 594/4 Vozran, Vagator* ☎ *832/727–4931* ⊕ *www.casaboutiquehotels.com/CasaVagator* ⤴ *11 rooms, 1 penthouse suite* ⊗ *Closed roughly June–mid-Sept.* ⦿ *Breakfast.*

$$$
B&B/INN
⌂ **Purple Valley Yoga Retreat.** Sitting inland, in the lush, quiet environs of Assagao, Purple Yoga is renowned the world over for its retreats, led by world-class yoga instructors. **Pros:** guests can pay extra for ayurvedic massage therapies. **Cons:** one- or two-week stay only. $ *Rooms from: Rs. 70000* ✉ *142, Bairo Alto, Assagao, Bardez* ☎ *0091/832–226–8364* ⊕ *www.yogagoa.com* ⤴ *25 rooms* ⦿ *All meals.*

$$$
HOTEL
⌂ **Sunbeam.** Owned by flamboyant Indian stylist Jivi Sethi, Sunbeam is a gorgeously redecorated Portuguese family home in one of North Goa's most charming villages. **Pros:** excellent food; beautiful family heirlooms and home-style touches; access to some of Goa's best beaches. **Cons:** powercuts; lack of light in the Old House rooms. $ *Rooms from: Rs. 7000* ✉ *E-13 Saunta Vaddo, Mapusa-Anjuna Rd., Assagao* ☎ *832/226–8525* ⤴ *3 rooms* ⦿ *All meals.*

ANJUNA BEACH

20 km (12 miles) northwest of Panaji.

Discovered by the hippies in the late 1960s, Anjuna and its palm-lined beaches have had many seasons of glory. Although Anjuna can get very crowded and boisterous, its beach is still not as commercial as Calangute and doesn't have the large-scale luxury resorts you'll find at Sinquerim Beach and in the south. With coconut trees framing the sands against jagged laterite cliffs and boulders, the beach is as popular as ever. Drugs are all too easily available here, too, but they are also highly illegal—even if they seem to be part of the atmosphere. Anjuna is known for its Wednesday night **flea market** where you can buy everything from jewelry and juice to art and antiques.

BEACHES

Anjuna Beach. This is Goa's original hippie haven. Those full-moon parties, now so synonymous with this beach state, first happened on the sands of Anjuna in the 1960s, and even today this northern beach is home to modern-day flower children, international travelers keen on sampling some of that hippie stardust, and everyone looking for a party. It's definitely not one of Goa's most beautiful beaches, but the steady influx of people means that it's got restaurants and bars galore. Anjuna's busiest on Wednesday, when the famed weekly Anjuna Flea Market takes place. The water is safe for swimming and you'll find lots of sunbathers and souvenir vendors year-round. **Amenities:** food and drink; water sports; parking. **Best for:** partiers; sunset; swimming; walking. ⊠ *Anjuna.*

WHERE TO EAT AND STAY

$
BAKERY
✕ **Baba Au Rhum.** This charming little French pizzeria and bakery, in a sleepy residential lane off the busy Anjuna road, is open all day, but it's best for breakfast. The croissants are buttery and fresh, and the pain au chocolat is far too good to be restricted to the morning. The menu also includes a concise selection of freshly squeezed juices, sandwiches, and salads, as well as fairly good pizzas and burgers, but it's with the sweet stuff that they really excel—try a strawberry and lemon tart or the chocolate passion fruit version, which sounds an unwise blend, but is actually delightful (with just a little kick). They're closed all monsoon, but tend to reopen their doors in October. $ *Average main: Rs. 300* ⊠ *Salim House, opposite Uttam Resorts, Arpora* ☎ *98/2207–8759.*

$
INDIAN
✕ **Biryani Palace.** The Palace's relaxed service, open-air seating and dependable North Indian food make this casual eatery a popular draw in Anjuna. The cook specializes in *biryanis* (Indian rice pilaf made with vegetables, spices, and a choice of seafood, chicken or meat), of course, but also barbecued seafood, mixed seafood grills, and Goan specialties. Soft lighting, mat ceilings, rattan chairs on a sandy floor, and no a/c set the mellow mood that is enhanced by classic sitar music—instead of the driving Goan trance played in most area restaurants. $ *Average main: Rs. 200* ⊠ *Anjuna Beach Rd., 500 yds. from beach, Anjuna* ☎ *93/2612–4699* ▭ *No credit cards.*

$$$
HOTEL
🏨 **Casa Anjuna.** History, style, and attitude combine to make spending time in this 200-year-old Portuguese mansion and its lush tropical

garden a rare pleasure. **Pros:** beautiful setting; antiques-filled rooms; peace and quiet. **Cons:** 10-minute walk to the beach. $⑤ Rooms from: Rs. 7000 ⊠ D'Mello Vaddo 66, Anjuna, Bardez ☎ 832/227–4123 ⊕ www.casaboutiquehotels.com/CasaAnjuna ⤴ 19 rooms, 2 suites, 3 penthouses ⦿⦿ Breakfast.*

$ ▦ **Hotel Bougainvillea (Granpa's Inn).** This hotel occupies a 200-year-old
HOTEL restored Portuguese country house on an inland lane. **Pros:** great value; funky; rural setting. **Cons:** too far to walk to the beach; no a/c in some rooms. $⑤ Rooms from: Rs. 2900 ⊠ Gaunwadi, Anjuna ☎ 832/227–3270, 832/227–3271 ⊕ www.granpasinn.com ⤴ 7 rooms, 7 suites ⊙ Closed July and Aug. ⦿⦿ Breakfast.*

$$ ▦ **Laguna Anjuna.** This upscale place to stay is less than a kilometer from
RESORT the beach, in a tree-lined residential area. **Pros:** quiet, relaxed setting. **Cons:** a bit removed from the main attraction. $⑤ Rooms from: Rs. 5500 ⊠ Soranto Vado, Anjuna ☎ 832/227–4131 ⊕ www.lagunaanjuna.com ⤴ 19 rooms, 6 suites ⦿⦿ Breakfast.*

NIGHTLIFE

Curlie's Bar. At the south end of Anjuna, Curlie's is something of an institution, organizing parties in season and *the* place for partiers to congregate year-round. With a great sea view and a basic menu, this is an essential pit stop for anyone who wants to sample the hard-partying side of Goa. ☎ 98/2216–8628.

Paradiso. This is one of Goa's most popular nightclubs, near Anjuna Beach atop a cliff with a fabulous view. ☎ 832/325–9999.

Primrose Music Club. Situated between Anjuna and Vagator, this is a favorite spot to get the night started. It started off as a favorite with the psychedelic trance crowd, and while those parties have moved indoors in keeping with new legislation, as is the case at most Goan night-spots, Primrose continues to be very popular in season (it is closed all monsoon).

Shore Bar. The most popular place to down beer, watch the dramatic sunset over the Arabian Sea, and listen to loud music until the wee hours is the Shore Bar on the beach. The steps of this place are usu-ally packed with people, especially on Wednesday after the flea mar-ket. Walk north from the market for about a kilometer to get here. ☎ 0091/9822383795.

BAGA BEACH

15 km (9 miles) northwest of Panaji; 2 km (1 mile) north of Calangute.

One of Goa's top party beaches, Baga is known for its hopping "shack life." If you're looking for a quiet spot to sunbathe, Baga probably isn't for you. But the many popular food and drink joints mean that it's a top spot for nighttime revelry, headlined by St. Anthony's for seafood and the legendary Tito's Bar and Café Mambo for club nights. During the day, and in season, there are plenty of water sports on offer as well, including parasailing, windsurfing, and Jet Ski rides.

The beach drops steeply to the shoreline, where fishing canoes make use of the easy boat-launching conditions to provide rides, including trips

The Flea Market at Anjuna

Getting to the Wednesday flea market at Anjuna can be half the fun; you can take a bus or a motorcycle taxi, or a fisherman's boat from Baga, which takes 15 minutes or so. (Going by road takes half an hour.) There are still some old-school foreigners around manning the stands, but it really isn't their market anymore. Now the markets are dominated by Lamani, Kashmiris, and Tibetans, who sell all kinds of trinkets while dressed in striking clothing and jewelry, as well as craftspeople from elsewhere in India. The market is a splash of red and orange in a flat area above the rocky beach. Bead and white-metal bangles, necklaces and earrings, silver toe rings, embroidered shoulder bags, silk and cotton sarongs, and ethnic footwear are among the more common products on sale. If you look carefully, there are all sorts of other things here as well, from used motorbikes of uncertain age to do-it-yourself *mehendi* henna-tattoo kits. Buy a crochet bikini, tops and skirts embroidered with tiny mirrors, or a tie-dye bandanna, or just sit back at the market bar and down a ridiculously cheap beer while someone braids your hair deftly or offers to tattoo, pierce, or otherwise mutilate various parts of your anatomy. Be careful not to bargain unfairly, because you run the risk of a sarcastic "take it for free?" from one of the tribal women. When your day's bargains have been struck (and getting things for a third or less of the quoted price is not uncommon), join the rest of Anjuna down at the shore. The market only appears during the tourist season; during the monsoon there's a smaller market in Anjuna just above the main town beach.

to the Wednesday market at Anjuna Beach just around the bend (the ride to Anjuna takes 15 minutes by sea, but twice as long by road). A few hundred meters down the beach, to the south of the point where the steep slope meets the sand, you'll find relatively less-crowded areas where you can spread out your towel and sunbathe. The beach gets its name from the Baga River, which meets the sea at the beach's northern end.

BEACHES

Baga Beach. This long, narrow (at high tide) beach is one of Goa's most popular, and Baga is where you'll find nonstop action, cocktails around the clock, innumerable water-sports vendors, as well as some of North Goa's best-loved party spots like Tito's ⇨ *See Nightlife listings* and Cavala (a short walk away from the beach). In the winter months this beach is filled with package tourists, so although you won't find peace at Baga, you will find everything else. **Amenities:** food and drink; water sports; lifeguards. **Best for:** partiers; sunset; windsurfing. ⊠ *Baga*.

WHERE TO EAT AND STAY

$ ✕ **Lila Café.** Cross the river, and you arrive at picturesquely situated
CAFÉ   Lila Café, by the banks of the Baga River. The daytime eatery is the perfect antidote to any late-night revelry and is famous for its freshly baked breads and jams, soups, omelets, and continental dishes—don't miss the hot croissants. This German café is among the top breakfast

places around; even locals happily make the trip from Panaji. $ *Average main: Rs. 150* ✉ *House no. 566, near Baga River, Arpora-Baga, Bardez* ☎ *0832/227–9843* ⊕ *www.lilacafegoa.com* ▭ *No credit cards* ☉ *Closed Tues. and June–Sept.*

$$
SEAFOOD ✕ **St. Anthony's.** This seaside restaurant, a bit above Baga's many beach shacks, serves an astonishing variety of fish dishes in a casual setting that draws big crowds due to its location at the mouth of the river. The tuna steaks and pomfret dishes are particularly good. They host very popular karaoke nights; if you're keen, it's worth ringing ahead to see when they're on. $ *Average main: Rs. 400* ✉ *Near Baga River* ☎ *832/645–2396* ▭ *No credit cards.*

$$$
HOTEL ⌂ **Casa Baga.** This rambling, boutique hotel is far and away the best place to stay in Baga—the lively beach scene is only two minutes away, and the friendly staff treat you like family, making up for any upkeep deficits. **Pros:** not on the noisy main road; exceptional staff. **Cons:** sketchy plumbing. $ *Rooms from: Rs. 7000* ✉ *40/7 Saunta Vaddo* ☎ *832/227–6957, 832/228–2930, 832/228–2931* ⊕ *www.casaboutiquehotels.com/CasaBaga/* ⇥ *14 rooms* �◯ *Breakfast.*

$
HOTEL ⌂ **Cavala.** Quality bargain accommodations are rare in this side of town, which makes this welcoming property, by a tropical garden near Baga beach, a cheery option. **Pros:** minutes to Baga beach, lively bar on hotel grounds. **Cons:** drab, less than thrilling rooms. $ *Rooms from: Rs. 2200* ✉ *Saunta Vaddo* ☎ *832/227–6090* ⊕ *www.cavala.com* ⇥ *21 rooms, 9 suites* ◯ *Breakfast.*

NIGHTLIFE

Tito's. Probably the best-known of all Goa's clubs, Tito's is always packed. Having undergone a recent refurbishment, this bar and club is bigger than ever, and while the management have now opened a slew of other venues across the beach state, the original on Baga Beach continues to be the main draw. Café Mambo, on the premises, is open 9:30 am–3:30 am daily, but the party crowd doesn't come in until close to midnight. Expect fashion shows, famous DJ mixers theme nights, popular dance music, and fairly expensive drinks. ☎ *832/227–5028, 832/227–9895.*

CALANGUTE BEACH, CANDOLIM AND AROUND

12 km (7 miles) northwest of Panaji.

Calangute is by far the most crowded of the northern beaches—it's an open stretch of white sand with an entrance area crammed with restaurants, stalls, and shops. The mood is especially festive during the high season in winter, when dozens of shacks serving inexpensive beer, mixed drinks, and seafood pop up on the beach.

The beach is accessible by concrete steps. △ **Note the sign warning that swimming is dangerous—there's a fairly strong undertow here.**

Beyond the beach are some of the area's best restaurants and shopping. You'll also find hundreds of shops, including roadside trinket stalls, branches of the Oxford Bookstore and Café Coffee Day, ATMs, travel agencies, and Malini Ramani's boutique, filled with vibrant clothes.

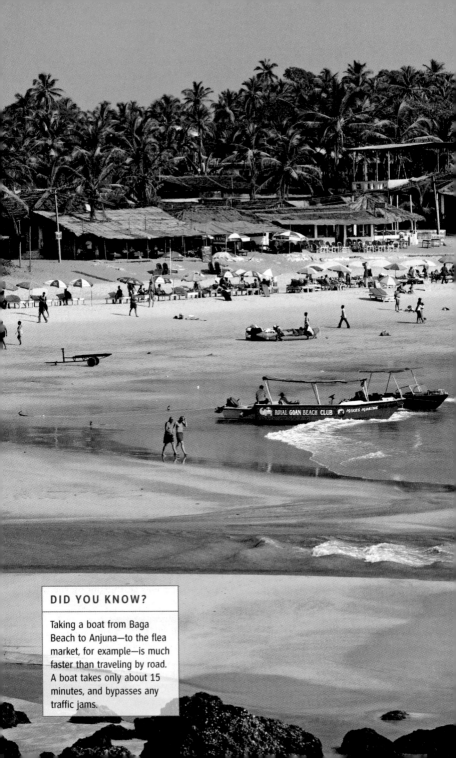

DID YOU KNOW?

Taking a boat from Baga Beach to Anjuna—to the flea market, for example—is much faster than traveling by road. A boat takes only about 15 minutes, and bypasses any traffic jams.

Most of these shops are on the stretch of road running from St. Anthony's Chapel, past a market, to Baga. Candolim Church was first built in 1560 and dedicated to Our Lady of Hope; it was repaired in 1661 and received its current cake-icing look when the village Communidade remodeled it thanks to contributions from Candolim parishioners.

GETTING HERE AND AROUND

Calangute is at the center of the Bardez Coast, bordered by Candolim Beach to the south and Baga to the north. From the airport, a pre-paid taxi costs around Rs. 600–Rs. 700.

LOOK BOTH WAYS

India is second only to China in traffic fatalities, a high percentage of which involve pedestrians. When walking on Goa's country lanes or potholed city streets, beware of vehicles coming at you from every possible direction. Indian drivers pass on curves, head down the wrong side of the road, and swerve to miss stray dogs, cows, and the occasional wild pig.

BEACHES

Calangute Beach. Crowded and dirty, particularly in the high season, Calangute Beach is a tourist trap and the main destination for every package tourist in Goa. The rampant commercialization means that visitors can take their pick of activities, from water sports to shopping, but space and quiet are harder to find. The beach is accessible by concrete steps. ⚠ Note the sign warning that swimming is dangerous—there's a strong undertow here. **Amenities:** food and drink; water sports; lifeguards. **Best for:** partiers; windsurfing. ⊠ *Calangute*.

WHERE TO EAT

$$$$
INTERNATIONAL

✕ **A Reverie.** As the name suggests, A Reverie has a dreamlike, elegant ambience: the space is painted in warm earthy tones but there are stylish overtones of bling. Dimmed lounge areas, crystal chandeliers, and wrought-iron decorative furniture accent this popular fine-dining restaurant where dishes are "re-visited, re-interpreted and re-invented." Flavors are truly fused and all the food is beautifully plated. You might start, for instance, with a wasabi-flavored guacamole or a lemongrass-scented seafood dashi consommé with seaweed; intricately prepared seafood, meat, and dessert options hit similarly nuanced notes. The cocktails are intriguing, too—try the Desi Caipirinha made with fresh sugarcane juice or a Goan pina colada with a hint of the local (very potent) feni liquor. There is a live jazz band on weekends. Reservations are recommended. ⑤ *Average main: Rs. 2000* ⊠ *Holiday St., next to Goan Heritage, Gaurovaddo* ☏ *91/2350–5550, 98/2317–4927* ⊕ *areverie.com* ⊗ *No lunch. Closed May–Oct.*

$$$$
ECLECTIC

✕ **I-95.** This open-air dinner lounge and restaurant is chic but casual, with red stone walls and soothing candle-lit ambience. The brainchild of two couples from Mumbai, I-95 is a hit for its well-executed dishes and flair for presentation. The menu is a mixed bag, with some Indian, seafood, and continental fare. The delectable dishes include the blue crab risotto with jalapeño, lime, and cilantro jelly, beef carpaccio with quail egg, and seared tiger prawns dusted with lemon rind. The restaurant has earned a reputation for its lobster creations, and there's also a rich hot-chocolate soufflé to cap a fine meal. $ *Average main: Rs. 3000* ✉ *Castello Vermelho, behind Art chamber, 1/115 A Gauravaddo, near Kamat's Holiday Homes* ☎ *832/227–5213, 98/8130–1184.*

$$$$ ✕ **Republic of Noodles.** Its chain restaurant name belies how good the
ASIAN food is here. Slightly more expensive than is the norm in Goa, this Pan-Asian eatery sends out excellent seafood *laksa* (spicey noodle soup) and Asian barbecue to a swanky crowd. The interior is all dark bamboo and sandstone with Indonesian accents, and diners can choose to sit at *teppanyaki* counters (with a built-in hotplate where the chef cooks and serves the food straight onto your plate) or at regular tables to tuck into their bowls of panfried noodles or Javanese duck curry. Try the excellent fresh watermelon margaritas to go with a steaming bowl of panfried Singapore noodles. $ *Average main: Rs. 2000* ✉ *Lemon Tree Amarante Beach Resort, Vadi, Calangute* ☎ *832/398–8188* ⊘ *No lunch Mar.–Oct.*

$$ ✕ **Souza Lobo.** Established in 1932, and now managed by the third gen-
INDIAN eration of the Lobo family, this large, airy no-frills restaurant on hectic Calangute Beach catches the exuberant sea breeze. The seafood is excellent, which means the place is always busy. The Goan masala fried prawns are exactly as they should be—with authentic red masala and fresh, perfectly deveined prawns. Other Goan specialties include the squid *amot tik* (a sour curry), kingfish steak *peri-peri* (in spicy, tangy red sauce), and prawn-stuffed pomfret. The restaurant also serves Western-style seafood with a good garlic butter sauce. There's live music every night. (Be warned: The toilet here is shabby.) $ *Average main: Rs. 500* ✉ *Calangute Beach, Bardez* ☎ *832/227–6463, 832/228–1234* ⊕ *www.souzalobo.com.*

WHERE TO STAY

$$$ 🏨 **Casa Britona.** On a bank of a tributary of the River Mandovi, this
HOTEL boutique hotel 10 km (6 miles) from Sinquerim comes with unique views of inland Goa, mangroves, and freshwater wildlife. **Pros:** lovely location; private, tranquil hideaway. **Cons:** a taxi or scooter is needed to reach the beach. $ *Rooms from: Rs. 7000* ✉ *H. No. 217 Salvador-do-Mundo, near Charmanos, Britona* ☎ *832/241–0962, 832/241–6737* ⊕ *casaboutiquehotels.com/CasaBritona* ⤵ *10 suites* ⦿ *Breakfast.*

$$$$ 🏨 **Fortune Select Regina.** In a quiet location off the main road near Can-
HOTEL dolim, this resort from the Fortune Hotels group is competent and professional in its service and facilities. **Pros:** tranquil location in a busy tourist area. **Cons:** pricey for this type of property; a taxi or scooter is needed to reach the beach. $ *Rooms from: Rs. 10000* ✉ *376 off Fort Aguada Rd., Candolim* ☎ *832/398–8444* ⊕ *www.fortunehotels.in* ⤵ *96 rooms, 6 suites* ⦿ *Breakfast.*

$$$$ 🏨 **Nilaya Hermitage.** Nilaya, which roughly translates to "a hidden dwell-
HOTEL ing," could not be more aptly named. **Pros:** fabulous tiled pool; dreamy theme rooms; day cruises on the wooden sailing dhow; on-site ayurvedic spa. **Cons:** remote, requires taxis to go anywhere. $ *Rooms from: Rs. 21998* ✉ *Off Main Calangute Rd., Arpora, Calangute* ☎ *832/226–9794* ⊕ *www.nilaya.com* ⤵ *14 rooms* ⦿ *Some meals.*

$$$$ 🏨 **Pousada Tauma.** This beautiful boutique hotel built of laterite (a
HOTEL local red-pitted stone) has old Portuguese floor tiles and an abundant,

Inner Peace

If there's anything that sums up the Goan attitude to life, it's *sussegado*, which means "take it easy." Even with the tourist influx exceeding the local population, the massive star resorts, and the party scene, there's a certain peace in Goa that is unlikely to ever be disturbed, because it comes from within. A part of this mood of daylong siesta can be attributed to a widespread love of excellent food and local alcohol—Goa brews its own *feni*, a potent and inexpensive concoction distilled from palm sap or cashew-fruit juice. If you're looking to imbibe the true spirit of Goa, try the coconut-palm feni—it smells less pungent than the cashew variety and goes down a little bit easier.

You can buy the alcohol from just about anywhere in Goa (but make sure it's bottled properly) and down it with classic tender coconut water. A morning in the waves, tiger prawns at a seaside shack, and a couple of fenis, and you will come to discover why people come back to Goa year after year to rejuvenate, even as they complain about how crowded and dirty it's getting. A week in the company of Goans, with their mellow attitude toward life and their legendary warmth—despite the heavy toll that tourism takes on their home state—and you may find yourself, for better or for worse, more than a little intoxicated by the Goan way.

leafy garden, giving it an earthiness and warmth that's especially welcome in this overcrowded part of town. **Pros:** secluded setting; full ayurvedic treatments available. **Cons:** pricey compared to similar hotels in this range. $ *Rooms from: Rs. 22300* ⊠ *Porba-Vaddo, Calangute* ☎ *832/227–9063* ⊕ *www.pousada-tauma.com* 🛏 *13 suites* ⫤ *Breakfast.*

SPORTS AND THE OUTDOORS

Sea Waves Water Sports. Sea Waves has the standard gamut of water activities, from windsurfing and jet-skiing to banana boat rides, on offer but they also have winchboat parasailing, which allows you to soar high above the water. ⊠ *Opposite Tito's, Calangute* ☎ *98/2317–4669.*

Hop aboard a dolphin- or crocodile-spotting tour, which winds past thick mangroves along the Zuari and Mandovi rivers, or take a ride on a banana boat.

MAPUSA

15 km (9 miles) north of Panaji.

Friday is the big market day in Mapusa (pronounced *map*-sa)—the main town in the Bardez district. People from adjoining villages and some transplanted hippies convene to sell everything from vegetables to blue jeans to handicrafts. It's an ideal place to buy souvenirs. Mapusa is not a place you'd want to stay for the night, and there's really nothing much to see here, but like Margao in the south, the town is good for brief forays to shop and take care of other necessities. Except for the lively Friday market, the town is a bit dreary.

SINQUERIM BEACH

10 km (6 miles) northwest of Panaji.

You can rent Windsurfers and water skis at Sinquerim and Bogmalo, also in the Bardez district. Equipment rental is fairly cheap, but always check the condition of the equipment you use and make sure life jackets are provided. If possible, shop around at the other places on the beach for your best offer. Stretched out in front of the luxury Taj hotel, this small, sandy beach can get crowded with tourists and vendors.

GETTING HERE AND AROUND

Sinquerim is the first beach you'll get to as you head northwest after crossing the Mandovi River from Panaji.

EXPLORING

Fort Aguada. Perched high on a hill, with wonderful views west across the Arabian Sea and east across Aquada Bay to Panaji, Fort Aguada was built in 1612 and named for the natural springs that supplied not only the fort but also passing ships. Surrounded by wild grass, the fort is in excellent condition. Inside, you can take a good look at the solid stone architecture and the old lighthouse. The fort's defenses actually enclosed a much larger area than the bastion at the top of the hill; a seaward bastion still juts into the Arabian Sea on Sinquerim Beach, near the Taj cluster of hotels. If you only have time for one of Goa's many forts, hit Aguada—it's the best preserved and most magnificent. Hire a taxi if time is a constraint; it's not an easy walk, as it's 4 km (2½ miles) south of Sinquerim Beach and at least half the way is a fairly steep uphill. ⊠ *Sinquerim, Candolim* ⊘ *Weekdays 10–5.30.*

BEACHES

Sinquerim Beach. Close to Panaji, Sinquerim is a quiet, well-kept beach and, with some of Goa's most expensive resorts in the area—including the Vivanta by Taj–Fort Aguada and the Taj Holiday Village ⇨ *See Where to Stay listings*—it tends to be a destination for well-heeled local tourists and older international travelers. Having said that, pockets of vendors and tourists can gather around some of the more populist beachfront hotels. Visitors can try their hand at water sports such as windsurfing to snorkeling, and while the water isn't crystal clear, it is clean and makes for a lovely afternoon of paddling about; consistent waves make for good bodysurfing. **Amenities:** lifeguards; water sports. **Good for:** snorkeling; sunrise; swimming. ⊠ *Bardez.*

WHERE TO EAT AND STAY

$$
\begin{array}{l}
\text{\$\$} \\
\text{SEAFOOD}
\end{array}
$$

✕**Morisco.** Excellent Goan food and a view of Fort Aguada are the draw at this seafood restaurant. Choose the catch of the day, marinated in Goan spices and served alongside local music. [$] *Average main: Rs. 400* ⊠ *Fort Aguada Beach Resort, Sinquerim Beach, Bardez* ☎ *832/664–5858* ⊘ *No lunch. Closed Mon.*

$$$$
HOTEL

⌸**Aashyana Lakhanpal.** This handsome, and sprawling, property provides an excellent base from which to explore North Goa. **Pros:** airy bedrooms and lots of open space; wonderful swimming pool; great food and attentive service. **Cons:** the dense foliage attracts mosquitoes so make sure to carry repellent; the attentive service might be

Saris and bathing suits at Calangute Beach

overbearing to some, the minimum stay requirement might be a deterrent for some. ⑤ *Rooms from: Rs. 16000* ✉ *Escrivao Vaddo, Candolim* ☎ *832/248–9225* ⊕ *www.aashyanalakhanpal.com* ↩ *5 rooms, 3 cottages* ⑩ *No meals.*

$$$
B&B/INN

🏠 **Marbella Guest House.** This heritage guesthouse is on one of North Goa's narrowest lanes, behind the massive Taj resorts. **Pros:** great location; oozing with charm. **Cons:** no phones in room. ⑤ *Rooms from: Rs. 7500* ✉ *Between Sinquerim and Candolim beaches, Bardez district* ☎ *832/247–9551* ⊕ *www.marbellagoa.com* ↩ *3 rooms, 3 suites* ⑩ *Breakfast.*

$$$$
RESORT

🏠 **Vivanta by Taj–Holiday Village.** The guest rooms at this resort are housed in charming Goan village–style cottages and villas that face lush gardens or the broad expanse of Sinquerim Beach. **Pros:** spectacular setting; sophisticated yet friendly service. **Cons:** lots of kids can mean lots of noise. ⑤ *Rooms from: Rs. 11900* ✉ *Sinquerim, Bardez* ☎ *832/664–5858* ⊕ *www.tajhotels.com* ↩ *133 rooms, 9 villa suites* ⑩ *Breakfast.*

$$$$
RESORT
Fodor's Choice
★

🏠 **Vivanta by Taj–Fort Aguada.** Constructed within the boundary and adjoining the ramparts of an old Portuguese fort built in 1612, this hotel has gorgeous views of the fort, sea, and beach. **Pros:** stunning location; beautifully furnished rooms. **Cons:** may be too formal for some guests. ⑤ *Rooms from: Rs. 11400* ✉ *Sinquerim Beach, Bardez* ☎ *832/664–5858* ⊕ *www.tajhotels.com* ↩ *121 rooms, 24 suites, 38 cottages, 15 villas* ⑩ *Breakfast.*

SPORTS AND THE OUTDOORS

John's Boat Tours. Dolphin-watching, snorkeling at Grand Island, croc-odile-spotting in the river backwaters and sea fishing are all available from John's. There are also jeep tours to nearby spice plantations, Dudhsagar Falls, and Hampi ruins in the neighboring state of Karnataka. ⊠ *Candolim Beach* ☎ *98/2218–2814, 98/2215–6543* ⊕ *www.digitalgoa.com/johnsboattours* ☉ *Closed June–Sept.*

Thunderwave Water Sports. On Sinquerim Beach, Candolim, this operator has been offering winchboat parasailing for nearly 20 years. ⊠ *Near Taj Holiday Village, Arambol Beach* ☎ *832/249–9779, 98/2217–6985, 98/2217–6986.*

PANAJI AND NEARBY

Panaji (also called Panjim) was once the capital of the former Portuguese colony and is now the state's capital. A scenic little city, it sits along the banks of the Mandovi River, about 29 km (18 miles) north of Goa's Dabolin airport. Apart from its own considerable charms—including the colonial architecture in the city's Fontainhas and Sao Tomé neighborhoods—the small city is a good base to explore Goa's Portuguese past, visible in the grand and ornate churches of Old Goa.

PANAJI

600 km (372 miles) south of Mumbai.

Fodor's Choice Panaji has somewhat less of the poverty and hustle and bustle of India's
★ other state capitals, and its palm-lined plazas, elegant Portuguese colonial architecture, and other sights are easy to explore. There are historic homes and churches, restaurants serving flavorful Goan cuisine, and many unique galleries and boutiques. The best way to see the older parts of the city is on foot—in fact, if you leave without having explored the backstreets at leisure, you haven't really seen the best it has to offer. For die-hard sun-and-sand lovers, there's the city beach at Dona Paula, but Panaji isn't recommended for its beaches, as they tend to be dirty and crowded.

GETTING HERE AND AROUND

Expect to pay about Rs. 500 for the 40-minute taxi ride to reach Panaji from Dabolim airport. After that, it's an easy stroll to reach the city's main attractions, which are all in a central part of town. Banks and ATMs, Internet cafés, tour operators, and airline offices are all generally found along the city's main arteries, in particular 18th June Road and 31st January Road.

ESSENTIALS

Visitor Information A good first stop for all visitors to the state. Staff are on-hand and happy to assist with queries regarding accommodation, transport, and safety for foreign visitors. They also have a stand at Dabolim airport. ⊠ *Paryatan Bhavan, Patto, Panaji, 2nd fl.* ☎ *0832/249–4200, 0832/243–8866* ⊕ *www.goa-tourism.com.*

EXPLORING

Church of Our Lady of Immaculate Conception. This grand shrine was a mere chapel before 1541. Soon after, in 1600, it became a parish, and its structure was rebuilt entirely. Now the church almost entirely presides over one of Panaji's squares. The building's distinctive zigzag staircases are a 19th-century addition, and the church's large bell was originally in the Church of St. Augustine in Old Goa. An annual December festival here draws huge crowds. At the other times of the year the square is a peaceful place to linger. ✉ *Near Municipal Gardens* 🎫 *Free* 🕐 *Mon.– Sat. 9–6, Sun. 10–6.*

Dr. Salim Ali Bird Sanctuary. Just a short distance from Panaji, this delightful bird refuge is on the tip of Chorao, an island in the Mandovi. The ferry jetty for Chorao is on Ribander jetty on the southern bank of the Mandovi River, between Panaji and Old Goa, and boats travel regularly to the island and back. A taxi can bring you to the jetty for the 15-minute ride across the river. The Forest Department in Panaji organizes guided tours to Chorao. The tiny sanctuary, full of mangroves, is named after a dedicated Indian ornithologist. Although October through March is the best time to view migratory birds, the sanctuary is open year-round. ✉ *3 km (2 miles) northeast* ☎ *832/222–4747.*

Fontainhas. The shady, narrow streets of this largely residential neighborhood do not seem Indian—they are clearly still Portuguese at heart. From tiny *balcaos* (colonnaded porches), inhabitants watch as their quiet, unchanging world goes by, and through the old windows you can hear people practicing the piano and violin. At the heart of Fontainhas is the little whitewashed Chapel of St. Sebastian, which dates only to the late 19th century—new by Goan standards. Its claim to fame is an old crucifix that was once housed in the infamous Palace of the Inquisition in Old Goa. ✉ *Between Ourem Creek and Altinho.*

The Old Secretariat. This heritage building, with sloping tiled roofs, wooden verandas, and carved stone coats of arms, occupies a pleasant spot by the Mandovi River and has several important associations. The first building on this site was the palace of the Sultan of Bijapur, who ruled Goa at the time of the Portuguese invasion. The building that the Portuguese erected in its place served as temporary quarters for the viceroys of Goa upon their arrival or departure from the territory until it became their permanent residence in the mid-18th century, when Old Goa was abandoned as the capital. In the early 20th century the Secretariat became a government office. It's slated to become a museum in the future, now that the legislature has moved to Porvorim. ✉ *Mandovi riverfront.*

Sao Tomé. This crumbling old neighborhood contains the General Post Office, a former tobacco trading house, and a maze of extremely narrow streets behind it. The tiny bars of this district are full of old-world character, and indeed you might need that drink to help banish the more grisly images of Goa's past—the area opposite the post office was once the site of Panaji's town executions. ✉ *Between M.G. Rd. and Emidio Gracia Rd.*

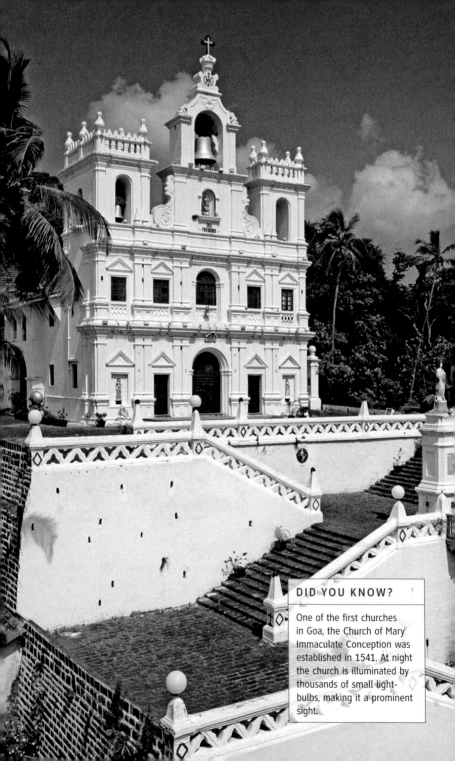

DID YOU KNOW?

One of the first churches in Goa, the Church of Mary Immaculate Conception was established in 1541. At night the church is illuminated by thousands of small light-bulbs, making it a prominent sight.

WHERE TO EAT

$$$$
ECLECTIC
✕**AZ.U.R.** The Goa Marriott's café and lounge, pronounced "As You Are," may be worth a visit for the bay views alone—fortunately, the quality of its limited yet choice menu won't disappoint, either. Western classics like croque monsieur or a BLT are great for either lunchtime or a late afternoon snack. There are also bar-food options such as calamari fritters and potato skins, as well as a selection of teas and coffees. After dark, the coffee shop morphs into a relaxed evening lounge bar. ⑤ *Average main: Rs. 1200* ✉ *Goa Marriott, Miramar* ☎ *832/246–3333.*

$$$$
BARBECUE
✕**Ernesto's Bistro.** Brothers Ernesto and Vasquito Alvares are at the helm of this Goan barbeque and bistro in the old town, in the protected heritage zone of the Latin Quarter. The menu is dominated by meaty fare, and you'll be in the company of locals and tourists alike, who come for the excellent barbecued ribs and burgers, as well as for Asian-inflected seafood. Wonderful desserts include their specialty, serradura—the name means "sawdust," but don't be deterred; the novel creation blends crushed cookies and sweetened cream. Inclement weather you can eat outdoors in the courtyard, and they are closed from July until the end of the monsoon. ⑤ *Average main: Rs. 1000* ✉ *6/49 Nanu Tarkar Pednekar Rd., below Maruti Temple, Fontainhas* ☎ *98/2301–5921.*

$$$
INDIAN
Fodor'sChoice
★
✕**Mum's Kitchen.** Smack-dab in the middle of Panjim, Mum's Kitchen, a Goan institution, is indisputably the best place in town for home-style Goan food. The menu's vast and enticing, so either visit as part of a large group, or when absolutely ravenous. Most of the regulars are locals, so the kitchen doesn't hold back on the spice. Try the *rawa* (semolina) fried Bombay duck and the spicy prawn *recheado* (a Portuguese-inspired masala). The milder sausage curry, served with fresh *poi* (the Goan bread that's similar to a ciabatta), is a real treat. Go prepared to wait for a table, although service is brisk so the wait shouldn't be too long. ⑤ *Average main: Rs. 600* ✉ *854 Martins Bldg., D.B. St., Panaji–Miramar Rd.* ☎ *098/2217–5559, 91/90110–95557* ⊕ *www.mumskitchengoa.com.*

$$
ECLECTIC
✕**Panjim Inn.** The veranda, up a flight of stairs at the historic Panjim Inn, is an atmospheric location for those seeking tasty Goan and continental fare, casual dining, and fair prices. The menu includes local favorites such as spicy Goan prawn curry served with rice, but also be sure to check the daily specials, particularly for seasonal seafood items. It's open from 7 am to 10 pm. ⑤ *Average main: Rs. 500* ✉ *E-212 31st January Rd., Fontainhas* ☎ *832/222–1122, 832/222–6523, 832/243–5628* ⊕ *www.panjiminn.com.*

$$
INDIAN
✕**Rio Rico.** The formal staff of this somewhat somber restaurant at the Hotel Mandovi serve tasty Goan specialties that include *rawa* (semolina) -fried fish and prawns and Portuguese-influenced seafood *caldeirada* (poached fish layered with potatoes and tomatoes and cooked with white wine). ⑤ *Average main: Rs. 300* ✉ *The Mandovi Hotel, D.B. Marg* ☎ *832/222–4405 to 09* ⊕ *www.hotelmandovigoa.com.*

$$$
INDIAN
✕**Ritz Classic.** You're likely to be the only foreigner in this family favorite—that is if you can find it. The restaurant may be drab and hidden away on the second floor of an anonymous block on the commercial 18th June Road, but it's certainly worth looking for. Goan specialties,

including grilled kingfish, pomfret *recheiado* (marinated in a blend of spices, then grilled), and chicken *xacuti* (coconut and tamarind curry), are prepared wonderfully and without any concession to international tolerance levels for spice. With lines going out the door, especially at lunch, service is quick and sometimes rushed amid the din. $ *Average main: Rs. 500* ⊠ *Wagle Vision Bldg., 18th June Rd., 2nd fl.* ☎ 832/242–6417, 832/664–4796, 832/222–1138.

$$$

NORTH INDIAN

✕**Sher-e-Punjab.** Locals and foreigners hungry for North Indian food seek this diner out for lunch, dinner, or a quick snack while taking a break from the intense shopping of 18th June Road. With an enticing selection of kebabs, tandoori items, and favorites like butter chicken, this is the place for a satisfying meal in a no-frills setting. House specialties include the Peshawari chicken and the mutton dry fry. $ *Average main: Rs. 500* ⊠ *18th June Rd., in front of Bombay Bazaar* ☎ 832/222–7204 ⊕ *www.hotelaromagoa.com.*

$

INDIAN

✕**Viva Panjim.** A walk down a narrow alley in the Fontainhas district brings you to one of the city's best-value restaurants. Featuring the award-winning cuisine of chef Linda De Souza, this cheery hideaway is crowded with locals and tourists. The maître d' is happy to make recommendations to anyone unfamiliar with Goan specialties such as kingfish vindaloo, and chicken *cafreal* (marinated and cooked with fresh cilantro, also known as coriander; green chillies, and ginger). Indoor seating can get cramped (there are just a handful of tables there), but tables are also available outside. Reliable Goan classics, conviviality, and bargain prices are the rule, and the prawn curry is possibly the best in the state. $ *Average main: Rs. 300* ⊠ *H. No. 178 31st January Rd., behind Mary Immaculate High School, Fontainhas* ☎ 832/242–2405, 98/5047–1363 ⊗ *No lunch.*

WHERE TO STAY

$$$

RESORT

🏨 **Goa Marriott Resort.** Walk into the lovely sea-facing lobby, where you can watch and listen to the crash of waves along the rocky shores, and you will find it hard to leave. **Pros:** courteous staff; beautiful location. **Cons:** city beach isn't the best; a bit pricey. $ *Rooms from: Rs. 9350* ⊠ *Miramar Beach Rd.* ☎ 832/246–3333 ⊕ *www.marriott.com* ⇆ *175 rooms, 5 suites* ◯❘ *Breakfast.*

$$

HOTEL

🏨 **Hotel Fidalgo.** At the corner of a crowded intersection on the bustling 18th June Road, this business hotel offers all the amenities you'd expect at relatively reasonable prices, and with the convenience of being in the center of town. **Pros:** good value for money. **Cons:** noisy commercial part of town; drab hallway carpets; pool faces a shabby building. $ *Rooms from: Rs. 4500* ⊠ *18th June Rd.* ☎ 832/222–6291 to 99 ⊕ *www.hotelfidalgo-goa.com* ⇆ *101 rooms, 7 suites* ◯❘ *Breakfast.*

$

B&B/INN

🏨 **Panjim Inn.** Travelers who appreciate a sense of place love the warmth of the Panjim Inn, a unique hotel in the center of historic Fontainhas that was built in the late 1800s and incorporates the former family home of the owner, Ajit Sukhija. **Pros:** great location in the center of the historic district; friendly staff; relaxed atmosphere. **Cons:** traffic noise; no phones in rooms. $ *Rooms from: Rs. 3693* ⊠ *E-212, 31st January Rd., Fontainhas* ☎ 832/222–6523, 98/2357–2035, 832/222–1122, 832/243–5628 ⊕ *www.panjiminn.com* ⇆ *24 rooms* ◯❘ *Breakfast.*

Along the streets of Panaji, Goa's capital

$$$ 🛏**Panjim People's.** Four-poster beds, carved rosewood dressers, and
HOTEL plenty of windows grace each of the four spacious rooms in this historic annex of the Panjim Inn (it's also home to the Gitanjali art gallery, on the ground floor). **Pros:** spacious rooms; old-world charm.
Cons: some windows overlook a dumpster below; no elevator, no room
phones. ⑤ *Rooms from: Rs. 9000* ✉ *E-212, 31 January Rd., Fontainhas*
☎ *832/222–6523, 832/243–5628, 832/222–1122, 98/2357–2035*
⊕ *www.panjiminn.com/panjim-peoples.html* ⤴ *4 rooms* ☉ *Breakfast.*

$ 🛏**Pousada Panjim.** On a quiet street across from the Panjim Inn is a
B&B/INN stylish property furnished with elegant antique cupboards and teak and
rosewood four-poster beds. **Pros:** quiet refuge in a noisy city; memorable, one-of-a-kind setting; exceptional value. **Cons:** no restaurant on
premises (there is one across the street though). ⑤ *Rooms from: Rs.*
2700 ✉ *E-212, 31 January Rd., Fontainhas* ☎ *832/222–6523, 832/243–*
5628, 832/222–1122, 98/2357–2035 ⊕ *www.panjiminn.com/panjim-*
pousada.html ⤴ *9 rooms* ☉ *Breakfast.*

$$$$ 🛏**Vivanta by Taj–Panaji.** This three-year-old Taj property is more busi-
HOTEL ness-oriented than other members of the group, with the added oomph
of high-tech features such as surround-sound home theater systems,
multimedia panels, and LCD screens in all rooms. **Pros:** top-notch
facilities. **Cons:** better suited to business travelers; no nearby beach
access. ⑤ *Rooms from: Rs. 11700* ✉ *D.B. Bandodkar Rd., St. Inez*
Junction ☎ *832/663–3687* ⊕ *www.tajhotels.com* ⤴ *158 rooms, 12*
suites ☉ *Breakfast.*

SPORTS AND THE OUTDOORS

Dive Goa. This operation offers diving instruction from a location near Panaji. Be warned that Goa's waters aren't particularly clear, so you're unlikely to see much marine life. ⊠ *Arambol Beach* ☎ *0091/9325030110* ⊕ *www.divegoa.com.*

BOAT CRUISES

Casino Carnival. Gambling, food, and drink can be enjoyed every night from 5 pm until 6 am aboard the Casino Carnival, a floating luxury casino that also has a TV/game room for those under 18, a toddlers' room with babysitters, and an open-air swimming pool. The dress code is smart-casual, which in India means no shorts, bikinis, or swimming trunks are allowed outside the pool area. ⊠ *Casino Carnival Front Desk, Goa Marriott Resort and Spa, Panjim* ☎ *0091/888885314 to 47* ⊕ *www.casinocarnival.in.*

Department of Tourism. In addition to several private operators, the Department of Tourism organizes river cruises, some with a Goan cultural show, music, and dinner. Most cruises depart from the Panaji jetty on the River Mandovi. ☎ *832/243–8750* ⊕ *www.goa-tourism.com.*

SHOPPING

Stores are open 10 am to 7 pm, and 18th June Road (named after an anti-colonial protest launched by a socialist leader in 1946) is the city's busiest shopping thoroughfare. It's worth a stroll if you are in the market for dried fruits, curry pastes, and powders, or for some examples of Goa's foot-thumping and lively Konkan folk music.

Barefoot. Trendy handcrafted and natural housewares, home furnishings, silk, cotton men's and women's clothing, and jewelry from different parts of the country are sold here. Their ceramic tea sets alone are worth a look. ⊠ *H. No. 1/26, 31st January Rd.* ☎ *832/243–6815* ☉ *Mon.–Sat. 10–8.*

Bombay Bazaar. Bombay Bazaar, a department store with a twist, is a gathering of dozens of vendors, each competing for business in the confines of a jam-packed two-story building. Wares include Indian- and Western-style clothing, saris and handicrafts, plus basic needs such as suitcases, shoes, and watches. Everything is well priced. ⊠ *18th June Rd.* ☎ *832/222–1985.*

Sinari's. This is the place to buy Indian music of all sorts, including Goan trance, devotional Hindi, Indian pop, and rap. It's in the shopping arcade next to Bombay Bazaar. ⊠ *Padmavati Towers, 18th June Rd.* ☎ *832/222–4842.*

Sosa's. Come here for high-end Indian designers, including Goan favorite Savio Jon. Expect bright colors, easy silhouettes, cotton and silk and all manner of resort wear. ⊠ *E-245 Rua de Ourem* ☎ *832/222–8063, 98/2338–1488* ☉ *Closed Sun.*

IT'S A STAKEOUT

Goan taxi drivers stake out tourists by waiting outside hotels and restaurants. As soon as you walk out the door, three or four of them are at your side asking you if you want a cab, and where you are going. They find it hard to believe you'd want to walk when you can afford to pay for a ride.

Take Home the Taste of Goa

If you haven't found your share of slippers, sarongs, bags and bangles at Anjuna or the shack-shops near the main beaches, pay a visit to a local grocery. Look carefully, and you'll find some great stuff to take home as a reminder of your stay in Goa or to give away as unusual epicurean gifts. There's high-quality *bebinca* (a rich, layered, dense 16-layer cake made of butter, sugar, egg yolk, and coconut) that has a long shelf life, making for easy packing; *feni* (Goan liquor) in fancy bottles (though it smells the same as the stuff in the downmarket bottles), which you'd be well advised to transport only in your carry-on baggage; *prawn balchao* (in a red chilli sauce) and *mackerel reicheado* (pickled prawns and mackerel soaked in red masala, which have to be fried once you get home); a variety of dried and wet *masalas* (spice mixes) from *cafreal* (green masala) and *vindaloo* (hot red masala) to *xacuti* (a masala with coconut and ground spices), and packets of *tendlim* (a pickled gourd). Chances are the storeowner will wrap it for you with a grin to acknowledge that you know a bit about Goa after all.

UK Dry Fruits. This store has an excellent selection of cashew nuts—Goa is famous for its cashew crop. There are exotic varieties such as Pudina Lime, Hot Masala, and Szechuan—sample a couple before buying. You will also find a great selection of Goan curry pastes, powders, and spice mixtures. ⊠ *18th June Rd.* ☎ *832/243–5455* ⊕ *www.ukdryfruits.com.*

Velha Goa Galleria. This is the store for *azulejos,* a traditional Portuguese style of hand-painted tiles and ceramics. In addition to a selection of tiles, frames, and other ceramics, they have the rights to sell the reproduced ceramic artwork of Goa's own celebrated cartoonist Mario Miranda. Fantastic for souvenirs and gifts. ⊠ *4/191 Rua de Ourem* ☎ *832/242–6628* ⊕ *www.velhagoa.com* ☉ *Closed Sun.*

OLD GOA

10 km (6 miles) east of Panaji.

Fodor'sChoice ★ Gorgeous Old Goa, with foliage creeping in around the ruins of old churches, served as the capital of the Portuguese colony until repeated outbreaks of cholera forced the government to move to Panaji in 1843. The shift out of Old Goa, however, had begun as early as 1695. It was a slow desertion—first the viceroy, then the nobility, then the customs. By the time the official declaration came, it was already a deserted, ruined city. There are several imposing and beautiful churches, convents, and monasteries that reveal its former glory. Most were begun at a time when European architectural styles were shifting toward the baroque. For anyone with an interest in religious architecture or Catholic history, Old Goa is a must-see destination, and merits a couple of hours of exploration.

GETTING HERE AND AROUND

Hop into a taxi or auto-rickshaw in Panaji to reach Old Goa. The 20-minute ride will cost Rs. 250 by taxi or Rs. 150 by auto-rickshaw. It's a small area, and you can walk easily from one sight to another. It's worth hiring an English-speaking guide for a one-hour walking tour—they tend to find you around the entrance of the Basilica of Bom Jesus.

EXPLORING

Archaeological Museum. A part of the Franciscan monastery behind the Church of St. Francis of Assisi, the Archaeological Museum has an intricately gilded and carved interior. The museum's collection is not entirely devoted to Catholic objets d'art; it also has bits and pieces from Goa's early Hindu history. It's worth a quick look around, if only to peruse the portrait gallery of Goa's viceroys. ⊠ *Across road from Basilica of Bom Jesus* ☎ *832/228–6133* ✉ *Rs. 5* ⊗ *Sat.–Thurs. 10–5.*

Basilica of Bom Jesus. Dedicated to the worship of the infant Jesus, the Basilica of Bom Jesus is also known throughout the Christian world as the tomb of St. Francis Xavier, patron saint of Goa, who was handed the task of spreading Christianity in the Portuguese colony. The saint's body has "survived" almost 500 years now without ever having been embalmed, and lies in a silver casket well out of reach of visitors. Built from local red stone around the turn of the 17th century, the tomb took the Florentine sculptor Giovanni Batista Foggini 10 years to complete. Once every 10 years the missionary's body is exposed to the public at close quarters, drawing thousands of pilgrims. ▣ *Free* ☾ *Mon.–Sat. 9–6:30, Sun. 10–6:30.*

Museum of Christian Art. Inside the Convent of St. Monica, the Museum of Christian Art has a number of objects of Christian interest, including paintings and religious silverware, some dating back to the 16th century. The convent was the first nunnery of its kind in the East, and functioned as one until the late 19th century. ✉ *Holy Mount Hill* ⊕ *www.museumofchristianart.com* ▣ *Rs 20* ☾ *Tues.–Sun. 9:30 am–5:30 pm.*

Sé (St. Catherine's) Cathedral. The imposing white Sé (St. Catherine's) Cathedral—the largest church in Old Goa—was built between 1562 and 1652 by order of the King of Portugal. Fine carvings depict scenes from the life of Christ and the Blessed Virgin over the main altar, which commemorates St. Catherine of Alexandria. Several splendidly decorated chapels are dedicated to St. Joseph, St. George, St. Anthony, St. Bernard, and the Holy Cross. Only one of the cathedral's two original majestic towers remains; the other collapsed in 1776. ✉ *Across road from Basilica of Bom Jesus* ▣ *Free* ☾ *Mon.–Sat. 9–6:30, Sun. 10–6:30.*

DUDHSAGAR FALLS

50 km (31 miles) southeast of Panaji.

These imposing waterfalls make a good day trip from Panaji or Calangute.

EXPLORING

Dudhsagar Waterfalls. With a name that means "sea of milk," these waterfalls are imposing, with water cascading almost 2,000 feet into a rock-ribbed valley. They are at their most impressive when the monsoons arrive, but this also makes the approach road inaccessible, so the ideal time for a trek here is between October and the end of April. Pack refreshments and beach towels, and plan to spend a morning here; monkeys, birds, bees, butterflies, and thick foliage complete the wild experience. The Goa Tourism Development Corporation runs tours from Panaji and Calangute (9 am–6 pm; around Rs. 700) in a nonair-conditioned bus, which include the falls and the nearby Tambdi Surla Hindu temple, built in the 13th century. You could also take a train to Dudhsagar from Margao and get there in an hour and a half. ✉ *Sanguem District.*

PONDA

29 km (18 miles) southeast of Panaji; 45 km (28 miles) from Dabolim Airport.

Ponda itself is an uninteresting town, but a number of the temples in the hills that surround it shouldn't be missed. The area came under Portuguese control relatively late, in 1764, about 250 years after the Portuguese conquered Goa—which explains why the temples were not destroyed.

Sé (St. Catherine's) Cathedral in Old Goa, the largest church in Asia

EXPLORING

Manguesh Temple. One of the chief attractions of Ponda is this temple in Priol, 7 km (4 miles) before you reach Ponda. With its domes and other eccentric, un-Hindu architectural features, the temple has evidence of Islamic and Christian influences. Other temples in the vicinity include the always-crowded Shantadurga temple, with its distinctive tower, the Mahalsa temple, with its gargantuan (41-foot-high) oil lamp, and the Lakshmi Narasimha and Naguesh temples, with their lovely temple tanks (large pools with steps leading into them, so that the faithful can bathe).

SOUTH GOA

Margao, about 7 km (4 miles) inland from the coast, is the main town in South Goa. There's a bustling market, and it's worth exploring for its shopping areas, but only if you happen to be passing through; there's no reason to stay here. If you want to check out the sights, make Colva or Benaulim your base, and get the benefit of the beach and the nightlife after your day out. Excursions include the villages of Loutolim and Chandor, which have beautiful ancestral homes, some of which date from the early 1600s. The beaches of the south are more

DRESS CODE REVISION

Almost anything goes at Western-style resorts, and bikinis are fine to wear on the beach. Throw on a cover-up if wandering around the streets or going in to a restaurant, although swimsuits are completely acceptable at the beach shacks.

relaxing than those of the north; people here are less prone to partying, although there is more shack life in the south now than there used to be. Some of the state's most luxurious and expensive resorts are in this area.

BOGMALO BEACH

24 km (15 miles) north of Margao; 25 km (16 miles) south of Panaji.

This tiny crescent of fine sand is perfect for swimming and sunning. It's near a low, verdant hill topped by a few modern buildings on one side and the Bogmallo Beach Resort on the other. Two tiny islands sit about 10 km (6 miles) out to sea. For the most privacy, walk down the beach to the far right—there are fewer fishing boats, shacks, and people. Another of Bogmalo's assets is its boating and water-sports facilities for diving and jet-skiing. For a lunch break, try the **Seagull,** a simple, thatched-roof shack on the beach—they serve some of the best prawn-curry rice in Goa. The airport is just a 4-km (2½-mile) ride away.

WHERE TO STAY

$$$
RESORT
🏨 **Bogmallo Beach Resort.** This six-story high-rise hotel seems to have ignored all the rules about being close to the beach. **Pros:** close to the airport. **Cons:** not much character. ⑤ *Rooms from: Rs. 9900* ☎ *832/253–8222 to 235* ⊕ *www.bogmallobeachresort.com* 🛏 *126 rooms, 15 cottages* ⑩ *Breakfast.*

$$
RESORT
🏨 **Coconut Creek.** On a dense coconut plantation, a two-minute walk (about 500 yards) **Pros:** private jungle setting; one of the nicest mid-range resorts in South Goa. **Cons:** only half the rooms have a/c, the rest have fans and are likely to be uncomfortable in summer. ⑤ *Rooms from: Rs. 4200* ☎ *832/253–8100* ⊕ *www.coconutcreekgoa.com* 🛏 *20 rooms* ⑩ *Breakfast.*

SPORTS AND THE OUTDOORS

Goa Diving. Scotsman Willie Downey offers casual diving as well as PADI open-water courses. ☎ *832/255–5117, 98/2210–0380* ⊕ *www. goadiving.com.*

CANSAULIM BEACH

10 km (6 miles) northwest of Margao.

This quiet, clean stretch of beach between Bogmallo and Colva has a fine location—it's conveniently close to both Dabolim Airport and Margao, and yet a good distance from the crowded north and the congested beaches around Colva. The only significant signs of life in these parts are the hotels and resorts in the vicinity, and a couple of sleepy villages.

WHERE TO EAT AND STAY

$$$$
ECLECTIC
✕ **The Village Plaza.** The Hyatt's food "village" adjacent to the expansive lobby has a number of interconnected restaurants: Da Luigi serves wood-fired pizzas and pasta; Casa Sarita has Goan specialties; Masala offers North and South Indian cuisine; and Café is a coffee shop that's open 24 hours. ⑤ *Average main: Rs. 3000* ✉ *Park Hyatt Goa Resort and Spa, Arossim Beach, Cansaulim* ☎ *832/272–1234.*

$$$$ 　⚅ **Park Hyatt Goa Resort and Spa.** In the very top bracket of the Goa
RESORT　resorts, the modern and sleek Hyatt has spacious rooms with unusual
Fodor'sChoice　pebble-floor and glass-wall bathrooms. **Pros:** ultraluxurious; impeccable
★　service; top notch spa and restaurants. **Cons:** very spread out; very
expensive. $ *Rooms from: Rs. 12000* ⊠ *Arossim Beach, Cansaulim*
☎ *832/272–1234* ⊕ *www.goa.park.hyatt.com* ⤳ *237 rooms, 12 suites*
○ *Breakfast.*

MAJORDA AND UTORDA

10 km (6 miles) from Margao.

Majorda and nearby Utorda, which both have a number of resorts, are
rapidly sacrificing peace and quiet to larger volumes of tourists. Just
north of Colva Beach, they are within cycling distance from Colva (5 km
[3 miles]) and Betalbatim (3 km [2 miles]), both known for restaurants
and shack life. If you stay here, you'll have yourself a good base from
which to explore the sights around Margao.

WHERE TO EAT AND STAY

$$ ✕ **Martin's Corner.** This famous family-run restaurant in a village near
INDIAN　Majorda grew out of a small shop that was set up with four tables about
20 years ago. With its lamps and cane bar, it still feels like a shack. Its
prices, however, are well above the average shack's, and with good rea-
son—Goan seafood dishes like the masala fried king crab are prepared
with great care by the acclaimed Mrs. Carafina, who runs the place with
her three sons. Pleasant retro music and the aromas of Goan cooking
fill the air at lunch and dinnertime. Try the sausage pulao, a delicious,
salty rice dish that's cooked with the fat of spicy Goan chouriço sau-
sages. $ *Average main: Rs. 500* ⊠ *Bin Waddo, Betalbatim, Salcette*
☎ *832/288–0061* ⊕ *www.martinscornergoa.com.*

$$$ ⚅ **Alila Diwa Goa.** Overlooking verdant rice plantations and the Arabian
RESORT　Sea, the Alila Goa is a cool open oasis of dark pitched roofs, breezy
verandas, and serene courtyards. **Pros:** free Wi-Fi; great service; gorgeous rooms. **Cons:** no direct beach access (it's about five minutes by
car or the hotel shuttle). $ *Rooms from: Rs. 9945* ⊠ *48/10 Adao Vado
Majorda, Salcette* ☎ *832/274–6800* ⊕ *www.aliladiwagoa.com* ⤳ *153
rooms, 18 suites* ○ *Breakfast.*

$$$$ ⚅ **The Kenilworth Beach Resort.** Lacking the frantic-to-please service typi-
RESORT　cal of some other hotels in Goa—the staff here is experienced and
calm—this large resort has a marble lobby with lots of quiet corners
for relaxing. **Pros:** all rooms have private balconies. **Cons:** sprawling
and crowded at times. $ *Rooms from: Rs. 11000* ⊠ *Utorda, Salcete*
☎ *832/669–8888* ⊕ *www.kenilworthhotels.com* ⤳ *101 rooms, 3 suites*
○ *Breakfast.*

$$$ ⚅ **Majorda Beach Resort.** An old favorite with tourists from Mumbai and
RESORT　Gujarat, this resort has an Ayurvedic ashram and spacious rooms. **Pros:**
good beach access; quiet surrounding areas. **Cons:** dark lobby; slightly
run-down; slow Wi-Fi. $ *Rooms from: Rs. 8000* ⊠ *Salcete* ☎ *832/288–
1111 to 1113* ⊕ *www.majordabeachresort.com* ⤳ *110 rooms, 10 cot-
tages* ○ *Breakfast.*

$$$
B&B/INN
Fodor's Choice
★

🏠 **Vivenda Dos Palhacos.** This 100-year-old restored Portuguese home—with a lovely front porch—has lots of pizzazz thanks to owners Simon and Charlotte Hayward. **Pros:** personalized, friendly service; rooms with character; free Wi-Fi. **Cons:** no TV or phones in rooms. ⑤ *Rooms from: Rs. 6000 ⊠ Costa Vaddo, Majorda, Salcette* ☎ *832/322–1119* ⊕ *www.vivendagoa.com* ↪ *6 rooms, 1 tent (seasonal)* ⑩ *Breakfast.*

COLVA

7 km (4 miles) west of Margao.

Colva Beach is the most congested beach in South Goa. Its large parking and entrance areas are crowded with shacks selling snacks and souvenirs and young men offering mopeds for rent. The first 1,000 feet of the beach are hectic—stuffed with vendors, cows, and fishing boats—but the sand, backed by palm groves, stretches in both directions, and promises plenty of quieter spots. The water is good for swimming and the restaurants and bar shacks are plentiful.

WHERE TO STAY

$$$
HOTEL

🏠 **Longuinhos Beach Resort.** This old Colva favorite is right on the beach, about a kilometer from the crowded village. **Pros:** great beach access; one of the best mid-range resorts in Colva. **Cons:** a bit run-down. ⑤ *Rooms from: Rs. 6000 ⊠ Salcete* ☎ *832/278–8068 to 69* ⊕ *www.longuinhosgoa.com/* ↪ *51 rooms, 2 suites* ⑩ *Breakfast.*

SPORTS AND THE OUTDOORS

Chris Water Sports. This company organizes parasailing and jet skiing off the shores of Colva beach. The more timid can go for a ride on a banana boat. ⊠ *Arambol Beach* ☎ *98/2214–2110.*

LOUTOLIM

10 km (6 miles) northeast of Margao.

Fodor's Choice
★

Loutolim is among Goa's prettiest villages, with lush paddy fields and tranquil village roads that lie under a canopy of forest trees. This is also a lovely area to view some fine examples of Goan-Portuguese architecture. There's not much by way of accommodations except for the charming Casa Susegad. If you are able to get a room, make Loutolim a stopover to experience nontouristy Goa and visit nearby spice plantations, the Brangaza house in Chandor, or the Miranda House—a well-preserved Goan country house. Lunch at one of Goa's most delightful restaurants, Fernando's Nostalgia, in the courtyard of the chef's house on the Ponda-Margao road, is a must if you venture this side.

WHERE TO EAT AND STAY

$$$
INDIAN
Fodor's Choice
★

✕ **Fernando's Nostalgia.** In the tranquil, slow-paced old village of Raia you'll find one of the best restaurants in the state. If you sit at certain tables you can catch glimpses of household life in the late chef Fernando's country house. Now run by his wife, the restaurant serves classic Goan and Portuguese-Goan dishes, such as salted ox tongue, *fofos* (fish cutlets mixed with mashed potatoes and spices, rolled in breadcrumbs and egg, and shallow-fried), *sopa de bretalha* (spinach soup), and prawn

7

almondegas (prawn cutlets), which are rarely found in restaurants; that probably explains why Nostalgia is where many Goans go. The restaurant comes to life in the evening, when the alcohol begins to flow and the band starts to play (Thursday through Sunday). ⑤ *Average main: Rs. 600* ✉ *608 Uzro, Raia, Salcete* ☎ *832/277–7098, 832/277–7054, 98/2210–3467* ⊕ *fernandosnostalgia.wordpress.com.*

$$$
B&B/INN

🏠 **Casa Susegad.** Loutolim's laid-back charm is captured in Norman and Carol Steele's warm and inviting country inn. **Pros:** very relaxing; lovely food; personalized service; yoga lessons available in season. **Cons:** 30-minute ride to the beach; there might be too many pets here for some. ⑤ *Rooms from: Rs. 6000* ✉ *Orgao Loutolim, Salcete* ☎ *832/648–3368, 098/2210–6341* ⊕ *www.casasusegad.com* ⇨ *5 rooms* ⦿ *All meals.*

CHANDOR

15 km (9 miles) east of Margao.

This small, sleepy village occupies the site of Chandrapur, ancient capital of the region from AD 375 to 1053.

Braganza House. The chief reason to visit Chandor is this 400-year-old house—a slice of living history. Two wings are occupied by two branches of the Braganza family, the Menezes Braganzas and the Braganza Pereiras. You can see the style in which the wealthy landed gentry must have lived until the land reformation that followed Independence in 1947; the great rooms are filled with treasures, including beautiful period furniture and Chinese porcelain. Although some parts of the house have been renovated and are in reasonably good shape, it takes a lot of effort to maintain the two wings, and contributions toward upkeep are expected. ☎ *832/278–4201, 832/278–4227* ✉ *Donations welcome* ⊙ *Usually 9–5, but call ahead for appointment.*

BENAULIM

9 km (6 miles) southwest of Margao.

Just 2 km (1 mile) south of Colva is the first of the beautiful, secluded beaches of South Goa—a far cry from the action-packed beaches of the north. Head to Benaulim and farther south only if you want to get away from it all. All this isolation comes at a price: the resorts are more expensive here.

GETTING HERE AND AROUND

Benaulim village has a small supermarket and is centered on a crossroads called Maria Hall. The beach is less than a kilometer from the village. There are some vendors, food shacks, and locals, but none of the crowds you'd find up north.

BEACHES

Benaulim beach. Despite its proximity to crowded Colva, Benaulim beach is a world apart. Still relatively quiet, an increasingly rare commodity on Goa's beaches, this long swathe of sand features only the odd souvenir hawker or stray dog, and is an excellent spot on which to park your beach towel. Of course there are beach shacks, if you'd prefer a steady supply of beer and snacks as well as the comfort of a sunbed, and while

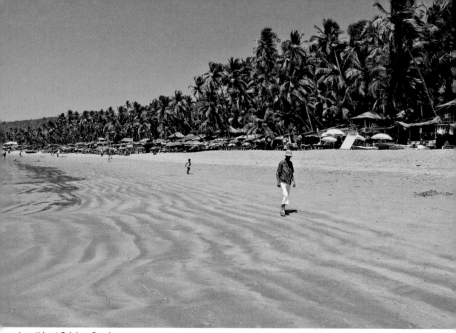

Low tide at Palolem Beach

it isn't as idyllic as Morjim or Mandrem further north, with still water and soft sand, Benaulim is a great pick for a day in the sun. **Amenities:** food and drink; lifeguards; water sports. **Best for:** solitude; swimming; walking. ⊠ *Benaulim beach.*

WHERE TO EAT AND STAY

\$\$\$\$
INDIAN
Fodor's Choice
★

✕ **Allegria.** This Goan restaurant in the Taj is reminiscent of an old-fashioned landlord's drawing room, with sepia photographs on the walls and carved wooden furniture. The variety of menu items makes an excellent introduction to local cuisine. Try the *kullanche mass kottnim* (crabmeat with onions, coriander, and garlic), and *sannas* (sweet, delicately flavored, steamed rice cakes) with an assortment of curries, such as classic pork vindaloo, pork *sorpotel* (curry simmered with Goan vinegar), and boneless chicken xacuti. If you want to be adventurous with dessert, try the *adsorachem merend,* a feni-infused coconut mousse with saffron sauce. Live singing accompanied by guitar and mandolin adds to the scene. ⓢ *Average main: Rs. 3000* ⊠ *Taj Exotica* ☎ *832/668–3333* ◿ *Reservations essential.*

\$\$
SEAFOOD

✕ **Joecons.** The highlight of this open-air restaurant, a short walk from the Taj Exotica and less than a kilometer from the village, is the well-prepared fresh seafood specialties, including exceptional grilled garlic prawns. The best part may be that you can custom order their fresh seafood with the spice and style of your choice. ⓢ *Average main: Rs. 500* ⊠ *Near Taj Exotica* ☎ *832/277–0099.*

\$\$\$\$
RESORT

⛺ **Taj Exotica.** Beside tranquil Benaulim Beach you'll find one of the most attractive places to stay in south Goa. **Pros:** great restaurants; gorgeous setting. **Cons:** very spread out; very expensive. ⓢ *Rooms from: Rs.*

14000 ✉ Calwaddo, Salcette ☎ 832/668–3333 ⊕ www.tajhotels.com ⤴ 140 rooms, 4 suites ⦿ Breakfast.

VARCA

14 km (8.7 miles) southwest of Margao.

The scenery at Varca is rural: there are deep fields on either side of the road, and you may get the distinct feeling that you're heading nowhere in particular. This is an illusion. There are a number of resorts close to Varca village that take advantage of its perfect, unspoiled stretch of beach. Stay at Varca for the beach and for the opportunity to take long walks through the green Goan countryside.

BEACHES

Varca beach. Another of the south's treasures, and only a short distance from Benaulim beach is Varca, a clean, quiet beach that manages the seemingly impossible feat of being nearly entirely hawker-free. Visitors from the area's resorts are treated to a quiet, palm-lined strip of beach that's perfect for unwinding with a good book. Beach shacks are thin on the ground in season, and nonexistent in the off-season, so plan to pack a picnic basket if you're headed there in the leaner months. **Amenities:** none. **Best for:** solitude; sunset; swimming; walking. ✉ *Varca Beach.*

WHERE TO EAT AND STAY

$$ ✕ **Carnaval.** Low-hung black lamps light a woven bamboo ceiling, and ECLECTIC Mario Miranda cartoons enliven the walls at this restaurant with excellent fusion food. Try the jerk potatoes *peri peri* (with hot chilli peppers), the tandoor-grilled tiger prawns with lemon mustard sauce, and the naan with pesto. After all this the dessert, such as crepes filled with *gajar ka halwa* (a sweet made from carrots), seems almost ordinary. ⑤ *Average main: Rs. 800* ✉ *Ramada Caravela, Varca Beach* ☎ *832/669–5000* ⊙ *No lunch.*

$$$ ⌷ **Ramada Caravela.** A casino, a fusion Indian-Mediterranean restau-
RESORT rant, and a Polynesian eatery on the beach add to the mix of this cheery beachfront resort, which is spread-out over 23 acres. **Pros:** refurbished rooms are a plus; very attentive and eager-to-please staff. **Cons:** public spaces could use a sprucing up; not ideally situated for those looking to go out. ⑤ *Rooms from: Rs. 9000* ✉ *Varca Beach, Salcete* ☎ *832/669–5000* ⊕ *www.caravelabeachresort.com* ⤴ *190 rooms, 4 suites, 5 villas* ⦿ *Breakfast.*

$$$ ⌷ **The Zuri White Sands.** This family-friendly hotel has a massive free-
RESORT form pool, more than 600 feet long, with a swim-up bar. **Pros:** the pool is a fun centerpiece for the resort; free Wi-Fi. **Cons:** no elevators. ⑤ *Rooms from: Rs. 8000* ✉ *Pedda, Varca, Salcete* ☎ *832/272–7282 to 84* ⊕ *www.thezurihotels.com* ⤴ *154 rooms, 4 suites* ⦿ *Breakfast.*

CAVELOSSIM

20 km (12 miles) southwest of Margao.

The last of the villages before the mouth of the Sal River, Cavelossim is also the end of the coastal road southward from Bogmalo. If you want to continue down the coast, you have to head back inland and take the national highway south, or take a country road up the river and use a ferry. Given that this is a rural area, Cavelossim is a surprisingly developed little place, with a shopping arcade; this is chiefly because of the presence of the Leela, arguably the most luxurious of the southern Goa resorts. The beach is clean and striking because it's at the mouth of the Sal River—serene and flanked by fields and coconut plantations.

This part of South Goa is an end in itself, and it's not a good base from which to explore the rest of the state (if you're keen on beach-hopping and other touristy activities, stay up north). It's the place to come when you want to relax, take up residence on the beach, and forget about everything, including trips to town.

GETTING HERE AND AROUND

From Dabolim Airport, it will take you about 45 minutes to reach Cavelossim.

BEACHES

Cavelossim Beach. One of Goa's lesser-known stretches, Cavelossim Beach is starting to come into its own. With a few swanky hotels in the area, including the Leela Goa ⇨ *See Where to Eat and Stay listings*, Cavelossim is primarily popular with older Indian visitors, due to the proliferation of upscale resorts in the area, and as a result is fairly clean, with soft white sand. If you're looking for swinging nightlife, this is not the beach for you, but it is worth a visit for those seeking relaxation, or perhaps some dolphin spotting—contact the area's boat operators who can organize sunset trips to spot the pods of dolphins that inhabit these waters. **Amenities:** food and drink; lifeguard; water sports. **Best for:** solitude; sunset; swimming. ⊠ *Cavelossim Beach.*

WHERE TO STAY

$$$
RESORT
⛱ **Holiday Inn.** The chief advantage of this international chain is its uniform service and friendly vibe, and the private access to Mobor Beach is a blessing after the crowded beaches of North Goa. **Pros:** well priced for its lovely beach location. **Cons:** could use an update. $ *Rooms from: Rs. 7000* ⊠ *Mobor Beach* ☎ *832/287–1303 to 312* ⊕ *www.holidayinngoa. com* ⤳ *200 rooms, 3 suites* ⫶◯⫶ *Breakfast.*

$$$$
RESORT
Fodor's Choice
★
⛱ **The Leela Goa.** For flat-out, over-the-top luxury and sophistication, nothing in Goa can top this well-planned 75-acre resort that includes a secluded beach and a magnificent view of cliffs and coves. **Pros:** quiet; excellent in-house restaurants; super spa. **Cons:** expensive Wi-Fi; not much to do in the areas surrounding the hotel. $ *Rooms from: Rs. 20000* ⊠ *Cavelossim, Mobor, Salcete* ☎ *832/662–1234* ⊕ *www.theleela. com* ⤳ *120 rooms, 66 suites* ⫶◯⫶ *All meals.*

PALOLEM BEACH

37 km (23 miles) southwest of Margao.

Fodor's Choice
★
Until recently, Goa's southernmost sandy stretch—nicknamed Paradise Beach—really was like a dream. The visitors who made their way to Palolem, in the Canacona district, were nature lovers, privacy seekers and the odd backpackers. It's no longer quiet or under the radar, and every year the number of shacks, hotels, and restaurants go up, although

it continues to have a negligible club scene. Also increasingly popular with Indian tourists, Palolem is not the quiet haven of years past, but this mile-long, crescent-shape stretch of white sand remains one of the most beautiful beaches in India. Compared to Goa's other beach strips, accommodation options are thin on the ground, and tend more toward beach shack–style low-budget accommodations that pop up in season and pack up for the monsoon, but visitors will spot lots of construction works underway, and in another couple of seasons, Palolem will likely be rife with resorts and high-end properties.

For visitors not keen on lower-budget living, at present your best bet might be at the Lalit Goa, a few kilometers south, at Raj Baga.

GETTING HERE AND AROUND
From Dabolim Airport, a prepaid taxi will cost you about Rs. 1,200 to make the 67-km (42-mile) trip, which will take roughly 90 minutes.

BEACHES
Palolem Beach. This once-deserted white-sand beach, backed by palm groves and low, green mountains, is still quieter than its northern counterparts, but Palolem is now a definite destination for sunseekers. It has a solid selection of cheap eateries and shacks, which have sprung up to cater to its bunch of hippie visitors. The farthest south of this coastline's developed beaches, it's no longer quite the idyll that first drew visitors this far south, but it is still very beautiful. **Amenities:** food and drink. **Best for:** solitude; swimming; walking.

WHERE TO STAY
$
B&B/INN
Ciaran's. Over the years Ciaran's has evolved from beachfront huts into proper cottages, all set around a small garden and with their own veranda. **Pros:** good, hearty breakfasts, right on the seafront. **Cons:** can be noisy in season; service slightly slow; rooms slightly gloomy in the daylight. $ *Rooms from: Rs. 3500* ✉ *233/A Palolem Beach, behind Old Syndicate bank, Canacona* ☎ *9/18322–643477* ⊕ *www.ciarans. com* ↪ *37 rooms* ⊗ *Breakfast.*

$$$
RESORT
The Lalit Goa. They don't get much bigger than this sprawling 85-acre all-suites resort. **Pros:** secluded; great for golf enthusiasts. **Cons:** it's quite a walk between all the amenities; not close to the beach. $ *Rooms from: Rs. 7200* ✉ *Raj Baga, Cancona, 3 km (2 miles) from Palolem Beach* ☎ *832/266–771* ⊕ *www.thelalit.com* ↪ *255 suites, 8 villas* ⊗ *Breakfast.*

$$$
B&B/INN
Lotus Yoga Retreat. Simon Low, one of Tri-Yoga London's founders, runs these in-season yoga holidays on Patnem beach. **Pros:** residents recieve a discount on holistic treatments. **Cons:** expensive; inclusive packages only. $ *Rooms from: Rs. 6500* ✉ *Gurawal 442, Agonda, Canacona* ⊕ *lotus-yoga-retreat.com.*

$
B&B/INN
The Nest. A stone's throw from the sea, and reasonably priced, the Nest is fairly emblematic of accommodations in Palolem. **Pros:** right on the beach; quiet; excellent views. **Cons:** very basic bathrooms. $ *Rooms from: Rs. 3000* ✉ *Ourem Rd., Mohanbagh, Canacona* ⊕ *www.thenestpalolem.com* ↪ *15 rooms* ⊗ *Breakfast.*

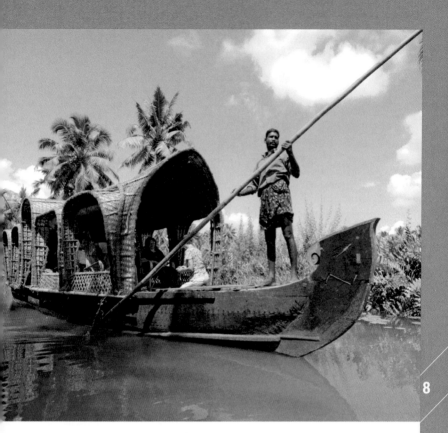

KERALA

WELCOME TO KERALA

TOP REASONS TO GO

★ **Ease your stress:** There's no place better than Kerala to get an ayurvedic oil massage and a yoga session. Let your tension melt away and your body kick back into equilibrium.

★ **Sail along the scenic backwaters:** Luxury houseboats come with hotel comforts, but the real attraction is the traditional village life you see drifting by.

★ **Lounge by the sea:** Relax along an isolated stretch of sand in North Kerala, access backwaters minutes from the beach at Marari, or party on Kovalam's Lighthouse Beach.

★ **Indulge your taste buds:** Whether its spicy, coconut-based curries, Portugese- and Dutch-influenced dishes, or North Kerala *biryani*, traditionally cooked in a hollow piece of bamboo, Kerala's extensive menu is sure to win over your taste buds.

★ **Tap into the past:** Reflect on Kerala's colonial past in Kochi, as you watch the sun set over the Fort area.

0   50 m

0   50 km

Arabia

1 Kochi. This colonial port city is packed with historical homes, churches, mosques, and a centuries-old synagogue where the city's small remaining population of Jews still worship.

2 Central Kerala. This region is blessed with natural beauty: beaches, the backwaters, stunning tea and spice plantations, and cool mountain wildlife preserves. It's also a busy tourist destination with crowds in season.

3 Southern Kerala. The main attractions here are the beaches in and around Kovalam and the laid-back atmosphere. It also holds the capital city of Thiruvananthapuram (also known as Trivandrum).

4 Northern Kerala. In this quiet area, you'll find long stretches of pristine sand and very few tourists.

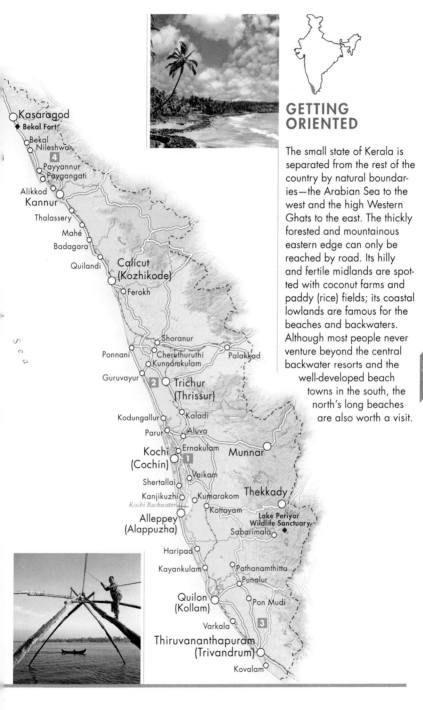

GETTING ORIENTED

The small state of Kerala is separated from the rest of the country by natural boundaries—the Arabian Sea to the west and the high Western Ghats to the east. The thickly forested and mountainous eastern edge can only be reached by road. Its hilly and fertile midlands are spotted with coconut farms and paddy (rice) fields; its coastal lowlands are famous for the beaches and backwaters. Although most people never venture beyond the central backwater resorts and the well-developed beach towns in the south, the north's long beaches are also worth a visit.

8

EATING WELL IN KERALA

The Kerala table is eclectic, savory, and adventuresome. Rice is the staple, coconut the essence, seafood the star, and spices the local zing.

(top left) Spicy fried chicken with curry leaves; (top right) Fish curry; (bottom right) *Idiyappam*

Kerala means "land of coconuts" in Malayalam, and its cuisine certainly bears that out. Keralan food, both sweet and savory, uses every part of the coconut, and its milk, meat, and oil.

Expect distinctive meat and fish dishes—rich beef or mutton stewed in coconut milk, seafood, chicken and mutton (goat) fried up dry and spicy, *biryanis* (often spelled *biriyanis* locally) cooked in an assortment of spices, and fish curries. Vegetarian dishes are plentiful, like the sumptuous vegetarian *thalis* or *sadya*, a platter of many choices served on banana leaves. Kerala is known for *iddiappa*, thin strands of dough formed into little nests that are steamed and served with coconut milk and sugar for breakfast or as an accompaniment to curries. *Appam*, similar to the rice-and-lentil *dosa*, is an oil-free coconut-and-rice pancake, thin and crispy on the edges with a steamed, raised center. *Puttu*, ground rice and coconut steamed in a bamboo cylinder is a common breakfast item unique to the area.

CHRISTIAN CUISINE

Kerala's Syrian Christian cuisine bears the stamp of all those who traversed its coasts. A typical day begins with *pallappam*, a rice pancake with Portuguese origins. Red meat is a major ingredient, with lamb *ishtew* (a stew with coconut milk), *urachi varutharachathu* (goat or beef cooked with ground coconut) and *ularthiyathu* (dry beef or goat with spices) all favorites.

MEEN POLLICHATHU

A central Kerala delicacy, **meen pollicha-thu** is a fragrant preparation of stuffed fish in a banana leaf. Any fish in season can be used, but the karimeen pearl spot is a freshwater local. The fish is marinated with various spices and a paste of diced tomatoes, onions, ginger, garlic, and coconut milk, then wrapped in a banana leaf sealed with a clove and cooked. This dish is available in almost every restaurant in Kerala.

MEEN PATHIRI

Malabar's stuffed fish pancakes, or **meen pathiri,** are found at almost every highway eatery in the northern part of the state. A *pathriri*—or *parota*, as it's often called—is a flat bread based on rice flour and coconut milk. This is filled with fish (usually kingfish, sardines, or pearl spot) that is shredded and cooked with spices, including chilli powder and turmeric. While some meen pathiri are so generously stuffed they look like a pie, in some parts of Malabar the pancake is flattened with a rolling pin after being stuffed. Chicken, egg, and mutton stuffings are also used.

IDIYAPPAM

String hoppers, or **idiyappam,** are made with rice flour and can be eaten with a curry, a stew, or at breakfast with *mutta* (egg) roast or simply with coconut milk. This Kerala staple can be sweet or savory and is a standard accompaniment to all

meals, often garnished with grated coconut. Most often you will find it served with chicken stew.

PAZHAM PORI

An evening snack available from street vendors, cafeterias, and train stations across the state, **pazham pori** are plantain fritters—deep-fried delights that are best when served hot. A ripe Kerala-grown banana, which is very similar to a plantain, is chopped and coated in a flour-based batter before it's fried. A similar fritter is made using yams.

MEEN MULAKITTATHU

Using the fresh catch of the day, **meen mulakittathu,** or fish curry, is a staple at the dinner table. Traditionally cooked in a brass pot, the gravy is a combination of coconut milk and spices that are all grown in Kerala—and freshly crushed when the dish is cooked in traditional homes. Different kinds of fish can be used, although the most popular are pearl spot and kingfish. The emphasis is on freshness. This dish is served with steamed red rice or with idiyappam.

PUTTU

Another specialty of the region, **puttu** is a puddinglike dish made from fresh-grated coconut and rice flour, molded into a cylindrical shape, and then steamed.

8

Updated by
Vaihayasi
Pande Daniel

From pristine beaches and backwaters to extensive stretches of tea and spice plantations and rolling hills, Kerala, the narrow state running 560 km (350 miles) along India's western coast, is a land of diverse natural beauty. The scenery changes across the breadth of the state, and is dotted with waterfalls, fresh springs, and forests full of the opportunity to spot unique species of birds and wildlife. It is also rich in history, with Hindu temples and Christian churches dating back hundreds or thousands of years and a culture that include dance, martial arts, and age-old ayurvedic treatments.

From the more recent past, coastal cities preserve colonial mansions and 19th-century godowns (warehouses) used to store spices and teas and coffee from the plantations. Outside of the historic, spice-trading city of Kochi, attractions are rustic: quiet beaches spiked with palm trees line the west coast; the hilly eastern interior is heavily forested. Kochi is the anchor of low-lying central Kerala, a region dominated by lazy inland waterways, broad lakes, rice fields, and fishing boats; the backwater lifestyle is best experienced from the deck of a slow-moving houseboat. Farther inland, you'll find tranquil tea and spice plantations as well as two national parks and a sanctuary. At Periyar Wildlife Sanctuary, near Thekkady, you can observe creatures in their native habitat from the comfort of a boat. Rajamala Wildlife Sanctuary, in the Evarikulam National Park near Munnar, is where you'll find the endangered *Nilgiri tahr*, a shy but sweet-tempered mountain goat. At Chinnar Wildlife Sanctuary you may have a better chance of seeing wild elephants or bison. The hills surrounding Thekkady and Munnar are lovely for trekking and rich in waterfalls and birdsong, especially in the rains. Southern Kerala is best known for the sparkling beaches near Kovalam, which lie south of the stately capital city, Thiruvananthapuram (Trivandrum), the home of the famous Padmanabhaswamy Temple. Undeveloped, conservative northern Kerala is the state's cultural heartland; you can witness some of the region's most spectacular festivals here. Kerala's Muslim community is concentrated in the north, and Christians are largely in the central and southern regions. Note that many of Kerala's low-slung, modest temples restrict entry to Hindus only.

PLANNING

WHEN TO GO

HIGH SEASON: OCTOBER TO MARCH

Although Kerala used to have a second dip in visitor numbers during October's monsoon, this month now marks the beginning of the high season for all hotels and tour operators, with foreign tourists flocking in to take advantage of "monsoon tourism" deals. December and January are the peak tourist months, so be prepared to pay top rates around Christmas and New Year's Eve. If you plan on visiting during that time be sure to book way ahead, as many hotels run on full occupancy. Because of Kerala's many Christians, this time of the year is quite festive and very enjoyable. The climate is ideal for the beach and backwaters, while the hills offer a cooler alternative.

LOW SEASON: MARCH TO JULY

By March the tourist season starts to wind down as temperatures soar to almost 40 degrees Celsius (105 Fahrenheit) and the air becomes humid. June brings in the monsoon season that lasts up to mid-August (in the last few years). This rainy season deters tourists bound for the beaches and the backwaters, but it's supposed to be the best time for ayurvedic treatments. At the start of the monsoon it can rain continuously for many days at a time. Otherwise you get intermittent showers with lovely days of sunshine in between. The landscape is a really rich green, tourists are few, and hotel discounts excellent. So planning a visit after the middle of the rains or beyond may make sense for travelers who can handle a little rain. The hills, including Munnar and Kannur, are still pleasant during this time and often cater to domestic tourists escaping the heat in the plains.

SHOULDER SEASON: AUGUST AND SEPTEMBER

By mid-August the monsoons are over and the temperature is cooler. The Onam Festival is celebrated across Kerala around this time, and the Nehru Cup Snake Boat Race is held on the backwaters on the second Saturday in August. With the exception of dates around those two events, tourists can find some of the best deals during this period, and domestic vacationers often take advantage of this. The cooler temperature and good prices make this an ideal time to visit, although, because August is the tail end of the monsoon and the sea is on high tide, swimming in the ocean is restricted on several beaches. This is also bug season, so insect repellents and a suitcase full of long pants is advisable to ward off the mosquitoes that can cramp evenings outside, and go easy on uncooked food or food cooked in less-than-trustworthy kitchens.

GETTING HERE AND AROUND

The most convenient way to get around Kerala is with a hired car and driver. The journey from Thiruvananthapuram to Kochi takes about five hours. Figure about Rs. 12 per km (½ mile) for a non-air-conditioned car and a halt charge of Rs. 150 per night. Shop around, and hire a car from a government-approved travel agency. There are prepaid taxi counters at both Thiruvananthapuram and Kochi airports. Figure on a minimum of about Rs. 1,600 per day for drives up to 150 km (93 miles) that take less than eight hours, in an air-conditioned medium-sized car; taxes and overnight halt charges are extra. The charge for driving in the city in an air-conditioned medium-size car for up to 80 km (50 miles) and eight hours is also about Rs. 1,600.

If you are doing a circular tour of Kerala it is best (and cheaper) to keep the same car and driver for the length of the trip. Drivers expect to be tipped at the end of each day. Additionally when you stop to eat somewhere offer to pay for him (though tourist-oriented restaurants often do feed drivers for free). Shop around, and hire a car from a government-approved travel agency or from your hotel (the latter will be more expensive).

In central Kerala boat cruises offer a fascinating look at the backwaters where people still live. Most houseboats are based in the Alleppey district. When booking an overnight stay on one, make sure it comes equipped with solar panels and air-conditioning or a fan, or you're in for a hot night. The going rate for a posh one-bedroom vessel with air-conditioning and meals is about Rs. 16,000 for two, for two nights and three days. Or Rs. 5,000 for one day on a one-bedroom boat and Rs. 9,500 for a two-bedroom boat.

AIR TRAVEL

Most international flights land in Thiruvananthapuram or Kochi, though Calicut airport also serves the Middle East and Sri Lanka. Air India, Jet Airways, Spice Jet, IndiGo, and Go Air cover domestic routes; most local carriers fly between Thiruvananthapuram, Kochi, and Calicut.

AIRPORT TRANSFERS Calicut's Karipur Airport is 23 km (14 miles) south of town; a cab will cost roughly Rs. 850 if it isn't air-conditioned and Rs. 950 if it is.

Kochi's international airport is about 40 km (25 miles) east of the city; abominable traffic can make it a two-hour trip. A taxi will cost about Rs. 990 (no a/c) and Rs 1,134 (a/c). The small airport in Thiruvananthapuram is 6 km (4 miles) west of the city center; taxis charge about Rs. 450 to get to the city and about Rs. 500 to reach Kovalam. Prepaid taxi booths operate in all three of these airports.

BOAT AND FERRY TRAVEL

A houseboat cruise is the quintessential way to experience Kerala. The District Tourism Promotion Council has houseboat information. Private companies, the K- Corporation (KTDC), and the Tourist Desk operate motorboat and houseboat tours from Alleppey; these only run when a minimum number of passengers has been reached. Prices range from Rs. 400 for one hour by motorboat to Rs. 7,000 for a 24-hour houseboat tour with meals. The Alleppey Tourism Development Cooperative

(ATDC) has had daily ferry trips between Alleppey and Quilon (Rs. 500), but it takes eight hours and isn't recommended. There is also a public ferry from Alleppey to Kottayam (close to Kumarakom) for Rs. 10.

Boat and Ferry Information **ATDC** ✉ *Municipal Library, Thathampally, 2nd fl., Alleppey* ☎ *91/477–2264462* ⊕ *www.atdcalleppey.com.* **District Tourism Promotion Council** ☎ *9400051796, 477/2251796, 477/2253308* ⊕ *www. keralatourism.org/dtpc.php.*

Houseboat Cruise. The Kuttanad, a 74-km-long (46-mile-long) network of beaches, lakes, canals, rivers, inland sea, islands, and brooks, links Alleppey, Marari, Quilon, Kochi, and beyond to Varkala, Kovalam, and Poovar. It's a tropical kingdom of coastal canals, sheltered by trees, that wanders past two houses-and-a-palm hamlets, mosques, temples, whitewashed chapels, flocks of ducks, floating bazaars, paddy farms, and bridges. Your camera will have a hard time keeping pace with the scenes flitting past.

Shaded by a woven bamboo canopy and fanned by cool breezes, you can drift past simple but often gorgeously colored, tile-roof houses with canoes moored outside; and people washing themselves, their clothes, their dishes, and their children in the river. A houseboat cruise provides a window into traditional local life. Graceful palms are everywhere, as are village walls painted with political slogans, the inevitable portrait of Che Guevara (worshipped in Kerala), and ads for computer-training courses. Backwater trips can be designed to suit any time constraint or budget. Motorized or punted canoes squeeze into narrow canals, taking you to roadless villages, and big ferries ply the eight-hour Quilon–Alleppey route as if it were a major highway. Romantic houseboats give you the opportunity to stay overnight on the water. Any travel agent, hotel, or the Kerala Tourism Development Corporation, can help you hire a private boat or plan a trip. Most cruises depart from Quilon, Alleppey, or Kumarakom. In addition, the Trident Hilton (Oberoir) in Kochi can book you a stateroom on the MV *Vrinda,* an eight-bedroom luxury cruise ship. ☎ *484/235–3234* KTDC ⊕ *www.ktdc.com.*

TAXIS AND AUTO-RICKSHAWS

Auto-rickshaws are a convenient and quick way to travel around town. In Thiruvananthapuram, figure Rs. 15 for the first 1½ km (1 mile) and Rs. 8 per additional kilometer—other cities will be slightly less. Don't be alarmed if your driver doesn't use the meter—it usually doesn't work (whether because it was intentionally broken or not is difficult to say). Make sure to agree on a fare before you get in, and don't trust a driver for unbiased shopping recommendations.

Auto-rickshaws (fix the price before you get in) are a good way to get around Fort Cochin; cabs are also a good option for longer distances around Kochi. Fares will run about Rs. 350 for an air-conditioned car for 25 km (15½ miles). Ask at any tourist office about the latest legal rates. Taxis hired at your hotel will have a slightly higher rate, but drivers are more likely to speak some English.

TRAIN TRAVEL

Rail journeys in Kerala can be scenic and more comfortable than traveling by car. The KK Express—which travels from Kanya Kumari, at India's southern tip, all the way up to New Delhi—is a good train to take through Kerala, as is the Kerala Express and the Jan Shatabdi. December is a major pilgrimage season, so you'll need to book tickets in advance if you're traveling during this period. Check with KTDC for the latest schedules and fares, or try ⊕ *www.indianrail.gov.in* or ⊕ *indiarailinfo.com*, and use a travel agent or your hotel's travel desk to make bookings, unless you don't mind standing in a sometimes-unruly line at the train station.

Train Information Ernakulam Junction ⊠ *Ernakulam* ☎ **131. Ernakulam Town Station** ⊠ *Ernakulam* ☎ *484/237–5431* ⊕ *indiarailinfo.com.* **Thiruvananthapuram Central Station** ⊠ *Thiruvananthapuram* ☎ *132* ⊕ *indiarailinfo.com.*

MONEY MATTERS

ATMS

ATMs are available in Kerala's major cities of Kochi, Thiruvananthapuram, and Calicut, as well as many smaller towns. Check for the Cirrus or Plus sign, as some local banks do not accept foreign cards. Make sure your PIN is four digits.

CURRENCY EXCHANGE

Most of the major hotels have currency exchange services, but it's wise to shop around for the best deal. Thomas Cook offers good rates. ANZ Grindlays and any branch of the Bank of India will cash traveler's checks and change hard currency. Traveler's checks sometimes get marginally higher rates than cash.

TRAVEL AGENTS AND TOURS

The Kerala Tourism Development Corporation (KTDC) has several inexpensive tours, including wildlife-spotting excursions to the Periyar Wildlife Sanctuary and one- to two-week trips that follow a pilgrim trail through Kerala's sacred shrines. Sita Travels can help with bookings and arrange a car and driver. The Great India Tour Company, one of Kerala's best travel agencies, has offices throughout South India. SATM Tours and Travel designs affordable packages around your particular interests. Thiruvananthapuram-based Tourindia created the houseboat phenomenon and offers unusual Kerala backwaters experiences, that is much more authentic than what you see elsewhere. One intriguing two- to three-day trip—created by Tourindia and the forestry department—sends you deep into the jungle with a local guide, an armed escort, and a naturalist. Destination Holidays specializes in Kerala tours, and has a good reputation among budget operators for good service and local knowledge.

Contacts Destination Holidays ⊠ *Pallath Bldgs., Kurisupally Rd., Ravipuram, Ernakulam, Kochi* ☎ *484/235–6497, 484/235–7316* ⊕ *www.destinationholidays. net.* **Great India Tour Company** ⊠ *Mullassery Towers, Vanross Junction, Trivandrum* ☎ *471/301–1500.* **Tourindia** ⊠ *136 M. G. Rd., Trivandrum* ☎ *471/233–0437, 471/233–1507.*

VISITOR INFORMATION

Excellent brochures, maps, pamphlets, and transportation information on all of Kerala's districts are available at any KTDC office. KTDC runs an around-the-clock tourist information toll-free number that can be dialed from within India. In Kochi, the office is open daily 10–6. Thiruvananthapuram's two KTDC offices—one in town and one at the airport—are open weekdays 10–5.

In Kochi, an alternative source of information is the Tourist Desk, a private, nonprofit organization that conducts moderately priced tours and provides clear, straightforward information about the state. In Kannur, the District Tourism Promotion Council is quite active. Central Kerala is well served by the ATDC. The Government of India Tourist Office in Ernakulam—open weekdays 9–5:30 and Saturday 9–1—has its own vehicles, boats, lodgings, and tours.

Tourist Offices ATDC. Details and plenty of friendly help and advice on houseboat and motorboat tours and on the ferries connecting different points on the backwaters are available from this tourist office. ⊠ *Komala Rd., Alleppey* ☎ *477/226–1693* ⊕ *www.atdcalleppey.com.* **Kannur District Tourism Promotion Council** ⊠ *Taluk Office Campus, Kannur* ☎ *497/270–6336* ⊕ *www. dtpckannur.com.*

RESTAURANTS

Until recently eating out was a relatively new concept in Kerala; the older generation viewed restaurants with a great deal of suspicion and the act of dining outside the home as some sort of tragedy. Most restaurants, as a result, catered to visitors and are often attached to hotels. (The word hotel, in fact, is often synonymous with restaurant.) But that has changed, and large cities and even roadside highway halts fairly bristle with places to eat.

In mid-2014, as part of a move to essentially ban alcohol consumption, the government of Kerala issued orders to close all bars that are not part of five-star hotels, and to begin closing 10% of all liquor stores each year. It is not yet clear if these closures will actually continue.

HOTELS

Many Kerala resorts make use of traditional regional architecture, from tribal-style huts to elaborate wooden manors. Heritage properties transplant or reassemble traditional teakwood homes, or *tharavads*, while other hotels are newly built in the old style, helping to support traditional carpentry.

In cities, most hotels have air-conditioning, but many resorts in less populated and cooler areas do not. Beach properties often rely on fan and sea breezes, and in the hilly interior, air-conditioning is usually unnecessary and rooms may not even have fans. Some buildings have no window screens, so if a cool and/or bug-free sleep is part of your plan, ask about both and request a mosquito net/curtains. Many resorts, even upscale establishments, don't have TVs in guest rooms. Outside of cities, power supply is tenuous. Most hotels, even small ones, have their own generators, but they take a few seconds to kick in. Don't be surprised if you're left in the darkness for a moment—it's unavoidable. Most rooms are equipped with flashlights or an emergency light.

Some lodgings charge a 10% service fee, and the state government tacks on another 6%–16%, depending on the facilities. In luxury places, count on paying up to 25% in taxes. You may be able to offset such fees with off-season discounts—around 50% during the monsoon season, from June to August. When booking during off seasons make sure you push hotels to give you the best possible rate; they discount quite a bit from the quoted rate or the rate on their websites. On the other hand, many hotels charge higher-than-usual rates in peak season, from mid-December to mid-January. *Hotel reviews have been shortened. For full information, visit Fodors.com.*

WHAT IT COSTS IN RUPEES			
	$	**$$**	**$$$**	**$$$$**
Restaurants	under Rs. 300	Rs. 300–Rs. 499	Rs. 500–Rs. 700	over Rs. 700
Hotels	under Rs. 4,000	Rs. 4,000–Rs. 5,999	Rs. 6,000–Rs. 10,000	over Rs. 10,000

Restaurant prices are the average cost of a main course at dinner or, if dinner is not served, at lunch. Hotel prices are the lowest cost of a standard double room in high season.

PLANNING YOUR TIME

The most convenient way to tackle Kerala is with a car and driver, allowing for the maximum amount of flexibility. Spend at least a day in Kochi, soaking in the beauty and the cultural offerings. A four-day itinerary can also include two days of ayurvedic massages and great local food in the resort town of Kumarakom and an overnight houseboat cruise through inland waterways. Drive inland to Thekkady or Munnar and spend two days viewing the wildlife in Thekkady's Periyar Wildlife Sanctuary (take the 4 pm boat cruise or a more adventurous jungle trek) and scenic Munnar, Kerala's Switzerland, with the added attractions of wild elephants and the Rajamala sanctuary. The Kochi-Munnar-Thekkady circuit forms a trips with roughly equal distances between each point. Some travelers arrive in Kerala by car from Madurai, in Tamil Nadu; if that's your plan, visit Idukki on your way west toward the coast. Another option is to travel south from Thekkady to Thiruvananthapuram, Kerala's capital. Explore its sights and quiet lanes before heading for the mellow beaches, palm-fringed lagoons, and rocky coves near Kovalam and Varkala beach. If you want to get away from the crowds, head for the rarely visited north to see the extraordinary Theyyam festivals of Kannur and the pristine beaches along the northern coast.

Keralan Culture

A charming myth explains the creation of Kerala. Parashurama, an avatar of Vishnu, performed a series of penances to atone for a grievous sin, and the god of the sea rewarded his devotion by reclaiming Kerala from the deep. The reality is a little more prosaic: In 1956 the Malayalam-speaking states of Kochi and Travancore joined with the district of Malabar to form Kerala. The new Indian state became the first place in the world to adopt a communist government in a free election, an event that caused global speculation. Today this tropical enclave between the western mountains and the Arabian Sea is one of India's most progressive states, with a literacy rate of well over 95.5% and a life expectancy far higher than the Indian average. Even in the shabbiest backwater "toddy shop," where locals knock back glasses of potent coconut liquor, you'll find a copy of the day's newspaper in Malayalam, the local language. However, despite Kerala's very real accomplishments, unemployment remains endemic: it's close to 7.5%, and higher than the national average. Its citizens depend to a large degree on remittances (money sent from abroad). To be able to provide for their families back home, many Keralan men and women must leave to work in the Middle East.

The Malayalis make up India's most highly educated population; many are conversant in English, Hindi, and Tamil, as well as Malayalam. In the nearly three millennia before the 1795 establishment of British rule, Phoenicians, Arabs, Jews, Chinese, and Europeans came in droves, attracted by the region's valuable cash crops: tea, rubber, cashews, teak, and spices—notably black pepper (Kerala's "black gold") and cardamom.

Kerala's diversity is a testament to all those who passed by during the last few centuries. This state is unique in that its Hindu population (56%) is joined by relatively large numbers of Muslims (25%) and Christians (19%) (India's three largest religious communities).

Since Independence, people have begun using the place names that were used prior to British colonization. The strong British presence here makes name changes particularly germane; hence, Alleppey/Alappuzha, Calicut/Kozhikode, Cochin/Kochi, Quilon/Kollam, Trichur/Thrissur, and Trivandrum/Thiruvananthapuram. Official maps and tourist brochures reflect these changes, but both versions are still commonly used.

8

KOCHI

1,380 km (860 miles) south of Mumbai.

Kochi, formerly and still commonly known as Cochin, is one of the west coast's largest and oldest ports. The streets behind the docks of the historic Fort Cochin and Mattancherry districts are lined with old merchant houses, godowns (warehouses), and open courtyards heaped with betel nuts, ginger, peppercorns, and tea. Throughout the second millennium this ancient city exported spices, coffee, and coir (the fiber made from coconut husks), and imported culture and religion from

Europe, China, and the Middle East. Today Kochi has a synagogue, several mosques, Portuguese Catholic and Syrian Christian (Saint Thomas Christian) churches, Hindu temples, and the United Church of South India (an amalgamation of several Protestant denominations).

The city is spread out over mainland, peninsula, and islands. Ernakulam, on the mainland 2 km (1 mile) from the harbor, is the commercial center and the onetime capital of the former state of Cochin. Willingdon Island, which was created by dredging the harbor, holds several luxury hotels as well as a navy base. The beautiful Bolghatty Island, north of Ernakulam, is a favorite picnic spot for locals. On it there's a government-run hotel in a colonial structure that was once used by the Dutch governor and later by the British Resident. Another local favorite is Cherai beach on Vypin Island, which is a 10-minute ferry ride from Fort Cochin but which takes about an hour total to reach. The Fort Cochin district, the area's historic center and the most important for area for sightseeing, is at the northern tip of the Mattancherry peninsula. Houses here often recall Tudor manors; some have been converted to hotels, others remain in the hands of the venerable tea and trading companies. South of Fort Cochin, in the Mattancherry district, is where you'll find the city's dwindling Jewish community. Their small neighborhood, called Jew Town, which is now dotted with cafés and shops selling curios and antiques, is centered on the synagogue. It's known for its antiques and curio shops.

GETTING HERE AND AROUND

Kochi is 212 km (132 miles) from Thiruvananthapuram and 193 km (120 miles) from Calicut. The efficient intercity express train Jan Shatabdi connects Ernakulam with Alleppey, Quilon, Thiruvananthapuram, and Calicut and is the quickest way to get to Kochi. There are slower trains connecting Kochi with Varkala and other smaller towns in Kerala. Express trains link Kochi with Mumbai, Bangalore, and Chennai. There are several flights a day from Delhi and Mumbai, Chennai, and Bangalore.

Cabs are a good option for getting around the city; public ferries and private boats go between Fort Cochin, Willingdon Island, and Ernakulam throughout the day. Ernakulam's main boat jetty is south of the Taj Residency hotel. Boats leave for Fort Cochin roughly every half hour, from 6 am to 9 pm. There are frequent ferries to Mattancherry, and limited service to Embarkation Jetty, on Willingdon Island's eastern tip. Ferry rides cost only a few rupees.

TIMING

Spend at least two days here to soak up the history and culture of the city, see all the sights, and enjoy some downtime relaxing by the harbor and dining on local delicacies.

ESSENTIALS

Tourist Offices **Government of India Tourist Office.** Another office is located in Ernakulam. ⊠ *Malabar Rd., Willingdon Island, Kochi* ☎ *484/266–8352, 1-800/425–4747 tourist information; toll-free in India* ⊕ *www.keralatourism.org/ information-offices.* **KTDC** ⊠ *Shanmugham Rd., Ernakulam, Kochi* ☎ *484/235–3234* ⊕ *www.ktdc.com* ⊠ *Museum Complex, LMS Vellayambalam Rd., Trivandrum*

Traditional Chinese fishing nets

☎ 471/232–2279 ⊕ www.ktdc.com. **Tourist Desk** ✉ Main Boat Jetty, Ernakulam, Kochi ☎ 484/237–1761 ⊕ www.touristdesk.in.

Travel Agents and Tours Great India Tour Company ✉ Ravipuram, Pithuru Smarana, Srikandath Rd., 1st fl., Ernakulam, Kochi ☎ 484/231–7004. **Sita Travels** ✉ Tharakan Bldg., M. G. Rd., Ernakulam, Kochi ☎ 124/470–3400 ⊕ www.sita.in. **Travelogics** ✉ Warriam Rd., Ernakulam, Kochi ☎ 484/236–5765 ⊕ www.travelogics.in.

EXPLORING

TOP ATTRACTIONS

Chinese Fishing Nets. The precarious-looking bamboo and wood structures hovering like cranes over the waterfront are Kochi's famous Chinese fishing nets. Although they've become identified with the city, they're used throughout central Kerala. Thought to have been introduced by Chinese traders in the 14th century, the nets and their catch can be easily seen from Fort Cochin's Vasco da Gama Square. There's lots going on at the square—cooking, hawking, gaping (by tourists)—and don't miss the artistically decked-out tree in the center with tiger face, clowns, and fish painted on it. You can watch the fishermen haul up the nets around 6 am, 11 am, and 4 pm. They're particularly striking at sunset or at any time when viewed from the deck of a boat. ✉ Vasco da Gama Sq., Fort Cochin.

Fodor's Choice **Dutch Palace** (*Mattancherry Palace*). Built by the Portuguese in the mid-
★ 16th century as a gift for the Rajas of Cochin, this two-story structure reflects elements of traditional design while still looking colonial. It was

A GOOD TOUR

The sleepy, tree-lined streets of Fort Cochin are perfect for a leisurely stroll. Start at the **St. Francis Church,** one of the earliest Indian churches to be built by Europeans. The Portuguese explorer Vasco da Gama was once buried here. Continue northeast along Church Street, passing colonial bungalows, to Vasco da Gama Square and the famed **Chinese Fishing Nets.** Follow River Road along the sea front past more colonial buildings. When you come to the end of the small Children's Park, take a right so that the edge of the park is on your right. At the park's far edge you'll hit tiny Princess Street—one of the first streets built in Fort Cochin, it's now crammed with shops, tour agencies, and modest European-style houses. The next major intersection is at Bastion Street. Take a left here and you'll soon see **Santa Cruz Cathedral** on your right. From here, hop in an auto-rickshaw to Mattancherry and visit the **Dutch Palace.** When you exit, take a right and follow the road as it turns a corner. Turn right again and you'll reach the **Synagogue.** In the afternoon browse in the antiques and spice shops that line Jew Town Road, or head back north to the jetty and catch a ferry to Ernakulam for shopping on Mahatma Gandhi (M.G.) Road.

TIMING

You can see Fort Cochin and Mattancherry in a day. Remember that all houses of worship close for a few hours around lunchtime. The Dutch Palace is closed on Friday, the synagogue is closed to visitors on Friday and Saturday, and many shops are closed on Sunday.

extended by the Dutch when they took control of the area. The rajas, in turn, added some of India's best mythological murals—the entire story of the *Ramayana* is told on the walls in a series of bedchambers, which also have inviting window seats. In the ladies' ground-floor chamber, you can see a colorful, mildly erotic depiction of Lord Krishna with his female devotees. The coronation hall near the entrance holds a series of portraits of monarchs (that interestingly show continuous familial resemblance) and some of the rajas' artifacts, like including maps, swords, and a fantastic palanquin covered in red wool. The palace has rare, traditional Kerala flooring, which looks like polished black marble but is actually a mix of burned coconut shells, charcoal, lime, plant juices, and egg whites. ✉ *Palace Rd., Mattancherry* 🕙 *Rs. 5* ☻ *Sat.–Thurs. 9–5.*

NEED A BREAK?

Kashi Art Café. A favorite hangout for artists and young tourists, Fort Cochin's Kashi Art Café is about as funky as Kerala gets. The front room hosts rotating exhibitions, primarily of South Indian contemporary art, and light continental fare and Western-style coffee is served in the garden café at the rear. The real treat is to experience this tiny little pocket of Kerala subculture. ✉ *Burgher St.* ☎ *484/221-6769* ⊕ *www.kashiartgallery.com* ☻ *Daily 8:30–7:30.*

Pardesi Synagogue. The first migration of Jews to Kerala is thought to have taken place in the 6th century BC, followed by a much larger wave in the 1st century AD, when Jews fleeing Roman persecution in Jerusalem settled at Cranganore (on the coast about 26 km [16 miles] north of Kochi). In the 4th century, the local king promised the Jews perpetual protection, and the colony flourished, serving as a haven for Jews from the Middle East and, in later centuries, Europe. When the Portuguese leader Afonso de Albuquerque discovered the Jews near Cochin in the 16th century, however, he destroyed their community, having received permission from his king to "exterminate them one by one." Muslim anti-Semitism flared up as well. The Jews rebuilt in Mattancherry but were able to live without fear only after the less-belligerent Dutch took control in 1663.

> **HEAD FOR WATER**
>
> Traffic on land and the city's many bridges can be abominable. Private launches and small ferries zip through the waterways, making the journey as enjoyable as the destination.

The rather small synagogue, built in 1568, houses four scrolls of the Torah kept in cases of silver and gold and is topped by an attractive clock tower that was added in 1760. Admire the collection of antique colonial Indian lights hanging from the center and the blue-and-white Chinese tiles on the floor (a gift from a Jewish businessman in the 18th century); no two tiles are alike. Also on view are the 4th-century copper plates that detail, in Malayalam, the king's decree that allowed the Jewish community to live in his kingdom. Before you enter the main synagogue there is a collection of paintings on the left highlighting the Jewish story in India. Photography and videography are not allowed in the synagogue. ✉ *Synagogue La., Jew Town, Mattancherry* 🎫 *Rs. 5* ⊗ *Sun.–Thurs. 10–1 and 3–5 (closed on Jewish holidays).*

WORTH NOTING

St. Francis Church. This stately church is the first European house of worship in India. The Portuguese flag first appeared in Fort Cochin in 1500, and Vasco da Gama arrived in 1502. The following year, Afonso de Albuquerque came with half a dozen ships full of settlers—he built the fort, and five friars in the crowd built this church in 1510. Da Gama returned in 1524 (his third trip) as Portuguese viceroy of the Indies, died that same year, and was buried in this church. You can still visit his gravestone inside the church, but his remains were shipped back 14 years later to Lisbon in 1538.

The church's history reflects the European struggle for colonial turf in India. It was a Catholic church until 1664, when it became a Dutch Reform church; it later became Anglican (1804–1947) and is now part of the Church of South India. Inside are beautifully engraved Dutch and Portuguese tombstones and the *doep boek,* a register of baptisms and marriages between 1751 and 1894; you can view a photographic reproduction—the original is too fragile. The first Portuguese was buried in 1562 and the first Dutch in 1664—their epitaphs are on view. ✉ *Church St., between Parade Rd. and Bastion St., Fort Cochin* ⊗ *Daily 9:30–5.*

Kochi

KEY

▶ 1 Exploring

1 Hotels & Restaurants

Exploring ▶

Chinese Fishing Nets **2**
Dutch Palace **4**
Pardesi Synagogue **5**
St. Francis Church **1**
Santa Cruz Cathedral **3**

Restaurants ▶

Arca Nova **18**
Bristow's Bistro **4**
David Hall **6**
The History **16**
Kayees Rahmathullah **19**
Mainland China **24**

Malabar Junction **2**
Menorah **9**
The Rice Boat **22**
Teapot Café **14**
Thai Pavilion **20**

Hotels ▶

Brunton Boatyard **17**
Delight **15**
Fort Heritage **14**
Koder House **13**
Le Meridien **23**
The Malabar House **5**

No. 18 .... **11**
The Old Courtyard **8**
Old Harbour Hotel **10**
Old Lighthouse Bristow ... **3**
Raintree Lodge **12**
The Tower House **7**
Vivanta by Taj-Malabar ... **21**

Laccadive Sea

Vembanad Lake

Santa Cruz Cathedral Basilica. This Gothic-looking basilica, set in spacious grounds, has an interior that's colorfully painted with scenes and decorations that some find gaudy and others find gorgeous. The king of Cochin granted the Portuguese permission to build a fort and later a church in 1505 for their assistance in defeating the Zamorins of Calicut. For a while that structure was used as a Dutch armory. It was razed by the British in 1795, and in 1904 the current structure was completed, with a pillar of the original church within. Pope Paul IV elevated the church to a cathedral in 1558, and Pope John Paul II made it a basilica in 1984. ⊠ *Parade and K. B. Jacob Rds., Fort Cochin* ☎ *484/221–5799* ⊕ *www. santacruzcathedralbasilica.org* ⊗ *Daily 9–1 and 3–5.*

> ## KOCHI BOAT TOURS
>
> From Ernakulam's High Court or Sealord Jetty you can hire private boats, usually for about Rs. 500 an hour. The Kerala Tourism Development Corporation (KTDC) conducts two inexpensive boat tours of Kochi each day; the 3½-hour trips depart at 9 am and 2 pm from the Sealord Jetty, opposite the Sealord Hotel, between the Main and High Court jetties.

WHERE TO EAT

As Kerala's premier city, Kochi offers the most options for dining out. Many top hotels open outdoor seafood grills in season (November to February), where you can pick from the day's catch and have it prepared as you like. Try *karimeen,* also known as the pearl spot, a bony but delicious fish found only in central Kerala, prepared with spices wrapped in a banana leaf. Keep an eye out for unusual Portuguese-influenced dishes and do try the rare, eclectic Kochi Jewish cuisine. Lots of hotel restaurants feature live music, especially during peak season.

$
SEAFOOD
✕ **Arca Nova.** Inside a budget hotel in a great location on the jetty, this simple, open-air restaurant doesn't skimp on quality or authenticity. The menu is almost entirely seafood—chicken and specialty items (like lobster) must be ordered in advance. Every dish is cooked to order and presented in a clay vessel. The Prawns Kerala—fried—and the braised seerfish are terrific. If you agonize over oil, tell the chef in advance. Note that service can be slow, and open-air dining isn't available during the monsoon. ⑤ *Average main: Rs. 150* ⊠ *Fort House Hotel, 2/6 A Calvathi Rd., Fort Cochin* ☎ *484/221–7103, 484/221–5221.*

$$$
ECLECTIC
✕ **Bristow's Bistro.** This restaurant offers a flavor of Fort Cochin both with its food, and with its location overlooking the beach and sea. The buffet spread is varied and the à la carte options include choice dishes such as the stuffed red snapper, seafood platters, and desserts like the *chakkara choru* (a Malabari rice pudding) and Mattancherry Sweet Spice Roll, made with grated coconut and jaggery (unrefined sugar). The restaurant is tastefully decorated. ⑤ *Average main: Rs. 600* ⊠ *Old Lighthouse Bristow Hotel, Beach Rd., Fort Cochin* ☎ *484/305–0102* ⊕ *www.oldlighthousehotel.com.*

$
SOUTH INDIAN
✕ **Chinese Fishing Nets stalls.** Fresh seafood is available, many times a day, at any of multiple food stalls behind the Chinese Fishing Nets, run by

enthusiastic fishing folk, some of them in aprons. A variety of entreaties will be made for you to visit just their stall. This is the most genuine way to sample Kerala seafood. You choose the seafood you would like, and it is fried up on the spot in local masalas. Tables are set up in the open air in front of the stoves. Be sure to fix the price for the seafood chosen before you sit down to dine. The area gets quite busy in high season. ⑤ *Average main: Rs. 200* ✉ *Chinese Fishing Nets, Fort Cochin* 🚫 *No credit cards.*

$$
CONTEMPORARY

✕ **David Hall.** This rambling former Dutch home is now an art gallery and spacious garden café run by the Casino Group. The front room displays the work of contemporary Indian artists and works from art camps held in villages across Kerala. Beyond this is the café, open from noon to 9 pm, which extends out to the back lawn; the place has a lovely atmosphere. Best known for its delicious Italian pizza (made in a traditional stone oven in front of you) and panini, the restaurant changes its menu regularly, depending on what ingredients are in season, making for interesting choices and dependable freshness. ⑤ *Average main: Rs. 300* ✉ *1/264 Princess St., opposite Parade Ground, Fort Cochin* ☎ *484/221–8298* 🚫 *No credit cards* ⊘ *Closed Mon.*

$$$$
INDIAN
Fodor'sChoice
★

✕ **The History.** The intriguing, extensively researched menu draws on the myriad international influences on Kochi's history. Alongside traditional fare you'll find unusual dishes bearing the stamp of the Middle East, Portugal, the local Jewish community, and the days of the British Raj. Some age-old recipes have been passed on to the restaurant by local communities. The lofty, elegant dining room is windowed on all sides, and capped with a gabled wooden ceiling (resembling an upturned ship) supported by massive wood beams. Live sitar and tabla music is performed every evening. Don't miss out on the railway mutton curry (from the British Raj era) or the *chuttuli meen*, grilled fish cooked in spices, which is a favorite of local Jewish cuisine. The Padua Duck Moilee is another Kerala dish worth trying. Vegetarians may want to try the bol, deep-fried flat breads made from rice served with lentils. Wind up with the *vattalappam*, a Syrian Christian version of caramel custard utilizing jaggery and coconut milk. ⑤ *Average main: Rs. 800* ✉ *Brunton Boatyard Hotel, River Rd., Fort Cochin* ☎ *484/221–5461* ⊘ *No lunch.*

$
INDIAN

✕ **Kayees Rahmathullah.** Known for its biryani, a rice dish cooked with meat and spices, this very modest restaurant is the original, and people say it's the best, with some of the most authentic and lip-smackingly good Kerala food you will find—be ready for serious spice. There's usually a line for lunch on weekdays, and the menu may become more limited if you arrive late—they run out. A variety of biryanis is on offer, with both local and other regional specialties, such as Malabar-style, with fish, as well as vegetarian. Other notable dishes include the prawn fry, mutton fry, and fried fish curry with flaky flat bread. Be sure to wash down your meal with Kayees' special *jeera* water (boiled with cumin seeds), an ayurvedically approved drink that aids digestion. The restaurant is open relatively late, until about 9:45 pm. Another branch is in Ernakulam (P484–235–4321); it's air-conditioned, but the one in Mattancherry is easier to get to. ⑤ *Average main: Rs. 200* ✉ *Durbar Hall Rd., Mattancherry.*

$$$
CHINESE
✕ **Mainland China.** If you happen to be in the Ernakulam area and are craving for some especially good Chinese, do head to Mainland China, part of an upscale Indo-Chinese chain popular all over India. Wood-paneled walls and wooden chains with bright-orange cushions everywhere add style here. Tuck into their black-pepper prawns or the chilli sea bass. The General Tao Chicken, diced and cooked in a brown oyster sauce, is done well here. Vegetarians can try the lettuce wraps, chilli-garlic noodles, or a selection of dim sum dishes. There's also a buffet option. ⑤ *Average main: Rs. 700* ✉ *Dream Hotel, S.A. Rd., Kadavanthra, Ernakulam* ☎ *484/412–9999* ⌦ *Reservations essential.*

$$$$
ECLECTIC
Fodor's Choice
★
✕ **Malabar Junction.** The mix of regional specialties and Mediterranean cuisine at this small, quirky restaurant in a very elegant setting with an open side facing a garden and swimming pool, isn't as crazy as it sounds—most dishes veer closer to one side or the other. A tasty mahimahi fillet for instance, is flavored with local spices. If you're craving Western food, the pastas, like the homemade cheese ravioli, are excellent. Some North Indian food also available, and there is a selection of snacks for between meals. Seafood is always fresh and perfectly cooked. Don't miss the chocolate-filled samosas in mango sauce, the restaurant's signature dessert. The *chickoo* (sapodilla) parfait is also excellent. The restaurant has a large selection of Indian wines, too. ⑤ *Average main: Rs. 1000* ✉ *The Malabar House, 1/268–1/269 Parade Rd., Fort Cochin* ☎ *484/221–6666.*

$$$
INDIAN
✕ **Menorah.** Menorah, a fine tribute to Cochin's rich Jewish history, is in the former mansion of one of the city's best-known Jewish families, and the waitstaff will elaborate on the history and the family if you ask. Traditional Cochin-Jewish cuisine is served—try the *chemeen ularth*, a prawn fry, or *plav*, a rice and chicken dish, and the *mutta* roast (eggs cooked with a variety of spices). The fine table linens and stately surroundings recall the royalty, prime ministers and dignitaries that once dined here. An excellent selection of pasta is also available. Sip a glass of wine while looking out onto the courtyard with a pool to complete the picture of a bygone era. ⑤ *Average main: Rs. 700* ✉ *Koder House, Tower Rd., Fort Cochin* ☎ *484/221–8485* ⊕ *www.koderhouse.com.*

$$$$
SEAFOOD
✕ **The Rice Boat.** A favorite of Kochi's well-to-do and considered one of Kerala's best restaurants, the plush Rice Boat has a prime location right on the harbor. The restaurant, which has windows on three sides, is long and shaped like a traditional wooden boat. The menu stresses seafood, as you might expect, with much of it often caught just a few hours ago in the Chinese fishing nets or in boats nearby. Kerala specialties are made with saltwater, and the local freshwater fish are grilled and cooked in traditional curries. Try the *meen pollichathu*, the local pearl spot cooked wrapped in banana leaf. The showpiece is an interactive kitchen where you can chat with the chef as he prepares your meal. ⑤ *Average main: Rs. 1200* ✉ *Vivanta by Taj–Malabar Hotel, Malabar Rd., Willingdon Island* ☎ *484/664–3000* ⌦ *Reservations essential.*

$
ECLECTIC
✕ **Teapot Café.** This quirky two-story café, off Princess Street and near the harbor, has teapots and kettles decorating every available space, including some dangling from the ceiling; some tables are made from wooden tea chests. It's almost like being in a tea museum. There's a

8

fair selection of both Indian and continental food—roast chicken and potatoes, prawn *moilee* (in a coconut curry), vegetable stew—but the café is best known for its sandwiches (do try their Indie rarebit) and freshly baked cakes—in particular the Death by Chocolate. The relaxed atmosphere and extensive range of teas makes this place popular with tourists and locals alike; it's wonderful to laze away an hour or so here. In season it stays open till 10 pm or so. ⑤ *Average main: Rs. 150* ✉ *Peter Celli St., Fort Cochin* ☎ *484/221–8035* ⊘ *No dinner.*

$$$$ ✕ **Thai Pavilion.** Don't be surprised if your waiter explains each dish to
THAI you when he brings it—this was, after all, Kerala's first Thai restaurant (it's still immensely popular). The menu features plentiful seafood, as well as Vietnamese and Chinese. The *pla rad prik* includes a very soft fish, nicely flavored with basil, and the spicy classic *tom yam goong* soup, made with prawns, doesn't disappoint. The Thai chicken or vegetable green curry is popular, as, too, is the Thai-style pork ribs. The dining room is done up in warm woods, with silver and rich red accents on the ceiling and chairs as well as colorful murals. Beveled glass windows give you a glimpse of the sea. ⑤ *Average main: Rs. 800* ✉ *Vivanta by Taj–Malabar Hotel, Malabar Rd., Willingdon Island* ☎ *484/664–3000* ⌕ *Reservations essential.*

WHERE TO STAY

$$$$ 🏨 **Brunton Boatyard.** Built in a combination of Dutch and Portuguese
HOTEL colonial styles, this elegant hotel is on the site of a former boatyard, fac-
Fodor'sChoice ing the Chinese Fishing Nets; it's a perfect location. **Pros:** all rooms and
★ bathrooms are sea-facing; swanky hotel bar is one of the few in Kochi stocked with foreign liquor; great restaurants; Wi-Fi in all rooms. **Cons:** pricey; doesn't offer no-smoking rooms. ⑤ *Rooms from: Rs. 16000* ✉ *Calvetty Rd., Fort Cochin* ☎ *484/221–5461* ⊕ *www.cghearth.com* ⌕ *26 rooms, 4 suites* ⧄*Breakfast.*

$ 🏨 **Delight.** This spotless homestay is wildly popular with budget travel-
B&B/INN ers, in no small part because of the warm, knowledgeable, and extraordinarily helpful hosts who can arrange for great English-speaking taxi and auto drivers. **Pros:** quiet location across from cricket field and a short walk from the Chinese Fishing Nets; great value; really homey. **Cons:** showers in the pretty tiled bathrooms aren't separate, so the floor gets wet; extra 1,000 rupees charged for a/c. ⑤ *Rooms from: Rs. 2000* ✉ *Parade Ground, Ridsdale Rd., Fort Cochin* ☎ *484/221– 7658, 484/221–6301* ⊕ *www.delightfulhomestay.com* ⌕ *6 rooms* ⧄*Breakfast.*

$$ 🏨 **Fort Heritage.** Each room in this restored 17th-century Dutch man-
B&B/INN sion is slightly different from the next, though all are enormous and have towering wooden ceilings, period reproduction furniture, and an eccentric feel. **Pros:** great location; good price; friendly atmosphere. **Cons:** ground-floor rooms open directly into the restaurant; no Internet access; no swimming pool; no views. ⑤ *Rooms from: Rs. 5500* ✉ *1/283 Napier St., Elphinstone Rd., Fort Cochin* ☎ *484/221–5333, 484/221– 5455* ⊕ *www.fortheritage.com* ⌕ *12 rooms* ⧄*Breakfast.*

$$ 🏨 **Koder House.** Unlike the sober, patrician Dutch mansions nearby,
B&B/INN the three-story Koder House sticks out because of its brick exterior's

An antique shop in Kochi

fire-engine color and slightly unusual, Portuguese-inflected architecture. **Pros:** atmospheric; good restaurant, Menorah, is attached. **Cons:** staff can sometimes seem a little distracted. $ *Rooms from: Rs. 5500* ✉ *Tower Rd., Fort Cochin* ☎ *484/221–8485* ⤴ *6 rooms* ⚇ *Breakfast.*

$$
HOTEL ⚇ **Le Meridien.** On 25 landscaped acres on the outskirts of Ernakulam, this imposing, green-tile-roofed complex houses a massive hotel and South India's largest convention center. **Pros:** world class amenities; plenty of entertainment options, including one of Kerala's few night-clubs; excellent value for money. **Cons:** several kilometers from anything worth seeing; tasteful, but lacks local flavor. $ *Rooms from: Rs. 5500* ✉ *Kundannur Junction, NH–47 Bypass, Maradu, Ernakulam* ☎ *484/270–5777* ⊕ *www.lemeridien.com/cochin* ⤴ *223 rooms, 4 suites* ⚇ *Breakfast.*

$$$
HOTEL ⚇ **The Malabar House.** Luxurious but homey, this early-18th-century Dutch villa once housed European traders and bankers. **Pros:** elegant; restaurant might be Kochi's best; deluxe rooms open into private garden; hotel staff is friendly and helpful. **Cons:** expensive. $ *Rooms from: Rs. 9000* ✉ *1/268 Parade Rd., Fort Cochin* ☎ *484/221–6666* ⊕ *www.malabarhouse.com* ⤴ *15 rooms, 1 suite* ⚇ *Breakfast.*

$$
HOTEL ⚇ **No 18.** Much like its name, this long, modern, and blocky hotel, close to the ferry jetty, is a bit bland. **Pros:** ideally located; good prices (try asking for a discount); three restaurants serving a range of cuisines; Wi-Fi in room. **Cons:** not atmospheric or with much that feels like a local experience. $ *Rooms from: Rs. 4000* ✉ *Near Fort Cochin bus terminal, Fort Cochin* ☎ *86/0604–7544* ⊕ *www.no18.co.in* ⤴ *28 rooms, 1 suite* ⚇ *No meals.*

$ ⊞ **The Old Courtyard.** Slightly decrepit but still charming, this late-18th-
B&B/INN   century refurbished mansion in the heart of Fort Cochin has eight rooms
overlooking a central courtyard. **Pros:** great location; friendly staff.
Cons: a little worn around the edges and not as charming as neighboring hotels; basic accommodations without phones or Internet; no
restaurant but a small attached coffee shop. ⑤ *Rooms from: Rs. 3000*
✉ *1/371 Princess St., Fort Cochin* ☎ *484/221–5035, 484/221–6302*
⊕ *www.oldcourtyard.com* ⇆ *6 rooms, 2 suites* ⑩ *Breakfast.*

$$$ ⊞ **Old Harbour Hotel.** Just opposite the Chinese Fishing Nets, this 1837
HOTEL   Dutch heritage building, a former brokerage house, reopened in 2006
after a two-year restoration by the same folks who designed Brunton
Boatyard. **Pros:** the airy and appealing restaurant serves very good Ker-
ala delicacies; very good off-season discounts. **Cons:** TVs only available
on request. ⑤ *Rooms from: Rs. 7900* ✉ *1/328 Tower Rd., Fort Cochin*
☎ *484/221–8006, 484/221–8007* ⊕ *www.oldharbourhotel.com* ⇆ *13
rooms, 3 cottages* ⑩ *Breakfast.*

$$ ⊞ **Old Lighthouse Bristow.** This tastefully decorated hotel is the former
HOTEL   home of the late Sir Robert Bristow, the architect of the modern port
of Kochi. **Pros:** spa offers a variety of ayurvedic massages; pool; Wi-Fi
in all rooms. **Cons:** service is somewhat lacking; can be noisy because
it's on the busy Fort Cochin beach; need to book in advance. ⑤ *Rooms
from: Rs. 5000* ✉ *Near INS Dronacharya, Beach Rd., Fort Cochin*
☎ *484/305–0102, 484/221–5103* ⊕ *www.oldlighthousehotel.com*
⇆ *11 rooms* ⑩ *Breakfast.*

$ ⊞ **Raintree Lodge.** At the quiet end of busy Petercelle Street, this simply
B&B/INN   furnished hotel inside a 1700s Dutch building has earned raves for its
reasonable rates and good-looking rooms, furnished with two-poster
beds, wood furniture, and interesting masks and art, with the attached
bathrooms tiled in mustard. **Pros:** great location; atmospheric rooms.
Cons: no restaurant; no breakfast; no fridge in the room. ⑤ *Rooms
from: Rs. 2000* ✉ *1/618 Petercelli St., Fort Cochin* ☎ *484/325–1489*
⊕ *www.fortcochin.com* ⇆ *5 rooms* ⑩ *No meals.*

$ ⊞ **The Tower House.** Converted from a rambling 17th-century house,
HOTEL   this hotel, directly opposite the Chinese Fishing Nets, strikes the right
balance between providing modern amenities and lovely shared spaces
while retaining the integrity of the historic building. **Pros:** reasonably
priced; in the heart of historic Fort Cochin; has a garden pool; good
home-style meals. **Cons:** service is not their strongest point; no TVs;
mattresses a bit hard; no in-room safes. ⑤ *Rooms from: Rs. 3000*
✉ *1/320 Tower Rd., Fort Cochin* ☎ *484/221–6962* ⊕ *neemranahotels.
com/tower-house* ⇆ *14 rooms* ⑩ *Breakfast.*

$$$ ⊞ **Vivanta by Taj–Malabar.** Isolated at the tip of Willingdon Island, this
RESORT   grand hotel offers a heritage sensibility and style, and absolute luxury,
including simply excellent dining experiences. **Pros:** unmatched water
views of the harbors and of frigates going by; spacious rooms and great
atmosphere in the public spaces; fantastic restaurants that are some of
the best in Kerala. **Cons:** isolated on an island with little to do that's
far from city landmarks; the heritage rooms, which are the ones to get
and the reason for staying here, aren't cheap. ⑤ *Rooms from: Rs. 6500*

✉ *Malabar Rd., Willingdon Island* ☎ *484/664–3000* ⊕ *www.tajhotels. com* ⤴ *95 rooms, 9 suites* ⑩ *Breakfast.*

NIGHTLIFE AND PERFORMING ARTS

NIGHTLIFE

BARS

Armoury Bar. Brunton Boatyard's bar and café is decorated, as its name suggests, with rifles and other such colonial-era weaponry, as well as chests and maritime artifacts. The rich wood rafters and views of the harbor make it an excellent place for a sundowner or a late night drink. A pleasingly wide variety of cocktails are available. ✉ *Calvetty Rd., Brunton Boatyard, Fort Cochin* ☎ *484/221–5465, 484/221–5465* ⊕ *www.cghearth.com/brunton-boatyard.*

Seagull. Popular with both locals and tourists, Seagull is Kochi's best option for a chilled beer by the sea—in fact, it's one of the few places that serves liquor. The restaurant offers a large selection of local seafood and other dishes, and though the interior is rather basic, its outdoor seating on the pier makes it the ideal place to enjoy a relaxing meal to the sound of the ocean. ✉ *Calvathy Rd., Fort Cochin* ☎ *484/221–8128.*

PERFORMING ARTS

DANCE

Dating back to the 17th century, Kathakali is an art form in which elaborately made-up and costumed dancers tell epic stories using stylized hand gestures. For centuries, Kathakali performances were the only after-dark entertainment in Kerala; shows began at sundown and lasted all night. Today, for the benefit of tourists, performances are often shortened to one or two hours. Many centers also offer the chance to watch dancers being made up, which can be as entertaining as the show. Larger hotels all over the state organize impromptu and abridged performances of Kathakali and Mohiniyattam on their premises, either for free or for a small fee.

Cochin Cultural Centre. Kathakali performances in the air-conditioned room of the Cochin Cultural Centre start daily at 6 pm, though you should arrive an hour before the show to see makeup being applied. ✉ *K.B. Jacob Rd., near police station, Fort Cochin* ☎ *484/221–6911* ⊕ *www.cochinculturalcentre.com.*

Kerala Kalamandalam. This revered arts academy is credited with the revival of traditional arts in Kerala, providing training in Kathakali, Mohiniattam, and at least 14 different native art forms. You're welcome to watch students in practice sessions, weekdays from 9 am to 12:30 pm. ✉ *Cheruthuruthy, 29 km (18 miles) north of Thrissur)*

BEYOND KATHAKALI

Although Kathakali is by far the best-known form of local dance, some 50 other classical, folk, and tribal dances survive in Kerala. Many are unique to a particular caste or temple. The graceful, swaying movements of Mohiniyattam, a dance that lies somewhere between Kathakali and classical Bharata Natyam, are thought to mimic the movement of coconut palms.

8

Kathakali dancers

near NH 17, Thrissur ☎ *944/642–6662, 488/426–2418* ⊕ *www.kalamandalam.org.*

Kerala Kathakali Centre. This is a pleasant outdoor venue, where makeup starts at 5 pm and Kathakali shows follow at 6 pm daily. Short-term dance courses are held Saturday at 8 am. ⊠ *River Rd., near bus stand, opposite Brunton Boatyard, Fort Cochin* ☎ *484/221–5827* ⊕ *www.kathakalicentre.com* ◻ *Performances Rs. 300.*

See India Foundation. The director here provides lively explanations of the Kathakali dance before every show, held 6:45–8 pm in season. Makeup starts at 6 pm. ⊠ *Kalthil Parambil La., Ernakulam* ☎ *484/237–6471* ◻ *Rs. 200.*

MARTIAL ARTS

Kerala's dramatic, high-flying martial art, Kalaripayattu, may be the oldest in Asia. Some think it started in the 12th century, others think it began earlier, and still others say later. Some scholars believe that Buddhist monks from India introduced Kalaripayattu to China along with Buddhism. Participants learn both armed- and unarmed-combat techniques. One of the more unusual skills involves defending yourself against a knife-wielding attacker using only a piece of cloth. In peak season, many hotels stage performances.

E.N.S. Kalari Centre. If you call in advance, you can watch Kalarippayattu practitioners here, before 5 pm daily. ⊠ *Nettoor, Ernakulam* ☎ *484/270–0810, 944/707–0081* ⊕ *www.enskalari.org.in.*

SHOPPING

The streets surrounding the synagogue in Mattancherry are crammed with stores that sell curios, and Fort Cochin's Princess Street, Prince Street, Rose Street, and Peter Celli Street have all sprouted small shops worth a browse. For more serious, exhaustive hunts for saris, gold jewelry, handicrafts, and souvenirs, head to M. G. Road in Ernakulam. Be suspicious of the word "antique" in all stores, and bargain hard.

Anokhi. This outlet of the popular and sophisticated Rajasthani handicrafts and clothing shop carries beautifully tailored women's clothing and linens for the home. It's closed Sunday from May through July. ⊠ *1/297 Parade Rd., near Lilly St., Fort Cochin* ☎ *484/312–7426* ⊕ *www.anokhi.com.*

KERALA CRAFTS

Look for cups, vases, spoons, and teapots carved from coconut shells and baskets, floor and table mats, and carpets hand-woven from coir (coconut fiber), and sleeping mats and handbags made of resilient, pliable kova grass. Other goods include brass lamps and other brassware, rosewood elephants, lacquered wooden boxes with brass fittings—traditionally used to store the family jewels—and metal polished assiduously to make mirrors from Aranmula, northeast of Thiruvananthapuram. Cinnamon, cloves, cardamom, and other spices are also sold throughout Kerala, as is coffee.

Cinnamon. This branch of the chic Bangalore boutique stocks stylish ethnic and modern housewares, silk scarves and purses, jewelry, and Indo-Western designer clothing. The store is closed Sunday. ⊠ *1/658 Ridsdale Rd., Parade Ground, Fort Cochin* ☎ *484/221–7124, 484/221–8124* ⊕ *www.cinnamonthestore.com.*

Cochin Gallery. Jewelry, carpets, cushion covers, bronze figurines, and wooden boxes are sold at this gallery. ⊠ *6/116 Jew Town Rd., Mattancherry* ☎ *484/222–1225, 484/221–0851.*

Crafter's. Local hotels often get their antiques here. The store is crammed with stone and wood carvings, pillars, and doors as well as such portable items as painted tiles, navigational equipment, and wooden boxes. Crafter's also has a café upstairs. ⊠ *6/141 Jew Town Rd., Mattancherry* ☎ *484/222–3346.*

Fabindia. Stop here for a range of colorful hand-printed cotton garments—skirts, pants, tops, kurtis, kurtas, men's shirts, and saris. Their white tops are lovely. ⊠ *Napier St., near Parade Ground, Fort Cochin* ☎ *484/221–7077* ⊕ *www.fabindia.com.*

Fort Royal. This is an expensive all-in-one shop with goods from all over India. You can find brocade work, marble inlay boxes, and Kashmiri carpets, plus local handicrafts and precious and semiprecious jewelry. ⊠ *1/258 Napier St., Fort Cochin* ☎ *484/221–7832.*

Idiom Books. Whether you're looking for a little information on Kerala or a little something to while away the hours, stop by Idiom Books, a small bookshop opposite the synagogue, or its branch in Fort Cochin. You can find an intriguing collection of recent Western and Indian fiction,

8

as well as books on history, culture, cooking, and religion. ⊠ *Jew Town Rd., Mattancherry* ☎ *484/222–5604* ⊙ *Closed Sun.* ⊠ *1/348 Bastion St., near Princess St., Fort Cochin , Kochi.*

Indian Arts and Curios. This is one of Kerala's oldest and most-reliable curio shops. ⊠ *6/189 Jew Town Rd., Mattancherry* ☎ *484/222–8049.*

Indian Industries Arts and Crafts. John Korula and his family have been running this shop for more than half a century. This shop's name is far more pedestrian than its contents—it's a virtual Aladdin's cave of curios and antiques—masks, statues, sculpture, Christian artifacts, and much more. And no one will follow you around the shop insisting you buy this or that, as does happen elsewhere. Note that it closes for a lunch break from about 1:30 to 3 pm. ⊠ *1/364 Princess St., Fort Cochin* ☎ *484/221–6448* ⊙ *Closed Sun.*

Jayalakshmi. A mind-blowing selection of saris (including the Keralan style), *lehangas* (long skirts with fitted blouses), and the like are on offer here, as well as Indian and Western clothes for men and children. ⊠ *M. G. Rd., near Rajaji Rd., Ernakulam* ☎ *484/408–9899.*

Kairali. A fixed-price government shop, Kairali has a good selection of local handicrafts and curios. It's closed on Sunday. ⊠ *M. G. Rd., near Jose Junction, Ernakulam* ☎ *484/235–4507.*

Malabar Sarees. Try this small shop for silks by the meter. You can also buy a gorgeous Kerala sari or *veshti* (the men's wraparound skirt) and have a nearby tailor make it into a top or dress for you in a day or less, especially in you have a good sample for him to follow. ⊠ *1/323 Church La., off Rose Rd., Fort Cochin* ☎ *484/221–5977.*

Surabhi. Run by the state's Handicrafts Cooperative Society, Surabhi has an impressive selection of local products. ⊠ *M. G. Rd., Ernakulam* ☎ *484/238–0144.*

Tribes India. Indian tribal artisan work is sold through this cooperative store, which benefits the crafters directly. There's an unusual selection of crafts, including clothing and knickknacks. ⊠ *Ministry of Tribal Affairs, Ridsdale Rd., Fort Cochin Head Post Office, Fort Cochin* ☎ *484/221–5077* ⊕ *tribesindia.com* ⊙ *Mon.–Sat. 10–6:30.*

CENTRAL KERALA

Between Kochi and Quilon (Kollam), to the south, is the immense labyrinth of waterways called *kayals,* through which much of the life of the Malayalee has historically flowed. From the vastness of Vembanad Lake to quiet streams just large enough for a canoe, the backwaters region, Kuttanad, has carried Kerala's largely coconut-based products from village to market for centuries, and continues to do so today. You can relax at some of Kerala's finest resorts, or briefly join the floating lifestyle by taking a boat cruise for a few hours or a few days. A houseboat cruise is one of the best ways to see the fascinating river village life of central Kerala and should not be missed. A day's worth is quite adequate, but a few days of cruising can be magical.

The terrain rises and the temperature drops as you move inland, up into the teak-forested hills of Thekkady and Munnar. Kerala's interior is elephant country—you'll find them roaming in Periyar Wildlife Sanctuary and even appearing in the mists of Munnar's tea plantations.

KUMARAKOM

80 km (50 miles) south of Kochi.

Some of Kerala's finest resorts are hidden in this tiny, rapidly developing area on the shores of Vembanad Lake. The quiet, rustic town of Kumarakom is a haven just outside the humming market town of Kottayam, deep in Central Kerala's wealthy and lush belt of rubber plantations, many of which have been owned for generations by Syrian Christians. The Christian population is quite noticeable here, with churches and Christian shrines popping up on the horizon every five minutes as you drive. Kerala Christians are particularly devout, and you will see more nuns and fathers here than in most of parts of the world—in fact, this area exports priests to the rest of the world. Christianity has been practiced in these parts longer than anywhere in the western world.

Novelist Arundhati Roy's birthplace, Ayemenem (featured in her 1997 novel *The God of Small Things*) is nearby; the Coconut Lagoon hotel is next to it. Birds abound in the backwaters, as well as in the sanctuary on the lake's eastern shore. Sailing the Vembanad Lake or exploring the canals is the most enjoyable exploring you could do while in Kumarakom, apart from visiting a selection of seafood restaurants. A small cruise of the lake and the shores nearest to your hotel may be enough to get the flavor of it. A larger part of your time should be devoted to roaming the backwater canals and peeking at a slice of Kuttanad life.

GETTING HERE AND AROUND

A prepaid cab from Kochi airport (Rs 1,900 for a non-a/c car, one-way) is the safest and most hassle-free way of reaching Kumarakom.

There are few auto-rickshaws in the Kumarakom area, so your best best it so either hire and car-and-driver from your hotel or a travel agency or to take a speedboat, houseboat, or a small, traditional, motor-run ketch (about Rs. 1,000 an hour if hired through a hotel).

WHERE TO EAT AND STAY

$$$
SOUTH INDIAN
✕ **Lakshmi Hotel.** Reliable local fare is on offer here, along with North Indian specialties, though the menu is not lengthy. A visit to this restaurant is a bit of an adventure and a chance to see how locals dine. Service can be slow, but the food is freshly prepared, and the air-conditioned dining room is clean and comfortable, with brightly colored interiors, thought still a bit grungy. The restaurant is known for its karimeen fish wrapped in a banana leaf, and its traditional Kerala seafood and vegetarian dishes. $ *Average main: Rs. 500* ✉ *Kottayam–Kumarakom Rd., Kumarakom North* ☎ *481/252–3313.*

$$$
HOTEL
🏨 **Abad Whispering Palms.** This hotel's setting, in a natural backwater on the banks of Vembanad Lake, is ideal even if the rooms lack special charm. **Pros:** friendly and helpful staff; nice views; well priced; ayurvedic rejuvenation center. **Cons:** rooms need an upgrade. $ *Rooms*

from: Rs. 6500 ✉ *New Nazarath Rd., Konchumada* ☎ *481/252–3820* ⊕ *abadhotels.com/lakeresort* ⌇ *53 rooms* ⏐⊙⏐ *Breakfast.*

$$$$ 🏨 **Coconut Lagoon.** This groundbreaking and much-imitated Vembanad
RESORT Lake resort put Kerala's backwaters on the map. **Pros:** good restau-
Fodor's Choice rants; kid-friendly; eco-friendly; staff naturalists lead tours of local
★ bird sanctuary and the hotel's butterfly garden; can only be accessed
by boat. **Cons:** pricey two-story mansions have bathroom and bedrooms on different floors (opt for a bungalow); can only be reached by
boat. $ *Rooms from: Rs. 13500* ✉ *Vembanad Lake* ☎ *481/252–5834*
⊕ *www.cghearth.com* ⌇ *42 rooms, 8 suites* ⏐⊙⏐ *Some meals.*

$$$ 🏨 **The Grove.** This sleek and modern resort, right on Vembanad Lake,
RESORT makes no attempt to create typical Kerala ambience though it does
have charm of its own. **Pros:** well priced; sparkling. **Cons:** does not
reflect local character; can be quite busy; no spa. $ *Rooms from: Rs.
8000* ✉ *New Nazareth Rd., Konchumada* ☎ *481/252–6252* ⊕ *www.
chakraresorts.com/#the_grove* ⌇ *24 rooms* ⏐⊙⏐ *Breakfast.*

$$$$ 🏨 **Kumarakom Lake Resort.** In the heritage section of this beautiful, lush
RESORT 25-acre lakefront property, the palatial traditional villas, reassembled
Fodor's Choice from old houses, are set around a network of canals and lawns dotted
★ with long black Kerala canoes filled with plants. **Pros:** amazing 820-
foot meandering infinity pool; gorgeous traditional setting; large and
varied buffet; pottery classes. **Cons:** pricey; large, less intimate resort
that can get noisy. $ *Rooms from: Rs. 13000* ✉ *Kumarakom North*
☎ *481/252–4900, 1800/425–5030* ⊕ *www.kumarakomlakeresort.in*
⌇ *33 rooms, 26 villas* ⏐⊙⏐ *Breakfast.*

$$$$ 🏨 **Vivanta by Taj–Kumarakom.** The main building of this tranquil, verdant
RESORT resort is an 1891 plantation house, set among rubber trees, built by the
son of an English missionary. **Pros:** trees are populated by winged resi-
dents of the nearby bird sanctuary; excellent seafood restaurant; nice
pool-facing gym; rooms have big tubs; plenty of activities for children.
Cons: not as carefully maintained as other Taj properties; pricey; very
little lakefront or backwaters view; staff can be slightly indifferent.
$ *Rooms from: Rs. 13000* ☎ *481/252–5711, 481/252–1116* ⊕ *www.
vivantabytaj.com* ⌇ *18 rooms* ⏐⊙⏐ *Breakfast.*

$$$ 🏨 **Zuri Kumarakom Resort and Spa.** The impressive, giant four-headed
RESORT statue of a Kathakali dancer in the gleaming lobby, the boat-shape
check-in desk, and the backwater setting all locate the property soundly
in Kerala, but guests checked into this luxurious resort could easily forget where they are as they indulge in the decidedly untraditional couple's
massage at the Maya spa or relax with a Havana stogie in the cigar bar.
Pros: standard rooms are a good value; enormous modern spa has both
ayurvedic and Western treatments. **Cons:** massage rates are rather high;
look elsewhere if you want a Kerala experience: lacks the elegance of
its neighbors, while its rates are still high. $ *Rooms from: Rs. 9500*
✉ *Karottukayal, Kumarokom* ☎ *481/252–7272* ⊕ *www.thezurihotels.
com/kumarakom* ⌇ *72 rooms* ⏐⊙⏐ *Breakfast.*

ALLEPPEY

35 km (22 miles) southwest of Kumarakom.

This city was once known as the Venice of India, though most residents have abandoned their canoes for cars. Alleppey (Alappuzha) is an important gateway to the backwaters—tour operators abound, and several resorts 30 minutes out of the town are a good alternative to the pricier properties in Kumarakom.

Alleppey, from the tourist's point of view, is essentially an access point to the backwaters and does not offer much in the way of sights. It's a lively, noisy town of bazaars, with a unattractive beach, and the administrative headquarters of the surrounding district, so most visitors hurry through on their way to the lagoons. However, if you are looking to hire a houseboat for a day or more, Alleppey is the best place to do it.

GETTING HERE AND AROUND

Alleppey is a one-hour drive from Kochi. Prepaid cabs booked and paid for at Kochi airport (Rs. 1,900 for a non-a/c taxi one-way and Rs. 2,150 for a/c taxi) are the safest and most hassle-free way of reaching your hotel outside Alleppey. The Jan Shatabdi express train connects Alleppey with Ernakulam, Quilon, Thiruvananthapuram, and Calicut and is the quickest way to get here. There are slower trains connecting Alleppey with Varkala and other smaller towns of Kerala. Alleppey has plenty of auto-rickshaws, but the best way to get about Alleppey is by houseboat or another water vessel—the scenery is gorgeous, and the canals are practically right at your door in nearly any hotel you're likely to stay at here.

EXPLORING

Kerala Kayaking. A four-hour kayak tour of the Alleppey backwaters is a very peaceful way to see the lagoons up close. Tours, which cost Rs. 1,500, begin at 6:30 am; they come with a guide as well as a backup boat. Longer tours as well as two-seater kayaks are available. Credit cards are available. ⊠ *Near Vazhicherry Bridge, opposite Indian Oil Petrol Pump, Sanathanam Ward* ☎ *984/658–5674, 854/748–7701* ⊕ *www.keralakayaking.com/home.*

Nehru Cup Snake Boat Race. On the second Saturday in August throngs of supporters line the shore to watch the annual Nehru Cup Snake Boat Race, which starts with a water procession and concludes dramatically as the boats (propelled by as many as 100 rowers) vie for the trophy. The best way to see the race is from a houseboat that you have booked far in advance. Several other snake-boat races take place in the area from mid-July to mid-September. Check with the Alleppey Tourism Development Cooperative (ATDC) for exact times and locations.

St. Andrew's Forane Church. At Arthunkal, 20 km (12 miles) north of Alleppey and 22 km (14 miles) south of Kumarakom, stands the ancient St Andrew's Forane Church. It was built in 1581 by Portuguese missionaries out of wood and coconut fronds, in honor of St Andrew the Apostle. This was done with the permission of the area's Hindu king and the cooperation of local Hindus; according to the church's history, the church was considered holy by Hindus as well, and the king

8

even visited the shrine. In 1584, the church was rebuilt in stone and then renovated some years later, too. It's one of the oldest and more impressive churches in a state where you can spot startling-looking church every few miles. You will pass through Arthunkal on your way to Alleppey from either Kochi or Kumarakom. The church makes for an interesting break. ⊠ *Arthunkal, Alleppey district, Cherthala* ⊕ *www. arthunkalchurch.org.*

WHERE TO EAT

Most of the best food in the area is likely to be what's served in the hotel or resort you're staying at.

$$
SOUTH INDIAN

✕ **Chakara.** Raheem Residency, on Alleppey's main beach, is in an elegant old British-built bungalow dating from the 19th century. Its partially alfresco restaurant serves a variety of cuisines—Kerala, North Indian, and some western dishes. Try the Alleppey fish curry, the Kerala prawns roast, or a chicken biryani (served only at lunch). Another good option is chicken *makhani* (in a creamy sauce), accompanied by either chapati or *puri* breads. From an upper floor here you can get a view of the buzzing beach. ⑤ *Average main: Rs. 350* ⊠ *Beach Rd.* ☎ *477/223–9767* ⊕ *www.raheemresidency.com/restaurant.html.*

WHERE TO STAY

$$
RESORT

🛏 **Abad Turtle Beach.** Although not as luxurious as some of its neighbors, this resort combines comfort with serenity. **Pros:** excellent location; bicycles for rent; ayurvedic center; well priced. **Cons:** busy in high season. ⑤ *Rooms from: Rs. 4000* ⊠ *Varankavala, Pollathai, Mararikulam* ☎ *478/218–6966, 478/218–6968* ⊕ *www.abadhotels.com/mararibeach* ⤼ *29 rooms* †◎† *Breakfast.*

$$$
HOTEL

🛏 **A Beach Symphony.** Each of these luxury private cottages, in a delightful beach garden hotel with coconut palms, has a spacious veranda where all meals are served, and some have their own private swimming pool (the others share a pool). **Pros:** high levels of privacy; cottages have Wi-Fi. **Cons:** gets booked up fast; might be too quiet and intimate for some; spa needs soundproofing; Marari Beach is not that pristine. ⑤ *Rooms from: Rs. 8900* ⊠ *Marari Beach Rd., Mararikulam* ☎ *91974/429–7123* ⊕ *www.abeachsymphony.com* ⤼ *4 cottages* †◎† *Some meals.*

$$$
RESORT

🛏 **Kayaloram Heritage Lake Resort.** Just steps from the backwaters, and set among about an acre of manicured gardens in a sunny coconut grove, this pleasant, small-scale hotel consists of tiny, simple cottages that surround the restaurant and reception area. **Pros:** quiet, intimate environment; cute and homey; splendid views. **Cons:** no TV; a/c is only on at night; hotel may lack enough creature comforts for some. ⑤ *Rooms from: Rs. 6100* ⊠ *Punnamada Lake* ☎ *477/223–2040* ⊕ *www.mirresorts.in/kayaloram-lake-resort-alleppey.html* ⤼ *12 cottages* †◎† *Breakfast.*

$
B&B/INN

🛏 **Keraleeyam.** This quaint and quirky waterfront property specializes in ayurvedic treatments. **Pros:** inexpensive; divinely pretty location; great deals on all-inclusive ayurvedic packages. **Cons:** very basic; spotty service; no TV or Internet in rooms; far from any main drag. ⑤ *Rooms* *from: Rs. 2257* ✉ *Thathampally* ☎*477/223–1468, 477/223–6950* ⊕ *www.keraleeyam.com* ⟿ *13 rooms* ❍❘ *No meals.*

$$$$
RESORT
⊡ **Marari Beach Resort.** With a private and unspoiled palm-fringed beach, an excellent ayurvedic center, and easy access to both Kochi and the backwaters, Marari packs a lot of Kerala into one bundle. **Pros:** spacious rooms; friendly and professional staff; ayurvedic spa; eco-friendly; pool, tennis courts, and volleyball; luxury villas have their own pools. **Cons:** no TVs; beach is closed during monsoons. ⑤ *Rooms from: Rs. 13000* ✉ *Mararikulam* ☎*478/286–3801* ⊕ *www.cghearth.com* ⟿ *52 villas* ❍❘ *Breakfast.*

$$$
RESORT
⊡ **Marari Villas.** An hour from Kochi, on the secluded Marari beach—considered one of Kerala's finest—this select set of villas (named Orchid, Hibiscus, Palm, and Bougainvillea) is run by a Russian-British couple who found a gap in the local hotel market: each villa has its own butler and chef. **Pros:** private setting on the beach; super-attentive service; payments can be made online. **Cons:** lacks the functionality of a hotel and might be too small for some; closed part of the year. ⑤ *Rooms from: Rs. 9000* ✉ *Marari Beach, Mararikulam, Pollethai* ☎*994/794–8707, 994/794–8868* ⊕ *www.mararivillas.com* ⟿ *4 villas* ⊙ *Closed mid-June–late July* ❍❘ *Breakfast.*

$
RESORT
⊡ **Palm Grove Lake Resort.** Simplicity rules the day at this coconut plantation hideaway near the starting point of the Nehru Cup Snake Boat Race. **Pros:** large, clean rooms; location, location, location. **Cons:** small hotel that might seem a little claustrophobic to some. ⑤ *Rooms from: Rs. 2250* ✉ *Punnamada* ☎*477/223–5004, 477/224–3474* ⊕ *www. palmgrovelakeresort.com* ⟿ *4 cottages, 2 suites* ❍❘ *No meals.*

$$$$
RESORT
⊡ **Punnamada Resort.** Drive 15 or 20 minutes out of the bustling, less appealing Alleppey and you hit the quiet green backwoods of Punnamada Lake, on the backwaters. **Pros:** beautiful lake views and serene atmosphere; relatively good value; safes in room. **Cons:** secluded location may be too quiet for some. ⑤ *Rooms from: Rs. 12000* ✉ *Punnamada Jetty Rd., Punnamada* ☎*477/223–3690, 477/223–3692* ⊕ *www. punnamada.com* ⟿ *26 rooms* ❍❘ *Breakfast.*

QUILON

71 km (44 miles) north of Thiruvananthapuram; 87 km (54 miles) south of Alleppey.

If you're coming up from Thiruvananthapuram, central Kerala starts here, with the peaceful waters of the eight-armed Ashtamudi Lake. The waterfront here is not nearly as developed as Vembanad Lake, and the few resorts are utterly peaceful and reasonably priced. Quilon itself is bustling and fairly nondescript, and most travelers pass through fairly quickly.

GETTING HERE AND AROUND

Quilon is about a two-hour drive from Thiruvananthapuram's airport. Prepaid cabs booked and paid for at Thiruvananthapuram airport (Rs. 1,900 for a non-a/c taxi one-way) are the best way of reaching your hotel outside Quilon. Kochi is nearly three hours away from Quilon and Alleppey two hours by road. The Jan Shatabdi express train connects Quilon with Thiruvananthapuram in the south and Alleppey, Ernakulam, and Calicut in the north and is the quickest way to get to Kollam. You can catch a ferry from Quilon (Kollam) in the morning and reach Alleppey eight hours later.

The distances in Quilon are too big to make using an auto-rickshaw practical, so get a car and driver from your hotel or from a travel agent.

THEKKADY

130 km (81 miles) east of Kumarakom; 195 km (121 miles) east of Kochi.

Due east of Kumarakom, Kottayam, and Kochi, this cool mountain town, thick with spice plantations, sits at 3,000 feet above sea level in the Cardamom Hills, midway between Kochi and the temple city of Madurai in Tamil Nadu. The hills are home to a range of wildlife, including (rarely spotted) tigers, as well as acres and acres of cardamom, cloves, allspice, vanilla, cocoa, and coffee. Most hotels and resorts are in Kumily town, about 4 km (2½ miles) from the Periyar Wildlife Sanctuary at Thekkady. Due to the high elevation, you don't need a room with air-conditioning here.

GETTING HERE AND AROUND

Thekkady is a six-hour drive from Kochi and five hours from Kumarakom. It can be an exhausting uphill drive, with many bends, and ideally it should be done in a good car, with a skilled driver and on an empty stomach. You can also reach Thekkady from Munnar (112 km or 70 miles; four hours). You will also need a hired car to get around the area, especially if you choose to stay outside Thekkady and Kumily town.

EXPLORING

Periyar Wildlife Sanctuary. In the vicinity of Thekkady, the Periyar Wildlife Sanctuary is one of India's best animal parks for spotting elephants, bison, wild boar, oxen, deer, black-faced Nilgiri langurs and lion-tailed macaques (two kinds of monkeys), and many species of birds. The best viewing period is March and April, when other watering holes have dried up and wildlife, including leopards and tigers, is forced to approach the lake to drink. Still, you have a good chance of seeing animals resident October through May.

Lake Periyar, its many fingers winding around low-lying hills, is the heart of the nearly 303-square-km (117-square-mile) sanctuary. Forget exhausting treks or long safaris. At this sanctuary, unlike any other in India, you lounge in a motor launch as it drifts around bends and comes upon animals drinking at the shores. ■TIP➜ Be prepared: Indian children (and adults) love to scream and shout at wildlife sightings. On a quiet trip, elephants hardly notice the intrusion, although younger pachyderms will peer at you out of curiosity and then run squealing back to their elders when your boat comes too close. If you're brave-hearted, you can spend a night doing a night trek (Rs. 1,000 per person), staying overnight in a jungle lodge. If you do go out in the forest, be prepared for leeches on the ground, especially during the monsoon. For information about treks in the park, which start at 7 every morning, contact the Wildlife Preservation Officer. The Kerala Tourism Development Corporation (KTDC), which has an office Ernakulam, Kochi, can also help you plan. ☎ 486/922–457 *Wildlife Preservation Officer, 484/235–3234 KTDC* ⊕ *idukki.nic.in/thekkady.htm and www.periyarfoundation.org* ✑ *Park entry Rs. 300. Boat safaris: Rs. 150; camera charge Rs. 25; video camera charge: Rs. 100* ⊗ *Boat safaris: daily at 7, 9:30, 11:30, 2, and 4. Book one day in advance with KTDC or at boat landing point in Thekkady* ⊗ *Park open daily 6–5.*

WHERE TO EAT

$ NORTH INDIAN ✕ **Ambadi.** Like the rest of the resort, the Ambadi's multicuisine restaurant has a rustic feel and is decorated with lots of wood. Head here for well-executed North Indian staples, such as kebabs and other tandoori dishes, butter chicken, and biryani, as well as Indo-Chinese options. Also on the menu are Kerala specials and Western dishes, including fish-and-chips and some pastas. ⑤ *Average main: Rs. 220* ⊠ *Ambadi Hotel, Kumily Rd.* ☎ 4869/222–193.

$$$ SOUTH INDIAN ✕ **The Tiffin Room.** This all-day hotel restaurant serves some of the best food in the area. You can choose to eat inside the thatched main building, decorated with a handsome and colorful selection of cattle masks, on a veranda overlooking the pool, or in the garden. North Indian dishes, pasta, pizza, sandwiches are all available, but the Kerala specialties are especially delicious and should not be missed—these include the *panni kurumulaku* roast, peppery roast pork, and the *malli meen pudhina*, grilled fish in a mint, coconut, and cilantro sauce. Ask for the pungent okra or green-banana pickle. Buffet lunches and dinners are also available. Another resort restaurant, 50 Mile Diet, serves food made only with local produce. ⑤ *Average main: Rs. 650* ⊠ *Spice Village, Kumily Rd., Kumily* ☎ 4869/224–514, 4869/222–315 ⊕ *www.cghearth.com/spice-village.*

WHERE TO STAY

$$ HOTEL ⊡ **Cardamom Club.** A fork in the road branches off to a 2-km-long (1-mile-long), bumpy ghost of a road (almost a track) that heads to the V & V Estate, a spice plantation that holds this small resort, which emerges like a little paradise from the undergrowth. **Pros:** great place to forget the rat race; good spa and excellent food. **Cons:** far away from any excitement; pricey. ⑤ *Rooms from: Rs. 5799* ⊠ *256 V & V Estate, Spring Valley, 66th mile, Kumily* ☎ 471/226–7333 ⊕ *www.niraamaya.in/thekkady.html* ⪢ *6 rooms* ⑪ *Breakfast.*

$$$$ HOTEL ⊡ **Hotel Lake Palace.** A ferry transports you to this former maharaja's hunting lodge on an island inside the Lake Periyar Wildlife Sanctuary, where you can spot wildlife from your balcony. **Pros:** attentive service; the best lodge in Thekkady for watching wildlife. **Cons:** bathrooms need updating, not very luxurious, given the rates; no safe in rooms; you need to book in advance; entry into the resort possible only between 6 am and 6 pm. ⑤ *Rooms from: Rs. 12000* ⊠ *Periyar Wildlife Sanctuary* ☎ 486/232–2023 ⊕ *www.lakepalacethekkady.com* ⪢ *6 rooms* ⑪ *All meals* ⑤ *Rooms from: Rs. 12000* ⊠ *Shanmugham Rd., Ernakulam, Kochi* ☎ 484/235–3234 ⊕ *www.ktdc.com.*

8

$$$
RESORT
FAMILY
🏯 **Muthoot Cardamom County.** Views from this steeply pitched resort are gorgeous, and on the grounds there's a fishpond where you can catch your own dinner. **Pros:** great ayurvedic massage center with a well-trained doctor; large swimming pool. **Cons:** fills up with package tourists; can be noisy; could be better priced. $ *Rooms from: Rs. 10000* ⊠ *Thekkady Rd., Kumily* ☎ *486/922–4501 to 4503* ⊕ *www.cardamomcounty.com* ⇨ *42 rooms, 2 suites* ⎜⊙⎜ *Breakfast.*

$$$
RESORT
🏯 **Shalimar Spice Garden.** This rustic retreat, inside a cardamom, allspice, and cloves plantation, lies 15 bone-jarring minutes and 6 km off the main road to Kumily, but once you're there, the emphasis is on serenity and relaxation; most guests come for ayurvedic treatment and yoga. **Pros:** gorgeous setting; rooms include complimentary slippers and heaters; pool. **Cons:** too isolated for some; rooms are somewhat small; not a place to venture to during the monsoon. $ *Rooms from: Rs. 7000* ⊠ *Kumily* ☎ *486/130–6352* ⊕ *www.shalimarkerala.net* ⇨ *20 rooms* ⎜⊙⎜ *Breakfast.*

$$$
RESORT
Fodor'sChoice
★
🏯 **Spice Village.** One of Thekkady's finest resorts, with top-notch service, Spice Village is also eco-friendly, running partially on solar energy and recycling all its waste within the premises. **Pros:** plenty of things to do; good location; chlorine-free pool; fantastic collection of animal masks. **Cons:** easy to get lost in this large resort, and cottages perhaps too close to each other in some parts. $ *Rooms from: Rs. 7500* ⊠ *Kumily Rd., Kumily* ☎ *486/922–2314, 486/922–2315* ⊕ *www.cghearth.com* ⇨ *52 rooms* ⎜⊙⎜ *Breakfast.*

$
B&B/INN
🏯 **The Wilderness.** Hardly a kilometer from the gates of the Periyar park stands a cute two-story cobblestone building with 10 cottage-style rooms. **Pros:** good value; intimate; decent Internet. **Cons:** no restaurant; might be too simple, with not enough creature comforts for some. $ *Rooms from: Rs. 3500* ⊠ *Thekkady Rd., Kumily* ☎ *4869/224–030, 4869/211–471* ⊕ *www.wildernest-kerala.com* ⇨ *10 rooms* ⎜⊙⎜ *Breakfast.*

MUNNAR

100 km (62 miles) north of Thekkady; 130 km (80 miles) east of Kochi.

On the drive from Thekkady to Munnar, a good road winds through lofty forests as well as spice and tea plantations. As you make the final climb to Munnar the hillside is richly carpeted with iridescent bushes and bushes of tea. Tea has been grown in Munnar for well over a hundred years, since about 1880. Like so many such areas in India, it reflects a long, virtually unchanged history—groups of workers heading out to pick the the leaves, overstuffed sacks of the leaves heading to the factory, sleepy shacks clustered around a tea factory.

The town of Munnar itself is small and unattractive, though its Christ Church, less than a kilometer above the main town and built of British planters, is worth a quick visit for its atmosphere and the old memorial plaques inside.

Most of the land around Munnar is owned by the tea section of the huge Tata Group, and a few smaller concerns, resulting in a kind of unspoiled hill station, with acres of tea, coffee, and cardamom plantations amid

A houseboat on the backwaters

hills, lakes, streams, and waterfalls. During your visit you can tour these plantations; arrange trekking, rock-climbing, paragliding, and river trips; or just sit on your hotel balcony with—what else?—a cup of tea, taking in the scenery. It's quite cool here, so you don't need to find a hotel with air-conditioning.

GETTING HERE AND AROUND

Munnar is easily accessed from Kochi or from Thekkady, both roughly four hours away using a car and driver. It should be done in a good, powerful car, with a skilled driver. The initial climb is a treat as you wind through ravines, thick tropical jungle that includes sandalwood forests, and across many rivers.

You will also need a hired car to get around Munnar, especially if you should choose to stay outside the town.

EXPLORING

Most lodgings can arrange a tea plantation tour, where you can walk through the steeply pitched, dense green hedges, and see how the leaf is processed.

You may like to also take a drive to see two of Munnar's lakes that have resulted in the area being compared to England's Lake District—the Sita Devi lake at Devikulum (7 km or 4 miles away) or Mattupetty Dam (13 km or 8 miles away). Cardamom plantations can be quite idyllic. The shade-loving spice needs plenty of forest cover, so a walk through a plantation feels like a stroll in the woods, complete with dappled sunlight, mountain streams, and birdsong.

Picking tea leaves

Visit the Rajamala Wildlife Sanctuary to catch a view of the rare Nilgiri tahr (mountain goat), and the Chinnar Wildlife Sanctuary (60 km or 37 miles) to see deer, bison, or elephants.

Rajamala Wildlife Sanctuary. This very well maintained 97-square-km (24,000-acre) sanctuary, 15 km (9 miles) northwest of Munnar, is home to the endangered Nilgiri tahr (*Nilgiritragus hylocrius*), an ibex-like goat that inhabits the highest, wettest reaches of the Western Ghats in Tamil Nadu and Kerala. It has lost numbers to poaching and shrinking habitat, leaving a population of just 1,300 in the park, roughly half of the world's total number. Here you can get quite close to this endearingly tame creature, pushed to the brink of extinction in part because of its utter lack of suspicion of humans. There are often long lines in season to buy your ticket, so it's a good idea to book in advance, or head early. From the entrance a park bus takes you about 7 km (4½ miles) into the hill, from which you can walk nearly 1½ km (1 mile) farther, to a higher lookout point. The craggy mountain views and gushing waterfalls in the monsoon add to the allure of this park. ■ TIP→ The sanctuary is closed for about 90 days during the calving season, roughly from February to April (check ahead of time) and occasionally for a day or so during the monsoons if there have been heavy rains. ✉ *Evarikulam National Park, Idukki District* ☎ *486/523–1587, 083/0102–4187* ⊕ *www.eravikulam. org* ✉ *Rs. 260; Rs. 25 for a camera; Rs. 200 for video* ☼ *Daily 8–4:30.*

Tata Tea Museum. At one of the only museums of its kind in India, you can learn about the history of local tea growing and view the antique furnishings of an estate manager's bungalow. Another highlight is the second-century-BC urn found at one of the tea estates nearby. You can also sample this area's famous blends in the tasting room. ⊠ *Kanan Devan Hills Plantations Company, Nalluthanni Estate, Idukki District* ☎ *4865/255–273* ⊕ *kdhptea.com/tea_museum.html* ⊠ *Rs. 80, camera Rs. 20* ☽ *Tues.–Sun. 9–4.*

Top Station. Take a drive to see the highest lookout points around Munnar, which offer great views of the tea estates below—one of the best is Top Station, 32 km (20 miles; 40 minutes) from Munnar town and 518 meters (1,700 feet) above sea level, across the border in Tamil Nadu, in the Kannan Devan hills. It gets its name from once being the highest point of a ropeway from which tea from Munnar was sent down to the town of Kottagudi. ⊠ *Idukki District.*

WHERE TO EAT

The best restaurants in Munnar are within the resorts. It is best to call ahead to notify them of your visit, because you might go a long way to find them closed, or not much available.

$$
INTERNATIONAL

✕ **Hill Spice.** The airy, glass-roofed Hill Spice, at the Tall Trees hotel, is a more elegant alternative to the restaurants in Munnar's main bazaar. Indian, Indo-Chinese (*hakka* noodles, chilli chicken) and continental food (fried fish, pasta) are all available, but the Kerala dishes are your best bet. The restaurant also offers thalis and buffet meals; there's alfresco seating and a grill at a terrace nearby when the weather is fine. ⑤ *Average main: Rs. 300* ⊠ *Tall Trees, Bison Valley Rd.* ☎ *4865/230–641* ⊕ *www.ttr.in.*

$
SOUTH INDIAN

✕ **Saravana Inn.** The hole-in-the-wall Saravana Inn, in the main town, serves South Indian delights—*dosa, idli, wada, sambar*—at great prices in simple surroundings. Although locals do call this Saravana Bhavan, it's not a branch of the popular international, Chennai-based chain. Still, the South Indian vegetarian fare here is undeniably good. ⑤ *Average main: Rs. 200* ⊠ *Munnar main market, M. G. Rd., near Gandhi statue* ☎ *4865/232–115.*

WHERE TO STAY

$$
HOTEL

🏨 **Blackberry Hills Retreat and Spa.** A seriously steep walk downhill through seriously green environs brings you to a clutter of whitewashed, terra-cotta-roofed cottages, clinging to the slope and with a bird's-eye view of tea plantations for miles around, including workers' settlements and a small blue-roofed church. **Pros:** not too far from the town (but not too close either); reasonably well-priced; Internet in room; spa; library. **Cons:** no room service or minibar in the room, though there is a hot water kettle; a new resort is being built nearby and may spoil the isolation; very steep climbs to the restaurant and reception. ⑤ *Rooms from: Rs. 5500* ⊠ *Bison Valley Rd., Pothamedu Viewpoint* ☎ *4865/232–978, 4865/232–979* ⊕ *www.blackberryresorts.com* ⤴ *18 rooms* ⑩| *Breakfast.*

$
B&B/INN

🏨 **Kaivalyam Retreat.** This is essentially a simple but beautifully maintained yoga retreat run by a couple who are both instructors. **Pros:** nice views; eco-friendly; very peaceful place. **Cons:** can get noisy with families around; isolated. ⑤ *Rooms from: Rs. 3200* ⊠ *Pallivasal Estate, opposite Workers Recreation Center, Moolakada,* ☎ *94/9582–1617* ⊕ *kaivalyamretreat.com* ⤴ *8 rooms* ⑩| *All meals.*

8

$$$ **Mountain Club.** Fluttering eucalyptus trees frame an alluring resort
HOTEL   of tile-roofed cobblestone cottages, some of them two-story. **Pros:** nice
ambience, TVs in the room, ayurvedic treatments available. **Cons:**
reaching the multicuisine restaurant is a climb; no Internet in the room,
far from the main town; popular, so expect crowds in high season.
[$] *Rooms from: Rs. 6000* ⊠ *Chinnakanal* ☎ *486/824–9978, 486/824–
9979* ⊕ *www.mountainclub.co.in* ⤴ *50 rooms* ↿⊙↾ *Breakfast.*

$$$ **The Tall Trees.** You can hardly spot the clapboard wood-and-stone
HOTEL   structures of this hushed, breezy resort on a 66-acre cardamom plan-
tation where the views are of trees, trees, and more trees. **Pros:** large
rooms; hotel arranges lots of activities. **Cons:** tiring walk uphill to the
restaurant; a lot to pay for relatively basic accommodations. [$] *Rooms
from: Rs. 7100* ⊠ *Bison Valley Rd.* ☎ *486/523–2717, 486/523–2716,
486/523–0593* ⊕ *www.ttr.in* ⤴ *19 cottages* ↿⊙↾ *No meals.*

$$$ **Windermere Estate.** Plantation life can be good when you're not work-
HOTEL   ing in the fields and are instead made to feel like the guest of a planter,
either in one of the five bedrooms of the main guesthouse, which has a
communal balcony, or in an individual cottage. **Pros:** service is warm
and personalized, and you are often eating the bounty of the plantation,
including sweet carrots, cardamom-flower infused honey, tree-tomato
juice, and fresh nutmeg pickle; great views, **Cons:** basic amenities, no
TVs or bar; pricey, electricity flucutates in the rain, but there is a backup
generator. [$] *Rooms from: Rs. 10000* ⊠ *Pothamedu* ☎ *484/242–5237
reservations, 486/523–0512* ⊕ *www.windermeremunnar.com* ⤴ *18
rooms* ↿⊙↾ *Some meals.*

SOUTHERN KERALA

The beaches near Kovalam are southern Kerala's main attraction—in
fact, they're what brought Western tourists to the state in the first place,
as the hippie scene from Goa moved down the coast. Parts of Kovalam
are now overdeveloped and remain full of touts selling cheap tie-dyed
clothes. There are, however, still some pleasant spots to relax within a
few miles of the main beach.

Kovalam's hippie vibe sets it apart from other more solemn beach places
in Kerala —the main drag on Lighthouse Beach is fairly lively, if a bit
seedy. Just a half hour from Kovalam is Kerala's capital city of Thiru-
vananthapuram (Trivandrum), the former home of the rajas of Travan-
core and now home to Kerala's primary international airport. Varkala,
slightly to the north of Thiruvananthapuram, has also gained tremen-
dous popularity as a beach town. The place has a slow charm that
grows on you. It's not as action-packed as Kovalam, but its numerous
thatched food stalls, an ever-increasing number of low-budget hotels,
and the pilgrims the town pulls in to see the Janardhana Swamy Temple
all add to a festive feeling.

THIRUVANANTHAPURAM (TRIVANDRUM)

222 km (138 miles) south of Kochi; 253 km (157 miles) southwest of Thekkady.

Built on seven low hills and cleansed by ocean breezes, Kerala's capital is surprisingly calm and pleasant, with wide avenues and some rather baronial buildings, a legacy of colonial times. Thiruvananthapuram's few sights and quiet lanes outside the town center make it an enjoyable place to spend part of a day or so, to have lunch, see a few landmarks, and shop a bit. Most leisure travelers decide to base themselves in any of the better-located hotels in Kovalam and then just make a visit to Thiruvananthapuram.

GETTING HERE AND AROUND

Thiruvananthapuram is 212 km (134 miles; about six hours or less) by road from Kochi. If you choose some of the coastal roads it is a lovely drive. The efficient intercity express train Jan Shatabdi connects Thiruvananthapuram with Quilon, Alleppey, Ernakulam, and Calicut in the north, and is the quickest way to get here. There are slower trains connecting Thiruvananthapuram with Varkala and other smaller towns in Kerala. Express trains also link Thiruvananthapuram with Mumbai, Bangalore, and Chennai. Flights arrive many times a day from Chennai, Bangalore, Delhi, and Mumbai, as well as a few international destinations.

It is easy to get around Thiruvananthapuram by auto-rickshaw, but be sure to fix the fare before you get in—no one goes by the meter rates, which are about Rs. 20 per kilometer. You can even take an auto-rickshaw from Kovalam into Thiruvananthapuram, but hiring a car from your hotel or a travel agent is the best option, both for getting here and then around the city.

EXPLORING

Kuthiramalika (Puthenmalika) Palace Museum. The 18th-century Kuthiramalika (Puthenmalika) Palace Museum, or Horse Palace, has carved rosewood ceilings and treasures of the royal family, including an ivory throne, weapons, paintings, and gifts from foreign dignitaries. Lifesize Kathakali figures stand in the dance room. Carved horses, for which the palace is named, line the eaves of an inner courtyard. Only one-third of the enormous compound is open to visitors; the entrance fee includes a knowledgeable guide. Also note that you must remove your shoes upon entering. ⊠ *Next to Padmanabhaswamy Temple, East Fort* ☎ *471/247–3952* ⬚ *Palace: Rs. 20* ☉ *Tues.–Sun. 8:30–1 and 3–5:30.*

FAMILY **Napier Museum and Trivandrum Zoo.** In an 80-acre park at the north end of M. G. Road are the many attractions of the Museum and Art Gallery Complex. Each part of the complex requires a special ticket. At the Natural History Museum, a musty collection of animal skeletons, dioramas, and stuffed birds, head straight to the second floor to see an interesting model of a traditional *nalakettu* home (the traditional home of the Nairs, a warrior clan), complete with costumed figurines and a full explanation. The art museum's collection of local arts and crafts—including bronze and stone sculptures, ivory ornaments, and musical instruments—is as noteworthy as the building itself, with its almost Cubist pattern of gables, European-style minarets, and a decorative interior. Built in 1874, it was designed by Robert Chisholm, a specialist in Indo-Saracenic design, and was named after Lord Napier, the governor of Madras. Memorabilia donated by the royal family, including a golden chariot used by the Maharaja of Travancore, is displayed in the tiny Sree Chitra Enclave. On the opposite side of the park, the Sree Chitra Art Gallery has an eclectic collection of paintings, including works of the Rajput, Mogul, and Tanjore schools as well as those of India's most famous oil painter, Raja Ravi Varma; copies of the Ajanta and Sigirya frescoes; and works from China, Japan, Tibet, and Bali, along with canvases by modern Indian painters. Trivandrum Zoo, one of India's oldest, occupies another 55 acres within the complex and showcases over 75 species. There's also a snake farm. ⊠ *Museum Rd.* ☎ *471/231–8294, 471/231–6275* 🖾 *Rs. 20 per section of museum; Rs. 40 for camera; Rs. 75 for video camera* ☉ *Tues. and Thurs.–Sun. 10–4:45, Wed. 1–5.*

Padmanabhaswamy Temple. The handsome Padmanabhaswamy Temple, dedicated to Vishnu, has a seven-story *gopuram* (entrance tower) that's as wide as it is tall to accommodate an unusual reclining statue of a very dark-skinned Vishnu (Padmanabha), lying in eternal slumber on a five-headed serpent. The date of its original construction has been placed at 3000 BC; legend has it that it was built by 4,000 masons, 6,000 laborers, and 100 elephants over the course of six months. In the main courtyard there's intricate granite sculpture, supplemented by more stonework on the nearly 400 pillars supporting the temple corridors. The complex is technically open only to Hindus and keeps erratic hours, so call ahead to be assured of entry into the temple courtyard and the main temple (although probably not the inner sanctum. The hours of opening reflect the eccentric uniqueness of this magnificent-looking and much revered house of worship: 3:30 am–4:45 am, 6:30 am–7 am, 8:30 am–10 am, 10:30 am–11:10 am, 11:45 am–noon, 5 pm–6:15 pm, 6:45 pm–7:20 pm, and a viewing of the lord can be booked online. You'll have to take off your shoes, and women should wear appropriate clothing (i.e., no shorts or sleeveless or revealing tops for women). Nearby there are little shops selling handicrafts. ⊠ *M. G. Rd., at Chali Bazaar* ☎ *471/245–0233, 471/246–6830* ⊕ *sreepadmanabhaswamy-temple.org* ☉ *3:30–4:45 am, 6:30–7 am, 8:30–10 am, 10:30–11:10 am, 11:45 am–noon, 5–6:15 pm, 6:45–7:20 pm.*

WHERE TO EAT AND STAY

$ — INDIAN — ✕ **Azad.** The food won't disappoint here, even if the interior isn't much to look at. Specialties include *biryani*, a flavorful rice cooked with chicken or mutton, and *kuthu paratha*, a Kerala Muslim delicacy of flat bread stuffed with minced fish and served from 4 pm onward. Azad has become a chain, but the branch at Vazhuthacaud may be the best. The biryani is ready around noon and runs out by early evening, so make sure you get there on time if that's what you're after. ⑤ *Average main: Rs. 135* ⊠ *Vazhuthacaud* ☎ *471/307–0603.*

$ — INDIAN — ✕ **Hotel Aryaas.** There's nothing fancy here—just simple, tasty, vegetarian food like *amma* (mom) would make. The air-conditioned restaurant

Thiruvananthapuram's Padmanabhaswamy Temple

is comfortable and clean, and menu options range from soups and salads to french fries. Opt for the traditional *thali*, a meal of rice and vegetable accompaniments, available from noon to 3—one extra-special thali comes with a whopping 18 dishes. There are always all the South Indian breakfast items, including dosa, idli, and vada, available from 7 to 10 am. ⑤ *Average main: Rs. 150* ⊠ *Subramaniam Rd.* ☎ *471/233–8999* ⊟ *No credit cards.*

$$$
ECLECTIC
✕ **Orion.** Although it offers a variety of cuisines, this restaurant has acquired a reputation with locals for its traditional Indian dishes. The South Indian lunch buffet (Rs. 575) features such Kerala specialties as *elisseri* (pumpkin with red beans), *avial* (mixed vegetables in a mild coconut gravy), and fish curry. ⑤ *Average main: Rs. 520* ⊠ *The Residency Tower, Press Rd.* ☎ *471/233–1661* ⊕ *www.residencytower.com.*

$$
HOTEL
🏨 **Hilton Garden Inn.** Rooms in this efficient, seven-story business hotel are large and come with wonderful views of the city. **Pros:** location; warm and helpful service; comfortable; contemporary; well priced. **Cons:** an ordinary, modern hotel with little in the way of local style. ⑤ *Rooms from: Rs. 5500* ⊠ *Punnen Rd.* ☎ *471/660–0000* ⊕ *hiltongardeninn3. hilton.com/en/hotels/india/hilton-garden-inn-trivandrum-trvgigi/ attractions/index.html* ⤶ *128 rooms, 6 suites* ⦿*No meals.*

$$$
HOTEL
🏨 **The South Park.** One of Trivandrum's better-known hotels, the South Park is large and well-located, right in the middle of town, and used primarily by business travelers. **Pros:** good location and online rates; in-room Wi-Fi. **Cons:** large and impersonal; on a noisy street; the beds are fixed to the ground in the twin-bedded rooms; in-person quoted prices aren't a great deal. ⑤ *Rooms from: Rs. 6050* ⊠ *Spencer Junction,*

M. G. Rd. ☎ *471/233–3333* ⊕ *www.fortunehotels.in* ⤳ *76 rooms* ⥄ *Breakfast.*

$$
B&B/INN

⬚ **Varikatt Heritage.** A 150-year-old tiled-roof colonial bungalow set in its own large garden, an oasis of calm and tradition in the heart of the city, is the location of this popular homestay run by an army colonel. **Pros:** charming, warm environment; well located. **Cons:** small; busy area, although the greenery helps shield the bustle. ⑤ *Rooms from: Rs. 4000* ⊠ *Punnen Rd.* ☎ *989/523–9055, 471/233–6057* ⊕ *www.varikattheritage.com* ⤳ *3 rooms, 1 suite* ⊟ *No credit cards* ⥄ *Breakfast.*

SHOPPING

Most shops are closed Sunday, and smaller shops occasionally shut down for a few hours at lunchtime on weekdays.

The Craft Shop. Crafts from all over India are available here. ⊠ *G. A. K Rd., off M. G. Rd.* ☎ *471/232–3335.*

Fabindia. This popular chain is a great spot to pick up any kind of quality Indian cottons, both as clothing and for your home. ⊠ *Anupama, 9/9/119 S. S. Kovil Rd., behind Tennis Club, Kowdiar* ☎ *471/3071–4441.*

Joyalukkas. The best and largest store in Trivandrum for gold and jewelry set with precious stones, including traditional Kerala-style ornaments. ⊠ *Attakulangara* ☎ *471/257–5035.*

Kalyan Silks. One of Kerala's largest stores for saris, and for cotton and gorgeous silk by the meter. Men's and women's traditional clothing is also available. ⊠ *M. G. Rd.* ☎ *471/233–8331.*

Karalkada. Weavers for Travancore's royal family sell traditional Kerala saris (made of plain white cotton) at Karalkada. ⊠ *Kaithamukku Junction* ☎ *471/247–2932.*

Natesan's. This is a respected and age-old art and antiques dealer. ⊠ *M. G. Rd.* ☎ *471/233–1594* ⊘ *Closed Sun.*

SMSM. For Kerala handicrafts and souvenirs, hit this government emporium. ⊠ *Statue Junction, off M. G. Rd.* ☎ *471/233–1668.*

KOVALAM

16 km (10 miles) south of Thiruvananthapuram.

Kovalam's numerous and delightfully clean and sandy beaches are lined with palm-fringed lagoons and rocky coves. Fishermen in *lungis* (colorful cloth wraps) drag in nets filled with the day's catch, then push their slender wooden boats out again with a Malayalam "Heave ho." Here you can spend the day loafing on warm sand or rocky outcroppings, watch the sun set, then sit back as the dim lights of distant fishing boats come on. In peak season, outdoor shacks come to life right on the beach—just point to the fish of your choice and specify how you'd like it prepared. ■**TIP**➔ Be sure to find out how much it's going to cost—a little discreet bargaining might be in order.

GETTING HERE AND AROUND

Kovalam is 235 km (146 miles; about six hours) by road from Kochi and 16 km (10 miles) from Thiruvananthapuram. It is easy to get around the town by auto-rickshaw. You can even take an auto-rickshaw from Kovalam into Thiruvananthapuram, but hiring a car from your hotel or a travel agent is the best option.

EXPLORING

Overdevelopment had nearly ruined Kovalam, but it's experiencing something of a revival, with hotel expansion under control and a variety of lodging, some it very luxury, coming to the area making it a place that attracts all kinds of tourists. The main beach, Lighthouse, has been cleaned up; the concrete promenade is lined with some interesting shops (selling mainly clothes), cheaper restaurants to catch a small bite, and budget hotels. It's well lighted at night, allowing for a pleasant evening stroll as well as some semblance of nightlife and lots of people-watching. For peace and solitude, however, stick to the secluded beaches in villages to the north and south of Kovalam town.

WHERE TO EAT

$ × **Cafe Spice Garden.** Most of the eating joints along Lighthouse Beach
CAFÉ   appear a bit dicey, although they display their freshly caught seafood in ice in front of the restaurant. Spice Garden, attached to the Neelakanta hotel, has a more pleasant atmosphere, with green tablecloths and bamboo furniture. Their menu is rather extensive—they have a dozen types of lassis, and many of fried rice, for instance. A good option is the seafood of the day, fried up with mild Kerala spice. The tiger prawns *buna* or the fish *pollichathi* are both good choices, or just come here for some *chai* (tea) and to watch the people shuffle past on the beach promenade from a less public vantage point. ⑤ *Average main: Rs. 250* ⊠ *Lighthouse Beach* ☎ *471/248–0321.*

$$ × **Hotel Rockholm Restaurant.** What might be Kovalam's best chef pre-
INDIAN   pares excellent international and local dishes. Try the seasonal seafood dishes, such as fried mussels or prawns Kerala-style, which are cooked in coconut oil with a variety of spices. You can eat indoors or on a terrace overlooking the ocean. They also serve Chinese, continental, and regional dishes; the owner suggests trying fish curry with rice, pickle (chutney), and a cracker-like papad. ⑤ *Average main: Rs. 400* ⊠ *Near Vizhinjam Fire Station, at end of Lighthouse Rd.* ☎ *471/248–0406, 471/248–0407.*

$$ × **Il Marinaio.** Come here, in a lane off Samudra Beach opposite Uday
ITALIAN   Samudra hotel and near the gates of the Taj Kovalam, to a pleasant garden restaurant that serves sample reasonably authentic Italian food (as well as some Indian dishes). Service is a bit slow, but the food is all freshly made and wholesome. Try the pastas or the pizzas. The vegetarian or meat lasagna is a good choice; it's made with homemade pasta. They have great soups as well, and an expansive breakfast menu expansive. Indian food is also available. An ATM is nearby, and there are a few handicraft shops nearby that are worth poking around in (be sure to bargain). ⑤ *Average main: Rs. 450* ⊠ *Samudra Rd., Samudra Beach* ☎ *471/248–1946* ➖ *No credit cards.*

$$$$ × **Tides.** The Leela's excellent seafood restaurant, Tides, is at sea level,
CONTEMPORARY   facing the beach in a breezy sort of pavilion. Here you can have seafood cooked in just about whatever style you like, including Indian, Chinese, Keralan, continental, Caribbean, and Middle Eastern. The Chinese wok-tossed lamb pepper comes recommended, as does the Singapore

8

chilli crab. Good vegetarian options are also available. $ *Average main: Rs. 950* ⊠ *The Leela Kovalam, Beach Rd.* ☎ *471/305–1234* ⊕ *www. theleela.com* ⌂ *Reservations essential.*

WHERE TO STAY

$ **Beach & Lake.** Sandwiched between the roar of the Arabian Sea and
RESORT the ripple of a backwater lagoon, this basic resort is 4 km (2½ miles) north of Kovalam, on the way to Thiruvanthapuram. **Pros:** cheap; gorgeous views and fantastic location; friendly staff. **Cons:** basic accommodations; no a/c; few eating options near the hotel, and it's far from Kovalam. $ *Rooms from: Rs. 2010* ⊠ *Pozhikkara Beach, Pachalloor Village* ☎ *471/238–2086* ⊕ *www.beachandlakeresort.com* ⤣ *26 rooms* ❑ *Breakfast.*

$$ **Coconut Bay.** In an undeveloped area about 2 km (1 mile) south of Kov-
HOTEL alam, this well-designed and maintained 3-acre property has a secluded beach and ayurvedic center. **Pros:** large, comfortable beds; it's pleasant and casual; pool. **Cons:** room decor is nothing to write home about. $ *Rooms from: Rs. 5000* ⊠ *Mulloor, Vizhinjam* ☎ *471/248–0566, 471/248–0668* ⊕ *www.coconutbay.com* ⤣ *33 rooms* ❑ *Breakfast.*

$ **Ideal Ayurvedic Resort.** This small, homey resort south of Kovalam has
RESORT specialized in ayurvedic treatment since 1997. **Pros:** friendly staff; little to distract guests from their treatment; well priced. **Cons:** few amenities; not on the beach, so a steep downhill walk; small hotel. $ *Rooms from: Rs. 1700* ⊠ *Just before Somatheeram, Chowara* ☎ *471/226–8632* ⊕ *www.idealayurvedicresort.com* ⤣ *33 rooms* ❑ *Some meals.*

$$$ **The Leela Kovalam.** The best-sited property in Kovalam is one of the
RESORT most luxurious and the largest, too. **Pros:** spectacular views; private beach area; lovely pool; good ayurvedic center. **Cons:** pricey; large and slightly impersonal; getting to the bars and restaurants on Lighthouse Beach is a bit of a walk. $ *Rooms from: Rs. 7700* ⊠ *Beach Rd.* ☎ *471/305–1234* ⊕ *www.theleela.com* ⤣ *174 rooms, 9 suites* ❑ *Breakfast.*

$$ **Manaltheeram.** Quieter and even closer to the water than its neigh-
HOTEL boring sister property, Somatheeram Beach Resort, Manaltheeram is quite charming. **Pros:** quiet, exclusive beachfront; some restaurant tables set up on the beach; lots of good handicraft, clothing, and knick-knack shops nearby. **Cons:** the ayurveda on offer is below average; a little short on amenities; dishes with meat are limited, and need to be requested; alcohol not permitted. $ *Rooms from: Rs. 4000* ⊠ *Chowara* ☎ *471/226–6222* ⊕ *www.manaltheeram.com* ⤣ *61 rooms* ❑ *Some meals.*

$ **Neelakanta.** This beachfront budget hotel, a large white low-rise right
HOTEL on Kovalam's slightly shabby but buzzing main drag, is popular with foreigners. **Pros:** beach views. **Cons:** building looks a bit drab; no elevators, and not very well-lit stairwells. $ *Rooms from: Rs. 3300* ⊠ *Lighthouse Beach* ☎ *471/248–0321* ⊕ *www.hotelneelakantakovalam.com* ⤣ *31 rooms* ❑ *Breakfast.*

$$$ **Nikki's Nest.** Among bougainvillea, coconut palms, banana trees,
HOTEL orchids, and acacia stand thatch-roof, circular cottages and traditional wooden houses, most with commanding sea views, making this hotel a popular choice. **Pros:** great hilltop beach views; good value. **Cons:**

uphill walk to the hotel from the beach; you must book in advance. ⑤ *Rooms from: Rs. 8000* ✉ *Azhimala Shiva Temple Rd., Chowara* ☎ *471/226–8822, 471/226–8821* ⊕ *www.nikkisnest.com* ⌇ *48 rooms* �101 *Breakfast.*

$$$$
RESORT
Fodor's Choice
★
☒ **Niraamaya – Surya Samudra.** Overlooking the sea, this rambling and simply beautiful resort, built along a hillside, has an exquisite beach, lovely views, and a great deal of peace (loud noise isn't allowed). **Pros:** top Kerala location; a good place for yoga or the spa; some massive rooms; a don't-miss infinity swimming pool cut out of rock, and with underwater sculptures. **Cons:** no television; no activities for children; pricey. ⑤ *Rooms from: Rs. 15000* ✉ *10 km (6 miles) south of Kovalam, Pulinkudi* ☎ *471/248–0413* ⊕ *niraamaya.in/kovalam.html* ⌇ *21 rooms, 4 suites* 101 *Breakfast.*

$$$
RESORT
☒ **Poovar Island Resort.** A speedboat ride up a sluggish backwater canal, through lots of eye-catching emerald scenery, brings you suddenly into a vast world of blue and white—ocean, spray, white waves, and sparkling beach—and to this resort, which is near the town of Poovar (100 km [62 miles] south of Quilon and 16 km [10 miles] south of Kovalam). **Pros:** amazing location; spacious grounds; boats take you to the beach and can be hired for excursions; reachable only by boat. **Cons:** reachable only by boat; buffet meals could stand improvement; land cottages in need of upkeep. ⑤ *Rooms from: Rs. 6500* ✉ *K.P. VII/911, Poovar* ☎ *894/333–8919, 471/221–2068, 471/221–2069* ⊕ *www. poovarislandresorts.com* ⌇ *16 floating cottages, 30 land cottages* 101 *Breakfast.*

$$$$
RESORT
Fodor's Choice
★
☒ **Vivanta by Taj–Kovalam.** Acres and acres of manicured gardens, set among hundreds of palms, facing the beach and the backwater, make the Taj's enormous resort easily one of the best places to stay in Kovalam. **Pros:** super location; two restaurants and a bar; top spa; handy to shops, a few local restaurants, and Lighthouse Beach. **Cons:** can be pricey in high season. ⑤ *Rooms from: Rs. 10399* ✉ *G. V. Raja Vattappara Rd., Samudra Beach* ☎ *471/661–3000* ⊕ *www.vivantabytaj. com/kovalam-kerala/overview.html* ⌇ *59 rooms, 9 suites* 101 *Breakfast.*

NIGHTLIFE AND PERFORMING ARTS

Wait and Watch. Hindustan Beach Retreat's rooftop cocktail lounge, five floors up, is a good place to come for a drink and a view. It opens at 5 pm and shuts at 10:30 pm year-round. You can also have snacks or dinner at the adjoining multicuisine restaurant. ✉ *Hindustan Beach Retreat, Varkala* ☎ *470/260–4254, 470/260–4255* ⊕ *www. hindustanbeachretreat.com.*

VARKALA

51 km (32 miles) north of Thiruvananthapuram, 59 km (37 miles) north of Kovalam

Varkala, a magically peaceful beach town, is on a small strip of coastline fringed by the sparkling Papanasam Beach, which stretches out below towering red cliffs.

Over the years, as Kovalam lost some its charm to overdevelopment and a flood of hippie tourists, quiet Varkala grew modestly. It's now considered one of Kerala's best beach destinations—one unmarred by the excessive bustle that haunts Kovalam at least some of the year. The relatively small number of hotels and the palm-thatched eateries that have sprung up along the beach and the Cliff (as it's known) haven't taken anything away from the rustic delightfulness of the place. There's a simple, laid-back air about Varkala—you can enjoy sun and sand and not be deprived of the liveliness of a seaside resort. Adding color and a festive feel are the many Hindu pilgrims who come to see Varkala town's ancient Sree Janardana Swamy temple. And an amble to the Cliff makes an interesting sundown excursion, as much for the people-watching as for finding out what's cooking at the stalls that are set up there.

GETTING HERE AND AROUND

Varkala is 50 km (31 miles; less than 90 minutes) from Thiruvananthapuram airport. Book a prepaid non-a/c taxi at Thiruvananthapuram airport for approximately Rs. 1,300 to reach here quickly and safely, without any hassles. Slower trains connect Varkala with Thiruvananthapuram and Kochi (check ⊕ *indiarailinfo.com*). There are not very large distances to negotiate in and around Varkala and most places are not that far on foot. But you can use auto-rickshaws (most fares, negotiated beforehand, would not come to more than Rs. 60), hire a motorbike or a bicycle, or else hire a car from the hotel or a local travel agency.

EXPLORING

Anchuthengu Beach and Anjengo Fort. The pristine Anchuthengu beach, 12 km (7½ miles) south of Varkala, is the location of a lighthouse and the ruins of the British Anjengo fort, built in 1695, which at various times was under Dutch and Portuguese attack. Anchuthengu ("Five Coconuts), was the site of the first trade settlement of the East India Company, and therefore the beginning of British India. It was also the site of the first rebellion against the British, when locals, unhappy with the conduct of the British traders, banded together to oust them. The fairly humble-looking fort has a few tombstones around it, was built in 1695. Like so many other areas of southern and central Kerala, the sea pleasantly merges with the backwaters here—be sure to bring a camera. ⊠ *Anchuthengu, Varkala.*

Odayam and Thiruvambady Beaches. Sparkling Odayam, the next beach north of Varkala, is considered part of the town but is about 2 km (1 mile) away. It's quieter and even prettier—well-worth visiting for an afternoon of sun or to watch a spectacular sunset. Thiruvambady Beach, still more tranquil, is a black-sand beach a climb down from the Cliff. ⊠ *Varkala.*

Sree Janardana Swamy Temple. Varkala is a major center for the worship of Vishnu—it's known as Dakshin Kashi, or the Varanasi of the south. At the Sree Janardana Swamy temple, you can see what happens at a popular Hindu pilgrimage destination—the prayers; the morning and evening *aarti* (devotions), when the gods are feted with oil lamps; and the customs of the devotees. You will probably not be allowed in the inner sanctum of the temple unless you are dressed in traditional clothes, but you can certainly view the architecture and soak up the atmosphere of this pretty and very busy temple. Note that photographs of the deity are not allowed, and there may be a charge for using a camera outside. Check with your hotel in case there is a change in temple times. ⊠ *Temple Rd.* ☉ *Daily 4 am–noon and 5 pm–8 pm.*

Varkala Beach. Varkala beach, a pristine strip of sand backed by a steep cliff, is probably one of South India's prettiest yet most happening beaches. Unlike many Goan beaches, its beauty has not been marred by overdevelopment, such as hotels that are too close to the water. At what's also known as Papanasam beach, which means "to wash away your sins," a dip here may be a chance to dissolve your life's regrets in the Arabian Sea. You are bound to see plenty of pilgrims doing just that. Plenty of vendors will also come by, offering coconut water or slices of fresh pineapple. There are a few rip currents in these waters, so obey the signs. From the beach you can climb up to the Cliff to have a bite or a cool drink or for some souvenir hunting. ⊠ *Varkala Beach.*

WHERE TO EAT

$ | ✕ **The Cliff.** In high season, the Cliff above Varkala's beach has more
SEAFOOD | than 100 thatched shacks serving a range of freshly cooked seafood. It's not fine dining, but there are great views, even at night, and lots of atmosphere. Caffé Italiano is known for its pasta, and Café Del Mar for spicy fried calamari, as well as for standard Italian and Indian dishes. Otherwise, you can head to the multicuisine restaurants in Varkala's one or two high-end hotels. $ *Average main: Rs. 200* ⊠ *The Cliff* ⊟ *No credit cards.*

$$$$ | ✕ **GAD.** Open all day, and with an open-air partio on the cliff, GAD
INTERNATIONAL | may just be Varkala's best restaurant. It serves all kinds of food, including regional and Kerala specialties. Don't miss the *karuvepilai* prawns, spicy and fried up with a lot of curry leaves, or the *meen polichathu*, fish fried in a wrapped banana leaf or *nadan meen charu*, a local kind of fish curry. Vegetarians can try the eggplant curry or stick to the well-cooked continental dishes. Their desserts are good, too. $ *Average main: Rs. 800* ⊠ *Gateway Hotel Varkala, Government Guest House* ☎ *470/667–3300* ⊕ *www.thegatewayhotels.com.*

WHERE TO STAY

$ | 🛏 **Clafouti Beach Resort.** At this homey and simple beach resort, the pic-
B&B/INN | turesque thatched cottages all face each other in a line, leading to the edge of the Cliff and the magnificent Arabian Sea below. **Pros:** decent value; quiet; ayurvedic center attached; billiards table. **Cons:** small rooms without TVs or phones; no room service, or a kettle to make tea or coffee; it's a walk down to the beach. $ *Rooms from: Rs. 2500* ⊠ *North Cliff* ☎ *470/260–1414, 470/302–1313* ⊕ *www.clafoutiresort. com* ➪ *10 rooms* ⭐ *No meals.*

$$ | 🛏 **Hindustan Beach Retreat.** Comfortable, large but somewhat bland
HOTEL | rooms are available in this modern block hotel a few yards from the sea. **Pros:** great location; well priced; pool. **Cons:** ordinary hotel lacking Kerala charm. $ *Rooms from: Rs. 4500* ⊠ *Varkala Beach* ☎ *470/260–4254* ⊕ *www.hindustanbeachretreat.com* ➪ *27 rooms, 3 suites* ⭐ *Breakfast.*

$$$ | 🛏 **Maadathil Cottages.** This small group of cottages is north of Varkala
B&B/INN | and close to both Odayam and Edava beaches. **Pros:** splendid isolation, but still within good distance of Varkala (it's 20 minutes and Rs. 150

8

by auto-rickshaw). **Cons:** might be too quiet for some; simple rooms. ⑤ *Rooms from: Rs. 6000 ⊠ Edava St., Manthara* ☎ *974/611–3495* ⊕ *www.maadathilcottages.com/index.php* ⤳ *10 rooms* ▭ *No credit cards* ⦾ *No meals.*

$ ⛌ **The Sanctum Spring Beach Resort.** The nicest hotel on Varkala's Cliff,
HOTEL Sanctum Spring offers modest rooms at decent prices, with spectacular views of the Arabian Sea. **Pros:** lot of action around here; decent value. **Cons:** maybe too much action; ordinary hotel. ⑤ *Rooms from: Rs. 2800 ⊠ Helipad* ☎ *470/260–6993* ⊕ *www.hotelsanctumspring.com* ⤳ *17 rooms, 3 suites* ⦾ *Breakfast.*

NIGHTLIFE AND PERFORMING ARTS

Many of the shacks along the Cliff, as well as a few of the restaurants facing the beach, stay open often beyond 11 pm offering drinks, beer and small dishes as well as a taste of Varkala's modest nightlife.

Terrace at Clafouti Beach Resort. This popular resort is known for its relaxed vibe and some of the freshest seafood around, including their butter-garlic crab. They serve wine, too, along with delightful seafood snacks in a terrace overlooking the roaring ocean. It is open throughout the year. Italian, Indian, and continental meals are also available. ⊠ *Clafouti Beach Resort, North Cliff* ☎ *470/260–1414, 470/302–1313* ⊕ *www.clafoutiresort.com.*

Varkala Kathakali Centre. Kathakali and Mohiniyattam performances take place here during the busy season, from 5 to 7 pm. Come early to see the elaborate preperformance makeup being applied. The KTDC office has exact details of the day's program. ⊠ *North Cliff* ☎ *470/260–2227.*

NORTHERN KERALA

If Kerala is unspoiled India, then Malabar—as the northern part of the state was once known—is unspoiled Kerala. Arab traders landed here long before Vasco da Gama; many trading families converted to Islam and this part of the state retains strong Muslim influences. Various conquerors built forts along spectacular stretches of coastline, and some of Kerala's most unique and colorful religious festivals take place in this region. With the exception of the hill station of Wyanad, tourism has yet to make major in-roads into the northern part of Kerala.

CALICUT

146 km (91 miles) northwest of Kochi.

This city doesn't hold much excitement in itself, but Calicut (Kozhikode) has an airport and is a good base for exploring several interesting sights nearby, including the lushly forested Wyanad district to the northeast. The city's historical ties with the Middle East are clearly apparent due to the strong Arab presence.

GETTING HERE AND AROUND

Calicut can be reached from Kochi by car or by train. The efficient Jan Shatabdi train connects Calicut with Ernakulam, Alleppey, Quilon, and Thiruvananthapuram in the south; this is the quickest way to get to

Calicut. You can fly into Calicut from Mumbai on Spice Jet, Jet Konnect, Air India, from Chennai on Air India and Spice Jet, and from Bangalore on Spice Jet. Several international flights connect Calicut with the Middle East. One can get around easily within town by autorickshaw, or by hiring a car.

EXPLORING

Tasara Center for Creative Weaving. You can see weavers working on giant hand looms here, and Tasara also hosts programs for artists-in-residence. Many different handloom products are also for sale. Call ahead to arrange a visit. ⊠ *10 km (6 miles) south of Calicut, Beypore North* ☎ *495/241–4832, 9446468832* ⊕ *www.tasaraindia.com.*

WHERE TO EAT AND STAY

$ ✕ **Kingsbay.** The friendly rubber planter who owns this restaurant has
SEAFOOD a passion for food that's much in evidence. The varied menu encompasses other regional and national cuisines, including South and North Indian, Thai, and continental. Most popular is the squid and prawn masala fry, while South Indian cuisine is represented by a mixed platter of six seafood specialties from nearby Mangalore. You won't find many vegetarian dishes on the menu. Located inside a bungalow, this is predominantly a family restaurant for well-heeled locals, and often hosts a lively crowd. Alcohol is not served. $ *Average main: Rs. 250* ⊠ *1414 Customs Rd., Vellayil* ☎ *495/405–4422* ⊘ *No lunch.*

$ ✕ **Mezban.** In the heart of the city, in a business hotel, this modern and
INDIAN comfortable restaurant serves a range of local, Chinese, North Indian, and continental dishes, which might include squid *tawa peralan* (a dry curry prepared with numerous spices), prawn biryani, and chicken malabar biriyani. The restaurant does not serve alcohol, which is common in this largely Muslim part of Kerala. The place gets busy at dinner, especially on weekends, and as a result waiting time can vary. Service can be slow. $ *Average main: Rs. 240* ⊠ *Hotel Asma Tower, Mavoor Rd.* ☎ *495/408–8000* ⊕ *www.asmatower.com/restaurant.*

$$ ✕ **Paragon.** It's not much to look at, and it can get noisy when crowded,
INDIAN but this Calicut stalwart serves up tasty food. The chicken and the prawn biryanis are both excellent, as is the unusual fried shrimp dish that goes very well with *parathas* (a flaky flat bread). Other favorites include the prawn pepper fry and tamarind fish curry. The biryanis may run out on the early side, but the restaurant is open quite late. $ *Average main: Rs. 320* ⊠ *Kannur Rd.* ☎ *495/276–1020, 495/276–7020* ⊕ *www.paragonrestaurant.net* ▭ *No credit cards.*

$ ✕ **Zain's Hotel Restaurant.** This brightly painted former house near the
SOUTH INDIAN beach is the place to go to for authentic Moplah (Kerala Muslim) dishes—it's one of Calicut's most popular restaurants. The family that owns it not only prepares dishes using family recipes passed down through the generations, but also creates innovative fusion dishes. With plastic chairs and tables laid out both indoors and outdoors, this is a no-fuss dining experience. The owner-chef, Zainabi Noor Mohammed, and her daughter Sherin Mustafa are usually there and are very hospitable. Head here for the biryani, *unnakkaya* (a sweet, banana- and coconut-based snack), mussel pie, and the different types of *pathiri* (North Kerala stuffed flat breads). $ *Average main: Rs. 160* ⊠ *Convent*

8

crossroads, behind Tagore Centenary Hall ☎ *495/236–6311.*

$$$
HOTEL
🛏 **Gateway Hotel, Calicut.** Calicut's premier hotel is frequented by airline crews and wealthy Omanis, who come for lengthy treatments at the well-regarded ayurvedic center. **Pros:** great pool. **Cons:** not much in the way of grounds. ⑤ *Rooms from: Rs. 7000* ⊠ *P. T. Usha Rd.* ☎ *495/276–5354* ⊕ *www. thegatewayhotels.com* 🛏 *74 rooms, 4 suites* ⑩ *Breakfast.*

$$$
RESORT
🛏 **Kadavu.** One of the first swank, world-class riverside and backwater resorts in the Calicut area, Kadavu signaled Malabar's foray into tourism. **Pros:** stunning river views; good value. **Cons:** Calicut is 26 km (16 miles) away. ⑤ *Rooms from: Rs. 9000* ⊠ *Off N. H. Bypass, Azhinjilam, Feroke* ☎ *483/283–0023, 483/283–0027* ⊕ *www.rphotels.in/HotelHome. aspx?hid=3* 🛏 *117 rooms* ⑩ *Breakfast.*

$$
HOTEL
🛏 **Westway.** Slim wooden pillars encircle the pleasant lobby of this modern red-stone business hotel, and there's a beautiful terra-cotta-tile atrium with a traditional brass lamp. **Pros:** rooftop pool with nice city views; mid-size rooms are comfortably furnished; Wi-Fi; great value, and centrally located. **Cons:** a little noisy; no safes in rooms. ⑤ *Rooms from: Rs. 4200* ⊠ *Kannur Rd.* ☎ *495/276–8888* ⊕ *www.westwayhotel. com* 🛏 *63 rooms, 3 suites* ⑩ *Breakfast.*

> **FESTIVAL TIME**
>
> January's Tiruvatira features folk dancing and singing by young Malayali women. In Trichur (Thrissur), the Pooram and Vela festivals (March and April) are among Kerala's best known. Thrissur Pooram is an eight-day spectacle with parades of decked-out elephants, music, and fireworks. In the north, Kannur and Kasargode are known for the extraordinary Theyyam (November–May), a religious dance of tribal origin. The harvest festival, Onam (late August–early September), which lasts up to 10 days in some locations, is celebrated with floral displays and snake-boat racing.

KANNUR

92 km (57 miles) northwest of Calicut.

The Kannur district is the heartland of the Moppilahs (Kerala's Muslim community). It's also a center for the hand-loom industry as well as the manufacture of *beedis*, potent hand-rolled cigarettes made from tobacco sweepings. The town itself was for many years at the center of the maritime spice trade. The ruling Kolathiri rajas profited from the spice trade as did the European colonists. Today Kannur is a good hub for visiting several coastal sights—to the north and the south—including forts and undeveloped beaches.

GETTING HERE AND AROUND

You can reach Kannur by road from Calicut in about two hours (93 km, 58 miles), either by bus or by a hired car. The Jan Statabdi and the Ernakulam–Kannur Intercity Express trains both go to Kannur, including from Kochi (a 5½-hour trip) or from Calicut (2 hours or less). The sights around Kannur are all fairly far out of town, and your best option is to hire a car.

EXPLORING

TOP ATTRACTIONS

Kanhirode Weaving Cooperative. The Kanhirode Weaving Cooperative is strewn with yarns of all colors, set out to dry after dyeing. You can watch the weavers at their giant, clackety-clacking looms, making bedsheets and upholstery for export as well as brightly colored saris. Cloth is available for purchase. ⊠ *Off Kannur–Mysore Rd., 13 km (8 miles) east of Kannur, Kanhirode* ☎ *497/285–7865* ⊕ *www.weaveco. com* ⌨ *Free* ⊙ *Mon.–Sat. 8:30–5:30.*

Sree Muthappan Temple. The unusual Sree Muthappan Temple, one of the largest shrines of its type, sits on the bank of the Valapattanam River at Parassinikkadavu, 18 km (11 miles) from Kannur. It's devoted not to a Vedic god, but to Sree Muthappan, a folk deity of the Thiya community. One school of Hindu thought claims that he is a combined manifestation of both Shiva and Vishnu, another believes he is simply another avatar of Shiva in the form of a tribal hunter. Several colorful legends about him exist. Worship does not take the form of paying homage to an idol but to enactment of the lord's life: the temple hosts such Theyyam performances almost every day of the year. Though it's not as colorful as traditional outdoor festivals, you can at least get a taste of this mystical local form of dance. Because Sree Muthappan is usually pictured with a hunting dog, there is a statue in honor of dogs on the premises; friendly mutts roam the sanctuary, and offerings at the shrine take the form of bronze dog figurines. The temple is also unusual for the fact that toddy (fermented palm sap) and fish are both offered to Sree Muthappan. ⊠ *Off NH–17, 18 km (11 miles) north of Kannur, Parassinikkadavu* ☎ *0497/278–0722* ⊕ *parassinikadavumuthappan. com* ⌨ *Free* ⊙ *Theyyams usually daily 5:30 am–8:30 am and 6:30 pm–8:30 pm.*

Theyyam. A unique regional draw is the spectacular dance called Theyyam. More than an art form, it's a type of worship that is tribal in origin and thought to predate Hinduism in Kerala. Theyyams aren't held in traditional temples, but rather in small shrines or family compounds. Dancers don elaborate costumes and terrifying makeup for the ritual dance, during which its believed they become possessed by the spirit of the deity they represent, allowing them to perform such feats as dancing with a 30-foot headdress, a flaming costume, or falling into a pile of burning embers. The ritual is accompanied by intense drumming, howling, and chanting. Theyyam season is from November to May.

WORTH NOTING

Fort St. Angelo (*Kannur Fort*). In 1505 the Portuguese built Fort St. Angelo, with the consent of the ruling Kolathiri Raja, in order to protect their interests in the area. After passing into Dutch and then British hands, it's now maintained by the Archaeological Survey of India. There are still a few British cannons intact, and lovely views of the fishing activity in Moppillah Bay. ⊠ *Off NH–17, 3 km (2 miles) north of Kannur* ⊕ *www.keralatourism.org/destination/st-angelo-fort-kannur/83* ⌨ *Free* ⊙ *Daily 8–6.*

WHERE TO EAT AND STAY

$
INDIAN ✗ **MVK.** It may not have much in the way of decor, but this Kannur institution attracts crowds, drawn by the authenticity of its outstanding biryanis. You first choice should be the mutton biryani. Otherwise go for the chicken or fish variants, the chicken 65 (made with deep-fried chicken nuggets), or the Kerala *parottas* (breads). Seating can be hard to get here, and the biryanis do run out from time to time, so try to come early, whether for lunch or dinner. ⑤ *Average main: Rs. 200* ✉ *Swami Madam Rd.* ☎ *497/276–7192* ▭ *No credit cards.*

$$$$
ALL-INCLUSIVE ⚏ **Ayisha Manzil.** A stay in this 1862 clifftop spice-estate home may be the best way to experience what North Kerala is all about—people come for the gorgeous sea views and the food, whipped up by TV host and chef Faiza Moosa, who's famous for her traditional Mopla (Kerala Muslim) dishes. **Pros:** taxes, great meals, and nonalcoholic drinks are all included in rates; great views. **Cons:** expensive. ⑤ *Rooms from: Rs. 18500* ✉ *Court Rd., Thalassery* ☎ *490/234–1590, 984/700–2340* ⊕ *www.ayishamanzil.com* ⇱ *7 rooms* ☽ *Closed Apr.– July* ⦿ *All-inclusive.*

$
HOTEL ⚏ **Mascot.** A terrific hillcrest location provides a great sea view, and a cliffside walkway leads to the large swimming pool and ayurvedic center. **Pros:** fantastic sea views from most rooms. **Cons:** the closest beach has been taken over by the navy. ⑤ *Rooms from: Rs. 3000* ✉ *Near Baby Beach, Burnassery* ☎ *497/270–8445* ⊕ *www.mascotresort.com* ⇱ *30 rooms* ⦿ *Breakfast.*

KOLKATA
(CALCUTTA)

WELCOME TO KOLKATA (CALCUTTA)

TOP REASONS TO GO

★ **Eclectic Architecture:** The city is packed with gorgeous temples, mosques, universities, and colonial mansions and monuments.

★ **Walking City:** Kolkata is best seen on foot: stroll along the river promenade, walk across the Howrah Bridge, explore the bazaars, or wander around the sprawling Maidan park.

★ **Cultural Capital:** Catch an Indian classical music concert; watch a locally produced play; go gallery-hopping or head to the Indian Museum, considered one of the country's best.

★ **Foodie's Paradise:** Kolkatans are obsessive about their food. A visit to a traditional sweetshop an absolute must, as is a sampling of the city's famous fish or Indo-Chinese dishes, created a century ago by Chinese immigrants.

★ **Book Bargains:** Kolkata's winter book fair is one of the biggest in the world, and year-round you can trust the stalls of College Street to surprise you with rare and cheap finds.

1 North Kolkata. The oldest part of the city harks back to a different era. It's filled with the crumbling mansions of the former gentry, narrow streets and quiet winding alleys, grand university campuses, and heated social and political debates at street corners over cups of tea. This is home to the famous College Street book stalls and the intriguing Marble Palace.

2 Central Kolkata. The bustling, unbelievably congested downtown is anchored by B. B. D. Bagh, where business and government buildings are concentrated. Many of the city's toniest shops and restaurants flank Park Street.

NORTH KOLKATA
1

CENTRAL KOLKATA
2

TANGRA

SOUTH KOLKATA
4

ALIPORE

3 The Maidan. This mammoth and very central park is not only a good place to see sheep grazing and Kolkatans at play, it's also where you'll see some of India's finest colonial buildings, including the Victoria Memorial across the street. Take a joyride in an old tramcar, a service that has been operation since 1902.

4 South Kolkata. You could say this neighborhood has two distinct identities. On one hand, it has the noisiest streets, with astonishing shopping in cheek-by-jowl kiosks. But it's also a leafy world of elegant homes, specialty restaurants, and tony clubs and condominiums.

GETTING ORIENTED

On the eastern bank of the Hooghly River, Kolkata is the commercial hub of Northeastern India. In the southern part of West Bengal, Kolkata is only about 72 km (44 miles) west of Bangladesh and about 80 km (49 miles) north of the Bay of Bengal. West Bengal borders Nepal to its north-west and the state of Assam and the country of Bhutan to its northeast; its western edge touches the states of Bihar and Jharkhand; Odisha is to its southwest.

9

EATING WELL IN KOLKATA

Food is a great passion for Bengalis, and they go to great lengths to ensure that every meal's a celebration. In addition to the great variety, eating out is also quite affordable, with even Kolkata's best restaurants cheaper than those in Delhi or Mumbai.

All over the city its narrow sidewalks are dominated by shanties, stalls, and carts serving breakfast, lunch, dinner, and snacks. Steaming-hot *luchi* (deep-fried puffy bread made of refined flour), curries, fried fish, fritters, samosas, rolls, kebabs, *momos* (Tibetan dumplings), chicken and mutton stew with unsliced flour bread, *chapatis* (flat bread) with chickpea curries, pastries, patties, and sweets—some streets resemble a smorgasbord for all the flavors, textures, and colors on view.

The street-food snack that scores over all others is the Calcutta (aka *kati*) roll, tender pieces of chicken or mutton wrapped in crisp and flaky parathas and served with onions and the occasional green chilli. Calcutta rolls are available at most roadside stalls, and every neighborhood has its favorite source, but Nizam's in New Market; Kusum in Park Street, and Campari, Bedouwin, and Nawab in Gariahat are some of the more famous. On the other end of the spectrum, Kolkata has always loved its continental food, and its colonial-era clubs and restaurants along Park Street are still putting their own spin on thermidors, Stroganoffs, and other classics. Of late, the city has also discovered a yen for French-style cafés and patisseries—they do a neat job of artisanal breads, quiches, pies, *choux* pastries, cookies, and cupcakes.

BIRYANI

This heavily flavored aromatic rice with meat and chicken in a rich gravy, with its roots in the Nawabi cuisine of Lucknow, takes on many forms—one very popular option is to get biryani accompanied by *chaap* or *champ*—marinated chicken or mutton slow-cooked in large, thick pans. Specialty restaurants serving their own takes on the dish are in every neighborhood of the city, but make sure you try it at a place that's popular, with lots of turnover. Shiraz, Rahmania, and Arsalan, with many branches throughout the city, are some of the more established options. Oudh 1590, in Deshpariya Park, near Gariahat, serves Nawabi cuisine in an upscale setting.

FISH

A much-loved and festive special is the *hilsa*, also called *ilish*, a delicate fish from the herring family that's found in fresh, salty, and brackish waters. Supplies have become limited, thanks in part to massive demand for its roe as well. The flesh is delicate, and in most restaurants it's served deboned. Another favorite dish is the prawn *malai* curry, made with coconut milk, and its many variations, including one served in the shell of a tender (green) coconut. A common Bengali way of cooking fish is in mustard oil and in a mustard paste, making it quite pungent. Most sophisticated restaurants are mindful about toning down the flavors to appeal to foreign palates.

BEGALI SWEETS

The mind-boggling array of sweets sold at every corner shop attests to their importance in the Bengali diet. No trip to Kolkata can be complete without tasting the two things that the city could stake a copyright on. *Mishti doi,* or *mitha dahi,* is delicately sweetened yogurt; *rashogolla* (*rasgulla*) are sugary, syrupy, spongy balls of soft curd cheese. Another specialty is a sweet made with *jaggery* (unrefined date-palm sugar)— *nolen gur.* This is produced in nearby villages, but only in the winter.

INDO-CHINESE FLAVORS

Calcutta is proud of its Chinese legacy and the community settled there is responsible for the city's abiding love for the hybrid cuisine served at most "Chinese" restaurants. The staples at most of these places are chilli chicken, chowmein-like *hakka* noodles, and mixed fried rice. The more authentic eateries in Tangra, Kolkata's Chinatown, serve Chimney Soup and pork dishes cooked in a unique style.

9

(top left) A classic Calcutta (kati) roll; (top right) a plate of Bengali sweets including rasgulla; (bottom right) samosas are favorite street-food snacks

Updated by
Chandrima Pal

Laid-back and vibrant, complacent and ambitious, politically charged but curiously indifferent, this is a city that contradicts itself at every turn of its famously winding alleys. A day in the life of Kolkata is India in all its colors, sound, chaos, and creativity—just one of the many reasons why a trip to the city is so essential.

Kolkata has been home to three Nobel Laureates—the authors and intellectuals Rabindranath Tagore and Amartya Sen, and Mother Teresa—as well as the world-famous director Satyajit Ray, and many other notable authors, filmmakers, musicians, actors, scientists, reformers, freedom fighters, and famous athletes. In its three centuries of existence, it has been a jewel in the crown of the British Empire, a muse for many artists, the heart of India's freedom movement, and a symbol of everything that was wrong with colonialism and politics of divisiveness. It is a home of the homeless, who sleep on the pavements at night, and some of India's richest, living in restored heritage mansions and condos in skyscrapers. Although the name was officially changed from Calcutta to Kolkata in 2001, both names are used more or less interchangeably.

It was here, as traders and landowners, that British entrepreneurs and adventurers began what would amount to the conquest of India and the establishment of the British Raj. More than any other city in India, including New Delhi, Kolkata is tied to the evolution and the British presence. Having embraced 19th-century European humanism, such Bengalis as the poet Rabindranath Tagore and others revived their indigenous culture and made the first organized efforts to oust the British. Emotions here ran high early on, and agitation in Bengal broke away from what would later be called Gandhian politics to choose terrorism—one reason the British moved their capital from Calcutta to Delhi in 1911.

Calcutta remained cosmopolitan and prosperous throughout the British period. But after Independence and Partition, in 1947, trouble began when the world's center of jute processing and distribution (Calcutta) was politically separated from its actual production center (the eastern

AMAZING FESTIVALS

The grandest Bengali festival of the year is the Durga Puja (Durga is an incarnation of Kali, Kolkata's patron goddess). The *pujas* (homage; literally, "worship") take place over several days in September or October. Thousands of devotees and revelers take to the streets, visiting different venues through the day and night. Food stalls, fairs, and live music stages come up in every corner. Colorful, sometimes handmade idols of Durga, sometimes more than 20 feet tall, are moved in large processions through the streets for several hours before reaching the river and being immersed there. The rites and processions blend tradition with innovation; themes at the puja venues are varied—war, tsunamis, film stars, and the White House and Obama have been faithfully re-created with local clay and other materials, lights, and sound effects.

Bengali hinterland). For Calcutta and the new East Pakistan, Partition was equivalent to separating the fingers of an industry from the thumb. Natural disasters—commonly cyclones and droughts, but also, as in 1937, earthquakes—had long sent millions from East Bengal (which later became East Pakistan) to Calcutta in search of shelter and sustenance; after Partition, a wave of 4 million political refugees from East Pakistan compounded and complicated the pressure. Conflict with China and Pakistan created millions more throughout the 1960s, and Pakistan's 1971 military crackdown alone sent 10 million temporary refugees into the city from what would soon become Bangladesh. By the mid-1970s, Calcutta was widely seen as the ultimate urban disaster. Riddled with disease and squalor, plagued by garbage and decay, the former heart of the British Raj, the "Paris of Asia," had quickly and dramatically collapsed.

However, the city kept on growing, and these days, greater Kolkata's entire metropolitan district covers more than 426 square km (264 square miles) and has more than 12 million people.

The change of regime to that of the All India Trinamool Congress, marked by the election of Mamata Banerjee to the position of Chief Minister of West Bengal in 2011, has brought a certain vigor and enthusiasm to the city. Buildings have received fresh coats of paint, and malls, IT hubs, restaurants, and small businesses seem invigorated. After a few unpardonable instances of violence against women, policing has been stepped up in certain areas, and the government is keen to put its best face forward.

Traffic policing may even be better than Mumbai and Delhi (motorists actually stop where they are supposed to at most signals) and police officers are able to fine errant motorists on the spot. Traffic signals in town play the music of Tagore, and some effort has been made to beautify the city, with varying results. In fact, some recent travelers have observed that in some ways Kolkata is cleaner, prettier, and less shabby than Mumbai, despite still being often used as the ultimate symbol of human strife. History may not always have been kind to the city, but Kolkata remains warm, rooted, thoughtful, and remarkably earnest.

9

CLOSE UP

Rickshaw Pullers

Kolkata is the last city on earth to use enormous Chinese-style rickshaws pulled by men on foot. The rickshaws were introduced in the 19th century by Chinese traders, and the British made it a legal form of transportation in 1919. Kolkata has about 6,000 licensed rickshaw operators, but at least as many operate without licenses. In 2005, the Communist government of West Bengal—concerned about its image as it positioned Kolkata as a technology hub—placed a ban on the human-powered vehicles. Government officials called the hand-pulled rickshaws "barbaric" and "inhuman" and vowed not to renew operators' licenses. But the rickshaw-puller union continues to fight the ban, saying the hand-drawn rickshaws are a symbol of the old city. Though cycle-rickshaws have taken over in most areas, you may still find the hand-drawn ones operating in some parts of town. Recently the Kolkata's mayor announced that the new government is keen to issue photo IDs to the licensed rickshaw pullers, most of who are from the neighboring, impoverished states of Bihar and Jharkhand.

PLANNING

MAKING THE MOST OF YOUR TIME

You can see most of Kolkata's major sights comfortably in three days. Morning is a good time to hit the Maidan park and see Kolkatans playing sports and enjoying the outdoors before the afternoon sun forces them inside. The Victoria Memorial across from the park is a good place to escape the heat; its art exhibitions are fabulous. Take a tram ride around the Maidan to get a feel of how people once commonly travelled; some still do. It is slow, but delightful. Visit the Indian Museum and then hang around the art galleries and auditoriums in the vicinity, where plays and concerts are held throughout the year. Later, shop at New Market, and then join the locals for dinner, drinks, and dancing at the restaurants and hotel nightclubs on and around Park Street. Or take a leisurely boat ride down the Hooghly to catch the sunset and watch the two gorgeous bridges here light up.

The next day, visit College Street and walk around the university area and the secondhand bookstalls. From College Street, you can walk to Nakhoda Mosque, the Marble Palace, and the Rabindra Bharati University Museum, filled with Bengal-school paintings and Rabindranath Tagore memorabilia. For a dose of Jain culture, take a cab to the Pareshnath Temple. Continue on to Kumartuli to see artists create clay icons by the river. Another cab ride will take you to the Belur Math Shrine, then cross back to the Dakshineshwar Kali Temple.

If you have still have time in town, you can taxi down to Nirmal Hriday to visit the late Mother Teresa's first charitable home. And finally, hit south Calcutta's shopping hub, Gariahat, for handicrafts, saris, and art galleries (and lots of noise). End your time here at one of the many restaurants serving traditional and fusion Bengali cuisine.

WHEN TO GO

Low Season: The hottest weather arrives in April and grows increasingly stifling through June, when the monsoon season begins. This runs through mid-September and cools Kolkata down, though the occasional downpour means you can expect a soaking or two.

> ### BAD DRIVING
>
> In response to the painful traffic situation, authorities have made many roads in Kolkata one-way, then the other way, then two ways at various times throughout the day and week.

Shoulder Season: After the monsoon, it's festival time. The biggest of all festivals is the Durga Puja, which takes place over two weeks in September or October. All of West Bengal virtually shuts down for four days; getting around may be difficult.

High Season: Around December the mild winter sets in and lasts until March. This is the best time to visit, but as a result making advance reservations for hotels, trains, and airplanes is essential. The annual book fair and several open-air, all-night music concerts featuring classical, jazz, and rock musicians enliven this time. If you visit around Christmas, you're likely to see such tangible signs of the season as Christmas lights and fruitcake-like puddings. The town of Shantiniketan has its major festival, the Poush Mela, around the same time.

GETTING HERE AND AROUND

AIR TRAVEL

All international and domestic airlines use Netaji Subhash Chandra Bose International Airport, colloquially called Dum Dum Airport, 15 km (9 miles) north of the city. The terminal has prepaid taxi services; a ride downtown takes about 30 minutes and costs around Rs. 400. You can also book online with some of the fleet operators for an airport pickup or drop-off. Air-conditioned Volvo buses also service the airport from various parts of the city; these cost Rs. 40 or more. Bus service runs from 8:30 am to 9:30 pm.

Airlines and Contacts Indigo Airlines ☎ *09910383838* ⊕ *https://book. goindigo.in.* **Jet Airways** ✉ *18/D Stephen Court Bldg., Park St., ground fl.* ☎ *011/2217–1344.*

Airport Netaji Subhash Chandra Bose International Airport (*Dum Dum Airport; CCU*). ✉ *Jessore Rd., Dum* ☎ *33/2511–8036, 33/2511–9720.*

BUS TRAVEL

Buses are slow, creaking, and unbearably crowded during rush hours. They will cost you next to nothing but will set you back in terms of time and comfort. The new air-conditioned buses are better. However, you should avoid them if you are have a lot of luggage.

HAND-DRAWN AND CYCLE-RICKSHAW TRAVEL

Kolkata is the only city in the world to still have hand-pulled rickshaws: they're an efficient form of transportation for short distances. However, being carried around by a poor, barefooted man may be unsettling for some. Rickshaw fares fluctuate depending on the distance and the amount of traffic; negotiate ahead of time, using Rs. 20 per 10 minutes

9

as a guide. Cycle-rickshaws, which are ubiquitous, offer a more comfortable ride for a similar price.

METRO TRAVEL

Kolkata's efficient metro system connects the airport with Garia, a South Kolkata locality that's the southernmost stop on the route. Tickets cost Rs. 5 for a 5-km (3-mile) ride and are available from machines and windows in every station. New routes have been added, with elevated lines joining the far-flung neighborhood of the expanding city to the airport and business district. Check ⊕ *www.kmrc.in* for the latest changes.

TAXI AND AUTO-RICKSHAW TRAVEL

The base fare for Kolkata taxis is Rs. 25, and then Rs. 12 for every kilometer. However, check with your hotel to confirm, because fares frequently change. If a driver refuses to turn the meter on, find another taxi. Traffic, unfortunately, plagues Kolkata, and it might bring your cab to a full stop amid humid air and diesel exhaust, so at rush hour you may just want to find a sweetshop and wait until it's over. Or better still, if your destination is along the metro's route, give the subway a try. A word of caution though—the office-hour crowd along the busy routes can be daunting even for those used to the rush-hour subway rush in places like New York.

Auto-rickshaws are cheaper (and sometimes dirtier) than taxis, but they're not as easy to find in the city center. Still, at rush hour they can be more efficient than taxis, which are more likely to get stuck in traffic.

The three-wheel auto-rickshaws used in Kolkata are often operated by unlicensed drivers and work much like buses, picking up passengers along fixed routes. Many taxi drivers are unfamiliar with the roads, so expect frequent stops for directions. Adding to the confusion is the haphazard way in which many streets have been renamed. Use your smartphone if possible to get around.

TRAIN TRAVEL

Howrah Junction, which sees tremendous amounts of train traffic every day, is divided into the neighboring Old and New Howrah stations. The main reservation office has a foreign-tourist section upstairs, open daily 9 am–1 pm and 1:30 pm–4 pm; you can buy tickets here with either foreign currency or a valid encashment certificate for rupees, so if you obtained your rupees from an ATM, go to the normal lines. There are also ticket offices on the first floor of Old Howrah Station, the second floor of New Howrah Station, and in Kalighat. Sealdah Station is used exclusively by trains to and from northern destinations such as Darjeeling. Tickets are sold on the platform level.

Getting to central Kolkata by taxi from here takes 20 to 40 minutes, depending on traffic. Once you get downtown, it's usually best to hire a car and driver, which you can do from the travel agencies and rental agencies. Expect to pay Rs. 1,000 for eight hours and 70 km (50 miles), with an hourly and per-kilometer rate beyond that. Hailing a plain old taxi can be cheaper. Take a cab to or from the area you're visiting, then walk or find a sturdy cycle-rickshaw.

Train Information Howrah Railway Junction ✉ *1 block south of west end of Howrah Bridge* ☎ *33/2638–2581, 33/2638–3542* ⊕ *www.irctc.co.in* ✉ *6 Fairlie Pl., North Kolkata* ☎ *33/2220–6811.* **Sealdah Station** ✉ *East end of Bepin Behari Ganguly St., North Kolkata* ☎ *33/2350–3535.*

RESTAURANTS

Kolkata has experienced a growth in its vibrant restaurant culture since the mid-1990s. Restaurants here cater to a varied sensibility: Asian, Mexican, Italian, and, of course, Bengali and other Indian cuisines. The service is largely friendly, and many places are crowded enough, especially on weekends, to warrant reservations. Eating out in Kolkata is cheaper compared to cities like Delhi and Mumbai—and every bit as good in terms of quality. Restaurants are generally open daily 12:30 to 3 for lunch and 7:30 to 11 for dinner.

HOTELS

Kolkata has seen the launch of several top-end five-star hotels and establishments over the years, besides medium and budget options mainly for business travelers.

Unless otherwise noted, hotels have air-conditioning, room TVs, and operate on the European meal plan (no meals included). Better hotels have foreign-exchange facilities, and most have rooms with bathrooms that have tubs. Some luxury hotels have exclusive floors with special privileges or facilities for the business traveler. *Hotel reviews have been shortened. For full information, visit Fodors.com.*

WHAT IT COSTS IN RUPEES			
	$	**$$**	**$$$**	**$$$$**
Restaurants	under Rs. 500	Rs. 500–Rs. 1,000	Rs. 1,001–Rs. 1,400	over Rs. 1,400
Hotels	under Rs. 6,000	Rs. 6,000–Rs. 9,000	Rs. 9,001–Rs. 13,000	over Rs. 13,000

Restaurant prices are the average cost of a main course at dinner or, if dinner is not served, at lunch. Hotel prices are the lowest cost of a standard double room in high season.

EMERGENCIES

General Emergencies Fire ☎ *101.* **Police** ☎ *100.*

Medical Care Bellevue Clinic ✉ *9 U. N. Brahmachari St., South Kolkata* ☎ *33/2287–2321* ⊕ *www.bellevueclinic.com.*

VISITOR INFORMATION

The West Bengal Tourist Office is open Monday through Saturday 10 to 5. The regional Government of India Tourist Office is well equipped to help baffled travelers; it's open Monday–Saturday 9–6. The Kolkata Information Centre is also helpful. The West Bengal Tourist Office is in the heart of Kolkata's business hub, but people here will only be able to give you information about destinations within the state. The Government of India Tourist Office, near the city center, gives more of an overall picture (including the state). The staff is friendly to boot.

Consulate U.S. Consulate ⊠ *5–1 Ho Chi Minh Sarani, Central Kolkata, Kolkata, West Bengal* ☎ *33/3984–2400.*

Tourist Offices Kolkata Information Centre ⊠ *Circus Ave., Gokhel Rd., Bhawanipur, South Kolkata* ☎ *33/2223–2451.* **Government of India Tourist Office** ⊠ *4 Birla Planetarium, Shakespeare Sarani, Elgin, Central Kolkata* ☎ *33/2282–7731.* **West Bengal Tourist Office** ⊠ *3/2 B. B. D. Bagh E, Central Kolkata* ☎ *33/2243–6440, 33/2248–8271* ⊕ *www.wbtourism.gov.in.*

TOURS

These agencies can arrange a car and driver for local sightseeing or help make long-distance travel arrangements.

Contacts Ashok Travel and Tours (ITDC) ⊠ *3 G Everest Bldg., 46 C J. L. Nehru Rd., Central Kolkata* ☎ *33/2290–9298, 33/2288–0901.* **Mercury Travels** ⊠ *Everest House, 46C Chowringhee Rd., Central Kolkata* ☎ *33/6626–8400* ⊕ *www.mercurytravels.co.in.* **Thomas Cook** ⊠ *378 Lake Gardens, Prince Anwar Shah Rd., South Kolkata* ☎ *33/6454–2160.*

WALKING TOURS

The most interesting tours in Kolkata are the walks through various neighborhoods led by Calcutta Walks.

Calcutta Walks. Half- and full-day walks with this company start at Rs. 2,500 for a minimum of two people. The company also organizes boat rides, bike tours, and stays in old houses with interesting stories that evoke the true spirit of the city. Contact them via email. ⊠ *9A Khairu Pl., Central Kolkata* ☎ *91/98301–84030* ⊕ *www.calcuttawalks.com.*

TELEPHONE NUMBERS

Phone numbers change with alarming frequency in Kolkata. Whenever you make a call and get a recorded message saying, "This telephone number does not exist," dial 1951 or 1952 or 197 to find out the new number. There are computerized as well as manual services.

EXPLORING KOLKATA

Kolkata and Howrah (also written as Haora) straddle the Hooghly River, with Kolkata on the east side, and Howrah on the west. Across the Hooghly from Kolkata's old quarter, the Howrah district—which holds Kolkata's massive train station—is a constantly expanding suburb. On the eastern side of town is Salt Lake City, a planned, upscale residential community.

In Kolkata itself, the Howrah Bridge spills into Burra Bazaar, the vibrant wholesale-market area that anchors the city's commerce. North Kolkata includes Burra Bazaar and Kolkata University and extends to the distant neighborhood of Chitpur and the Jain Temple in Tala. The heart of Central Kolkata remains B. B. D. Bagh (Binoy Badal Dinesh Bagh, formerly Dalhousie Square), where commerce and government have been concentrated since British times. Central Kolkata also holds the expansive Maidan park, the crowded bazaar at New Market, and the upmarket shops and restaurants on Park Street. At the south end of the Maidan are the Victoria Memorial and Kolkata's racecourse. South

Kolkata has the Kali Temple and the late Mother Teresa's hospice in Kalighat and the National Library and zoo in Alipore, a posh residential community. To the east of the city is the Eastern Metropolitan Bypass (known simply as "the bypass"), which links south Kolkata to the north. The expanding city now stretches well beyond the bypass, which is now lined with five-star hotels, exclusive condominiums, malls, and parks that overlook vast stretches of agricultural lands and fisheries. The Chinese settlement in Tangra, famed for its Indo-Chinese cuisine, is a popular dining destination.

NORTH KOLKATA

The streets in northern Kolkata are more crowded and narrower than those elsewhere in the city. This is where hand-pulled rickshaws still run along winding, skinny alleys, and old mansions seem to brood over the past. This—the old village of Sutanuti—is also where the Indians lived while the British spread their estates east and south of Fort William and Dalhousie Square (B. B. D. Bagh). The architecture reflects Italian and Dutch influences.

North Kolkata's attractions are somewhat scattered. You'll need to take taxis at least sporadically. The bazaar areas surrounding Mahatma Gandhi Road, universally known as M. G. Road, are at once intensely commercial and residential; tourists are only occasional, despite the fascinating sights and vibe. You may attract some curious stares, but anyone you stop and speak to is bound to be friendly and welcoming.

EXPLORING
TOP ATTRACTIONS
Belur Math Shrine. This is the headquarters of the Ramakrishna Mission, a reform movement inspired by the mystic Ramakrishna Paramahansa, who died in 1886. Having forsaken his privileged Brahmin heritage, Ramakrishna preached the unity of religious faiths and an adherence to altruistic values for all people. His disciple, Swami Vivekananda, established the mission in 1898. The serene Belur Math Shrine, on the banks of the Hooghly, resembles a church, a temple, or a mosque, depending on where you're standing. Somber *aarti* (chants and hymns) are sung in the immense prayer hall every evening; visitors are more than welcome. Simple vegetarian meals, offered at the shrine, are then served to visitors who make a nominal donation. ✉ *Belur Rd., Howrah, 2 km (1 mile) south of 2nd Hooghly Bridge (Vivekananda Setu)* ☎ *33/2654–1144, 33/2654–5391* ⊕ *www.belurmath.org* ☉ *Daily 6:30– noon and 3:30–7:30.*

Dakshineshwar Kali Temple. Far north along the Hooghly, this 19th-century complex with 13 temples is a major pilgrimage site for devotees of Kali, as well as other deities. The variety of temples makes this site a good introduction for the uninitiated to the Hindu pantheon. It was here that the 19th-century mystic Ramakrishna had the vision that led him to renounce his Brahmin caste and propound altruism and religious unity. His most famous disciple, Swami Vivekananda, went on to be a major force in the intellectual and spiritual growth of Kolkata, and founded the Ramakrishna Mission, headquartered in the Belur Math Shrine.

9

9

Calcutta to Kolkata

In 2001, Calcutta's name was officially changed to Kolkata. This transformation, like similar ones in India, was supposed to contribute to ridding the city of its colonial past. The two names are used interchangeably. Streets, too, have been renamed. Although some maps and street signs have only the new names, you're more likely to see just the old or both. Taxis and rickshaws use the names interchangeably, but old names are still favored, as most of the new names are ridiculously long and obscure. Here are a few of the most important name changes:

■ Chowringhee Road/Jawaharlal Nehru (J.L. Nehru) Road

■ Ballygunge Circular/Pramathesh Barua Sarani

■ Bowbazar/B.B. Ganguly Street

■ Harington Street/Ho Chi Minh Sarani

■ Lansdowne Road/Sarat Bose Road

■ Lower Circular Road/A.J.C. Bose Road

■ Rippon Street/Muzaffar Ahmed Street

■ Theatre Road/Shakespeare Sarani

Ramakrishna's room here is a museum. Don't miss the chance to spend some quiet moments on the banks of the river. Stalls selling local fast food line the busy street up to the temple. ⊠ *P. W. D. Rd., near Second Hooghly Bridge (Vivekananda Setu)* ⊕ *www.dakshineswarkalitemple. org* ✉ *Free* ⊙ *Daily dawn–10 pm.*

Fodor's Choice ★ **Kumartuli.** Home to hundreds of clay artists, this neighborhood is the most famous producer of idols of popular deities in the Hindu pantheon. The skilled craftsmen are especially in demand during the immense Durga Puja, which is usually held in the autumn. A walk around the maze of potters' settlements can be full of surprises. ⊠ *Chitpur Rd., between Bidhan Sarani and Jatindra Mohan.*

Fodor's Choice ★ **Marble Palace.** One of the strangest buildings in Kolkata was the inspiration of Raja Rajendra Mullick Bahadur, a member of Bengal's landed gentry. Mullick built the palace in 1855, making lavish use of Italian marble. It's behind a lawn cluttered with sculptures of lions, the Buddha, Christopher Columbus, Jesus, the Virgin Mary, and Hindu gods. Near a small granite bungalow (where Mullick's descendants still live), a large pool houses some exotic birds with large headdresses. The palace has an interior courtyard, complete with a throne room where a peacock often struts around the seat of honor. The upstairs rooms are downright baroque: enormous mirrors and paintings cover the walls (including works by Reynolds, Rubens, and Murillo), gigantic chandeliers hang from the ceilings, and hundreds of statues and Far Eastern urns populate the rooms. The floors bear multicolored marble inlay on a giant scale, with a calico effect. Even the lamps are detailed creations, especially those on the staircases, where metal women are entwined in trees with a light bulb on each branch. Movie producers use the palace for shooting films. Make sure to tip your guide here. ⊠ *46 Muktaram Babu St., opposite Ram Mandir, Jorasanko* ☎ *33/2269–3310* ✉ *Free;*

you must obtain pass from West Bengal Tourist Office 24 hrs in advance ⊙ *Tues., Wed., and Fri.–Sun. 9:30–3:30.*

WORTH NOTING

College Street. This erudite destination smells of old books and history. This was the hotbed of the Bengal Renaissance movement, and it eventually became a symbol of revolutionary ideals and radical youth movements. Several walking tours are available around the elite Presidency College University, Kolkata University, Sanskrit College, Baptist Mission, Theosophical Society and Hindu School. The pavements are dominated by bookstalls that are treasure troves for those with the inclination and time to discover a rare (and usually quite inexpensive) title. At Indian Coffee House, at 15 Bankim Chatterjee Street, you can grab a quick bite over a leisurely cup of coffee and get a whiff of the languid airs of the historic neighborhood. Heritage walks of the Renaissance neighborhood are organized by both Calcutta Walks and Kolkata Magic. ⊠ *North Kolkata* ⊕ *www.calcuttawalks.com or www. kolkatamagic.com.*

Howrah Bridge. One of the most enduring icons of the city, the Howrah Bridge was commissioned and built by the British between 1936 and 1943. The tall cantilevered bridge links Kolkata to Howrah and its bustling railway station, which serves as a gateway to the northeast of India. The web of girders stretches 1,500 feet over the Hooghly, crisscrossed with small and big fishing boats, ferries, and steamers. Now renamed Rabindra Setu, after Nobel laureate Rabindranath Tagore, who hailed from the city, the Howrah has fascinated poets, painters, writers, filmmakers and tourists.

Bordered by thin walkways, the bridge's eight lanes of chaotic traffic bear 2 million people each day in buses, rickshaws, cars, scooters, bicycles, and pushcarts. A walk across the bridge provides terrific people-watching.

Nakhoda Mosque. This massive red sandstone mosque, which can hold 10,000 worshippers, was built in 1926 by the Sunni Muslim community as a copy of Akbar's tomb in Agra. Each floor has a prayer hall. The top floor has views of the streets below, which are crowded with stalls selling everything from paperback Korans to kebabs. The tailors in the bazaar are known for their skillful embroidery and can turn out traditional kurtas on short notice. ⊠ *M. G. Rd. and Rabindra Sarani* 🖾 *Free* ⊙ *Daily sunrise–8 pm.*

Pareshnath Temple. Built in 1867 and dedicated to Pareshnathji, the 23rd of the 24 Jain *tirthankaras* ("perfect souls," meaning sages who have achieved Nirvana), this Jain temple is an uncharacteristically ostentatious one, with inlaid-mirror pillars, stained-glass windows, floral-pattern marble floors, fountains, a gilded dome, colorful fish in sparkling reservoirs, and chandeliers from 19th-century Paris and Brussels. The garden holds blocks of glass mosaics depicting European figures and statues covered with silver paint. ⊠ *Badridas Temple St., near Raja Dinendra St.* ⊙ *Daily sunrise–noon and 3–7.*

Prinsep Ghat-Babu Ghat Promenade. The promenade between the restored Prinsep Ghat (steps leading into the river), north to Outram Ghat and then Babu Ghat, has been spruced up to attract tourists and others seeking some spectacular photo ops. You'll find it under Vidyasagar Setu, the newer bridge that crosses the Hooghly. The stretch has sweeping views of the riverbanks, old warehouses, the beautiful cable bridge, and steamers and smaller ships. There's a park at one end, with some food stalls favored by families; privacy-starved couples head to the quieter sections. The area is well policed and illuminated in the evenings, so if you feel adventurous, try a joyride in an oar-boat, as much an icon of the old city as the Howrah Bridge itself. Avoid late nights, though—stick to sunsets and sunrises. ⊠ *Prinsep Ghat, Strand Rd.*

Rabindra Bharati University and Tagore Museum. Rabindranath Tagore's sprawling and well-maintained mansion is a pilgrimage site for his fans and followers. A poet, philosopher, and Renaissance man, Tagore won the Nobel Prize for Literature in 1913. Inside, the university fosters cultural activities and maintains a display of paintings by artists of the Bengal School of Art. The nerve center of Calcutta's intellectual activity around the turn of the 20th century, Tagore's abode now holds memorabilia, including beautiful sepia photographs of the poet, his family, and his contemporaries. A 40-minute sound-and-light show takes visitors through Tagore's life and the movement he spearheaded. ⊠ *6–4 Dwarkanath Tagore La., Jorasanko* ☎ *33/2269–5241, 33/2218–1744* ⊕ *museum.rbu.ac.in* ⊠ *Rs. 100* ☉ *Sound-and-light show: Nov.–Jan., daily 6 pm; Feb.–June, daily 7 pm.*

Tiretta Bazaar/Old Chinatown. Chinese settlers in Kolkata have given the city a few things to fall in love with, and the breakfast served at Tiretta Bazaar is one of them. Every morning, kiosks come up along the streets, catering to the dwindling Chinese population, as well as call-center employees, pub crawlers, and foodies. With the younger generation of Chinese migrants leaving the city, the market has shrunk considerably, as has the menu, though you can expect meatballs, fish soup, pork buns, and Chinese sausages. There are plans of reviving the neighborhood and turning it into a tourist hub. Until that happens, a quick trip here is a great way to sample authentic, even if a tad rustic, Chinese fare. Note that the vendors all disappear by 10 am. ⊠ *Tiretta Bazar La., Tiretti, Central Kolkata.*

Town Hall. Built with Doric columns in 1813, Town Hall was where Europeans of British India met to socialize. After India's Independence, the structure (and its paintings and statues) were thrown open to the public and subjected to rampant misuse. Thankfully, in the late 1990s, the Town Hall was restored and today houses the Kolkata Panorama museum, showcasing some of the city's cultural and historic milestones. ⊠ *4 Esplanade Row (West), B. B. G. Bagh* ☎ *33/2248–3085* ⊠ *Weekends: Rs. 15; weekdays, Rs. 10* ☉ *Tues.–Sun., 11–6.*

CENTRAL KOLKATA AND THE MAIDAN

The British first built Fort William in the middle of a dense jungle. When disagreements led the local Bengali ruler, Siraj ud-Daula, to attack and destroy it, the British response was a quick and decisive battle led by Robert Clive. The Battle of Plassey (some 160 km [100 miles] north

Calcutta's Anglo-Indians

Calcutta, once the capital of British Raj, is home to the country's largest population of Anglo-Indians, a fast-vanishing group of native English-speakers who are of mixed European and Indian ancestry. Anglos thrived under the British, who set aside important government jobs for them, especially ones having to do with the railways. Many others were successful teachers, secretaries, nurses, and singers. But after Independence many Anglo-Indians left for North America, England, and Australia, fearing hostility from other Indians, who identified them with the former rulers.

The exodus continues, but the dwindling community works hard to maintain its identity. Younger generations marry outside the community and are gaining familiarity with the Bengali language and culture. But at home, they eat chicken *jalfrezi* (with tomatoes and green chillies) and other Anglo-Indian dishes, attend the community's churches, and speak English with little trace of an Indian accent. At Christmas, Anglo-Indians from around the world come to dance, sing, and party on the narrow street that anchors Bow Barracks, a century-old neighborhood of Anglo-Indians behind Bowbazar Police Station in Central Calcutta. Among the most famous Anglo-Indians are singers Engelbert Humperdinck and Cliff Richard, who spent his early childhood in Calcutta. The moving documentary *A Calcutta Christmas* (1998) covers the lives of some elderly Anglo-Indians living in a home, in a city that's much different than the one they grew up in.

of town), transformed the British from traders into a ruling presence in 1757—after it, the forest was cut down in order to provide a clear line for cannon fire in case of attack. It's really from the year 1757 that modern Kolkata traces its history, and from the impenetrable Fort William (completed in 1773) that the city began its explosive growth.

Starting about 1 km (½ mile) north of the fort, central Kolkata became the commercial and political heart of the city. It was here that the British conducted business, and here that they built their stately homes. The immense area cleared for British cannons is now Kolkata's 3-square-km (2-square-mile) park, the Maidan, and central Kolkata now goes beyond the Maidan to B. B. D. Bagh square and most of the commercial and residential areas to the east of the giant park.

EXPLORING
TOP ATTRACTIONS
Chowringhee. North Kolkata may be the city's intellectual heart, but the slick commercial area east of the Maidan is the city's spinal cord. Now technically called Jawaharlal (or J. L.) Nehru Road, Chowringhee runs along the east side of the Maidan, with shops, hotels, and old Victorian buildings lining the other side of the wide pavement. In the evening, hawkers do their best with potential shoppers, and at night, the homeless bed down. ⊠ *Central Kolkata.*

Indian Museum. India's oldest museum has one of the largest and most comprehensive collections in Asia, including one of the best natural-history collections in the world. It's known locally as Jadu Ghar, the "House of Magic." The archaeology section has representative antiquities from prehistoric times to the Moghul period, including relics from Mohenjo Daro and Harappa, the oldest excavated Indus Valley cities. The southern wing includes the Bharhut and Gandhara rooms (Indian art from the 2nd century BC to the 5th century AD), the Gupta and medieval galleries, and the Moghul gallery.

The Indian Museum also houses the world's largest collection of Indian coins; ask at the information desk for permission to see it. Gems and jewelry are on display. The art section on the first floor has a good collection of textiles, carpets, wood carving, papier-mâché figures, and terracotta pottery. A gallery on the third floor contains exquisite Persian and Indian miniature paintings, and banners from Tibetan monasteries. The anthropology section on the first floor is devoted to cultural anthropology, though the museum plans to establish India's first comprehensive exhibit on physical anthropology; some interesting specimens are an Egyptian mummy donated in 1880 by an English seaman, a fossilized 200-million-year-old tree trunk, the lower jaw of a 26-meter (84-foot) whale, and meteorites dating back 50,000 years. ⊠ *27 J. L. Nehru Rd., Dharmatala* ☎ *33/2286–1699* ⊕ *indianmuseumkolkata.org* ☞ *Rs. 150* ⊙ *Mar.–Nov., Tues.–Sun. 10–5; Dec.–Feb., Tues.–Sun. 10–4:30.*

NEED A BREAK?

Flury's Tea Room. For breakfast or tea with sandwiches, try Flury's Tea Room, which serves nostalgia in a new, contemporary setting. Kolkata's first Swiss confectioner opened in the 1920s and is now an institution. You can get a chicken or cheese omelet, croissants, vegetable patties, beans on toast, tea in a pot, and coffee for Rs. 500. ⊠ *18 Park St.* ☎ *33/4000–7453* ⊕ *www.flurysindia.com* ⊙ *Daily 7:30 am–8 pm.*

The Maidan. Maidan, the green lungs of the city, and loved and prized by its people, stretches from the Governor's house in the north to the National Library in the south, the Hooghly in the West, and the iconic Victoria Memorial in the east. The historic fields were created when the forests around the water bodies in the area were cleared out for the British army stationed at Fort William. The Maidan is now home to cricket fields, Eden Gardens, clubhouses of popular football (soccer) leagues, stadiums, monuments, statues of both British generals and Indian leaders, and a racecourse. Mornings see fitness enthusiasts and sports teams take to the grounds, while evenings are for families and couples enjoying the pony rides and fountains. ⊠ *Just south of B. B. D. Bagh to northern border of Alipore, and from Hooghly River to J. L. Nehru Rd. and shops of Park St..*

South Park Street Cemetery. The graves and memorials here form a repository of British imperial history. People who lived within the Raj from 1767 on are buried here, and in the records of their lives you can see the trials and triumphs of the building of an empire. ⊠ *Park St. at Rawdon St.* ⊙ *Daily sunrise–sunset.*

Fodor's Choice ★

Victoria Memorial. This massive white-marble monument was conceived in 1901 by Lord Curzon and built over a 20-year period. Designed in a mixture of Italian Renaissance and Saracenic styles, surrounded by

Cricket matches are a favorite pastime in the central Maidan, the green lungs of Kolkata.

extensive, carefully manicured gardens, and preceded by a typically sober statue of Victoria herself, it remains a major symbol of the British Raj as well as that of Kolkata itself. Inside the building is an excellent museum of the history of Kolkata (there's a lot to read, but it will really sharpen your sense of the British-Bengali relationship) and various Raj-related exhibits, including Queen Victoria's writing desk and piano, Indian miniature paintings, watercolors, and Persian books. Cameras and electronic equipment must be left at the entrance. In the evenings there's a sound-and-light show, with narration in English, about Kolkata's history. The lawns are used by locals, especially in winter, for family picnics and joyrides on horse-drawn carriages. ⊠ *Queen's Way* ☎ *33/2223–1890* ⊡ *Monument Rs. 150, sound-and-light show Rs. 20* ⊙ *Tues.–Sun. 10–4:30; sound-and-light show Tues.–Sun. 7:15 (Oct.–Feb.) and 7:45 (Mar.–June).*

WORTH NOTING

B. B. D. Bagh. With wide, buzzing streets lined with late-Victorian buildings and pavements taken over by vendors selling rice-based meals, snacks, fruits, clothes, accessories, books, magazines, and electronic devices, this square remains the heart of the city. Still referred to by its Colonial name, Dalhousie Square, the regal buildings were built around a sprawling tank (water reservoir), Lal Dighi, for civil employees. Now they are home to international banks, and the state secretariat and other public offices. After office hours, the square falls silent; that's a good time to visit if you're interested in taking a closer look at its architectural and historic landmarks. ⊠ *East of Hooghly River, 2½ km (1½ mile) south of Howrah Bridge.*

Fort William. The irregular heptagon south of the Eden Gardens in the Maidan is surrounded by a moat almost 50 feet wide. Begun in 1757 after Robert Clive's victory at Plassey over Siraj ud-Daula, Fort William was designed to prevent any future attacks. The fort's walls, as well as its barracks, stables, and Church of St. Peter, have survived to this day chiefly because the fort has, in fact, never been attacked. The Indian government still uses the fort, but it's closed to the public. ⊠ *Strand Rd..*

General Post Office (*GPO*). Built in 1864 and still in use as Kolkata's main post office, this building's massive white Corinthian columns rest on the site of the original Fort William, where the British were attacked in 1756 and many officers were imprisoned by Siraj ud-Daula in the infamous "Black Hole of Calcutta" a tiny space that caused most of the group to suffocate. A postal museum, founded in 1884, has artifacts and stamps. The Philatelic Bureau is situated at the southwestern end of the building. ⊠ *Netaji Subhash Rd., near B. B .D. Bagh* ☎ *33/2242–1572* ⊘ *Weekdays 10–5:30.*

Ochterlony Monument (*Shaheed Minar*). On the north end of the Maidan stands a 148-foot pillar commemorating Sir David Ochterlony's military victories over the Nepalese in the border war of 1814–16. Built in 1828, the impressive monument has a curious design: the base is Egyptian, the column is Syrian, and the cupola is Turkish. Now officially called the Shaheed Minar (Martyr's Tower), it has been the site of many political rallies and student demonstrations during Calcutta's turbulent post-Independence history. ⊠ *J. L. Nehru Rd..*

St. Paul's Cathedral. Completed in 1847, the cathedral now has a steeple modeled after the one at Canterbury; previous steeples were destroyed by earthquakes in 1897 and 1934. Florentine frescoes, the stained-glass western window, and a gold communion plate presented by Queen Victoria are prize possessions. Birds congregate in the interior eaves. The lawns and the Parish Hall are a popular venue for marriages and other functions. ⊠ *Cathedral Rd., east of Victoria Memorial* ☎ *33/2223–0127* ⊘ *Mon.–Sat. 9–noon and 3–6, Sun. 7–12:30 and 3–7.*

Writers' Building. The original "writers" were the clerks of the British East India Company. Now a government office building, this dramatically baroque edifice is closed to the public. ⊠ *North side of B. B. D. Bagh.*

SOUTH KOLKATA

Calcutta's rich and powerful moved consistently south as the city grew more and more crowded and unpleasant. Here you'll see an interesting mix of large colonial homes, modern hotels and businesses, open space, and crowded temple areas.

EXPLORING

TOP ATTRACTIONS

Indian Botanical Gardens (*Acharya Jagadish Chandra Bose Indian Botanic Garden*). Across the Second Hooghly Bridge (Vivekananda Setu) in Howrah are these sprawling botanical gardens, first opened in 1786. Darjeeling and Assam teas were developed here. The gardens' banyan tree has one of the largest canopies in the world, covering a mind-boggling 1,300 square feet. On Sundays and holidays, locals turn out in droves to enjoy their day off. The winters are excellent for bird-watching. ⊠ *Between Andul Rd. and Kurz Ave., Shibpur, Howrah* 🕾 *33/2668–0554* 📷 *Rs. 100, Rs. 20 extra for cameras* ☉ *Daily 1 hr after sunrise–1 hr before sunset.*

Kalighat Kali Temple. Built in 1809, the Kali temple is one of the most significant pilgrimage sites in India, with shrines to Shiva, Krishna, and Kali, the patron goddess of Kolkata. Human sacrifices were reputed to be commonly practiced here on special days during the 19th century, but only goats are slaughtered now, then offered to the goddess with *bhang* (marijuana). The building rewards a close look: you'll see thin, multicolored layers of painted trim and swaths of tilework. Only Hindus are allowed in the inner sanctum, but the lanes and brilliant flower markets surrounding the temple are lovely in themselves. Beware of touts and aggressive priests. ⊠ *Kalighat Rd.* ☉ *Daily sunrise–sunset.*

WORTH NOTING

National Library. Once the house of the lieutenant governor of Calcutta, this hefty neo-Renaissance building has miles of books and pleasant reading rooms. The rare-book section holds some significant works, adding to the importance of this 2-million-volume facility. There are no displays, but you can take a short walk through the grounds. ⊠ *Belvedere Rd., near Taj Bengal hotel, Alipore* ⊕ *www.nationallibrary.gov.in* ☉ *Weekdays 9–8, weekends 9:30–6.*

Nirmal Hriday (*Pure Heart*). Mother Teresa's first home for the dying is now one of 300 affiliated organizations worldwide that care for people in the most dire need. Mother Teresa is buried in this building, which was her home for 44 years, until her death in 1997. ⊠ *Next to Kali Temple, Kalighat Rd., Kalighat* 🕾 *33/2464–4223* ☉ *Fri.–Wed. 3–6.*

Missionaries of Charity. Awarded the Nobel Peace Prize in 1979 and beatified in 2003, Mother Teresa founded the Missionaries of Charity in Kokata in 1950. Today the group works in 133 countries. The Charity's work for those who have contracted HIV/AIDs, leprosy, and tuberculosis, including mobile dispensaries and shelters for orphans, draws volunteers and donors through the year. The headquarters has information on the Missionaries' work and opportunities to volunteer with the various initiatives. ⊠ *10 Park St., Mullick Bazar* 🕾 *33/2249–7115.*

WHERE TO EAT

NORTH KOLKATA

$$$$ ✕ **PanAsian.** This sleek, modern restaurant with massive ceilings is
ASIAN bathed in blacks and browns. As the name suggests, the menu here
Fodor'sChoice covers a broad variety of dishes from all over Asia. The menu's three
★ sections are divided into Japan, Mongolia, and Korea; Thailand; and China. The sushi, grilled dishes, and Thai curries seem to be the favorites here. The Sunday brunch, with an option for unlimited alcohol and champagne, is the latest crowd-puller at this haunt, loved by many

The city's best street food can be discerned from the busiest stalls.

expats. Reservations are a good idea. $ *Average main: Rs. 1500* ✉ *ITC Hotel the Sonar, 1 Haldane Ave., Bypass and beyond* ☎ *33/84449–69514* ⚞ *Reservations essential* ☾ *No lunch weekdays.*

CENTRAL KOLKATA AND THE MAIDAN

$$
ECLECTIC
✕ **Peter Cat.** Along with the nearby Mocambo, this is one of the city's oldest restaurants, with an atmosphere that harkens back to its early days in the 1960s. (Some of the staff may actually date from those times, too.) The Chelo kebab here—a simple dish plated to resemble a cello with buttered saffron rice, a fried egg, two pieces of mutton (goat) kebabs, and one chicken kebab—is wildly popular in Kolkata for reasons best known to the loyals. The dining room is intimate, thanks to the small tables, with white stucco walls, and somewhat tired, as with most restaurants in the vicinity, with Tiffany-style lamps and soft lighting. The restaurant is always packed, so book your table in advance. $ *Average main: Rs. 500* ✉ *18 Park St.* ☎ *33/2229–8841* ⚞ *Reservations essential.*

$$
ECLECTIC
✕ **Tangerine.** This is perhaps one of the better places with a multi-cuisine menu in Kolkata. Small and cozy, with minimalist furniture and plate-glass windows, this restaurant is run by a friendly, helpful staff, and it serves great food. Don't-miss choices include prawn salad, fish-and-chips, lobster thermidor, and chilli crab. $ *Average main: Rs. 600* ✉ *2–1 Outram St.* ☎ *33/2281–5450* ⚞ *Reservations essential.*

$$
MODERN INDIAN
✕ **Veda.** Designed by the "bad boy" of Indian design, Rohit Bal, the flamboyant interiors of this Park Street restaurant set the stage for the classic and trendy Indian dishes served here. The menu is clearly

BEST BETS FOR KOLKATA DINING

Fodor'sChoice ★	$$	BENGALI
6 Ballygunge Place, p. 518	Arsalan, p. 518	Bohemian, p. 518
Bohemian, p. 518	Mainland China, p. 518	6 Ballygunge Place, p. 518
Chinoiserie, p. 518	Oh! Calcutta, p. 519	Oh! Calcutta, p. 519
Mrs Magpie, p. 519		
Oh! Calcutta, p. 519	$$$$	DESSERTS
PanAsian, p. 515	Chinoiserie, p. 518	Mrs Magpie, p. 519
	PanAsian, p. 515	
By Price	**By Cuisine**	EUROPEAN
		Peter Cat, p. 516
$	ASIAN	Tangerine, p. 516
6 Ballygunge Place, p. 518	Chinoiserie, p. 518	INDIAN
Bohemian, p. 518	Mainland China, p. 518	Zaranj, p. 517
Momo Plaza, p. 519	Momo Plaza, p. 519	HOT SPOT
Mrs Magpie, p. 519	PanAsian, p. 515	Veda, p. 516

inspired by dishes served at starred Indian restaurants in New York or London, with an occasional nod to local flavors and ingredients. While the food and service have received a mixed response, the lounge, on the lower floor, has been grabbing lots of attention for its high-profile celebrity parties and live music performances. Try their signature dishes, dal Veda (long-simmered black lentils with cream and tomatoes) and Death by Rabri, a sweet, rich dessert. $ *Average main: Rs. 700* ⊠ *Park Mansion, 57A Park St.* ☎ *033/2229–9999* ⊕ *www.vedarestaurants.com* ⚑ *Reservations essential.*

$$

INDIAN ✕**Zaranj.** Opulent, if a little over the top, with a fountain, ornate furniture, and red tablecloths and upholstery, Zaranj remains popular for its North Indian and tandoori classics. A major standout is the Zaranji *raan*, a whole leg of goat marinated in Indian spices and slowly grilled—it takes a good 30 minutes to prepare, but it melts in your mouth. $ *Average main: Rs. 800* ⊠ *26 J. L. Nehru Rd.* ☎ *33/2249–0369* ⚑ *Reservations essential.*

$$

ASIAN ✕**Zen.** Art deco meets postmodern in the sleek lines of this Southeast Asian restaurant, which serves cuisines from Japan to Indonesia. Their standout dishes include the various sushi dishes, pork with pineapple and ginger, and Thai curries. $ *Average main: Rs. 900* ⊠ *Park Hotel, 17 Park St.* ☎ *33/2249–7336* ⊕ *www.theparkhotels.com/kolkata/kolkata.html* ⚑ *Reservations essential* ⊘ *No lunch.*

9

SOUTH KOLKATA

$ ╳ **6 Ballygunge Place.** This well-liked restaurant is known for its tradi-
INDIAN   tional and contemporary Bengali cuisine. Try the prawns or the *hilsa*
Fodor's Choice   (a local fish), wrapped in banana leaves and steamed in a mustard and
★   coconut marinade. The buffet here is one of the best you can get in the
city—it's a great introduction to Bengali dishes. There's another branch
in Salt Lake Sector 1. $ *Average main: Rs. 400* ⊠ *6 Ballygunge Pl., Bal-
lygunge* ☎ *990/397–5614* ⊕ *www.savourites.in/flagship.asp* ⌲ *Reservations essential.*

$$ ╳ **Arsalan.** The city's love affair with *biryani*—aromatic and spiced rice
NORTH INDIAN   usually cooked with chicken or mutton (goat)—is legendary. Although
every neighborhood has its favorite biryani destination, Arsalan has
emerged as one of the most popular and successful destinations for
it in recent years. The restaurants are basic, the queues are often long
and serpentine, and service is brisk—you are expected to finish your
meal and quickly make way for those waiting outside. The biryani in
Calcutta is closer to the Awadhi variant of Lucknow and is served with
chunky, golden potatoes and often a piece of hard-boiled egg. You can
order it to go here, too. $ *Average main: Rs. 500* ⊠ *Marina Garden
Court, 7 Point Crossing, Park Circus Rd.* ☎ *28/448–556, 32/918–297*
⊕ *www.arsalanrestaurant.in* $ *Average main: Rs. 500* ⊠ *119A Muzaf-
far Ahmed St., Ripon St.* ☎ *33/2227–7493 to 7494* $ *Average main: Rs.
500* ⊠ *28 Circus Ave., 033-2* ☎ *33/2281–3921 through 3928.*

$ ╳ **Bohemian.** In a residential neighborhood to the south, this tiny, thread-
MODERN INDIAN   bare restaurant is making all the right noises with its global-Bengali
Fodor's Choice   cuisine. The menu, created by Chef Joy Bannerjee, takes the best and
★   most unique ingredients and flavors of Bengali cuisine, and gives them
a contemporary twist. So, crab cakes come with mustard sauce and are
baked with local greens in small clay saucers, river prawns are simmered
in a coconut gravy with grapes, and desserts are delicately flavored with
gondhoraj, a close cousin of the Kaffir lime used in Thai dishes. The
restaurant is packed on most days, so book ahead. $ *Average main:
Rs. 400* ⊠ *32/4 Old Ballygunge 1st La., Ballygunge* ☎ *33/4001–9005*
⌲ *Reservations essential.*

$$$$ ╳ **Chinoiserie.** Popular with locals and visitors, this place serves such
CHINESE   delicacies as Peking duck, crispy spinach, and a selection of corn dishes.
Fodor's Choice   The food is delectable, though the menu holds few surprises. Try the
★   kung pao pork ribs, steamed scallop morsel, or the crispy lamb. The ele-
gant interiors, with old mirrors and paintings, and the attentive service
make it a pleasant experience. $ *Average main: Rs. 1500* ⊠ *Taj Bengal,
34B Belvedere Rd., Alipore* ☎ *33/2223–3939* ⌲ *Reservations essential.*

$$ ╳ **Mainland China.** Kolkata's popular Chinese restaurant, now one in
CHINESE   a national chain, is known for efficient service and spacious interi-
ors with minimalist but comfortable furniture. The Szechuan menu is
extensive. Try their fish and prawn dishes. They also serve an elaborate
and reasonably priced buffet. $ *Average main: Rs. 700* ⊠ *Uniworth
House, 3A Gurusaday Rd.* ☎ *33/2283–7964* $ *Average main: Rs. 700*
⊠ *South City Mall, Prince Anwar Shah Rd.* ☎ *8820408933* $ *Average
main: Rs. 700* ⊠ *3rd fl., Silver Arcade, EM Bypass, Bypass and beyond*
☎ *8820362457.*

$ × **Momo Plaza.** Momos, dumplings with chicken or meat filling that are
ASIAN served with a spicy red chutney and a thin soup, were introduced to the
city by the large Tibetan community that settled here. Thanks partly to
the low prices, the no-frills eateries and street stalls that serve the dish
are popular with students and young officegoers. While legendary eateries such as Momo Plaza and Humro Momo (Sambhunath Pandit Street),
continue to do brisk business, the Blue Poppy (*4/1, Middleton Street,
Elgin*) and Ecstasea (*Lake Road*) have acquired loyal followings as well.
Wow!Momo, with 25 outlets across the city, serve innovative momos,
including some with chocolate or seafood fillings. The latter also serves
a momo burger if you are adventurous enough to try it. $ *Average
main: Rs. 50* ⊠ *2A Suburban Hospital Rd.* ⊟ *No credit cards.*

$ × **Mrs Magpie.** This pretty café is always buzzing with patrons lined
EUROPEAN up for pretty-as-a-picture cupcakes, tiered cakes, quiches, and pies,
FAMILY all served with some excellent coffee and a flourish. Service is prompt
Fodor'sChoice and attentive, and the prices are reasonable. Try the apple brandy,
★ or the sweet and salty chocolate mini cupcakes. There's also a hearty
breakfast, and a high tea, which comes with scones, finger sandwiches,
and fine Darjeeling for Rs. 450. The music is mostly European, with
just the right decibels to encourage relaxed conversation. $ *Average
main: Rs. 200* ⊠ *570, Lake Terrace Rd., Hindustan Park, Gariahat*
☎ *86977–31491.*

$$ × **Oh! Calcutta.** Started in 2002, this is one of the most successful chains
INDIAN for traditional Bengali cuisine in upscale settings. All-time favorites
Fodor'sChoice here include river prawns, cooked in coconut milk and served in ten-
★ der coconut shells; their fish dishes in mustard sauce are also clas-
sic. During festivals they tweak their menu to include interesting and
unusual dishes. $ *Average main: Rs. 500* ⊠ *Forum Mall, 10/3 Elgin
Rd.* ☎ *33/2283–7161* ⊕ *www.speciality.co.in/oh_calcutta* ◬ *Reserva-
tions essential.*

WHERE TO STAY

NORTH KOLKATA

$$ ▦ **ITC Hotel The Sonar.** Although this is essentially a business hotel, the
HOTEL Sonar feels like a resort, with a picturesque pond of lotuses that are
set in lush landscaped gardens, and architecture inspired by that of
the Pala dynasty, which once ruled Bengal. **Pros:** guests-only spa has
soothing water views; exclusive floor for female travelers; proximity
to airport. **Cons:** restaurants are pricey (though good); close to busy
intersection with chaotic traffic. $ *Rooms from: Rs. 8000* ⊠ *1 Haldane
Ave., Bypass and beyond* ☎ *33/2345–4545* ⊕ *www.itcwelcomgroup.in*
⇥ *231 rooms, 8 suites* �❑ *No meals.*

$$ ▦ **Swissôtel.** A modern hotel catering to the white-collar professionals
HOTEL and other business travelers in the new satellite town of Rajarhat, this
property is more about efficiency than style. **Pros:** close to the airport;
next to a mall and multiplex; efficient. **Cons:** cut off from the rest of
the city. $ *Rooms from: Rs. 8500* ⊠ *Plot-11/5, Action Area 2 D, City*

BEST BETS FOR KOLKATA LODGING

Fodor's Choice ★	Oberoi Grand, p. 520	BEST FOR KIDS
Taj Bengal, p. 521	$$$	Hotel Hindustan International, p. 521
By Price	Taj Bengal, p. 521	
	By Experience	BEST HOTEL BAR
$		Park Hotel, p. 521
Fairlawn, p. 520	BEST FOR BUSINESS	BEST LOCAL FLAVOR
$$	Kenilworth, p. 520	Fairlawn, p. 520
ITC Hotel The Sonar, p. 519	The Lalit Great Eastern Hotel, p. 520	Oberoi Grand, p. 520
The Lalit Great Eastern Hotel, p. 520	Swissôtel, p. 519	BEST LOCATION
		Oberoi Grand, p. 520

Center, New Town, Rajarhat ☎ 033/6626–6626 ⊕ www.swissotel.com/hotels/kolkata ⬎ 147 rooms ⦿ No meals.

CENTRAL KOLKATA

$ **Fairlawn.** If you want a taste of life in the Raj, stay in this Kolkata
HOTEL landmark that dates from 1801 and is in a neighborhood now popular with backpackers and volunteers. **Pros:** atmosphere of yesterday. **Cons:** neighborhood is a little seedy. $ *Rooms from: Rs. 2000* ⊠ *13A Sudder St.* ☎ *33/2252–1510* ⊕ *www.fairlawnhotel.com* ⬎ *20 rooms* ⦿ *No meals.*

$$ **Kenilworth.** Popular with repeat visitors to Kolkata, this hotel has
HOTEL two attractive wings and pretty gardens. **Pros:** suites are a good value; digital safes in rooms. **Cons:** service can be a little indifferent. $ *Rooms from: Rs. 6000* ⊠ *1–2 Little Russell St.* ☎ *33/2282–3939* ⊕ *www.kenilworthhotels.com* ⬎ *98 rooms, 7 suites* ⦿ *Breakfast.*

$$ **The Lalit Great Eastern Hotel.** In the heart of Kolkata's business district,
HOTEL this 19th-century heritage property had fallen into disrepair before an Indian company turned it into a classy business hotel in 2014. **Pros:** beautifully restored heritage property. **Cons:** in the heart of a chaotic commercial district, which can be unnerving during office hours. $ *Rooms from: Rs. 7000* ⊠ *1–3 Old Court House St.* ☎ *4444–7777* ⊕ *www.thelalit.com* ⬎ *244 rooms* ⦿ *No meals.*

$$ **Oberoi Grand.** One of most elegant hotels in the country, this Vic-
HOTEL torian landmark in the center of town is rich in its marble and dark-wood interiors. **Pros:** no-tipping policy; old-world charm in the bar decorated with artifacts from the British Raj. **Cons:** faces a noisy street in the city's busiest shopping and commercial district. $ *Rooms from: Rs. 9000* ⊠ *15 J. L. Nehru Rd.* ☎ *33/2249–2323* ⊕ *www.oberoihotels.com* ⬎ *204 rooms, 9 suites* ⦿ *No meals.*

$$ 🏨 **Park Hotel.** The location, good service, and trippy interiors have made
HOTEL this into one of the busiest hotels in Kolkata. **Pros:** great location; some
of the hippest bars in town. **Cons:** the area directly near the hotel's
entrance gets a little seedy late at night. ⑤ *Rooms from: Rs. 9000* ⊠ *17
Park St.* ☎ *33/2249–9000* ⊕ *www.theparkhotels.com* ⥅ *132 rooms,
17 suites* ⦾ *No meals.*

SOUTH KOLKATA

$$ 🏨 **Hotel Hindustan International.** You won't feel cramped inside this
HOTEL family-run hotel. **Pros:** good value for money. **Cons:** not as luxurious
as most hotels in its class. ⑤ *Rooms from: Rs. 6000* ⊠ *235–1 A. J. C.
Bose Rd.* ☎ *33/4001–8000* ⊕ *www.hhihotels.com* ⥅ *176 rooms, 8
suites* ⦾ *Breakfast.*

$$$ 🏨 **Taj Bengal.** A fusion of traditional and contemporary Indian aesthet-
HOTEL ics, this hotel on the edge of the city center comes with spectacular views
Fodor'sChoice of the Maidan and the Victoria Memorial. **Pros:** gorgeous lobby with
★ a well-stocked tea lounge; very good location. **Cons:** expensive; like
many hotels in this class, the lobby is more impressive than the rooms;
service can be inconsistent; coffee-shop's food sometimes just so-so.
⑤ *Rooms from: Rs. 10000* ⊠ *34B Belvedere Rd., Alipore* ☎ *33/6612–
3939* ⊕ *www.tajhotels.com* ⥅ *216 rooms, 29 suites* ⦾ *No meals.*

NIGHTLIFE AND PERFORMING ARTS

NIGHTLIFE

After a spell of gloom, the nightlife scene has been looking up, largely
due to the city's deathless love for music, theater, and food. Venues in
Park Street, Ballygunge, and even the satellite city of Salt Lake host local
bands with a loyal following. They perform until midnight, which is
late by the city's (and most of India's) standards.

During Durga Puja, the city remains up all night. Lounges, *sheesha*
(hookah) bars, and discos all draw well-heeled young entrepreneurs,
fashion designers, models, and professionals. Cabs run late into the
night and are usually considered safe. Be cautious while traveling on
your own, however, especially late at night.

BARS AND LOUNGES

Park Street boasts of the most popular bards and lounges, most of
them situated in hotels, except the local favorite Olympia, aka Oly Pub
(unbelievably cheap drinks and service that follows a sort of secret code;
waiters may refuse to serve you if you don't play by their rules). How-
ever, there are several new places all around town where you can have
a drink too many, provided you have something to munch on as well.

Big Ben. Local professionals congregate in this pub, which has skilled
bartenders. Coming from the speakers is a mix of rock, pop, and Bol-
lywood music. Midweek theme nights and special offers on sangria
pitchers help pack 'em in. ⊠ *Kenilworth Hotel, 1–2 Little Russell St.,
Central Kolkata* ☎ *33/2282–3939.*

9

Plush. The Astor Hotel may have fallen out of favor with travelers due to the glitzier and younger competition, but its lounge remains a top draw with party animals. The spacious interior—a rarity in city nightspots—draws a suitably well-heeled crowd that also comes for the food. The spicy glazed prawns, the clay-oven barbecued chicken, and the Caribbean chicken skewers all come recommended. The drinks are less amazing. ⊠ *The Astor Hotel, 15, Shakespeare Sarani, Theatre Rd., Central Kolkata* ☎ *9830/122–203* ⊕ *www.astorkolkata.com.*

Fodor's Choice **Someplace Else.** Kolkata's favorite pub is compact and always packed—it
★ hosts nine hours of live music every day. Besides talented and popular local bands playing rock, blues, alternative, and jazz, the venue hosts top international acts frequently. It's a great place to bond with musicians and music lovers—the city is teeming with both. ⊠ *The Park Hotel, 17 Park St., Central Kolkata* ☎ *33/249–7336.*

NIGHTCLUBS

Kolkata's clubs are technically open only to members and hotel guests, but you can get in for either a cover charge or a smile, depending on the doorman. All clubs retain good DJs for a mixture of Indian pop and Western dance music.

Aafra. A popular hangout for young professionals and those on a date, this *sheesha* (hookah) lounge also serves a Sunday brunch and has a menu of Japanese, Mediterranean and continental cuisine. ⊠ *7th fl., Block G, City Centre Mall, Salt Lake, Bypass and beyond* ☎ *33/88205–85182.*

Tantra. Despite newer, younger venues around town, Tantra still draws the hottest crowd to its dance floor. Favored by those in their 20s, Tantra is where film stars and models let their hair down. ⊠ *The Park Hotel, 17 Park St., Central Kolkata* ☎ *33/2249–7336.*

PERFORMING ARTS

Kolkata takes as much pride and interest in its vibrant, artistic present as it does its glorious past. Concerts, exhibitions, plays, book fairs, and literary and cultural festivals are held throughout the year. To find out what is happening, check ⊕ *bookmyshow.com,* ⊕ *timescity.com,* ⊕ *zomato.com,* ⊕ *burrp.com,* ⊕ *10times.com,* ⊕ *explocity.com,* and similar websites.

ART GALLERIES

Akar Prakar Art Gallery. At one of the newer galleries in the city, you can view works of both young and legendary artists. Exhibits are innovatively curated, and their display is top-notch. ⊠ *P 238 Hindusthan Park, Gariahat, Central Kolkata* ☎ *33/2464–3843* ⊕ *www.akarprakar.com.*

CIMA. The Centre for International Modern Art displays works by Indian and international artists. ⊠ *Sunny Towers, 43 Ashutosh Choudhury Ave., South Kolkata* ☎ *33/2485–8717* ⊕ *www.cimaartindia.com.*

Fodor's Choice **Gallery Experimenter.** This buzzy venue is where you will find works
★ of award-winning contemporary artists from around the world. Bani Abidi, Nadia Kaabi-Linke, and Ayesha Sultana have all shown here. Experimental films and video art are also shown from time to time.

✉ *2/1 Hindusthan Rd., Dover Terrace, South Kolkata* ☎ *033/400–2289* ⊕ *www.experimenter.in.*

FILM

The latest Bollywood, Hollywood, and Bengali films are shown at all the multiplexes in town, which are often inside malls. Check ⊕ *bookmyshow.com* for tickets and showtimes; local English-language newspapers all carry listings, too.

Nandan. Nandan, the state-run theater in the Rabindra Sadan complex, shows art-house and independent films. ✉ *A. J. C. Bose Rd. and Cathedral Rd. junction, Central Kolkata* ☎ *33/2223–9917.*

VENUES

Many auditoriums host regular performances of music, dance, and theater—the most Bengali of the performing arts.

Academy of Fine Arts. This center of art and creative discourse was established in 1933 by Lady Ranu Mookerji, a close associate of Tagore who was known for her beauty and her patronage of the arts and beauty. In addition to the permanent collection of paintings and Tagore manuscripts, the Academy hosts live acts and theater festivals throughout the year. It's a popular meeting ground for the city's intellectuals, especially in winter. ✉ *2 Cathedral Rd., Central Kolkata, Kolkata, West Bengal* ☎ *33/2223–4302.*

Birla Academy of Art and Culture. The nondescript venue has some art on display, but the main draw is the auditorium, where some very talented musicians and dancers perform. Winters are especially favored for classical concerts. ✉ *108–109 Southern Ave., South Kolkata* ☎ *33/2466–6802* ⊕ *www.birlaart.com.*

Kalamandir. Theatrical and musical events are often staged here. ✉ *48 Shakespeare Sarani, Central Kolkata* ☎ *33/2247–9086.*

Rabindra Sadan. A popular venue for music, dance, and theater. ✉ *Cathedral Rd., Central Kolkata* ☎ *33/2248–9917.*

SPORTS AND THE OUTDOORS

Kolkata still puts class first when it comes to sports, with the result that you need to be a member's guest to enter the golf and racing clubs. But if you'd like to just see a little cricket, head to the Maidan: on nice days it can sometimes seem like one big cricket pitch.

Calcutta Cricket and Football Club. Whether you want to watch or play, get cricket information from the Calcutta Cricket and Football Club. Rugby, tennis, and swimming are also done here. ✉ *19–1 Gurusaday Rd., South Kolkata* ☎ *33/2461–5060.*

Calcutta Polo Club. Established in 1862, Calcutta Polo Club is one of the oldest running polo clubs still in operation. Matches are played against the picturesque backdrop of the Victoria Memorial. ✉ *31 J. L. Nehru Rd., Central Kolkata* ☎ *33/2282–2311* ⊕ *www.calcuttapolo.com.*

SHOPPING

Shopping in Kolkata bazaars is an adventure, and a test of your ability to shake off touts. In general, most shops are open six days a week and closed Sunday. Hours tend to be 10:30–8.

Kolkata has never been the place for trendy shopping, so you may want to concentrate on getting hand-loomed cloth, handicrafts, and artistic jute and metal gifts, most of which will cost you next to nothing. Things to look out for include long-necked terra-cotta Bankura horses, dokra metalwork, and Bengal saris, made in crisp cottons and luscious silks. And many galleries sell very affordable art.

NORTH KOLKATA

JEWELRY AND ACCESSORIES

Bowbazar. Some of the country's most skilled goldsmiths and jewelry designers hail from Kolkata. And in Bowbazar, east of Chitpur Road, is where you will find them. The cheek-by-jowl shops that line the busy street sell good-quality traditional gold and silver jewelry, but there are also more trendy and chic designs in platinum, with diamonds and other precious and semiprecious stones. Prices are reasonable, because labor charges are less here than in other Indian cities. Each shop has an astrologer on hand to help you find the most auspicious stone based on your sign and birthdate. ⊠ *Near College St., parallel to Chittaranjan Ave. and bounded by Mahatma Gandhi Rd. and Vivekananda Rd., Calcutta Medical College, and Presidency College* ⊗ *Closed Sun.*

CENTRAL KOLKATA

AUCTIONS

Russell Exchange. On Sunday auctions take place along Russell Street. A trip to the oldest auction house, the Russell Exchange, run by brothers Anwar and Arshad, or any of its neighbors is invariably entertaining. Goods auctioned range from antiques and period furniture to crockery and cutlery. On Thursday, there's a sale of vintage clothes. ⊠ *12C Russell St.* ☎ *33/2229–8974.*

BAZAARS AND SHOPPING MALLS

New Market. The century-old New Market, officially Sir Stuart Hogg Market, houses about 2,500 stores under one roof, selling cotton saris, Bankura clay horses, brassware, leather bags from Shantiniketan, silk from Murshidabad, *khadi* (handmade cotton) cloth, clothes for kids, wigs, poultry, cheeses, nuts, and other foods. The neighborhood is also home to several air-conditioned malls, department stores, restaurants and stand-alone shops, while the sidewalks are taken over by street-food vendors and knickknack stalls. It's definitely the busiest shopping district in the region. ⊠ *19 Lindsay St., off J. L. Nehru Rd., behind Oberoi Grand* ⊗ *Weekdays 10:30–7, Sat. 10:30–2*

BOOKSTORES

Oxford Bookstore-Gallery. The café overlooking the chic street below serves teas and snacks at this store, one of the city's favorite spaces for books and book parties. There's a wide range of titles in English, as well as some in Indian languages and in French. Gifts and a DVD section round out the offerings. ⊠ *17 Park St.* ☎ *33/2229–7662.*

CRAFTS

Central Cottage Industries. For curios in a hurry and at fixed prices, head to Central Cottage Industries. It may seem a tad musty and salespeople may seem disinterested, but you may just find a good bargain. ⊠ *7 J. L. Nehru Rd.* ☎ *33/2228–4139.*

Konark Collectables. Quaint little Konark Collectables carries handicrafts, curios, antiques, period furniture, and gift items. ⊠ *Humayun Court, 20 Lindsay St.* ☎ *33/2249–7273* ⊕ *www.konarkcollectables.com.*

SOUTH KOLKATA

BAZAARS AND SHOPPING MALLS

Gariahat. South Kolkata's most popular and very congested shopping district is home to chic boutiques and bustling shops selling saris in all kinds of styles and prices. The pavements are taken over by hawkers selling clothes, toys, accessories, and handcrafted jewelry—it can be challenging to negotiate the crowd during peak hours. Intense bargaining is de rigueur on the street, but the air-conditioned shops offer respite from the heat as well the haggling. The lanes away from Gariahat Road itself—Hindusthan Park Road, Dover Lane, Southern Avenue—are quieter and more upscale. Here, among the elegant homes of Kolkata's upper classes are where you will find art galleries, quirky and traditional Bengali restaurants, specialty shops, boutiques, and quaint cafés that are local favorites. Visit By Loom for handloomed saris, jewelry, and a cozy café. Bunkari sells saris, stoles, and scarves; Weaver's Studio has handloomed textiles. For a bite of Kolkata's famous kati rolls, try Bedouwin or Badshah, where crisp parathas are wrapped around succulent pieces of meat and finely chopped onions and served piping hot. For traditional Bengali meals, try 6 Ballygunge Place, Sholo Ana, Tero Parbon, or Bhojohori Manna. Le Petit De La Maison, The Bistro, Wise Owl, and French Loaf are some of the European-style eateries in the area. If the shopping and the crowds get to you, head to the Ramakrishna Mission, in Gol Park, for some quiet reflection. ⊠ *Gariahat Rd. connects Ballygunge Phari with Prince Anwar Shah Rd. and Raja SC Mullick Rd. near Jadavpur police station on southern part of Kolkata.*

Quest. Kolkata's newfound love affair with malls is reflected in this massive and high-end example of the genre, home to Paul Smith, Emporio Armani, Canali, Fendi, Gucci, Michael Kors—some 130 brands in all. Restaurants include SeraFina and Irish House. ⊠ *33 Syed Amir Ali Ave..*

South City Mall. By some measures this is the largest mall in the region—there's parking for 1,800 vehicles. A huge number of major brands are available on its five floors, and there's also a sprawling food court and a multiplex. ⊠ *375 Prince Anwar Shah Rd.* ⊕ *southcitymall.in.*

9

BOOKSTORES

Seagull. Specializing in art, social sciences, theater, and politics, this publishing imprint has a cozy store, which manages to devote space to art and literary discussions as well as an expansive and eclectic stock of books. ⊠ *31A SP Mukherjee Rd.* ☎ *33/2476–5865* ⊕ *www.seagullindia. com.*

CLOTHING AND TEXTILES

Dakshinapan. For those who want to browse through handicrafts and hand-loomed cloth and clothing from around the country, this no-fuss, no-frills mall is a good destination. Discovering gems in this sea of government shop may leave you parched, though. Head for Dolly's Tea Shop, on the ground floor, for refreshing hot and cool blends of the finest teas, handpicked by the owner, Dolly Roy, the world's first female tea auctioneer and India's first female tea-taster. ⊠ *Near Dhakuria Bridge.*

Fodor's Choice ★ **Sabyasachi.** Sabyasachi Mukherji, one of India's most well-known fashion designers, is from Kolkata; a trip to his flagship store is a crash course in Indian textiles and craftsmanship. Known for his saris and wedding clothes, Sabya (as he's popularly known) dresses many of India's top film stars and celebrities. ⊠ *P 545 Lake Terrace Rd., near Vivekananda Park* ☎ *98300–05953* ⊕ *www.sabyasachi.com.*

UNDERSTANDING INDIA

Books and Movies

BOOKS AND MOVIES

Books
Nonfiction

The best **general surveys** of Indian history are John Keay's recently updated *India: A History* and Stanley Wolpert's *New History of India* (6th ed.), with Keay focusing more on antiquity. Three sparkling **introductions to the modern nation** are *India: From Midnight to the Millennium*, by Shashi Tharoor; *India Unbound: From Independence to the Global Information Age*, by Gurcharan Das; and *The Idea of India*, by Sunil Khilnani.

Mark Tully's books, including *No Full Stops in India* and *India in Slow Motion* (with Gillian Wright), **combine travel with social analysis**. William Dalrymple's *The Age of Kali* is a collection of incisive essays on aspects of the modern subcontinent, as are Gita Mehta's *Snakes and Ladders* and Octavio Paz's *In Light of India*, by the Nobel Laureate and former Mexican ambassador. Elisabeth Bumiller's *May You Be the Mother of a Hundred Sons* is an American reporter's take on the varied lives of Indian women. Santosh Desai's *Mother Pious Lady* deals with some of the numerous facets of modern Indian life through a series of witty yet poignant vignettes. **Urban subculture** is explored narrowly but amusingly in Palash Krishna Mehrotra's *The Butterfly Generation*. *Freedom at Midnight*, by Larry Collins and Dominique Lapierre, is a spellbinding account of India's break from Britain; *City of Joy*, by the same authors, is a powerful portrait of Calcutta. Nirad Chaudhuri's classic *Autobiography of an Unknown Indian* recounts the Bengali author's youth in **colonial India**, with insightful descriptions of Indian customs, castes, and relations with the British. James Cameron's *An Indian Summer* is a glib but loving memoir by a British journalist who lived in India during and after the Raj. Sudha Koul's *The Tiger Ladies* recalls life in beautiful Kashmir before it became a war zone in the late 1980s. While not his best writing, *India: A Million Mutinies Now* is the most optimistic of Nobel Laureate V.S. Naipaul's three books on India.

The **classic works on early India** are A.L. Basham's *The Wonder That Was India* and Romila Thapar's *History of India*, Volume I. India's first prime minister, Jawaharlal Nehru, was a peerless writer and left some inspiring works including his autobiography and *The Discovery of India*, a unique rendition of the country's history. William Dalrymple's *White Mughals* illuminates the bicultural lives of British traders in Hyderabad during the 18th century. Among the great **Sanskrit texts**, the best translations of the *Bhagavad-Gita* are Barbara Stoler Miller's and Eknath Easwaran's; Easwaran has also translated the sacred *Upanishads*. The epics known as the *Mahabharata* and *Ramayana* are available in countless translations, the most popular of which are Krishna Dharma's and Eknath Easwaran's. **Classical Hindu myths** are retold in prose form in *Gods, Demons, and Others*, by the master writer R. K. Narayan, and more recently in *Ka*, by Roberto Calasso. Diana Eck's *Banaras: City of Light* is an engaging profile of the holy city.

Stuart Cary Welch's *India: Art and Culture, 1300–1900* is a lavishly illustrated catalog by a great connoisseur, while Vidya Dehejia's *Indian Art* is a good textual survey. *Myths and Symbols in Indian Art and Civilization*, by Heinrich Zimmer (edited by Joseph Campbell) is helpful to the art or mythology buff. The famously erotic *Kama Sutra* has been freshly translated by A.N.D. Haksar. The colorful minibook *India and the Mughal Dynasty*, by Valérie Berinstain, makes a great pocket companion in much of North India, and William Dalrymple's *City of Djinns* brings Mughal Delhi to life. Royina Grewal's *In Rajasthan* is an excellent **travelogue** by an Indian. For ravishing **photographs**, see *A Day in the Life of India*, people going about their business;

Living Faith, Dinesh Khanna's renditions of sacred spaces and scenes; *India Modern,* a contemporary treatment of **traditional buildings and crafts;** and any of several collections by Raghubir Singh, Raghu Rai, and Henri Cartier-Bresson.

Fiction

Indian novelists took the literary world by storm in the 1980s and '90s, and the flood has not abated. **Vikram Seth's** mesmerizing *A Suitable Boy* portrays middle-class life in the 1950s through a timeless story of young love. **Rohinton Mistry's** novels center on the Parsi community of Bombay; his masterpiece, *A Fine Balance,* is an extraordinary study of the human condition as experienced by a motley group in the 1970s, and *Family Matters* and *Such a Long Journey* weave poignant tales of family ties and personal misfortune. Another fine Bombay novel, **Manil Suri's** *The Death of Vishnu,* features an old homeless man whose neighbors squabble over the best way to deal with him. *Love and Longing in Bombay,* by **Vikram Chandra,** is a collection of short stories with a single narrator. **Aravind Adiga's** Booker Prize-winning *The White Tiger* addresses social divisions in modern India with a rags-to-riches tale from the perspective of a hired chauffeur from a small town who wants to make it big in the city.

Midnight's Children, by **Salman Rushdie,** is the epic tale of a boy who was born the moment India gained independence. Rushdie's *The Moor's Last Sigh,* narrated by a young man of mixed heritage, paints incomparably sensual portraits of Bombay and Cochin. **Arundhati Roy's** *The God of Small Things,* set in 1960s Kerala, tells a disturbing story of brother-and-sister twins raised by a divorced mother. Roy has since become a political activist in New Delhi. **David Davidar's** *The House of Blue Mangoes* is a South Indian family saga.

Amit Chaudhuri's short novel *A Strange and Sublime Address* (published in the United States with Chaudhuri's *Freedom Song*) is a gorgeous story of a 10-year-old boy's stay with relatives in Calcutta. **Anita Desai's** *Fasting, Feasting* concerns an Indian family whose son goes off to college in the United States. **Khushwant Singh's** *Delhi* is a bawdy but ultimately moving romp through Delhi's tumultuous history. *The Impressionist,* a picaresque novel by **Hari Kunzru,** shows the adventures of a half-English, half-Indian boy in both countries in the early 20th century. **Upamanyu Chatterjee's** *English, August* is a funny account of a rookie in the Indian Civil Service. *The Lowland* by **Jhumpa Lahiri** is the story of two brothers from Kolkata, one of whom moves to the U.S. while the other joins India's Maoist Naxalite movement.

Bengali poet and Nobel Laureate **Rabindranath Tagore** wrote some enduring novels including *Gora* and *Home and the World*; to read his poetry in translation, look for *Gitanjali.* **Rudyard Kipling's** *Kim* is still one of the most intimate works of Western fiction on India; in **E. M. Forster's** *A Passage to India* the conflict between Indians and their British rulers is played out in the story of a man accused of rape. **Ahmed Ali's** 1940 novel *Twilight in Delhi* gives a poignant account of 19th-century urban Muslim society. The 19 short stories that make up **R.K. Narayan's** *Malgudi Days* are some of the most celebrated tales in India, and were turned into a popular TV series in the 1980s.

Not all good Indian writing has been published in the West. In India you'll find plenty of English-language fiction and nonfiction on the issues of the day. **Janice Pariat's** *Boats on Land* is a collection of short stories that provide a glimpse into India's little talked-about Northeastern states. Reading fiction from other languages is another way to penetrate India's regional cultures; top writers available in translation include **Sunil Gangopadhyay** (Bengali), **Nirmal Verma** (Hindi), **Intizar**

Husain and **Ismat Chugtai** (Urdu), **U. R. Ananthamurty** (Kannada), **Vaasanthi** and **Ambai** (Tamil), and **Paul Zacharia** (Malayalam).

Films

Indian films can be roughly divided into Bollywood fare—**musical romances** from Bombay's prolific industry—and **independent art films**. A prime example of classic costume melodrama is *Aan* (1952), directed by Mehboob, a story of royalty tamed by peasants. The late Satyajit Ray adapted and directed the internationally known *Pather Panchali* (1955), *Aparajito* (1956), and *The World of Apu* (1959), a breathtaking trilogy depicting poverty and tragedy in the life of a Bengali boy. *Salaam Bombay* (1988), directed by Mira Nair, is a heartbreaking fictionalized exposé of Bombay's homeless and slum children. Roland Joffe's *City of Joy* (1992), starring Patrick Swayze, is based on Dominique Lapierre's book about Calcutta. Deepa Mehta's best-known films are *Fire* (1996), in which two beautiful but neglected sisters-in-law turn to each other for love, and *Earth* (1999), an adaptation of Bapsi Sidhwa's novel on the partition of India and Pakistan, *Cracking India*. Another Mira Nair film, *Monsoon Wedding* (2001), takes on several contemporary issues in the context of a high-class Punjabi wedding. Although not set in India, Gurinder Chadha's *Bend It Like Beckham* (2002) is worth watching for its funny, life-affirming portrait of a soccer-loving Punjabi girl in London. Aparna Sen's *Mr. and Mrs. Iyer* (2002) won accolades for its sensitive treatment of interfaith relations.

Bollywood's exuberant musicals are now widely available on DVD. Blockbusters include *Dilwale Dulhania Le Jayenge* (1995), a love story set in London and Switzerland and one of the most successful Bollywood films of the modern era, *Kal Ho Naa Ho* (2003), which places a fetching Bollywood cast in photogenic New York; *Dil Chahta Hai* (2001),

a romantic comedy set in Bombay; and *Lagaan* (2001), featuring a 19th-century cricket match with the British. Although not a huge success in India, *Dil Se* (1998) went on to become one of the most popular Bollywood films in the United States and United Kingdom; the film's song *Chaiyya Chaiyya* went on to become one of the most popular Bollywood tunes of all time.

Films set in India by Western directors are numerous. The excellent *Shakespeare Wallah* (1965), written by Ruth Prawer Jhabvala and James Ivory and directed by Ivory, fictionalizes the experience of the Kendal family's traveling theater troupe. Ivory's *Heat and Dust* (1982), an adaptation of Jhabvala's novel, re-creates the past through a young woman's discovery of a series of her grandmother's letters. *Phantom India* (1969), directed by Louis Malle, is an epic documentary of Indian life. Richard Attenborough's *Gandhi* (1982) traces the adult life of the leader of India's independence movement. *A Passage to India* (1984), based on E. M. Forster's novel, was directed by David Lean. *The Jewel in the Crown* (1984), an epic TV series based on part of Paul Scott's *Raj Quartet*, features a romance between a British woman and an Indian man in the waning years of British rule. The multiple Oscar-winning *Slumdog Millionaire* (2008), directed by Danny Boyle, is an adaptation of Vikas Swarup's novel, *Q & A*, which explores the life of a Mumbai youth and his success on a TV quiz show. Most recently, *The Best Exotic Marigold Hotel* (2012) tells the story of a few British retirees who move to a retirement hotel in India.

TRAVEL SMART
INDIA

GETTING HERE AND AROUND

The major international tourist hubs are Delhi, in the north, and Mumbai, 1,407 km (874 miles) to the south. All the major cities are connected by a national highway system, air service, and trains.

Road travel is definitely an easy way to take in local color in a leisurely way. Unfortunately, most roads still have just two lanes and are in poor condition, and progress can be painstaking. However, that's changing as India continues to work on its modernization project, which has already produced the "Golden Quadrilateral," a massive four-lane highway network, similar to those in America, that connects Delhi, Kolkata, Chennai, and Mumbai.

An onslaught of domestic airlines competing for business has made air travel throughout the subcontinent relatively hassle-free and convenient. It's the best option for those who are on a tight schedule, although flight delays—due to congestion and weather (usually fog or monsoon rains)—are common. Always be prepared for flights to be delayed or even canceled.

The Indian train system is an intricate network shuttling millions of people across the country every day. It's very reliable, if run-down, and practically every point of interest in the nonmountainous areas of India has a train station nearby. Train travel is also likely to be the cheapest option for going long distances, making it perfect for travelers on a budget and those who want to travel the way many Indians do.

Common terms for the word "road" in local languages (India has many) include *marg, galli, rasta, salai, peth,* and *sarani.* Many streets and roads have an older British name and a newer, post-Independence name. Residents often refer to roads by their old names or use abbreviated versions of cumbersome names. Mumbai and its pre-Independence name, Bombay,

FINDING YOUR WAY

Indian addresses are often haphazard. Building numbers may appear in postal addresses, but they don't always appear prominently on the buildings themselves. Some neighborhoods use lettered block systems—each block has a corresponding letter and each house a number (i.e., B-139 is house number 139 in B block). In some towns and some residential areas, houses are not numbered sequentially—number 45/234 could be next to 32/342. This makes neighborhood names and landmarks, often included in urban addresses, very important. Addresses in small villages may include the name of the district or nearest large town or city. Postal codes play a big part in ensuring that letters reach their destinations.

are used interchangeably. The city's Netaji Subhash Chandra Marg is still called by its old, easy-to-remember name of Marine Drive, and Jay Prakash Road is referred to as J.P. Road. And many cities have a main drag that's now called M.G. (for Mahatma Gandhi) Road. In Delhi, however, M.G. Road stands for Mehrauli-Gurgaon Road.

▮ AIR TRAVEL

Flying to and within India has become easier in recent years with new international routes and the emergence of several new low-cost Indian domestic airlines. Flying from Delhi to Mumbai, for example, is just about as easy as flying between two major cities in America. Domestic tickets can generally be purchased through traditional travel agents, airline websites, travel websites, and even at Indian airports if you've decided to make a last-minute trip.

Security in Indian airports, however, often requires considerable time. You'll need to attach blank luggage tags (provided at the check-in counter) to all of your hand luggage (including purses). When you clear screening, these tags will be rubber stamped and reverified by a police officer or airline staff member at the time of boarding. Passengers are routinely patted down at security, irrespective of whether the metal detector goes off. Women are frisked in a separate dressing-room-like box by female security guards, whereas men are checked out in the open. Because of these time-consuming procedures, it's a good idea to check in at least two hours before a flight within India.

Flight time from New York is 14 hours to Delhi, 15 hours to Mumbai. Flight time from Chicago to Delhi is 14.5 hours.

Airline Security Issues Transportation Security Administration. Answers for almost every question that might come up are available here. ⊕ *www.tsa.gov.*

AIRPORTS

India's two major international gateways are Indira Gandhi International Airport (DEL) in New Delhi and Chhatrapati Shivaji International Airport (BOM) in Mumbai. Delhi is best for all the major tourist spots in the north, including Rajasthan. Mumbai is more convenient for Goa and Kerala. Both airports are reasonably close to the city centers and to the train stations if that's your next mode of travel.

The airports in Delhi and Mumbai, which also accommodate domestic flights, are as comfortable as those in the United States or Europe, but with fewer shopping and dining options. In 2010 a new, ultramodern international terminal, T3, opened at the Delhi airport, which has vastly improved the experience for everyone passing through.

Airport Information Chhatrapati Shivaji International Airport (Mumbai) ☏ *22/6685–1010* ⊕ *www.csia.in.* **Indira Gandhi International Airport (Delhi)** ☏ *124/337–6000* ⊕ *www.newdelhiairport.in.*

GROUND TRANSPORTATION

The best way to get to and from India's major international airports is by taxi or auto-rickshaw (the latter if you're feeling adventurous and don't have that much luggage). Your hotel can also arrange for a private pickup at the airport, in which case the driver will be holding a sign with your name at the exit point. Hotel pickups are considerably more expensive than any other option and vary greatly in price (expect a charge of at least Rs. 1,000 in big cities).

If you are on a budget, you can also arrange a basic, usually non-air-conditioned taxi at the prepaid, government-approved stands beyond immigration and customs. In most cities, you'll state your destination, pay in advance, and be given a voucher to give to your driver when he drops you off. He may need to take it from you when leaving the airport parking lot, to show to the parking attendant who will record the voucher number and your name in a log. If you want an air-conditioned car, you can book through one of the private taxi companies whose desks resemble those of car-rental companies. These are all reputable companies and they will either charge you a preset or a metered fair, depending on your destination. Luggage room is ample in taxis in Delhi, but many of the cars used in Mumbai are older and smaller, with less room. Taxi drivers might try to charge you an extra fee (around Rs. 10–Rs. 20) per bag, but again, this varies from city to city.

TRANSFERS BETWEEN TERMINALS

If you need to transfer between terminals (for example, between domestic and international) you can use the airport-run terminal transfer bus for free, provided you have a ticket for a departing flight from the destination terminal.

FLIGHTS

TO INDIA

International companies are constantly reevaluating their service to South Asia. Call the air carriers listed here to confirm their flights and schedules, or work with a travel agent who's knowledgeable about the region. You can get to India, usually with a stop in Europe, on many international carriers. Those offering daily direct flights include United Airlines (Newark to Delhi or to Mumbai) and Air India (New York JFK to Mumbai and Delhi, and Chicago to Delhi).

WITHIN INDIA

India's domestic airline scene has boomed since the millennium, although the world economic downturn in 2008 has taken some of the wind out of future expansion plans. In addition to the so-called legacy carriers, Jet Airways and Air India, which both also fly internationally, there is a newer crop of carriers—including ones you've probably never heard of—each with its own quirks.

Jet Airways is often the most expensive carrier, but provides excellent service. Air India, the government carrier, can be a little stodgy and prices a bit high. Popular low-cost, no frills carriers include Spice-Jet, IndiGo, and GoAir.

Airline Contacts Air India ☎ *800/223–7776 in U.S., 800/160–1407 in India* ⊕ *www.airindia. com.* **American Airlines** ☎ *800/433–7300 in U.S., 124/256–7222 in India* ⊕ *www.aa.com.* **British Airways** ☎ *800/247–9297 in U.S., 1860/180–3592 in India* ⊕ *www.britishairways. com.* **Delta Airlines** ☎ *800/241–4141 in U.S., 800/180–0099 in India* ⊕ *www.delta.com.* **Luftansa** ☎ *800/645–3880 in U.S., 124/488– 8888 in India* ⊕ *www.lufthansa.com.* **United Airlines** ☎ *800/864–8331 in U.S., 124/431– 5500 in India* ⊕ *www.united.com.*

Within India Air India ☎ *800/160–1407 in India, 800/223–7776 in U.S.* ⊕ *www.airindia. com.* **IndiGo** ☎ *99/1038–3838, 124/661–3838* ⊕ *www.goindigo.in.* **Jet Airways** ☎ *800/225– 522 in India, 877/835–9538 in U.S.* ⊕ *www. jetairways.com.* **SpiceJet** ☎ *800/180–3333* ⊕ *www.spicejet.com.*

▌BUS TRAVEL

Bus travel isn't the safest or most comfortable way to travel in India, especially at night. Service within cities, especially in Delhi, is crowded and dangerous for women, with men literally hanging outside the bus (if they can manage to grab hold while the bus is still moving). The situation is a bit better in Mumbai, but a lack of published bus schedules and routes makes the city bus experience best left to locals or those who have time to figure it out. If you decide on bus travel between cities, try to take the most luxurious privately run air-conditioned coaches, (often Volvo buses, which are associated with high quality in India), and have a local travel agent make the arrangements. Buses rarely if ever have restrooms on board, but they usually stop every 2–4 hours at restaurants or roadside cafés so that passengers can use the restrooms and drink a cup of tea. It's a good idea to bring earplugs or earphones, as many play Bollywood movies or music at high volumes.

▌CAR TRAVEL

Travel by car in India isn't for the faint of heart, but if you can get over India's extremely different road philosophy, it can be an enjoyable, never boring way to see the country and get from one city to the next.

ROAD CONDITIONS

Roads in India may be wide and smooth in big cities, but they're usually narrow and terribly maintained in the countryside. Traffic in major cities is so erratic and abundant that it is hard to pin down local rush hours. Roads are filled with countless cars at all times of the day and even late at night, especially around the airports (international flights tend to arrive in the wee morning hours). Always be ready for some kind of traffic jam or other road drama if traveling by car.

Traffic is multifarious: you'll see slow-moving cyclists, bullock carts, cows, herds of goats, and even camels or elephants sharing the road with speeding, honking, quick-to-pass, ready-to-brake-for-animals vehicles of all shapes and sizes. Barring a few principal routes and highways built under the continuing modernization project, Indian roads are often dilapidated and become worse during monsoon season. Speed limits, set according to road conditions, are frequently ignored. Road signs, when they exist, are often just in Hindi or the local language.

FROM DELHI TO	DISTANCE	
City	Distance in kilometers	Distance in miles
Agra	203	126
Jaipur	258	160
Mumbai	1,407	874
Goa	1,912	1,188

Because of Britain's historic influence in India, traffic circles are common in newer sections of cities. Older parts of cities are generally made up of extremely narrow, winding streets. Old Delhi's streets tend to be one-way, although you won't be able to tell which way that is unless you simply look at the traffic. Locals drive fast when they can and show little regard for pedestrians.

In rural areas two-way roads are often only one-lane wide, so vehicles frequently dodge oncoming traffic for hours on end. Some roads also serve as innovative extensions to farms, with grain laid out to dry on the pavement or sisal rope strung over the route so that vehicles tramp the grain or rope down. Driving is on the left-hand side of the road.

RULES OF THE ROAD

Hard copies of road regulations are difficult to come by in India, and many Indians either ignore or genuinely aren't aware of road rules across the subcontinent. Take, for instance, speed limits. They aren't always posted, and different states have different speed limits on their respective stretches of the national highways. Any speed less than 100 km (about 60 miles) per hour is probably legal. Locals drive faster than that if not stifled by gridlock, and punishment for speeding is spotty at best. On the off chance that you're driving and you get stopped for speeding, you might have to pay a fine (which is often really just a bribe) depending on the officer's mood.

There are also laws requiring the use of seat belts and laws against using your cell phone while driving. However, you'll be hard-pressed to find any local who wears a belt religiously or gets punished if he doesn't. People do seem to be more aware of restrictions on cell-phone use, and talkers in cities like Delhi and Mumbai, especially foreigners, do get singled out by the cops—it's best not to use your cell phone behind the wheel. The most serious offense—drunk driving—is taken very seriously (when enforced) and is punishable by jail time.

The website ⊕ *www.indiandrivingschools. com* has a fairly comprehensive outline of basic Indian traffic regulations. Nevertheless, it's not too much of a stretch to call Indian roads a free-for-all where traffic rules are theoretical at best.

HIRING A CAR AND DRIVER

Don't rent a self-drive car. The rules and road conditions are probably like nothing you've ever experienced, so taking taxis or hiring a car and driver are the best choices. The good news: hiring a car and driver is affordable by Western standards, and even Indians use this option for weekend getaways. However, the price can add up for long trips, so be sure to establish terms, rates, and surcharges in advance. Drivers are usually paid by the company they work for, and every company has unique policies. It's not uncommon for you to pay for the whole trip in advance, or to pay for half at the front end while settling the balance at the end of the trip. Rates generally include gasoline.

Shorter trips are usually priced by kilometer. Figure around Rs. 15 per km for a non-air-conditioned Ambassador—a hefty, roomy car designed by the British in the 1950s. Ambassadors, which sometimes come with air-conditioning, are not as universal as they used to be, and now the most economic rates often get you a Tata Indica, a small but also practical choice. Indicas are not quite as comfortable as the Ambassador, as these are lighter cars that get bounced about on pot-holed roads. In some locations a higher rate gets you a diesel Sumo jeep or an air-conditioned Cielo or Contessa; still more cash gets you a Toyota, a minivan, or, at some agencies, even a Mercedes-Benz or a BMW.

On longer trips one price usually covers a certain number of hours and kilometers; beyond that you pay extra. Expect to pay at least Rs. 1,000–Rs. 1,500 a day to have a driver at your disposal—more if you're using an expensive hotel car. Add to this a "night halt charge" of Rs. 200 to Rs. 300 per night for overnight trips. Some companies also charge a driver's fee for an eight-hour day.

Arrange a car and driver only through a reputable travel agency or licensed, government-approved operator or, for quite a bit more money, through your hotel. Be sure to discuss your itinerary up front—what seems like a reasonable day's drive on a map can often take much longer in reality. Roads in some areas—wildlife sanctuaries, for example—require a jeep; better to iron out all the details than to miss sights because you don't have the right sort of vehicle. On long journeys, decide in advance where and when you'll stop for tea or meal breaks. The daredevil road maneuvers that are the norm in India can be unsettling. Ask the driver to travel slowly, or have the operator inform the driver of your request.

▍TAXI AND AUTO-RICKSHAW TRAVEL

Probably the best way to get around an Indian city is by taxi or motorized auto-rickshaw. Auto-rickshaws, especially, are fast and cheap, although not as comfortable as an air-conditioned taxi.

Auto-rickshaws are practically everywhere and are easy to flag down. Taxis are also easy to hail on the street in Mumbai, but harder to find in Delhi. One drawback is that most drivers don't speak much English. If your driver can't understand your pronunciation of a landmark or hotel, pen and paper may do the trick. Bystanders are also often helpful in getting from point A to B.

Most important, find out in advance the approximate fare for the distance you will be going—someone at your hotel can give you a ballpark figure. This is crucial, because even if your taxi or rickshaw has a meter, the driver might not use it. In Delhi, it's common for rickshaw drivers to quote outrageous fares and claim that the meter is "broken." Don't fight the system—just have an idea of a fair price before you get in, and expect that negotiation will usually be part of the game. A good rule of thumb is that no rickshaw ride should cost more than Rs. 150 (most are much less), and no taxi ride should cost more than Rs. 600, unless you are going really, really far away. In Mumbai, drivers are good about using the meter and rate conversion cards that are used to convert the rates on outdated meters to current, government-approved norms. Once you're at your destination, the card shows how much you should pay based on the figure displayed on the meter. If you think you're going to a place that may not have vehicles for the return journey (you will probably know for sure only when you reach your destination, unfortunately), then when you arrive, negotiate a waiting fare and a return fare with the driver.

Remember that there are prepaid taxi and auto-rickshaw counters at airports and train stations in major cities, as well as at some top tourist spots. You tell the clerk your destination and pay for it in advance. He may ask you how much luggage you have—paying an extra Rs. 10 is the norm for each large bag or suitcase. The clerk will give you a receipt, at which point you might have to stand in line for the taxi or rickshaw. The driver might also be standing next to you and escort you to his vehicle. Do not get waylaid by aggressive drivers who try to persuade you to come to them instead of going to the counter; they'll certainly charge you more than the published rate. At your destination, do not pay the driver anything extra, even if he claims you gave the wrong destination to the counter clerk (unlikely) or gives other excuses.

Drivers in areas popular with tourists supplement their incomes by offering to find you a hotel or to take you shopping at the "best" stores, which means they'll get a commission if you get a room or buy anything. The stores are usually very expensive, so if you don't want this kind of detour, you must be very firm. Finally, taxis close to luxury hotels are notorious for swindling customers who hire them outside the hotel. Establish beforehand, with the help of the doorman, that the taxi driver will follow his meter or rate card, or negotiate the fare in the presence of the doorman. Or, better yet, walk a block or two away from the hotel's entrance.

▮ TRAIN TRAVEL

Traveling by train in India can be a fine experience if you plan it well. Trains connect the tiniest places across the subcontinent, and train journeys are a terrific way to see off-the-beaten-track India. Traveling on second-class non-air-conditioned trains can be tough, but you'll get better views of the countryside, because the windows are wide open, not sealed, and don't have a smoky film on them, as they do in air-conditioned cars. On the other hand, air-conditioned trips are much more comfortable. Trains, especially on smaller routes, can often be late, so be prepared to cope with delays.

Like its international airports, India's train stations are rather chaotic—though highly entertaining to observe. Hawkers sell everything a typical traveler would want: hot *puris* (deep-fried whole wheat bread), boiled eggs, squeaky toys, and hot tea and coffee made on a crude portable stove. Porters, also known as coolies, weave in and out, balancing unimaginable configurations of trunks and bags on their heads. Invariably, when one person sets out on a journey, five come to see him off. The platforms swirl with crowds and luggage. You need to be careful to hang on to your possessions and keep your bearings so you don't get bumped or swept away. Plan to be early, and keep your tickets safe. If the train is delayed or has not yet arrived, try to find a waiting room. Though usually drab and not very comfortable, these places are safe and might have attached bathrooms. Many large train stations have restaurants or at least snack counters where you can take a break, too.

Train ticket prices vary greatly depending on where and how you're traveling. The *Shatabdi* and *Rajdhani* expresses are fast and have air-conditioned cars and either reclining seats (in *Shatabdis*) or berths (in *Rajdhanis*), but only offer services between major cities. The next-fastest trains are called "mail" trains. "Passenger" trains, which usually offer only second-class accommodations, make numerous stops, and are crowded. Even on the best trains in this group, seats can be well worn and lavatories less than pleasant. But traveling by air-conditioned first class makes for a leisurely and fun journey.

The *Bhopal Shatabdi Express* (train 2002 or 2002A) and *Taj Express* (train 2280) travel between Delhi's Hazrat

Nizamuddin station (NZM) and Agra's Cantonment station (AGC). (Many other trains also travel between the two cities daily.) Both expresses leave early in the morning from Delhi; the *Shatabdi* takes about two hours, the *Taj* 2½ hours. Either option allows for a full day of sightseeing before returning to Delhi on a similar express. There are also express trains connecting Delhi with Mumbai and other major cities. The website of the Indian Railway system has comprehensive schedules of every train running across India.

For long train rides, buy a meter-long chain with loops and a padlock to secure your luggage. (You might find a vendor on the platform at a large train station.) After you've locked your bag and stowed it in its place, loop the chain through its handle and attach it to a bar or hinge below the seat. Be sure to chain your luggage as soon as possible; a lot of small bag thefts take place at the beginning and ends of journeys. Your trip will be more pleasant if you bring along packaged snacks, sandwiches, juice, and bottled water, which aren't always available on board. Long-distance trains provide meals as part of the tariff, and you can expect a number of the items on a food tray to be pre-packaged.

Trains have numerous classes. The air-conditioned cars consist of first-class air-conditioned (also known as 1AC; lockable compartments with two or four sleeping berths), second-class air-conditioned (also known as 2AC; two or four berths that convert to sleepers, but no lockable compartments), and third-class air-conditioned (also known as 3AC; just like 2AC but with six berths in each seating bay). Ordinary first class are the non-air-conditioned lockable compartments with two or four sleeping berths. The a/c chair car (AC chair class) is a comfortable way to go on day trips, with rows of two or three seats on each side. Seats are covered in either vinyl or cloth. Any of the previous classes are adequate, although 3AC can make for slightly cramped quarters.

Sleeper class is laid out just like the 3AC car without the air-conditioning. Finally there's second seating, the cheapest because no reservations are required. But it's not recommended for long distances—the car has an open-air plan with rows of padded or plain wood benches.

Berths are in configurations of four or six in an open coupe arrangement on one side of a train car. On the other (corridor) side, berths are against the wall, in pairs of two; corridors run parallel past these "side" berths and bring in noise and traffic, but have more room to sit up in than the other berths. You'll find two kinds of lavatories, the Western-style commode lavatory and the Indian-style toilet (essentially a hole over which you squat). Although it can be hard to get used to Indian-style facilities, they're actually more sanitary in the sense that there's no contact. Definitely bring enough toilet paper (and some hand sanitizer)—you won't find it on most trains.

In large cities you may be able to buy tickets with major credit cards. Elsewhere, expect to pay cash. Most local travel agents can get train tickets for you.

You must reserve seats and sleeping berths in advance, even with a rail pass. If your plans are flexible, you can make reservations once you arrive in India. To save time, use a local travel agent (who may need to photocopy your passport); otherwise, head to the train station and prepare for long lines and waits. Large urban stations have a special office for foreigners, where you can buy "tourist quota" tickets. (Every train reserves a few seats for tourists who haven't made reservations.) If you arrive early in the morning—around 8—getting a ticket shouldn't take you more than half an hour; however, in peak season tourist quotas fill quickly, and you may have to change your dates altogether. When it's time to travel, arrive at the station at least half an hour before departure so you have enough time to find your seat. Sleeper and seat numbers are displayed on the platform and on each car, along with a list of passengers' names and seat assignments.

If you are not buying from the tourist quota and are booking during nonpeak season, booking online is a convenient option. You can buy e-tickets, which must be printed out and can often be bought on the day of travel, at ⊕ *www.irctc.co.in.* A good resource for train schedules is ⊕ *www.indianrail.gov.in.*

LUXURY TRAINS

In recent years India has expanded its range of luxury trains. They all offer elaborate meals from a variety of cuisine types and luxury quarters as well as excellent (albeit extremely busy) itineraries. Packages, which are very expensive, include food, bus tours from stations (after you disembark you're loaded onto a luxury bus for sightseeing), rail travel, and more. High-season rates for seven- or eight-day tours on some of the trains start at around $3,000, based on double occupancy, but the *Maharajas' Express*, introduced in 2010, is much more: around $6,000 for a weeklong trip. Tickets on

some trains are cheaper in the off-season (March–October).

Rajasthan's *Palace on Wheels*, the original luxury train, and the *Royal Rajasthan on Wheels* both depart from Delhi and in their most popular routes have nearly identical destinations, passing through such tourist hot spots as Jaipur, Jaisalmer, Jodhpur, Udaipur, and Agra. The *Maharajas' Express and the Deccan Odyssey* operate several different thematic routes and depart from either Delhi or Mumbai.

Luxury Trains *Deccan Odyssey* ☎ 11/4777–3400 in India ⊕ www.thedeccanodysseyindia.com. *Maharajas' Express* ☎ 97176–35915 in India ⊕ www.the-maharajas.com. **Palace on Wheels** ☎ 800/103–3500 toll-free in India ⊕ www.rtdc.in. **Royal Rajasthan on Wheels** ☎ 11/2338–6069 ⊕ www.royalrajasthanonwheels.com.

Train Information Indian Railways ⊕ www.indianrail.gov.in. **Indian Railways International Tourist Bureau** ✉ New Delhi Railway Station, Paharganj side, 2nd fl. ☎ 11/4262–5156 ⊗ Mon.–Sat. 8–8, Sun. 8–2.

ESSENTIALS

▮ ACCOMMODATIONS

Staying in India can be a pleasure, regardless of whether you've paid top price at a world-class luxury hotel or gone the no-frills route at a local hostel. For average accommodations somewhere in the middle, you often can expect to pay significantly less than what you'd pay at a comparable hotel in America, which makes getting the bill a pleasant surprise. Whether a room has plush carpets and chairs or a simple bed and table, most tend to be clean and neat.

The lodgings we list are the cream of the crop in each price category. We always list the facilities that are available, but we don't specify whether they cost extra. When pricing accommodations, always ask what is and isn't included. Properties are assigned price categories based on the rate for a standard double room in the high season, which in most of India is approximately October through March, peaking at Christmas and New Year's, when even higher rates apply. When you book a room at a hotel, however (especially an expensive hotel), ask for their best rate and push them to include breakfast and a station or airport pickup. Be a hard bargainer; consider asking them to knock the rate down further, even after they have given you a discount. You can always shop around and come back.

Try to secure all room reservations before arrival, especially during peak season and in the major cities and popular tourist destinations such as Mumbai, Delhi, Agra, and Goa. But give yourself a little leeway to make plans on arrival, especially if you have more than two weeks. In the off-season and in smaller cities it's often fairly easy to change plans at the last minute. This is especially true during monsoon season (late June through August) when many hotels have vacancies and deep discounts. Indians vacation during school holidays in April, May, and early June; for a few days in October or November (for Diwali, or, in eastern India, Durga Puja); and for 10 days between Christmas and the New Year. Reservations are extra-difficult to secure during these times.

Room rates can be extremely expensive in business-oriented cities like Mumbai and Delhi. Urban hotels rarely have off-season discounts, though some international chains have incentive programs for frequent guests. In other areas, hotels may be seeking guests, so you may be able to negotiate your price. When you reserve, ask about additional taxes and service charges, which increase the quoted room price. Do not agree to an airport pickup or breakfast without asking whether these services involve extra costs. Airport pickups organized by luxury hotels are generally overpriced.

As in restaurants, practically every hotel in India will gladly put up with children running around. Most allow children under a certain age to stay in their parents' room at no extra charge or for a nominal fee, but others charge for them as extra adults. Confirm the cutoff age for children's discounts. Only in the more upscale hotels will you find extra special accommodations like a cot or a crib. The same goes for structured children's programs: Oberoi and Taj hotels offer pretty reliable plans for kids with staff supervision, but programs vary from hotel to hotel, so you'll need to ask when making reservations. Most Oberoi hotels also have a library of kid-friendly DVDs. Beyond the luxury realm, however, there's nothing that kids will find particularly spectacular about the average Indian hotel—that is, no over-the-top playgrounds. You're better off trying to impress them with the sights.

Most hotels and other lodgings require you to give your credit-card details before they will confirm your reservation. If you don't feel comfortable using the Internet for this information, give it over the phone or ask if you can fax it (some places even prefer faxes). However you book, get confirmation in writing and have a copy of it handy when you check in.

Be sure you understand the hotel's cancellation policy. Some places allow you to cancel without any kind of penalty—even if you prepaid to secure a discounted rate—if you cancel at least 24 hours in advance. Others require you to cancel a week in advance or penalize you the cost of one night.

CATEGORY	COST
$$$$	over Rs. 10,000
$$$	Rs. 6,000–Rs. 10,000
$$	Rs. 4,000–Rs. 5,999
$	under Rs. 4,000

All prices are in rupees for a standard double room in high season, with no meals, excluding tax and service charges, which vary by region.

GOVERNMENT LODGING
The state-government-run tourism departments and the forestry department manage inexpensive accommodations throughout India. Most of these facilities are poorly maintained, and government employees and officials receive priority booking. Some states, including Rajasthan and Maharashtra run fairly competent hotels—and some are in former palaces or other heritage buildings. For more information, contact the tourist office in the capital of the state you plan to visit.

HERITAGE HOTELS
The Indian government has an excellent incentive program that encourages owners of traditional *havelis* (mansions), forts, and palaces to convert their properties into hotels or bring existing historic hotels up to government standards. (But do be careful where you stay, because "government standards" aren't always ideal for Westerners.) Many of these official heritage hotels—noted in reviews throughout this guide—are well outside large cities. Their architecture and style are authentically Indian, not Western. If this type of lodging appeals to you, contact one of the Indian tourist offices for more information. There are more than 60 such establishments in Rajasthan and a smattering elsewhere in India.

HOTELS AND GUESTHOUSES
Hotels and guesthouses are easy to find in most cities. Hotels include chains, company-run, and privately owned properties—anything from a bare-bones budget hotel at a train station to a lavish palatial property in the choicest part of town or a luxurious beach resort. Overall, they tend to be larger, more formal, and more expensive than guesthouses. The term guesthouse refers to small, independent budget digs that usually lack some of the standard hotel amenities (TVs and in-room telephones, for example). Especially popular with foreign backpackers, they often have fewer rooms than hotels and the owners tend to live on-site. Room service is available in most guesthouses, although meals are not generally included in the rates.

India's tourism department approves and classifies hotels based on a rating system of five stars (the fanciest) to no stars (no frills). The ratings are based on the number of facilities and on hotel and bedroom size. Hotels without pools or those that serve only vegetarian food or that don't have a 24-hour restaurant—including some historic, charming, comfortable properties—don't qualify for five-star status but are often just as luxurious as those that do. The rating system also fails to take service and other important intangibles into account. Although these ratings can be misleading, tour operators often use them, so ask what a star rating means when booking.

If a room you're taking looks a little dingy, chances are the staff will clean it again for you. Make sure the door locks and that the bathroom's plumbing works.

LOCAL DO'S AND TABOOS

CUSTOMS OF THE COUNTRY

In India, food and food-related hospitality is very important. Indians believe in showing their warmth by feeding a guest endless cups of tea, snacks, and meals. If you refuse entirely to eat a meal or have a cup of tea you may offend your host. Indians also believe in offering food over and over again, to make sure the guest has had enough, in case he or she is too shy to ask for more. So if you don't want more of something, be firm but polite in your refusals.

Higher-income households in the big cities are increasingly more westernized, so you might not feel too out of place if you're invited to such a home. However, if you're invited to an extremely traditional Indian home, you should observe certain customs. Men often sit separate from women. Sometimes, when the men entertain a foreign visitor (even a woman), the women of the house keep their distance or don't emerge; they may not speak English, or may be shy. Don't be surprised if the woman of the house serves you but doesn't join the gathering. Don't protest, and don't follow her into the kitchen—in some "upper-caste" Hindu homes the kitchen is frequently off-limits—just accept her behavior as the tradition of this particular home. Often, shoes are taken off before entering, so be sure to inquire, or watch what the family does.

Numerous customs govern food and the partaking of meals. In many households you arrive, sit and talk, and then have your meal; after you eat, the evening is over. Consequently, the meal might not start until 10 pm or later. When you eat in remote areas, you may not be given utensils; eat only with your right hand, as the left is considered unclean. (Left-handers can use utensils if available.) If you want a second helping or are buying openly displayed food, don't help yourself with your hands, which is considered by some as "polluting" the food. Let your host or vendor serve you.

GIFTS

If you visit someone's home for dinner or you're staying with an Indian family, it's a kind gesture to bring a gift from abroad. If there are youngsters in the home, bring something for them. Toys, cosmetics, perfume, and aftershaves are all good options, as is liquor if you're sure that your guests are drinkers—many Indians are not.

GREETINGS

People in India are not overly ceremonious on a day-to-day basis. The common greeting is a simple hello or *namaste* in Hindi or the more formal *namaskaar*. In formal situations and in more traditional circles, people say *namaste/namaskaar* with their hands pressed together in a prayer position. A firm handshake has become common, especially in professional contexts in Delhi, Mumbai, and Bangalore, although outside of the office world, men and women generally don't shake hands. Hugging and European-style cheek kissing is increasingly common among the young urban elite although strictly frowned upon in rural areas and in middle class communities. However, you may see young men walking down the street holding hands or with arms intertwined—this is an expression of friendship, not romance. For safety's sake, foreign women are better off not making eye contact with or smiling at men on the street—it could be perceived as flirtation or an invitation for more communication. When you're leaving, a simple goodbye or expression of thanks will do.

HONORIFICS

It's common for people in India to address their elders as uncle or auntie, even if they are complete strangers. To show extra respect, you tack the suffix –*ji* onto auntie or uncle or simply address your interlocateur as *ji*. This is commonly translated into "sir" in English.

Similarly, people of around the same age in Hindi-speaking parts of the country may call strangers *bhaiya* or *bhai* (which means elder brother but doesn't imply that the person is older than you) or the female form, *didi*. If you want to show extra respect, you can address men around your age *bhai-saab* and women *behen-ji* (but calling someone "a *behen-ji*" is offensive, as it implies she's homely).

SIGHTSEEING

Religious monuments demand respect. Remove your shoes before entering a temple or shrine, even if it appears to be in ruins (this is also the case in many Christian churches in South India). All religions forbid smoking, alcohol consumption, and loud talking on the premises. Some temples and mosques are off-limits to foreigners who don't practice the faith (or, in the case of Hindu temples, of non-Indian descent), or to unaccompanied women; don't try to bribe your way inside. Women should dress modestly—no shorts or tank tops—and should cover their heads before entering a mosque. Both men and women must cover their heads before entering a Sikh temple. Cameras and video cameras are not always permitted.

On rare occasions a Hindu or Muslim festival involves animal sacrifice; do a little research on the festival rituals ahead of time if you are worried this may upset you or your child. Some Hindu and Jain temples don't allow any leather products inside their premises— and the prohibition includes wallets, purses, shoes, belts, and camera cases. Some temples also expect you to purify yourself by washing your hands and feet in a nearby tap or tank before you enter. In Sikh temples, don't point your feet toward the Holy Book or step over anyone sitting in prayer or meditation. Play it safe in both Hindu and Sikh temples: if you sit on the floor, sit cross-legged or with your feet tucked beneath you. In some shrines the sexes are separated;

look around (or follow instructions) and let the situation govern what you do. Step into the courtyards of mosques with your right foot first.

Many well-meaning travelers commit an unforgivable sacrilege when they visit a Buddhist monastery. You're welcome to spin any prayer wheel, but just as you must circumambulate the interior and exterior of a monastery, *stupa*, or *mani* wall in a clockwise direction, you must spin prayer wheels clockwise only. Inside the monastery, cushions and chairs are reserved for *lamas* (monks), so sit on the steps outside or on the floor. If you meet a *rimpoche* (head lama) or a respected monk, it's polite not to turn your back on him when you leave. Also remove your hat and lower your umbrella in the confines of a monastery and in the presence of a lama.

LANGUAGE

Try to learn a little Hindi or the local language. You need not strive for fluency; even just mastering a few basic words and terms is bound to make chatting with the locals more rewarding.

Contrary to popular belief, English is not spoken fluently by the majority of Indians. The country does function in English alongside Hindi and other local languages, however, so barring rural areas, you aren't likely to experience too much of a language barrier, especially in cities and tourist hubs where a working command of English is widespread. Hindi is the national language, but India isn't truly unified linguistically, and many Indians don't speak Hindi at all. Most states and countless smaller areas have their own unique tongues that bear no resemblance to the national language. For example, the languages of South India have completely different scripts and origins from those of the north—one reason why a command of both Hindi and English comes in handy.

If you opt for room service outside a luxury hotel, here are a few things to keep in mind: Tea or coffee usually comes pre-mixed—ask to have a pot of tea or coffee with the milk, sugar, and tea bags or instant coffee brought separately. You can probably get food cooked according to your preferences, but you have to make the request. Ask for fruit juice without ice (you may or may not be successful in getting it without added sugar). Make sure any bottled water you plan to consume is sealed, and do not use water from pitchers in the room unless you are certain it's safe.

■ COMMUNICATIONS

INTERNET

High-speed Internet access is available almost everywhere in India at Internet cafés and hotels, and connection speeds often approach what you're used to at home. Upscale private cafés in major cities often offer Wi-Fi free to customers. Hotel service is generally more reliable, but it's also usually more expensive—business-class hotels may charge as much as Rs. 1,000 or more a day. Rates at Internet cafés are very cheap (around Rs. 30–Rs. 50 for an hour), so it's probably best to leave your computer at home unless you absolutely need it.

If you plan to bring a laptop to India, remember to never plug your computer into a socket before asking about surge protection—some hotels don't have built-in current stabilizers, and extreme electrical fluctuations can damage your adapter.

Contacts Cybercafes. More than 4,000 Internet cafés worldwide are listed here. ⊕ *www.cybercafes.com.*

PHONES

Calling from a hotel is almost always the most expensive option; hotels usually add huge surcharges to all calls, particularly international ones. You can phone from public call offices (PCOs), roadside shops, or even the post office. Calling cards usually keep costs to a minimum, but only if you purchase them locally. And then there are cell phones, which are more prevalent than landlines in some areas; as expensive as cell-phone calls can be, they are still usually a much cheaper option than calling from your hotel.

Using landlines as well as cell phones in India can be frustrating—sometimes the connections are great, sometimes they're lousy, and you'll sometimes have to repeat yourself at least once because connections aren't always clear.

A few peculiarities to keep in mind: Indian businesses usually have a series of phone numbers instead of just one, because networks can get congested. If a number reads "562/331701 through 331708," for example, you can reach the establishment using any number between 331701 and 331708. Some of the numbers may be telefax numbers, so if you're trying to send a fax and someone answers, ask them to put the fax machine on. Homes may also have two (or more) phone lines, although this is becoming less common with the near-universality of cell phones, especially among young urbanites.

There is no standard number of digits in landline phone numbers across the country. The norm, however, is 10 digits, which includes a city code of two or three digits. Cell-phone numbers are always 10 digits and start with the number 8 or 9. If the cell number is from another state, you'll need to dial 0 first.

The country code for India is 91, after which you dial the city code, and then the phone number. Delhi's city code is 11, and Mumbai's is 22. Some city codes are three digits, such as the code for Amritsar, which is 183.

CALLING WITHIN INDIA

If you're calling long distance within India to any of the landline numbers listed in this book, dial a zero, then the city code, then the phone number. You only have to dial a zero before a 10-digit cell-phone number—there is no city code. When calling from a cell phone to another one in a different city, the call is considered long distance.

Aside from the quality of connections at times, the local telephone system is adequate for getting in touch when you need to. All phone numbers can be dialed directly from pretty much every public access phone, eliminating the need for an operator.

If you don't have a cell phone, the easiest option is to make a call from one of the ubiquitous public call offices (PCOs), easily identifiable by their bright yellow signs. They're not really offices so much as open-air booths, and they're pretty much on every street corner in Indian cities and in small villages, too, as well as in airports and train stations. PCOs are equipped with ISD/STD capabilities, meaning you can make international and long-distance domestic calls in addition to local ones. (ISD stands for "international subscriber dialing," STD for "subscriber trunk [direct distance] dialing.") You'll make a call from a regular telephone connected to a meter that keeps track of the call duration. Once you hang up, an attendant will give you a receipt with the meter reading and tell you how much you owe. Rates are on a per-minute basis, and there is no surcharge. At less than Rs. 10 per minute, domestic calls won't break the bank. It's much more expensive to call internationally, though, so inquire about current rates to different countries. Still, if you just want to call home quickly, calling from a PCO is convenient and usually hassle-free. Try to avoid making calls from hotels. They often come with huge surcharges, and it's just as convenient to use the PCO down the street.

Directory assistance is spotty in India. The private company JustDial (⊕ *www. justdial.com*) is reliable and has numbers all over the country. Two national numbers—6999 and 9999—can be called for assistance from anywhere in India.

CALLING OUTSIDE INDIA

International calls can be subject to long delays, but most hotels, airports, train stations, post offices, and PCOs are connected to the ISD system. Simply dial 00, followed by the country code, the area code, and the number. If calling from a public phone stall, you'll be handed a receipt with the number of minutes and an attendant will calculate how much you owe. Remember that hotels add an enormous surcharge to international calls and faxes; in addition, they sometimes charge a fee per call made on your calling card. Find out what the charges are before you dial. To avoid the surcharge, make your calls at a PCO. There are no reduced-rate calling hours for international calls. Some Internet cafés are set up to let you use an Internet-based calling service such as Skype. This allows very inexpensive international rates.

The country code for the United States is 1.

Using an AT&T access code to reach an operator can be helpful if you absolutely must use your own calling card from home or want to have charges billed to your personal account. However, it's usually more trouble than it's worth, and calling cards bought locally are guaranteed to be cheaper. Some hotels might not let you use the access number, and surcharges are always involved.

Access Codes AT&T USADirect ☎ *000–117 in India* ⊕ *www.att.com.*

CALLING CARDS

Calling cards for use within India are fairly common. The Indian cell phone service providers Reliance, and Vodafone sell international prepaid calling cards that you can use to call domestically, too. International rates are less than Rs. 10 per minute. The cards work on cell phones and landlines, including at PCOs, and can be bought at practically any stall or shop selling cell phone services. Remember that there might be a surcharge for connecting with these cards on hotel phones.

CELL PHONES

If you have an unlocked multiband phone (some countries use different frequencies from those used in the United States) and your service provider uses the world-standard GSM network (as do T-Mobile, AT&T, and Verizon), you can probably use your phone abroad. Roaming fees can be steep, however: 99¢ a minute is considered reasonable. And overseas you normally pay the toll charges for incoming calls. It's almost always cheaper to send a text message than to make a call, since text messages have a very low set fee (often less than 5¢).

If you just want to make local calls, consider buying a new SIM card and a prepaid service plan in the destination. You'll then have a local number and can make local calls at local rates.

Note that your home provider may have to unlock your phone for you to use a different SIM card. Cell phone technology is excellent in India, and whether you have your own phone or rent one, you'll likely be connected wherever you go because of extensive network coverage all over the country—even in small towns.

If you're based in Europe or another Asian country, your unlocked cell phone will probably work in India. Many American cell phones, especially smartphones, have international roaming capabilities, so inquire with your provider. It's a good idea to confirm how much the provider charges per minute for international roaming, which can be unless you have a special plan.

If you are planning on staying several weeks, it may be worth your while (and the least hassle) to simply buy a prepaid local SIM card. In most cities there are cell phone shops on just about every corner, and they often sell good-quality used phones as well as inexpensive new ones.

As an anti-terrorism measure, Indian cell-phone shops are required to have a proof of address for anyone buying a new SIM card or cell phone. Although not all shops are stringent about this, the law does mean that buying a card or phone for a short trip may be more trouble than it's worth. If you do find a shop that's willing to work with you, you'll have to provide a copy of your passport, two passport-size photos, and your local address (normally that of your hotel) to register for a SIM card. You'll usually be up and running with a phone number in less than 15 minutes. Some upscale hotels also offer phone rentals to their guests.

You will have to pay a certain number of rupees in advance to get talk time. Non-residents do not have the option of "post-pay" plans. Rates are generally around Rs. 1 per minute, depending on who you are calling. When you've run out of minutes, you can easily recharge your phone at a cell phone service shop. Airtel and Vodafone are the country's two largest cell phone service providers.

Contacts Cellular Abroad. You can rent and buy GMS phones and buy SIM cards that work in many countries from Cellular Abroad. ☎ 800/287–5072 ⊕ www.cellularabroad.com. **Mobal.** This company rents mobiles and sells GSM and satellite phones (starting at $7/day) that work in more than 190 countries. Per-call rates vary throughout the world. ☎ 888/888–9162 ⊕ www.mobalrental.com. **Planet Fone.** You can rent cell phones here starting at $21/week, but the per-minute rates are expensive. ☎ 888/988–4777 ⊕ www.planetfone.com.

▮ CUSTOMS AND DUTIES

You're allowed to bring goods of a certain value back home without having to pay any duty or import tax. There's a limit on the amount of tobacco and liquor you can bring back duty-free, and some countries have separate limits for perfumes; for exact figures, check with your customs department. The values of duty-free goods are included in these amounts. When you shop abroad, save all your receipts, as customs inspectors may ask to see them as well as the items you purchased. If the total value of your goods is more than the duty-free limit, you'll have to pay a tax (most often a flat percentage) on the value of everything beyond that limit.

The customs process at the international gateways isn't difficult, although the line you have to wait in is likely to be long. If you're entering India with dutiable or valuable articles, you must mention this when you stop at customs. Officials may ask you to fill out a Tourist Baggage Re-Export Form (TBRE), as such articles must be taken with you when you leave India. You'll have to pay a duty on anything listed on the TBRE that you plan to leave in India. Depending on the attitude of the customs official, you may have to list your laptop computer, camera or video equipment, and cell phone on a TBRE form. It's a good idea, though, not to go searching for forms or a customs official unless someone questions you.

Among other things, you may bring the following into India duty-free: personal effects (clothing and jewelry); a camera, a video camera, a laptop computer, a cell phone, 200 cigarettes or 50 cigars or 250 grams of tobacco, up to two liters of alcohol, and gifts not exceeding a value of Rs. 8,000 (about US$175). You may *not* bring in illegal drugs, firearms, Indian currency (although a small amount is unlikely to cause any trouble, especially if you don't declare it), pornographic material, gold or silver that's not jewelry, counterfeit or pirated goods, or antiquities. Consult India's Central Board of Excise and Customs website for complete details.

LEAVING INDIA

Rupees aren't technically allowed out of India; you must exchange them before you depart, although you are unlikely to be questioned or searched for a few small bills you may have kept for a coffee in the airport. Foreign-exchange facilities are usually in the same airport halls as the check-in counters, but there's no access to these facilities once you pass through immigration. Tourists cannot take out more foreign currency than they brought in. There is no limit on gold jewelry.

All animal products, souvenirs, and trophies are subject to the Wildlife Protection Act of 1972. The export of ivory (unless you can prove it's antique) and the skins of protected species aren't allowed. Export of exotic birds, wildlife, orchids, and other flora and fauna is forbidden as well.

In general, items more than 100 years old cannot be exported without a permit from the Archaeological Survey of India (ASI), which has offices in many cities, including Delhi and Mumbai. Reputable shops will provide you with the necessary permit or help you get it.

Information in India Central Board of Excise and Customs ⊕ *www.customs.gov.in.*

U.S. Information U.S. Customs and Border Protection ☎ *877/227–5511* ⊕ *www.cbp.gov.*

▌EATING OUT

Indian culture definitely revolves around food, and there are plenty of restaurants serving international cuisine, fast food, and regional specialties, especially in big cities. There are numerous cafés and food stalls, especially in market areas—these are especially popular with locals looking for a small snack in between meals. If you choose to try out street food, be wary of hygiene issues—look for stalls popular with families and avoid shaved ice or anything containing cold water. India is also a haven for vegetarians, with plenty of pure-veg restaurants that don't serve any meat, fish, poultry, or eggs. Even "non-veg" places usually have delicious meatless options.

⇨ *For information on food-related health issues, see Health below.*

Almost all restaurants in India are family-friendly, even many of the fancier ones in top hotels. If your child doesn't like Indian food, it's almost always possible to order things like sandwiches and pizzas.

American fast food is widely available in larger cities, most of which have branches of McDonald's, Pizza Hut, and Domino's

Pizza. Nirula's is a well-known fast-food chain in Delhi and other points in the north, and they serve Indian fast food, burgers, and ice cream. In villages and smaller towns across the subcontinent such eateries are nonexistent. In that case, an order of plain bread such as *naan* and lentils may be just the ticket.

MEALS AND MEALTIMES

A regular Indian meal consists of some rice or bread, served with spiced vegetables, meat, and lentils. Accompaniments to the meal can include *chaas* (spiced buttermilk), *lassi* (a sweet or salty yogurt drink), pickle, *papad* (a deep-fried or dry roasted savory wafer made from lentil or rice), chutney, and *raita* (spiced yogurt). A sweet, usually very sugary and milk-based, is the last course. At the end of the meal, *paan* (a stimulating concoction of sugar and various spices wrapped in the leaves of the betel pepper plant), *supari* (plain betel nut), rock sugar, or aniseed may be served as a breath-freshener/digestive.

Although lots of Indians eat cornflakes or toast to start the day, traditional Indian breakfasts are often much heavier. They can consist of any of the following South Indian foods: *idlis* (steamed rice and lentil cakes) with chutney; *rasam wada* (deep-fried lentil fritters served with a hot, spicy watery lentil curry); *dosas* (a crisp pancake, made with a fermented ground-rice-and-lentil batter); *upma* (light semolina, also known as farina, with vegetables); or *aloo poha* (spicy potatoes mixed with rice flakes).

A good portion of the Indian population is vegetarian for religious reasons, and while milk is part of the typical vegetarian diet in India, eggs are not. Many people who eat meat don't do so every day (and certainly not at every meal). Most Hindus consider the cow sacred and do not eat beef. Muslims (and many Hindus) do not touch pork. Some Hindus eat only chicken and seafood and stay away from red meat. Many Jains are not only vegetarian but also don't eat any vegetable grown under the ground—one reason may be that plucking up the root destroys life in the soil. As you travel through India, expect to encounter folks who don't eat meat on Tuesday (in honor of Hanuman, the monkey-god servant of Rama); much of India's religious and ethical life, indeed, revolves around food.

Although South Indian restaurants often start serving lunch early, in North India people tend to eat lunch later in the afternoon than in the United States, sometimes around 2 or 3 pm. Restaurants in cities normally stay open until 11 pm or midnight, as Indians are known for starting dinner quite late (past 10 pm). In other areas, expect an earlier dinner in restaurants (finished by 9 pm) unless you're staying in a luxury hotel. Coffee shops in urban luxury hotels are often open 24 hours.

Snacking is also popular, and common treats include samosas, white-bread sandwiches, *jalebis* (deep-fried bright yellow flour fritters soaked in sugar syrup), and the fudgelike milk sweets. *Masala chai* (spiced milk tea) and ginger tea are extremely popular and are often consumed four to five times a day. But as you go south, coffee becomes increasingly important and is served boiling hot, creamy, and foamy (sort of like a sugary latte).

Unless otherwise noted, the restaurants listed in this guide are open daily for lunch and dinner.

RESERVATIONS AND DRESS

Most restaurants don't require reservations, except for upscale establishments in big cities. We only mention reservations when they are essential or when they are not accepted. For popular, high-end restaurants, book as far ahead as you can (often 30 days), and reconfirm as soon as you arrive in India. (Large parties should always call ahead to check the reservations policy.)

Very few restaurants require formal attire. By and large India is very casual about dress codes. However, certain clubs do not allow anyone—even in daylight hours—to wear shorts or men to wear sandals.

WINES, BEER, AND SPIRITS

India produces many kinds of liquor, and exorbitant duties make imported spirits unaffordable to all but the wealthiest of its citizens. Its locally produced versions of international brands of rum, vodka, and gin are adequate but generally unmemorable. The sweet local red rum, Old Monk, is worth a try. Kingfisher beer is ubiquitous, refreshing, and bland. With every year more and more Indian wine is produced, and much of it is good, although not overly complex. Scotch whisky is by far the most popular kind of hard liquor in India: Director's Special is a mild and reliable brand.

Alcohol at luxury hotels is vastly marked up. Consider buying your own liquor and having it in your room—you can always call room service for glasses and mixers. If you're a woman traveling alone, drinking in your room is probably a better option in any case.

Indian customs may appear prudish toward drinking—but open a bottle and you may make some instant friends. According to proper Indian etiquette, alcohol is excluded from many occasions. When you visit someone's house you may not be offered a drink even in the evening, and the strongest beverage you may get is tea. At some Hindu and virtually all Muslim weddings and at festival time, alcohol may not be served. Women are infrequent drinkers, at least in public. Don't be surprised if you encounter quite a few male teetotalers.

Dry days—when alcohol isn't available anywhere in the country—are observed on January 26, August 15, October 2, and on certain festival dates. Some states observe additional dry days, which are usually on or around election days; others prohibit everything but beer.

■ ELECTRICITY

Blackouts lasting anywhere from 30 minutes to 12 hours are a part of everyday Indian life, particularly in summer when the load is high. But if you're staying at a mid- to high-end hotel, there will, no doubt, be a generator that can restore electricity within seconds. Storms can play havoc with electricity, and low-voltage electricity and surges are problems. It's always a good idea to have a flashlight or a small handheld fan if you plan on being in rural, rugged areas for any length of time.

The electrical current in India is 220 volts, 50 cycles alternating current (AC). There are two types of wall outlets in India: large, three-pronged ones used for large appliances such as refrigerators and air-conditioners, and smaller ones that take plugs with two round prongs, like those used in continental Europe.

Consider making a small investment in a universal adapter, which has several types of plugs in one lightweight, compact unit. Most laptops and mobile phone chargers are dual voltage (i.e., they operate equally well on 110 and 220 volts), so they require only an adapter. These days the same is true of small appliances such as hair dryers. Always check labels and manufacturer instructions to be sure. Don't use 110-volt outlets marked "for shavers only" for high-wattage appliances such as hair-dryers.

Contacts **Help for World Travelers Global & Electric Phone Directory.** This directory has information on electrical plugs and telephones around the world. ⊕ *www.kropla.com.*

■ EMERGENCIES

Delhi's 24-hour East West Medical Center has a referral list of doctors, dentists, pharmacists, and lawyers throughout India. Its staff can arrange treatment wherever you are in the country. It also provides air ambulances that can evacuate you from remote areas in the case of a medical emergency. Note: You must pay the center when you receive assistance—credit cards are accepted—and then apply for reimbursement by your insurance company later. It's necessary to get in touch with East West first so that they can verify your policy details. This can take anywhere from a few hours to a day, depending on the day of the week and whether the details are in order; at that point East West will organize payment.

Contact Meera Rescue, based in Delhi with branches in Mumbai and Goa, if international evacuation is necessary. (Whatever happens, don't go to a government hospital. In a grave emergency, contact your embassy.) Meera Rescue is a professional evacuation service recognized by international insurance companies; the company evacuates from anywhere in the country to hospitals in major cities and overseas if necessary; it's open 24 hours. Like East West, you must pay Meera and be reimbursed by your insurance company.

Consulates and Embassies Indian Consulate General ⊕ *www.indiacgny. org.* **Indian Embasssy** ☎ *202/939–7000* ⊕ *www.indianembassy.org.* **U.S. Consulate (Mumbai)** ✉ *Bandra Kurla Complex, C-49, G-Block, Bandra East, Mumbai, Maharashtra* ☎ *22/2672–4000* ⊕ *mumbai.usconsulate.gov.* **U.S. Embassy** ✉ *Shantipath, Chanakyapuri, New Delhi* ☎ *11/2419–8000* ⊕ *newdelhi. usembassy.gov.*

General Emergency Contacts East West Medical Center ✉ *28 Greater Kailash 1, New Delhi* ☎ *11/2464–1494* ⊕ *www.eastwestassist. com.* **Meera Rescue** ✉ *112 Jor Bagh, New Delhi* ☎ *11/2465–3170, 11/2465–3175* ⊕ *www.meera-rescue.com.*

▌ HEALTH

No vaccination certificate or inoculations are required to enter India from the United States, Canada, or the United Kingdom unless you're coming via certain parts of sub-Saharan Africa, in which case you'll need proof of vaccination against yellow fever. Without such proof, you could be quarantined on arrival in dismal government facilities.

Ultimately you must decide what vaccinations are right for you before you travel to India; it's wise to consult your doctor at least three months before departure. The Centers for Disease Control and Prevention (CDC) maintain a list of recommended vaccinations for the Indian subcontinent on their website; these include hepatitis A and typhoid fever.

In areas where malaria and dengue fever—both carried by mosquitoes—are prevalent, use mosquito nets, wear clothing that covers the body, apply repellent containing DEET, and use spray for flying insects in living and sleeping areas. When you arrive in India, consider purchasing repellents that plug into the wall and release a mosquito-repelling scent. These are effective in keeping rooms mosquito-free and can be found in most general stores. You may want to consider taking malaria prophylactics, as the disease exists in many regions of India. There's no vaccine to combat malaria or dengue, and mosquitoes can pass on other infections, such as the Chikungunya virus, so preventing bites should always be your first line of defense.

While traveling in remote areas or in small towns, it's a good idea to have a medical kit containing a pain reliever, diarrhea medication, moist towelettes, antibacterial skin ointment and skin cleanser, antacids, adhesive bandages, and any prescription medications.

The precautions you take for yourself in India are the same ones you should take for your child. Make sure they have all their vaccinations, and consult a pediatrician about antimalaria medication. Bring a mosquito repellent spray from home that you know to be safe for children. And only give them bottled water to help guard against stomach problems that could spoil a short trip.

The most common types of illnesses are caused by contaminated food and water. If you have problems, mild cases of traveler's diarrhea may respond to Imodium (known generically as loperamide) or Pepto-Bismol. Be sure to drink plenty of fluids; if you can't keep fluids down, seek medical help. Infectious diseases can be airborne or passed via mosquitoes and ticks and through direct or indirect physical contact with animals or people. Some, including Norwalk-like viruses that affect your digestive tract, can be passed along through contaminated food. Speak with your physician and/or check the CDC or World Health Organization websites for health alerts, particularly if you're pregnant, traveling with children, or have a chronic illness.

SPECIFIC ISSUES IN INDIA

The major health risk in India is traveler's diarrhea, caused by eating contaminated fruit or vegetables or drinking contaminated water, so it's important to watch what you eat. Avoid ice, uncooked food, and unpasteurized milk and milk products, and **drink only bottled water or water that has been boiled for at least one minute.** Avoid tap water, ice, and drinks to which tap water has been added. **You may want to turn down offers of "filtered" water**; it may have been filtered to take out particles but not purified to kill parasites. Water purified through an Aquaguard filter system, however, is generally safe (as long as the filter has been maintained correctly). You'll be fine at most places catering to foreign tourists. **When buying bottled water, make sure that the cap hasn't been tampered with.** Bottles are sometimes refilled with tap water. However, moves to encourage people to refill bottles with Aquagard water to help reduce the country's mountain of plastic waste is blurring this issue. Many mid-range tourist hotels offer free or very cheap boiled or filtered water. Soft drinks, in bottles or cans, and packaged fruit juices are safe, readily available options. And always **keep at least one bottle of water in your hotel room** for brushing your teeth as well as for drinking.

If your stomach does get upset, try to drink plenty of purified water or tea—ginger tea (*adrak chai*) is a good folk remedy. In severe cases, rehydrate yourself with a salt-sugar solution—½ teaspoon salt (*namak*) and 4 tablespoons sugar (*shakar or cheeni*) per quart of water.

Avoid raw vegetables and fruit outside of fancy restaurants, even those that have been peeled, unless it was you who did the cutting and peeling. Make sure that all meats are thoroughly cooked. It's not necessary to go vegetarian, and to do so would mean missing out on some delicious dishes. Just choose restaurants with care, and eat hot foods while they're hot. A little bit of personal hygiene can also go a long way in preventing stomach upsets. Wash your hands before you eat anything, and carry moist towelettes or hand sanitizer. **Locally popular, worn-looking restaurants often serve the safest food.** Such restaurants often can't afford refrigeration, so the cooks prepare food acquired that day—not always the case with the upscale places. Some hotel chefs buy in bulk and, thanks to temperamental electricity, a refrigerator may preserve more than just foodstuffs. That said, digestion problems often are due more to the richness and spice of Indian cuisine than to the lack of hygiene. Many hotel restaurants cook Indian dishes with quite a bit of oil. If you have a sensitive stomach, order carefully and don't overdo things, especially in your first few days when your body is getting used to the new flavors. Fried foods from street vendors often look delicious, but inspect the oil: if it looks as old as the pot, it could be rancid.

Stomach issues are what tend to scare first-time visitors the most, and if you're only going to be in India for a short time, it makes sense to take as many precautions as possible so sickness won't cut into your vacation. However, if you're going to be in India for a longer period, try to acclimate yourself to things like street food, filtered water, ice, and the wonderful abundance of fresh-squeezed juices, because avoiding every single thing that could possibly make you sick in India is not only impractical, but also limiting. Chances are that your body will simply adjust and become resistant to most stomach problems.

All Indian cities are heavily polluted, though serious efforts have been going on for years to reduce vehicle pollution. Mumbai and Delhi require their taxis to run on compressed natural gas (CNG), which has considerably reduced the smog. People with breathing problems, especially asthma, should **carry the appropriate respiratory remedies.** India's heat can dehydrate you, and dust can irritate your throat, so **drink plenty of liquids.** Dehydration will make you weak and more susceptible to other health problems. Seek air-conditioned areas when possible, and plan your day so you're visiting tourist sites in the early morning or late afternoon, when the sun is less strong.

If you travel into jungle areas during or right after the monsoon, you may fall victim to the disgusting but generally nondangerous plague of leeches, which lie in wait on damp land. Help protect yourself by covering your legs and carrying salt. Applying DEET and strong-smelling chemicals such as deodorant to your skin and pants will also help make your flesh less appealing. Don't wear sandals. If a leech clings to your clothing or skin, dab it with a pinch of salt and it will fall off.

For bedbug bites, buy a bar of Dettol soap (available throughout India) and use it when you bathe to relieve itching and discomfort. If you're staying in a dubious hotel, **check under the mattress** for bedbugs, cockroaches, and other unwanted critters. Use Flit, Finit, or one of the other readily available spray repellents on suspicious-looking furniture and in mosquito-infested rooms. Mosquito coils (*kachua*), which you must light, and Good Knight pellets, which are plugged into an outlet, are fairly effective at "smoking" mosquitoes

away. On the road, **treat scratches, cuts, and blisters immediately.** If you're trekking, save the bottle and cap from your first bottled water so you can refill it with water that you purify yourself.

Beware of overexposure even on overcast days. To avoid sunburn, **use a sunscreen** with a sun-protection factor of at least 30. To play it safe, **wear a wide-brimmed hat.**

OVER-THE-COUNTER REMEDIES

You don't necessarily need to lug a medicine cabinet with you to India—**practically every over-the-counter medication and medical supply under the sun is available** in the big cities should you need them. The pharmacies, or "chemists"—which are also abundant—will carry a wide variety of both recognizable name brands and Indian versions. If you're not sure what you need to make yourself feel better, shopkeepers can usually make good recommendations.

CHILDREN IN INDIA

Bringing your kids to India may seem daunting, but most children love it. India is like a giant circus, with color, chaos, and a sideshow every minute. Kids are warmly welcomed everywhere except, perhaps, in the stuffiest of restaurants, and most Indians will bend over backward to help you with a child-related need. In fact, so much affection is lavished on children here—everyone wants to pick them up, pinch their cheeks, talk to them—that your little ones may even get overwhelmed.

There are a couple of things to remember: Many diseases are prevalent in India that no longer exist elsewhere, so **check with your pediatrician first** and make sure your child's immunizations are current. It's easiest to bring an infant (who cannot yet crawl, and who is still dependent on breast-feeding or formula) or children who are a bit older and can walk on their own.

Something you might find strange is the fact that no one really uses car seats in India; even educated women think nothing of holding infants in their arms while sitting in the front seat of a moving vehicle (or on the back of a motorbike). So if you plan on getting a car and driver, **don't expect to get a car seat**—bring your own (don't expect, either, that seat belts will always work).

Health Warnings National Centers for Disease Control & Prevention (*CDC*). ☎ *800/232-4636* ⊕ *www.cdc.gov/travel.* **World Health Organization** (*WHO*). ⊕ *www. who.int.*

▌ HOURS OF OPERATION

Most banks are open weekdays 10–2 and Saturday 10–noon, and most ATMs are open around the clock. International airports and some top hotels have 24-hour currency-exchange facilities, and the major American Express branches have extended hours for check cashing. Post offices are generally open Monday–Saturday 10–5.

Gas stations are usually open daily 6 am–10 pm. In larger cities, some stay open 24 hours.

Most museums are closed on Monday. Site museums (adjoining archaeological monuments) are normally closed on Friday.

Pharmacies are usually open daily 9:30–8, though in cities there are some 24-hour establishments. In some places you can also buy medications from the 24-hour pharmacies at large hospitals. (Note that in India pharmacies are called "chemists.")

Outside the major metropolitan areas, many shopkeepers close their establishments for lunch and an afternoon siesta. Some stores are closed Sunday.

Bars and nightclubs in the big cities are usually done by 2 am, although some local laws mandate much earlier closing times, sometimes as early as 11 pm.

HOLIDAYS

India's fixed date national holidays are January 26 (Republic Day), August 15 (Independence Day), October 2 (Gandhi's birthday), and December 25 (Christmas). Endless festivals enliven—and shut down—different parts of the country throughout the year. Festivals often affect availability of travel connections or the time needed to reach the airport, so look into the holidays that are coming up as you plan your itinerary.

▌ MAIL

The Indian postal system is fairly reliable, and stamps can be bought in post offices and various other shops. Airmail letters and postcards take a week to 10 days to reach most destinations from India. Postal delays are caused by holiday rushes (during Diwali and the Christmas season) and strikes.

Airmail letters (weighing 20 grams, or 0.7 ounce) to Australia, New Zealand, United States, Canada, South Africa, or Europe cost Rs. 20; postcards cost Rs. 12. Aerograms to anywhere in the world are Rs. 15. Although your postcards are likely to arrive, they may take a very long time to do so.

SHIPPING PACKAGES

There are many options for shipping gifts and other purchases home. Many stores—especially those that cater to tourists—ship items using courier services or other private methods. It's usually reliable and fast, but reconsider shipping anything special that you would absolutely hate to lose. You can send parcels home "surface air lifted" (SAL), a special service provided by the Indian postal department that's cheaper than airmail. A letter or parcel of 250 grams or less costs Rs. 465 to the United States and Rs. 620 to Canada. Each additional 250 grams cost Rs. 101. Different rates apply for other countries.

▌ MONEY

A trip to India can be as luxurious and expensive—or as bare-bones and cheap—as you want it to be. The economy has really spiked since 2000, along with domestic travel and international foot traffic, and as a result, room rates at fancy urban hotels are comparable to those in New York, London, or Paris. You'll pay substantially more for everything in popular tourist spots and big cities compared with the rest of the country, although certain goods (including soda, cigarettes, chips) have a maximum retail price (MRP) printed on their packaging. It's illegal to sell such products for more than the printed amount, although sometimes vendors try to charge foreigners more, assuming they are unaware of this price regulation.

If you're willing to stay at modest hotels and eat where the locals do, you might find that the most expensive part of your trip turns out to be the international airfare ($1,000–$2,000, depending on when you go). It's possible to find decent hotels for less than US$70 a night, and the cheapest run less than US$20 (sometimes a lot less). You could also conceivably eat every meal for less than US$2.

Many merchants, even in big cities, still only accept payment in cash. Always carry sufficient rupees as well as a credit card in your wallet. (Although it's possible to cash traveler's checks in big cities, it's rarely convenient to do so.) Shopkeepers appreciate it when people pay with the exact amount, or as close to it as possible. In fact, they balk at giving change in general. The 1,000 rupee note should definitely not be used to pay for, say, something that costs Rs. 100, because merchants might not even have that much change on hand. It's advisable to stick to denominations of Rs. 100 or less, and don't flaunt Rs. 500 and Rs. 1,000 notes.

A cup of tea from a stall costs about Rs. 5–Rs. 10 (US9¢–US17¢), but in top hotels it can cost more than Rs. 80 (US$1.30).

A 650-ml bottle of beer costs about Rs. 75 (US$1.25) in a shop, and upward of Rs. 250 (US$4.15) without taxes in a top hotel. A 6-km (4-mile) air-conditioned taxi ride in Delhi is supposed to cost about Rs. 73 (US$1.22), though it may cost more; taxi drivers often do not want to use their meters and try to charge higher prices for tourists.

ITEM	AVERAGE COST
Cup of Coffee	Rs. 10–Rs. 50, fancy Rs. 80
Glass of Wine	Rs. 250–Rs. 500
Glass of Beer	Rs. 250 in a bar or hotel
Sandwich	Rs. 40–Rs. 80
Museum Admission	Rs. 200–Rs. 250 (foreigner rates)

Prices throughout this guide are given for adults. Substantially reduced fees are almost always available for children, students, and senior citizens.

ATMS AND BANKS

Your home bank will probably charge a fee for using ATMs abroad; the foreign bank you use may also charge a fee. Nevertheless, you'll usually get a better rate of exchange at an ATM than you will at a currency-exchange office or even when changing money in a bank. And extracting funds as you need them is a safer option than carrying around a large amount of cash.

▌TIP➡ PINs with more than four digits are not recognized at ATMs in many countries. If yours has five or more, remember to change it before you leave.

There are only a few cash machines in smaller towns in India, but larger cities are dotted with ATMs. Look for ICICI, HDFC, Citibank, or HSBC ATMs, which generally accept foreign cards. Other ATMs might only accept Indian cards, especially in smaller towns. If you know you'll be traveling to a rural area, it's crucial to have enough cash on hand.

If you think you'll need cash from your bank account or cash advances through your credit card, make sure that your bank and credit cards are programmed for ATM use in India before you leave home, and inform your bank that you'll be using your cards in India. All ATMs function in English, and most have security guards.

CREDIT CARDS

It's a good idea to inform your credit-card company before you travel, especially if you're going abroad and don't travel internationally very often. Otherwise, the issuing company might put a hold on your card due to unusual activity. Record all your credit-card numbers—as well as the phone numbers to call if your cards are lost or stolen—in a safe place, so you're prepared should something go wrong. Both MasterCard and Visa have general numbers you can call (collect if you're abroad) if your card is lost, but you're better off calling the number of your issuing bank, since MasterCard and Visa usually just transfer you to your bank.

If you plan to use your credit card for cash advances, you'll need to apply for a PIN at least two weeks before your trip. Although it's usually cheaper (and safer) to use a credit card abroad for large purchases (so you can cancel payments or be reimbursed if there's a problem), note that some credit-card companies *and* the banks that issue them add substantial percentages to all foreign transactions, whether they're in a foreign currency or not. Check on these fees before leaving home, so there won't be any surprises when you get the bill.

■TIP➔ Before you charge something, ask the merchant whether he or she plans to do a dynamic currency conversion (DCC). In such a transaction the credit-card processor (shop, restaurant, or hotel, not Visa or MasterCard) converts the currency and charges you in dollars. In most cases you'll pay the merchant a 3% fee for this service in addition to any credit-card company and issuing-bank foreign-transaction surcharges.

Dynamic currency conversion programs are becoming increasingly widespread. Merchants who participate in them are supposed to ask whether you want to be charged in dollars or the local currency, but they don't always do so. And even if they do offer you a choice, they may well avoid mentioning the additional surcharges. The good news is that you *do* have a choice.

Credit cards are widely accepted in large Indian cities, especially at the retail chain stores and the upscale restaurants. Smaller merchants and street stalls, however, are likely to take only cash. It's a good idea to keep at least Rs. 1,000 (in small denominations) in your wallet at all times in the cities, along with your credit card, so you'll always have both options. In rural India, don't ever count on being able to pay with a credit card, and always have enough cash to see you through.

American Express is rarely accepted in India, Diners Club is not widely accepted, and Discover isn't accepted at all.

Reporting Lost Cards American Express ☎ 800/528–4800 in U.S., 124/280–1800 in India ⊕ www.americanexpress.com. **Diners Club** ☎ 800/263–5018 in U.S., 303/799–1504 collect from abroad ⊕ www.dinersclub. com. **MasterCard** ☎ 800/627–8372 in U.S., 636/722–7111 collect from abroad ⊕ www. mastercard.com. **Visa** ☎ 800/847–2911 in U.S., 800/100–1219 in India ⊕ www.visa.com.

CURRENCY AND EXCHANGE

The units of Indian currency are the *rupee* and the (rare) *paisa*—100 paise equal one rupee. Paper money comes in denominations of 2 (also rare), 5, 10, 20, 50, 100, 500, and 1,000 rupees. Coins are worth 5, 10, 20, 25, and 50 paise (all rare), 1 rupee, 2 rupees, 5 rupees, and 10 rupees, but it's unlikely that you'll see anything less than 1 rupee. At this writing, the rate of exchange is approximately US$1 to Rs. 60, so that a 500-rupee note is worth just over $8. The price of big-ticket items, such as real estate or cars, is usually given in units of *lakh* or *crore*. A lakh is equal to 100,000, and a crore is equal to 100 lakh. Therefore, 1 lakh rupees is equal to roughly $1,700, and 1 crore is $170,000. India has strict rules against importing or exporting its currency. The currency-exchange booths at the international airports are always open for arriving and departing overseas flights. When you change money, remember to get a certain amount in small denominations (in 10s is best) to pay taxi drivers and such. Reject torn, frayed, taped, or soiled bills, as many merchants, hotels, and restaurants won't accept them, and it's a hassle to find a bank to get them exchanged.

Always change money from an authorized moneychanger and ask for a receipt, known as an encashment slip. Some banks now charge a nominal fee for this slip, which you might need if you want to reconvert rupees into your own currency on departure from India. Don't be lured by illegal street hawkers who offer you a higher exchange rate.

For the most favorable rates, change money at banks. Although ATM transaction fees may be higher abroad than at home, ATM rates are excellent because they're based on wholesale rates offered only by major banks. India's state-run banks can take a long time to cash traveler's checks. If you must use them, save time and use an American Express office or the foreign-exchange service at your hotel. Rates will be slightly lower, but you'll save irritation and time. Rates are also unfavorable in airports, at train and bus stations, and at restaurants, hotels, and stores.

TRAVELER'S CHECKS AND CARDS

Fewer establishments accept traveler's checks these days than ever before. Nevertheless, they're a cheap and secure way to carry extra money, particularly on trips to urban areas. Thomas Cook, Citibank (under the Visa brand), and American Express issue traveler's checks in the United States, but Amex is better known

and more widely accepted; you can also avoid hefty surcharges by cashing Amex checks at Amex offices. Whatever you do, keep track of all the serial numbers in case the checks are lost or stolen.

You can use traveler's checks in India, but in most cases it's just not that convenient to cash them. Cash (both brought in and withdrawn from an ATM) and credit cards are better options. You can cash traveler's checks only in big cities, and most merchants, whether urban or rural, don't accept them. Lost or stolen checks can usually be replaced within 24 hours. To ensure a speedy refund, buy your own traveler's checks—don't let someone else pay for them, as the purchaser is the only one able to request a refund. Don't leave traveler's checks in your hotel room, and keep the counterfoil with the check numbers separate from the checks.

Contacts American Express ☎ *800/528–4800 in U.S., 124/280–1800 in India* ⊕ *www.americanexpress.com.*

▌ PACKING

India is full of beautiful, colorful, over-the-top fashions, but your visit here probably shouldn't include lots of fancy things from your own closet. Make it a point to buy Indian statement pieces during your travels if that's your thing, keeping the original contents of your suitcase simple: shirts made of plain cotton or cotton-synthetic blends and a couple of pairs of comfortable pants—all of which can be washed easily and worn again throughout your trip. Avoiding completely synthetic fabrics that don't breathe is key, since much of India is hot year-round, with temperatures topping 110 degrees or more in the summer months. Delicate fabrics just don't respond well to vigorous Indian washing and powerful detergents, let alone profuse amounts of sweat. Dry cleaning is available across every city and in all major hotels, but even if you think it's a safe bet, quality can vary significantly among dry cleaners, and they tend to use harsh chemicals.

Don't worry about looking too casual—India is not a dressy society. If an upscale function or fancy dinner at a big-city restaurant is on the itinerary, men can often get away with just a formal shirt and pants. Women can wear a simple dress or a dressier blouse with pants and heels.

Bring sunglasses, a bottle of high-SPF sunblock (the amount of protection in sunblock sold in India is questionable) and two good pairs of footwear—sandals with rubber soles and lightweight walking shoes are smart options. Skip anything that's difficult to maneuver in, such as hiking boots—unless you'll be trekking in the north—since you'll often be required to remove your shoes to enter religious sites.

It's especially important is to dress modestly, particularly at sacred sites. In such places, long pants are appropriate for men; women are advised to stick to below-the-knee skirts, dresses, or neat pants. T-shirts are fine, but the male topless look should be left to wandering *sadhus* (Hindu ascetics). Women may want to avoid wearing tight tank tops or tops that are sheer or have plunging necklines, except in nightclubs and upscale restaurants, as even moderately revealing clothing can attract unwanted attention. Longer shorts are more socially acceptable than short shorts when not at the beach, except for children. You'll attract stares if you wear a long Indian tunic as a dress or a midriff-baring sari blouse as a top. One-piece bathing suits are the norm for women at public pools frequented by Indians, but bikinis are common at beach resorts and large hotels that cater to a foreign clientele.

Things to keep handy at all times are toilet paper and moist towelettes or hand sanitizer, especially on long train trips. Few public restrooms provide toilet paper or a way to wash your hands thoroughly. In any case, there probably won't be any hand towels, so a handkerchief for drying your hands is also useful. Consider also carrying a money pouch or belt, a basic first-aid kit, and a small flashlight. Good sanitary napkins are sold in India, but women should pack their own tampons unless they don't mind using ones without applicators, which are generally the only kind available in India.

If you visit in monsoon season, bring a collapsible umbrella. Instead of bringing your own rain boots, buy a cheap pair once you arrive, or just don some flip-flops. Locals call rain boots gum shoes. In winter, bring a sweater or a light jacket for cool evenings.

WITH CHILDREN

If you have a young child, it's probably not worth the bother of packing a stroller: sidewalks in Indian cities often have cracks or even holes, and in any case they don't usually have enough space for them. Be extra careful in Delhi and Mumbai, as streets are crowded and cars unforgiving. **Pack all necessary medications as well as rash creams, zinc oxide, sunscreen, diapers, and diaper wipes.**

Although major brands of disposable diapers, as well as Nestlé instant baby cereals, are available in most cities, they can be hard to find. Powdered milk produced by such companies as Amul and Nestlé is readily available, as is sterilized (UHT) milk sold in sealed boxes. Use those products instead of looking for fresh milk, which needs to be boiled properly—in fact, it's a wise precaution to boil UHT milk as well. If you run out of formula, Lactogen is a reliable Indian brand. Bottled mineral water and packaged snacks—potato chips, cookies, chocolate bars, fruit juices, and soft drinks—are sold throughout India. Though not nutritious, such snacks are often preferable to food that may be spicy or not entirely hygienic. If you're heading out for a day of sightseeing, ask your hotel staff if they can pack a lunch for your child. A small hot pot or kettle can be useful for making instant soup or noodles, which are widely available throughout India.

If you'll be taking any air-conditioned trains, bring a few pieces of warm clothing, as the cars get very cold. Leggings help protect against mosquitoes in the evening, hats shade faces from the sun, and rubber slippers or sandals are always practical. A few pairs of socks can come in handy. If you plan to travel by car **bring a portable car seat.** *See the transportation section (above) for further information.* Choose accommodations that are air-conditioned or have rooms equipped with mosquito netting to protect your child from mosquito bites. **Pack plenty of insect repellent as well as a 3-square-foot piece of soft cloth netting** (available in fabric stores), which you can drape over a carriage or car seat to shield your child from insects. Pellet repellents that plug into the wall and release a mosquito-repelling scent are available in stores across India, and are effective in keeping a room mosquito-free. It's a good idea to purchase such a gizmo on arrival (try Good Knight or ALLOUT).

∎ PASSPORTS AND VISAS

Unless you hold an Indian passport or are a citizen of Nepal or Bhutan, you need a visa to enter India. This applies to children and infants as well.

Information Cox & Kings Global Services ⊕ www.in.ckgs.us.**Travisa** ⊕ *indiavisa. travisaoutsourcing.com.*

PASSPORTS

U.S. passports are valid for 10 years. You must apply in person if you're getting a passport for the first time; if your previous passport was lost, stolen, or damaged; or if your previous passport has expired and was issued more than 15 years ago or when you were under 16. All children under 18 must appear in person to apply for or renew a passport. Both parents must accompany any child under 14 (or send a notarized statement with their permission) and provide proof of their relationship to the child.

∎**TIP→ Before your trip, make two copies of your passport's data page (one for

someone at home and another for you to carry separately). You can also scan the page and email it to someone at home and/or yourself.

There are 26 regional passport offices and thousands of passport acceptance facilities in post offices, public libraries, and other governmental offices. If you're renewing a passport, you can do so by mail. Forms are available at passport acceptance facilities and online.

The cost to apply for a new passport is $135 for adults, $105 for children under 16; adult renewals are $110. Allow up to six weeks for processing, both for first-time passports and renewals. For an expediting fee of $60 you can reduce this time to about three weeks. If your trip is less than two weeks away, you can get a passport even more rapidly by going to a passport office with the necessary documentation. Private expediters can get things done in as little as 48 hours, but charge hefty fees for their services.

VISAS

A visa is essentially formal permission to enter a country. India no longer handles visa applications directly, except on an emergency basis. Instead, you must go to the website of to submit an application and pay electronically. A standard, multiple-entry six-month tourist visa costs US$80 for American citizens. Non-U.S. citizens pay different fees. If you're traveling on business or as a student or journalist, you require a different (and more expensive) visa.

Cox & Kingshas offices in Washington, New York, Chicago, San Francisco, Atlanta, and Houston, and you can submit your passport in person at those locations. Refer to the website for detailed instructions. Your Indian visa should be processed within five days from the time receives your passport, but start the process at least two weeks before your departure to allow for glitches. Your visa is valid from the date of issue, not the day you arrive in India. You must enter and leave during the specified time period, and your passport must have a remaining validity of at least six months.

As of July 2014, plans to unveil an electronic visa-on-arrival system for nationals of most developed countries were underway. Under the new system, applicants would be able to apply for permission to visit India online and receive approval within a few days, without having to submit their passports for processing. Once approved, applicants would be eligible for a visa on arrival at any of India's major ports, valid for one month from the date of entry.

If you need to extend your visa, go to the Foreigners' Regional Registration Office (FRRO) in one of the major cities. But beware—the Indian government makes it extremely difficult to extend a visa for any reason, and if you overstay your visa, you may be required to get clearance from India's Ministry of Home Affairs to leave the country. Punishment can range from heavy fines to actually being jailed. Bottom line: Follow the visa rules and don't expect exceptions to be made, even if you think you have a good excuse.

U.S. Passport Information U.S. Department of State ☎ 877/487–2778 ⊕ travel.state.gov/content/passports/english.html.

U.S. Passport and Visa Expediters A. Briggs Passport & Visa Expeditors ☎ 800/806–0581, 202/338–0111 ⊕ www.abriggs.com. **American Passport Express** ☎ 800/455–5166 ⊕ www.americanpassport.com. **Passport Express** ☎ 800/362–8196 ⊕ www.passportexpress.com. **Travel Document Systems** ☎ 800/874–5100 Washington D.C., 877/874–5104 New York, 888/874–5100 San Francisco, 866/797–2600 Houston, 888/424–8472 Los Angeles ⊕ www.traveldocs.com. **Travel the World Visas** ☎ 202/223–8822 ⊕ www.world-visa.com.

▌ RESTROOMS

When you need a restroom, ask for the "loo," the washroom, or the toilet. Two types of toilets are available wherever you go in India. Traditional Indian toilets are holes in the ground—a squat variety with two steps in which to put your feet. There are also Western-style toilets, but the toilet seat, except in luxury hotels and better restaurants, may be messy. In many bathrooms you'll see a faucet, a small hand-held showerhead, and/or a bucket with a plastic cup or other small vessel; Indians use these to rinse, bidet-style, after using the toilet. Sinks are either inside or right outside the bathroom. Outside of hotels, malls, and some restaurants, public restrooms are rarely clean, and ideally avoided. On long road journeys, finding any public restroom—let alone a clean one—is difficult. Always use the restroom before you set out and ration your fluid intake during a long journey. Be on the lookout for a decent hotel or opt for the outdoors. Luxury hotels and fancier restaurants usually have clean bathrooms.

Nicer hotels and restaurants provide toilet paper, but you can't depend on this, as most Indians don't use the stuff (they use their left hand and running water to clean themselves, which is why this hand is considered unclean). And often soap and paper towels are not available for washing up afterward. Keep toilet paper and towelettes with you at all times, which are readily available in pharmacies and grocery stores in large cities. Never throw anything other than a small amount of toilet paper in a toilet; India's septic systems clog easily.

Find a Loo The Bathroom Diaries. This site has a searchable map of restrooms the world over—each one located, reviewed, and rated. ⊕ www.thebathroomdiaries.com.

▌ SAFETY

There are no generalizations that can be made regarding potential dangers for all tourists in India, but urban areas do have their particular crime patterns, and everyone is vulnerable in bad parts of town. For example, Delhi is known to be dangerous for women at night and has more crime in general than other big cities in India. Mumbai is safer for women, with fewer violent crimes taking place, although it's important to be vigilant wherever you are.

Scams for targeting foreigners abound. One of the better-known, yet not that common, scams comes from the shoe shiners at Delhi's Connaught Place, who furtively sling mud at your feet and then point out how badly your shoes need to be cleaned. Just be cautious everywhere you go, and know that in a country in which most tourists stand out—and that is filled with locals vying for their business—you're always a potential target.

Theft in hotels is not common, but you should never leave money, traveler's checks, passports, or jewelry in plain sight. If your hotel has a safe, definitely use it, but if there's nothing to lock up valuables, you may wish to take them with you. Follow the lead of locals: avoid wandering around late at night, especially in smaller towns where shutters close early, and avoid road journeys after dark. As anywhere, never leave suitcases unattended in airports or train stations. The most visible police officers are traffic cops, clad in white and khaki; they can usually help out, even with a nontraffic problem (though taxis are in their jurisdiction). Otherwise, look for a regular police officer, in a khaki uniform.

Avoid strangers who offer their services as guides or moneychangers, and do not agree to be taken anywhere with anyone. In crowds, be alert for pickpockets—wear a money belt, and/or keep your purse close to your body and securely closed. If you travel by train, you may want to avoid accepting food or beverages from fellow passengers. There have been a few cases in which train travelers (usually Indians) are given food laced with sedatives and then robbed once the drug takes effect. It's likely that you will be offered food on a train; Indians feel uncomfortable eating meals in front of another without sharing, but it's safest to offer an excuse and refuse. In train stations, ignore touts who tell you that your hotel of choice is full or has closed; they hope to settle you into a place where they get a kickback for bringing in business. Do not agree to carry a parcel for anyone.

Women need to take extra precautions. If you're alone, don't travel late at night, especially in Delhi. Avoid seedy areas, touts volunteering their services, or over-friendly strangers and jostling crowds of men. Also, never get into a taxi or auto-rickshaw if a second man accompanies the driver. If you find yourself in a tricky situation—a taxi driver demanding a king's ransom, a hawker plaguing you, a stranger following you—head straight for a police officer or at least threaten to do so, which often works just as well. Don't hesitate to protest loudly if you're harassed.

Overnight trains are safe for women traveling alone provided they take sleeper class or better, where you'll be in an open compartment packed with other people. Just remember to chain your luggage to the loops provided below your sleeping berth (luggage chains and locks are available at every major train station). You may want to avoid first-class air-conditioned trains, because on those you're locked in a room with three others—who may all be male. However, this is also the most comfortable compartment and chances are that your fellow travelers—irrespective of their gender—will be educated and respectful.

It's easy to get upset by the number of beggars who beseech you for spare rupees, motioning from hand to mouth to indicate they have nothing to eat. Most disturbing are the children, as young as three years old, roaming in between cars on busy streets with no adult figure in sight. Sometimes, especially in big cities, such beggars are part of a ring and may not be as destitute as they look. If you give a beggar money, a dozen more may immediately spring up, and you may feel pressured to provide for all; it can also be difficult to get the first beggar, or the entire group, off your tail. Be firm and do not allow a beggar to follow you—a raised voice or mild threats usually work. If you're not firm, expect to be followed by a pack for a while—they do not give up easily.

If you want to contribute, seek out an established charity that's in a position to substantially help those in need. It also doesn't hurt to pass out small trinkets or candy to child beggars if you really can't stand the thought of ignoring them—but do it discreetly.

Hawkers and touts can also be a tremendous nuisance. If you're not interested in what a hawker is offering, give him a firm, polite no and ignore him after that. If he persists, tell him to clear off and employ some mock anger or else he will follow you for blocks. Do not encourage touts at all.

GOVERNMENT ADVISORIES

As different countries have different worldviews, look at travel advisories from a range of governments to get more of a sense of what's going on out there. And be sure to parse the language carefully. For example, a warning to "avoid all travel" carries more weight than one urging you to "avoid nonessential travel," and both are much stronger than a plea to "exercise caution." A U.S. government travel warning is more permanent (though not necessarily more serious) than a so-called public announcement, which carries an expiration date.

The U.S. Department of State's website has more than just travel warnings and advisories. The consular information sheets issued for every country have general safety tips, entry requirements (though be sure to verify these with the country's embassy), and other useful details. By registering on the site, you can have the DOS email you travel warnings as they are posted.

The U.S. Department of State generally does not list broad travel warnings for India because the majority of the country is safe for tourists. Still, there are a few unstable areas, and riots and other disturbances can arise quickly in otherwise-safe areas. It's always a good idea to know where the closest consulate or embassy is.

General Information and Warnings U.S. **Department of State** ☎ *888/407-4747 in U.S., 202/501-4444 from overseas* ⊕ *www. travel.state.gov.*

▌ TAXES

Airport departure tax is Rs. 500 for non-Indians, and it's included in the price of your ticket. The tax is the same no matter which country you fly to.

V.A.T., or Value-Added Tax, can be 1%, 4%, 12.5%, or nothing depending on the item purchased and the state where it was purchased. The V.A.T. is included in the listed price of items, except at restaurants and some hotels. For your hotel room, you will probably pay a service tax (around 12%), V.A.T. (12.5% and included in rates) and possibly even a luxury tax (10%). Rates differ from state to state.

▌ TIME

There are no time changes from region to region in India and India does not observe daylight saving time. The entire country operates on Indian Standard Time, which is 5½ hours ahead of Greenwich Mean Time, 10½ hours ahead of Eastern Standard Time (9½ hours during daylight saving), 13½ hours ahead of Pacific Standard Time (12½ hours during daylight saving), 4½ hours behind Australian Eastern Standard Time (5½ hours during daylight saving), and 7½ hours behind Auckland time (8½ hours during daylight saving).

▌ TIPPING

It's true that much of India runs on tips, but you can get a skewed understanding of the system if you stay only in top hotels, where wealthy tourists and businesspeople are the majority of the clientele. In those situations, hotel employees have come to appreciate modest tips. In smaller towns, however, tipping is less institutionalized and not expected in many instances. Always trust your instincts and reward good service accordingly wherever you are. Some guidelines:

Always tip in cash. You should leave up to 10% on any restaurant bill, 15% for exceptional service. At some large luxury hotel chains, such as Oberoi, tips to individuals are not encouraged, but they ask you to leave one tip at the end of your stay, which management then divides among staff. At other hotels, you won't go wrong if you tip your room valet Rs. 20 per night. Bellboys and bell captains should be paid Rs. 10 per bag. For room service, tip 10% of the bill. Tip the concierge about Rs. 10 if he gets you a taxi, or consider a Rs. 100 tip at the end of your stay if he has helped you in several situations. Train-station porters should be paid Rs. 40 or more per bag, depending on the weight, plus Rs. 40 per 30 minutes waiting fees, if applicable. Set the rate before you let him take your bags (a sign may be posted with official rates). Taxi drivers don't expect tips unless they go through a great deal of trouble to reach your destination; in such a case Rs. 10–Rs. 20 is fair. Some taxi and auto-rickshaw drivers may ask for Rs. 10 per piece of luggage over and above the meter charge. If you hire a car and driver, tip the driver about Rs. 50–Rs. 100 per day, depending on the distance traveled and about Rs. 50 for each lunch or dinner; also give him a larger amount at the end of the journey if you have been using him for many days. Tip local guides 10% of the price of the tour.

TIPPING GUIDELINES FOR INDIA	
Bartender	10% percent of bill
Bellhop	Rs. 10 per bag
Hotel Concierge	Depends on level of service. At least Rs. 10–Rs. 20 for getting a car or taxi
Hotel Doorman	Rs. 10 if he opens car door
Room Valet	Rs. 20 per day
Hotel Room-Service Waiter	10% of bill
Porter at Train Station	Negotiate price before accepting service. Official rates start at Rs. 40 per bag
Skycap at Airport	Same as porter
Taxi Driver	None, or up to Rs. 40
Tour Guide	Depends on extent of tour. 10% of total price is acceptable
Valet Parking Attendant	Rs. 10–Rs. 20
Waiter	10% at a regular restaurant. 15% at high-end and five-star hotel restaurants. Make sure service has not been added to the bill
Hired Driver	Rs. 50–Rs. 100 per day

▌ TOURS

A package tour to India can help tremendously when you have a short amount of time and want to pack in as much as possible. You'll save time by not having to arrange everything yourself or learn too much about the great Indian art of haggling, and you'll also know in advance what you're getting. The downside is that you'll often end up paying much more. Because tour companies assume, in general, that foreigners traveling to India expect Western standards of accommodations and dining, they'll often book you in business-class or luxury hotels and have you eating pricey meals. This approach often neglects a more authentic understanding of India, where independent travel and exploration can be very fulfilling—not to mention much cheaper—if you're willing to do a little research and branch out from the typical tourist spots.

Organizations American Society of Travel Agents (*ASTA*). ☎ *800/275–2782* ⊕ *www.asta. org*. **United States Tour Operators Association** (*USTOA*). ☎ *212/599–6599* ⊕ *www.ustoa. com*.

■TIP→ Local tourism boards can provide information about lesser-known and small-niche operators that sell packages to only a few destinations.

GUIDED TOURS

Guided tours are a good option when you don't want to do it all yourself. You travel along with a group (sometimes large, sometimes small, sometimes just your party and the guide), stay in prebooked hotels, eat with your fellow travelers (the cost of meals is sometimes included in the price of your tour, sometimes not), and follow a schedule.

A knowledgeable guide can take you places that you might never discover on your own, and you may be pushed to see more than you would have otherwise. Tours aren't for everyone, but they can be just the thing for trips to places where making travel arrangements is difficult or time-consuming (particularly when you don't speak the language).

Whenever you book a guided tour, find out what's included and what isn't. A "land-only" tour includes all your travel (by bus, in most cases) in the destination, but not necessarily your flights to and from or even within it. Also, in most cases prices in tour brochures don't include fees and taxes. And remember that you'll be expected to tip your guide (in cash) at the end of the tour.

The number of tours to India is overwhelming. Quality and price vary greatly, but the ones listed here have proven track records. Overseas Adventure Travel offers

a good, "classic" tour of India in which you'll visit points in Rajasthan as well as Agra, Khajuraho, and Varanasi. OAT tends to attract older Americans who can afford a high standard of travel—standards reflected in the tours' cost. Tours usually cost somewhere around $200 a day (including international airfare).

Four Wheel Drive India is a Jaipur-based tour company that provides several tour options, including honeymoon and wildlife packages. The major advantage here is that if you don't see the exact tour you want, they can customize one for you and help coordinate every aspect. Siddharth Travels Interserve, based in Delhi, is a responsive company that has many suggested tours that can also be personalized. Compass Tours and Travel offers a dizzying array of options all over the subcontinent, from four-day jaunts in Goa to luxury tours of Rajasthan at all price points. Djoser offers the opportunity of traveling with small groups of Europeans (mostly Dutch) and caters to a more independent-minded traveler. Their tours lack the cookie-cutter features of more mainstream tour companies.

Recommended Companies Compass India ☎ *877/772–6672* ⊕ *www.compasstours. com*. **Djoser** ☎ *877/356–7376, 484/595–0480* ⊕ *www.djoserusa.com*. **Four Wheel Drive India** ☎ *950/993–5599* ⊕ *www. fourwheeldriveindia.com*. **Overseas Adventure Travel** ☎ *800/955–1925* ⊕ *www. oattravel.com*. **Siddharth Travels Interserve** ☎ *11/4656–5500* ⊕ *www.siddharthtravels.com*.

CULTURE TOURS

Both Smithsonian Journeys and National Geographic Expeditions have tours that come with highly educated guides, lodging in high-end hotels, and hefty price tags. Their tours will involve you in local culture, as in having dinner in an Indian family's house or a visit to an ashram. Alumni associations are another source for interesting (albeit also often expensive), culturally oriented trips to India.

Contacts **National Geographic Expeditions** ☎ 888/966–8687 ⊕ www. nationalgeographicexpeditions.com. **Smithsonian Journeys** ☎ 855/330–1542 ⊕ www. smithsonianjourneys.org.

PHOTO TOURS

Photo Safari India, run by photographer Vandit Kalia, can put together custom tours whose destinations maximize the chances of getting great shots of wildlife. (Group tours to national parks—Ladakh, Goa, and Arunachal Pradesh—are also run on occasion.) *National Geographic* takes advantage of its publication's traditional strength by offering a 10-day tour tailored to photographers.

Contacts **Photo Safari India** ⊕ www. photosafariindia.com.

VOLUNTOURISM

Transitions Abroad, a clearinghouse for creative ways to travel at low cost, lists many organizations that accept volunteers for their programs in India.

Contact **Transitions Abroad** ⊕ www. transitionsabroad.com.

▮ VISITOR INFORMATION

The America-based Indian tourism offices can send brochures and help with plans, but it's better to call or visit the website for information—trying to get a response by email usually doesn't work.

Contacts **Ministry of Tourism** ☎ 11/2371–0518 in India, 212/586–4901 in U.S. ⊕ www. incredibleindia.org.

For travelers spending more than a few days in Delhi, Mumbai, or another vast, rapidly changing Indian city, the Eicher series of maps is useful. National English-language newspapers include *Indian Express* (⊕ *www.indianexpress. com*) and *Hindustan Times* (⊕ *www. hindustantimes.com*). The Indian answer to 411, JustDial (☎ 22/6999–9999) helps callers find out about local businesses and answers lots of other questions. Listings can be text messaged to a cell phone. (The prefix in the phone number dials Mumbai, but substituting other local area codes will work equally well.) They also run a search engine (⊕ *www.justdial.com*) of their listings, which is useful for locals and visitors in urban areas alike. Google works pretty well, too. Rediff (⊕ *www.rediff. com*) dissects current events and pop culture across India.

INDEX

PHOTO CREDITS

Front cover: Igor Plotnikov/Shutterstock [Description: Houseboat, Kerala]. 1, cmittman, Fodors.com member. 2, Inikep | Dreamstime.com. 5, Dinodia/ age fotostock. Chapter 1, Experience India: 8-9, Luca Tettoni / age fotostock. 11 (left), Sreeganesha, Fodors.com member. 11 (right), Joan Saba, Fodors.com member. 14, AbhijeetRane/Flickr. 15 (left), thefinalmiracle/Shutterstock. 15 (right), NCPA Photo/ Narendra Dangia. 16, h0usep1ant/Jeff Karpala/Flickr. 17 (left), Oberoi Hotels & Resorts. 17 (right), R-photos/Shutterstock. 18 (top middle), Rafal Cichawa/Shutterstock. 18 (bottom), Terraxplorer/iStockphoto. 18 (top right), anneblock, Fodors.com member. 19 (top), Taj Hotels Resorts and Palaces. 19 (bottom), Polly Ryan, Fodors.com member. 19 (right), Steven Miric/ iStockphoto. 20, Pangfolio.com/Shutterstock. 21 (left), emin kuliyev/Shutterstock. 21 (right), highviews/Shutterstock. 22, Günter Gollnick/ age fotostock. 23, RABOUAN Jean-Baptiste / age fotostock. 24, Anne Clark/iStockphoto. 25 (left), paul prescott/Shutterstock. 25 (right), Caroline Gaines, Fodors.com member. 26, Dana Ward/Shutterstock. 27, Taj Hotels Resorts and Palaces. 28, mcgregorjn, Fodors. com member. 30, Jeremy Richards/iStockphoto. 31 (left), Mikhail Nekrasov/Shutterstock. 31 (right), Aleksandar Todorovic/Shutterstock. 32-33, Ian Cumming / age fotostock. 34, Navin Mistry / Alamy. 35, Neil Barclay / age fotostock. 36 (top), Dinodia / age fotostock. 36 (middle), Lukas Hlavac/Shutterstock. 36 (bottom), Ben Sutherland/Flickr. 37, Boaz Rottem / age fotostock. 38 (both), Dinodia / age fotostock. 39 (top), 2010 SuperStock. 39 (bottom), ARCO / Therin-Weise / age fotostock. 40, Dana Ward/Shutterstock. 41, Kharidehal Abhirama Ashwin/Shutterstock. 42 (left), Christian Haugen/Flickr. 42 (right), Terraxplorer/iStockphoto. 43, Honza Soukup/Flickr. 44, Taka / age fotostock. Chapter 2, Portrait of India: 45, Photosindia.com / age fotostock. 46, Kulpreet_Photography/iStockphoto. 47, James Burger / age fotostock. 48, Marco Cristofori / age fotostock. 49 (bottom left), Teresa Zau, Fodors.com member. 49 (top right), Nikhil Gangavane/iStockphoto. 50, Nick Hanna / Alamy. 51, Vikram Raghuvanshi/iStockphoto. 52, Ivan Vdovin / age fotostock. 53 (bottom left), Alan Lagadu/ iStockphoto. 53 (top right), Rafal Cichawa/Shutterstock. 54, Jan S./Shutterstock. 55, Walter Bibikow / age fotostock. 56, Wikimedia Commons. 57 (bottom left), paul prescott/Shutterstock. 57 (top right), AJP/Shutterstock. 58, Lebedinski Vladislav/Shutterstock. 59, paul prescott/Shutterstock. 60, Christophe Boisvieux / age fotostock. 61 (bottom), JeremyRichards/Shutterstock. 61 (top), AJP/Shutterstock. 62, Matthias Rosenkranz/Flickr. 63 (bottom), Vassil/Wikimedia Commons. 63 (top), jaimaa/Shutterstock. 64, Dinodia / age fotostock. 65, saiko3p/Shutterstock. 66, Joe Gough/iStockphoto. 67 (bottom), Jehangir Hanafi /iStockphoto. 67 (top), Monkey Business Images/Shutterstock. 68, Joe Gough/iStockphoto. 69, Colin & Linda McKie/iStockphoto. 70, WITTY234/Shutterstock. 71, Bartosz Hadyniak/ iStockphoto. 72, JTB Photo / age fotostock. 73 (bottom), Sid B. Viswakumar/Shutterstock. 73 (top), RABOUAN Jean-Baptiste / age fotostock. 74, Ian Cumming / age fotostock. 75, Wikimedia Commons. 76, M Balan / age fotostock. 77 (bottom), testing/Shutterstock. 77 (top), NCPA Photo/ Harkiran Singh Bhasin. 78, Eitan Simanor / age fotostock. Chapter 3, Delhi: 79, Arco Images/age fotostock. 80, Rajibnandni/Wikimedia Commons. 81 (top right), Terra plorer/iStockphoto. 81 (top left), Dana Ward/Shutterstock. 81 (bottom), indigreen.co.in. 82 and 83 (bottom), highviews/Shutterstock. 83 (top), sanskarshan/Wikimedia Commons. 84, Varun Shiv Kapur/Flickr. 85 (bottom), Kylelovesyou/Wikimedia Commons. 85 (top), Russ Bowling/Flickr. 86, Sreeganesha, Fodors.com member. 93, Helene Rogers / age fotostock. 96, Massimo Pacifico / age fotostock. 101, Dinodia /age fotostock. 102, Mel Longhurst / age fotostock. 105, The Print Collector / age fotostock. 108, ARCO / Therin-Weise / age fotostock. 111, McPHOTOs / age fotostock. 115, Tibor Bognar / age fotostock. 116, Oriental Touch / age fotostock. 137, Edmund Sumner/VIEW / age fotostock. 143, Varun Shiv Kapur/Flickr. Chapter 4, Side Trips from Delhi: 147, Alexander Pöschel/ age fotostock. 148, Polly Ryan, Fodors.com member. 149 (top left), NGail, Fodors.com member. 149 (top right), Rudolf Tepfenhart/Shutterstock. 149 (bottom), jennyt/Shutterstock. 150, paul prescott/Shutterstock. 151 (both), Bon Appetit / Alamy. 152, Guillermo Garcia/Shutterstock. 162, Mel Longhurst / age fotostock. 166-67, Redtigerxyz/Wikimedia Commons. 166, J Hauke / age fotostock. 168 (bottom left), Mark Henley / age fotostock. 168 (top left), Hashim/ Wikimedia Commons. 168 (top center), Gavin Hellier / age fotostock. 168 (bottom right), Wikimedia Commons. 168 (top right), Samir Luther/Wikimedia Commons. 169, Dinodia / age fotostock. 170, John Henry Claude Wil / age fotostock. 171 (top), Rafal Cichawa/Shutterstock. 171 (second), William Donelson/Wikimedia Commons. 171 (third), Alexey Fateev/Shutterstock. 171 (fourth), Galyna Andrushko/Shutterstock. 171 (bottom), JeremyRichards/Shutterstock. 178, Tibor Bognar / age fotostock. 185, Richard Ashworth / age fotostock. 188-89, Jose Fuste Raga / age fotostock. 196-97, Aleksandar Todorovic/Shutterstock. 198 (left), Christopher Soghoian/Flickr. 198 (right), Rumi Arpita-devi/ Flickr. 199 (top left), Lebedinski Vladislav/Shutterstock. 199 (bottom), Aleksandar Todorovic/Shutterstock. 199 (top center), Ken Wieland/Wikimedia Commons. 199 (top right), JeremyRichards/Shutterstock. 200 (top left), Jon Larson/iStockphoto. 200 (bottom left), Igor Plotnikov/Shutterstock. 200 (top right), Sequoy/Shutterstock. 200 (center right), Arindam Banerjee/iStockphoto. 200 (bottom right), Bartosz Hadyniak/iStockphoto. 201 (top left), Jeremy Edwards/iStockphoto. 201 (center left), selimaksan/iStockphoto. 201 (bottom left), Aleksandar Todorovic/Shutterstock. 201 (center), Arindam Banerjee/iStockphoto. 201 (bottom right), oksana.perkins/Shutterstock. 201 (top right), Regien Paassen/Shutterstock. Chapter 5, Rajasthan: 211, Steven Caudill, Fodors.com member. 212, gpsaba, Fodors.com member. 213 (top left), Joan Saba, Fodors.com member. 213 (top right), Martapallares, Fodors.com member. 213 (bottom), Steven Caudill, Fodors.com member. 214, Simon Reddy / Alamy. 215 bottom, Dinodia / age fotostock. 215 (top), Shoko Muraguchi/Flickr. 216, paul prescott/Shutterstock. 217 (bottom), ErickN/Shutterstock. 217 (top), brytta/iStockphoto. 218, Kris Ubach / age fotostock. 219 (bottom), Igor Plotnikov/Shutterstock. 219 (top), Rafal Cichawa/Shutterstock. 220, graham klotz/iStockphoto. 221 (bottom), Michael Wade/Flickr. 221 (top), Jack Macilwinen/iStockphoto. 222, Maria Gioberti/Shutterstock. 229, Tibor Bognar / age fotostock. 237, José Fuste Raga / age fotostock. 238, Tolo Balaguer / age fotostock. 241, Bob Turner / age fotostock. 243, Alvaro Leiva / age fotostock. 246, David Dunning Anokhi Archives. 251, Kris Ubach / age fotostock. 257, Dennis Albert Richardson/Shutterstock. 260, Dinodia / age fotostock. 265, Philippe Michel / age fotostock. 266, Jose Fuste Raga / age fotostock. 270-71, Alvaro Leiva / age fotostock. 272, Oberoi Hotels & Resorts. 279, Kris Ubach / age fotostock. 281, Philippe Michel / age fotostock. 289, Ajay Onkar Garg / age fotostock. 295, Dennis Cox / age fotostock. Chapter 6, Mumbai: 301, RABOUAN Jean-Baptiste / age fotostock. 302, Christian Haugen/Flickr. 303 (top left), Kristin Koop, Fodors.com member. 303 (top right), blcktiebombshell, Fodors.com member. 303 (bottom), Nichalp/Wikimedia Commons. 304, foodanddrinkphotos co / age fotostock. 305 (bottom), Colin & Linda McKie/iStockphoto. 305 (top), Meen Kadri/Flickr. 306, Helio San Miguel. 307 (bottom), chiragndesai/Flickr. 307 (top), York Winery. 308, Dinodia / age fotostock. 309 (bottom), Rakesh Krishna Kumar/Flickr. 309 (top), Nick Gray/Flickr. 310, Alexanderpf/Flickr. 316, Dinodia / age fotostock. 318, Christophe Bluntzer / age fotostock. 323, Johnny Stockshooter / age fotostock. 328, Günter Gollnick / age fotostock. 339, Christophe Boisvieux / age fotostock. 354, Helio San Miguel. 365, RABOUAN Jean-Baptiste / age fotostock. 376, Dinodia Photos / Alamy. 377, JeremyRichards/Shutterstock. 378, Dinodia / age fotostock. 379, David Evison/Shutterstock. 380 (top), JeremyRichards/Shutterstock. 380 (center), Ivan Vdovin / age fotostock. 380 (bottom), Luca Tettoni / age fotostock. 381, Rafal Cichawa/Shutterstock. 382-83 (all) and 384 (top), JeremyRichards/Shutterstock. 384 (bottom), Y.Shishido/Wikimedia Commons. 385 (top), JeremyRichards/Shutterstock. 385 (bottom), Wikimedia Commons. Chapter 7, Goa: 389, raffaele meucci /age fotostock. 390, rfh, Fodors.com member. 391 (left), Steven Miric/iStockphoto. 391 (right), Mikhail Nekrasov/Shutterstock. 392, Joe Gough/Shutterstock. 393 (bottom), Monkey Business Images/Shutterstock. 393 (top), Amanda Fernandes/Flickr. 394, Andrey Lukashenkov/Shutterstock. 395 (bottom), Mishakov/Shutterstock. 395 (top), Ridinghag/Wikimedia Commons. 396, vicspacewalker/Shutterstock. 406, Achim Schmidt / age fotostock. 410-11, Alvaro Leiva /age fotostock. 414, Walter Bibikow / age fotostock. 419, World Pictures/Phot / age fotostock. 422, Dinodia / age fotostock. 425, Alvaro Leiva / age fotostock. 430, Jordí Camí / age fotostock. 435, Andrey Lukashenkov/Shutterstock. Chapter 8 Kerala: 439, Balan Madhavan / age fotostock. 440 (top and bottom), Helio San Miguel. 441 (top), Pikoso.kz/Shutterstock. 441 (bottom), Daniel Bhim-Rao/iStockphoto. 442, Paul Cowan/iStockphoto. 443 bottom, Manubahuguna | Dreamstime.com. 443 (top), Kgtoh | Dreamstime.com. 444, Helio San Miguel. 453, Philippe Michel / age fotostock. 461, Helio San Miguel. 464, Zzvet / Dreamstime.com. 475, f9photos/Shutterstock. 476, Aleksandar Todorovic / Shutterstock.com. 481, Alan Lagadu/iStockphoto. Chapter 9, Kolkata: 493, Sanjay Marathe / India Photo Stock / Alamy. 494 and 495 (top), Radiokafka / Shutterstock. 495 (bottom), neelsky / Shutterstock. 496, PIFood / Alamy. 497 (top), UrbanZone / Alamy. 497 (bottom), pzAxe / Shutterstock. 498, AJP / Shutterstock. 513, National Geographic Image Collection / Alamy. 516, DINODIA / age fotostock. Back cover (from left to right): Aleksandar Todorovic/Shutterstock; infinity21/Shutterstock; Terraxplorer/iStockphoto. Spine: Kulpreet_Photography/iStockphoto. About Our Writers: All photos are courtesy of the writers except for the following: Malavika Bhattacharya, courtesy of Nisha Jha.

NOTES

ABOUT OUR WRITERS

 Margot Bigg has lived and worked in India for many years and has written for a number of Indian publications, including local editions of *Rolling Stone, Condé Nast Traveller,* and *Time Out.* She's also the author of *Moon Living Abroad in India* and *Moon Taj Mahal, Delhi & Jaipur.* Margot contributed to the first edition of *Fodor's Essential India* and for this edition she updated the Experience, Portrait of India, and Travel Smart chapters. Find out more about her at ⊕ *www. margotbigg.com.*

 Malavika Bhattacharya is an independent travel journalist based New Delhi. Her work has appeared in publications such as *National Geographic Traveler, Conde Nast Traveler,* and CNN. com. Armed with a degree in Mathematics, she stumbled into journalism while seeking out the remote Himalayan villages and hidden beaches of her country. For this edition, Malavika updated the Side Trips from Delhi chapter.

Vaihayasi Pande Daniel is an editorial director at ⊕ *www.rediff.com,* a popular website for Indians all over the world. She writes on current affairs, travel, food, and more. The granddaughter of Estonian and Indian freedom-fighters, Vaihayasi was born in Montreal, grew up in Baltimore, married a Tamil Christian, and has lived in India ever since. Peripatetic tendencies draw her and her daughters all over India and elsewhere, but she prefers Mumbai to any other place in the world. For this edition, she updated the Rajasthan and Kerala chapters.

Snigdha Poonam is the arts editor at *The Caravan,* a Delhi-based magazine of narrative nonfiction. She writes on culture and society, and has been published in the *New York Times,* the *Guardian* and other publications in India and elsewhere. For this edition of *Fodor's Essential India,* Snigdha updated the Delhi chapter.

 Michael Edison Hayden is an American writer currently living in Mumbai. A recipient of two prestigious Pulitzer Grants, his work as a journalist as appeared in the *New York Times,* the *Wall Street Journal, Slate,* and *Al Jazeera America,* among others. Michael recently finished his first novel, and updated the Mumbai chapter for this edition.

 Chandrima Pal is a feature writer who covers everything from politics to high society, Bollywood to social issues, for some of India's biggest media houses. Her first novel, *A Song for I* (Amaryllis) was published in 2012; she is working on her second for Harper Collins, India. For *Fodor's Essential India,* Chandrima has updated and added to the Kolkata chapter.

 Vandana Verma is the editor of *Motherland,* a quarterly magazine on contemporary and emerging Indian culture. She also manages The India Tube, a travel website. Formerly the Food & Drink and Lifestyle editor at *Time Out Delhi,* Vandana has a degree in journalism from the University of London. For this edition of *Fodor's Essential India,* Vandana updated the Goa chapter.